# EDMUND HUSSERL AND HIS CRITICS

# AN INTERNATIONAL BIBLIOGRAPHY (1894-1979)

# BIBLIOGRAPHIES OF FAMOUS PHILOSOPHERS

The Philosophy Documentation Center is publishing a series of "Bibliographies of Famous Philosophers," Richard H. Lineback, general editor. **HENRI BERGSON: A BIBLIOGRAPHY** was the first bibliography in the series. **JEAN-PAUL SARTRE AND HIS CRITICS: AN INTERNATIONAL BIBLIOGRAPHY (1938-1975)** was the second, **ALFRED NORTH WHITEHEAD: A PRIMARY-SECONDARY BIBLIOGRAPHY** was the third, and **EDMUND HUSSERL AND HIS CRITICS. AN INTERNATIONAL BIBLIOGRAPHY (1894-1979)** is the fourth.

# EDMUND HUSSERL AND HIS CRITICS

# AN INTERNATIONAL BIBLIOGRAPHY (1894-1979)

Preceded by a Bibliography
of Husserl's Writings

**François Lapointe**

Published by

**PHILOSOPHY DOCUMENTATION CENTER
BOWLING GREEN STATE UNIVERSITY
BOWLING GREEN, OHIO 43403
U.S.A.**

Library of Congress Card Number: 80-83172

ISBN 0-912632-42-9

# CONTENTS

# INTRODUCTION

Although Husserl's work has been widely read and reviewed, and has exerted a significant influence on contemporary thought, no comprehensive and up-to-date bibliography of the wide range of critical response to his writings has yet appeared in book form to date. Since bibliography is an essential tool at some stage of most scholarly endeavors, and certainly is an essential tool of philosophy and the human sciences as a kind of scholarship, it is hoped that this compilation of primary and secondary materials will give Husserl scholars and students some assistance.

With thousands of titles devoted to Husserl, surely a Husserl bibliography needs no lengthy justification. I have long been aware of the need for a full, detailed, and accurate list of the reactions of Husserl's critics. There can be little doubt that Husserl has received, and is still receiving, the sort of attention given only to great thinkers. The works listed here show that Husserl's ideas are constantly being examined in new ways, in new contexts, and using new resources uncovered by investigations in a variety of fields. This bibliography provides continuing proof that Husserl's work is still found fresh and exciting by a new generation of scholars and students.

The following bibliography is intended to be as complete as is technically feasible. The purpose is to provide an accurate, reasonably complete and useful arrangement of materials. Although no bibliography can claim to be exhaustive, every attempt at completeness and accuracy has been made. All of the standard reference works known and available to me were consulted, and many periodicals and books were searched individually. Previous bibliographies (and the reader/user may find those listed in items 945 to 958) have been incorporated. Items through December 1979 are included. Admitedly the coverage is less than complete for items that have appeared in the last year or so. The coverage is fairly complete for journals, but, regrettably, much less so for discussions that occur in the body of a book. I should be most grateful for any help from scholars in making good some of the omissions.

Although every effort has been made to compile an accurate, up-to-date, and reasonably complete bibliography, I am fully aware of the provisional nature of my work and feel no obligation to apologize for this. As is well known to bibliographers, publication constitutes a stage in the movement toward completeness, a more or less 'complete' starting point for further work. My hope is that eventually I can come closer to my ideal of completeness in a second edition, which will continue this one beyond 1979, and which will include earlier important items I was regrettably unable to include in this edition, as well as corrections of possible errors. My hope is also to include in a second edition many critical annotations. Effort in this direction has already been made.

Bibliography always serves a utilitarian purpose. Some kind of order has to be imposed. To compile as complete a collection of items as possible is one thing. To provide a useful arrangement of this collection is quite another thing. The major task of the bibliographer should be to bring some kind of order out of the chaos of alphabetic or chronological listings. After long deliberation, it has been decided to distribute the material in two parts. Part One contains an exhaustive bibliography of Husserl's writings and publications. Part Two contains the bibliography of secondary sources, and is subdivided into seven sections. Section 1 contains books devoted to Husserl (or almost exclusively so), including all available reviews, and the books are classified by language. Section 2 lists dissertations and theses, also indicating the entries, when available, in *Dissertation Abstracts International.* Section 3 lists items by proper names. This section includes material in which Husserl is being compared, or contrasted with major figures in philosophy and science. Section 4 lists items arranged by subjects. In Section 5 we have grouped studies that involved a general discussion of Husserl. Section 6 comprises studies and reviews devoted to a single work of Husserl, beginning with *Philosophie der Arithmetik,* and following the chronological order of publication. The last section contains discussion of phenomenology with incidental reference to Husserl. Entries that arrived too late to be included in the body of the manuscript are grouped in Part Three, the Appendix. Part Four is an index of authors and editors.

It is impossible in an extensive bibliography to remove all errors and make good all gaps of information. Since as I mentioned above, I intend to issue a revised edition, I urgently solicit the help of those who might use this bibliography, to send corrections, leads, and information.

I wish to thank the staff of the Philosophy Documentation Center for their help and especially Barbara J. Sharp for her preparation of the manuscript.

François Lapointe
Department of Psychology
Tuskegee Institute,
Alabama 36088, U.S.A.

# PART ONE
# BIBLIOGRAPHY OF EDMUND HUSSERL'S
# WRITINGS AND PUBLICATIONS

## Husserl's Writings and Publications

Part One, devoted to Husserl's writings and publications, comprises the following sections: A) The Husserl Archives and the *Husserliana,* B) Works and publication by year, C) Texts and translations since 1950, D) Anthologies, E) Conversations, Correspondence, F) Husserl's editorial activities.

### A) The Husserl Archives and the *Husserliana*

The Husserl Archives at Louvain (and now also in New York at the New School for Social Research) contain approximately 40,000 pages of Husserl's manuscripts. Detailed information concerning the Husserl Archives can be found in Part Two, see items 918 to 933.

Of the greatest importance for the future of phenomenology was a visit to Freiburg im Bresgau by the Belgian Franciscan Herman Leo Van Breda in 1938, a few months after Husserl's death. Father Van Breda's search for materials for his doctoral dissertation led, after some episodes worthy of a "suspense" novel, and which he has described in "Le sauvetage de l'héritage husserlien et la fondation des Archives Husserl" (see item no. 932), to the transfer of Husserl's entire manuscript remains (over 40,000 pages) and his library to Louvain, where the Husserl Archives soon became the center of all Husserl studies and editions.

Under the direction of Father Van Breda, the publications of these manuscripts, as well as definitve edition of previously published works of Husserl, started in 1950. The new collection of Husserl's works is called *Husserliana* and is published in The Hague by Martinus Nijhoff.

Here is a list of all the *Husserliana* volumes published to date. Most of the volumes are preceded by important and substantial introductions.

### *Husserliana*

Volume I. *Cartesianische Meditationen und Pariser Vorträge.* Herausgegeben und eingeleitet von Prof. Dr. S. Strasser, 1950, 224 p. 2. Auflage, 1963. [Text and development of lectures given at La Sorbonne in 1929. Appendix contains remarks by Roman Ingarden, and sent to Husserl in 1932]

Volume II. *Die Idee der Phänomenologie. Fünf Vorlesungen.* Herausgegeben und eingeleitet von Walter Biemel, 1950, 94 p. 2. Auflage 1958. [Text of the 5 lectures given at Göttingen in 1907]

Volume III. *Ideen zu einer reinen Phänomenologie und phänomenologischen Philosophie. Erstes Buch: Allgemeine Einführung in die reine Phänomenologie.* Neue, auf Grund der Handschriftlichen Zusätze des Verfassers erweiterte Auflage. Herausgegeben von Walter Biemel, 1950, 484 p. [Text of the first volume of *Ideen* published in 1913. Also contains additional material written by Husserl between 1914 and 1929 and the analytical index prepared by Ludwig Landgrebe.]

Volume IV. *Ideen zu einer reinen Phänomenologie und phänomenologischen Philosophie. Zweites Buch: Phänomenologische Untersuchungen zur Konstitution.* Herausgegeben von Marly Biemel, 1952, 426 p. [Second volume of *Ideen* which had remained unpublished]

Volume V. *Ideen zur einer reinen Phänomenologie und phänomenologischen Philosophie. Drittes Buch: Die Phänomenologie und die Fundamente der Wissenschaften.* Herausgegeben von Marly Biemel, 1952, 168 p.

Volume VI. *Die Krisis der Europäischen Wissenschaften und die Transzendentale Phänomenologie. Eine Einleitung in die phänomenologische Philosophie.* Herausgegeben von Walter Biemel, 1954, 557 p. 2. Auflage, 1962. [Only the first part had been published in *Philosophia (Belgrade)], vol. I, 1936, 77-176.*

Volume VII. *Erste Philosophie (1923/24).* Erster Teil: Kritische Ideengeschichte. Herausgegeben von Rudolf Boehm, 1956, 468 p. [Not published before]

Volume VIII. *Erste Philosophie (1923/24).* Zweiter Teil: Theorie der phänomenologischen *Reduktion.* Herausgegeben von Rudolf Boehm, 1959, 594 p.

Volume IX. *Phänomenologische Psychologie.* Vorlesungen Sommersemester 1925. Herausgegeben von Walter Biemel, 1961, 650 p. 2. Auflage, 1968.

Volume X. *Zur Phänomenologie des inneren Zeitbewusstseins* (1893-1917). Herausgegeben von Rudolf Boehm, 1966, 484 p.

Volume XI. *Analysen zur passiven Synthesis.* Aus Vorlesungs- und Forschungsmanuskripten 1918-1926. Herausgegeben von Margot Fleischer, 1966, 530 p.

Volume XII. *Philosophie der Arithmetik.* Mit ergänzenden Texten (1890-1901). Herausgegeben von Lothar Eley, 1970, 586 p.

Volume XIII. *Zur Phänomenologie der Intersubjecktivität.* Texte aus dem Nachlass *Erster* Teil: 1905-1920. Herausgegeben von Iso Kern, 1973, 546 p.

Volume XIV. *Zur Phänomenologie der Intesubjektivität.* Texte aus dem Nachlass. Zweiter Teil: 1921-1928. Herausgegeben von Iso Kern, 1973, 624 p.

Volume XV. *Zur Phänomenologie der Intersubjektivität.* Texte aus dem Nachlass. Dritter Teil: 1929-1935. Herausgegeben von Iso Kern, 1973, 741 p.

Volume XVI. *Ding und Raum.* Vorlesungen 1907. Herausgegeben von Ulrich Claesges, 1973, 432 p.

Volume XVII. *Formale und transzendentale Logik. Versuch einer Kritik der logischen Vernunft.* Mit Ergänzenden Texten. Herausgegeben von Paul Janssen, 1974, 432 p.

Volume XVIII. *Logische Untersuchungen.* Erster Band: *Prologemena zur reinen Logik.* Text der 1. und der 2. Auflage. Herausgegeben von Elmar Holenstein, 1975, 288 p.

## B) Works and Publications by Year

The student desiring to follow the development of Husserl's works and publications must consult the detailed, month by month chronique published by Karl Schuhmann, *Husserl-Chronik. Denk- und Lebensweg Edmund Husserls.* The Hague: Martinus Nijhoff, 1977, xxi-516.

### 1882

Beiträge zur Variationsrechnung. Doctral Dissertation (unpublished), Vienna, 1882

### 1887

*Ueber den Begriff der Zahl.* (Habilitationsschrift). Halle: F. Beyer, 1887
  "Über den Begriff der Zahl Psychologische Analysen," in *Husserliana,* vol. XII, 289-338, 1970. "On the concept of number: Psychological analysis," Dallas Willard (trans.), *Philosophica Mathematica,* vol. IX, 1972, 44-52, and vol. X, 1973, 37-87. *see also:* 2741. "Sur le concept de nombre. Analyses psychologiques," in Edmund Husserl, *Philosophie de l'arithmétique. see* year below 1891

### 1891

*Philosophie der Arithmetik, I. Psychologische und logische Untersuchungen.* Halle: Pfeiffer, 1891, xvi-324. [Only the first volume was ever published]
  *Philosophie der Arithmetik.* Mit ergänzenden Texten (1890-1901). Herausgegeben von Lothar Eley, *Husserliana,* XII, 1970, xxix-585.
  *Philosophy of Arithmetic,* José Huertas-Jourda (trans.). The Hague: Martinus Nijhoff, forthcoming.
  *Philosophie de l'arithmétique. Recherches psychologiques et logiques.* Traduction, notes, remarques et index par Jacques English. [En annexe:] Sur le concept de nombre. Analyses psychologiques (Epiméthée). Paris: Presses Universitaires de France, 1972, xiv-464.
"Folgerungskalkül und Inhaltslogik." *Vierteljahrsschrift für Wissenschaftliche Philosophie,* vol. 15, 1891, 168-189, 351-356.
  "The deductive calculus and the logic of contents." *The Personalist,* vol. 60, Jan. 1979, 7-25, Dallas Willard (trans.).
"Besprechung: E. Schröder, *Vorlesungen über die Algebra der Logik, I.*" *Göttingische Gelehrte Anzeigen,* 1891, 243-278.
  "Review of Ernst Schroder's *Vorlesungen über Die Algebra der Logik.*" *The Personalist,* vol. 59, April 1978, 115-143. Dallas Willard (trans.).

## 1890-1913

*Articles sur la logique (1890-1913)*. Traduction, notes, remarques et index par Jacques English (Epiméthée). Paris: Presses Universitaires de France, 1975, 586 p.

## 1893

"A. Voigts Elementare Logik und meine Darlegungen zur Logik der logischen Calculs." *Vieteljahrsschrift für Wissenschaftliche Philosophie*, vol. 17, 1893, 111-120, 508-511.

"A. Voigt's "Elemental Logic" in relation to my statement on the logic of the logical calculus." *The Personalist*, vol. 60, no. 1, Jan. 1979, 26-35. Dallas Willard (trans.).

## 1894

"Psychologische Studien zur elementaren Logik." *Philosophische Monatshefte*, vol. XXX, 159-191.

"Psychological studies in the elements of logic." *The Personalist*, vol. 58, Oct. 1978, 297-320. Dallas Willard (trans.).

## 1897

"Bericht über deutsche Schriften zur Logik aus dem Jahre 1894."

*Archiv für Systematische Philosophie*, vol. III, 1897, 216-244. [Discusses works of Wundt, Glogau, Flügel, Husserl, Jerusalem, Marty, Cornelius, Lipps, Rickert, Erdmann, Mach, Biedermann and Henrici]

## 1900-1901

*Logische Untersuchungen*, Bd. I, 1900, Bd. II, 1901. Halle: Max Niemeyer.

Selbstanzeige: *Vierteljahrsschrift für Wissenschaftliche Philosophie*, Bd. 24, 1900, 511, Bd. 25, 1901, 260-263.

"Selbstanzeigen," Philip J. Bossert and Curtis Peters (trans.), *Introduction to the Logical Investigations*. The Hague: Martinus Nijhoff, 1975. An earlier translation appears in *The Foundation of phenomenology: Edmund Husserl and the quest for a rigorous science of philosophy*, by Marvin Farber. Cambridge: Mass.: Harvard University Press, 1943, 101-102.

*Logische Untersuchungen*. 2 vol.

*Volume I: Prolegomena zur reinen Logik*, Second revised edition, Halle: Max Niemeyer, 1913.

*Volume II: Untersuchungen zur Phänomenologie und Theorie der Erkenntnis.* Second, revised edition, issued in two parts, with the following subtitles:

*Volume II, Part I: Untersuchungen zur Phänomenologie und Theorie der Erkenntnis.* Halle: Max Niemeyer, 1913.

*Volume II: Part 2: Elemente einer phänomenologischen Aufklärung der Erkenntnis.* Halle: Max Niemeyer, 1921.

*Logische Untersuchungen.* Bd. I: *Prolegomena zur reinen Lokik.* Text der I. und der 2. Auflage, Herausgegeben von Elmar Holenstein, *Husserliana* XXVIII, The Hague: Martinus Nijhoff, 1975, liv-289 p.

V. *Logische Untersuchung. Über intentionale Erlebnisse und ihre "Inhalte".* Nach dem Text der I. Auflage von 1901 Herausgegeben, eingeleitet und mit Registern vers. von Elisabeth Ströker (Philosophische Bibliothek, 209). Hamburg: Felix Meiner, 1975, xxxviii-162 p.

*Logical investigations, I-II.* J. N. Findlay (trans.) from the second German edition of *Logische Untersuchungen* (International library of philosophy and scientific method). London: Routledge and Kegan Paul; New York: The Humanities Press, 1970, xviii-435-878 p.

*Introduction to the logical investigations.* A draft of 'A preface to the *Logical investigations*' (1913). Eugen Fink (ed.). Philip J. Bossert and Curtis H. Peters (trans.). The Hague: Martinus Nijhoff, 1975, xxx-61 p.

"The task and the significance of the *Logical Investigations*," in *Readings on E. Husserl's Logical Investigations.* J. N. Mohanty (ed. & trans.). The Hague: Martinus Nijhoff, 1978, 197-215.

*Recherches logiques.* Traduit de l'allemand par Hubert Elie.

T. I: *Prolégomèmens à la logique pure* (Epiméthée. Essais philosophiques. Coll. dirigée par Jean Hyppolite). Paris: Presses Universitaires de France, 1959, xx-286. 2e éd. refondue et corrigée, par Hubert Elie, Arion L. Kelkel et René Schérer. Paris: Presses Univesitataires de France, 1969, xx-304.

T. II: *Recherches pour la phénoménologie et la théorie de la connaissance.* Première partie: (Recherches I et II). Traduit par Hubert Elie avec la collaboration de Lothar Kelkel et René Schérer. Paris: Presses Universitaries de France, 1961, 284 p.

Deuxième partie: *Recherches III, IV et V.* 2e ed. revue et corrigée, Paris: Presses Universitaires de France, 1972, 392 p.

T. III: *Eléments d'une élucidation phénoménologique de la conaissance.* Recherche VI, 2e éd. revue et corrigée, Paris: Presses Universitaires de France, 1974, 322 p. Traduit par Hubert Elie, Arion Lothar Kelkel et René Schérer.

*Investigaciones lógicas.* Trad. por Manuel G. Morrente y José Gaos. 2a ed. Madrid: Revista de Occidente, 1967, 2 vols. 525 p., 571 p. 3a ed. 1976, 784 p.

I: Prolegómenos a las lógica pura. II: Investigaciones para la fenomenología y teoría del conocimiento (Investigaciones I y II). III: Investigaciones para la fenomenología y teoría del conocimiento (Investigaciones III, IV, V). IV: Elementos de un esclarecimiento fenomenológico del conocimiento (Investigacion VI).

"Tarea y significación de las *Investigaciones lógicas.* Trad. de Raúl Velozo F. *Revista Venezolana de Filosofía,* no.4, 1976, 175-203.

*Investigaçñes lógicas.* Sexta investigaçao. Trad. de Z. Loparic. Sao Paulo: Abril Cultural, 1975.

    Vol. I, E. A. Bernstein (Russian trans.), St. Petersburg, 1909.

"Ueber psychologische Begründung der Logik," [Vortrag in der Philosophischen Gesellschaft Halle, 2. Mai 1900.] *Zeitschrift für Philosophische Forschung,* 1959, 346-348.


## 1903

"Bericht über deutsche Schriften zur Logik 1895-1898." *Archiv für Systematische Philosophie,* vol. IX, 1903, 113-132, 237-259, 393-408, 523-543. [Discusses works by A. Marty, J. Bergmann, L. Rabus, R. Heilner, Th. Elsenhans, R. Wrzecionko, H. Gomperz, W. Jerusalem, W. Kinkel, J. von Kries]


## 1904

"Bericht über deutsche Schriften zur Logik 1895-1899." *Archiv für Systematische Philosophie,* vol. X, 1904, 101-125.


## 1906

"Remarks on the articles "Faculté," "Fait," "Fantasie," in Lalande, *Vocabulaire philosophiques." Bulletin de la Société française de philosophie,* 1906, 293, 296, 299.


## 1907

*Die Idee der Phänomenologie. Fünf Vorlesungen.* (Husserliana II). The Hague: Martinus Nijhoff, 1950, xi-97 p.

*The idea of phenomenology.* William P. Alston and George Nakhnikian (trans.). Introduction by George Nakhnikian. The Hague: Martinus Nijhoff, 1964, xxiv-60. Also in *Readings in twentieth century philsophy,* William P. Alston and George Nakhnikian (trans.). London: The Free Press of Glencoe, Collier-Macmillan, 1963, 621-677.

*L'idée de la phoménologie.* Cinq leçons. Traduit de l'allemand par Alexandre Lowit (Epiméthée). Paris: Presses Universitaires de France, 1970, 136 p.

"La idea de la fenomenología. Primera lección. Trad. del alemán por Ricardo G. Maliandi." *Revista de Filosofía,* La Plata, no. 18, 1967, 79-87.

## 1909

"Remarks on the articles "Invididu," and "Intention," in A. Lalande, *Vocabulaire philosophique.*" *Bulletin de la Société française de Philosophie*, 1909, 235, 236.

## 1910-1911

*Grundprobleme der Phänomenologie 1910/11.* Herausgegeben von Iso Kern. The Hague: Martinus Nijhoff, 1977, xiv-136 p.

## 1911

"Philosophie als strenge Wissenschaft." *Logos*, Vol. I, 289-341. Erste deutsche Buchausgabe. Mit Inhaltsanalyse, Nachwort und Anhang vom Herausgegeben Wilhelm Szilasi (Quellen der Philosophie. Texte und Probleme. Herausgegeben von Rudolf Berlinger, I). Frankfurt am Main: Vittorio Klostermann, 1965, 107 p.

*Philosophy as rigorous science.* Quentin Lauer (trans.), in Edmund Husserl, *Phenomenology and the crisis of philosophy.* New York: Harper Torchbooks, 1965, 71-148.

*La philosophie comme science rigoureuse.* Traduction de Quentin Lauer. Paris: Presses Universitaires de France, 1955, 199 p. [Contains an Introduction by Q. Lauer, 1-50]

*La filosofía como sciencia estricta.* Buenos Aires: Universidad de Buenos Aires, 1951, 98 p.; Buenos Nova, 1962, 142 p.

*La filosofia come scienza rigorosa.* Trad., intr. e commento a cura di Filippo Costa (Biblioteca di filosofia e pedogogia). Torino: G. B. Paravia, 1958, xliii-84 p.

## 1913

*Ideen zu einer reinen Phänomenologie und phänomenologischen Philosophie.* I. Teil. *Jahrbuch für Philosophie und phanomenologische Forschung*, Vol. I, Halle, Niemeyer, 1913, 1928. Ausfürliches Index von Gerda Walther, 1923.

*see: Husserliana*, III, IV, V.

*Ideen zu einer reinen Phänomenologie und phänomenologischen Philosophie.* Buch I: *Allgemeine Einführung in die reine Phänomenologie.* Neu herausgegeben von Karl Schumann. I. Halbband. Text der I.-3 Auflage. 2. Halbband: Ergänzende Texte (1912-1929). (Husserliana, III, 1-2). The Hague: Martinus Nijhoff, 1976, lviii-476 p., vii, 477-708 p.

*Ideas.* General introduction to pure phenomenology. W. R. Boyce Gibson (trans.). New York: Macmillan, 1931; London: Allen, 1952, 465 p. ("Muirhead Library of Philosophers"). New York: Collier Books, 1962, 446 p. paper.

[A forthcoming translation, prepared by Fred Kersten, with the assistance of Dorion Cairn's unfinished translation, is entitled *Ideas pertaining to a pure phenomenology and to a phenomenological philosophy: Introduction, Book One, Epilogue.* New York-London: Macmillan.] [The 1931 trans. was preceded by an original Preface of Husserl, later published in German, without serious revisions, under the title "Nachwort zu meinen *Ideen...* (See below for 1930)]

*Idées directrices pour une phénoménologie et une philosophie phénoménologique pures.* Tome premier, Introduction générale à la phénomáologie pure. Traduction de Paul Ricoeur. Paris: Gallimard, 1950, xxxix-561 p. [Contains an important introduction by Ricoeur, a glossary, and Landgrebe's analytical index], 3e ed. 1963.

*Ideas relativas a una fenomenología pura y una filosofía fenomenológica.* Traducción del alemán por José Gaos. México: Fondo de Cultura Económica, 1949, 446 p. 2a ed. México-Buenos Aires: Fondo de Cultura económica, 1962, 529 p.

*Idee per una fenomenologia pura e per una filosofia fenomenologica.* Libro primo: Introduzione generale alla fenomenologia pura. Libro secondo: Ricerche fenomenologiche sopra la costituzione. Libro terzo: La fenomenologia e i fondamenti delle scienze. A cura di Enrico Filippini (Biblioteca di cultura filosofica). Torino: G. Einaudi, 1965, xlv-982 p. Einaudi reprints, 72-74. Facs. dell'ed di Torino del 1965, 1976, xlv, xviii, 982 p.

## 1917

"Die reine Phänomenologie, ihr Forschungsgebiet und ihre Methode. Freiburge Antrittsvorlesung [Herausgegeben und mit Vor Bemerkung von Samuel IJsseling]. *Tijdschrift voor Filosofie,* vol. 38, 1976, 363-378 p.

    "Pure phenomenology, its method and its field of investigation," ("Antrittsrede: May 3, 1917")," Robert Welch Jordan (trans.), in *Life-world and consciousness:* Essays for Aron Gurwitsch, Lester E. Embree (ed.). Evanston, Ill.: Northwestern University Press, 1972, 4-18 p.

"Adolf Reinach. Ein Nachruf." *Frankfurter Zeitung,* Dec. 6, 1917

## 1919

"Erinnerungen an Franz Brentano," in Oskar Krauss, *Franz Brentano.* Munich, 1919, 153-167 p.

"Adolf Reinach. Ein Nachruf." *Kantstudien,* vol 23, 1919, 147-149 p. "Adolf Reinach." Lucinda V. Brettler (trans.). *Philosophy and Phenomenological Research,* vol. 35, 1974-1975, 571-574 p.

## 1922

"Syllabus of a course of four lectures on 'Phenomenological method and phenomenological philosophy'." (M ll3b/2b-11b) *Journal of the British Society for Phenomenology,* vol. 1, no. 1, 1970, 18-23 [Lectures were delivered at University College, London, June 6, 8, 9, 12, 1922]

## 1923

"Erneuerung. Ihr Problem und ihre Methode." Japanische Zeitschrift *Kaizo,* 1923, 84-92.

"Die Idee einer philosophischen Kultur." *Japanisch-deutschen Zietschrift für Wissenschaft und Technik,* 1923, 1, 45-51.

> [Full title is:] "Die Idee einer philosophischen Kultur. Ihr erste Aufkeimen in der grieshischen Philosophie." *Japanisch-deutschen Zeitschrift für Wissenschaft und Technik,* 45-51.

## 1923-1924

*Erste Philosophie* (1923/34). Erster Teil: *Kritische Ideengeschichte.* Herausgegeben von Rudolf Boehm (Husserliana, VII). The Hague: Martinus Nijhoff, 1956, xxxiv-468. *Zweiter Teil: Theorie der phänomenologischen Reduktion.* Herausgegeben von Rudolf Boehm (Husserliana, VIII). The Hague: Martinus Nijhoff, 1959, xliii-594 p.

*Philosophie première,* (1923-24). Première partie: *Histoire critique des ids;* Deuxième partie: *Théorie de la réduction phénoménologique,* traduit de l'allemand par Ariel L. Kelkel. Paris: Presses Universitaires de France, 1970 et 1972, 2 vols. 374 et xlvi-328. [Pages VII-XLVI of volume II, contains an important "Avant-propos du traducteur" locating these lectures in the evolution of Husserl from *Ideen* to *Krisis.*

## 1924

"Die Methode der Wesenforschung," *Kaizo,* Heft 2, 1924, 107-116.

"Erneuerung als individualethisches Problem." *Kaizo,* Heft, 3, 1924, 2-31.

## 1925

*Phänomenologische Psychologie.* Vorlesungen Sommersemester 1925. Herausgegeben von Walter Biemel (Husserliana, IX). The Hague: Martinus Nijhoff, 1962, xxvii-652.

*Phenomenological psychology.* Lectures, Summer semester, 1925. John Scanlon (trans.). The Hague: Martinus Nijhoff, 1977, xvi-186 p.

"Über die Reden Gotama Buddhos." *Piperbot,* Frühling 1925, II/1, 8-19.

## 1918-1926

*Analysen zur passiven Synthesis.* Aus Vorlesungs- und Forschungsmanuskripten 1918-1926. Herausgegeben von Margot Fleischer (Husserliana, XI). The Hague: Martinus Nijhoff, 1966, xxiv-532.

## 1927

"Phenomenology." *Encyclopedia Britannica,* 1927, 14th ed. vol. XVII, 699-702. Richard E. Palmer (trans.). *Journal of the British Society for Phenomenology,* vol. 2, 1971, 77-90. An earlier "translation," by Christopher V. Salmon, appears in the *Encyclopedia Britanica,* 14th ed., vol. XVII, col. 699-702.

The original German text, "Phänomenologie," appears in *Husserliana,* IX, 1962.

"Die Phänomenologie und Rudolf Eucken." *Die Tatwelt,* 1927, 10-11.

## 1928

"Vorlesungen zur Phänomenologie des inneren Zeitbewusstseins. Herausgegeben von Martin Heidegger." *Jahrbuch für Philosophie und phänomenologische Forschung,* vol. IX, 1928, 367-497. An offprint appeared in Halle: Niemeyer, 1938

*Zur Phänomenologie des inneren Zeitbewusstseins* (1893-1917). Herausgegeben von Rudolf Boehm (Husserliana, X). The Hague: Martinus Nijhoff, 1966, xliv-484.

*The phenomenology of internal time-consciousness.* Martin Heidegger (ed.). James S. Chruchill (trans.). Introduction by Calvin O. Schrag. The Hague: Martinus Nijhoff, 1964, 188 p. Bloomington: Indiana University Press, 1964, 188 p.

*Leçons pour une phénoménologie de la conscience intime du temps.* Traduit de l'allemand par Henri Dussort. Préface de Gérard Granel (Epiméthée. Essais philosophiques. Coll. dirigée par Jean Hyppolite). Paris: Presses Universitaires de France, 1964, xii-208.

*Fenomenología de la conciencia del tiempo inmanente.* Trad. directa de Otto E. Langfelder. [Estudio preliminar sobre] "El Tiempo en Husserl y en Heidegger," por Ivonne Picard. Trad. de Elsa Tabernig (Col. La vida del espiritu). Buenos Aires: Edit. Nova, 1959, 212 p.

## 1929

*Formale und transzendentale Logik. Jahrbuch für Philosophie und Phänomenologische Forschung* vol. X, 1929, xi-298.

*Formale und transzendentale Logik. Versuch einer Kritik der logischen Vernunft.* Mit ergänzenden Texten herausgegeben von Paul Janssen (Husserliana, XVII). The Hague: Martinus Nijhoff, 1974, xlv-512.

*Formale und transzendentale Logik, I-II.* Versuch einer Kritik der logischen Vernunft. Herausgegeben von Paul Janssen. The Hague: Martinus Nijhoff, 1977, xii-146.

*Formal and transcendental logic.* Dorion Cairns (trans.). The Hague: Martinus Nijhoff, 1969, xx-340.

*Logique formelle et logique transcendentale.* Essai d'une critique de la raison logique. Traduit de l'allemand par Suzanne Bachelard (Coll. "Epiméthée"). 2e éd. Paris: Presses Universitaires de France, 1965, 448 p. ["Introduction" by S. Bachelard, 1-25]

*Logica formale e trascendentale.* Saggio di critica della ragione logica. Traduzione, avvertenza, nota aggiunta e note a cura di Guido D. Neri. Prefazione di Enzo Paci (Classici della filosofia moderna). Bari: Laterza, 1966, xvi-432.

*Pariser Vortäage.* [Lectures at La Sobonne, 1929] See *Husserliana* I.

*Pariser Vorträge. Husserliana,* I. The Hague: Martinus Nijhoff, 1950.

*The Paris lectures.* Peter Koestenbaum (trans. from German). With an introductory essay. The Hague: Martinus Nijhoff, 1964, lxxvii-39 2e ed. 1967.

"Syllabus for the Paris Lectures or "Introduction to transcendental phenomenology." [Husserls Inhaltsübersicht im Urtext," in *Husserliana,* vol. I, 1950]," Herbert Spiegelberg (trans.), *Journal of the British Society for Phenomenology,* 1975.

*Meditazioni cartesiane e i Discorsi parigini.* Traduzione e introduzione di Filippo Costa ("Idee muove, XXXI). Milano: V. Bompiani, 1960, xiv-216.

### 1930

"Nachwort zu meinen *Ideen zu einer reinen Phänomenologie." Jahrbuch für Philosophie und phänomenologische Forschung,* vol. XI, 1930, 549-570. Published in Halle: Niemeyer, 1930.

"Postface à mes '*Idées directrices pour une phénoménologie pure'*. Traduction et notes par L. Kelkel." *Revue de Métaphysique et de Morale,* vol. 62, no. 4, 1957, 369-398.

"Stephan Strasser's "Introduction" to *Husserliana,* Vol. I, Thomas Attig (trans.), *Journal of the British Society for Phenomenology,* vol. 7, no. 1, Jan. 1976, 12-17.

"Husserl's Syllabus for his Paris Lectures on "Introduction to transcendental phenomenology," Introduction by Herbert Spiegelberg (18-20), and text, 20-24. *Journal of the British Society for Phenomenology,* vol. 7, no. 1, Jan. 1976, 18-24.

*Cartesianische Meditationen* und *Pariser Vorträge.* Herausgegeben von eingeletet von S. Strasser (Husserliana, I). The Hague: Martinus Nijhoff, 1950, xxxii-249.

*Cartesianische Meditationen. Eine Einleitung in die Phänomenologie.* Herausgegeben, eingel. u. mit Registern versehen von Elisabeth Ströker (Philosophische Bibliothek, 291). Hamburg: Felix Meiner Verlag, 1977, xxxiv-174.

*Cartesian meditations. An introduction to phenomenology.* Dorion Cairns (trans.). New York: Humanities Press, 1966, 157 p. The Hague: Martinus Nijhoff, 1966. 3rd impression. The Hague: Martinus Nijhoff, 1969.

*Méditations cartésiennes. Introduction à la phénoménologie.* Paris: A. Colin, 1931. Paris: J. Vrin, 1947. Gabrielle Pfeiffer and Emmanuel Levinas (trans.). Paris: J. Vrin, 1969, viii-136.

*Meditazioni y cartesiane e i Discorsi parigini.* Traduzione e introduzione di Filippo Costa ("Idee nuove, 31). Milano: V. Bompiani, 1960, xvi-216. 2a edizione riveduta, 1970.

"Textes tirés du groupe E et lettre à Misch de 1930," *Les Etudes Philosophiques,* July-Sept. 1954.

## 1933

"Vorwort," Eugen Fink, *Studien zu Phänomenologie 1930-1939.* (Phaenomenologica, 21). The Hague: Martinus Nihoff, 1966.

## 1935

"Die Krisis des europäischen Menschentums und die Philosphie," in *Husserliana, VI,* 1954. Jean T. Wilde and William Kimmel (trans.), "The crisis of European humanity and Philosophy," in *The Search for Being: Essays from Kierkegaard to Sartre on the problem of existence,* Jean T. Wilde and William Kimmel (eds.). New York: Twayne, 1962, 378-413.

"Philosophy and the crisis of European man" in *Phenomenology and the crisis of philosophy.* Philosophy as rigorous science and Philosophy and the crisis of European man. With notes and an introduction Quentin Lauer (trans.), (Harper Torchbooks. The Academy Library. TB 1170). New York: Harper & Row, 1965, 192 p.

*La crise de l'humanité européenne et la philosophie.* Traduit de l'allemand par Paul Ricoeur. Préface de Stephan Strasser (Conférence prononcée à Vienne le 7 mai 1935. Reproduit en fac-similé d'un extrait de la *Revue de Métaphysique et de Morale,* 1950, no. 3, 225-258). (Republications Paulet, 2). Paris: Paulet, 1968, 225-260. Also, Paris: La Pensée sauvage: L'Impensé radical, 1975, xxi-31.

*La crise de l'humanité européenne et la philosophie.* Edition bilingue. Traduction: Paul Ricoeur. Préface du Dr. S. Strasser, avec, en postface, un essai de J.-M. Guirao: Contribution à la constitution d'une Grammaire de Husserl (La Philosophie en poche). Paris: Aubier Montaigne, 1977, 176 p.

## 1936

"Brief an den VIII. internationalen Kongress für Philosophie in Prag," in *Proceedings of the Eighth International Congress of Philosophy,* Prague, 1936, xli-xlv. *Travaux du VIIIe Congrés international de Philosophie,* Prague, 1936.

"Die Krisis der europäischen Wissenschaften un die transzendentale Phänomenologie," I. Teil. Philosophia, *Belgrad,* Vol. I, 1936, 77-176.

*Die Krisis der europäischen Wissenschaften und die transzendentale Phänomenologie. Eine Einleitung in die phänomenologische Philosophie.* Herausgegeben von Walter Biemel (Husserliana, VI), xxii-559.

*Die Krisis der europäischen Wissenschaften und die transzendentale Phänomenologie. Eine Einleitung in die phänomenologische Philosophie.* Herausgegeben, eingeleitet und mit Registern versehen von Elisabeth Ströker (Philosophische Bibliothek, 292). Hamburg: Felix Meiner Verlag, 1977, xxxii-120.

*The crisis of European sciences and transcendental phenomenology. An introduction to phenomenological philosophy.* With an introduction by David Carr (trans.), (Studies in phenomenology and existential philosophy). Evanston, Ill.: Northwestern University Press, 1970, xliii-406.

"La crise des sciences européennes et la phénoménologie transcendentale." Traduction française, Gaston Berger. *Etudes Philosophiques,* vol. 4, 1949, 127-157, 229-301. [Text from *Philosophia,* I, 1936]

*La crise des sciences européennes et la phénoménologie transcendentale.* Traduit de l'allemand et préfacé par Gérard Granel (Bibliothèque de Philosophie). Paris: Gallimard, 1976, ix-589.

"La crise des sciences européenes, para. 21 à 24. Traduction française de G. Granel." *Annales de l'Université de Toulouse-Le Mirail,* 1973, vol. 9, no. 6, 1973, 23-31.

*La crisi delle scienze europee e la fenomenologia transcendentale.* Introduzione alla filosofia fenomenologica. A cura di Walter Biemel. Traduzione di Enrico Filippini. Avvertenza di Enzo Paci (Collano "La Cultura," 35). Milano: Il Saggiatore, 1961, 548.

## 1939

*Erfahrung und Urteil. Untersuchungen zur Genealogie der Logik.* Ausgearbeitet und herausgegeben von Ludwig Landgrebe. Prag: Academia-Verlag, 1939, xxiv-478. Reprinted Hamburg: Claasen & Goverts, 1948.

*Erfahrung und Urteil.* Mit Nachwort und Reister von Lothar Eley (Philosophische Bibliothek, 280). Hamburg: Felix Meiner Verlag, 1972, xxviii-532.

*Experience and judgment.* Investigations in genealogy of logic. Ludwig Landgrebe (Rev. and ed.). James S. Churchill and Karl Ameriks (trans.). Introduction by James S. Churchill. Afterword by Lothar Eley (Northwestern University Studies in phenomenology and existential philosophy). Evanston, Ill.: Northwestern University Press, 1973, xxxi-443. London: Routledge & Kegan Paul, 1973, xxvii-444.

*Expérience et jugement. Recherches en vue d'une généalogie de la logique.* Traduit de l'allemand par D. Souche (Epiméthée). Paris: Presses Universitaires de France, 1970, 500.

*Experienza e giudizio.* Ricerche sulla genealogia della logica. Pubblicate e redatte da Ludwig Landgrebe. Trad. ital. di F. Costa (Collana filosofica). Milano: Silva, 1960, 469. 2a ed. Milano: Silva, 1965, xx-469.

"Entwurf einer Vorrede zu den *Logischen Untersuchungen." Tijdschrift voor Filosofie,* vol.I, 1939, 319-320.

*Introduction to the "Logical Investigations,"* Philip J. Bossert and Curtis Peters (trans.). A draft of "A preface to the *Logical Investigations* (1913). Eugen Fink (ed.). The Hague: Martinus Nijhoff, 1975, xxx-6l.

"Die Frage nach dem Ursprung der Geometrie als intentional-historisches Problem (Introduction by Eugen Fink)." *Revue Internationale de Philosophie,* vol. I, no. 2, 1938-1939, 203-225. Reprinted in *Husserliana,* VI, 365-386.

J, Derrida, *Edmund Husserl's 'Origin of geometry';* An introduction. John P. Leavey, Jr. (trans.). Stony Brook, N.Y.: Nicolas Hays, i978. [*see also:* 2748]

*L'origine de la géométrie.* Traduction et introduction par Jacques Derrida. (Epiméthée). Paris: Presses Universitaires de France, 1962, iv-220. 2e éd. Revue 1974.

*Over de oorsprong van de meetkunde.* Vertaald door dr. j. Duytschaever. Ingeleid en geannoteerd dor dr. Rudolf Boehm (Dixit). Baarn: Het Wereldvenster, 1977, 127 p.

## 1940

"Grundlegende Untersuchungen zum phänomenologischen Ursprung der Räumlichkeit der Natur," in *Philosophical essays in memory of Edmund Husserl,* Marvin Farber (ed.). Cambridge, Mass.: Harvard University Press, 1940, 305-326. [Manuscript composed around May 1934. The manuscript is continued by "Notizen sur Raumkonstitution." *see below*

"Notizen sur Raumkonstitution." *Philosophy and Phenomenological Research,* vol. I, 1940-1941, 23-37, 217-226. [With a preface by Alfred Schuetz 21-23] [Manuscript written in May 1934. It continues the above manuscript composed at the same time and treating of the same topic]

## 1941-1942

"Phänomenologie und anthropologie." *Philosophy and Phenomenological Research,* vol. II, 1941-42, 1-14. [Lectures given in the Kantgesellschaft of Frankfurt (1 June 1931), also in Berlin (l0 June 1931) and in Halle (16 June 1931)]

"Phenomenology and anthropology," Richard G. Schmitt (trans.), in *Realism and the background of phenomenology,* Roderick M. Chisholm (ed.). Glencoe: The Free Press, 1960, 129-142. [Lectures given in the Kantgesellschaft of Frankfurt (1 June 1931), also in Berlin (10 June 1931) and in Hale (16 June 1931)]

**1945-1946**

"Die Welt der lebendigen Gegenwart und die Konstitution der ausserleiblichen Umwelt," Alfred Schuetz (ed.). *Philosophy and Phenomenological Research,* vol. 6, 1946, 323-343.

**1949**

"Husserl." (Article written by Eugen Fink but submitted by Husserl himself). *Philosophenlexikon,* herausgegeben von W. Ziegenfuss. Berlin: Walter de Gruyter, T. I 1949, 569-576.

### C) Texts and Translations Published Since 1950

"La philosophie comme prise de conscience de l'humanité." *Deucalion,* no. 3, 1950, 116-127. [Traduction d'un inédit par Paul Ricoeur, avec introduction de Walter Biemel, 109-115]

"Réflexions (Introduction par W. Biemel, traduction de P. Ricoeur)." *Esprit et Vie,* Dec. 1950, 446-449.

"Shaw und die Lebenskraft des Abandlandes." *Hamburger Akademische Rundschau,* vol. 3, 1950, 743-744.

"Rapport entre la phénoménologie et les sciences." *Les Etudes Philosophiques,* vol. 4, 1949, 3-7. [According to W. Biemel, this would be a sort of introduction to *Ideen* III]

"The course of my life," ("Lebenslauf"), A. D. Osborn (trans.), in *Edmund Husserl and his Logical investigations,* 2nd. ed. by A. D. Osborn, Cambridge, Mass.: Harvard University Press, 1949, 110 p.

"Ueber psychologische Bergründung der Lokig." Ein unveröffentlichter Eigenbericht Husserls über einen von ihm gehaltenen Vortrag, herausgegeben von Hans Reiner." *Zeitschrift für Philosophische Forschung,* vol. 13, no. 2, 1959, 346-348.

"Anmerkungen zu Begriffsschrift G. Freges," in Gottlob Frege, *Bergriffschrift und andere Aufsätze.* 2. Aufl. Mit E. Husserl und H. Scholz' Anmerkungen herausgegeben von Ignacio Angelelli. Hildesheim: Olms, 1964.

"Dal manoscrito inedito K III 28. Dal manoscrito inedito K III 26." *Archivio di Filosofia,* no.1, 1954, 168-175.

"Du manuscrit inédit K III 28," and "Du manuscrit inédit K III 26," in *La philosophie de l'histoire de la philosophie.* Roma: Istituto di Studi Filosofici; Paris: J. Vrin, 1956, 124-129, 129-131.

(Deux textes de Husserl sur la méthode et le sens le sens de la phénoménologie). I. Marche de la pensée phénoménologique 1907 [traduction de *Husserliana* II, 3-14] II. Avant-propos à la suite de la '*Crisis*' (1937) [traduction de *Husserlina* VI, 435-445] Textes traduit et présentés par Henri Dussort." *Revue Philosophique de la France et de l'Etranger,* vol. 84, 1959, no. 4, 433-462.

"L'esprit collectif (Extrait des 'Inédits" de Husserl) [traduit par R. Toulemont]."
Cahiers Internationaux de Sociologie, vol. 27, 121-130.

"Universale teleologie (Inedito E III 5). Testo e trad. italiana a cura di E. Paci." Archivio
di Filosofia, no. 1, 1960, 13-16. Also in Enzo Paci, Tempo e verità nella
fenomenologia di Husserl. Bari, 1961, (Husserliana, XV, 1973).

"Universal teleology," Severin Schurger (trans.). Telos, no. 4, 1969, 176-180.
[Translation of Manuscript E III 5 written by Husserl in the 1930's]

"La fenomenologia." Semirrecta, vol. i, no. 3, 1952-53, 3-9.

"A reply to a critic of my refutation of logical psychologism." Dallas Willard (trans.).
The Personalist, vol. 53, 1972, 5-13. Reprinted in Readings on E. Husserl's Logical
investigations, J. N. Mohanty (ed.). The Hague: Martinus Nijhoff, 1978, 33-42.

"Kant and the idea of transcendental philosophy." Ted E. Klein and William E. Pohl
(trans.). Southern Journal of Philosophy, vol. 5, 1974, 9-56. ["Kant und die Idee
der Transzendentalphilosophie," VII, 1956] [An expanded version of a lecture
Husserl gave at Freiburg on May 1, 1924, at a celebration of the 200th anniversary
of Kant's birth. It was first published in German as a "Supplementary text" to
Erste Philosophie 1923/24.]

"The Method of clarification" ("Die Methode der Klarung," in Husserliana V, 1952),
Ted E. Klein and William E. Pohl (trans.). Southwestern Journal of Philosophy,
vol. 5, 1974, 57-67. [Translation of Chapter IV of Husserl's Ideen, Volume III.
It is based upon a manuscript of 1912, published in Husserliana V]

"Il problema de la negatividad." Revista Venezolana de Filosofía, 1976, 175-203.

### D) Anthologies

La fenomenologia trascendentale Antologia a cura di Alfredo Marini (Pensatori antichi
e moderni, 89). Firenze: La Nuova Italia, 1974, xlviii-318.

Logica, psicologia, filosofia. Pagine scelte e tradotte da A. Masullo. Napoli: Edizione
Il Tripode, 1961, 160 p.

La fenomenologia. A cura di Carlo Sini (Filosofi e scienziati, 3). Palermo: Palumbo,
1966, 156 p.

Edmund Husserl. Selection of articles. Hugo Bergman and Nathan Rotenstreich (eds.).
(Philosophical Classics) [in Hebrew]. Jerusalem: At Magnes Press, The Hebrew
University, 1952, xi-186.

### E) Conversations, Correspondence, Reminiscences

Conversations with Husserl and Fink, by Dorion Cairns. The Hague: Martinus Nijhoff,
1976, xiv-114. [Edited by the Husserl-Archives in Louvain. With a foreword by
Richard M. Zaner (Phaenomenologica, 66).

"Excerpts from a 1928 Freiburg diary by W. R. Boyce Gibson," Herbert Spiegelberg
(ed.). Journal of the British Society for Phenomenology, vol. 2, 1971, 63-81.

Husserl, Edmund. "Reminiscences of Franz Brentano," in *The Philosophy of Brentano.* With an introduction by Linda L. McAlister (ed.). London: G. Duckworth, 1976, 47-56.

### F) Letters from Husserl

"Brief an Dorion Cairns (21. März 1930)," in *Edmund Husserl 1859-1959* (Phaenomenologica, 4). The Hague: Martinus Nijhoff, 1959, 283-285.

Dilthey-Husserl. "En torno a la filosofía como ciencia estricta y al alcance del historicismo. Correspondencia entre Dilthey y Husserl de 29 junio, 5/6 julio y 10 julio de 1911 (Edición, introducción y notas por Walter Biemel)." *Revista de Filosofía de la Universidad de Costa Rica,* vol. 1, no. 2, 1957, 101-124.

"Letter to Marvin Farber" ("Brief an Marvin Farber"), Marvin Farber (trans.), in "Edmund Husserl and the background of his philosophy," by Marvin Farber, *Philosophy and Phenomenological Research,* vol. I, 1940, 13 p.

"The Frege-Husserl correspondence," J. N. Mohanty (trans.). [Letter to Frege: July 18, 1891 ("Brief an Frege"). *Southwestern Journal of Philosophy,* vol. 5, 1974, 83-95, [86-87].

Frege, Gottlob. *The Philosophical and mathematical correspondence.* Brian McGuiness (ed.), Hans Kaal (trans.). Basil Blackwell Pub., Oxford, 1979. [Draws together all the extant letters of Frege and his correspondents that bear upon Frege's mathematical work. Husserl, Hilbert, Peano are among the correspondents whose letters appear here].

"Letter to Aron Gurwitsch: April 15, 1932," Lester E. Embree (trans.), in *Life-world and consciousness:* Essays for Aron Gurwitsch, Lester E. Embree (ed.). Evanston, Ill.: Northwestern University Press, 1972, xv p.

"Letter to G. Dawes Hicks: March 15, 1930," Wolfe Mays (trans.), in "Husserl on Ryle's review of *Sein und Zeit,*" by Wolfe Mays. *Journal of the British Society for Phenomenology,* vol. 1, 1970, 14,15.

*Briefe an Roman Ingarden* mit Erläuterungen und Erinnerungen an Husserl. Herausgegeben von Roman Ingarden (Phaenomenologica, 25). The Hague: Martinus Nijhoff, 1968, ix-186.

"Drei unveröffentlichte Briefe von Husserl an Ingarden." *Zeitschrift für Philosophische Forschung,* vol. 13, no. 2, 1959, 349-351.

"Letter to Roman Ingarden: November 19, 1927 [from *Briefe an Roman Ingarden*], Theodore Kisiel (trans.), in "On the dimensions of a phenomenology of science in Husserl and the young Dr. Heidegger," by T. Kisiel, *Journal of the British Society for Phenomenology,* vol. 4, 1973, 228 p.

"Ein Brief Husserl an Theodor Lipps," Karl Schuhmann, *Tijdschrift voor Filosofie,* vol 39, March 1977, 141-150.

"Ein Brief Edmund Husserls an Ernst Mach," Joachim Thiele, *Zeitschrift für Philosophische Forschung*, vol. 19, 1965, 134-138.

"Ein Brief Edmund Husserls von 1919 [an Arnold Metzger auf Grund eines von Metzger gesandten, unveröffentlichten Manuskriptes: *Die Phänomenologie der Revolution* (1919)] *Philosophisches Jahrbuch*, vol. 62, no. 1, 1953, 195-200.

"A letter to Arnold Metzger." Introduced by Erazim V. Kohak (trans.). *The Philosophical Forum*, vol. 21, 1963-1964, 48-68.

"Letter to Arnold Metzger: September 4, 1919," Paul Senft (German-English trans.), with an introduction. *Human Context*, vol. 4, 1972, 244-249, 249-263.

"Letter to Hugo Münsterberg ("Brief an Hugo Münsterberg"), Hugo Münsterberg (trans.), in *The Peace and America*, by Hugo Münsterberg. New York: D. Appleton, 1915, 222-224.

"Ein Brief von Husserl an Stoltenberg (Faksimile-Wiedergabe)." *Zeitschrift für Philosophische Forschung*, vol. 13, no. 2, 179-180.

"Letter to E. Parl Welch: June 17-21, 1933," ("Brief an E. Parl Welch"), Herbert Spiegelberg (German-English trans.), in "Husserl's way into phenomenology for Americans," by H. Spiegelberg, in *Phenomenology: Continuation and criticism*, Fred Kersten and Richard Zaner (eds.). The Hague: Martinus Nijhoff, 1973, 171-181.

### G) Editorial Work

*Jahrbuch für Philosophie und Phänomenologische Forschung.* In Gemeinschaft mit M. M. Geiger (München), A. Pfänder (München), A. Reinach (Göttingen), M. Scheler (Berlin), herausgegeben von E. Husserl. Halle a. s.,: M. Niemeyer-Verlag.

I. Bd., 1913, xii-847. E. Husserl, *Ideen* I. A. Pfänder, *Zur Psychologie der Gesinnungen* I. M. Geiger, *Beiträge zur Phänomenologie des ästetischen Genusses.* M. Scheler, *Der Formalismus in der Ethik und die materiale Wertethik* I. A. Reinach, *Die apriorischen Grundlagen des bürgerlichen Rechtes.*

II. Bd., 1916, viii-478. P. F. Linke, Phänomenologie und Experiment in der Frage der Bewegungsuaffassung. M. Scheler, Der Formalismus in der Ethik und die materiale Wertethik II.

III. Bd., 1916, vi-542. A. Pfänder, Zur Psychologie der Gesinnungen. D. v. Hildebrand, Die Idee der sittlichen Handlung. H. Ritzel, Ueber analytische Urteile. H. Conrad-Martinus, Zur Ontologie und Erscheinungslehre der realen Ausswelt.

IV. Bd., 1921, x-499. M. Geiger, Fragment über den Begriff des Unbewussten und die psychische Realität. A. Pfänder, Logik. J. Hering, Bemerkungen über d. Wesen, die Wesenheit und die Idee. R. Ingarden, Ueber die Gefahr einer Petitio principii in der Erkenntnistheorie.

V. Bd., xvi-628. E. Stein, Beiträge zur philosophischen Begründung der Psychologie und der Geisteswissenschaften. R. Ingarden, Intuition und Intellekt bei H. Bergson. D. v. Hildebrand, Sittlichkeit und ethische Werturteile. A. Koyré, Bermerkungen zu den Zenonischen Paradoxen.

VI. Bd., 1923, x-571. G. Walther, Zur Ontologie der sozialen Gemeinschaften. H. Conrad-Martius, Realtontologie. Fritz London, Ueber die Bedingungen der Möglichkeit einer deduktiven Theorie. O. Becker, Beiträge zur phänomenologischen Begründung der Geometrie und ihrer physikalischen Anwendungen. H. Lipps, Die Paradoxien der Mengenlehre.

VII. Bd., 1925, x-770. E. Stein, Eine Untersuchung über den Staat. R.Ingarden, Essentiale Fragen. Ein Beitrag zu dem Wesensproblem. D. Mahnke, Leibnizens Synthese von Universalmathematik und Individualmetaphysik. A. Metzger, Der Gegenstand der Erkenntnis. Studien zur Phänomenologie des Gegenstandes, I. Teil.

VIII. Bd., 1927, xii-810. M. Heidegger, Sein und Zeit I. O. Becker, Mathematische Existenz.

IX. Bd., 1928, x-498. Fritz Kaufmann, Die Philosophie des Grafen P. Yorck von Wurtenburg. L. Landgrebe, W. Diltheys Theorie der Geisteswissenschaften. E. Husserl, Vorlesungen zur Phänomenologie des inneren Zeitbewusstseins (herausgegeben M. Heidegger).

X. Bd., 1929, xvii-569. E. Husserl, Formale und transzendentale Logik. C. V. Salmon, The central problem of David Hume's philosophy.

*Festschrift E. Husserl zum 70. Geburtstag gewidmet.* Ergänzungsband zum *Jahrbuch für Philosophie und Phänomenologische Forschung,* 1929, 370 p. H. Ammann, Zum deutschen Impersonale. O. Becker, Von der Hinfälligkeit des Schönen und der Abenteuerlichkeit des Künstlers. L. Claus, Das Verstehen des sprachlichen Kunstwerks. M. Heidegger, Vom Wesen des Grundes. G. Husserl, Recht und Welt. R. Ingarden, Bemerkungen zum Problem "Idealismus-Realismus." Fritz Kaufmann, Die Bedeutung der künstlerischen Stimmung. A. Koyré, Die Gotteslehre J. Bömes. H. Lipps, Das Urteil. Fr. Neumann, Die Sinneinheit des Satzes und das indogermanische Verbum. E. Stein, Husserls Phänomenologie und die Philosophie des heil. Thomas V. Aquino. H. Conrad-Martius, Farben. Ein Kapitel aus der Realontologie. XI. Bd., 1930, x-570. H. Spiegelberg, Ueber das Wesen der Idee. E. Fink, Vergegenwärtigung und Bild. H. Mörchen, Die Einbildungskraft bei Kant. O. Becker, Zur Logik der Modalitäten. E. Husserl, Machwort zu meinen 'Ideen zu reinen Phänomenologie und phänomenologische Philosophie.

# PART TWO
# BIBLIOGRAPHY ON HUSSERL

## Section 1
### Books Devoted to Husserl

#### Books in English

1    *Analecta Husserliana.* The Yearbook of Phenomenological Research. Anna-Teresa Tymieniecka (ed.). Dordrecht: D. Reidel, vol. 1, 1971. [*see* 0060]

2    Bachelard, Suzanne. *A study of Husserl's Formal and Transcendental Logic.* Lester E. Embree (trans.), (Northwestern University Studies in Phenomenology and Existential Philosophy). Evanston, Ill.: Northwestern University Press, 1968, ix-230.
**Book Reviews:**
P. McCormick, *Journal of the British Society for Phenomenology,* vol. 2, 1971, 87-92.
A. Medina, *New Scholasticism,* vol. 45, 1971, 632-634.
G. J. Stack, *Journal of the History of Philosophy,* vol. 10, 1972, 105-107.
A. W. Wood, *Philosophical Review,* vol. 80, 1971, 267-273.

4    Berger, Gaston. *The cogito in Husserl's philosophy.* Kathleen McLaughlin (trans.). With an introduction by James M. Edie (Northwestern University Studies in Phenomenology and Existential Philosophy). Evanston, Ill.: Northwestern University Press, 1972, xxvii-159.

5    Bossert, Philip, ed. *Phenomenological perspectives.* Historical and systematic essays in honor of Herbert Spiegelberg (Phaenomenologica, 62). The Hague: Martinus Nijhoff, 1975.

6    Cairns, Dorion. *Guide for translating Husserl* (Phaenomenologica, 55). The Hague: Martinus Nijhoff, 1973, x-145.
**Book Reviews:**
D. Carr, *Journal of the British Society for Phenomenology,* vol. 7, Jan. 1976, 65-66.
R. Sokolowski, *Review of Metaphysics,* vol. 27, 1973-1974, 787-788.

Dorion Cairns, *Conversations with Husserl and Fink.* Edited by the Husserl-Archives in Louvain. With a foreword by Richard M. Zaner (Phaenomenologica, 66). The Hague: Martinus Nijhoff, 1976, xiv-114.

David Carr, *Phenomenology and the problem of history.* A study of Husserl's transcendental philosophy (Northwestern University Studies in Phenomenology an Existential Philosophy). Evanston, Ill.: Northwestern University Press, 1974, xxvi-283.

**Book Reviews:**

T. Attig, *Journal of the British Society for Phenomenology,* vol. 7, Jan. 1976, 66-67.

J. L. Marsh, *Modern Schoolman,* vol. 54, 1976-1977, 67-69.

Sang-Ki Kim. *Philosophy and Phenomenological Research,* vol. 36, 1975-1976, 578-580.

R. Sokolowski, *Review of Metaphysics,* vol 28, March 1975, 547-548.

P. Tummons, *Telos,* no. 23, Spring 1975, 185-187.

J. J. Valone, *International Philosophical Quarterly,* vol. 17, March 1977, 109-111.

9      Cunningham, Suzanne. *Language and the phenomenological reductions of Edmund Husserl* (Phaenomenologica, 70). The Hague: Martinus Nijhoff, 1976, x-102.

**Book Reviews:**

M. Lavoie, *Laval Théologique et Philosophique,* vol. 33, Oct. 1977, 321-326.

C. O. Schrag, *Review of Metaphysics,* vol. 31, Dec. 1977, 314-315.

10     de Muralt, André. *The idea of phenomenology.* Husserlian exemplarism. Gary L. Breckon (trans.), (Northwestern University Studies in Phenomenology and Existential Philosophy). Evanston, Ill.: Northwestern University Press, 1974, xxiii-411.

11     Derrida, Jacques. *Speech and phenomena, and other essays on Husserl's theory of signs.* With an introduction by David B. Allison (trans.). Preface by Newton Garver (Northwestern University Studies in Phenomenology and Existential Philosophy). Evanston, Ill.: Northwestern University Press, 1973, xlii-166.

**Book Reviews:**

P. Clifford, *Journal of the British Society for Phenomenology,* vol. 6, 203.

R. Sokolowski, *Review of Metaphysics,* vol. 27, 1973-1974, 123-124.

12     Dreyfus, Hubert L. *Husserl's phenomenology of perception* (Northwestern University Studies in Phenomenology and Existential Philosophy). Evanston, Ill.: Northwestern University Press, 1978.

13     Elliston, Frederick A., and McCormick, Peter (eds.). *Husserl. Expositions and appraisals.* Notre Dame, Ind. and London: University of Notre Dame Press, 1977, xvii-378. Contents:

Editor's Introduction, 2-9.

Dallas Willard, "The paradox of logical psychologism," 10-17.

J. N. Mohanty, "Husserl's theory of meaning," 18-37.

H. Pietersma, "Husserl's views on the evident and the true," 38-53.

D. Welton, "Structure and genesis in Husserl's phenomenology," 54-69.

E. S. Casey, "Imagination and phenomenological method," 70-82.

J. B. Brough, "The emergence of an absolute consciousness in Husserl's early writings on time-consciousness," 83-100.

L. Landgrebe, "Phenomenology as transcendental theory of history," 101-113.

H. L. Van Breda, "A note on reduction and authenticity according to Husserl," 124-125.

I. Kern, "The three ways to the transcendental phenomenological reduction in the philosophy of Husserl," 126-149.

J. Patocka, "The Husserlian doctrine of eidetic intuition and its recent critics," 150-159.

F. A. Olafson, "Husserl's theory of intentionality in contemporary perspective," 160-167.

R. C. Solomon, "Husserl's concept of the noema," 168-181.

C. Van Peursen, "The horizon," 182-201.

D. Carr, "Husserl's problematic concept of the life-world," 202-212.

F. A. Elliston, "Husserl's phenomenology of empathy," 213-231.

G. B. Madison, "Phenomenology and existentialism: Husserl and the end of idealism," 247-268.

J. J. Kockelmans, "Husserl and Kant on the pure ego," 269-285.

W. Biemel, "Husserl's *Encyclopaedia Britannica* article and Heidegger's remarks thereon," 286-303.

M. W. Wartofsky, "Consciousness, praxis, and reality: Marxism vs. phenomenology," 304-313.

G. Frege, "Review of Dr. E. Husserl's *Philosophy of arithmetic,*" 313-324.

E. Tugendhat, "Phenomenology and linguistic analysis," 325-337.

G. Küng, "Phenomenological reduction as epoché and explication," 338-349.

P. McCormick, "Phenomenology and metaphilosophy," 350-365.

14  Elveton, R. O. (ed.). *The phenomenology of Husserl.* Selected critical readings. With an introduction by R. O. Elveton (ed. & trans.). Chicago: Quadrangle Books, 1970, 305 p. Contents:

R. O. Elveton, "Introduction," 3-39.

O. Becker, "The philosophy of Edmund Husserl," 40-72.

E. Fink, "The phenomenological philosophy of Edmund Husserl and contemporary criticism," 73-147.

W. Biemel, "The decisive phases in the development of Husserl's philosophy," 148-173.

R. Boehm, "Husserl's concept of the 'absolute'," 174-203.

H. Wagner, "Critical observations concerning Husserl's posthumous writings," 204-258.

L. Landgrebe, "Husserl's departure from Cartesianism," 259-303.

15      Embree, Lester E. (ed.). *Life-world and consciousness.* Essays for Aron
        Gurwitsch (Northwestern University Studies in Phenomenology and
        Existential Philosophy). Evanston, Ill.: Northwestern University Press,
        1972, xxx-610. Contents:

        E. Husserl, "Translation of letter from Edmund Husserl to Aron Gurwitch.
        Lester E. Embree (trans.), xv.

        E. Husserl, Husserl's inaugural lecture at Freiburg im Breisgau. H. L. Van
        Breda (ed.). Robert Welsh Jordan (trans.), 3-18.

        D. Cairns, "The many sense and denotations of the word *Bewusstsein*
        ("consciousness") in Edmund Husserl's writings," 19-31. L. Landgrebe,
        "The problem of the beginning of philosophy in Husserl's phenomenology,"
        José Huertas-Jourda (trans.), 33-53.

        R. Sokolowski, "Husserl's protreptic," 55-82.

        E. G. Ballard, "On the method of phenomenological reduction, its
        presuppositions, and its future," 101-123.

        J. Sallis, "On the ideal of phenomenology," 125-133.

        H. Dreyfus, "The perceptual noema: Gurwitsch's crucial contribution,"
        135-170.

        G. Chiara Moneta, "The foundation of predicative experience and the
        spontaneity of consciousness," 171-190.

        L. E. Embree, "Toward a phenomenology of theoria," 191-207.

        R. M. Zaner, "Reflections on evidence and criticism in the theory of
        consciousness," 209-230.

        J. M. Edie, "Husserl's conception of *The grammatical* and contemporary
        linguistics," 233-261.

        N. Rotenstreich, "The forms of sensibility and transcendental
        phenomenology," 389-405.

        H. Spiegelberg, "What William James knew about Edmund Husserl. On
        the credibility of Pitkin's testimony," 407-422.

        H. Blumemberg, "The life-world and the concept of reality," 425-444,
        Theodore Kisiel (trans.).

        W. Marx, "The life-world and Gurwitsch's *Orders of existence,*" 445-460.

        E. Paci, "Life-world, time and liberty in Husserl," 461-468.

**Book Reviews:**

        H. G. Pleydell-Pearce, Jr. *Journal of the British Society for Phenomenology,*
        vol. 5, 1974, 266-272.

        G. J. Stack, Modern Schoolman, vol. 52, 1974-1975, 97-105.

16      Farber, Marvin. *Phenomenology as a method and a philosophical discipline.*
        Buffalo, 1928.

17    Farber, Marvin. *Philosophical essays in memory of Edmund Husserl.* Cambridge, Mass.: Harvard University Press, 1940, xiii-332.

18    Farber, Marvin. *The foundation of phenomenology.* Edmund Husserl and the quest for a rigorous science of philosophy. Cambridge, Mass.: Harvard University Press, 1943, xi-505. 2d ed., with introduction "After twenty-five years." (Paine-Whitman studies in social science and social theory). New York: Paine-Whitman Pub., 1962, xv-585. Rev. 3rd. ed. Alblany, N.Y.: State University of New York Press, 1968, xv-585.

**Book Reviews:**

P. L. de Ambroggio, *Sapientia,* vol. 12, 1957, 70-71.

L. Dupré, *New Scholasticism,* vol. 45, 1971, 152-154.

19    Farber, Marvin. *The aims of phenomenology.* The motives, methods, and impact of Husserl's thought. New York: Harper & Row, 1966, 240 p.

**Book Reviews:**

S. A. Erickson, *Journal of History of Philosophy,* vol. 6, 1968, 404-406.

P. Kurtz, *Journal of History of Philosophy,* vol. 7, 1969, 74-78.

R. W. Sellars, *Philosophy and Phenomenological Research,* vol. 29, 125-129.

20    Farley, Edward. *Ecclesial man.* A social phenomenology of faith and reality. Philadelphia, Fortress Press, 1975.

**Book Reviews:**

R. Williams, Ecclesial man: a radical approach to theology through Husserl's phenomenology." *Philosophy Today,* vol. 19, 1975, 369-376.

21    Fuchs, Wolfgang Walter. *Phenomenology and the metaphysics of presence.* An essay in the philosophy of Edmund Husserl (Phaenomenologica, 69). The Hague: Martinus Nijhoff, 1976, vi-98.

22    Gurwitsch, Aron. *Phenomenology and the theory of science* (Northwestern University Studies in Phenomenology and Existential Philosophy). Evanston, Ill.: Northwestern University Press, 1974, xi-272.

**Book Reviews:**

P. Jakobson, "'Dirty work': Review of *Phenomenology and the theory of science,* by Aron Gurwitsch." *Research in Phenomenology,* vol. 6, 1976, 191-204.

F. Kersten, *Philosophy and Phenomenological Research,* vol. 36, 1975-1976, 129-131.

J. J. Kockelmans, *Studi Int. di Filosofia,* vol. 7, 1975, 207-208.

23    Hines, Thomas J. *The later poetry of Wallace Stevens.* Phenomenological parallels with Husserl and Heidegger. Lewisburg, Pa.: Bucknell University Press, 1976, 298 p. London: Associated University Presses.

24    Ihde, Don and Zaner, Richard M. (eds.). *Interdisciplinary phenomenology* (Selected studies in phenomenology and existential philosophy, 6). The Hague: Martinus Nijhoff, 1977, 187 p.

25     Ingarden, Roman. *On the motives which led Husserl to transcendental idealism.*
        Arnos Hannibalsson (trans.). The Hague: Martinus Nijhoff, 1975.
        **Book Reviews:**
        R. Sokolowski, *Journal of Philosophy,* vol. 74, March 1977, 176-180.

26     Kersten, Fred and Zaner, Richard M. (eds.). *Phenomenology. Continuation
        and criticism.* Essays in memory of Dorion Cairns (Phaenomenologica, 50).
        The Hague: Martinus Nijhoff, 1973, xii-266. Contents:

        D. Cairns, "My own life," 1-13.

        C. Hartshorne, "Husserl and Whitehead on the concrete," 90-104.

        R. W. Jordan, "Being and time. Some aspects of the ego's involvement in
        his mental life," 105-113.

        F. Kersten, "Husserl's doctrine of noesis-noema," 114-144.

        V. J. McGill, "Evidence in Husserl's phenomenology," 145-166.

        H. Spiegelberg, "Husserl's way into phenomenology for Americans. A letter
        and its sequel (German original and translation)," 168-191.

        R. M. Zaner, "The art of free phantasy in rigorous phenomenological
        science," 192-219.

        D. Cairns, "An approach to Husserlian phenomenology [Published under
        the title, An approach to phenomenology, in *Philosophical essays in memory
        of Edmund Husserl,* Marvin Farber (ed.). Cambridge, Mass.: Harvard
        University Press, 1940]," 223-238.

        D. Cairns, "The ideality of verbal expression [Reprinted from *Philosophy
        and Phenomenological Research,* vol. 1, 1940]," 239-250.

        D. Cairns, "Perceiving, remembering, image-awareness, feigning
        awareness," 251-262.

27     Kim Sang-Ki. *The problem of the contingency of the world in Husserl's
        phenomenology* (Philosophical currents, 17). Atlantic Highlands, N.J.:
        Humanities Press, 1977, 102 p.
        **Book Reviews:**
        R. D'Amico, *Philosophy and Phenomenological Research,* vol. 38, March 1978,
        434-436.

28     Kockelmans, Joseph J. *Phenomenology and physical science.* Pittsburgh, Pa.:
        Duquesne University Press, 1966, 208 p.
        **Book Reviews:**
        G. M. Gutting, *Modern Schoolman,* vol. 45, 1967-1968, 178-179.

        T. Kisiel, *Philosophy and Phenomenological Research,* vol. 28, 1967-1968,
        138-139.

        C. Vansteenkiste, *Angelicum,* vol. 44, 1967, 535-537.

29     Kockelmans, Joseph J. and Kisiel, Theodore (eds.). *Phenomenology and the
        natural sciences* (Northwestern University Studies in Phenomenology and

Existential Philosophy). Evanston, Ill.: Northwestern University Press, 1970.

**Book Reviews:**

G. Gutting, *New Scholasticism,* vol. 49, no. 2, 1974, 253-266.

N. E. Wetherich, *Journal of the British Society for Phenomenology,* vol. 5, 1974, 165-167.

30    Kockelmans, Joseph J. *A first introduction to Husserl's phenomenology.* Pittsburgh, Pa.: Duquesne University Press, 1967, xxiii-372. Louvain: E. Nauwelaerts.

31    Kockelmans, Joseph J. *Edmund Husserl's phenomenological psychology.* A historico-critical study. Bernd Jager (trans. from the Dutch) and revised by the author (Duquesne studies. Psychological series, 4). Pittsburgh, Pa.: Duquesne University Press, 1967, 359 p.; Louvain: E. Nauwelaerts.

**Book Reviews:**

A. M. *Review of Metaphysics,* vol. 22, 1969, 573.

32    Kockelmans, Joseph J. (ed.). *Phenomenology.* The philosophy of Edmund Husserl and its interpretation. Garden City, N.Y.: Doubleday & Co. Inc. A Doubleday Anchor Original, A 585, 1967, 555 p. Contents:

Preface.

Part I: The phenomenology of Edmund Husserl

I. What is Phenomenology? Some fundamental themes of Husserl's phenomenology, Joseph J. Kockelmans, 5-36.

II. Husserl and philosophic radicalism. The ideal of a presuppositionless philosophy, Marvin Farber, 37-57.

III. Phenomenological reduction. ''Hussserl's transcendental-phenomenological reduction," Richard Schmitt, 58-67.

"The thesis of the natural standpoint and its suspension," Edmund Husserl, 67-79.

IV. Essences and Eidetic reduction. "Intuition of essences," Emmanuel Levinas, 83-104.

"On eidetic reduction," Edmund Husserl, 105-117.

V. Intentionality, Constitution, and Intentional Analysis. "On the intentionality of consciousness," Aron Gurwitsch, 118-136.

"Intentional and constitutive analyses," Joseph J. Kockelmans, 137-146.

"Some results of Husserl's investigations," Dorion Cairns, 147-150.

VI. Evidence.

"On evidence," Quentin Lauer, 150-157.

"Phenomenology of reason," Edmund Husserl, 158-167.

VII. Intersubjectivity.

"The other explained inentionally," Quentin Lauer, 167-182.

VIII. Transcendental idealism.

"Toward a descriptive science of man," Joseph J. Kockelmans, 533-555.

33    Kolakowski, Leszek. *Husserl and the search for certitude.* New Haven, London: Yale University Press, 1975, vi-85.
**Book Reviews:**
A. Z. Bar-On, *Iyyun,* vol. 26, Jan., July 1975, 172-173.

Sang-Ki Kim, *Philosophy and Phenomenological Research,* vol. 38, no. 4, June 1978, 583-584.

W. Mays, *Philosophical Books,* vol. 17, May 1976, 70-72.

34    Laszlo, Erwin. *Beyond scepticism and realism.* A constructive exploration of Husserlian and Whiteheadian methods of inquiry. The Hague: Martinus Nijhoff, 1966, 238 p.
**Book Reviews:**
G. Helal, *Dialogue,* vol. 5, 1966-1967, 671-673.

35    Lauer, J. Quentin. *The triumph of subjectivity.* New York: Fordham University Press, 1958. Published in 1966 under the title of *Phenomenology: Its genesis and prospect.* New York: Harper & Row, Harper Torchbook, 1965, vii-185.
**Book Reviews:**
F. J. Crosson, *Philosophical Studies,* vol. 8, 1958, 207-209.

L.-B. Geiger, *Bulletin thomiste,* vol. 10, 1957-1959, 23*-24*.

R. C. Hinners, *Thought,* vol. 34, 1959, 136-139.

V. J. McGill, *Journal of Philosophy,* vol. 56, 1959, 626-631.

J. V. McGlynn, *Philosophy and Phenomenological Research,* vol. 20, 1959-1960, 564.

T. Ogiermann, *Scholastik,* vol. 35, 1960, 123-124.

36    Levin, David Michael. *Reason and evidence in Husserl's phenomenology* (Northwestern University Studies in Phenomenology and Existential Philosophy). Evanston, Ill.: Northwestern University Press, 1970, xxv-232.
**Book Reviews:**
W. Mays, *Philosophical Books,* vol. 12, no. 2, 1971, 14-16.

D. W. Smith, Journal of Philosophy. vol. 70, no. 12, 1973, 356-363.

W. J. Stohrer, *Modern Schoolman,* vol. 49, 1971-1972, 177-179.

37    Levinas, Emmanuel. *The theory of intuition in Husserl's phenomenology.* André Orlanne (trans.), (Northwestern University Studies in Phenomenology and Existential Philosophy). Evanston, Ill.: Northwestern University Press, 1973, xxxvi-163. [Originally: *La théorie de l'intuition dans la phénoménologie de Husserl.* Paris: Alcan, 1932]

38    Mall, R. A. *Experience and reason.* The phenomenology of Husserl and its relation to Hume's philosophy. The Hague: Martinus Nijhoff, 1973, 154 p.

39    Marx, Werner. *Reason and world.* Between tradition and another beginning. Thomas V. Yates (trans. from German). The Hague: Martinus Nijhoff, 1971, xii-113.

**Book Reviews:**

A. Gibbon, *Review of Metaphysics,* vol. 26, 1972-1973, 360-361.

40    McIntyre, R., and Woodruff Smith, D. *Intentionality via intensions:* Husserl's phenomenology and the semantics of modalities. (Synthese Library) Dordrecht: D. Reidel, 1978.

41    Mays, Wolfe and Brown, S. C. (eds.). *Linguistic analysis and phenomenology.* Lewisburg, Pa.: Bucknell University Press, 1972.
**Book Reviews:**

E. Pivcevic, *Mind,* vol. 83, 1974, 139-140.

42    Mohanty, J. N. *Edmund Husserl's theory of meaning* (Phaenomenologica, 14). The Hague: Martinus Nijhoff, 1964, xii-148. 2nd ed. 1969.
**Book Reviews:**

Y. Bar-Hillel, *Philosophical Quarterly,* vol. 16, 1966, 184-185.

J. Derrida, *Etudes Philosophiques,* vol. 19, 1964, 417-419.

J. Edie, *International Philosophical Quarterly,* vol. 6, 1966, 673-675.

D. Föllesdal, *Foundations of Language,* vol. 2, 1966, 266-268.

J. M. Hems, *Mind,* vol. 75, 1966, 449-450.

H. James John, Sr. *New Scholasticsm,* vol. 40, 1966, 242-243.

R. Schmitt, *Philosophical Review,* vol. 75, 1966, 394--395.

R. Sokolowski, *Philosophy and Phenomenological Research,* vol. 27, 1966-1967, 447-448.

D. H. Salman, *Revue des Sciences Philosophiques et Théologiques,* vol. 49, 1965, 417-418.

A.-T. Tymieniecka, *Philosophische Rundschau,* vol. 14, 1966-1967, 191-193.

L. Villoro, *Crítica,* vol. 1, no. 2, 1967, 117-122.

43    Mohanty, J. N. *The concept of intentionality.* St. Louis: Warren H. Green, 1972, 213 p.
**Book Reviews:**

R. J. Deveterre, *International Philosophical Quarterly,* vol. 13, 1973, 583-586.

J. M. Edie, *Southwestern Journal of Philosophy,* vol. 5, 1974, 205-218.

F. Kersten, *Philosophy and Phenomenological Research,* vol. 33, 1972-1973, 582-584.

L. C. Rice, *Modern Schoolman,* vol. 50, 1972-1973, 241-243.

44    Mohanty, J. N. (ed.). *Readings on Edward Husserl's Logical investigations.* With introd, by J. N. Mohanty. The Hague: Martinus Nijhoff, 1977, 220 p. Contents:

Frege, Gottlob. "Review of Dr. E. Husserl's *Philosophy of arithmetic.*" E. W. Kluge (trans.) [Repr. *Mind,* vol. 81, 1972, 321-337], 6-21.

Mohanty, J. N. "Husserl and Frege. A new look at their relationship," [Repr. *Research in Phenomenology,* vol. 4, 1974, 51-62], 22-32.

Husserl, Edmund. "A reply to a critic of my refutation of logical psychologism." Dallas Willard (trans.), [Repr. *Personalist,* vol. 53, 1972, 5-13], 33-42.

Willard, Dallas. "The paradox of logical psychologism. Husserl's way out" [Repr. *American Philosophical Quarterly,* vol. 9, 1972, 94-100], 43-54.

Natorp, Paul. "On the question of logical method in relation to Edmund Husserl's *Prolegomena to pure logic,*" J. N. Mohanty (trans.), 55-66.

Naess, Arne. "Husserl on the apodictic evidence of ideal laws" [Repr. *Theoria,* vol. 20, 1954, 53-64], 66-75.

Mohanty, J. N. "Husserl's thesis of the ideality of meanings," 76-82.

Atwell, John E. "Husserl on signification and object" [Repr. *American Philosophical Quarterly,* vol. 6, 1969, 312-317], 83-93.

Sokolowski, Robert. "The logic of parts and wholes in Husserl's *Investigations,*" [Repr. *Philosophy and Phenomenological Research,* vol. 28, 1967-1968, 537-553], 94-111.

Bar-Hillel, Yehoshua. "Husserl's conception of a purely logical grammar," [Repr. *Philosophy and Phenomenological Research,* vol. 17, 1956-1957, 362-369], 128-136.

Edie, James M. "Husserl's conception of 'the grammatical' and contemporary linguistics," [Repr. from L. E. Embree (ed.), *Life-world and consciousness.* Evanston, Ill.: Northwestern University Press, 1972], 137-161.

Downes, Chauncey. "On Husserl's approach to necessary truth," [Repr. *Monist,* vol. 49, 1965, 87-106], 162-178.

Patzig,Günther. "Husserl on truth and evidence," J. N. Mohanty (trans.), 179-196.

Husserl, Edmund. "The task and the siginificance of the *Logical Investigations,*" J. N. Mohanty (trans.), 197-215.

45      Natanson, Maurice (ed.). *Essays in phenomenology.* The Hague: Martinus Nijhoff, 1966, viii-240.

**Book Reviews:**

T. Langan, *Philosophy and Phenomenological Research,* vol, 29, 1968-1969, 129-130.

Contents: M. Natanson, "Introduction," 1-22.

A. Schutz, "Some leading concepts of phenomenology," 23-39.

A. Gurwitsch, "The phenomenological and the psychological approach to consciousness," 40-57.

J. S. Fulton, "The Cartesianism of phenomenology," 58-78.

H. M. Chapman, "Realism and phenomenology," 79-115.

H. Spiegelberg, "How subjective is phenomenology?" 137-143.

F. Kaufman, "Art and phenomenology," 144-156.

46 Natanson, Maurice. *Edmund Husserl: philosopher of infinite task* (Northwestern University in Phenomenology and Existential Philosophy). Evanston, Ill.: Northwestern University Press, 1973, xx-227.
**Book Reviews:**

L. J. Goldstein, *Studia Internazionale di Filosofia,* vol. 6, Fall 1974, 232-233.

H. B. Hall, *Journal of Philosophy,* vol. 72, 18 Dec. 1975, 819-822.

J. L. Marsh, *Modern Schoolman,* vol. 53, Nov. 1975, 79-82.

J. N. Mohanty, *Journal of History of Philosophy,* vol. 13, Oct. 1975, 542-545.

A. van Schoenborn, *International Philosophical Quarterly,* vol. 15, June 1975, 234-237.

47 Osborn, Andrew D. *Edmund Husserl and his logical investigation.* Cambridge, Mass.: Harvard University Press, 2nd ed. 1949.
**Book Reviews:**

M. Farber, *Philosophical Review,* Sept.1936.

48 Pettit, Philip. *On the idea of phenomenology.* Dublin: Scepter Books, 1969, 99 p.
**Book Reviews:**

J. Daly, *Philosophical Studies* (Maynooth), vol. 20, 1970, 269-272.

J. B. O'Malley, *Journal of the British Society for Phenomenology,* vol. 2, 1971, 94-95.

R. C. Poole, *Philosophy,* vol. 45, 1970, 167-168.

49 Pivcevic, Edo. *Husserl and phenomenology.* London: Hutchinson University Library, 1970.
**Book Reviews:**

P. Pettit, *Journal of the British Society for Phenomenology,* vol. 2, 1971, 95-97.

50 Ricoeur, Paul. *Husserl.* An analysis of his phenomenology. Edward G. Ballard and Lester E. Embree (trans.), (Northwestern University Studies in Phenomenology and Existential Philosophy). Evanston, Ill.: Northwestern University Press, 1967, xxii-238.
**Book Reviews:**

J. Daly, *Philosophical Studies,* (Maynooth), vol. 20, 1970, 310-312.

L. Dupré, *New Scholasticism,* vol. 45, 1971, 191-193.

J. M. Edie, *Journal of Philosophy,* vol. 65, 1968, 403-409.

51 Sinha, Debabrata. *Studies in phenomenology* (Phaenomenologica, 30). The Hague: Martinus Nijhoff, 1969, vii-136.
**Book Reviews:**

W. Halfbass, *Erasmus,* vol. 22, 1970, 649-651.

S. Poggi, *Rivista di Filosofia,* vol. 61, 1970, 327-328.

G. J. Stack, *Modern Schoolman,* vol. 49, 1971-1972, 184-187.

52     Sokolowski, Robert. *The formation of Husserl's concept of constitution* (Phaenomenologica, 18). The Hague: Martinus Nijhoff, 1965, xii-250.
**Book Reviews:**

A. Brunner, *Salzburger Zeitschrift,* vol. 176, 1964-1965, 473-474.

J. Collins, *Modern Schoolman,* vol. 43, 1965-1966, 187-188.

J. Derrida, *Etudes Philosophiques,* vol. 20, 1965, 557-558.

L. Dupré, *New Scholasticism,* vol. 40, 1966, 206-212.

W. McMahon, *Bijdragen,* vol. 27, 1966, 453.

53     Sokolowski, Robert. *Husserlian meditations.* How words present things (Northwestern University Studies in Phenomenology and Existential Philosophy). Evanston, Ill.: Northwestern University Press, 1974, xx-296.
**Book Reviews:**

T. Attig, *Journal of the British Society for Phenomenology,* vol. 7, Oct.1976, 212-214.

P. J. Bossert, *Modern Schoolman,* vol. 53, March 1976, 307-308.

J. B. Brough, *Review of Metaphysics,* vol.28, 1974-1975, 136-137.

G. Gutting, *New Scholasticism,* vol. 49, Aut. 1975, 516-520.

L. Henning, *International Philosophical Quarterly,* vol. 16, March 1976, 125-128.

F. Kersten, *Man and World,* vol. 10, no. 3, 1977, 351-361.

J. L. March, *Modern Schoolman,* vol. 54, Jan. 1977, 188-190.

H. L. Meyn, *International Philosophical Quarterly,* vol. 16, 1976, 125-128.

J. N. Mohanty, *Philosophy and Phenomenological Research,* vol. 35, March 1975, 427-428.

W. F. Vallicella, *Cultural Hermeneutics,* vol. 4, Nov. 1976, 93-106.

P. Widulski, *Aitia,* vol. 4, Spring 1976, 29-32.

E. Winance, *Journal of History of Philosophy,* vol. 14, July 1976, 380-381.

M. E. Zimmerman, *Thomist,* vol. 41, July 1977, 442-446.

54     Son, B. H. *Science and persons.* A study on the idea of 'Philosophy as rigorous science in Kant and Husserl. Assen: Van Gorcum, 1972, 188 p.

U.-U. Hoche, *Archiv für Geschichte der Philosophie,* vol. 57, 1975, 226-230.

E. Schaper, *Journal of the British Society for Phenomenology,* vol. 6, 1975, 202-203.

55     Spiegelberg, Herbert. *The phenomenological movement.* A historical introduction. Vol. I-II (Phaenomenologica, 5). The Hague: Martinus Nijhoff, 1960, xxxii-391, ix-p. 395-735.
**Book Reviews:**

P. Chiodi, *Rivista di Filosofia,* vol. 54, 1963, 236-238.

H.-G. Gadamer, *Philosophische Rundschau,* vol. 11, 1963, 2-12.

S. L. Hart, *Philosophical Review,* vol. 73, 1964, 113-116.

J. Héring, *Revue d'Historie et de Philosophie Religieuses,* vol. 42, 1962, 74-76.

A. Jacob, *Etudes Philosophiques,* vol. 16, 1961, 473.

Th. Langan, *Modern Schoolman,* vol 39, 1961-1962, 267-269.

Q. Lauer, *Erasmus,* vol. 15, 1963, 65-68.

W. Long, *The Personalist,* vol, 43, 1962, 549-550.

V. J. McGill, *Philosophy and Phenomenological Research,* vol. 22, 1961-1962, 587-592.

J. V. McGlynn, *New Scholasticism,* vol. 36, 1962, 388-391.

M. Natanson, *Journal of History of Philosophy,* vol. 1, 1963, 115-124.

R. Schmitt, *Review of Metaphysics,* vol. 15, 1961-1962, 450-479.

Ch. Taylor, *Mind,* vol. 71, 1962, 546-551.

S. Vanni Rovighi, *Rivista di Filosofia Neo-Scholastica,* vol. 55, 1963, 535.

J. Villard, *Studia Philosophica,* vol. 23, 1963, 207-211.

F. Voltaggio, *Giornale Critico della Filosofia Italiana,* vol. 40, 1961, 532-537.

E. Weil, *Critique,* vol. 18, no. 185, 1962, 906-909.

56      Stevens, Richard. *James and Husserl: the foundations of meaning* (Phaenomenologica, 60). The Hague: Martinus Nijhoff, 1974, vii-191.
**Book Reviews:**

M. G. Rawl, *Modern Schoolman,* vol. 53, March 1976, 330-331.

B. W. Wilshire, *International Studies in Philosophy,* vol. 7, Fall 1975, 260-261.

57      Straus, Erwin W. (ed.). *Phenomenology: pure and applied.* The first Lexington conference. Pittsburgh, Pa.: Duquesne University Press, 1964, vii-208.

58      Sukale, Michael. *Comparative studies in phenomenology.* The Hague: Martinus Nijhoff, 1976, x-154.

59      Tymieniecka, Anna-Teresa (ed.). *For Roman Ingarden.* Nine essays in phenomenology. The Hague: Martinus Nijhoff, 1959.
**Book Reviews:**

D. Deledalle, *Etudes Philosophiques,* vol. 15, 1960, 286.

G. Piana, *Archivo di Filosofia,* no. 1, 1960, 99-103.

60      Tymieniecka, Anna-Teresa (ed.). *Analecta Husserliana.* The Yearbook of Phenomenological Research, Vol. I. Dordrecht: D. Reidel, 1970, ix-208.
Contents:

A.-T. Tymieniecka, "Die phänomenologische Selbstbesinnung, I: Der Leib und die Transzendentalität in der gegenwärtigen phänomenologischen und psychiatrischen Forschung," 1-10.

J. J. Kockelmans, "World-constitution. Reflections on Husserl's transcendental idealism," 11-35.

R. Ingarden, "Die vier Begriffe der Transzendenz und das Problem des Idealismus in Husserl,: 36-74.

A. Lingis, "Intentionality and corporeity," 75-90.

U. Claesges, "Intentionalität und Transzendenz. Zur Konstitution der materiellen Natur," 91-99.

J. N. Mohanty, "Husserl's concept of intentionality," 100-132.

E. Ströker, "Das Problem der *epoché* in der Philosophie Edmund Huserls," 170-185.

K. Kuypers, "Die Wissenschaften vom Menschen und Husserls Theorie von zwei Einstellungen," 186-196.

D. Laskey, "Embodied consciousness and the human spirit," 197-207.

61    Tymieniecka, Anna-Teresa (ed.). *The later Husserl and the idea of phenomenology.* Idealism-realism, historicity and nature. Papers and debate of the International and Phenomenological Conference held at the University of Waterloo, Canada, April 9-14, 1969. *Analecta Husserliana,* vol. 2, 1972. Dordrecht: D. Reidel, 1972, 374 p. Contents:

A.-T. Tymieniecka, "Phenomenology reflects upon itself, II: The ideal of the universal science: the original project of Husserl reinterpreted with reference to the acquisitions of phenomenology and the progress of contemporary science," 3-17.

R. Ingarden, "What is new in Husserl's *Crisis.*" Rolf George (trans. from the German text, 23-47.

D. Laskey, "Ingarden's criticism of Husserl," 48-54.

F. Kersten, "On understanding idea and essence in Husserl and Ingarden," 55-63.

J. J. Kockelmans, "Phenomenologico-psychological and transcendental reductions in Husserl's *Crisis,*" 78-89.

A. Póltawski, "Constitutive phenomenology and intentional objects," 90-95.

A. Lingis, "Hyletic data," 96-101.

G. Brand, "The material *apriori* and the foundation for its analyses in Husserl," 128-148.

H. L. van Breda, "The actual state of the works on Husserl's *inedita:* achievements and projects," 149-159.

H.-G. Gadamer, "The science of the life-world," 173-185.

K. Kuypers, "The sciences of man and the theory of Husserl's two attitudes," 186-195.

E. Ströker, "Edmund Husserl's phenomenology as foundation of natural science," 245-257.

H. Elkin, "Towards a developmental phenomenology: transcendental-*ego* and body-*ego,*" 258-263.

E. Eng, "Body, consciousness, and violence," 267-277.

H. Pietersma, "The concept of horizon," 278-282.

U. Claesges, "Intentionality and transcendence. On the constitution of material nature," 283-291.

J. N. Mohanty, "A note on the doctrine of noetic-noematic correlation," 317-321.

Th. De Boer, "The meaning of Husserl's idealism in the light of his development," 322-332.

L. Ely, "*Life-world* constitution of propositional logic and elementary predicate logic," 333-353.

R. Ingarden, "Roman Ingarden's letter to Edmund Husserl. A.-T. Tymieniecka (ed.), 357-374.

62    Tymieniecka, Anna-Teresa (ed.). *Analecta Husserliana,* vol. 3, 1974. Contents:

J. N. Mohanty, "The life-world and a priori in Husserl's later thought," 46-65.

R. T. Murphy, "The transcendental a priori in Husserl and Kant," 66-79.

M. Sancipriano, "The activity of consciousness: Husserl and Bergson," 161-167.

D.Souche-Dagues, "Le platonisme de Husserl," 335-360.

R. M. Zaner, "Passivity and activity of consciousness in Husserl," 199-202. [Discussion, 202-226]

63    Tymieniecka, Anna-Teresa (ed.). *Analecta Husserliana,* vol. 4: *Ingardeniana,* 1976.

R. Ingarden, "Probleme der Husserlschen Reduktion," 1-71.

A.-T. Tymieniecka, "Beyond Ingarden's idealism/realism controversy with Husserl--The new contextual phase of phenomenology," 241-418.

R. Ingarden, "The letter to Husserl about the VI [*Logical] investigation* and 'idealism'," 418-438.

64    Tymienieckka, Anna-Teresa (ed.). *Analecta Husserliana,* vol. 5: *The crisis of culture,* 1976, 382 p. [Papers and discussions at the Third International Conference held by the International Husserl and Phenomenological Research Society] Contributors:

A.-T. Tymieniecka, Claude Levesque, Robert D. Sweeney, David Carr, Serge Morin, Wladyslaw Stronzewski, Michel Masson, Henning L. Meyn, Albert Shalom, M. C. Dillon, Kenley R. Dove, Louis Dupré, Mildred Bakan, Mikel Dufrenne, Philibert Secretan, David M. Rasmussen, Kardinal K. Wojtyla, Francis F. Seeburger, Angela Bello, Efraim Shumueli.

D. M. Rasmussen, "The quest for valid knowledge in the context of society [Marx and Husserl]," 259-268 [Discussion, 296-302].

E. Shmueli, "Consciousness and action: Husserl and Marx on theory and praxis," 343-382.

**Book Reviews:**

65    Van Peursen, Cornelis. *Phenomenology and analytical philosophy* (Duquesne Studies. Philosophy Series, 28). Pittsburgh, Pa.: Duquesne University Press, 1972, 190 p.

**Book Reviews:**

C. B. Breslin, *Review of Metaphysics,* vol. 26, 1972-1973, 768-769.

H. L. Meyn, *International Philosophical Quarterly,* vol. 13, 1973, 592-595.

66    Van Peursen, Cornelis. *Phenomenology and reality.* Pittsburgh, Pa.: Duquesne University Press, 1972.

**Book Reviews:**

W. S. Hamrich, *Modern Schoolman,* vol. 54, Jan. 1977, 177-182.

K. Schuhmann, *Tijdschrift voor Filosofie,* vol. 35, 1973, 416-417.

67    Welch, E. Parl. *Edmund Husserl's phenomenology* (The University of Southern California Studies in Philosophy, series 4). Los Angeles: The University of Southern California Press, 1939, 100 p.

68    Welch, E. Parl. *The philosophy of Edmund Husserl.* The origin and development of his phenomenology. New York: Columbia University Press, 1941; 2nd. ed., 1948. Reprint, New York: Octagon Books, 1965, xxiv-337.

## Books in French

69    Bachelard, Suzanne. *La logique de Husserl.* Etude sur *'Logique formelle et logique transcendentale'* ("Epiméthée"). Paris: Presses Universitaires de France, 1957, 316 p.

**Book Reviews:**

R. Allers, *Erasmus,* vol. 12, 1959, 131-133.

Anonymous. *Revue de Métaphysique et de Morale,* vol. 55, 1960, 112-114.

R. Champigny, *Journal of Philosophy,* vol. 54, 1957, 825-826.

J. Collins, *Cross Currents,* vol. 9, 1959, 187.

F. Dagognet, *Revue Internationale de Philosophie,* vol. 11, 1957, 472-475.

A. de Muralt, *Studia Philosophica,* vol. 17, 1957, 140-149.

J. Deveterre, *Revue des Questions Scientifiques,* vol. 19, 1958, 480.

H. Duméry, *Revue Générale des Sciences Pures et Appliquées,* vol. 64, 1957, 323-324.

H. Dussort, *Revue de Philosophie de la France et de l'Etranger,* vol. 84, 1959, 556-557.

J. Ecole, *Etudes Philosophiques,* vol. 13, no. 1, 1958, 76.

J. Fragata, *Revista Portuguesa de Filosofia,* vol. 3, 1958, 292, suppl bib.

Q. Lauer, *Philosophy and Phenomenological Research,* vol. 19, 1958-1959, 126-127.

F. Russo, *Etudes,* no. 298, 1958, 130-131.

F. Voltaggio, *Rassegna di Scienze Filosofiche,* vol. 7, no. 3, 1957, 280-289.

70 Berger, Gaston. *Le cogito dans la philosophie de Husserl.* Paris: Aubier, 1941. Réimpression, Paris: Aubier, Editions Montaigne, 1950.
**Book Reviews:**

A. de Waelhens, *RNP,* 1940-Aug. 1945, no. 67-68, 329-332.

A. Gurwitsch, *Revue Internationale de Philosophie,* vol. 1, 1939, 342-353.

A. Gurwitsch, *Philosophy and Phenomenological Research,* vol. 1, 1940-1941, 127-129.

A. Gurwitsch, "G. Berger. *Das cogito in Husserls Philosophie,*" [aus dem Englischen übersetzt von Ursual Beul, in *Husserl.* Herausgegeben von H. Noack (Wege der Forschung, 40). Darmstadt: Wissenschaftliche Buchgesellschaft, 1973, 222-230.

A. Gurwitsch, *Philosophy and Phenomenological Research,* vol. 7, 1946-1947, 649-654. [German trans. in Noack, *see above*]

71 Christoff, Daniel. *Husserl ou le retour aux choses.* Présentation, choix de textes, bibliographie (Coll. "Philosophies de tous les temps," 30). Paris: Seghers, 1966, 192 p.
**Book Reviews:**

A. Guy, *Etudes Philosophiques,* vol. 22, 1967, 461-462.

J.-P. Leyvraz, *Revue de Théologie et de Philosophie,* vol. 101, 1968, 62-63.

P. Schérer, *Journal de Psychologie Normale et Pathologique,* vol. 64, 1967, 346-347.

72 de Muralt, André. *L'idée de la phénoménologie.* L'exemplarisme husserlien. Edition augmentée d'un index (Bibliothèque de philosophie contemporaine. Histoire de la philosophie et philosophie générale). Paris: Presses Universitaires de France, 1958, 400 p.
**Book Reviews:**

J. M. Alejandro, *Pensamiento,* vol. 16, 1960, 487.

H. Dussort, *Revue Philosophique de la France et de l'Etranger,* vol. 84, 1959, 557-558.

J. M. Edie, *Philosophy and Phenomenological Research,* vol. 22, 1961-1962, 278-281.

A. Jacob, *Etudes Philosophiques,* no. 4, 1959, 381-382.

Q. Lauer, *Erasmus,* vol. 12, 1959, 579-581.

G. Morel, *Etudes,* vol. 305, 1960, 127.

J.-C. Piguet, *Revue de Théologie et de Philosophie,* 1959, 282-283.

X. Tilliette, *Etudes,* vol. 304, 1960, 265-266.

73　　Derrida, Jacques. *La voix et le phénoméne*. Introduction au problème du signe dans la phénoménologie de Husserl (Epiméthée). Paris: Presses Universitaires de France, 1967, x-120. 2e édition, 1972.
**Book Reviews:**

A. Jacob, *Etudes Philosophiques*, 1968, 224-225.

W. Mays, *Philosophy*, vol. 44, 1969, 77-79.

J.-D. Robert, *Revue Philosophique de Louvain*, vol. 66, 1968, 309-324.

C. M. R. *Review of Metaphysics*, vol. 22, 1968, 142-143.

K. Schümann, *Tijdschrift voor Filosofie*, vol. 30, 1968, 159-163.

F. J. Smith, *Philosophy Today*, Summer 1967.

74　　Elie, Hubert. *Etude logico-grammaticale sur les 'Logische Untersuchungen' de Husserl* [extrait de *Studia Philosophica*, vol. 23, 1963, 51-89]. Basel: Verlag für Recht und Gesellschaft, 1963.

76　　Fink, Eugen. *De la phénoménologie*. Traduit de l'allemand par Didier Franck. Avant-propos d'Edmund Husserl (Collection Arguments). Paris: Editions de Minuit, 1974, 245 p. Contents:

"Re-présentation et image. Contributions à la phénoménologie de l'irréalité," 15-93. "La philosophie phénoménologique d'Edmund Husserl face à la critique contemporaine," 95-175. "Que veut la phénoménologie?" 177-198. "Le problème de la phénoménologie d'Edmund Husserl," 199-242.

77　　Granel, Gérard. *Le sens du temps et de la perception chez Edmund Husserl* (Bibliothèque). Paris: Gallimard, 1968, 282 p.

78　　Gurvitch, Georges. *Tendances actuelles de la philosophie allemande:* E. Husserl, M. Scheler, E. Lask, M. Heidegger. Paris: Vrin, 1930.

79　　Halda, Bernard. *Thématique phénoménologique et implications.* Husserl, Edith Stein, Merleau-Ponty. Louvain: Nauwelaert; Paris, Diffusion Vander-Oyez, 1976, 71 p.

80　　*Husserl* (Cahiers de Royaumont. Philosophie no. III) (Troisième Colloque philosophique de Royaumont, 23 au 30 avril 1957. L'oeuvre et la pensée de Husserl). Paris: Les Editions de Minuit, 1959, 438 p. Contents:

E. Minkowski, "Introduction à la conférence de M. Tatarkiewicz," 14-15.

V. Tatarkiewicz, "Réflexions chronologiques sur l'époque oú a vécu Husserl," 16-26 [Discussion, 27-31].

W. Biemel, "Les phases décisives dans le Développement de la philosophie de Husserl," 32-62 [Discussion, 63-71].

K. Kuypers, "La conceptiion de la philosophie comme science rigoureuse et les fondements des sciences chez Husserl," 72-83 [Discussion, 83-94].

E. Levinas, "Réflexions sur la 'technique' phénoménologique," 95-107 [Discussion, 108-119].

J. Wahl, "Au sujet des jugements de Husserl sur Descartes et sur Locke," 119-131 [Discussion, 132-142].

A. de Waelhens, "Commentaire sur l'idée de la phénoménologie," 143-156 [Discussion, 157-169].

S. Strasser, "Misère et grandeur du 'fait': une méditation phénoménologique," 170-184 [Discussion, 185-195].

C. A. van Peursen, "La notion du temps et de l'Ego transcendental chez Husserl," 196-207 [Discussion, 208-213].

E. Fink, "Les concepts opératoires dans la phénoménologie de Husserl," 214-230 [Discussion, 231-241].

R. Ingarden, "Le problème de la constitution et le sens de la réflexion constitutive chez Edmond Husserl," 242-264 [Discussion, 265-270].

J. Wild, "L'anthropologie philosophique et la crise des sciences européennes," 271-292 [Discussion, 293-306].

H. L. Van Breda, "La réduction phénoménologique," 307-318 [Discussion, 319-333].

A. Schütz, "Le problème de l'intersubjectivité transcendentale chez Husserl," 334-365 [Discussion, 366-381].

Ph. Merlan, "Idéalisme, réalisme, phénoménologie," 382-410.

A. Banfi, "Husserl et la crise de la civilisation européenne," 411-427.

J. Wahl, "Clôture du Colloque phénoménologique," 428-432.

**Book Reviews:**

J. Ecole, Etudes Philosophiques, vol. 15, 1960, 284-285.

H.-G. Gadamer, *Philsophische Rundschau,* vol. 11, 16-33.

K. K. *Algemeen Nederlands Tijdschrift voor Wijsbegeerte en Psychologie,* vol. 53, 1960-1961, 35.

B. Rochot, *Revue de Synthèse,* vol. 81, 1960, 135-136.

J. Taminiaux, *Revue Philosophique de Louvain,* vol. 55, 1957, 381-384.

L. A. Schuwer, *Tijdschrift voor Filosofie,* vol. 19, 1957, 524-544.

81    *Husserl et la pensée moderne. Husserl und das Denken der Neuzeit* (Actes du deuxiéme Colloque International de Phénomenologie, Krefeld, 1-3 novembre 1956, édités par les soins de H. L. Van Breda et J. Taminiaux. Akten des zweiten Internationalen Phänomenologischen Kolloquiums, Krefeld, 1-3 November 1956, herausgegeben von H. L. Van Breda und J. Taminiaux) (Phaenomenologica, II). The Hague: Nijhoff, 1959, 250 p. Contents:

H. L. Van Breda, "Le sauvetage de l'héritage husserlien et la fondation es Archives-Husserl."

F. J. J. Buytendijk, "La signification de la phénoménologie husserlienne pour la psychologie actuelle."

A. De Waelhens, "Le idée phénoménologique d'intentionalité."

E. Fink, "Monde et histoire" (Traduit par J. Ladrière et J. Taminiaux).

J. Hyppolite, "L'idée fichtéenne de la doctrine de la science et le projet husserlien."

R. Ingarden, "De l'idéalisme transcendental chez E. Husserl" (Traduit par Jacques Taminiaus).

L. Landgrebe, "La signification de la phénoménologie de Husserl pour la réflexion de notre époque." (Traduit par J. Taminiaux).

K. H. Volkmann-Schluck,, "La doctrine de Husserl au sujet de l'idealité de la signification en tant que problème métaphysique," (Traduit par J. Ladrière).

**Book Reviews:**

S. Breton and H. Rousseau, *Revue Thomiste,* vol. 57, 1957, 115-128.

J. Ecole, *Etudes Philosophiques,* vol. 15, 1960, 284-285.

H.-G. Gadamer, *Philosophische Rundschau,* vol. 11, 16-33.

S. L. Hart, *Philosophy and Phenomenological Research,* vol. 22, 1961-1962, 429-431.

H. Hohl, *Philosophisches Jahrbuch,* vol. 69, 1961, 206-208.

H. D. Mandrioni, *Revista de Filosofía* (La Plata), no. 10, 1961, 122-126.

J. H. Nota, *Bijdragen,* vol. 22, 1961, 229, & *Ibid.,* vol. 18, 1957, 71-76.

H. Ogiermann, *Scholastik,* vol. 36, 1961, 140-141.

C. Sini, *Il Pensiero,* no. 2, 1961, 203-215.

S. Vanni-Rovighi, *Rivista di Filosofia Neo-Scholastica,* vol. 55, 1963, 526-527 & *Ibid.,* vol. 49, 1957, 259-263.

J. Wahl, *Revue de Métaphysique et de Morale,* vol. 65, 1960, 339-343.

K. K. *Algemeen Nederlands Tijdschrift voor Wijsbegeeret en Psychologie,* vol. 53, 1960-1961, 35.

L. Van Haecht, *Revue Philosophique de Louvain,* vol 64, 1956, 660-664.

82 *Edmund Husserl 1859-1959.* Recueil commémoratif publié à l'occasion du centenaire de la naissance du philosophe (Phaenomenologica, IV). The Hague: Martinus Nijhoff, 1959, xii-306. I portrait hors texte. Contents:

W. E. Hocking, "From the early days of the *Logische Untersuchungen,"* *1-11.*

W. Schapp, "Erinnerungen an Husserl," 12-25.

J. Hering, "Edmund Husserl. Souvenirs et réflexions," 26-28.

H. Plessner, "Bei Husserl in Göttingen," 29-39.

F. Kaufmann, "Bei Husserl in Göttingen," 40-47.

K. Löwith, "Eine Erinnerung an E. Husserl," 49-55.

H. Spiegelberg, "Perspektivenwandel: Konstitution eines Husserlbildes," 56-63.

L. Binswanger, "Dank an Edmund Husserl," 64-72.

E. Levinas, "La ruine de la représentation," 73-85.

A. Schutz, "Husserl's importance for the social sciences," 86-98.

E. Fink, "Die Spätphilosophie Husserls in der Freiburger Zeit," 99-115.

H. L. Van Breda, "Geist und Bedeutung des Husserl-Archivs," 116-122.

M. Yamamoto, "Why I am interested in phenomenology," 122-133.

H. Reiner, "Sinn und Recht der phänomenologischen Methode," 133-147.

S. Strasser, "Intuition und Dialektik in der Philosophie Edmund Husserls," 148-153.

M. Farber, "On the meaning of radical reflections," 167-174.

Q. Lauer, "The subjectivity of objectivity," 167-174.

H. Conrad-Martius, "Die transzendentale und die ontologische Phänomenologie," 175-184.

S. Vanni-Rovighi, "Edmund Husserl e la perennità della filosofia," 185-194.

M. Merleau-Ponty, "Le philosophe et son ombre," 195-220.

A. de Waelhens, "Réflexions sur une problématique husserlienne de l'inconscient. Husserl et Hegel," 221-237.

**Book Reviews:**

M. de Mullewie, *Tijdschrift voor Filosofie,* vol. 23, 1961, 159-161.

H.-G. Gadamer, *Philosophische Rundschau,* vol. 11, 16-33.

H. Hohl, *Philosophisches Jahrbuch,* vol. 69, 1961, 205-206.

J. Nota, *Bijdragen,* vol. 22, 1961, 340.

H. Ogiermann, *Scholastik,* vol. 36, 1961, 139-140.

W. Schwanz, *Philosophy and Phenomenological Research,* vol. 21, 1960-1961, 576-577.

S. Vanni-Rovighi, *Rivista di Filosofia Neo-Scholastica,* vol. 55, 1963, 523-526.

J. Wahl, *Revue de Métaphysique et de Morale,* vol. 65, 1960, 327-328.

W. H. Werkmeister, *The Personalist,* vol. 42, 1961, 97-98.

K. K., *Algemeen Nederlands Tijdschrift voor Wijsbegeerte en Psychologie,* vol. 53, 1960-1961, 35-36.

83 Jeanson, Francis. *La phénoménologie* (Notre Monde). Paris, 1951.

**Book Reviews:**

A. de Waelhens, *Revue Philosophique de Louvain,* vol. 50, 1952, 160-162.

84 Kelkel, Lothar, et Schérer, René. *Husserl.* Sa vie, son oeuvre, avec un exposé de sa philosophie (Coll. "Philosophes"). Paris: Presses Universitaires de France, 1964, 144 p. 2e ed. mise à jour. 1971, 148 p.

**Book Reviews:**

I. Meyerson, *Journal de Psychologie Normale et Pathologique,* vol. 62, 1965, 473-474.

G. Morel, *Etudes,* no. 320, 1964, 864.

R. Sánchez, *Aporía,* vol. l, 1964, 102.

E. Sturani, *Rivista di Filosofia,* vol. 56, 1965, 384-385.

85    Kouropoulos, Pétros. *Remarques sur le temps de l'homme selon Heidegger et Husserl* (Les Cahiers du Centre d'Etudes et de recherches marxistes). Paris: Centre d'Etudes et de Recherches marxistes, 1967, 33.

86    Lauer, Quentin. *Phénoménologie de Husserl.* Essai sur la genèse de l'intentionalité (Epiméthée. Essais philosophiques). Paris: Presses Universitaires de France, 1955, xvi-444. Bibliographie, 431-441.
      **Book Reviews:**
      J. Collins, *Modern Schoolman,* vol. 33, 1956, 281-284.
      J. de Vries, *Scholastik,* vol. 36, 1961, 448-449.
      J. Ecole, *Etudes Philosophiques,* vol. 10, 1955, 517-518.
      H.-G. Geyer, *Philosophische Rundschau,* vol. 4, 1956, 158-166.
      J. Gilbert, *Nouvelle Revue de Théologie,* vol. 78, 1956, 320-322.
      V. J. McGill, *Journal of Philosophy,* vol. 53, 1956, 843-849.
      G. Morel, *Etudes,* no. 288, 1956, 291.
      M. Natanson, *Philosophical Review,* vol. 65, 1956, 563-567.

87    Levinas, Emmanuel. *La théorie de l'intuition dans las phénoménologie de Husserl.* Paris: Alcan, 1930.

88    Levinas, Emmanuel. *En découvrant l'existence avec Husserl et Heidegger.* Paris: Vrin, 1949, ll p. *En découvrant l'existence avec Husserl et Heidegger* (Bibliothèque d'histoire de la philosophie). 3e éd. conforme à la Ière éd., suivie d'essais nouveaux. Paris: J. Vrin, 1974, 239 p.
      **Book Reviews:**
      R. Schérer, *Revue Internationale de Philosophie,* no. 103, 1970, 61.

89    Miguelez, J. *Sujet et histoire.* Ottawa: Presses de l'Université d'Ottawa, 1975.
      **Book Reviews:**
      M. Corvez, *Revue Thomiste,* vol. 75, 1975, 299-30l.
      J. L. Dumas, *Revue de Métaphysique et de Morale,* vol. 80, 1975, 269-270.
      J. N. Kaufman, *Dialogue,* vol. 15, March 1976, 515-519.

90    *Phénoménologie-Existence.* Recueil d'études par Henri Birault, H. L. Van Breda, Aron Gurwitsch, Emmanuel Lévinas, Paul Ricoeur, Jean Wahl (Publications de la *Revue de Métaphysique et de Morale*). Paris: Armand Colin, 1953, 208 p.

91    *La phénoménologie.* En colloboration. Juvisy, 12 septembre 1932. Ed. du Cerf, Paris, 1932. Journées d'Etudes de la Société Thomiste.
      **Book Reviews:**
      A. Kojevnikoff, *Recherches Philosophiques,* vol. 3, 1935, 429-431.
      L. Landgrebe, *Kantstudien,* 1933, 357.

92    Autour de la phénoménologie. En collaboration *Revue de Métaphysique et de Morale,* vol. 62, no. 4, 1957, 369-488). Paris: Librairie A. Colin, 1958.

93    *Philosophes d'aujourd'hui en présence du droit.* Sartre, Husserl, Gabriel, Marcel, Teilhard de Chardin, Ernst Bloch, Reinach (*Archives de philosophie du droit,* 10). Paris: Sirey, 1965, viii-375.

94    Robberechts, Ludovic. *Husserl* (Classiques du XXe siècle, 66). Paris: Editions Universitaires, 1964, 128 p.
**Book Reviews:**
C. Bosch, *Revista de Ideas Estéticas,* vol. 24, no. 95, 1966, 254-257.
H. Delhougne, *Revue Philosophique de Louvain,* vol. 65, 1967, 561-562.
R. Vander Gucht, *Revue Nouvelle,* vol. 41, 1965, 443.

95    Rollin, France. *La phénoménologie au départ.* Husserl, Heidegger, Gaboriau (Trident, 3). Paris: P. Lethielleux, 1967, 200 p.

96    Saraiva, Maria Manuela. *L'imagination selon Husserl* (Phaenomenologica, 34). The Hague: Martinus Nijhoff, 1970, xvi-280.
**Book Reviews:**
Br. Danhier, *Revue Philosophique de Louvain,* vol. 70, 1972, 304-305.

J. B. O'Malley, *Human Context-Le Domaine Humain,* vol. 6, Sum. 1974, 449-453.

René Schérer, *La phénoménologie des 'Recherches logiques' de Husserl* (Epiméthée). Paris: Presses Universitaires de France, 1967, 372 p.
**Book Reviews:**
J.-M. Benoîst, *Etudes Philosophiques,* no. 4, 1969, 525-528.

M. Dambuyant, *Journal de Psychologie Normale de Pathologique,* vol. 67, 1970, 228-229.

J.-L. Galay, *Studia Philosophica,* vol. 28, 1968, 216-218.

W. Halbfass, *Erasmus,* vol. 20, 1968, 450-453.

D. Herrera, *Franciscanum,* vol. 12, 1970, 115-116.

98    Souche-Dagues, D. *Le développement de l'intentionalité dans la phénoménologie husserliene* (Phaenomenologica, 52). The Hague: Martinus Nijhoff, 1972, vi-306.
**Book Reviews:**
J. Danek, *Laval Thélogique et Philosophique,* vol. 30, 1974, 88-90.

S. Valdinci, *Revue de Métaphysique et de Morale,* vol. 82, 1977, 123-131.

99    Taminiaux, Jacques. *Le regard et l'excédent* (Phaenomenologica, 75). The Hague: Martinus Nijhoff, 1977, xii-182.

100   Thévenaz, Pierre. *De Husserl à Merleau-Ponty.* Qu'est-ce que la phénoménologie? (Coll. "Etre et penser," 52). NeuchÂtel: Editions de la Baconnière, 1966, 120 p.

101   Toulemont, René. *L'essence de la société selon Husserl* (Bibliothèque de philosophie contemporaine). Paris: Presses Universitaires de France, 1962, 348 p.

**Book Reviews:**

H. Bernard-Maître, *Revue de Synthèse,* vol. 54, 1963, 545.

L. Geldsetzer, *Philosphischer Literaturanzeiger,* vol. 17, 1964, 103-107.

M. Natanson, *Philosophy and Phenomenological Research,* vol. 25, 1964-1965, 603-604.

Ph. Secrétan, *Revue de Théologie et de Philosophie,* vol. 13, 1963, 90.

102    Tran Duc Thao. *Phénoménologie et matérialisme dialectique.* Paris: Mink-Tan, 1951, 308 p.

**Book Reviews:**

Anonymous, *Revue de Métaphysique et de Morale,* vol. 58, 1953, 310-315.

A. Flew, *British Journal of Philosophy of Science,* 1952-1953, 290-291.

A. de Waelhens, *Critique,* vol. 8, no. 56, 1952, 85-88.

103    Van Breda, Hermann Leo (ed.) *Problèmes actuels de la phénoménologie.* Textes de P. Thévenaz, H. J. Pos, P. Ricoeur, E. Fink, M. Merleau-Ponty, J. Wahl. Edités par H. L. Van Breda. *Actes du Colloque International de Phénoménologie,* Bruxelles, avril 1951 (Collection "Textes et Etudes philosophiques"). Paris: Desclée de Brouwer, 1952, 165 p.

**Book Reviews:**

R. Boehm, *Zeitschrift für Philosophische Forschung,* vol. 7, 1953, 598-605.

E. Brisbois, *Nouevlle Revue de Théologiie,* vol. 75, 1953, 768.

R. Ceñal, *Pensamiento,* vol. 8, 1952, 533-534.

D. M. De Petter, *Tijdschrift voor Filosofie,* vol. 14, 1952, 596.

R. Drudis Baldrich, *Revista de Filosofía* (Madrid), vol. 13, 1954, 194-195.

G. Ducoin, *Etudes,* no. 281, 1954, 265.

J. Ecole, *Etudes Philosophiques,* vol. 9, 1953, 187.

C. Fabro, *Divus Thomas,* Piacenza, vol. 55, 1952, 456.

J. Fragata, *Revista Portuguesa de Filosofia,* Supl. bib. vol. 2, 1953, 32-33.

R. Francès, *Journal de Psychologie Normale et Pathologique,* vol. 46, 1953, 233-235.

J. Gérard, *Revue Internationale de Philosophie,* vol. 7, no. 1-2, 1953, 160-161.

R. Gradi, *Sapienza,* vol. 6, 1953, 343-344.

F. Kaufmann, *Philosophical Review,* vol. 63, 1954, 279-285.

J. L. Lorenzi, *Ciencia y Fe,* vol. 8, 1952, 177-178.

V. J. McGill, *Journal of Philosophy,* vol. 50, 1953, 74-79.

M. Nédoncelle, *Revue des Sciences Religieuses,* vol. 26, 1952, 422-424.

J. Nota, *Bijdragen,* vol. 14, 1953, 104.

D. F. Pró, *Humanitas* (Tucumá), vol. 1, no. 2, 1953, 415-420.

R. Schaerer, *Revue de Théologie et de Philosophie,* vol. 3, 1953, 300-30l.

F. Valentini, *Rassegna di Scienze Filosofiche,* vol. 2, 1953, 280-284.

H. Van Lier, *Revue Nouvelle*, vol. 19, 1954, 440-441.

L. Van Haecht, *Revue Philosophique de Louvain*, vol. 51, 1953, 150-152.

L. Vander Kerken, *Katholiek Cultureel Tijdschrift Streven*, vol. 6, 1952-1953, 291.

C. Viano, *Rivista di Filosofia*, vol. 44, 1953, 89-91.

J. H. Walgrave, *Kultuurleeven*, vol. 20, 1953, 398-399.

Anonymous, *Civiltà Cattolica*, 104, III, 1953, 411-412.

104     Van Breda, Hermann-Leo (ed.) *Vérité et vérification. Wahrheit und Verifikation.* (Actes du quatrième Colloque International de Phénoménologie,, Schwabisch Hall (Baden-Wurttemberg). 8-11, septembre 1969 édités par les soins de H.-L. Van Breda) (Phanomenologica, 61). The Hague: Martinus Nijhoff, 1974, 225 p. Contents:

E. Fink, "Grussansprache," 1-2.

G. Funke, "Bewusstseinwissenschaft," 3-58.

E. Paci, "Vérification empirique et transcendence de la vérité," 59-70.

A. Pazanin, "Wahrheit und Lebenswelt beim späten Husserl," 71-116.

S. Bachelard, "Logique husserlienne et sémantique," 117-131.

S. Strasser, "Probleme des "Verstehens" in neuer Sicht," 132-189.

P. Ricoeur, "Conclusions," 190-209.

H.-G. Gadamer, "Zusammenfassender Bericht," 210-223.

**Book Reviews:**

A. Babolin, *Rivista di Filosofia Neo-Scolastica*, vol. 61, 1969, 743-749.

105     Vancourt, Raymond. *La phénoménologie et la foi* (Coll. "Le Monde et la foi"). Tournai: Desclee de Brouwer, 1953, 128 p.

**Book Reviews:**

B. Baudoux, *Antonianum*, vol. 30, 1955, 338.

G. Ducoin, *Etudes*, vol. 286, 1955, 119.

A. Fabrat, *Estudios Ecclesiasticos*, vol. 29, 1955, 397-398.

A. González Alvarez, *Arbor*, vol. 29, 1954, 346-347.

P. Pacifique, *Etudes Franciscaines*, vol. 6, 1955, 241-242.

H. Van Lier, *Revue Nouvelle*, vol. 21, 1955, 210.

106     Waelhens, Alphonse de. *Phénoménologie et vérité*. Essai sur l'évolution de la vérité chez Husserl et Heidegger (Collection "Epiméthée"). Paris: Presses Universitaires de France, 1953, 168 p.

**Book Reviews:**

D. Campanele, *Rivista Critica di Storia della Filosofia*, vol. 8, 1955, 350-352.

M. de Mullewie, *Kultuurleeven*, vol. 21, 1954, 705-706.

J. Ecole, *Etudes Philosophiques*, vol. 10, 1955, 131.

J. Gérard, *Revue Internationale de Philosophie*, vol. 9, 1955, 156-157.

G. Ladrille, *Salesianum*, vol. 17, 1955, 179-182.

A. Voekke, *Studia Philosophica,* vol. 15, 1955, 232-233.

K. K., *Algemeen Nederlands Tijdschrift voor Wijsbegeerte en Psychologie,* vol. 47, 1954-1955, 97-98.

107    Wahl, Jean. *Les aspects qualitatifs du réel,* I: Introduction, la philosophie de l'existence. II: Début d'une étude sur Husserl. III: La philosophie de la nature de Nicolai Hartman (Les Cours de Sorbone). 3 fasc. Paris: Centre de documentation universitiare, 1955.

108    Wahl, Jean. *Husserl, I-II* (Coll. "Cours photolithographiés"). Paris: Centre de documentation universitaire, 1958.

109    Wahl, Jean. *L'ouvrage posthume de Husserl: la Krisis.* La crise des sciences sciences européennes et la phénoménologie transcendante (Coll. "Cours photolithographieés"). Paris: Centre de documentation universitaire, 1958.

110    Wahl, Jean. *Husserl, la "Philosophie permière," erste Philosophie* (Les Cours de Sorbonne). Paris: Centre de documentation universitaire, 1961, 144 p.

## Books in German

111    Abra, Boris. *Vor-und Selbstzeitigung als Versuch der Vermenschlichung in der Phänomenologie Husserls* (Monographien zur philosophischen Forschung, 104). Meisenheim am Glan: Hain, 1972, 161 p.
**Book Reviews:**
R. Beck, *Salzburger Jahrbuch für Philosophie,* vol. 20, 1975, 153-154.

112    Adorno, Theodor W. *Zur Metakritik der Erkenntnistheorie.* Studien über Husserl und die phänomenologischen Antinomien. Stuttgart: W. Kohlhammer, 1956, 251 p. Reprinted, Edition Suhrkamp, 590, Frankfurt am Main: Suhrkamp, 1972, 245 p.
**Book Reviews:**
R. Boehm, *Revue Philosophique de Louvain,* vol. 57, 1959, 259-260.

G. Brand, *Philosophische Rundschau,* vol. 8, 1960, 261-267.

L. Eley, *Zeitschrift für Philosophische Forschung,* vol. 13, 1959, 351-357.

K. Meyer, *Etudes Philosophiques,* vol. 13, 1958, 60.

H. Ryffel, *Studia Philosophica,* vol. 20, 1961, 216-218.

H.-J. Schüring, *Zeitschrift für Philosophische Forschung,* vol. 12, 1958, 473-477.

J. Wahl, *Erasmus,* vol. 11, 1958, 2-5.

113    Adriaanse, Hendrik Johan. *Zu den Sachen selbst.* Versuch einer Konfrontation der Theologie Karl Barths mit der phänomenologischen Philosophie Edmund Husserls. s'Gravenhague: Mouton, 1974, xii-247.

114    Aguirre, Antonio. *Genetische Phänomenologie und Reduktion.* Zur Letztbegründung der Wissenschaft aus der radikalen Skepsis im Denken Husserls (Phaenomenologica, 38). The Hague: Martinus Nijhoff, 1970, xxiv-198.

**Book Reviews:**

G. Brand, *Philosophische Rundschau*, vol. 20, 1973, 65-70.

G. Hoyos, *Pensamiento*, vol. 28, 1972, 207-210.

J. San Martín, *Anales del Seminario de Metafísica*, 1971, 121-123.

115 Almeida, Guido Antonio de. *Sinn und Inhalt in der genetischen Phänomenologie Edmund Husserls* (Phaenomenologica). The Hague: Martinus Nijhoff, 1972, 230 p.

116 Anzenbacker, Arno. *Die Intentionalität bei Thomas von Aquin und Edmund Husserl.* München: Oldenburg, 1972, 234 p.

117 Asemissen,, Hermann Ulrich. *Strukturanalytische Probleme der Wahrnehmung in der Phänomenologie Husserls* (Kantstudien. Ergäzungshefte, 83). Köln: Kölner Universität-Verlag, 1957, 100 p.

**Book Reviews:**

R. Boehm, *Revue Philosophique de Louvain*, vol. 57, 1959, 258-259.

G. Brand, *Philosophische Rundschau*, vol. 8, 1960, 275-280.

J. Ell, *Freiburger Zeitschrift für Philosophie und Theologie*, vol. 7, 1960, 72-73.

J. Héring, *Revue d'Histoire et de Philosophie Religieuses*, vol. 38, 1958, 217-218.

C. Nink, *Scholastik*, vol. 35, 1960, 1124-1125.

118 Bannes, J. *Versuch einer Darstellung und Beurteilung der Grundlagen der Philosophie Edmund Husserls.* Breslau: Borgmeyer, 1930.

119 Bergman, Hugo. *Edmund Husserl.* Davar, 1938, 513 p.

120 Boehm, Rudolf. *Vom Gesichtspunkt der Phänomenologie.* Husserl-Studien (Phaenomenologica, 26). The Hague: Martinus Nijhoff, 1968, xxii-266. Contents:

"Die Philosophie als strenge Wissenschaft," 1-17.

"Husserl und der klassische Idealismus," 18-71.

"Das Absolute und die Realität," 72-105.

"Das Konstitutionsproblem und das Zeitbewusstsein," 106-118.

"Die phänomenologische Reduktion," 119-140.

"Immanenz und Transzendenz," 141-185.

"Die *Erste Philosophie* und die Wege zur Reduktion," 186-216.

"Der Phänomenologie der Geschichte," 237-259.

**Book Reviews:**

A. Mercier, *Journal of the British Society for Phenomenology*, vol. 2, 1971, 92-94.

R. Sokolowski, *Philosophy and Phenomenological Research*, vol. 32, 1971-1972, 135-139.

H. Steinbeck, *Philosophischer Literaturanzeiger*, vol. 22, 1969, 214-218.

121    Brand, Gerd. *Welt, Ich und Zeit.* Nach unveröffentlichten Manuskripten
       Edmund Husserls (Phaenomenologica). The Hague: Martinus Nijhoff,
       1955, xiv-147.
       **Book Reviews:**
       R. Boehm, *Etudes Philosophiques,* vol. 11, 1956, 105-106.
       H.-G. Geyer, *Philosophische Rundschau,* vol. 4, 1956, 82-89.
       H. Keinz, *Studia Philosophica,* vol. 17, 1957, 178.
       A. Pinto de Caralho, *Kriterion* (Brazil), vol. 11, no. 45-46, 1958, 591-592.
       X. Tilliette, *Archives de Philosophie,* vol. 19, no. 4, 1956, 141-142.

122    Brand, Gerd. *Welt, Geschichte, Mythos* (Trierer Universitätsreden, Bd. 8).
       Trier: NCO-Verlag, 1977, 89 p. Contents:
       Die wichtigsten Grundlagen der Phänomenologie Husserls;
       Interpretationen von Husserls Ansätzen zu Praxis und Geschichte; Die
       phänomenologische Analyse der mythologischen Seinsweise des Menschen.

123    Broekman, Jan M. *Phänomenologie und Egologie.* Faktisches und
       transzendentales Ego bei Edmund Husserl (Phaenomenologica, 12). The
       Hague: Martinus Nijhoff, 1963, x-224.
       **Book Reviews:**
       S. L. Hart, *Philosophy and Phenomenological Research,* vol. 25, 1964-1965,
       604.
       F. H. Heinemann, *Philosophy,* vol. 40, 1965, 166-167.
       H. Künz, *Studia Philosophica,* vol. 24, 1964, 254-258.
       H. Steinback, *Philosophischer Literaturanzeiger,* vol. 18, 1965, 82-86.

124    Brueck, Maria. *Uber das Verhältnis Edmund Husserls zu Franz Brentano,*
       vornehmlich mit Rücksicht auf Brentanos Psychologie. Würzburg, 1933,
       118 p.

125    Celms, Theodor. *Der phänomenologische Idealismus Husserls.* Riga: Acta
       Universitatis Latviensis, 1928.

126    Claesges, Ulrich. *Edmund Husserls Theorie der Raumkonstitution*
       (Phaenomenologica, 19). The Hague: Martinus Nijhoff, 1964, ix-148.
       **Book Reviews:**
       Th. de Boer, *Tijdschrift voor Filosofie,* vol. 27, 1967, 182-183.
       M. S. Frings, *Philosophy and Phenomenological Research,* vol. 26, 1965-1966,
       298-299.
       J. J., *Review of Metaphysics,* vol. 19, 1965-1966, 370.
       B. Lemaigre, *Revue des Sciences Philosophiques et Théologiques,* vol. 50, 1966,
       156-158.
       R. Sokolowski, *Journal of the History of Philosophy,* vol. 6, 1968, 305-307.

127    Claesges, Ulrich und Held, Klaus, hrsg. *Perspektiven*
       *Transzendentalphänomenologischer Forschung.* Für Ludwig Landgrebe

zum 70. Geburtstag von seinem Kölner Schülern. (Phaenomenologica, 49). The Hague: Martinus Nijhoff, 1972. Contents:

I. Zum Programm der Phänomenologie Husserls.

K. Held, "Das Problem der Intersubjektivität und die Idee einer phänomenologischen Transzendentalphilosophie," 3-60.

G. Hoyos, "Zum Teleologiebegriff in der Phänomenologie Husserls," 61-84.

U. Claesges, "Zweideutigkeiten in Husserls Lebenswelt-Befriff," 85-101.

A. Aguirre, "Transzendentalphänomenologischer Rationalismus," 102-128.

R. A. Mall, "Phenomenology of reason," 129-143.

II. Zur Neueren Wissenschaftstheorie.

P. Janssen, "Ontologie, Wissenschaftstheorie und Geschichte im Spätwerk Husserls," 145-163.

L. Eley, "Zeitlichkeit und Protologik," 164-188.

H.-U. Hoche ''Gegenwart und Handlung. Eine sprachanalytisch-phänomenologische Untersuchung," 189-224.

K. Düsing, "Das Problem der Denkökonomie bei Husserl und Mach," 225-254.

de Almeida, Guido Antonio. *see:* Almeida.

128    de Oliveira, Manfredo Araujo. *Subjektivität und Vermittlung.* Studien zur Entwicklung d. transzendentalen Denkens bei I. Kant, E. Husserl und H. Wagner. München: Fink, 1973, 329 p.

129    Diemer, Alwin. *Edmund Husserl.* Versuch einer systematischen Darstellung seiner *Phänomenologie* (Monographien zur philosophischen Forschng, Band 15). Meisenheim am Glan: Anton Hain, 1956, vii-337.

**Book Reviews:**

R. Allers, *Erasmus,* vol. 12, 1959, 452-455.

W. Cerf, *Philosophy and Phenomenological Research,* vol. 18, 1957-1958, 569-570.

E. Coreth, *Zeitschrift für Katholische Theologie,* vol. 79, 1957, 225-226.

L. Kelkel, *Etudes Philosophiques,* vol. 13, no. 1, 1958, 71.

130    Drüe, Hermann. *Edmund Husserls System der phänomenologischen Psychologie* (Phänomenologisch-psychologische Forschungen, 4). Berlin: Walter de Gruyter, 1963, xvi-326.

**Book Reviews:**

A. F. Aguirre, *Archiv für Geschichte der Philosophie,* vol. 48, 1966, 109-112.

L. Gilen, *Scholastik,* vol. 39, 1964, 112-114.

E. Heinteil, *Wiener Jahrbuch für Philosophie,* vol. 2, 1969, 298-300.

H.-P. Hempel, *Philosophische Literaturanzeiger,* vol. 1, 1964, 138-144.

H. Hülsmann, *Salzburger Jahrbuch für Philosophie,* vol. 8, 1964, 274-276.

H. W. Jager, *Psyche,* vol. 72, 1964-1965, 235-236.

J. Kijm, *Bijdragen,* vol. 26, 1965, 247.

Th. Langan, *Modern Schoolman,* vol. 43, 1965-1966, 75-76.

B. Mangus, *International Philosophical Quarterly,* vol. 4, 1964, 488-490.

H. Niel, *Archives de Philosophie,* vol. 28, 1965, 473-474.

H. Ogiermann, *Scholastik,* vol. 39, 1964, 471-472.

D. H. Salman, *Revue des Sciences Philosophiques et Théologiques,* vol. 47, 1963, 652-653.

W. H. Werkmeister, *The Personalist,* vol. 46, 1965, 149-150.

131    Ehrlich, W. *Kant and Husserl.* Kritik der transzendentalen und phänomenologischen Methode. Halle, 1923.
**Book Reviews:**

Egon von Petersdorff, *Kantstudien,* vol. 28, 1924.

132    Eigler, Günter. *Metaphysische Voraussetzungen in Husserls Zeitanalysen* (Monographien zur philosophischen Forschung, 24). Meisenheim am Glan: Hain, 1961, 117 p.
**Book Reviews:**

H. Hohl, *Philosophisches Jahrbuch,* vol. 69, 1962, 415-416.

W. H. Werkmeister, *The Personalist,* vol. 43, 1962, 138-139.

133    Eley, Lothar. *Die Krise des Apriori in der transzendentalen Phänomenologie Edmund Husserls* (Phaenomenologica, 10). The Hague: Martinus Nijhoff, 1962, viii-146.
**Book Reviews:**

J. Collins, *Modern Schoolman,* vol. 40, 1962-1963, 424-425.

Q. Lauer, *Dialogue,* vol. 2, 1963, 242.

C. Nink, *Scholastik,* vol. 38, 1963, 93-94.

134    Fein, Hubert. *Genesis und Geltung in Edmund Husserls Phänomenologie* (Kritische Studien zur Philosophie). Frankfurt am Main: Europäische Verlagsanstalt, 1970, 123 p., Wein: Europa-Verlag.

135    *Festschrift Edmund Husserl.* Zum 70. Geburtstag gewidmet. 2., unveränd. Aufl. Tübingen: Niemeyer, 1974, 370 p. [i. Aufl. als: *Jahrbuch für Philosophie und phänomenologischen Forschung,* 10, Erg. -Bd., 1929]

136    Fink, Eugen. *Sein, Wahrheit, Welt.* Vor-Fragen zum Problem des Phänomenologischen Begriffes (Phaenomenologica, 1). The Hague: Martinus Nijhoff, 1958.
**Book Reviews:**

R. Boehm, *Etudes Philosophiques,* vol. 14, 1959, 367-368.

E. Braun, *Archives de Philosophie,* vol. 22, 1959, 621-624.

H. Kuhn, *Philosophische Rundschau,* vol. 7, 1959, 9-12.

C. Nink, *Scholastik,* vol. 34, 1959, 262-267.

J. Wahl, *Revue de Métphysique et de Morale,* vol 65, 1960, 187-194.

137    Fink, Eugn. *Studien zur Phänomenologie 1930-1939* (Phaenomenologica, 21). The Hague: Martinus Nijhoff, 1966, 235 p. Contents:

Vergegenwartigung und Bild. Beiträge zur Phänomenologie der Unwirklichkeit (1930), 1-77.

Die Phänomenologische Philosophie Edmund Husserls in der Gegenwärtigen Kritik (1933), 78-156.

Was Will die Phänomenologie Edmund Husserls (Die phänomenologische Grundlegungsidee), 157-178.

Das Problem der Phänomenologie Edmund Husserls (1939), 179-225.

**Book Reviews:**

F. Bosio, *Il Pensiero,* vol. 13, 1968, 330-332.

J. Derrida, *Etudes Philosophiques,* vol. 22, 1967, 549-550.

Y. Gauthier, *Dialogue,* vol. 6, 1967-1968, 278-280.

M. Kerkhoff, *Diálogos,* vol. 4, no. 8-9, 1967, 148-150.

W. H. Werkmeister, *The Personalist,* vol. 47, 1966, 577.

138    Fink, Eugen. *Nähe und Distanz.* Phänomenologische Vorträge und Aufsätze, hrsg. von Franz-Anton Schwarz. Freiburg-München: Karl Alber, 1976, 331 p. Contents:

Die Idee der Transzendentalphilosophie bei Kant und der Phänomenologie (Erstveröffentlichung).

Die Entwicklung der Phänomenologie Husserls (Erstveröffentlichung).

Husserl (1859-1938) (Erstveröfftntlichung).

Philosophie als Überwindung der "Naivität"; Zum Problem der ontologischen Erfahrung.

Die intentionale Analyse und das Problem des spekulativen Denkens.

Welt und Geschichte; Operative Begriffe in Husserls Phänomenologie.

Die Spätphilosophie Husserls in der Freiburger Zeit. Phänomenologie und Dialektik (Erstverröffentlichung).

Phänomenologische Probleme der Verfremdung (Erstveröffentlichung).

Weltbezug und Seinsverständnis. Bewusstseinalytik und Weltprolem. Reflexionen zu Husserls phänomenologische Reduktion.

139    Fisch, M. P. *Husserls Intentionalitäts- und Ureilslehre.* Bale, 1942.

140    Föllesdal, Dagfinn. *Husserl und Frege.* Ein Beitrag zur Beleuchtung der Entstehung der phänomenologischen Philosophie (Vid.-Akad. Skr. II. H.-F. Kl. 1958, no.2). Oslo: Aschehoug, 1958, 60 p.

141    Folwart, Helmut. *Kant, Husserl, Heidegger.* Breslau, 1936.

142    Fritsch, W. *Die Welt "einklamern",* eine philosophische Frage an Edmund Husserl. Reclams Universum, 1931.

143     Funke, Gerhard. *Zur Transzendental Phänomenologie.* Bonn: Bouvier Verlag,
        1957, 147 p.
        **Book Reviews:**
        R. Boehm, *Revue Philosophique de Louvain,* vol. 57, 1959, 257.
        G. Brand, *Philosophische Rundschau,* vol. 8, 1960, 271-275.
        W. H. Müller, *Philosophia Naturalis,* vol. 5, 1958-1959, 113-114.

144     Gorsen, Peter. *Zur Phänomenologie des Bewusstseinsstroms.* Bergson, Dilthey,
        Husserl, Simmel und die Lebensphilosophischen Antinomien
        (Abhandlungen zur Philosophie, Psychologie und Pädogogik, 33). Bonn:
        Bouvier, 1966, 243 p.

145     Grünewald, Bernward. *Der phänomenologische Ursprung des Logischen.* Ein
        krit. Analyse d. phänomenologische Grundlegugn d. Logik in Edmund
        Husserls *Logischen Untersuchungen.* Kastellaun: Henn, 1977, 184 p.

146     Hartmann, Klaus. *Husserls Einfühlungstheorie auf monadologischer
        Grundlage.* Bonn: Bouvier, 1953.

147     Hegg, Hans. *Das Verhältnis der phänomenologischen Lehre von Husserl zur
        empirischen Psychologie* Heidelberg: Hahn, 1919, 59 p.

148     Heim, Klaus. *Psychologismus oder Antipsychologismus?* Berlin: 1902.

149     Held, Klaus. *Lebendige Gegenwart.* Die Frage nach der Seinsweise des
        transzendentalen Ich bei Edmund Husserl, entwickelt am Leitfaden der
        Zeitproblematik (Phaenomenologica, 23). The Hague: Martinus Nijhoff,
        1966, xvii-190.
        **Book Reviews:**
        S. Danglemayr, *Erasmus,* vol. 22, 1970, 449-452.

150     Herrmann, Friedrich-Wilhelm von. *Husserl und die Meditationen des
        Descartes* (Antrittsvorlesung) (Wissenschaft und Gegenwart.
        Geisteswissenschaft. Reihe H.48). Frankfurt am Main: V. Klostermann,
        1971, 29 p.

151     Hoche, Hans-Ulrich. *Nichtempirische Erkenntnis.* Analytische und
        synthetische Urteile a priori bei Kant und bei Husserl. Meisenheim am
        Glan: Anton Hain, 1964, 208 p.
        **Book Reviews:**
        S. Decloux, *Revue Philosophique de Louvain,* vol. 65, 1967, 136-137.
        R. Delfino, *Stromata,* vol. 21, 1965, 44-45.
        H. Delius, *Philosophical Quarterly,* vol. 16, 1966, 183-184.
        H. Ogiermann, *Theologie und Philosophie,* vol. 41, 1966, 142-143.

152     Hohl, Hubert. *Lebenswelt und Geschichte.* Grundzuge der Spätphilosophie
        Edmund Husserls (Symposium, 7). Freiburg-München: Karl Alber, 1962,
        122 p.

Book Reviews:

Fr. Bosio, *Il Pensiero*, vol. 7, 1962, 410-413.

J. Derrida, *Etudes Philosophiques*, vol. 18, 1963, 95-96.

H.-G. Gadamer, *Philosophiche Rundschau*, vol. 11, 1963, 33-35.

A. Korínek, *Gregorianum*, vol. 45, 1964, 172-175.

H. Kunz, *Studia Philosophica*, vol. 22, 1962, 217-219.

H. Ogiermann, *Scholastik*, vol. 38, 1963, 1131-1132.

153    Holenstein, Elmar. *Phänomenologie der Assoziation*. Zur Struktur und
       Funktion eines Grundprinzips der passiven Genesis bei Edmund Husserl
       (Phaenomenologica, 44). The Hague: Martinus Nijhoff, 1972, xxvi-370.
       Book Reviews:

E. Eng, *Journal of Phenomenological Psychology*, vol. 5, 1974-1975, 113-123.

J. N. Kaufmann, *Dialogue*, vol. 13, 1974, 424-428.

154    Hoyos Vasquéz, Guillermo. *Intentionalität als Verantwortung*.
       Geschichtsteleologie und Teleologie der Intentionalität bei Husserl
       (Phaenomenologica, 67). The Hague: Martinus Nijhoff, 1976, viii-212.

155    Hülsmann, Heinz. *Zur Theorie der Sprache bei Edmund Husserl* (Salzburger
       Studien zur Philosophie, 4). München: Pustet, 1964, 255 p.
       Book Reviews:

E. Albrecht, *Deutsche Zeitschrift für Philosophie*, vol. 14, 1966, 121-124.

C. Verhaak, *Bijdragen*, vol 26, 1965, 247.

B. Waldenfels, *Philosophische Rundschau*, vol. 15, 1968, 44-50.

155    *Husserl et la pensée moderne. Husserl und das Denken der Neuzeit* (Actes du
       deuxième Colloque International de Phénoménologie. Krefeld, 1-3
       novembre 1956, édités par les soins de H. L. Van Breda et J. Taminiaux.
       Akten des zweiten Internationalen Phänomenologischen Kolloquiums,
       Krefeld, 1-3 November 1956, herausgegeven von H. L. Van Breda und J.
       Taminiaux) (Phaenomenologica, 2). The Hague: Martinus Nijhoff, 1959,
       x-250. Contents:

       H. L. Van Breda, "Die Rettung von Husserls Nachlass und die Gründung
       des Husserl-Archivs (Übersetzt von Rudolf Boehm)

       F. J. J. Buytendijk, "Die Bedeutung der Phänomenologie Husserls für die
       Psychologie der Gegenwart"

       A. de Waelhens, "Die phänomenologische Idee der Intentionalität,"
       (Übersetzt von Rudolf Boehm)

       E. Fink, "Welt und Geschichte"

       H. Hyppolite, "Die fichtesche Idee der Wissenschaftslehre und der Entwurf
       Husserls (Übersetzt von Walter Biemel und E. Ch. Schröder)

       R. Ingarden, "Über den transzendentalen Idealismus bei E. Husserl"

L. Landgrebe, "Die Bedeutung der Phänomenologie Husserls für die Selbstbesinnung der Gegenwart"

K. H. Volkmann-Schluck, "Husserls Lehre von der Idealität der Bedeutung also metaphysisches Problem"

**Book Reviews:**

see: *Husserl et la pensée moderne,* no. 81.

156     Husserl, Edmund. *Briefe an Roman Ingarden mit Erläuterungen und Erinnerungen* an Husserl. Hrsg. von Roman Ingarden (Phaenomenologica, 25). The Hague: Martinus Nijhoff, 1968, ix-186.

**Book Reviews:** .

P. Gorner, *Journal of the British Society for Phenomenology,* vol. 2, 1971, 84-87.

S. L. Hart, *Philosophy and Phenomenological Research,* vol. 31, 1970-1971, 145-146.

G. Kalinowski, *Archives de Philosophie,* vol. 33, 1970, 161-162.

G. Kalinowski, *Etudes Philosophiques,* no. 3, 1969, 405-406.

157     Illeman, Werner. *Husserls vorphänomenologische Philosophie.* (Mit einer monographischen Bibliographie Husserls). Leipzig: Hirzel, 1932, 88 p. (Studien und Bibliographien zur Gegenwärtsphilosophie).

**Book Reviews:**

O. Becker, *Deutsche Literaturzeitung,* 1934.

A. Kovevnikoff, *Recherches Philosophiques,* vol. 3, 1933.

L. Landgrebe, *Kantstudien,* 1933.

158     Janssen, Paul. *Geschichte und Lebenswelt.* Ein Beitrag zur Diskussion von Husserls Spätwerk (Phaenomenologica, 35). The Hague: Martinus Nijhoff, 1970, xxii-218.

**Book Reviews:**

J. Borg, *Revue Philosophique de Louvain,* Vol. 71, 1973, 597-603.

W. H. Werkmeister., *Journal of History of Philosophy,* vol. 11, 1973, 427-429.

159     Janssen, Paul. *Edmund Husserl.* Einführung in seine Phänomenologie. Freiburg-München: Karl Alber, 1976, 184 p.

160     Kern, Iso. *Husserl und Kant.* Eine Untersuchung über Husserls Verältnis zu Kant und zum Neukantianismus (Phaenomenologica, 16). The Hague: Martinus Nijhoff, 1964, xxiv-448.

**Book Reviews:**

E. Garulli, *Il Pensiero,* vol. 9, 1964, 125-146.

K. Hartman, *Kantstudien,* vol. 58, 1967, 370-375.

H. Hülsmann, *Salzburger Jahrbuch für Philosophie,* vol. 10-11, 1966-1967, 462-464.

A. L. Kelkel, *Revue de Métaphysique et de Morale,* vol. 71, 1966, 154-198.

A. Marini, *Aut Aut,* no. 111, 1969, 73-90.

H. Pietersma, *Dialogue,* vol. 5, 1966-1967, 630-633.

R. Sokolowski, *Philosophy and Phenomenological Research,* vol. 26, 1965-1966, 132-134.

W. H. Werkmeister, *Journal of History and Philosophy,* vol. 6, 1968, 97-98.

161    Kraft, Julius. *Von Husserl zu Heidegger.* Kritik der phänomenologischen Philosophie, Leipzig, 1932. 2 erweiterte Auflage. Frankfurt am Main: Verlag 'Oeffentliches Leben', 1957, 147 p. 3 Aufl. Hamburg: Meiner, 1977, 151 p.

**Book Reviews: (1932):**

V. Springmeyer, *Kantstudien,* vol. 37, 281-284.

**Book Reviews (1957):**

A. Brunner, *Salzburger Zeitschrift,* vol. 163, 1958-1959, 313-314.

162    Krämer, Ernst. *Benno Erdmanns Wahrheitsauffassung und ihre Kritik* durch Husserl. Blaubeuren, 1930.

163    Landgrebe, Ludwig, and Patocka, Jan. *Edmund Husserl zum Gedächtnis. Schriften des Prager philosophischen Cercles.* Prag, I, 1938, 287-321. Nachdr. d. Ausg. Prag. Academic Verlagsbuchhandlung, 1938.

164    Landgrebe, Ludwig. *Phänomenologie und Geschichte.* Gütersloh: Gütersloher Verlaghaus G. Mohn, 1967, 206 p.

**Book Reviews:**

W. Cerf, *Review of Metaphysics,* vol. 5, 1951-1952, 125-144.

H. Kolleritsch, *Philosophy and History,* vol. 2, 1969, 40-41.

M. A. Presas, *Revista de Filosofía* (La Plata), no. 21, 1969, 112-114.

165    Lapp, Adolf. *Versuch über den Wahrheitsbegriff mit besonderer Berücksichtigung von Rickert, Husserl und Vaihinger.* Erlangen, 1912.

166    Lübbe, Hermann. *Bewusstsein in Geschichten.* Studien zur Phänomenologie der Subjektivität: Mach, Husserl, Schapp, Wittgenstein (Rombach-Hochschulpaperback, 37). Freiburg: Verlag Rombach, 1972, 174 p.

**Book Reviews:**

G. Pfafferott, *Archiv für Geschichte der Philosophie,* vol. 57, 1975, 114-118.

167    Marbach, Eduard. *Das Problem des Ich in der Phänomenologie Husserls* (Phaenomenologica, 59). The Hague: Martinus Nijhoff, 1974, xvi-3348.

**Book Reviews:**

J. Collins, *Modern Schoolman,* vol. 53, March 1976, 323-324.

168    Maxsein, Agnes. *Die Entwicklung des Begriffs a priori von Bolzano über Lotze zu Husserl und den von ihm beeinflussten Phänomenologen.* Fulda, 1933.

169 Misch, Georg. *Lebensphilosophie und Phänomenologie.* Eine Auseinandersetzang d. Diltheyschen Richtung mit Heidegger und Husserl. Mit ein Nachwort z. 3. Aufl. Unveränd. Nachdr. d.2. Aufl. Leipzeg-Berlin, 1931. Stuttgart: Teubner, 1967, x-328.
**Book Reviews (1931):**
A.Kojevnikoff, *Recherches Philosophiques,* vol. 2, 1934, 470-475.
A. Spaier, *Recherches Philosophiques,* vol. 3, 1935, 431-432.

170 Müller, Wolfgang Hermann. *Die Philosophie Edmund Husserls nach den Grundzügen ihrer Entstehung und ihrem systematischen Gehalt.* Bonn: Bouvier, 1956, 92 p.
**Book Reviews:**
G. Brand, *Philosophische Rundschau,* vol. 8, 1960, 268-271.
W. Cerf, *Philosophy and Phenomenological Research,* vol. 18, 1957, 569-570.

171 Müller, Severin. *Vernunft und Technik:* d. Dialektik d. Erscheinung bei Edmund Husserl (Alber-Broschur Philosophie). Freiburg im Bresgau: Karl Alber, 1976, 349 p.

172 Noack, Hermann. Hrgs. *Husserl* (Wege der Forschung, 40). Darmstadt: Wissenschaftliche Buchgesellsachft, 1973, x-340. Contents:
P. Natorp, "Zur Frage der logischenMethode. Mit Beziehung auf Edmund Husserls *Prolegomena zur reinen Logik,*" 1-15.
W. Schuppe, "Zur Psychologismus und zum Normcharakter der Lokig. Eine Ergänzung zu Husserls *Logischen Untersuchungen,*" 16-35.
P. Natorp, "Husserls *Ideen zu einer reinen Phänomenologie,*" 36-60.
E. Stein, "Husserls Phänomenologie und die Philosophie des Hl. Thomas v. Aquino. Versuch einer Gegenüberstellung," 61-86.
E. Lévinas, "Über die *Ideen* Edmund Husserls (Aus dem Französischen übersetzt von H. Backes)," 87-128.
O. Becker, "Die Philosophie Edmund Husserls. Anlässlich seines 70. Geburtstags dargestellt," 129-167.
R. Ingarden, "Rezension von: Edmund Husserls, *Formale und transzendentale Logik* (1929)," 168-173.
H.Kuhn, "Rezension von: Edmund Husserl, *Méditations cartesiennes.* Introduction à la phénoménologie (1931)," 174-187.
A. de Waelhens, "Descartes und das phänomenologische Denken. Aus dem Französischen übersetzt von Klaux Stickweh," 188-209.
G. Berger, "Husserl und Hume. Aus dem Französischen übersetzt von Katharina Arndt," 210-222.
A. Gurwitsch, "Rezension von: Gaston Berger, *Das cogito in Husserls Philosophie* (1941)," "Aus dem Englischen übersetzt von Ursula Beul, 222-230.

P. Ricoeur, "Husserl und der Sinn Geschichte. Aus dem Französischen übersetzt von Klaus Stichweh," 231-276.

H.-L. Van Breda, "Husserl und das Problem der Freiheit. Aus dem Französischen übersetzt von Katharina Arndt," 277-281.

W. Biemel, "Husserls *Encyclopedia-Britannica*-Artikel und Heideggers Anmerkungen dazu," 282-315.

L. Landgrebe, "Ist Husserls Phänomenologie eine Transzendental-philosophie?" 316-324.

"Bibliographie," 325-331.

**Book Reviews:**

K. Schuhmann, *Tijdschrift voor Filosofie,* vol. 37, 1975, 143-147.

173    Orth, Ernst Wolfgang. *Bedeutung, Sinn, Gegenstand.* Studien zur Sprachphilosophie Edmund Husserls und Richard Hönigswald (Conscientia, 3). Bonn: Bouvier, 1967, xiv-269.

174    Passweg, Salcia. *Phänomenologie und Ontologie.* Husserl, Scheler, Heidegger. Zürich: Heitz, 1939, viii-215.

175    Pazanin, Ante. *Wissenschaft und Geschichte in der Phänomenologie Edmund Husserls* (Phaenomenologica, 46). The Hague: Martinus Nijhoff, 1972, xii-192.

**Book Reviews:**

M. Di Cintio, *Giornale Critico della Filosofia Italiana,* vol. 53, 1974, 147-150.

176    Pöll, M. *Wesen und Wesenserkenntnis.* Untersuchungen mit besonderer Berücksichtigung der Phänomenologie Husserls und Schelers. Munchen, 1936, x-207.

177    *Phänomenologie, Lebendig oder tot?* Zum 30. Todesjahr Edmund Husserls. Von Eugen Fink u. a. (Veröffentlichungen der Katholischen Akademie der Erzdiözese Freiburg, 18). Karlsruhe: Badenia-Verlag, 1969, 48 p.

178    *Phänomenologie und Praxis.* Einleitung: Ernst Wolfgang Orth. Beiträge: Ludwig Landgrebe, Hermann Lübbe, Peter Schwankl, Ulrich Wienbruch, Ante Fazanin, Stephan Strasser, (Phänomenologische Forschungen, 3). Freiburg im Bresgau: Verlag Karl Alber, 1976, 180 p.

179    Pivcevic, Edo. *Von Husserl zu Sartre.* Auf. d. Spuren d. Phänomenologie. Aus d. Engl. von Anne Edwards (List--Taschenbücher der Wissenschaft, 1643: Philosophie). München: List, 1972, 254 p.

180    Rang, Bernhard. *Kausalität und Motivation.* Untersuchungen zum Verhältnis von Perspektivität und Objektivität in der Phänomenologie Edmund Husserls (Phaenomenologica, 53). The Hague: Martinus Nijhoff, 1973, viii-248.

181    Rechtenwald, Friederike. *Die phänomenologische Reduktion die Edmund Husserl.* München, 1929, 30 p.

182    Reenpää, Yrjö. *Über die Lehre vom Wissen.* Darstellung und Kommentar der Wissenslehren von Edmund Husserl and Viktor von Weizsäcker sowie

Hinweis auf diejenigen von Richard B. Braithwaite, unsere zeitzentrierte Theorie und die Theorie von Gotthard Günther (Annales Academiae Scientiarum Fennicae, ser. B. tom. 145, 1). Helsinki: Soumalainen Tiedakatemai, 1966, 114 p.

183     Robberechts, Ludovic. *Edmund Husserl*. Ein Einführung in seine Phänomenologie. Aus dem Französischen von Klaus und Margret Held. Mit ein Nachwort von Klaus Held (Claassen-Cargo). Hamburg: Claassen, 1967, 162 p.

**Book Reviews:**

H.-G. Eschke, *Deutsche Zeitschrift für Philosophie*, vol. 17, 1969, 1271-1275.

184     Rosen, Klaus. *Evidenz in Husserls deskriptiver Transzendentalphilosophie* (Monographien zur philosophischen Forschung, 153). Meisenheim am Glan: Hain, 1977, 170 p.

185     Roth, Alois. *Edmund Husserls ethische Untersuchungen*. Dargestellt anhand seiner Vorlesungsmanuskripte (Phaenomenologica, 7). The Hague: Martinus Nijhoff, 1960, xviii-171.

**Book Reviews:**

P. Chiodi, *Rivista di Filosofia*, vol. 54, 1963, 488-492.

H. Declève, *Revue Internationale de Philosophie*, vol. 18, 1964, 140-142.

M. Farber, *Philosophy and Phenomenological Research*, vol. 24, 1963-1964, 552-560.

E. Przywara, *Etudes Philosophiques*, vol. 18, 1963, 232.

H.-J. Schuering, *Mind*, vol. 71, 1962, 579-582.

S. Vanni-Rovighi, *Rivisti di Filosofia Neo-Scholastica*, vol. 55, 1963, 535.

Fr. J. Vogt, *Philosophischer Literaturanzeiger*, vol. 14, 1961, 206-208.

186     Röttges, Heinz. *Evidenz und Solipsismus in Husserls Cartesianischen Meditationen* (Philosophie als Benziehungswissenschaft, 9) (Eidos, 12). Frankfurt am Main: Heiderhoff, 1971, 23 p.

187     Schuhmann, Karl. *Die Fundamentalbetrachtung der Phänomenologie*. Zum Weltproblem in der Philosophie Edmund Husserls (Phaenomenologica, 42). The Hague: Martinus Nijhoff, 1971, xlvii-201.

**Book Reviews:**

A. Aguirre, *Pensamiento*, vol. 32, 1976, 107-111.

M. Fischer, *Philosophisches Jahrbuch*, vol. 80,1973, 435-437.

188     Schuhman, Karl. *Die Dialektik der Phänomenologie*, Vol. I: *Husserl über Pfänder*. Vol. II: *Reine Phänomenologie und phänomenologische Philosophie*. Historischanalytische Monographie über Husserls *Ideen I* (Phaenomenologica, 56-57). The Hague: Martinus Nijhoff, 1973, x-211, viii-197.

Book Reviews: I

H. Spiegelberg, *Tijdschrift voor Filosofie*, vol. 36, 1974, 565-573.

Book Reviews: II

R. Sokolowski, *Review of Metaphysics*, vol. 28, 1974-1975, 566-567.

H. Spiegelberg, *Journal of the British Society for Phenomenology*, vol. 5, 1974, 273-276.

189    Schuhmann, Karl. *Husserl-Chronik.* Denk- und Lebensweg Edmund Husserls (Husserliana. Dokumente, I). The Hague: Martinus Nijhoff, 1977, xii-516.

190    Schümmer, Heinz. *Die Wahrnehmungs- und Erkenntnismetaphysik Max Schelers in den Stadienihrer Entwicklung.* Unter besonderer Berücksichtigung der Beziehungen Schelers zu Husserl. Bonn: Bouvier Verlag, 1954.

191    Seebohm, Thomas. *Die Bedingungen der Mölichkeit der Transzendental-Philosophie.* Edmund Husserls transzendental-phänomenologischer Ansatz, dargestellt im Anschluss an seine Kant-Kritik (Abhandlungen zur Philosophie, Psychologie und Pädogogik, 24). Bonn: H. Bouvier und Co. Verlag, 1962, 202 p.

Book Reviews:

J. Berger, *Philosophisches Jahrbuch*, vol. 71, 1963-1964, 415-418.

Fr. Bosio, *Il Pensiero*, vol. 7, 1962, 406-410.

A. Brunner, *Salzburger Zeitschrift*, vol. 172, 1962-1963, 466-468.

H.-G. Fritzsche, *Theologische Literaturzeitung*, vol. 89, 1964, 940-941.

H.-G. Gadamer, *Philosophische Rundschau*, vol. 11, 1963, 35-41.

I. Kern, *Revue Philosophique de Louvain*, vol. 61, 1963, 692-694.

H. Kunz, *Studia Philosphica*, vol. 24, 1964, 1250-1253.

G. Mende, *Deutsche Literaturzeitung*, vol. 84, 1963, 555-557.

A. F. Morajao, *Documentación Crítica Iberoamerica de Filosofía y Ciencias Afines* (Sevilla), vol. 2, 1965, 318-329.

H. Ogiermann, *Scholastik*, vol. 38, 1963, 122-123.

C. Verkaak, *Bijdragen*, vol. 24, 1963, 106-107.

192    Seigfried, Thomas. *Phänomenologie und Geschichte.* Kairos, 1926, 92-231.

193    Szilasi, Wilhelm. *Einführung in die Phänomenologie Edmund Husserls.* Tübingen: Max Niemeyer, 1959, 142 p.

Book Reviews:

G. Beschin, *Giornale di Metafisica*, vol. 21, 1966, 408-409.

W. von Del Negro, *Philosophischer Literaturanzeiger*, vol. 14, 1961, 183-186.

L. M., *Pensamiento*, vol. 17, 1961, 221.

H. Ogiermann, *Scholastik*, vol. 36, 1961 449-450.

K. Schilling, *Deutsche Literaturzeitung*, vol. 82, 1961, 300-303.

194	Temuralq, T. *Ueber die Grenzen der Erkennbarkeit bei Husserl und Scheler.* Berlin, 1937, 174 p.

195	Tugendhat, Ernst. *Der Wahrheitsbegriff bei Husserl und Heidegger.* Berlin: Walter de Gruyte, 1967, xxi-416. (2. unveränd. Aufl., 1970).
	**Book Reviews:**
	G. Brand, *Philosophische Rundschau,* vol. 17, 1970, 77-94.

	R. Ceñal, *Pensamiento,* vol. 25, 1969, 295-297.

	J. de Vries, *Theologie und Philosophie,* vol. 44, 1969, 305-307.

	C. F. Gehlmann, *Zeitschrift für Katholische Theologie,* vol. 93, 1971, 462-465.

	G. Guzzoni, *Il Pensiero,* vol. 16, 1971, 91-93.

	K. Hartmann, *Philosophy and History,* vol. 1, 1968, 53-55.

	E. Heintel, *Wiener Jahrbuch für Philosophie,* vol. 2, 1969, 300-303.

	S. IJsseling, *Tijdschrift voor Filosofie,* vol. 31, 1969, 771-785.

	B.-M. Lemaigre, *Revue des Sciences Philosophiques et Théologiques,* vol. 52, 1968, 293-296.

	O. Pöggeler, *Psyche,* vol. 76, 1968-1969, 376-385.

	M. A. Presas, *Revista de Filosofía* (La Plata), no. 2, 1970, 141-143.

	M. A. Presas, *Nord,* no. 10, 1968, 137-139.

196	Van Breda, H. L., hrsg. *Vérité et vérification. Wahrheit und Verifikation.* (Phaenomenologica, 61). The Hague: Martinus Nijhoff, 1974, 225 p.
	Contents:
	E. Fink, "Grussansprache," 1-2.

	G. Funke, "Bewusstseinswissenschaft," 3-58.

	E. Paci, "Vérification empirique et transcendance de la vérité," 59-70.

	A. Pazanin, "Wahrheit und Lebenswelt beim späten Husserl," 71-116.

	S. Bachelard, "Logique husserlienne et sémantique," 117-131.

	S. Strasser, "Probleme des 'Verstehens' in neuer Sicht," 132-189.

	P. Ricoeur, "Conclusion," 190-209.

	H.-G. Gadamer, "Zusamenfassender Bericht," 210-223.

197	Vollmer, R. *Beiträge zur Kritik der phänomenologische Methode vom Standpunkte der Friesschen Schule aus.* Yena, 1929.

198	Waldenfels, Bernhard. *Das Zwischenreich des Dialogs.* Socialphilosophische Untersuchungen in Anschluss an Edmund Husserl (Phaenomenologica, 41). The Hague: Martinus Nijhoff, 1971, xiv-428.
	**Book Reviews:**
	D. Howard, *Erasmus,* vol. 25, 1973, 69-73.

	W. Steinbeck, *Philosophischer Literaturanzeiger,* vol. 25, 1972, 5-7.

199	Weidauer, Friedrich. *Kritik der Transcendentalphänomenologie Husserls.* I. Teil einer Kritik der Gegenwärtsphilosophie (Studien und Bibliographien zur Gegenwäwrtsphilosophie, H. 2). Leipzig, 1933, xx-132.

**Book Reviews:**

A. Kojevnikoff, *Recherches Philosophiques,* vol. 3, 1935, 429.

L. Landgrebe, *Kantstudien,* vol. 39, 1934, 60-61.

200    Wewel, Meinolf. *Die Konstitution des transzendenten Etwas im Vollzug des Sehens.* Eine Untersuchung im Anschluss and die Philosophie von Hans Lipps und in Auseinandersetzung mit Edmund Husserls Lehre vom "intentionalen Bewusstseinskorrelat." Düsseldorf: M. M. Wewel, 1968, 166 p.

201    Wundt, Wilhelm. *Kleine Schriften,* vol. 1, Leipzig, 1910, 511-634.

202    Zocher, R. *Husserls Phänomenologie und Schuppes Logik.* Ein Beitrag zur Kritik des intuitionistischen Ontologismus in der Immanenzidee. München, 1932, 280 p.

**Book Reviews:**

A. Kojevnikoff, *Recherches Philosophiques,* vol. 2, 1934, 477-480.

### Books in Italian

203    Adorno, Theodor W. *Sulla metacritica della gnoseologica.* Studi su Husserl e sulle antinomie fenomenologiche. Trad. it. di Alba Burger Cori. Milano: Sugar, 1964, 248 p.

**Book Reviews:**

A. Martini, *Giornale di Metafisica,* vol. 23, 1968, 487-490.

A. Negri, *Giornale Critico della Filosofia Italiana,* vol. 44, 1965, 454-458.

204    Ales Bello, Angela. *Edmund Husserl e la storia.* Parma: Nuovi Quaderni, 1972, xv-186.

**Book Reviews:**

G. Drago, *Giornale di Metafisica,* vol. 29, 1974, 275-276.

F. Liverzioni, *Incontri Culturali,* vol. 8, 1975, 379-381.

M. Malestata, *Rivista Critica di Storia della Filosofia,* vol. 26, 1973, 171-176.

C. Pacchioni, *Bolletino Filosofico,* vol. 7, 1973, 60-61.

F. Rizzo, *Rivista di Studi Crociani,* vol. 11, 1974, 235-238.

A. M. S., *Sapienza,* vol. 26, 1973, 242-244.

C. Terzi, *Filosofia,* vol. 25, 1974, 86-89.

205    Altamore, Giovanni. *Dalla fenomenologia all'ontologia.* Saggio interpretativo su Edmund Husserl (Il Pensiero moderno. S. III, 6). Padova: CEDAM, 1969, 184 p.

**Book Reviews:**

G. A. De Vici, *Sophia,* vol. 37, 1969, 127-129.

206     Baratta, Giorgio. *L'idealismo fenomenologico di Edmund Husserl* (Publicazioni dell'Università di Urbino. Testi e saggi). Urbino: Argalia, 1969, 244 p.

**Book Reviews:**

M. Corvez, *Revue Thomiste,* vol. 75, 1975, 296-299.

C. Aniz, *Estudios Filosóficos* (Santender), vol. 20, 1971, 197-198.

A. Medina, *Review of Metaphysics,* vol. 26, 1972-1973, 151-152.

G. Pennisi, *Sophia,* vol. 38, 1970, 274-275.

A. Ponselto, *Civiltà Cattolica,* vol. 122, I, 1971, 192-193.

207     *Bilancio della fenomenologica e dell'esistenzialismo.* Relazioni di E. Garin, E. Paci, P. Prini. Università di Padova, Facoltà di Magistero. Padova: Liviana Editrice, 1960, 160 p. [E. Garin, "Introduzione storica," 7-47; Interventi, risposte e chairimenti, 47-72].

**Book Reviews:**

E. Renzi, *Il Verri,* no. 4, 1960, 123-130.

208     Biral, Alessandro. *L'nità del sapere in Husserl* (Publicazioni dell Scuola di Perfezionamento in Filosofia dell'Università di Padova, 8). Padova: CEDAM, 1967, 136 p.

**Book Reviews:**

G. B. Bacchin, *Giornale di Metafisica,* vol. 23, 1968, 582-585.

M. Olivieri, *Bolletino Filosofico,* vol. 1, 1967-1968, 118-122.

A. Vincenti, *Giornale di Metafisica,* vol. 24, 1969, 337-339.

209     Brand, Gerd. *Mondo, io e tempo nei manoscritti inediti di Husserl.* Introduzione di Enzo Paci (Idee nuove, 30). Milano: V. Bompiani, 1960, 254 p.

**Book Reviews:**

R. Franchini, *Il Pensiero,* vol. 6, 1961, 105-109.

M. Sancipriano, *Filosofia e Vita,* no. 4, 1960, 73-80.

M. Sancipriano, *Humanitas* (Brescia), vol. 16, 1961, 85-86.

210     Bosio, Franco. *Fondazione della logica in Husserl* (Biblioteca di filosofia e di cultura, 3). Milano: Lampugnani Nigri, 1966, 232 p.

**Book Reviews:**

G. Forni, *Giornale di Metafisica,* vol. 22, 1967, 767-772.

211     *Il compito della fenomenologia.* Scritti di G. Alliney, F. Bianco, S. Breton, C. Fabro, G. Funke, M. de Gandillac, R. Ingarden, R. Lazzarini, A. Plebe, E. Przywara, R. Pucci. (*Archivio di Filosofia,* no. 1-2, 1957). Padova: CEDAM, 1957, 276 p. Contents:

E. Przywara, "Phänomenologie, Realogie, Relationologie," 9-26.

E. Przywara, "Fenomenologia, realogia, relazionologia," 27, 36.

R. Lazzarini, "Fenomenologia, intentionalità e problematica degli status," 37-57.

S. Breton, "Essai d'une phénoménologie de l'exigence et des attitudes métaphysiques," 59-93.

R. Pucci, "Significato e compito della fenomenologia," 95-115.

G. Funke, "Transzendental-phanomenologische Untersuchung über "Universalen Idealismus," "Intentionanalyse," und "Habitusgenese," 117-154.

G. Funke, "Ricerca trascendentale-fenomenologica su 'idealismo universale', 'analisi intenzionale' e 'origine dell'habitus'," 155-185.

F. Bianco, "Metodo fenomenologico ed intepretazione del mito," 199-216.

R. Ingarden, "Ueber die gegenwärtigen Aufgaben der Phaenomenologie," 229-241.

R. Ingarden, "I compiti attuali della fenomenologia," 243-249.

**Book Reviews:**

J. G., *Nouvelle Revue de Théologie,* vol. 81, 1959, 890.

212    Costa, Filippo. *La filosofia come scienza rigorosa.* Saggio su Husserl. Milano: Silva ed., 1961, 412 p.

213    Costa, Filippo. *Cos'é la fenomenologia.* Husserl e la corrente filosoficapiú attuale e rigorosa (I nuovi, I). Milano: Silva ed. [1963?], 416 p.

**Book Reviews:**

Anonymous, *Revue de Métaphysique et de Morale,* vol. 69, 1964, 476-477.

214    Dentoni, Francesco. *La formazione e la problematica filosofica del primo Husserl*(Il primo progetto husserliano di filosofia della matematica). Roma: Luciano Lucarini, 1977, 211 p.

215    Derrida, Jacques. *La voce e il fenomeno.* Introduzione al problema del segno nella fenomenologia di Husserl. A cura di G. Dalmasso (Saggi, 15). Milano: Jaca Book, 1968, vii-150.

216    D'Ippolito, Bianca Maria. *Ontologia e storia in Edmund Husserl* (Saggi, I). Salerno: Rumma, 1968, 354 p.

**Book Reviews:**

P. Cosenza, *Logos,* no. 1, 1972, 241-242.

217    Faggiotto, Pietro. *L'interpretazione husserliana del pensiero moderno.* Guida alla lettura della parte I e II dalla *Crisi.* Padova: Gregoriana, 1971, 54 p.

218    Farber, Marvin. *Prospettive della fenomenologiac.* Bilancio del pensiero di Husserl. Trad. di Stefano Poggi. Firenze: Sansoni, 1969. [Trans. di *The aims of phenomenology,* 1966].

**Book Reviews:**

A. Babolin, *Incontri Culturali,* vol. 3, 1970, 232-233.

219     Ferrari, M. V. *Dalla fenomenologica pura alla trascendenza assoluta* (Husserl e San Tamasso d'Aquino). Roma: Edit. Universita Lateranense, 1968, 100 p.

221     Garulli, Enrico. *Coscienza e storia in Husserl.* Urbino: S. T. E. U., 1964, 180 p.

221     Giulietti, Giovanni. *La filosofia del profondo in Husserl e in Zamboni* (Uno studio comparativo). Treviso: Libreria Editrice Canova, 1965, 122 p.
        **Book Reviews:**
            A. Franchi, *Giornale di Metafisica,* vol. 21, 1966, 729.

222     Jacobelli Isoldi, Angela Maria. *Il tempo in Kant e suoi sviluppi in Husserl e in Heidegger.* Anno accademico 1962-1963 (Università delgi studi di Roma, Facoltà di magistero). Roma, Editr. E. de Santis, 1963, 168 p.

223     Kelkel, Lothar and Schérer, René. *Husserl.* La vita e l'opera. Traduzione e appendice bibliografica a cura di Emilio Renzi (Coll. "I Gabbiani), 43). Milano: Il Saggiatore, 1966, 182 p.

224     *La fenomenologia.* Atti del'XI Convengo del Centro di Studi Filosofici tra Professori Universitari: Gallarate, 1955. Brescia: Morcelliana, 1956, 285 p.
        **Book Reviews:**
            A. Carlini, *Giornale di Metafisica,* vol. 12, 1957, 131-133.
            R. Ceñal, *Revista de Filosofía* (Madrid), vol. 17, 1958, 98-101.

225     Landgrebe, Ludwig. *Itinerari della fenomenologia.* Trad. e nota a cura di Giovanni Piacenti (Classici del pensiero moderno e contemporaneo, 8). Torino: Marietti, 1974, 307 p.
        **Book Reviews:**
            F. De Natale, *Filosofia,* vol. 26, 1975, 221-224.

226     Lazzarini, Renato. *Intenzionalità e istanza metafisica* (Pubblicazioni dell' Istututo di Studi Filosofici - Roma. Serie II, N.3). Romas: Fretelli Bocca, 1954, 482 p.
        **Book Reviews:**
            A. Bausola, *Rivista di Filosofia Neo-Scolastica,* vol. 48, 1956, 252-266.
            G. Cives, *Archivio di Filosofia,* N. 1, 1956, 288-293.
            St. Deandrea, *Angelicum,* vol. 33, 1956, 315-332.
            G. Gianini, *Humanitas,* (Brescia), vol. 11, 1955, 585-588.
            A. Hayen, *Nouvelle Revue de Théologie,* vol. 80, 1958, 373-378.
            E. Riverso, *Sapienza,* vol. 8, 1955, 373-378.
            M. F. Sciacca, *Giornale di Metafisica,* vol. 10, 1955, 797-798.

227     Masullo, Aldo. *La comunità come fondamento.* Fichte, Husserl, Sartre (Filosofia e pedogogia). Napoli: Libreria Scientifica Editrice, 1965, 468 p.

**Book Reviews:**

E. Garulli, *Il Pensiero,* vol. 11, 1966, 254-258.

G. Martano, *Giornale Critico della Filosofia Italiana,* vol. 46, 1967, 154-158.

228    Masullo, Aldo. *Lezioni sull'intersoggettività, I: Fichte e Husserl.* Napoli: Libreria Scientifica Editrice, 1964, 140 p. [litografato].

229    Melandri, Enzo. *Logica ed esperienza in Husserl.* Bologna, 1960.
**Book Reviews:**

F. B., *Aut Aut,* no. 71, 1962, 420-423.

S. Vanni Rovighi, *Rivista di Filosofia Neo-Scholastic,* vol. 55, 1963, 531-532.

230    Minozzi, Bruno. *L'idealismo fenomenologico di Edmund Husserl.* Bologna: Soc. editrice "Il Mulino," 1962, 32 p.

231    Oggioni, Emilio. *La fenomenologia di Husserl e il pensiero contemporaneo* (Scienze filosofiche). Bologna: R. Pàtron, 1963, x-182.

232    *Omaggio a Husserl.* Saggi di A. Banfi, E. Filippini, G. Guzzoni, L.Lugarini, E. Melandri, G. D. Neri, E. Paci, G. Pedroli, R. Pucci, G. Semerari, S. Vanni-Rovighi. A cura di Enzo Paci (La Cultura, 9). Milano: Il Saggiatore, 1960, 320 p. Contents:

E. Paci, "Husserl sempre di nuovo," 7-27.

S. Vanni-Rovighi, "Una fonte remota della teoria husserliana dell'intenzionalità," 47-65.

G. D. Neri, "La filosofia come ontologia universale e le obiezioni del relativismo scettico in Husserl," 67-79.

E. Melandri, "I paradossi dell'infinito nell'orizzonte fenomenologico," 81-120.

G. Semerari, "La 'filosofia come scienza rigorosa' e la critica fenomenologica del dogmatismo," 121-161.

L. Lugarini, "La fondazione trascendentale della logica in Husserl," 163-194.

G. Pedroli, "Realtà e prasi in Husserl," 195-211.

E. Filippini, "Ego ed alter-ego nella *'Krisis' di Husserl,"* *213-225.*

G. Guzzoni, "Di una posizione 'storicamente' positiva respetto alla fenomenologia di Husserl," 263-289.

R. Pucci, "Fenomenologia e psicologia," 227-262.

I. Bona, "Bibliografia," 296-316.
**Book Reviews:**

G. Guzzoni, *Kantstudien,* vol. 53, 1961-1962, 114-115.

R. M. Kunz, *Philosophy and Phenomenological Research,* vol. 21, 1960-1961, 589-590.

L. Lugarini, *Il Pensiero,* vol. 5, 1960, 115-121.

G. Piana, *Il Verri,* no. 4, 1960, 117-123.

233      Pacchiani, Claudio. *L'idea della scienza in Husserl* (Pubblicazioni della Scoula di Perfezionamento in Filosofia dell'Università di Padova. Quaderni di Storia della Filosofia, 5). Padova: CEDAM, 1973, 124 p.

**Book Reviews:**

E. Namer, *Revue Phil. de la France et de l'Etranger,* 1975, (100), 457-458.

D. Rambaudi, *Giornale di Metafisica,* vol. 31, 1976, 199-200.

234      Paci, Enzo. *Il problema del tempo nella fenomenologia di Husserl.* Corso di filosofia teoretica. Anno accademico 1959-1960 (Università delgi studi di Milano, Facultà di lettere e filosofia). Milano: La Goliardica, 1960, 232 p.

235      Paci, Enzo. *Tempo e verità nella fenomenologica di Husserl* (Biblioteca di cultura moderna, 559). Bari: Laterza, 1961, 280 p.

**Book Reviews:**

F. Fanizza, *Giornale Critico della Filosofia Italiana,* vol. 41, no. 3, 1962, 405-417.

G. Gallino, *Filosofia,* vol. 13, 1962, 332-338.

E. Garulli, *Revue de Métaphysique et de Morale,* vol. 67, 1962, 384-390.

C. Sini, *Il Pensiero Critico,* vol. 3, no. 2-3, 1961, 132-140.

S. Vanni-Rovighi, *Rivista di Filosofia Neo-Scholastica,* vol. 55, 1963, 530-531.

236      Paci, Enzo. *Fenomenologia e antropologia.* Corsi di filosofia teoretica. Anno accademico 1961-1962. Appendice: Carlo Sini *Lezioni introduttive al pensiero di Husserl.* Milano: La Goliardica, 1962, 190-xcviii.

237      Paci, Enzo. *La formazione del pensiero di Husserl e il problema della costituzione della natura materiale e della natura animale.* Corso di filosofia teoretica. Anno accademico 1966-1967. (Università degli studi di Milano). Milano: La Goliardica, 1967, 201 p.

238      Pantaleo, Pasquale. *La direzione coscienza-intenzione nella filosofia di Kant e Husserl.* Bari: Arti grafiche Laterza e Polo, 1967, 363 p.

239      Pedroli, Guido. *La fenomenologia di Husserl* (Collezione di filosofia, 14). Torino: Taylor, 1958, 212 p.

**Book Reviews:**

P. Bertolini, *Rivista Rosminiana di Filosofia e di Cultura,* vol. 53, 1959, 150-151.

A. Deregibus, *Giornale di Metafisica,* vol. 15, 1960, 211-213.

A. Kockelmans, *Revue Philosophique de Louvain,* vol. 57, 1959, 252-254.

F. Sirchia, *Rivista di Filosofia Neo-Scolastica,* vol. 52, 1960, 484-489.

240      Penati, Giancarlo. *Alienazione e verità.* Husserl, Hartmann, Heidegger e l'ontologia come liberazione (Studi filosofici, 7). Brescia: Paideia, 1972, 206 p.

241 Piana, Giovanni. *Esistenza e storia negli inediti di Husserl.* Prefazione di Enzo Paci (Biblioteca di filosofia e di cultura, 2). Milano: Lampugnani Nigri, 1965, xvi-114.
**Book Reviews:**
G. Forni, *Filosofia,* vol. 18, 1967, 546-550.
P. F. T., *Studi Urbinati,* vol. 40, 1966, 292.

242 Poggi, Stefano. *Husserl e la fenomenologia* (Scuola aperta. Scienze umane). Firenze: Sansoni, 1973, 106 p.

243 Pucci, Raffaele. *Io trascendentale e mondo della vita nella fenomenologia di Husserl.* Napoli: Libreria scientifica editrice, 1962, 26 p.

244 Raggiunti, Renzo. *Husserl.* Dalla logica alla fenomenologia (Istituto di Filosofia dell'Università di Pisa). Firenze: F. Le Monnier, 1967, 328 p.
**Book Reviews:**
Anonymous, *Giornale di Metafisica,* vol. 23, 1968, 631-634.
L. d'A., *Rivista Internazionale di Filosifa del Diritto.*
A. Marietti, *Etudes Philosophiques,* no. 2, 1969, 257.
E. Namer, *Revue de Métaphysique et de Morale,* vol. 75, 1970, 254.
E. Namer, *Revue Philosophique de la France et de l'Etranger,* vol. 95, 1970, 254-255.

245 Ruggenini, Mario. *Verità e soggettività.* L'idealismo fenomenologico di Edmund Husserl (Quaderni veronesi di varia letteratura, 8). 1972, vii-110. Verona: Fiorini, 1972.

246 Sancipriano, Mario. *Il logos di Husserl.* Genealogia della logica e dinamica intenzionale. Torino: Bottega d'Erasmo, 1962, 440 p.
**Book Reviews:**
M. T. Antonelli, *Giornale di Metafisica,* vol. 19, 213-215.
G. Bortolaso, *Civiltà Cattolica,* vol. 117, no. 1, 1966, 159-160.
F. B., *Aut Aut,* no. 74, 1963, 104-107.
A. Pattin, *Revue de l'Université d'Ottawa,* vol. 34, 1964, 207.
E. Riverso, *Rivista Critica di Storia della Filosofia,* vol. 16, 1963, 379-380.
C. Rossi, *Filosofia,* vol. 14, 1963, 432-433.
C. Solaguren, *Verdad y Vida,* vol. 21, 1963, 485.
A. Tomasi, *Rivista Rosminiana di Filosofia e di Cultura,* vol. 57, 1963, 282-285.
S. Vanni-Rovighi, *Rivista di Filosofia Neo-Scholastica,* vol. 55, 1963, 536.

247 Sancipriano, Mario. *L'ethos di Husserl.* Communicazione intersoggettiva ed etica sociale, I. Torino: Giappichelli, 1967, 136 p.
**Book Reviews:**
V. Agosti, *Giornale di Metafisica,* vol. 25, 1970, 760-761.

248 Sciacca, Giuseppe Maria. *Esistenza e realtà in Husserl.* Palermo: Palumbo, 1960, 126 p.

**Book Reviews:**

B. Bertè, *Rivista Rosminiana di Filosofia e di Cultura,* vol. 55, 1961, 364-366.

N. Dazzi, *Scientia,* vol. 96, 1961, 392-393.

M. Schiavone, *Giornale di Metafisica,* vol. 18, 1963, 714.

249     Scrimieri, Giorgio. *I problemi della logica.* Studio sui *Prolegomena zur reinen Logik di Edmund Husserl.* Alla luce dei manoscritti inediti delgi Archivi Husserl di Louvain. Bari: Tip. Levante, 1958, 124 p.

250     Scrimieri, Giorgio. *Problemi di logica.* Studio sui *Prolegomena zur reinen Logik* di Edmund Husserl. Con l'ausilio dei manoscritti inediti delgi Archivi di Louvain. Bari: Levante, 1959, 160 p.

251     Scrimieri, Giorgio. *La matematica nel pensiero giovanile di Edmund Husserl.* Bari: F. Cacucci, 1965, 296 p.

252     Scrimeri, Giorgio. *La formazione della fenomenologia di Edmund Husserl.* La *Ding-Vorlesung* del 1907. Bari: Edizioni Levante, 1967, viii-494.

**Book Reviews:**

E. Namer, *Revue de Métaphysique et de Morale,* vol. 75, 1970, 254-255.

E. Namer, *Revue Phil. de la France et de l'Etranger,* vol. 95, 1970, 255-256.

253     Sini, Carlo. *Lezioni introduttive al pensiero di Husserl,* in Enco Paci, *Fenomenologia e antropologia.* Corsi di filosofia teoretica. Ano accademico 1961-1962. Milano: La Goliardica, 1962, 190-xcvii.

254     *Tempo e intenzionalità.* Husserliana. Scritti di E. Husserl, E. Paci, P. Caruso, E. Renzi, F. Bosio, V. Fagone, G. Piana, W. Biemel, L. Lugarini, A. Plebe, F. Bianco, J. Wyrsch. (*Archivio di Filosofia,* no. 1, 1960). Padova: CEDAM, 1960, 200 p. Contents:

E. Paci, "Commento al Manoscritto E III 5 (della teologia di Husserl)," 17-22.

E. Paci, "Tempo e relazione intenzionale in Husserl," 23-48.

P. Caruso, "L'Io trascendnetale come 'durata esplosiva'. Intenzionalità e tempo nella fenomenologia di Husserl," 49-72.

F. Bosio, "Constituzione statica e constituzione genetica," 73-88.

255     Thévenaz, Pierre. *La fenomenologia.* Husserl, Heidegger, Sartre, Merleau-Ponty. Trad.di G. Mura. Roma: Città Nuova, 1968, 102 p.

256     Toldo, Sisto. *Ontologia trascendentale e antropologia in Edmund Husserl* (Collona di studi filosofici, 25). Padova: Gregoriana, 1973, 189 p.

257     Vanni-Rovighi, Sofia. *Husserl* (Maestri del pensiero). Brescia: La Scuola, 1947, 176 p.

258     Vanni-Rovighi, Sofia. *La filosofia di Edmund Husserl* (Pubblicazioni dell' Università di Milano, 31). Milano: 1949, 173 p.

259     Vanni-Rovighi, Sofia. *La fenomenologia di Edmund Husserl.* Appunti delle lezioni (Dispense, 26). Milano: Celuc, 1973, 190 p.

**Book Reviews:**

A. Prezioso, *Sapienza*, vol. 28, 1975, 219-228.

A. Prezioso, *Rivista Critica di Storia della Filosofia*, vol. 27, 1974, 383-387.

260    Voltaggio, Franco. *Fondamenti della logica di Husserl* (Saggi di cultura contemporanea, 65). Milano: Edizioni di Comunità, 1965, 237 p.

**Book Reviews:**

G. Forni, *Filosofia*, vol. 18, 1967, 550-553.

F. V., *De Homine*, no. 19-20, 1966, 305-306.

261    Zecchi, Stefano. *Fenomenologia dell'esperienza*. Saggio su Husserl (Pubblicazioni dell Facoltà di Lettere e Filosofia dell'Università di Milano, 66. Sezione a cura dell'Instituto di Filosofia, I). Firenze: La Nuova Italia Editrice, 1972, xix-152.

## Books in Spanish

262    Astrada, Carlos. *Idealismo fenomenológico y metafísica existencial.* Buenos Aires, 1936.

263    Bascuñana, López. *Exposición y critica de la fenomenología de Edmund Husserl.* Barcelon, 1940, 61 p.

264    Caso, Antonio. *El acto ideario y la filosofía de Husserl.* México: Porrúa, 1946.

265    Cruz Hernández, Miguel. *La doctrina de la intencionalidad en la fenomenología* (Acta Salmanticensia. Filosofía y Letras, tome XIV, 2). Salamanca: Universidad de Salamanca, 1958, 116 p.

**Book Reviews:**

F. Ruiz, *Augustinus*, vol. 4, 1959, 436.

266    de Muralt, André. *La idea de la fenomenología.* (Filosofía contemporánea, 9). México: Universidad Nacional Autonoma de México, 1963, 492 p.

**Book Reviews:**

T. Sandin, *Studium*, vol. 6, 1966, 565-566.

267    Díaz Hernández, Carlos. *La intencionalidad en la fenomenología de Husserl* (Extracto de tesis). Madrid: Facultad de Filosofíía y Letras de al Universidad, 1970.

267    Díaz Hernández, Carlos. *Intencionalidad y fenomenología* (Biblioteca Promoción del Pueblo, Serie P., 40). Algorta: Edit. Zero, 1971, 128 p.

268    Farber, Marvin. *Husserl.* Trad. pro J.M. Coco Ferraris. Buenos Airs: Ediciones Losange, Colección Filósofos y Sistemas, 1956. [Trans. of *The Foundations of phenomenology:* Edmund Husserl and the quest for a rigorous science], 75 p.

269    *Husserl.* Tercer coloquio filosófico de Royaumont (Cahiers de Royaumont) (Col. Biblioteca de filosofía, serie mayor, 4). Buenos Aires: Paidós, 1968, 372 p.

270 Kogan, Jacobo. *Husserl* (Enciclopedia del pensamiento esencial). Buenos Aires: Centro Ed. de América Latina, 1967, 123 p.

271 Kolakowski, Leszek. *Husserl y la búsqueda de la certeza.* Trad. Adolfo Murguia Zuriarrain. Madrid: Alianza Editorial, 1977, 72 p.

272 Landgrebe, Ludwig. *El camino de la fenomenología* (Col. Biblioteca de filosofía). Buenos Aires: Sudaméricana, 1968, 320 p.
**Book Reviews:**

C. Cullen, *Stromata,* vol. 24, 1970, 373-374.

M. Danieri, *Sapientia,* vol. 24, 1969, 230-232.

273 Landgrebe, Ludwig. *Fenomenología y historia.* Caracas: Monte Avila, 1975, 233 p.

274 Martínez Bonati, Félix. *La concepción del lenguaje en la filosofíía de Husserl* (Serie negra, 6). Santiago/Chile: Ediciones de los Anales de la Universidad de Chile, 1960, 98 p.

275 Mayz Vallenilla, Ernesto. *Fenomenología del conocimiento.* El problema de la constitución del objeto en la filosofía de Husserl (Coleccion de tesis doctorales, 1). Caracas, Facultad de Humanidades y Educación, Universidad Central de Venezuela [Buenos Aires: Imprenta López, 1956], 372 p.
**Book Reviews:**

R. Boehm, *Revue Philosophique de Louvain,* vol. 57, 1959, 254-255.

J. D. Garcia Bacca, *Episteé* (Caracas), vol. 1, 1957, 505-510.

E. Nicol, *Philosophy and Phenomenological Research,* vol. 19, 1958-59, 274-277.

E. Ramírez, *Revista de Filosofía* (Madrid, vol. 19, 1960, 284-286.

J. Rodriquez, *Crisis,* vol. 5, 1958, 139-140.

L. Villoro, *Diánoia,* vol. 3, 1957, 379-383.

276 Millan Puelles, Antonio. *El problema del ente ideal.* Un examen a traves de de Husserl y Hartmann. Madrid: Instituto Luis Vivés, C.S.I.C. 1948, 196 p.
**Book Reviews:**

C. París, *Revista de Filosofíía* (Madrid), vol. 8, 1949, 135-136.

277 Palacios, Leopoldo. *Ideología pura y fenomenología pura.* De Balmes a Husserl. Madrid: Ateneo, 1952, 30 p.

278 Peligero Escudero, Fernando Luís. *Objectividad e idealidad en Husserl.* Madrid: Autor [Inocencio Fernández, 36, Madrid-35], 1976, 88 p.

279 Pérez Espejo, Sergio. *La reducción trascendental y el problema del alter ego en las 'Meditaciones cartesianas' de Husserl* (Colección "Lectio philosóphica"). Cartagena: Athenas Ediciones, 1959, 33 p.

280 Robberechts, Ludovico. *El pensamiento de Husserl* (Col. Breviarios, 198). México: Porrúa, 1968, 115 p.

281 Rodríquez Sández, José Luis. *El ser absoluto de la conciencia.* Un análisi de su sentido en la filosofía de Edmund Husserl. Madrid: Edit. Gredos, [s.a.], 30 p.

282 Schérer, René. *La fenomenología de las 'Investigaciones lógica' de Husserl.* Trad. del francés por Jesús Díaz (Biblioteca hispanica de filosofía, 59). Madrid: Gredos, 1969, 348 p.

**Book Reviews:**

A. Pintor-Ramos, *Naturaleza y Gracia,* vol. 17, 1970, 165-177.

M. T. A., *Estudios Filosóficos,* vol. 19, 1970, 445-446.

283 *Symposium sobre la noción husserliana de la "Lebenswelt".* Por José Gaos, Ludwig Landgrebe, Enzo Paci, John Wild (XIII Congreso Internacional de Filosofía). México: Universidad Nacional Autónoma de México, Centro de Estudios Filosóficos, 1963, 94 p. Contents:

L. Villoro, "Presentación," 7-18.

J. Gaos, "La *Lebenswelt* de Husserl," 19-24.

L. Landgrebe, "Das Methodenproblem der transzendentalen Wissenschaft vom lebensweltlichen Apriori," 25-49.

E. Paci, "Die Lebensweltwissenschaft," 51-75.

J. Wild, "Husserl's life-world and the lived body," 77-93.

284 Szilasi, Wilhelm. *Introducción a la fenomenología de Husserl.* Trad. Ricardo Maliandi (Col. Biblioteca de filosofiía). Buenos Aires: Amorrotu Ed., 1973, 188 p.

285 Vela, Fernando. *Abreviatura de Investigaciones lógicas de Edmund Husserl.* Buenos Aires: Revista de Occidente, Argentina, 1949, 507 p.

286 Villoro, Luis. *Estudios sobre Husserl* México: Universidad Nacional Autonoma de México, 1975, 179 p. (Opuscúlos, 83. Serie Investigación). Contents:

1. Los antecedentes de la reducción fenomenológica.

2. La reducción a la inmanencia.

3. La constitución de la realidad en la ciencia pura.

4. Ciencia radical y sabiduria.

5. La filosofía primera.

6. Fenomenología y filosofía analítica.

287 Virasoro, Rafael. *Introducción al estudio de la fenomenología de Husserl* (Symposium sobre existencialismo, 8). Rosario: Universidad del Litoral - Instituto de Filosofía, 1955, 47 p.

288 Xirau, Joaquín. *La filosofía de Husserl* (Biblioteca de filosofía) Buenos Aires: Troquel, 1966, 297 p.

## Books in Other Languages

289 Beerling, R. F. *De transcendental vreemdeling.* Een studie over Husserl, fenomenologie en sociale wetenschappen. Hilversum-Amsterdam: W. Dehaan & J. M. Meulenhoff, 1965, 175 p.
**Book Reviews:**

O. D. Duinter, *Wijsgerig Perspectief op Maatschappij en Wetenschap,* vol. 6, 1965-1966, 299-300.

S. Strasser, *Algemeen Nederlands Tijdschrift voor Wijsbegeerte en Psychologie,* vol. 58, 1966, 105-107.

290 de Boer, Theodorus. *De ontwikkelingsgang in het denken van Husserl.* Die entwicklung im Denken Husserls (mit deutscher Zusamenfassung). Assen: Van Gorcum, 1966, xxiv-632.
**Book Reviews:**

R. Boehm, *Algemeen Nederlands Tijdschrift voor Wijsbegeerte en Psychologie,* vol. 59, 1967, 243-250.

R. Boehm, *Philosophische Rundschau,* vol. 15, 1968, 283-290.

J. H. Nota, *Bijdragen,* vol. 30, 1969, 221-222.

S. U. Zuidema. *Philosophia Reformata,* vol. 32, 1967, 179-187.

291 Fragata, Júlio, S.J. *Problemas da fenomenologia de Husserl* (Coleccao "Filosofia," 19). Braga: Livraria Cruz, 1962, 202 p.
**Book Reviews:**

Anonymous, *Ciencia y Fe,* vol. 18, 1962, 412-413.

V. Capánaga, *Augustinus,* vol. 7, 1962, 48.

G. de Sotiello, *Naturaleza y Gracia,* vol. 11, 1964, 361.

P. DurÂo, *Revista Portuguesa de Filosofia,* vol. 19, 1963, 316-317.

R. Maliandi, *Philosophischer Literaturanzeiger,* vol. 16, 1963, 135-137.

T. Montull, *Estudios Filosoficos,* vol. 11, 1962, 352-353.

J. Roig Ginorella, *Espíritu,* vol. 13, no. 49, 93.

J. Roig Gironella, *Espíritu,* vol. 15, no. 53, 1966, 85-86.

T. Sandín, *Studium,* vol. 4, 1964, 391.

J. Santalo, *Arbor,* vol. 56, 1963, 319-320.

292 Fragata, Julio, S.J. *A fenomenologia de Husserl como fundamento da filosofia* ("Filosofia." Estudos publicados pela Faculdade de Filosofia de Braga). Braga: Livraria Cruz, 1959, 288 p.
**Book Reviews:**

P. Arbousse-Bastide, *Etudes Philosophiques,* vol. 14, 1959, 369.

V. Capánaga, *Augustinus,* vol. 5, 1960, 133.

D. Díaz, *Revista de Filosofía* (Madrid), vol. 19, 1960, 283-284.

J. Iriarte, *Razon y Fe,* vol. 160, 1959, 498-499.

J. C. Scanone, *Ciencia y Fe,* Vol. 15, 1959, 351-354.

B. Turiel, *Studium,* vol. 4, 1960, 392.

A. A. A., *FL,* vol. 6, 1959, 144-146.

A. de L., *Revista Portuguesa de Filosofia,* vol 16, 1960, 490-491.

293     Ingarden, Roman. Edmund Husserl, in *Z badan nad filosofia wspólczesna* (Dziela filozoficzne). Warszawa: Pantstwowe Wydawnictwo Naukowe, 1963, 664 p. 381-628.

294     Ingarden, Roman. *Innforing i Edmund Husserls fenomenologi.* 10 Oslo-forelesninger 1957. Oversatt fra tysk av Per Fr. Christiansen. Oslo: Johan Grundt Tanum Forlag, 1970, 366 p.

295     Ingarden, Roman. *Wstep do fenomenologii Husserla.* Wyklady wygloszone na Uniwersytecia w Oslo 15-IX-17,XI 1967 w jezyku niemieckim. Trad Andrzej Póltawski. Warszawa: Panstwowe Wydawnictwo Naukowe, 1974, 238 p.

**Book Review:**

J. Kowalski, *Revue Philosophique de Louvain,* vol. 74, 1976, 311-317.

296     Kockelmans, A. *Edmund Husserl.* Een inleiding tot zijn fenomenologie (Denkers over God en Wereld, 5). Tielt, The Hague: Lannoo, 1963, 128 p.

**Book Reviews:**

D. M. De Petter, *Tijdschrift voor Filosofie,* vol. 26, 1964, 720-721.

K. De Voght, *Collectanea Mechliniensia,* vol. 48, 1963, 410.

B. Klein Wasskink, *Nederlands Theologisch Tijdschrift,* vol. 18, 1963-1964, 420-421.

A. Poncelet, *Streven,* vol. 17, 1963-1964, 288.

J. H. Nota, *Bijdragen,* vol 28, 1967, 104.

H. van der Leew, *Streven,* vol. 17, 1963-1964, 185.

297     Kockelmans, J. J. G. A. *De fenomenologische psychologie volgens Husserl.* Een historisch-kritische studie (Randgebieden, 10). Tielt, Lannoo; 's-Grevenh. Anna Paulownastraaat, 73, 1964, 397 p.

**Book Reviews:**

K. Schuhmann, *Tijdschrift voor Filosofie,* vol. 30, 1968, 175-177.

F. Vandenbussche, *Streven,* vol. 19, 1965-1966, 183.

R. Vander Gucht, *Revue Nouvelle,* vol. 46, 1967, 251-252.

298     Lee Kwei-Liang, *Edmund Husserl's phenomenology* [in Chinese]. Taiwan, 1963.

299     Linschoten, J. *Op weg naar een fenomenologische psychologie.* Husserl en James. Utrecht, 1959.

**Book Reviews:**

J. M. Kijn, *Streven,* vol. 13, 1959-1960, 590.

J.H. van der Berg, *Algemeen Nederlands Tijschrfit voor Wijsbegeerte en Psychologie,* vol. 52, 1959-1960, 261-263.

300     Martel, Karol. *U podstaw fenomenologii Husserla.* Warszawa: Ksiazka i Widza, 1967, 254 p.

301     Micic, Zagorka. *Fenomenologija Edmunda Husserla.* Studija iz savremene filozofije, Belgrad, 1937, 176 p.

302     Morujó, Alexandre Fradique. *A doutrina da intencionalidade na fenomenologia* de Husserl (Das Investigacoes lógica as meditacoes cartesianas). Coimbra: Universidade de Combra, 1955.

**Book Reviews:**

A. V. V., *Kriterion* (Brazil), vol. 11, no. 45-46, 1958, 588-591.

B. T., *Filosofia (Lisboa), vol. 2, no. 8, 1956, 274-275.*

303     MorujÂo, Alexandre Fradique. *Mundo e intencionalidade.* Ensaio sobre o conceito de mundo na fenomenologia de Husserl (Instituto de Estudos filosóficos. Série de Filosofia). Combra: Universidade de Coimbra, 1961, 274 p.

**Book Reviews:**

J. Fragata, *Revista Portuguesa de Filosofia,* vol. 18, 1962, 92-93.

304     Petrescu, Camille. *Husserl,* o introducera ên la filosofia fenomenologia. Société Roumaine de Philosophie, Bucarest, 1938, 56 p.

305     Póltawski, Andrzej. *Swiat, spostrzetenie, swiadomosc, Fenomenologiczna koncepcja swiadmosci a realizm.* Warszawa: Panstwowe Wydawnictwo Naukowe, 1973, 474 p.

306     Sjestow, Leo. *Krisis der zerkerheden.* Pascal-Dostojewsky-Husserl. [Uit: *Na wesach iowa en Potestas clavium*]. Vert. uit. het Russisch door C. I. Spruit, 2e dr. (Parthenon-reeks). Bussum, Moussault, 1958, 220 p.

307     Spet, G. *Javlenie i Smysl.* Fenomenologij kak osnovnaja nauka i jeja problemy. Moskva, 1914, 219 p.

308     Uygur, Nermi. *Edmund Husserl'de Baskasinin ben'i problemi.* Transzendental fenomenologie ile transzendental felsefenin özune giris. Istanbul Üniversitesi Edebiyat Fakültesi Yayinlari: 791. Istanbul, 1958, 152 p.

308     Vajda, Mihaly. *Záójelbe tett tudomány.* A husserli fenomenológia tudományfelfogásanák brálatahoz. Budapest: Akadémiai Kiadó, 1968, 175 p.

310     Van Peursen, Cornelis A. *De tijd bij Augustinus en Husserl.* Groningen: J. B. Wolters, 1953, 20 p.

311     Veloso, Agostinho, S.J. *Nas encruzihadas do pensamento.* Vol. II: Sob o signo de Husserl. Porto: Livraria Apostolado da Impresa, 1956, 400 p.

**Book Reviews:**

D. Díaz. *Revista de Filosofía* (Madrid), vol. 17, 1958, 519.

M. Azevedo, *Revista Portuguesa de Filosofia,* vol. 14, 1958, 100-102.

Barata Tavarez, *Filosofia* (Lisboa), vol. 4, no. 14, 1957, 151-152.

# Section 2

# Doctoral Dissertations

312    Adorno, Theodor W. "Die Transzendenz des Dinglichen und Noematischen in Husserls Phänomenologie." Frankfurt, 1924.

313    Allen, Jeffner M. "Husserl and intersubjectivity: A phenomenological investigation of the analogical structure of intersubjectivity." Duquesne University, 1973, 590 p. *Dissertation Abstract Int.,* vol. 34, no. 12, June 1974, 7816-A.

314    Allison, David B. "Derrida's critique of Husserl: The philosophy of presence." The Pennsylvania State University, 1974, 201 p. *Dissertation Abstracts Int.,* vol. 35, no. 6, Dec. 1974, 3803-A.

315    Almeida, Guido Antonio de. "Sinn und Inhalt in der genetischen Phänomenologie Husserls." Freibug im Bresgau, 1970.

316    Attig, Thomas W. "Cartesianism, certainty and the cogito in Husserl's *Cartesian Meditations.*" Washington University, 1973, 342 p. *Dissertation Abstracts Int.,* vol. 34, no. 12, June 1974, 7817-A.

317    Atwell, John E. "A critical exposition of Edmund Husserl's first two *Logical investigations.*" University of Wisconsin, 1964, 208 p. *Dissertation Abstracts Int.,* vol. 25, no. 6, Dec. 1964, 3616-A. London: University Microfilms international, 1976.

318    Banja, John D. "Ego and reduction: A key to the development of Husserl's phenomenology." Fordham University, 1975, 281 p. *Dissertation Abstracts Int.,* vol. 37, no. 2, Aug. 1976, 1017-A.

319    Bannes, Joachim. "Versuch einer Darstellung und Beurteilung der Philosophie E. Husserls." Breslau, 1930, 118 p.

320    Baseheart, Sister Mary Catharine. "The encounter of Husserl's phenomenology and the philosophy of St. Thomas in selected writings of Edith Stein." University of Notre Dame, 1960, 210 p. *Dissertation Abstracts Int.,* vol. 21, no. 3, Sept, 1960, 646-A. London: University Microfilms Int., 1977.

321    Bernet, Rudolf. "Phänomenologische Erkenntnistheorie und Semantik. Eine Untersuchung zu Husserls Lehre von der noematischen Intentionalität." Louvain, 1976.

322    Bodnar, Joanne. "Bolzano and Husserl: Logic and phenomenology," SUNY
       at Buffalo, 1976, 172 p. *Dissertation Abstracts Int.,* vol. 37, no. 8, Feb. 1977,
       5178-A.

323    Bossert, Philip J. "The origin and early development of Husserl's method of
       phenomenology reduction." Washington University, 1973, 277 p.
       *Dissertation Abstracts Int.,* vol. 34, no. 5, Nov. 1973, 2692-A.

324    Brand, Gerd. "Der Rueckgang auf das welterfahrende Leben und die
       Zeitlichkeit als seine Ur-Form. Nach unveroeffentlichten Manuskripten
       Edmund Husserls." Louvain, 1950, viii-208.

325    Brough, John Barnett. "A study of the logic and evolution of Edmund
       Husserl's theory of the constitution of time-consciousness, 1893-1917."
       Georgetown University, 1970, 503 p. *Dissertation Abstracts Int.,* vol. 31, no.
       5, Nov. 1970, 2433-A. London: University Microfilms Int., 1977.

326    Bruzina, Ronald Charles. "Logos and eidos: A study in the phenomenological
       meaning of concept according to Husserl and Merleau-Ponty." University
       of Notre Dame, 1966, 256 p. *Dissertation Abstracts Int.,* vol. 27, no. 6, Dec.
       1966, 1862-A.

327    Burke, John P. "The concept of world in Husserl's transcendental
       phenomenology." University of California at San Diego, 1974, 495 p.
       *Dissertation Abstracts Int.,* vol. 35, no. 2, Aug. 1974, 1154-A.

328    Bush, Charles Peter. "Concerning Husserl's apparent metaphysical idealism:
       A critique of Roman Ingarden." University of Southern California, 1977.
       *Dissertation Abstracts Int.,* vol. 38, no. 10, April 1978, 6163-A.

329    Butts, Robert E. "Husserl's criticisms of Hume's theory of knowledge."
       University of Pennsylvania, 1957, 254 p. *Dissertation Abstracts Int.,* vol. 17,
       no. 11, May 1958, 2639-A.

330    Chandler, Albert R. "Plato's theory of ideas in the light of Husserl's theory
       of universals." Harvard University, 1913.

331    Cunningham, Suzanne M. "Language and intersubjectivity in the
       phenomenology of Edmund Husserl." The Florida State University, 1972,
       155 p. *Dissertation Abstracts Int.,* vol. 33, no. 5, Nov. 1972, 2432-A.

332    Debus, Ite Irmgard. "A critical analysis of Husserl's *Ideen I.*" The Johns
       Hopkins University, 1971, 250 p. *Dissertation Abstracts Int.,* vol. 32, no. 5,
       Nov. 1971, 2741-A. London: University Microfilms Int., 1977.

333    Devers Johnson, Guillermo. "Bases fundamentales de la ontología
       fenomenológica." Universidad Nacional Autonoma de México, 1946.

334    Dougherty, Charles J. "Phenomenological critique of empiricism: A study in
       the philosophies of Husserl and Peirce." University of Notre Dame, 1975,
       245 p. *Dissertation Abstracts Int.,* vol. 36, no. 3, Sept. 1975, 1576-A.

335    Downes, Chauncey B. "Husserl's theory of other minds. A study of the
       *Cartesian meditations.*" New York University, 1963, 345 p. *Dissertation
       Abstracts Int.,* vol. 25, no. 1, July 1964, 536-A. Ann Arbor, Mich., London:
       University Microfilms Int, 1976.

336     Dreyfus, Hubert L. "Husserl's phenomenology of perception. From
        transcendental to existential phenomenology." Harvard University, 1964,
        153 p. Ch. 1, 1-17 reprinted in *Phenomenology and existentialism,* Robert
        C. Solomon (ed.). New York: Harper & Row, 1972, 196-210.

337     Drummond, John J. "Presenting and kinaesthetic sensations in Husserl's
        phenomenology of perception." Georgetown University, 1975, 295 p.
        *Dissertation Abstracts Int.,* vol. 36, no. 9, March 1976, 6144-A.

338     Engel, W. "Zur Kritik der Phänomenologie Husserls." Prag, 1929.
        Manuskript mit gedruckter Inhaltangabe im *Jarhuch der philos. Fakultät,*
        1929.

339     Fischer, Gilbert R. "A study in the philosophy of Husserl." University of
        Chicago, 1962, 160 p.

340     Folwart, Helmut. "Kant, Husserl, Heidegger (Kritizismus, Phänomenologie,
        Existenzialontologie)." Habilit.-Schrift, Breslau, 1936, 281 p.

341     Füchs, Wolfgang W. "Phenomenology and the metaphysics of presence. An
        essay in the philosophy of Edmund Husserl." The Pennsylvania State
        University, 1971, 148 p. *Dissertation Abstracts Int.,* vol. 32, no. 9, March
        1972, 5283-A.

342     Gehlen, Arnold. "Wirklicher und unwirklicher Geist. Eine philosophische
        Untersuchung in der Methode der absoluten Phänomenologie."
        Habilit-Schrift, Leipzig, 1932.

343     Gotesky, Rubin. "Logic as an independent science. An examination of E.
        Husserl's conception of pure logic in the *Prolegomena zur reinen Logik*
        (First volume of the *Logische Untersuchungen*)." New York University,
        1939, 246 p. Ann Arbor, Michigan, London: Univeristy Microfilms Int.
        1977.

344     Graumann, Heinz. "Versuch einer historisch-kritischen Einleitung in die
        Phänomenologie des Verstehens." München, 1924.

345     Grundwaldt, H. H. "Ueber die Phänomenologie Husserls. Mit besonderer
        Berücksictigung der Wesenschau und der Forschungsmethode Gailieo
        Galileis." Berlin, 1927, 81 p.

346     Gurwitsch, Aron. "Phänomenologie der Thematik und des reinen Ich-Studien
        über Beziehungen von Gestalttheorie und Phänomenologie." Göttigen,
        1929. Published in *Psychologische Forschng,* 1929, 279-381.

347     Haddock, G. E. Rosado. "Edmund Husserls Philosophie der Logik und
        Mathematik im Lichte der gegenwartigen Logik und
        Grundlagensforschung." Bonn, 1973.

348     Hartjes, John F. "The critique of the 'given' in Wilfrid Sellars and Edmund
        Husserl." The Catholic University of America, 1974, 280 p. *Dissertation
        Abstracts Int.,* vol. 35, no. 3, Sept. 1974, 1701-A.

349     Heber, Johannes. "Die phänomenologisches Methode in der
        Religionsphilosophie. Ein Beitrag zur Methodologie der
        Wesensbestimmung der Religion." Leipzig, 192, 59 p.

**Book Reviews:**
R. Winkler, *Blätter für deutsche Philosophie,* vol. 5, 1931-1932, 148-150.

350    Hegg, Hans. "Das Verhältnis der phänomenologischen Lehre von Husserl zur emprischen Psychologie." Bern, 1919, 59 p.

351    Hemmendinger, David. "Husserl's phenomenological program: A study of evidence and analysis." Yale University, 1973, 270 p. *Dissertation Abstracts,* vol. 34, no. 5, Nov. 1973, 2699-A.

352    Heyde, G. "Von philosophische Ausgang. Die Grundlegung der Philosophie untersucht am Beispiel der Lehre von J. Rehmke, H. Driesch, E. Husserl, J. Volkelt, H. Rickert." Leipzig.

353    Hofmann, H. "Ueber den Empfindungsbegriff." Götti<sub>n</sub>gen, 1913. (*Archiv fur die gesammte Psychologie,* vol. 26, 1913).

354    Holveck, Eleanore Walkowski. "Edmund Husserl's concept of the ego in the *Cartesian meditations.*" University of North Carolina at Chapel Hill, 1970, 179 p. *Dissertation Abstracts Int.,* vol. 31, no. 11, June 1971, 6111-A. Ann Arbor, Michigan, London: University Microfilms Int., 1977.

355    Hoy, Ronald C. "Time and the mental: An examination of Broad's and Husserl's theories of temporal consciousness." Univeristy of Pittsburgh, 1974, 215 p. *Dissertation Abstracts Int.,* vol. 35, no. 2, Aug. 1974, 1160-A.

356    Huertas-Jourda, José. "On the threshold of phenomenology. A study of Edmund Husserl's *Philosophie der Arithmetik.*" New York University, 1969, 209 p. *Dissertation Abstracts Int.,* vol. 30, no. 8, Feb. 1970, 3502-A.

357    Iturrate, Miguel. "Existential psychoanalysis: A phenomenological essay." Fordham University, 1976, 298 p. *Dissertation Abstracts Int.,* vol. 37 no. 6, Dec. 1976, 2941-2942-A.

358    Janssen Paul. "Geschichte und Lebenswelt. Ein Beitrag zur Diskussion der Husserlschen Spätphilosophie (Inaugural-Dissertation zur Erlangung des Doktorgrades der philosophischen Fakultät der Universität Köln). Koln, 1964, 239 p.

359    Kelly, Francis J. "The structural and the developmental aspects of the formulation of categorial judgments in the philosophy of Edmund Husserl." Georgetown University, 1978, 399 p. D.A. 39:11 May 1979, 6810A.

360    Kersten, Frederick I. "Husserl's investigations toward a phenomenology of space." New School for Social Research, 1964, 259 p. *Dissertation Abstracts Int.,* vol. 25, no. 10, April 1965, 5988-A.

361    Kim, Hong-Woo. "Phenomenology and political philosophy: A study of the political implications of Husserl's account of the life-world." University of Georgia, 1975, 240 p. *Dissertation Abstracts Int.,* vol. 37, no. 2, Aug. 1976, 1023-A.

362    Kim, Sang-Ki. "The problem of contingency of the world in Husserl's phenomenology." SUNY at Buffalo, 1973, 173 p. *Dissertation Abstracts Int.,* vol. 34, no. 9, March 1974, 6045-A.

363    Klein, Theodore Ernest, Jr. "The world as horizon. Husserl's constitutional theory of the objective world." Rice University, 1967, 198 p. *Dissertation Abstracts Int.,* vol. 28, no. 4, Oct. 1967, 1469-A. Ann Arbor, Michigan, London: University Microfilms Int. 1977.

364    König, Josef. "Der Begriff des Intuition." Göttingen, Halle, 1926, 420 p. [bes. 290-367].

365    Krämer, Ernst. "Bruno Erdmanns Warheitsauffassung und ihre Kritik durch Husserl." München, 1930, 68 p.

366    Kroner, R. "Ueber logische und ästhetische Allgemeingültigkeit." Freiburg, 1906, xiii-99.

367    Kynast, Reinhard. "Intuitive Erkenntnis." Breslau, 1919.

368    Langdorf, Lenore. "Husserl on judging. A critique of the theory of ideal objects." SUNY at Stony Brook, 1977, 304 p. *Dissertation Abstracts Int.,* vol. 38, no. 6, Dec. 1977, 3560-A.

369    Lapp, A. "Versuch über den Wahrheitsbegriff." Erlangen, 1912.

370    Larrabee, Mary J. "Static and genetic phenomenology: A study of two methods in Husserl's philosophy." University of Toronto, 1974. *Dissertation Abstracts Int.,* vol. 37, no. 5, Nov. 1976, 2944-A.

371    Leavy, John Peter. "Undecidables and old names: Derrida's deconstruction and "Introduction" to Husserl's *The Origin of geometry.*" Emory University, 1976. *Dissertation Abstracts Int.,* vol. 37, no. 9, March 1977, 5886-A.

372    Lenzen, Wilhelm. "Der Intentionsgadanke in der Phänomenologie und die erkenntnistheoretische Repräsentation." Bonn, 1929.

373    Levin, David Michael. "A critique of Edmund Husserl's theory of adequate and apodictic evidence." Columbia University, 1967, 360 p. *Dissertation Abstracts Int.,* vol. 28, no. 10, April 1968, 4213-A. Ann Arbor, Michigan, London: University Microfilms Int., 1977.

374    Madden, Robert E. "Husserl and the problem of hidden reason: Intentionality as accomplished life." Duquesne University, 1973, 435 p. *Dissertation Abstracts Int.,* vol. 34, no. 12, June 1974, 7824-A.

375    Margolin, Julius. "Grundphänomene des intentionalen Bewusstseins." Berlin, 1929, 88 p.

376    McCarthy, Thomas Anthony. "Husserl's phenomenology of the theory logic." University of Notre Dame, 1968, 336 p. *Dissertation Abstracts Int.,* vol. 29, no. 9, March 1969, 3184-A. Ann Arbor, Michigan, London: University Microfilms Int., 1976.

377    McIntyre, Ronald T. "Husserl and referentiality. The role of the noema as an intensional entity." Stanford University, 1970, 197 p. *Dissertation Abstracts Int.,* vol. 31, no. 11, May 1971, 5288-A. Ann Arbor, Michigan, London: University Microfilms Int., 1977.

378    Mertens, Paul. "Zur Phänomenologie des Glaubens." Bonn, 1927.

379     Meyn, Henning Ludwig. "Husserl's transcendental logic and the problem of its justification." Brown University, 1971, 102 p. *Dissertation Abstracts Int.,* vol. 32, no. 9, March 1972, 5288-A. Ann Arbor, Michigan, London: University Microfilms Int., 1977.

380     Morgenstern, Georg. "Der Begriff der Existenz in der modernen Philosophie." Leipziger Dissertation, Weida, 1971.

381     Morriston, Barbara W. "Husserl and other minds." Northwestern University, 1974, 197 p. *Dissertation Abstracts Int.,* vol. 35, no. 6, Dec. 1974, 3815-A.

382     Murphy, Richard T. "Phenomenology and the dialectic of pre-reflexive consciousnes in the phenomenological theories of Husserl, Sartre, and Merleau-Ponty." Fordham University, 1963, 294 p. *Dissertation Abstracts Int.,* vol. 24, no. 2, Aug. 1963, 779-A. Ann Arbor, Michigan, London: University Microfilms Int., 1977.

383     Muth, Franz. "Edmund Husserl und Martin Heidegger in ihrer Phänomenologie und Weltanschauung." Münchener Dissertation, 1931.

384     Nissim-Sabat, Marilyn. "Husserl's theory of motivation." De Paul University, 1977, 266 p. *Dissertation Abstracts Int.,* vol. 37, no. 9, March 1977, 5887-A.

385     Oberlander, George E. "Reflection and Husserl's transcendental phenomenological epoche." The University of Texas at Austin, 1972, 169 p. *Dissertation Abstracts Int.,* vol. 33, no. 7, Jan. 1973, 3715-A.

386     Orianne, André Paul. "Husserl's theory of meaning. A commentary on the first *Logical investigation.*" University of California at Berkeley, 1971, 265 p.

387     Osborn, Andrew D. "The philosophy of Edmund Husserl in its development from his mathematical interests to his first conception of phenomenology in *Logical investigations.*" Columbia University, 1934.

388     Overhold, Gary Edon. "Husserl and the science of philosophy." Claremont Graduate School and University Center., 1966, 272 p. *Dissertation Abstracts Int.,* vol. 28, no. 2, Aug 1967, 730-A. Ann Arbor, Michigan, London: University Microfilms Int., 1977.

389     Pazanin, Ante. "Das Problem der Philosophie als strenger Wissenschaft in der Phänomenologie Edmund Husserls." (Inaugural-Dissertation zur Erlangung der Koktorgrages der Philosophischen Fakultät der Universität zu Köln). 1962, 186 p.

390     Pietersma, Henry. "Edmund Husserl's concept of philosophical clarification: Its development from 1887 to 1913." University of Toronto, 1962, 162 p.

391     Pinkard, Terry P. "The foundations of transcendental idealism: Kant, Hegel, Husserl." SUNY at Stony Brook, 1975, 426 p. *Dissertation Abstracts Int.,* vol. 36, no. 2, Aug. 1975, 938-A.

392     Rauch, Leo. "Intentionality and its development in the phenomenological psychology of Edmund Husserl." New York University, 1968, *Dissertation Abstracts Int.,* vol. 29, no. 3, Sept. 1968, 933-A. Ann Arbor, Michigan, London: University Microfilms Int., 1976.

393    Rawlinson, Mary C. "Identity and differing: Husserl's doctrine of self-constitution." Northwestern University, 1978.

394    Reiman, Jeffrey H. "Time and the epoché of Husserl." Pennsylvania State University, 1968, 206 p. *Dissertation Abstracts Int.,* vol. 30, no. 3, Sept. 1969, 1205-A. Ann Arbor, Michigan, London: University Microfilms Int., 1977.

395    Reeder, Harry P. "Public and private aspects of language in Husserl and Wittgenstein." University of Waterloo (Canada), 1977. *Dissertation Abstracts Int.,* vol. 38, no. 5, Nov. 1977, 2852-A.

396    Reiner, Hans. "Freiheit, Wollen und Aktivität. Phänomenologische Untersuchungen in der Richtung auf das Problem der Willensfreiehti." Freiburg, Halle, 1927, vi-172.

397    Ricci, Louis M. "Independent existence in Royce, Perry and Husserl." SUNNY at Buffalo, 1970, 172 p. *Dissertation Abstracts Int.,* vol. 31, no. 9, March 1971, 4844-A.

398    Scanlon, John D. "Husserl's conception of philosophy as a rigorous science." Tulane University, 1968, 304 p. *Dissertation Abstracts Int.,* vol. 29, no. 5, Nov. 1968, 1573-A. Ann Arbor, Michigan, London: University Microfilms Int., 1976.

399    Schmidt Degener, H. "Proeve eener vergelijkende studie over Plato en Husserl." Groningen, 1924.

400    Schmitt, Richard G. "Husserl's phenomenology. Reconstruction in empiricism." Yale University, 1956.

401    Schönrock, W. "Das Bewusstsein. Ein psychologisch-phänomenologischer Versuch." Erlangen, 1924.

402    Schräder, H. "Die Theorie des Denkens dei Külpe und bei Husserl." Münster, 1924.

403    Seltzer, Edward C. "The problem of objectivity. A study of objectivity reflected in a comparison of the philosophies of Ernst Cassierer, Jean Piaget, and Edmund Husserl." New School for Social Research, 1969, 196 p. *Dissertation Abstracts Int.,* vol. 30, no. 11, May 1970, 5031-A. Ann Arbor, Michigan, London: University Microfilms Int., 1977.

404    Simoes Saraiva, Maria Manuela. "L'imagination selon Husserl." Université Catholique de Louvain, Institut Supérieur de Philosophie, 1963, 365 p.

405    Sinn, Dieter. "Die transzendentale Interjubjektivität bei Edmund Husserl mit ihren Seishorizonten." Heidelberg, 1958.

406    Smith, Barry. "The ontology of reference: Studies in logic and phenomenology." Manchester University, 1976.

407    Smith, David Woodruff. "Intentionality, noemata, and individuation. The role of individuation in Husserl's theory of intentionality." Stanford University, 1971, 267 p. *Dissertation Abstracts Int.,* vol. 32, no. 2, Aug. 1971, 1023-A. Ann Arbor, Michigan, London: University Microfilms Int., 1977.

408 Smith, Quentin P. "The phenomenology of feeling: A critical development of the theories of feeling in Husserl, Scheler, and Sartre." Boston College, 1977, 479 p. *Dissertation Abstracts Int.,* vol. 38, no. 3, Sept, 1977, 1457-A.

409 Spencer, James C. "Husserl's conception of the transcendental: A critical analysis." SUNY at Buffalo, 1974, 216 p. *Dissertation Abstracts Int.,* vol. 35, no. 3, Sept. 1974, 1710-A.

410 Ssalagoff, Leo. "Vom Begriff des Geltens in der modernen Logik." Heidelberg, 1910.

411 Stein, Edith. "Zum Problem der Einfühlung." Freiberg, Halle, 1917.

412 Stephens, James W. "Phenomenology and realism: An essay on Husserl's *Logical investigations." Princeton University, 1978. Dissertation Abstracts Int.,* vol. 39, no. 4, Oct. 1978, 2345-A.

413 Sternfeld, Robert. "Contemporary philosophies of experience: Philosophic method in Dewey, Bradley, and Husserl." University of Chicago, 1948, 127 p.

414 Stone, Robert V. "The self as agent-in-the -world. An alternative to Husserl's and Sartre's accounts of the ego." University of Texas at Austin, 1972, 240 p. *Dissertation Abstracts Int.,* vol. 34, no. 9, March 1974, 6051-A. Ann Arbor, Michigan, London: University Microfilms Int., 1977.

415 Stratton, Melville J. "The immanent and the transcendent in Husserl's *Cartesian meditations." SUNY at Buffalo, 1970, 273 p. Dissertation Abstracts Int.,* vol. 31, no. 9, March 1971, 4846-A. Ann Arbor, Michigan, London: University Microfilms Int., 1977.

416 Taylor, Darrell D. "Husserl and Merleau-Ponty and the problem of the cultural studies." University of Southern California, 1966, 424 p. *Dissertation Abstracts Int.,* vol. 27, no. 2, Aug. 1966, 508-A. Ann Arbor, Michigan, London: University Microfilms Int., 1977.

417 Uhler, Kathleen J. "A clarification of Husserl's distinction between phenomenological psychology and transcendental phenomenology." Geogetown University, 1975, 163 p. *Dissertation Abstracts Int.,* vol. 37, no. 1, July 1976, 388-A.

418 Van Breda, Hermann Leo. "De transcendenteel phenomenologische reductie in de Husserl's laatste periode (1920-1938)." Louvain, 1941.

419 Watson, Lawrence. "A study of the origins of formal logic in Husserl's *Formal and transcendental logic." De Paul University, 1973, 201 p. Dissertation Abstracts Int.,* vol. 34, no. 2, Aug. 1973, 826-A.

420 Welton, Donn C. "The temporality of meaning. A critical study of the structure of meaning and temporality in Husserl's phenomenology." Southern Illinois University, 1973, 314 p. *Dissertation Abstracts Int.,* vol. 34, no. 9, March 1974, 6053-A.

421 Wilhelm, Frederick E. "Theory of knowing in Husserl's phenomenology." University of California at Los Angeles, 1974, 592 p. *Dissertation Abstracts Int.,* vol. 35, no. 3, Sept. 1974, 1363-A.

422    Wilming, Josef. "Husserls Lehre von den intentionellen Erlebnissen." Leipzig, 1925. Manuscript m. Auszug im Jahrbuch der Fakultät.

423    Winter, Michael F. "Lived time in Husserl and Whitehead: A comparative study." Northwestern University, 1975, 165 p. *Dissertation Abstracts Int.,* vol. 36, no. 7, Jan. 1976, 4568-A.

424    Wolf, Alan E. "Husserlian phenomenology. Translated and adapted as a possible analytic technique for communication scholars." Pennsylvania State University, 1972, 238 p. *Dissertation Abstracts Int.,* vol. 33, no. 10, April 1973, 5874-A.

425    Yee, Stevan T. "Husserl's idea of phenomenological psychology and the problem of its relation to transcendental phenomenological philosophy." Pennsylvania State University, 1976, 286 p. *Dissertation Abstracts Int.,* vol. 37, no. 11, May 1977, 7169-A.

### Additional Items

426    Harlan, Robert M. "The I and the other: A reformulation of Husserl's Fifth *Cartesian meditation.*" New School for Social Research, 1978.

427    McCluskey, Frank B. "The perceptual basis of phenomenology in Husserl and Hegel." New School for Social Research, 1978.

428    Mensch, James R. "The quest of being in Husserl's *Logical investigations.* " University of Toronto, *Dissertation Abstracts Int.,* vol. 39, no. 4, Oct. 1978, 2340-A.

# Section 3

## Items Arranged By Proper Names

ANCESCHI, Luciano

429    Barilli, L. "L'estetica fenomenologica di Anceschi." *Aut Aut,* no 83, 1964, 53-61.

ARISTOTLE

430    Berger, Herman. *Op zoek naar identiteit.* Het Aristotelisch substantiebegrip en de mogeltjicheid van een hedendaagse metafysiek. Nijmegen: Dekker & Van de Vegt, 1968, 259 p.

431    Drummond, John J. "On the nature of perceptual appearances, or is Husserl an Aristotelian?" *New Scholasticism,* vol. 52, Winter 1978, 1-22.

AUGUSTINE

432    Cilleruelo, L. "San Agustín, genio de Europa, IX [Husserl]." *Religion y Cultura,* vol. 7, no. 27, 1962, 392-406.

433    Van Peursen, Cornelis A. *De tijd bij Augustinus en Husserl.* Groningen: J. B. Wolters, 1953, 20 p.

434     Van Peursen, Cornelis A. "Augustine's phenomenology of time," in his
        *Phenomenology and reality*. Pittsburgh, Pa.: Duquesne University Press,
        1972, 113-133.

BALMES

435     Palacios, Leopoldo. "De Balmes a Husserl (Ideogía pura y fenomenología
        pura)." *Revista de Filosofía* (Madrid), vol. 7, 1948, 821-832.

436     Palacios, Leopoldo. *Ideología pura y fenomenología pura*. De Balmes a
        Husserl. Madrid: Ateneo, 1952, 30 p.

BARTH, Karl

437     Adriaanse, Hendrik Johan. *Zu den Sachen selbst*. Versuch einer Konfrontation
        der Theologie Karl Barths mit der phänomenologisch Philosophie Edmund
        Husserls. 's-Gravenhague: Mouton, 1974, xii-247.

BERGSON, Henri

438     Berger, Gaston. "Le progrès de la réflexion chez Bergson et Husserl," in *Henri
        Bergson*. NeuchÂtel: La Baconnière, 1943, 257-263.

439     De Marneffe, J. "Bergson's and Husserl's concepts of intuition." *Philosophical
        Quarterly A.*, vol. 33, 1960-1961, 169-180.

440     Gorsen, Peter. *Zur Phänomenologie des Bewusstseinsstroms*. Bergson, Dilthey,
        Husserl, Simmel und die lebensphilosophischen Antinomien
        (Abhandlungen zur Philosophie,Psychologie und Pädagogik, 33). Bonn,
        Bouvier, 1966, 243 p.

441     Sancipriano, Mario. "Henri Bergson e Edmund Husserl." *Humanitas*
        (Brescia), vol. 14, no. 11, 1959, 792-799.

442     Sancipriano, Mario. "The activity of consciousness: Husserl and Bergson."
        *Analecta Husserliana*, vol. 3, 1974, 161-167.

443     Xirau, Joaquín. "A crisis. Husserl and Bergson." *The Personalist*, 1946, 27-33,
        and 269-294.

BINSWANGER, Ludwig

444     Cargnello, D. "Dal naturalismo psicoanalitico alla fenomenologia
        antropologica della Daseinsanalyse. Da Freud a Binswanger." *Archivio di
        Filosofia*, no. 3, 1961, 127-198.

BLONDEL, Maurice

445     Maréchal, Joseph, S.J. "Phénoménologie pure ou phénoménologie de
        l'action," in *Mélanges Maréchal*. Bruxelles: Museum Lessianum; Paris:
        Desclée de Brouwer, 1950, t. I, 181-206. [Intéressante étude sur Husserl,
        avec comparaison finale avec Blondel].

BOLZANO, Bernard

446     Bodnar, Joanne. "Bolzano and Husserl: Logic and phenomenology." Ph.D.
        Dissertation, SUNY at Buffalo, 1976, 172 p. *Dissertation Abstracts Int.*, vol.
        37, no. 8, Feb. 1977, 5178-A.

447    Bolzano, Bernard. *Wissenschaftslehre* (4 tomes), reedited Leipzig, 1929-1931.

448    Danek, Jaromir. *Die Weiterentwicklung der Leibnizschen Logik bei Bolzano.* Meisenheim am Glan: Anton Hain, 1970, vii-160.

449    Fels, H. "Bolzano und Husserl." *Philosophisches Jahrbuch,* 1926, 410-418.

450    Neemann, U. "Husserl und Bolzano." *Allgemeine Zeitschrift für Philosophie,* vol. 2, no. 2, 1977, 52-66.

451    Preti, G. "I fondmenti della logica formale pura nella *Wissenschaftslehre* di B. Bolzano e nelle *Logische Untersuchungen* di E. Husserl." *Sophia,* vol. 3, 1935, 187-194, and 361-376.

## BONAVENTURA

452    Russo, Rocco. "Riduzione bonaventuriana e Riduzione husserliana." *Miscellanea Francescana,* vol. 75, 1975, 733-744.

## BRADLEY

453    Sternfeld, Robert. "Contemporary philosophies of experience: Philosophic method in Dewey, Bradley, and Husserl." Ph.D. Dissertation, University of Chicago, 1948, 127 p.

## BRENTANO, Franz

454    Breuck, Maria. *Ueber das Verhältnis Edmund Husserls zu Franz Brentano,* vornehmlich mit Rücksicht auf Brentanos Psychologie. Würzburg, 1933, 118 p.

455    Del Negro, Walter. "Von Brentano über Husserl zu Heidegger." *Zeitschrift für Philosophische Forschung,* vol. 7, 1953, 571-585.

456    Dussort, Henri. "Brentano et Husserl [revue critique]." *Revue Philosophique de la France et de l'Etranger,* vol. 84, no. 4, 1959, 553-559.

457    Fagone, Virgilio. "Tempo e intenzionalità. Brentano, Husserl, Heidegger." *Archivio di Filosofia,* no. 1, 1960, 105-131.

458    Husserl. Edmund. "Reminiscences of Franz Brentano," in *The philosophy of Brentano,* with introduction by Linda L. McAlister (ed.). London: G; Duckworth, 1976, 47-56.

459    Kastil, Alfred. "Brentano und der Psychologismus." *Zeitschrift für Philosophische Forschung,* vol. 12, no. 3, 1958.

460    Kraus, Oskar. *Franz Brentano.* Zur Kenntnis seines Lebens und seiner Lehre. München, 1919.

461    Mayer-Hillebrand, Franziska. "Franz Brentanos ursprüngliche und spätere Seinslehre und ihre Beziehungen zu Husserls Phänomenologie." *Zeitschrift für Philosophische Forschung,* vol. 13, no. 2 [Ed. Husserl], 1959, 316-339.

462    Mayer-Hillebrand, Franziska. "Franz Bretanos Einfluss auf die Philosophie seiner Zeit und der Gegenwart." *Revue Internationale de Philosophie,* vol. 20, fasc. 4, [no. 78] [Franz Brentano], 1966, 373-394.

463    Morrison, James C. "Husserl and Brentano on intentionality." *Philosophy and Phenomenological Research,* vol. 31, 1970-1971, 27-46.

464    Murphy, Richard T. "Consciousness in Brentano and Husserl." *Modern Schoolman,* vol. 45, 1967-1968, 227-241.

465    Staue Alvarez, A. *La doctrina de la intencionalidad en Franz Brentano.* Barcelona: C.S.I.C. Instituto Luis Vives de Filosofía, 1961, 228 p.
       **Book Reviews:**
       A. Guy, *Etudes Philosophiques,* vol. 18, 1963, 480.

466    Spiegelberg, Herbert. "'Intention' und 'Intentionalität' in der Scholastik, bei Brentano und Husserl." *Studia Philosophica,* vol. 29, 1969, 189-216. "'Intention' and 'intentionality' in the Scholastics, Brentano and Husserl," (trans. from the German by Linda L. McAlister and Margarate Schlate) in *The philosophy of Brentano,* ed. with an introduction by Linda McAlister. London: G. Duckworth and Co., 1976, 108-127.

BROAD, D. C.
467    Hoy, Ronald C. "Time and the mental: An examination of Broad's and Husserl's theories of temporal consciousness." Ph.D. Dissertation, University of Pittsburgh, 1974, 215 p. *Dissertation Abstracts Int.,* vol. 35, no. 2, Aug. 1974, 1160-A.

CAIRNS, Dorion
468    Cairns, Dorion. "A letter to John Wild about Husserl." *Research in Phenomenology,* vol. 5, 1975, 155-181.

CAMUS, Albert
469    Curtius, Jerry L. "A Camus commentary: Sartre's debt to Husserl." *South Atlantic Bulletin,* vol. 40, no. 4, 1975, 1-6.

CASSIRER, Ernst
470    Seltzer, Edward C. "The problem of objectivity: A study of objectivity reflected in a comparison of the philosophies of E. Cassirer, J. Piaget, and E. Husserl." Ph.D. Dissertation, New School for Social Research, 1969, 196 p. *Dissertation Abstracts Int.,* vol. 30, no. 11, May 1970, 5031-A.

CAVILLÈS, Jean
471    Campbell, R. "Essai sur la philosophie des mathématiques selon Jean Cavaillès." *Critique,* Jan. 1953, 48-66.

CHESTOV, Leo
472    Déchet, F. "Chestov on Husserl." *Giornale di Metafisica,* vol. 30, March-June 1975, 209-243.

CHRIST
473    Oesterreicher, John M. *Sept philosophes juifs devant le Christ* [H. Bergson, E. Husserl, A. Reinach, M. Scheler, P. Landsberg, M. Picard, E. Stein]. (Collection "Foi vivante"). Paris: Editions du Cerf, 1955, 616 p.

COSTA RICA

474     Malavassi, G. "Presencia de Husserl en Costa Rica." *Revista de Filosofía de la Universidad de Costa Rica,* vol. 3, 1962, 275-278.

DERRIDA, Jacques

475     Allison, David B. "Derrida's critique of Husserl: The philosophy of presence." Ph.D. Dissertation, The Pennsylvania State University, 1974, 201 p. *Dissertation Abstracts Int.,* vol. 35, no. 6, Dec. 1974, 3803-A.

476     Dauenhauer, Bernard. "On speech and temporality: Derrida and Husserl." *Philosophy Today,* vol. 18, Fall 1974, 171-180.

477     Leavy, John P. "Undecidables and old names: Derrida's deconstruction and 'Introduction' to Husserl's *The Origin of geometry.*" Ph.D. Dissertation, Emory University, 1976. *Dissertation Abstracts Int.,* vol. 37, no. 9, March 1977, 5886-A.

478     Schuhmann, Karl. "Verschijning en niet-tegenwoordigheid. Derrida over metafysica en fenomenologie." *Tijdschrift voor Filosofie,* vol. 30, March 1968, 159-163.

479     Smith, F. Joseph. "Jacques Derrida's Husserl interpretation." *Philosophy Today,* vol. 12, Summer 1967, 101-123.

DESCARTES, René *see also:* Husserl, *Cartesian meditations*

480     Campanale, Domenico. "L'interpretazione husserliana di Cartesio," (Pubblicato in *Rassegna di Scienze Filosofiche,* no. 3-4, 1952), in his *Problemi epistemologici da Hume all'ultimo Wittgenstin* (Università di Bari. Pubblicazioni dell'Istituto di Filosofia, 4). Bari: Adriatica Editrice, 1961, 241-278.

481     De Muralt, André. "Epoché-Malin génie-Théologie de la toute-puissance divine. [Husserl, Descartes, Occam]." *Studia Philosophica,* vol. 26, 1966, 159-191.

482     Landgrebe, Ludwig. "Husserls Abschied vom Cartesianismus [Edm. Husserl, *Erste Philosophie,* II]." *Philosophische Rundschau,* vol. 9, no. 2-3, 1961-1962, 133-177. Reprinted in his *Den Weg der Phänomenologie.* Gütersloh: Gerd Mohn, 1967, 163-206. "Husserl's departure from Cartesianism," in *The Phenomenology of Husserl,* R. O. Elveton (ed. and trans.). Chicago: Quadrangle Books, 1970, 259-306.

483     Laporte, Jean-Marie. "Husserl's critique of Descartes." *Philosophy and Phenomenological Research,* vol. 23, 1962-1963, 335-352.

484     Lowit, Alexandre. "L'epoché' de Husserl et le doute de Descartes." *Revue de Métaphysique et de Morale,* vol. 62, no. 4, 1957, 399-415.

485     Meyer, Rudolf. "Descartes, Valéry, Husserl." *Hambürger Akademische Rundschau,* 1950, 753-769.

486     Miévile, H. "Le cogito de la phénoménologie de Husserl et le cogito de Descartes." *Schweizer Philosphische Gesellschaft,* vol. 1, 1941.

487    Pos, H. J. "Descartes en Husserl." *Algemeen Nederlands Tijdschrift voor Wijsgebeerte en Psychologie,* vol. 31, 1938, 23-38.

488    Reymond, A. "A propos du cogito de Descartes." *Annales de la Société Suisse de Philosphie,* vol. 2, 1942, 78-84.

489    Romero, Fr. "Descartes y Husserl," in *Memor de Descartes.* La Plata, 1938.

490    Semerari, Giuseppe. *Esperienze del pensiero moderno.* Urbino: Argalia, 1969, 297 p. [Tema cartesiana nella fenomenologia di Husserl]

491    Thévenaz, Pierre. "La question du point de départ radical chez Descartes et Husserl," in *Problèmes actuels de la phénoménologie.* Paris: Desclée de Brouwer, 1952, 9-30.

492    Vanni-Rovighi, Sofia. "Il 'cogito' di Cartesio ed il 'cogito' di Husserl." *Cartesio,* vol. 1, 1937.

493    Waelhens, Alphonse de. "Descartes et la pensée phénoménologique." *Revue Néo-scolastique de Philosophie,* vol. 41, 1938, 571-589. "Descartes und das phänomenologische Denken," (aus dem Französischen übersetzt von Kalus Stichweh), in *Husserl,* (Wege der Forschung, 40). Hrsg. von H. Noach. Darmstadt: Wissenschaftliche Buchgesellschaft, 1973, 188-209.

494    Wahl, Jean. "Au sujet des jugements de Husserl sur Descartes et sur Locke," in *Husserl* (Cahiers de Royaumont, 3). Paris: Les Editions de Minuit, 1959, 119-131. [Discussion, 132-142].

495    Weiler, G. "Yahaso shel Husserl le Descartes [The relationship of Husserl to Descartes]. [In Hebrew]." *Iyyun,* vol. 4, no. 3, 149-161.

DEWEY, John

496    Farber, Marvin. "The idea of a naturalistic logic [Husserl and Dewey]." *Philosophy and Phenomenological Research,* vol. 29, 1968-1969, 598-601.

497    Mathur, D. C. *Naturalistic philosophies of experience.* W. James, J. Dewey, M. Farber against the background of Husserl's phenomenology. St. Louis: Warren H. Green, 1971, 158 p.

498    Sternfeld, Robert. "Contemporary philosophies of experience: Philosophic method in Dewey, Bradley, and Husserl," Ph.D. Dissertation, University of Chicago, 1948 127 p.

499    Vircillo, Domenico. "I problemi della psicologia e l'unità del sapera in Dewey e Husserl." *Teoresi,* vol. 24, 1969, 83-105.

DILTHEY, Wilhelm

500    Biemel, Walter. "Der Briefwechsel Dilthey-Husserl." *Man and World,* vol. 1, Aug. 1968, 428-446.

501    *Dilthey-Husserl.* "En torno a la filosofía como ciencia estricta y al alcance del historicismo. Correspondencia entre Dilthey y Husserl de 29 junio, 5/6 julio y 10 de 1911 (Edición, introducción y notas por Walter Biemel). *Revista de Filosofía de al Universidad de Costa Rica,* vol. 1, no. 2, 1957, 101-124.

502    Gorsen, Peter. *Zur Phänomenologie des Bewusstseinstroms. see* BERGSON, no. 440.

503     Misch, Georg. *Lebensphilosophie und Phänomenologie:* Ein Auseinandersetzung der Diltheyschen Richtung mit Heidegger und Husserl. Leipzig-Berlin: Teubner, 1931. 3. Aufl. Stuttgart: Teubner, 1967, x-328. Mit e. Nachw.

504     Tilman, Mary Katherine. "Dilthey and Husserl." *Journal of the British Society for Phenomenology,* vol. 7, May 1976, 123-130.

(Meister) ECKHART

505     Caputo, John D. "The nothingness of the intellect in Meister Eckhart's ' Parisian questions'." *The Thomist,* vol. 39, Jan. 1975, 85-115.

ELIOT, T. S.

506     Kumar, Jitendra. "Consciousness and its correlatives: Eliot and Husserl." *Philosophy and Phenomenological Research,* vol. 28, 1967-1968, 332-367.

ENGLAND

507     Spiegelberg, Herbert. "Husserl in England. Facts and lessons." *Journal of the British Society for Phenomenology,* vol. 1, no. 1, 1970, 4-14 [Postscript, 15].

ERDMANN, Bruno

508     Krämer, Ernst. "Bruno Erdmanns Warheitsauffassung und ihre Kritik durch Husserl." Dissertation, München, 1930, 68 p.

FARBER, Marvin

509     Berger, Gaston. "L'établissement de la phénoménologie par Marvin Farber." *Revue Philosophique de la France et de l'Etranger,* vol. 138, 1948, 92-95.

510     Mathur, D. C. *Naturalistic philosophies of experience.* St. Louis: Warren H. Green, 1971, 158 p. *see:* DEWEY

FICHTE

511     Hyppolite, Jean. "De l'idée fichtéenne de la doctrine de la science et le projet husserlien," in *Husserl et la pensée moderne* (Phaenomenologica, 2). The Hague: Martinus Nijhoff, 1959. Reprinted in his *Figures de la pensée philosophique. Ecrits (1931-1968).* (Epiméthée). Paris: Presses Universitaires de France, Vol. I, 21-31, 1970. "Die fichtesche Idee der Wissenschaftslehre und der Entwurf Husserls," in *Husserl et la pensée moderne* (see above). "The Fichtean idea of the science of knowledge and the Husserlian project." *Auslegung,* 1-2, 1973-1975, 77-84.

512     Masullo, Aldo. *Lezioni sull'intersoggettivatà, I: Fichte e Husserl.* Napoli: Liberia Scientifica Editrice, 1964, 140 p. [litografato].

513     Masullo, Aldo. *La comunità come fondamento.* Fichte, Husserl, Sartre (Filosofia e pedagogia). Napoli: Libreria Scientifica Editrice, 1965, 468 p.

514     Mohanty, J. N. "Fichte's 'Science of knowledge' and Husserl's phenomenology." *Philosophical Quarterly A.,* vol. 25, 1952, 113-121.

FINDLAY, J. N.

515    Spiegelberg, Herbert. "Remarks on Findlay's translation of Edmund Husserl's
       *Logical Investigations.*" *Journal of the British Society for Phenomenology,*
       vol. 3, 1972, 195-196.

FOUCAULT, Michel

516    Flynn, Bernard Charles. "Michel Foucault and the Husserlian problematic of
       a transcendental philosophy of history." *Philosophy Today,* vol. 22, no. 4,
       Fall 1978, 224-238.

517    Valdinoci, S. "Les incertitudes de l'archéologie: archè et archive." *Revue de
       Métaphysique et de Morale,* vol. 83, no. 1, 1978, 73-101.

FREGE, Gottlob

518    Aquila, Richard E. "Husserl and Frege on meaning." *Journal of the History
       of Philosophy,* vol. 12, 1974, 377-383. [Review of Follesdal, "Husserl's
       notion of noema [*Journal of Philosophy,* vol. 66, 680-687] and D. W. Smith,
       Intentionality and intensions].

519    Angelelli, Ignacio. *Studies on Frege and traditional philosophy.* Dordrecht,
       Reidel, 1967.

520    Bernet, R. "Phänomenologische Erkenntnistheorie und Semantik: Eine
       Untersuchung zu Husserls Lehre von der noematischen Intentionalität."
       Dissertation, Louvain, 1976.

521    Dreyfus, Hubert L. "*Sinn* und Intentional object," 1-17 to "Husserl's
       phenomenology of perception." Ph.D. Dissertation, Harvard University,
       1963. [To be published by Northwestern University Press, 1979]. Reprinted
       in *Phenomenology and existentialism,* Robert C. Solomon (ed.). New York:
       Harper & Row, 1970, 196-210.

522    Dreyfus, Hubert L. "The perceptual noema: Gurwitsch's crucial
       contribution," in *Life-world and consciousness.* Essays in honor of Aron
       Gurwitsch, Lester E. Embree (ed.). Evanston, Ill.,: Northwestern
       University Press, 1972,.

523    Föllesdal, Dagfinn. *Husserl und Frege.* Ein Beitrag zur Beleuchtung der
       Entstehung der phänomenologischen Philosophie (Vid.-Akad. Skr. II. H-F.
       Kl. 1958, no. 2). Oslo: Aschehoug, 1958, 60 p.

524    Föllesdal, Dagfinn. "Husserl's notion of noema." *Journal of Philosophy,* vol.
       66, 1969, 680-687. Reprinted in *Phenomenology and existentialism,* Robert
       C. Solomon (ed.). New York: Harper & Row, 1970.

525    *Frege-Husserl* correspondence. *Southwestern Journal of Philosophy,* vol. 5, no.
       3, 1974, 83-95.

526    Frege, Gottlob. *Begriffsschrift und andere Aufsätze.* 2 Aufl. Mit. Edmund
       Husserls und H. Scholzs Anmerkungen. Hrsg. von I. Angelelli. Hildeshiem:
       G. Olms, 1964, 124 p.

527     Hintikka, J. "Die Intentionen der Intentionalität." *Neue Hefte für Philosophie,* vol. 8, 1975, 65-95. English translation in his *The intentions of intentionality and other new models for modalities* (Synthese Library). Dordrecht: Reidel, 1975

528     Küng, Guido. *Ontologie und logistiche Analyse der Sprache,* 1963 revised English translation by E. C. M. Mays. Dordrecht: Reidel, 1967.

529     Küng, Guido. "The role of language in phenomenological analysis." *American Philosophical Quarterly,* vol. 6, 1969, 330-334.

530     Küng, Guido. "The world as noema and as referent." *Journal of the British Society for Phenomenology,* vol. 3, 1972, 15-26.

531     Küng, Guido. "Noema and Gegenstand," in *Jenseits von Sein und Nichtsein,* R. Haller (ed.). Graz: Akademische Druck-und Verlagsanstalt, 1972.

532     Küng, Guido. "Husserl on pictures and intentional objects." *Review of Metaphysics,* vol. 26, 1973, 670-680.

533     Küng, Guido. "The phenomenological reduction as *epoché* and as explication." *The Monist,* vol. 59, 1975, 63-80.

534     McIntyre, R. "Husserl and referentiality: The role of the noema as an intensional entity." Ph.D. Dissertation, Stanford University, 1970.

535     McIntyre, R. and Woodruff Smith, D. "Intentionality via intensions." *Journal of Philosophy,* vol. 68, 1971, 541-561.

536     McIntyre, R. and Woodruff Smith, D. "Husserl's identification of meaning and noema." *The Monist,* vol. 59, 1975, 115-132.

537     McIntyre, R. and Woodruff Smith, D. *Intentionality via intensions:* Husserl's phenomenology and the semantics of modalities (Synthese Library). Dordrecht: Reidel, 1978.

538     Mohanty, J. N. "Husserl and Frege: A new look at their relationship." *Research in Phenomenology,* vol. 4, 1974, 51-62.

539     Mohanty, J. N. *Edmund Husserl's theory of meaning.* The Hague: Martinus Nijhoff, 1964. (Phaenomenologica, 14), xii-148. 2nd ed., 1969.

540     Mohanty, J. N. "Frege-Husserl Correspondence," translated into English with notes." *Southwestern Journal of Philosophy,* vol. 5, 1974, 83-95.

541     Mohanty, J. N. "On Husserl's theory of meaning." *Southwestern Journal of Philosophy,* vol. 5, 1974, 229-244.

542     Morscher, E. "Von Bolzano zu Meinong: Zur Geschichte der logischen Realismus," in *Jenseits von Sein und Nichtsein,* R. Haller (ed.). Graz: Akademische Druckund Verlagsanstalt, 1972.

543     Mortán, Günter. "Einige Bemerkungen zur Überwindung des Psychologismus durch Gottlob Frege und Edmund Husserl," in *Atti XII Congresso* internazionale di Filosofia, XII: Storia della filosofia moderna e contemporanea. Firenze: Sansoni, 1961, 327-334.

544     Pivcevic, Edo. "Husserl versus Frege." *Mind,* vol. 76, 1967, 155-165. [a translation of extracts from Ch. VIII of Husserl 1891].

545     Pietersma, Henry. "Husserl and Frege." *Archiv für Geschichte der Philosophie,* vol. 49, 1967, 298-323.

546     Smith, Barry. "The ontology of reference. Studies in logic and phenomenology." Ph.D. Dissertation, Manchester, 1976.

547     Smith, Barry. "Frege and Husserl: The ontology of reference." *Journal of the British Society for Phenomenology,* vol. 9, May 1978, 111-125. [Includes a detailed bibliography.]

548     Smith, B. "An essay in formal ontology." *Grazer Philosophische Studien,* vol. 4, 1978.

549     Solomon, Robert C. "Sense and essence: Frege and Husserl." *International Philosophical Quarterly,* vol. 10, 1970, 379-401. Reprinted in his *Phenomenology and existentialism,* Robert C. Solomon (ed.). New York: Harper & Row, 1970.

550     Thiel, C. *Sinn und Bedeutung in der Logik Gottlob Freges,* 1965. English trans. *Sense and reference in Frege's logic.* Dordrecht: Reidel, 1968.

551     Willard, D. "The paradox of logical psychologism: Husserl's way out." *American Philosophical Quarterly,* vol. 9, 1972, 94-99.

552     Willard, D. "Concerning Husserl's view of number." *Southwestern Journal of Philosophy,* vol. 5, 1974, 97-109.

553     Woodruff Smith, D. "Intentionality, noemata and individuation: The role of individuation in Husserl's theory of intentionality." Ph.D. Dissertation, Stanford University, 1970.

FREUD, Sigmund

Cargnello, D. *see* BINSWANGER, 444

554     Casey, Edward S. "The image/sign relation in Husserl and Freud." *Review of Metaphysics,* vol. 30, Dec. 1976, 207-225.

555     Demetz, P. "Kafka, Freud, Husserl. Probleme einer Generation." *Zeitschrift für Religion und Geistesgeschicte,* vol. 7, no. 1, 59-69.

GALILEO

556     Agosti, Villorio. "Galillei vista da Heidegger." *Giornale di Metafisica,* vol. 19, 1964, 779-796.

557     Bondanese, Maria Antonietta. "Galilei nell'opera di Husserl, Banfi, Della Volpe." *Giornale Critico della Filosofia Italiana,* vol.55, July-Sept. 1976, 416-455.

558     Grundwaldt, H. H. "Ueber die Phänomenologie Husserls. Mit besonderer Berücksichtigung der Wesenschau und der Forschungsmethode Galileo Galileis." Dissertation, Berlin, 1927, 81 p.

559     Gurwitsch, Aron. "Husserlian perspectives on Galilean physics," in his *Phenomenology and the theory of science.* Evanston, Ill.: Northwestern University Press, 1974, 33-59.

GEIGER, Moritz

560    Métraux, Alexandre. "Edmund Husserl und Moritz Geiger," in *Die Münchener Phänomenologie*. Vorträge des internationalen Kongresses en München 13-18 April 1971. Hrsg. von Helmut Kuhn et. al. (Phaenomenologica, 65). The Hague: Martinus Nijhoff, 1975, 139-157.

GELB-GOLDSTEIN

561    Gurwitsch, Aron. "Geld-Goldstein's concept of 'concrete' and 'categorial' attitude and the phenomenology of ideation." *Philosophy and Phenomenological Research*, vol. 10, 1949-1950, 172-196. Reprinted in his *Studies in Psychology and phenomenology*. Evanston, Ill.: Northwestern University Press, 1964.

GRAMSCI

562    Nemeth, Thomas. "Husserl and Gramsci. The life world and common sense." *Independent Journal of Philosophy*, vol. 1, no. 1, 1977, 65-68.

GURWITSCH, Aron

563    Dreyfus, Hubert L. "The perceptual noema: Gurwitsch's crucial contribution," in *Life-world and consciousness*. Essays for Aron Gurwitsch, Lester E. Embree (ed.). Evanston, Ill.: Northwestern University Press, 1972, 135-170.

564    Kersten, Frederick. "The originality of Gurwitsch's theory of intentionality." *Research in Phenomenology*, vol. 5, 1975, 19-27.

565    Null, Gilbert T. "Generalizing abstraction and the judgment of subsumption in Aron Guwitsch's version of Husserl's theory of intentionality." *Philosophy and Philosophy Research*, vol. 38, June 1978, 469-488.

566    Sokolowski, Robert. "The work of Aron Gurwitsch." *Research in Phenomenology*, vol. 5, 1975, 7-10.

HABERMAS, Jürgen

567    Menéndez Ureña, Enrique. "Teoría y praxis en la fenomenologia trascendental (E. Husserl) y en teoría crítica (J. Habermas)." *Pensamiento*, vol. 31, 1975, 231-244.

568    Schrader-Klebert, Karin. "Der Begriff des Transcendentalen bei Jürgen Habermas." *Soziale Welt*, vol. 19, no. 3-4, 1968, 342-359.

569    Widmer, Hans. "Conocimiento e interes en Jürgen Habermas." *Pensamiento*, vol. 32, July-Sept. 1976, 281-301.

HARE

570    Compton, John J. "Hare, Husserl and philosophic discovery." *Dialogue*, vol. 3, no. 1, 1964, 42-51.

HARTMANN, Nicolai

571    Hülsmann, H. *Die Methode in der Philosophie Nicolai Hartmanns.* Düsseldorf, 1959.

572 Landmann, Michael. "Nicolai Hartmann and phenomenology." *Philosophy and Phenomenological Research,* vol. 3, 1942-1943.

573 Millán Puelles, A. *El problema del ente ideal.* Un examen através de Husserl y Hartmann. Madrid: Instituto 'Luis Vives', C. S. I. C., 1947, 194 p.

574 Penati, Giancarlo. *Alienazione e verità.* Husserl, Hartmann, Heidegger e l'ontologia come liberazione (Studi filosofici, 7). Brescia: Paideia, 1972, 206 p.

HEGEL

575 Castro López, O. "Dos puntos de partida en el filosofar: Hegel y Husserl." *La Palabra y el Hombre* (Xalappa, México), vol. 7, 1964, 35-44.

576 Hyppolite, Jean. *Genése et structue de la "phénomenologie de l'esprit de Hegel".* Paris: Aubier, 1946.

577 Kuspit, D. B. "Hegel and Husserl on the problem of the difficulty of beginning philosophy." *Journal of the British Society for Phenomenology,* vol. 2, no. 1, 1971, 52-57.

578 Ladrière, Jean. "Hegel, Husserl, and reason today." *Modern Schoolman,* vol.37, 1959-1960, 171-195.

579 Lauer, Quentin. "Phenomenology: Hegel and Husserl," in *Beyond epistemology.* New Studies in the philosophy of Hegel, Frederick G. Weiss (ed.). The Hague: Martinus Nijhoff, 1974.

580 McCluskey, Frank Bryce. "The perceptual basis of phenomenology in Husserl and Hegel." Ph.D. Dissertation, New School for Social Research, 1978.

581 Orth, Ernest W. "Husserl und Hegel. Ein Beitrag zum Problem des Verhältnisses historischer und systematischer Forschung in der Philosophie," in *Die Welt des Menschen. Die Welt der Philosophie.* Festschrift fur Jan Patocka, Hrsg. von Walter Biemel (Phaenomenologica, 72). The Hague: Martinus Nijhoff, 1976, 213-250.

582 Pazanin, Ante. "Das Problem der Geschichte bei Husserl, Hegel und Marx," in *Phänomenologie heute.* Festschrift für Ludwig Landgrebe (Phaenomenologica, 51). The Hague: Martinus Nijhoff, 1972, 173-203.

583 Pinkard, Terry P. "The foundations of transcendental idealism: Kant, Hegel, Husserl." Ph.D. Dissertation, SUNY at Stony Brook, 1975, 426 p. *Dissertation Abstracts Int.,* vol. 36, no. 2, Aug. 1975, 938-A.

584 Puligandla, Ramakrishna. "Similarities between the phenomenologies of Hegel and Husserl." *Philosophical Quarterly* (India), vol. 18, 1965, 127-143.

585 Strenger, Irineu. "Hegel e Husserl: duas fenomenlogias?" *Revista Brasileira de Filosofia,* vol. 20, 1970, 453-459.

586 Waelhens, Alphonse de. "Phénoménologie husserlienne et phénoménologie hégélienne." *Revue Philosophique de Louvain,* vol. 52, 1954, 234-249.

587 Werkmeister, William H. "Husserl and Hegel," in *Akten XIV International Kongress für Philosophie,* VI, 553-558. Vienna: Herder, 1972.

HEIDEGGER, Martin

588 Beaufret, Jean. "Husserl et Heidegger," in his *Dialogue avec Heidegger:* (III) Approche de Heidegger. Paris: Editions de Minuit, 1974, 241 p.

589 Biemel, Walter. "Husserl's *Encyclopedia Britannica* article and Heidegger's remarks thereon," in *Husserl. Expositions and appraisals,* by F. Elliston (ed.) and P. McCormick. Notre Dame, Ind., London: University of Notre Dame Press, 1977, 286-303. "Husserls *Encyclopedia Britannica* Artikel und Heideggers Anmerkungen dazu." *Tijdschrift voor Filosophie,* vol. 12, 1950, 2462-80. Reprinted in *Husserl.* Hrsg. von H. Noack (Wege der Forschung, 40). Darmstadt: Wissenschaftliche Buchgesellsachft, 1973,

590 Cerf, Walter H. "An approach to Heidegger's ontology." *Philosophy and Phenomenological Research,* vol. 1, 1940-1941.

591 Chiodi, Pietro. "Husserl e Heidegger." *Rivista di Filosofia,* no. 2, 1961, 192-211.

592 Delfgaauw, Bernard. "La phénoménologie chez Martin Heidegger." *Etudes Philosophiques,* 1954, 50-56.

593 Del-Negro, Walter. "Von Brentano über Husserl zu Heidegger." *Zeitschrift für Philosophische Forschung,* vol. 7, 1953, 571-585. Also in *Zeitschrift für Religions-und Geistesgeschichte,* vol. 7, 1955, 59-69.

594 Dreyfus, Hubert L. "The priority of *the* world to *my* world: Heidegger's answer to Husserl (and Sartre)." *Man and World,* vol. 8, May 1975, 121-130.

595 Dreyfus, Hubert L., and Haugeland, John. "Husserl and Heidegger: Philosophy's last stand," in *Heidegger and modern philosophy.* Critical essays, by Michael Murray (ed.). New Haven-London: Yale University Press, 1978, 222-238.

596 Ertel, Christian. "Von der Phänomenologie und jüngeren Lebensphilosphie zur Existentialphilosophie M. Heideggers." *Philosophisches Jahrbuch,* vol. 51.

597 Ferrari, Oward. "El ser en la fenomenología de Husserl y de Heidegger." *Philosophia,* no. 35, 1969, 65-110.

598 Filippini, E. "Nota su Husserl e Heidegger." *Rivista de Filosofia,* no. 2, 1961, 212-216.

599 Folwart, Helmut. "Kant, Husserl, Heidegger (Kritizismus, Phänomenologie, Existenzialontologie)." Habilit-Schrift. Breslau, 1936, 281 p.

600 Granel, Gérard. "La gigantomachie." in *Traditionis traditio. Essais.* Paris: Gallimard, 1972, 315 p. [Une analyse du rapport entre *Sein und Zeit* et la phénoénologie husserlienne].

601 Granel, Gérard. "Remarques sur le rapport de *Sein und Zeit* et de la phénoménologie husserlienne," in *Durchbliche: Martin Heidegger zum 80. Geburtstag.* Frankfurt am Main: v. Klostermann, 1970, 350-368.

602     Grasselli, G. "La fenomenologia di Husserl e l'ontologia di M. Heidegger."
        *Rivista di Filosofia,* 1928, 330ff.

603     Heidegger, Martin. "The idea of phenomenology. With a letter to Edmund
        Husserl (1927)," Thomas J. Sheehan (trans.). *Listening,* vol. 12, 1977, no.
        3, 111-121.

604     Heidegger, Martin. "Only a god can save us: *Der Spiegel's* interview with
        Heidegger." *Philosophy Today,* vol. 20, Winter 1976, 267-284.

605     Herrmann, Friedrich-Wilhelm von. *Subjekt und Dasein.* Interpretation zu '
        *Sein und Zeit.* Frankfurt am Main: Klostermann, 1974, 91 p.

606     Herrmann, Friedrich-Wilhelm von. "Lebenswelt und In-der-Welt-sein. Zum
        Ansatz des Weltproblem bei Husserl und Heidegger," in *Weltaspekte der
        Philosophie.* Rudolph Berlinger zum 26. Oktober 1972. Herausgegebon von
        Werner Beierwalters und Wiebke Schrader. Amsterdam: Rodopi N. V.,
        1972, 123-141.

607     IJselling, Samuel. "Heidegger en de fenomenologie (Zusammenfassung:
        Heidegger und die Phänomenologie, p. 534)." *Tijdschrift voor Filosofie,* vol.
        38, Dec. 1976, 511-534.

608     Kisiel, Theodore. "On the dimensions of a phenomenology of science in
        Husserl and the young Dr. Heidegger." *Journal of the British Society for
        Phenomenology,* vol. 4, 1973, 217-234.

609     Kraft, Julius. *Von Husserl zu Heidegger.* Kritik der phänomenologischen
        Philosophie. Leipzig, 1932; Frankfurt, 1957.

610     Marino, Luigi. "Husserl e Heidegger: dialogo fencondo fra prospettive
        irriducibili," in *Atti dell'Accademia delle Scienze di Torino* (Cl. Sc. mor.,
        stor., e filol.) vol. 99, 1964-1965, 777-810.

611     Mays, Wolfe. "Husserl on Ryle's review of *Sein und Zeit.*" *Journal of the
        British Society for Phenomenology,* vol. 1, 1970, 14-15.

612     McGaughey, Douglas. "Husserl and Heidegger on Plato's cave allegory: A
        study of philosophical influence." *International Philosophical Quarterly,*
        vol. 16, Sept. 1976, 331-348.

613     Merlan, Philip. "Time consciousness in Husserl and Heidegger." *Philosophy
        and Phenomenological Research,* vol. 8, 1947-1948, 23-54.

614     Misch, Georg. *Lebensphilosophie und Phänomenologie.* Eine
        Auseinandersetzung der Diltheyschen Richtung mit Heidegger und
        Husserl. Leipzig-Berlin: Teubner, 1931. Mit e. Nachw. z. 3. Aufl. Stuttgart:
        Teubner, 1967, x-328.

615     Montero Moliner. Fernando. "La teoría de la significación en Husserl y
        Heidegger." *Revista de Filosofía* (Madrid), vol. 12, 1953, 393-426.

616     Muth, Franz. "Edmund Husserl und Martin Heidegger in ihrer
        Phänomenologie und Weltanschauung." Mäunchener Dissertation,
        Temeswar-Timisoara (Rumanien), 1931.

617 Nieto Arteta, Luis Eduardo. "Husserl y Heidegger: La fenomenología y la analítica de la existencia." *Universidad de Antioquia* (Medellín), no. 114, 1953, 243-262.

618 Nieto Arteta, Luis Eduardo. "Husserl y Heidegger." *Ciencia Fe,* vol. 8, no. 31-32, 1952, 29-39.

619 Olafson, Frederick A. "Consciousness and intentionality in Heidegger's thought." *American Philosophical Quarterly,* vol. 12, April 1975, 91-103.

620 Pantaleo, Pasquale. *La direzione coscienza-intenzione nella filosofia di Kant e Husserl.* Bari: Arti grafiche Laterza e Palo, 1967, 363 p.

621 Passweg, Salcia. *Phänomenologie und Ontologie.* Husserl, Scheler, Heidegger. Dissertation, Basel. Zürich: Heitz, 1939, viii-215.

622 Picard, Yvonne. "Le temps chez Husserl et chez Heidegger." *Deucalion,* vol. 1, 1946, 93-124.

623 Prsywara,Erich. "Husserl et Heidegger." *Etudes Philosophiques,* vol. 16, 1961, 55-62.

624 Ricoeur, Paul. "Kant et Heidegger." *Kantstudien,* vol. 46, 1954-1955, 44-67.

625 Rollin, France. *La phénoménologie au départ.* Husserl, Heidegger, Gaboriau (Trident, 3). Paris: P. Lethielleux, 1967, 200 p.

626 Schacht, Richard. "Husserlian and Heideggerian phenomenology." *Philosophical Studies* (Dordrecht), vol. 23, 1972, 293-314.

627 Schneider, Robert O. "Husserl and Heidegger: An essay on the question of intentionality." *Philosophy Today,* vol. 21, Winter 1977, 368-375.

628 Seeburger, Francis F. "Heidegger and the phenomenological reduction." *Philosophy and Phenomenological Research,* vol. 36, Dec. 1975, 212-221.

629 Sheehan, Thomas J. "Heidegger's early years: Fragments for a philosophical biography." *Listening,* vol. 12, Fall 1977, 3-20.

630 Smith, F. Joseph. "Being and subjectivity: Heidegger and Husserl," in *Phenomenology in perspective.* The Hague: Martinus Nijhoff, 1970, 122-156.

631 Taminiaux, Jacques. "Le regard et l'excédent. Remarques sur Heidegger et les *Recherches logiques* de Husserl." *Revue Philosophique de Louvain,* vol. 75, 1977. Reprinted in his *Le regard et l'excédent* (Phaenomenologica). The Hague: Martinus Nijhoff, 1978.

632 Theunissen, Michael. "Intentionaler Gegenstand und ontologische Differenz. Ansätze sur Fragestellung Heideggers in der Phänomenologie Husserl." *Philosophisches Jahrbuch,* vol. 70, 1963, 344-362. "Objeto intencional y differencia ontológica. Inicios del planteamiento de Heidegger en la fenomenología de Husserl." (Traducción de Ramón Castilla Lázaro). *Diálogos,* vol. 1, no. 2, 1964, 35-59.

633 Trépanier, Emmanuel. "Phénoménologie et ontologie: Husserl et Heidegger." *Laval Théologique et Philosophique,* vol. 28, 1972, 249-265.

634 Tugendhat, Ernst. *Der Wahrheitsbegriff bei Husserl und Heidegger.* Berlin: Walter de Gruyter, 1967, xii-416.

635     Waelhens, Alphonse de. "Husserl, Heidegger, Sartre," in *Les philosophes célèbres.* Paris: Mazenod, 1956, 322-350.

HODGSON, Shadworth

636     Schuhmann, Karl. "Husserl and Hodgson. Some historical remarks." *Journal of the British Society for Phenomenology,* vol. 3, 1972, 63-65.

637     Spicker, Stuart F. "Shadworth Hodgson's reduction as an anticipation of Husserl's phenomenological psychology." *Journal of the British Society for Phenomenology,* vol. 2, no. 2, 1971, 57-73.

H]RBIGER, Hans

638     Erckmann, R. "Husserl und Hans Hörbiger." *Schlüssel zum Weltgeschehen,* vol. 5, 1919, 150-154, 184-188.

HUME, David

639     Berger, Gaston. "Husserl et Hume." *Revue Internationale de Philosophie,* no. 2, 15 janvier 1939, 342-353. "Husserl und Hume," [Aus dem Französischen übersetz von Katharina Arndt], in *Husserl.* Hrsg. von H. Noack (Wege der Forschung, 40). Darmstadt: Wissenschaftliche Buchgesellschaft, 1973, 210-222.

640     Bossert, Philip J. "Hume and Husserl on time and time-consciousness." *Journal of the British Society for Phenomenology,* vol. 7, Jan. 1976, 44-52.

641     Butts, Robert E. "Husserl's criticisms of Hume's theory of knowledge." Ph.D. Dissertation, University of Pennsylvania, 1957, 254 p. *Dissertation Abstracts Int.,* vol. 17, no. 11, May 1958, 2639-A.

642     Butts, Robert E. "Husserl's critique of Hume's notion of *distinctions of reason.* " *Philosophy and Phenomenological Research,* vol. 20, 1959-1960, 213-221.

643     Mall, R. A. *Experience and reason.* The phenomenology of Husserl and its relation to Hume's philosophy. (Phaenomenologica). The Hague: Martinus Nijhoff, 1973, x-153.

644     Mall, R. A. "Der Induktionsbegriff. Hume und Husserl." *Zeitschrift für Philosophische Forschung,* vol. 29, 1975, 34-62.

645     Sauer, Friedrich. "Ueber das Verhältnis der Husserlschen Phänomenologie zu David Hume." *Kantstudien,* vol. 35, 1931, 151-182.

646     Schermann, H. "Husserls II. *Logische Untersuchung* und Meinongs Hume-Studien I," in *Jenseits von Sein und Nichtstein.* Beträge zur Meinong-Forschung, Hrsg. von Rudolf Haller. Graz: Akademische Druck.-und Verlagsanstalt, 1972, 103-115.

HUYGENS

647     Westfall, Richard S. "Huygens's rings and Newton's rings, periodicity and seventeenth century optics." *Ratio,* vol. 10, June 1968, 64-77.

INGARDEN, Roman

648     Hempolinski, Michal. "Epistemologie und Metaphysik bei Husserl und Ingarden." *Deutsche Zeitschrift fur Philosophie,* vol. 24, 1976, 1546-1555.

649    Husserl, Edmund. "Drei unveröffentlichte Briefe von Husserl an Ingarden."
       *Zeitschrift für Philosophische Forschung,* vol. 13, no. 2, [Husserl], 1959,
       349-351.

650    Ingarden, Roman. "The letter to Husserl about the VI [*Logical] investigation
       and 'idealism',"* Helmut Girndt (trans. from the German [With Ingarden's
       own introduction, conclusion and comments to the same letter,
       A.-T.Tymieniecka (trans.)]," in *Ingardeniana. Analecta Husserliana,* vol.
       4, 1976, 418-438.

651    Laskey, Dallas. "Ingarden's criticism of Husserl." *Analecta Husserliana,* vol.
       2, 1972, 48-54. [*See:* R. Ingarden, in *Ibid.,* 23-47].

652    Mostroshilova, N. V. "The problem of the cognitive subject as viewed by
       Husserl and Ingarden." *Dialectics and Humanism,* vol. 2, Summer 1975,
       no. 3, 17-31.

653    Rieser, Max. "The philosophy of Roman Ingarden in a critical light."
       *Dialectics and Humanism,* vol. 2, Spring 1975, 89-94.

654    *Studiow Filozoficznych,* ed. *Fenomenologia Romana Ingardena.* Wydanie
       specjalne [The phenomenology of Roman Ingarden. Special number of
       *Philosophical Studies*] Warszawa: Instytut Filozofii i Socjologii PAN, 1972,
       506 p. [Part II: The controversy of R. Ingarden with Husserl: Z. M.
       Kahanadie, J. Tischner, Guido Küng, A. Póltawski].

655    Tarnowski, Karol. "Roman Ingarden's critique of transcendnetal
       constitution." *Dialectics and Humanism,* vol. 3, Winter 1976, 111-119.

656    Tymieniecka, Anna-Teresa. "Beyond Ingarden's idealism/realism controversy
       with Husserl--The new contextual phase of phenomenology," in
       *Ingardeniana.* A spectrum of specialised studies established the field of
       research. *Analecta Husserliana,* vol. 4, 1976, 241-418. Dordrecht-Boston:
       D. Reidel, 1976.

JAKOBSON

657    Holenstein, Elmar. "Jakobson und Husserl. Ein Beitrag zur Genealogie des
       Strukturalismus." *Tijdschrift voor Filosofie,* vol.35, 1973, 560-607.

658    Holenstein, Elmar. "Jakobson and Husserl: A contribution to the genealogy
       of structuralism." *Human Context-Le Domaine Humain,* vol. 7, Spring
       1975, 61-83.

659    Holenstein, Elmar. *Jakobson ou le structuralisme phénoménologique.* Paris:
       Seghers, 1974, 247 p.

660    Holenstein, Elmar. "Jakobson und Husserl. Ein Beitrag zu Genealogie des
       Strukralismus," in *History of Linguistic thought and contemporary
       linguistics,* Herman Parret (ed.). Berlin-New York, Walter de Gruyter,
       1976, 772-810.

JAMES, William

661    Kessler, Gary E. "Pragmatic bodies versus transcendental egos." *Transaction
       of the Peirce Society,* vol. 14, Spring 1978, 101-119.

662    Linschoten, Johannes. *Auf dem Wege zu einer phänomenologischen Psychologie.* Die Psychologie von William James. Ins Deutsche übertragen von Franz Mönks (Phänomenologisch-psychologische Forschungen, 3, herausgegeben von C. F. Graumann und J. Linschoten). Berlin: Walter De Gruyter und Co., 1961, vii-254.

663    Spiegelberg, Herbert. "What William James knew about Edmund Husserl," in *Life-world and consciousness.* Essays for Aron Guwitsch, Lester E. Embree (ed.). Evanston, Il.: Northwestern University Press, 1972, 407-423.

664    Stevens, Richard. *James and Husserl.* The foundations of meaning (Phaenomenologica, 60). The Hague: Martinus Nijhoff, 1974, vii-191.

JOYCE, James

665    Fleming, R. "Dramatic involution: Tate, Husserl, and Joyce." *Sewanee Review,* vol. 60, no. 3, 1952, 445-464.

666    Garcia Bacca, Juan David. "Edmund Husserl and James Joyce. Theory and practice of the phenomenological attitude." *Philosophy and Phenomenological Research,* vol. 9, 1948-1949, 588-594.

KAFKA, Franz

667    Demetz, Peter. "Kafka, Freud, Husserl. Probleme einer Generation." *Zeitschrift für Religions-und Geistesgeschichte,* vol. 7, 1955, 59-69.

KANT, Immanuel

668    Baumgardt, David. "Das Möglichkeitsproblem der Kritik der reinen Vernunft, der modernen Phänomenologie und der Gegenstandstheorie." *Kantstudien,* 1920, Ergänzungshefte.

669    Danek, Jaromir. "Kant, Husserl et l'histoire de la logique." *Dialogue,* vol. 12, 1973, 110-115.

670    de Oliveira, Manfredo Arujo. *Subjektivität und Vermittlung.* Studien zur Entwicklung d. transzendentalen Denkens bei I. Kant, E. Husserl u H. Wagner. München: Fink, 1973, 329 p.

671    Dussort, Henri. "Husserl juge de Kant." *Revue Philosophique de la France et de l'Etranger,* vol. 84, no. 4, [Ed. Husserl], 1959, 527-544.

672    Folwart, Helmut. *Kant, Husserl, Heidegger.* Breslau, 1936.

673    Gallagher, Kenneth T. "Kant and Husserl on the synthetic *a priori.*" *Kantstudien,* vol. 63, 1972, 341-353.

674    Garulli, Enrico "Husserl, Kant e i neokantiani nell'interpretazione di Iso Kern [I. Kern, *Husserl und Kant*]." *Il Pensiero,* vol. 9, 1964, 125-146.

675    Gurwitsch, Aron. "Der Begriff des Bewusstseins bei Kant und Husserl." *Kantstudien,* vol. 55, 1964, 410-427. "The Kantian and Husserlian conception of consciousness," in his *Studies in Phenomeonolgy and psychology.* Evanston, Ill.: Northwestern University Press, 1966, 148-174. [Richard M. Zaner (trans.)].

676    Hartmann, Klaus. "Husserl und Kant." *Kantstudien,* no. 3, 1967, 370-375.

677    Hoche, Hans-Ulrich. *Nichtempirische Erkenntnis.* Analytische und synthetische Urteile bei Kant und bein Husserl (Monographien zur philosophischen Forschung, 35). Meisenheim am Glan: Anton Hain, 1964, 208 p.

678    Ingarden, Roman. *"A priori* knowledge in Kant versus *a priori* knowledge in Husserl," Ewa Hoffmann Szcepanek (trans.). *Dialectics and Humanism,* 1973, 5-18.

679    Jacobelli Isoldi, Angela Maria. *Il tempo in Kant e suoi sviluppi in Husserl e Heidegger.* Anno accademico 1962-1963 (Università delgi studi di Roma. Facoltà di maigstero). Roma: Editr. E. De Santis, 1963, 168 p.

680    Kelkel, Arion L. "Husserl et Kant. Réflexions à propos d'une thèse récente [I. Kern, *Husserl und Kant].* Revue de Métaphysique et de Morale,* vol. 71, 1966, 154-198.

681    Kern, Iso. *Husserl und Kant.* Eine Untersuchung über Husserls Verhältnis zur Kant und zum Neukantianismus (Phaenomenologica, 16). The Hague: Martinus Nijhoff, 1964, xxiv-448.

682    Kockelmans, Joseph J. "Husserl and Kant on the pure ego," in *Husserl. Expositions and appraisals,* F. Elliston and P. McCormick (eds.). Notre Dame, Ind., London: University of Notre Dame Press, 1977, 269-285.

683    Klein, Ted. "Husserl's Kantian meditations." *Southwestern Journal of Philosophy,* vol. 5, no. 3, 1974, 69-82.

684    Kuspit, Donald B. "The continuity between Kant and Husserl," in *Proceedings VIIth Interamerican Convention of philosophy,* II. Quebec: Les Presses de l'Universite Laval, 1968, II, 282-287.

685    Mall, Ram Adhar. "Husserl's criticism of Kant's theory of knowledge." *Journal of the Indiana Academy of Philosophy,* vol. 6, 1967, 21-31.

686    Murphy, Richard T. "The transcendental *a priori* in Husserl and Kant." *Analecta Husserliana,* vol. 3, 1974, 66-79.

687    Pantaleo, Pasquale. *La direzione coscienza-intenzione nella filosofia di Kant e Husserl.* Bari: Arti grafiche Laterza e Polo, 1967, 363 p.

688    Ricoeur, Paul. "Kant et Husserl." *Kantstudien,* vol. 46, 1954-1955, 44-67. "Kant and Husserl." *Philosophy Today,* vol. 10, Fall 1966, 145-168. Reprinted in *Husserl.* An analysis of his phenomenology, Edward G. Ballard and Lester E. Embree (trans.). Evanston, Ill.: Northwestern University Press, 1967, 175-201.

689    Sala, Javier San Martín. "La teoría del yo transcendental en Kant y Husserl." *Anales del Seminar de Metafísica,* vol. 9, 1974, 123-143.

690    Seebohm, Thomas. *Die Bedingungen der Möglichkeit der Transzendental-Philosophie.* Edmund Husserls transzendental-phänomenologischer Ansatz, dargestellt im Anschluss an seine Kant-Kritik (Abhandlungen zur Philosophie, Psychologie und Pädägogig, 24). Bonn: H. Bouvier u. Co. Verlag, 1962, 202 p.

691     Son, B. H. *Science and persons.* A study on the idea of philosophy as rigorous science in Kant and Husserl. Assen: Van Gorcum, 1972, 188 p.

692     Wallton, Roberto J. "Asociación y sintesis pasiva." *Cuadernos de Filosofía,* vol. 13, 1973, 433-446.

693     Yamanoto, Manjiro. "Husserls Ansicht über Kant." [In Japanese]. *Philosophy* (Tokyo), no. 34, 1958, 1-21 [Summary in German, 22-23].

KIERKEGAARD, Sören

694     Valori, Paolo. "Husserl e Kierkegaard," in *Kierkegaard e Nietzsche,* (Scritti di E. Paci, C. Fabro, F. Lombardi, G. Masi, P. Valori, et al.) *Archivo di Filosofia,* no. 2, 1953, 191-200.

695     Vancourt, R. "Deux conceptions de la philosophie: Husserl et Kierkegaard." *Mélanges de Sciences Religieuses,* vol. 1, 1944, 193-240.

KÜLPE, Oswald

696     Schräder, Herta. "Die Theorie des Denkens bei Külpe und Husserl." Dissertation, Münster, i. W., 1924, 46 p.

LASK, E.

697     Lukács, Georg. "Nachruf fur E. Lask." *Kantstudien,* vol. 22, 1918, 349-361.

LEIBNIZ

698     Ehrhardt, Walter E. "Die Leibniz-Rezeption in der Phänomenologie Husserls," in *Akten des Internationalen Leibniz-Kongresses,* Hannover, 14-19 November 1966. Band V: Geschichte der Philosophie (*Studia Leibnitiana,* Suppl. vol. 5). Wiesbaden: F. Steiner, 1971, 146-155.

699     Van Breda, Herman Leo. "Leibniz' Einfluss auf das Denken Husserls," in *Akten des Internationalen Leibniz-Kongresses* [*see:* 1265], 124-145.

LENIN, V.

700     Lozinski, Jerzy. "On the problems of the relation between Marxism and phenomenology: Truth and revolution--Husserl and Lenin." *Dialectics and Humanism,* vol. 3, Winter 1976, 121-133.

LEVINAS, Emmanuel

701     Strasser, Stephan. "Antiphénoménologie et phénoménologie dans la philosophie d'Emmanuel Levinas." *Revue Philosophique de Louvain,* vol. 75, Feb. 1977, 101-125.

702     Wyschogrod, Edith. *Emmanuel Levinas.* The problem of ethical metaphysics. The Hague: Martinus Nijhoff, 1974, 222 p.

LIPPS, Hans

703     Wewel, Meinoff. *Die Konstitution des transzendental Etwas im Vollzug des Sehens.* Eine Untersuchung im Anschluss an die Philosophie von Hans Lipps und in Auseinandersetzung mit Edmund Husserls Lehre vom 'intentionalen Bewusstseinskorrelat'. Düsseldorf: M. Wewel, 1968, 166 p.

LIPPS, Theodor

704 Schuhmann, Karl. "Ein Brief Husserls and Theodor Lipps." *Tijdschrift voor Filosofie,* vol. 39, March 1977, 141-150.

LOCKE, John

705 Wahl, Jean. "Au sujet des jugements de Husserl sur Descartes et sur Locke," in *Husserl* (Cahiers de Royaumont, 3). Paris: Editions de Minuit, 1959, 119-131 [Discussion, 132-142].

LONERGAN, Bernard

706 Ryan, William F. J., S.J. "Intentionality in Edmund Husserl and Bernard Lonergan." *International Philosophical Quarterly,* vol. 13, 1973, 173-190.

MACH, Ernst

707 Düsing, Klaus. "Das Problem der Denkökonomie bei Husserl und Mach," in *Perspektiven transzendentalphänomenologischer Forschuung* (Phaenomenologica, 49). Hrsg. von U. Claesges und K. Held. The Hague: Martinus Nijhoff, 1972, 225-254.

708 Lübbe, Hermann. "Positivismus und Phänomenologie (Mach und Husserl)," in *Beiträge zu Philosophie und Wissenschaft.* Wilhelm Szilasi zum 70. Geburtstag. München: Francke Verlag, 1960, 161-184.

709 McGinn, Colin. "Mach and Husserl." *Journal of the British Society for Phenomenology,* vol. 3, 1972, 146-157.

710 Thiele, Joachim. "Ein Brief Edmund Husserls an Ernst Mach." *Zeitschrift für Philosophische Forschung,* vol. 19, 134-138.

MALLARMÉ, Stéphane

711 Oxenhandler, Neal. "The quest for pure consciousness in Husserl and Mallarmé," in *The quest for imagination,* O. B. Hardison (ed.). Press of Case Western Reserve University, 1971, 149-166.

MAO Tse-Tung

712 Jung, Hwa Yol. "The hermeneutics of political ideology and cultural change: Maoism as the sinicization of Marxism." *Cultural Hermeneutics,* vol. 3, Aug. 1975, 165-188.

MARCEL, Gabriel

713 Ricoeur, Paul. "Gabriel Marcel et la phénoménologie [E. Husserl]," in *Entretiens autour de G. Marcel,* 53-74. [Discussion: G. Marcel, J. Parain-Vial, P. Ricoeur, M. Déglise, M. de Gandillac, J. Cornu, H. Gouhier, B. Schwarz, R. Bouveresse, G. de Champaux, R. Poirier, E. Tréves, E. Hattori, R. Sevigny, P. Cheetham, M. Belay, M. Charpy, H. Mavit,, J. Chenu, 75-94].

MARCUSE, Herbert

714     Steigerwald, Robert. *Herbert Marcuses dritter Weg.* Berlin: Akademie Verlag, 1969.

MARITAIN, Jacques

715     Brugnaro, F. G. "Jacques Maritain e la fenomenologia husserliana." *Humanitas* (Brescia), vol. 27, no. 8-9, 1972, 694-704.

MARTY, Anton

716     Kurda, S.-Y. "Edmund Husserl, *Gramaire générale et raisonnée* and Anton Marty." *Foundations of Language,* vol. 10, 1973, 169-195.

717     Parret, H. "Le débat de la psychologie et de la logique concernant le langage: Marty et Husserl," in *History of linguistic thought and contemporary linguistics* (Foundations of communications). Berlin-New York: Walter de Gruyter, 1976, 732-771.

MARX, Karl

718     Naville, Pierre. "Marx et Husserl." *Revue Internationale de Philosophie,* 1946, 227-243, et 445-454.

719     Paci, Enzo. "Il significato dell'uomo in Marx e in Husserl." *Aut Aut,* no. 73, 1963, 10-21.

720     Paci, Enzo. "Fenomenologia e obiettivazione [Husserl-Marx]." *Giornale critico della Filosofia Italiana,* vol. 40, 1961, 143-152.

721     Shmueli, E. "Consciousness and action: Husserl and Marx on theory and praxis." *Analecta Husserliana,* vol. 5, 1976, 343-382.

722     Pazanin, Ante. "Das Problem der Geschichte bei Husserl, Hegel und Marx," in *Phänomenologie heute.* Festschrift fur Ludwig Landgrebe (Phaenomenologica, 51). The Hague: Martinus Nijhoff, 1972, 173-203.

723     Rasmussen, D. M. "The quest for valid knowledge in the context of society [Marx and Husserl]." *Analecta Husserliana,* vol. 5, 1976, 259-268 [Discussion: 296-302].

724     Trans-Duc-Thao. *Phénoménologie et matérialisme dialectique.* Paris: Editions Minh-Tan, 1951, 368 p.

MASARYK

725     Jirasek, Josef (ed.). "Masarykovy dopisy Husserlovi." *Sb. Pr. Filos. Fak. Bratislava,* (19) B. 17, 1970, 157-164.

MEAD, George H.

726     Ames, Van Meter. "Mead and Husserl on the self." *Philosophy and Phenomenological Research,* vol. 15, 1954-1955, 320-331.

MEINONG

727     Schermann, Hans. "Husserls II. *Logische Untersuchung* und Meinongs Hume-Studien I," in *Jenseits von Sein und Nichtsein.* Beiträge zur

Meinong-Forschung. Hrsg. von Rudolf Haller. Graz: Akademische Druck.-udn Verlagsanstalt, 1972, 103-115.

MERLEAU-PONTY, Maurice

728    Bruzina, Ronald C. "*Logos* and *eidos:* A study in the phenomenological meaning of concept according to Husserl and Merleau-Ponty." Ph.D. Dissertation, University of Notre Dame, 1966, 259 p. *Dissertation Abstracts,* vol. 27, no. 6, Dec. 1966, 1862-A.

729    Devettere, Raymond. Merleau-Ponty and the Husserlian reductions." *Philosophy Today,* vol. 17, 1973, 297-310.

730    Dolgov, K. M. "The philosophy and aesthetics of Maurice Merleau-Ponty." *Soviet Studies in Philosophy,* vol. 14, Winter 1975-1976, 67-92.

731    Fanizza, F. "Motivi estetici nella fenomenologia di Merleau-Ponty." *Aut Aut,* no. 66, 1961, 516-538.

732    Halda, Bernard. *Thématique phénoménologique et implications.* Husserl, Edith Stein, Merleau-Ponty. Louvain: Nauwelaerts; Paris: Diffusion Vander-Oyez, 1976, 71 p.

733    Kwant, Remy C. *From phenomenology to metaphysics.* An inquiry into the last period of Merleau-Ponty's philosophical life. Pittsburgh, Pa.: Duquesne University Press, 1966.

734    Lowry, Atherton C. "Merleau-Ponty and fundamental ontology." *International Philosophical Quarterly,* vol. 15, Dec. 1975, 397-409.

735    Marini, A. "Psicologia e fenomenologia in Husserl e in Merleau-Ponty." *Aut Aut,* no. 66, 1961, 539-551.

736    Merleau-Ponty, Maurice. *Les sciences de l'home et la phénoménologie.* Paris: Les cours de Sorbonne, 1958. "Phenomenology and the sciences of man," John Wild (trans.) in *The primacy of perception,* with an intro. by James M. Edie (ed.). Evanston, Ill.: Northwestern University Press, 1964, 43-95.

737    Murphy, Richard T. "Phenomenology and the dialectic: A study of pre-reflexive consciousness in the phenomenological theories of Husserl, Sartre, and Merleau-Ponty." Ph.D. Dissertation, Fordham University, 1963, 294 p. *Dissertation Abstracts,* vol. 24, no. 2, Aug. 1963, 779-A.

738    Murphy, Richard T. "A metaphysical critique of method, Husserl and Merleau-Ponty." *Boston College Studies in Philosophy,* vol. 1, 1966, 175-207.

739    Pirella, A. "Fenomenologia e scienza (Husserl, Merleau-Ponty, Paci)." *Rendiconti* (Bologna), no. 1, 1961, 36-40.

740    Semerari, G. "Esistenzialismo e marxismo nella fenomenologia della percezione." *Rivista di Filosofia,* no. 2, 1961, 167-191 and *Ibid.,* no. 3, 331-353.

741    Semerari, G. "Scienza e filosofia nella fenomenologia della percezione." *Aut Aut,* no. 66, 1961, 481-497.

742    Semarari, G. "Critica e progetto dell'uomo nella fenomenologia di M. Merleau-Ponty." *Il Pensiero,* no. 3, 1960, 329-359.

743 Semarari, G. *Da Schelling a Merleau-Ponty.* Bologna, 1962.

744 Siméon, J.-P. "Maurice Merleau-Ponty et l'ideéalisme." *Revue de Métaphysique et de Morale,* vol. 82, July-Sept. 1977, 296-311.

745 Spiecker, Stuart F. "Inner time and lived-through time: Husserl and Merleau-Ponty." *Journal of the British Society for Phenomenology,* vol. 4, 1973, 235-247.

746 Taylor, Darrell D. "Husserl and Merleau-Ponty and the problem of the cultural studies." Ph.D. Dissertation, University of Southern California, 1966, 424 p. *Dissertation Abstracts,* vol. 27, no. 2, Aug. 1966, 508-A.

747 Trogu, G. "Merleau-Ponty e la fenomenologia della percezione." *Il Pensiero Critico,* no. 4, 1960, 65-78.

748 Van Breda, Herman Leo. "Maurice Merleau-Ponty et les Archives-Husserl à Louvain." *Revue de Métaphysique et de Morale,* vol. 67, 1962, 410-430.

749 Vircillo, Domenico. "Le scienze umane e la fenomenologia da Husserl a Merleau-Ponty." *Teoresi,* vol. 25, 1970, 235-273.

750 Waelhens, Alphonse de. *Une philosophie de l'ambigüité.* L'existentialisme de Maurice Merleau-Ponty. Louvain: Publication Universitaires de Louvain, 1951.

METZGER, Arnold

751 Husserl, Edmund-Metzger, A. "Ein Brief Edmund Husserl von 1919 [an Arnold Metzger auf Grund eines von Metzger gesandten, unveröffentlichten Manuskriptes: *Die Phänomenologie der Revolution* (1919)]." *Philosophisches Jahrbuch,* vol. 62, no. 1, [Deutung der Gegenwart], 1953, 195-200. "E. Husserl's letter. A. Metzger's letter. Introution by Paul Senft [English, German and French text]." *Human Context--Le Domaine humain,* vol. 4, 1972, 244-263.

MOTROSILOVA, N. V.

752 Blakeley, T. J. "N. V. Motrosilova on Husserl." *Studies in Soviet Thought,* vol. 10, 1970, 50-52.

NABERT, J.

753 Robberechts, Ludovic. "Réflexion phénoménologique et réflexion éthique [J. Nabert et E. Husserl]." *Etudes Philosophiques,* vol. 17, 1962, 403-420.

NATANSON, Maurice

754 Forrest, William. "Doubt and phenomenological reduction. An appendix to the Natanson-Amers controversy." *Philosophy and Phenomenological Research,* vol. 18, 1957-1958, 379-381.

NATORP, Paul

755 Pos, H. J. "Methodisch verschil tusschen Natorp en Husserl inzake de subjectiviteit." *Algemeen Nederlands Tijdschrift voor Wijsgeberte en Psychologie,* vol. 18, 1925.

NEO-HUMBOLDTIANS

756    Parret, Herman. "Husserl and the neo-Humboldtians on language."
       *International Philosophical Quarterly*, vol. 12, 1972, 433-68.

NEO-KANTIANISM

757    Stapleton, Timothy J. "Husserl and neo-Kantianism." *Auslegung*, vol. 4, Fall
       1977, 81-104.

NIETZSCHE, Friedrich

758    Boehm, Rudolf. "Deux points de vue: Husserl et Nietzsche," in *Pascal e
       Nietzsche*. Scritti di E. Castelli, et al (*Archivio di Filosofia*, no. 3, 1962).
       Padova: CEDAM, 1962, 167-178. "Husserl und Nietzsche," in his Vom
       Gesicktspunkt der Phänomenologie. Husserl Studien (Phaenomenologica,
       26). The Hague: Martinus Nijhoff, 1968, 217-236.

ORETGA Y GASSET, José

759    López Quintá, Alfonso. "Santayana, Husserl y Ortega. Necesidad de una
       revisión metodológica." *Arbor*, vol. 82, 1972, 287-298.

760    Ortega y Gasset, José. "Notes on thinking: its creation of the world and its
       creation of God," in his *Concord and liberty*. New York: Norton, 1968.

PACI, Enzo

761    Garulli, Enrico. "La phénoménologie de Husserl vue par Enzo Paci." *Revue
       de Métaphysique et de Morale*, vol. 67, 1962, 384-390.

PARSON, Talcott

762    Robert, Carl. "Husserlian phenomenology and Parsonian functionalism in
       juxtaposition." *Dialogue* (P.S.T.), vol. 18, April 1976, 60-65.

PEIRCE, C. S.

763    Dougherty, Charles J. "Phenomenological critique of empiricismm: A study
       in the philosophies of Husserl and Peirce." Ph.D. Dissertation, University
       of Notre Dame, 1975, 245 p. *Dissertation Abstracts*, vol. 36, no. 3, Sept.
       1975, 1576-A.

764    Spiegelberg, Herbert. "Husserl's and Peirce's phenomenology: Coincidence or
       interaction?" *Philosophy and Phenomenological Research*, vol. 17,
       1956-1957, 164-195.

PERRY, Ralph B.

765    Ricci, Louis M. "Independent existence in Royce, Perry, and Husserl." Ph.D.
       Dissertation, SUNY at Buffalo, 1970, 172 p. *Dissertation Abstracts*, vol. 31,
       no. 9, March 1971, 4844-A.

PFÄNDER, Alexander

766    Pettit, Philip. "Is the reduction necessary for phenomenology: Husserl and
       Pfänder's replies. A reply to Herbert Spiegelberg." *Journal of the British
       Society for Phenomenology*, vol. 5, 1974, 16-19.

767    Schuhmann, Karl. *Die Dialektik der Phänomenologie.* Vol. I: Husserl uber Pfänder (Phaenomenologica, 56). The Hague: Martinus Nijhoff, 1973, x-211.

768    Spiegelberg, Herbert. "Is the reduction necessary for phenomenology? Husserl's and Pfänder's replies." *Journal of the British Society for Phenomenology,* vol. 5, 1974, 315.

769    Spiegelberg, Herbert. "Neues Licht auf die Beziehungen zwischen Husserl und Pfänder. Bemerkungen und Ergänzungen anlässlich von Karl Schuhmanns *'Husserl über Pfander'.*" [*see:* 335]. *Tijdschrift voor Filosofie,* vol. 36, 1974, 565-573.

PETRESCU, Camil

770    Tertulian, Nicolas. "Camil Petrescu e la fenomenologia di Husserl." *Aut Aut,* no. 112, 1969, 71-86.

PIAGET, Jean

771    Marbach, E. "Husserls reine Phänomenologie und Piagets genetische Psychologie." *Tijdschrift voor Filosofie,* vol. 39, March 1977, 81-103.

772    Mays, Wolfe. "Genetic analysis and experience: Husserl and Piaget." *Journal of the British Society for Phenomenology,* vol. 8, Jan. 1977, 51-55.

773    Seltzer, Edward C. "The problem of Objectivity: A study of objectivity reflected in a comparison of the philosophies of E. Cassirer, J. Piaget, and E. Husserl." Ph.D. Dissertation, New School for Social Research, 1969, 196 p. *Dissertation Abstracts,* vol. 30, no. 11, May 1970, 5031-A.

PICASSO, Pablo

774    Piwocki, K. "Husserl and Picasso," in *Aesthetics in twentieth century Poland,* J. G. Harrell and A. Wierzbianka (eds.). Lewisburg, Pa.: Bucknell University Press, 1973, 143-163.

PLATO

775    Berl, H. E. "Husserl oder die Judaisierung des Platonismus," *Menorah,* vol. 10, 1932 [Wien].

776    Burnyeat, M. F. "Protagoras and self-refutation in Plato's Theaetetus." *Philosophical Review,* vol. 85, April 1976, 172-195.

777    Chandler, Albert R. "Plato's theory of ideas studied in the light of Husserl's theory of universals." Ph.D. Dissertation, Harvard University, 1913, 167 p.

778    McGaughey, D. R. "Husserl and Heidegger on Plato's cave allegory: A study of philosophical influence." *International Philosophical Quarterly,* vol. 16, Sept. 1976, 331-348.

779    Schmidt, Degener H. "Proeve eener vergelijkende studie over Plato en Husserl." Ph.D. Dissertation, Groningen, 1924.

PLOTINUS

780    Blanco, Julio Enrique. "Una vez má Husserl y Plotino." *Universidad Bolivariana,* 12, 1946, 471-490.

PROUST, Marcel

781    Huertas-Jourda, José. "Structures of the 'living present': Husserl and Proust," in *The study of time,* II, Proceedings of the second conference of the International Society for the study of time, J. T. Fraser and N. Lawrence (eds.). Berlin-New York: Springer Verlag, 1975, 163-195.

REINACH, Adolf

782    Husserl, Edmund. "Adolf Reinach," Lucinda V. Brettler (trans.). *Philosophy and Phenomenological Research,* vol. 35, 1974-1975, 571-574.

RICOEUR, Paul

783    Ihde, Don. *Hermeneutic phenomenology.* Evanston, Ill.: Northwestern University Press, 1971.

784    Renzi, E. "Ricoeur e l'Einfühlung husserliana." *Il Verri,* no. 4, 1960, 131-138.

ROYCE, Josiah

785    Ricci, Louis M. "Independent existence in Royce, Perry, and Husserl." Ph.D. Dissertation, SUNY at Buffalo, 1970, 172 p. *Dissertation Abstracts,* vol. 31, no. 9, March 1971, 4844-A.

RYLE, Gilbert

786    Hoche, Hans-Ulrich. "Phänomenologie und Sprachanalyse. Bemerkungen zu Wittgenstein, Ryle, und Husserl," in *Aufgaben und Wege des Philosphieunterrichts,* Hrsg. von Friedrich Borden. Neue Folge, Heft 4: Beiträge zu verschiedenen philosophischen Themen, 1972.

787    Mays, Wolfe. "Husserl on Ryle's review of ' *Sein und Zeit*." *Journal of the British Society for Phenomenology,* vol. 1, 1970, 14-15.

SANTAYANA, George

788    Ashmore, Jerome. "Essence in recent philosophy: Husserl, Whitehead, Santayana." *Philosophy Today,* vol. 18, Fall 1974, 198-210.

789    López Quintás, Alfonso. "Santayana, Husserl y Ortega. Necesidad de uan revisión metodológica." *Arbor,* vol. 82, 1972, 287-298.

SARTRE, Jean-Paul

790    Borrello, O. "L'intuizione nella psicologia fenomenologica di J.-P. Sartre." *Rivista di Filosofia,* no. 2, 1962, 128-158.

791    Brunet, Christian. "Husserl y Sartre frente al problema del conocimiento." *Diánoia* (México), 1955, 311-349.

792    Curtius, Jerry L. "A Camus commentary: Sartre's debt to Husserl." *South Atlantic Bulletin,* vol. 40, no. 4, 1975, 1-6.

793     Doran, Robert M., S.J. "Sartre's critique of the Husserlian ego." *Modern Schoolman,* vol. 44, 1966-1967, 307-317.

794     Dreyfus, Hubert L. "The priority of *the* world to *my* world: Heidegger's answer to Husserl (and Sartre)." *Man and World,* vol. 8, May 1975, 121-130.

795     Fanizza, F. "Il nuovo umnesimo di J.-P. Sartre." *Ricerche Filosofiche,* Dec. 1961, 10-21.

796     Gurwitsch, Aron. "A non-egological conception of consciousness." *Philosophy and Phenomenological Research,* vol. 1, 1940-1941, 325-338. Reprinted in his *Studies in phenomenology and psychology.* Evanston, Ill.: Northwestern University Press, 1966, 287-300.

797     Hoche, Hans-Ulrich. "Bemerkungen zum Problem der Selbst- und Fremderfahrung bei Husserl und Sartre." *Zeitschrift für Philosophische Forschung,* vol. 25, 1971, 172-186.

798     Masullo, Aldo. *La comunitá come fondamento.* Fichte, Husserl, Jean-Paul Sartre. Napoli: Libreria Scientifica Editrice, 1965, 468 p.

799     Natanson, Maurice. "Phenomenology and existentialism: Husserl and Sartre on intentionality." *Modern Schoolman,* vol. 37, 1959-1960, 1-10. Reprinted in his *Essays in phenomenology, literature and social sciences.* The Hague: Martinus Nijhoff, 1966.

800     Pivcevic, Edo. *Husserl and phenomenology.* London: Hutchinson University Library, 1970. [Chapters 12 and 13].

801     Prezioso, Antonio F. "Immagine, coscienza de io in Sartre." *Sapienza,* vol. 29, April-June 1976, 206-217.

802     Scanlon, John D. "Consciousness, the streetcar, and the ego: *pro* Husserl, *contra* Sartre." *Philosophical Forum,* vol. 2, 1970-1971, 332-354.

803     Stamps, Ann. "Shifting focus from Sartre to Husserl." *Journal of Thought,* vol. 8, Jan. 1973, 51-53.

804     Stone, Robert V. "The self as agent-in-the-world. An alternative to Husserl and Sartre's accounts of the ego." Ph.D. Dissertation, University of Texas at Austin, 1972, 272 p.

805     Sukale, Michael. "The ego and consciousness in rival perspectives. A study of Husserl and the early Sartre [in Hebrew]." *Iyyun,* vol. 22, 1971, 193-214. [Summary, 274-276].

806     Theunissen, Michael. "Die destruierende Wiederholung der transzendentalen Intersubjektivitätstheorie Husserls in der Sozialontologie Sartres," in *Der Andere: Studien zur Sozialontologie der Gegenwart.* Berlin: Walter de Gruyter, 1965, 187-240.

SAUSSURE

807     Parret, Herman. "Expression et articulation. Une confrontation des points de vue husserlien et saussurien concernant la langue et la discours." *Revue Philosophique de Louvain,* vol. 71, 1973, 72-112 [Résumé, 113].

SCHELER, Max

808    Guthrie, Hunter. "Max Schelers's epistemology of the emotions." *Modern Schoolman,* vol. 16, 1939.

809    Kranzlin, Gerhard. *Max Schelers phänomenologische Systematk.* Leipzig ( *Studien* und Bibliographien zur Gegenwartsphilosophie, 3, 1934, 103) [über Husser Abt. A].

810    Landgrebe, Ludwig. "Geschichtsphilosophische Perspektiven bie Scheler und Husserl," in *Max Scheler im Gegenwartsgeschehen der Philosophie.* Hrsg. von Paul Good. Bern-München: A. Francke Verlag, 1975, 79-90.

811    Métraux, Alexandre. *Max Scheler ou la philosophie des valeurs.* Présentation, choix de textes, bibliographie. Paris: Seghers, 1973, 160 p.

812    Pöll, M. *Wesen und Wesenserkenntnis.* Untersuchungen mit besondeer Berücksichtigung der Phänomenologie Husserls und Schelers. München, 1936, x-207.

812    Schümmer, Heinz. *Die Wahrnehmungs- und Erkenntnismetaphysik Max Schelers in den* Stadien ihrer Entwicklung. Unter besonderer Berücksichtigung der Beziehungen Schelers zu Husserl. Bonn, 1954.

813    Smith, Quentin P. "The phenomenology of feeling: A critical development of the theories of feeling in Husserl, Scheler and Sartre." Ph.D. Dissertation, Boston College, 1977, 479 p. *Dissertation Abstracts,* vol. 38, no. 3, Sept. 1977, 1457-A.

814    Temuralq, T. *Ueber die Grenzen der Erkennbarketi bei Husserl und Scheler.* Berlin, 1937.

SCH]NBERG, Arnold

815    Sini, Carlo. "Prospettive fenomenologiche nel 'Manuale' di Schönberg." *Aut Aut,* no. 79-80, 1964, 67-85.

SCHUPP

816    Zocher, R. *Husserls Phänomenologie und Schuppes Logik.* München, 1932.

SCHÜTZ, Alfred

817    Wagner, Helmut. "Phenomenology and contemporary sociological theory. The contribution of Alfred Schutz." *Sociological Focus,* vol. 2, no. 3, Spring 1969, 73-86.

SCIACCA, Michele F.

818    Gonzalo Casas, Manuel. "La idea de un saber adecuado a la condición humana en Husserl y Sciacca," in *Michele F. Sciacca.* In occasione del 30 anno di cattedra universitario (1938-1968). Milano:Marzorati, 1968, 229-234.

SELLARS, Wilfrid

819    Hartjes, John F. "The critique of the 'given' in Wilfrid Sellars and Edmund Husserl." The Catholic University of America, 1974, 280 p. *Dissertation Abstracts,* vol. 35, no. 3, Sept. 1974, 1701-A.

SESTOV, Leo

820     Déchet, Ferrucio. "Sestov critico di Husserl." *Giornale di Metafisica*, vol. 30, 1975, 209-243. [*see:* Chestov].

SIMMEL, Georg

821     Gorsen, Peter. *Zur Phänomenologie des Bewusstseinsstroms.* Bergson, Dilthey, Husserl, Simmel und die lebensphilosophischen Antinomien. Bonn: Bouvier, 1966, 243 p.

821     [Simmel, George]. "Simmels Briefs an Paul Ernst, Adolf von Harback, Edmund Husserl, Heinrich Rickert, an und von Rainer Maria Rilke, Auguste Rodin, Margarete Susman, Max und Marianne Weber," in *Buch des Dankes an G. Simmel.* Briefe, Erinnerungen, Duncker & Humblot, 1958, 67-135.

STEIN, Edith

822     Ales Bello, Angela. *see:* Thomas Aquinas 828.

823     Baseheart, M. C. "The encounter of Husserl's phenomenology and the philosophy of St. Thomas in selected writings of E. Stein." [*see:* Thomas Aquinas]

824     Ingarden, Roman. "Edith Stein on her activity as an assistant of Edmund Husserl (Extracts from the Letters of Edith Stein with a commentary and introductory remarks) (English translation by Janina Makota)." *Philosophy and Phenomenological Research*, vol. 23, 1962-1963, 155-175.

STEVENS, Wallace

825     Hines, Thomas J. *The later poetry of Wallace Stevens.* Phenomenological parallels with Husserl and Heidegger. Lewisbug, Pa.: Bucknell University Press, 1976, 298 p. London: Associated University Presses, 1976.

STRAUSS, Leo

826     Jung, Hwa Yol. "The life world, historicity and truth: Reflections on Leo Strauss's encounter with Heidegger and Husserl." *Journal of the British Society for Phenomenology*, vol. 9, Jan. 1978, 11-25.

STRAWSON

827     Gorner, Paul. "Husserl and Strawson." *Journal of the British Society for Phenomenology*, vol. 2, no. 1, 1971, 2-9.

THOMAS AQUINAS

828     Ales Bello, Angela. "A proposito della 'Philosophia perennis', Tommaso d'Aquino e Edmund Husserl nell'interpretazione di E. Stein." *Sapienza*, vol. 27, July-Dec. 1974, 441-451.

829     Baseheart, M. C. "The encounter of Husserl's phenomenology and the philosophy of St. Thomas in selected writings of Edith Stein." Ph.D. Dissertation, University of Notre Dame, 1960, 210 p. *Dissertation Abstracts*, vo. 21, no. 3, Sept. 1960, 646-A.

830      Abustan, R. L. "Edmund Husserl's epoché and St. Thomas" metaphysical abstraction." *Unitas* (Manilla), vol. 44, no. 4, 1971, 56-94.

831      Anzenbacker, Arno. *Die Intentionalität bei Thomas von Aquin und Edmund Husserl.* " *München: Oldenburg, 1972, 234 p.*

832      Breton, Stanislas. "Etudes phénoménologiques. Conscience et intentionalité selon saint Thomas et Brentano." *Archives de Philosphie,* vol. 19, cahier 2, janvier 1956, 63-87.

833      Cerri, Stefano. "La nozione di intenzionalità in Husserl e S. Tommaso. Appunti per un esame comparativo." *Rivista di Filosofia Neo-Scholastica,* vol. 59, 1967, 700-725.

834      Ferrari, M. V. *Dalla fenomenologia pura alla trascendenza assoluta* (Husserl e San Tommaso d'Aquino). Roma: Edit. Universita Laterense, 1968, 100 p.

835      Gironella, Juan Roig. "Un capítulo de filosofía del lenguaje: La metafísica de Santo Tomás y la transcendenica del pensamiento, planteada por la fenomenología." *Espíritua,* vol. 70, 1974, 131-147.

836      Gironella, Juan Roig. "Fenomenología de las formas y filosofía de las metamáticas a través del comentario de Tomás de Aquino a la metafísica." *Pensamiento,* vol. 30, July-Sept. 1974, 251-288.

837      Hufnagel, A. *Intuition und Erkentnis nach Thomas von Aquin.* Münster, 1932.

838      Stein, Edith. "Husserls Phänomenologie und die Philosophie des heiligen Thomas von Aquino. Versuch einer Gegenüberstelug," in *Husserl.* Hrsg. von H. Noack (Wege der Forschung, 40). Darmstadt: Wissenschaftliche Buchgesellschaft, 1973, 61-86.

839      Van Riet, Georges. "Reálisme thomiste et phénoménologie husserlienne." *Revue Philosophique de Louvain,* vol. 55, 1957, 58-92.

UNITED STATES

840      Edie, James M. "Phenomenology in the United States [1974]." *Journal of the British Society for Phenomenology,* vol. 5, Oct. 1974, 199-211.

URSS

841      de Virovich, Silvana. "Husserl in URSS [due libri]." *Aut Aut,* no. 107, 1968, 104-106.

VEDANTA

842      Reboul, Jean. "Husserl et le Védanta." *Revue de Métaphysique et de Morale,* vol. 64, 1959, 320-336.

VICO, Giambattista

843      Jordan, Robert W. "Vico and Husserl: History and historical science." in *Giambattista Vico's view of humanity,* Giorgio Tagliacozzo (ed.). Baltimore: The Johns Hopkins University Press, 1976, 251-261.

WEIERSTRASS, Karl

844    Biermann, K.-R. "Did Husserl take his doctor's degree under Weierstrass' supervision?" *Organon* (Warszawa), no. 6, 1969, 261-264.

WIEZSÄCKER, Viktor von

845    Reenpää, Yrjö. *Über die Lehre vom Wissen.* Darstellung und Kommentar der Wissenslehren vom Edmund Husserl und Viktor von Weizsäcker sowie Hinweis auf diejenigen von Richard B. Braithwaite, unsere zeitzentrierte Theorie und die Theorie von Gotthard Günther (Annales Academiae Scientiarum Fennicae, ser. B. tom. 145, 1). Helsinki: Soumalainen Tiedakatemia, 1966, 114 p.

WHITEHEAD, Alfred N.

846    Ashmore, Jerome. "Essence in recent philosophy: Husserl, Whitehead, Santayana." *Philosophy Today,* vol. 18, Fall 1974, 198-210.

847    Bennett, John B. "Husserl's *Crisis* and Whitehead's process philosophy." *The Personalist,* vol. 56, Summer, 1975, 289-300.

848    Hartshorne, Charles. "Husserl and Whitehead on the concrete," in *Phenomenology. Continuation and criticism,* F. Kersten and R. M. Zaner (eds.) (Phaenomenologica, 50). The Hague: Martinus Nijhoff, 1973, 90-104.

849    Laszlo, Erwin. *Beyond scepticism and realism.* A constructive exploration of Husserlian and Whiteheadian methods of inquiry. The Hague: Martinus Nijhoff, 1966, 238 p.

850    Paci, Enzo. "Whitehead e Husserl." *Aut Aut,* no. 84, 1965, 7-18.

851    Paci, Enzo. "Über einige Verwandtschaften zwischen der Philosophie Whiteheads und der Phänomenologie Husserls." *Revue Internationale de Philosophie,* vol. 15, no. 56-57 [Whitehead], 1961, 237-250.

852    Rovatti, Pier Aldo. "Whitehead e Husserl: una relazione." *Man and World.* vol. 1, 1968, 587-603.

853    Martin, Gottfried. "Neuzeit und Gegenwart in der Entwicklung des mathematischen Denkens [Husserl, Whitehead]." *Kantstudien,* vol. 45, 1953-1954, 155-165. Reprinted in his *Gesammelte Abhandlungen.* Band I (*Kantstudien,* Ergänzungshefte, 81). Koln: Kolner Universitats-Verlag, 1961, 138-150.

854    Winter, Michael F. "Lived time in Husserl and Whitehead: A comparative study." Ph.D. Dissertation, Northwestern University, 1975, 165 p. *Dissertation Abstracts,* vol. 36, no. 7, Jan. 1976, 4568-A.

WITTGENSTEIN, Ludwig

855    Copleston, Frederick C. "Wittgenstein frente a Husserl." *Revista Portuguesa de Filosofia,* vol. 21, 1965, 134-149.

856    Dufrenne, Mikel. "Wittgenstein et Husserl," in his *Jalons* (Phaenomenologica, 20). The Hague: Martinus Nijhoff, 1966, 188-207.

857     Hems, John M. "Husserl and/or Wittgenstein." *International Philosophical Quarterly,* vol. 8, 1968, 547-578.

858     Hoche, Hans-Ulrich. "Phänomenologie und Sprachanalyse. Bemerkungen zu Wittgenstein, Ryle und Husserl," in *Aufgaben und Wege des Philosophieunterrichts.* Hrsg. von Friedrich Bordon. Neue Folge, Heft 4: Beiträge zu verschiedenen philosophischen Themen, 1972.

859     Malmgren, H. "Internal relations in the analysis of consciousness." *Theoria,* vol. 41, 1975, 61-83.

860     Nyiri, J. C. "Beim Sternenlicht der Nichtexistierenden: Zur ideologierkritischen Interpretation des Platonisierenden Antipsychologismus." *Inquiry,* vol. 17, Winter 1974, 399-433.

861     Reeder, Harry P. "Public and private aspects of language in Husserl and Wittgenstein." Ph.D. Dissertation, University of Waterloo (Canada), 1977. *Dissertation Abstracts,* vol. 38, no. 5, Nov. 1977, 2852-A.

862     Ricoeur, Paul. "Husserl and Wittgenstein on languge," in *Phenomenology and existentialism,* N. Lee and M. Mandelbaum (eds.). Baltimore: The Johns Hopkins University Press, 1967, 207-217.

863     Solomon, Robert C. "Husserl's private language." *Southwestern Journal of Philosophy,* vol. 5, Fall 1974, 203-228.

864     Van Peursen, Cornelis. "Edmund Husserl and Ludwig Wittgenstein," in his *Phenomenology and reality.* Pittsburgh, Pa.: Duquesne University Press, 1972, 189-213.

865     Van Peursen, Cornelius. "Edmund Husserl and Ludwig Wittgenstein." *Philosophy and Phenomenological Research,* vol. 20, no. 2, 1959-1960, 180-198. [Symposium on the 100th anniversary of the birth of Edmund Husserl, 147-265].

ZAMBONI, Giuseppe

866     Giulietti, Giovanni. *La filosofia del profondo in Husserl e in Zamboli* (Uno studio compartivo). Treviso: Libreria Editrice Canova, 1965, 122 p.

867     Picard, Novato. "Gnoseologia pura e fenomenologia trascendentale [Husserl-Zamboni]," in *Studie sul pensiero di Giuseppe Zamboni.* Milano: Marzorati, 1957, 675-688.

868     Valori, Paolo. "Il punto di partenza della filosofia in Giuseppe Zamboni ed Edmund Husserl," in *Studi sul pensiero di Giuseppe Zamboni.* Milano: Marzorati, 1957, 667-674.

ZEN

869     Bossert, Philip J. "Paradox and enlightenment in Zen dialogue and phenomenological description." *Journal of Chinese Philosophy,* vol. 3, June 1976, 269-280.

ZUBIRI, Xavier

870    Riaza, Maria. "El enfreantamiento de Zubiri con la fenomenología de Husserl," in *Homeanje a Xavier Zubiri,* II. Madrid: Ed. Moneda y credito, 1970, 559-584.

871    Savignano, Armando. "Il pensiero fenomenologico di Edmund Husserl secondo Xavier Zuribi." *Aquinas,* vol. 20, 1977, 3-42.

# Section 4

# Items Arranged By Subjects

## ABSOLUTE

872    Beerling, R. F. "Husserl de geschiedenis enhet absolute." *Tijdschrift voor Filosofie,* vol. 29, 1967, 353-394 [Zusammenfaussung: Husserl. Die Geschichte und das Absolute, 395].

873    Boehm, Rudolf. "Zum Begriff des 'Absoluten' bei Husserl." *Zeitschrift für Philosophische Forschung,* vol. 13, no. 2, [Husserl], 1959, 214-242. Reprinted with the title "Das Absolute und die Realität," in his *Vom Gesichtspunkt der Phänomenologie.* Husserl Studien (Phaenomenologica, 26). The Hague: Martinus Nijhoff, 1968, 72-105. "Husserl's concept of the 'absolute'," in *The phenomenology of Husserl,* R. O. Elveton (ed. and trans.). Chicago: Quadrangle Books, 1970, 174-203.

874    de Boer, Theodor. "Die Begriffe 'absolut' und 'relativ' bei Husserl." *Zeitschrift für Philosophische Forschung,* vol. 27, 1973, 514-533.

## ABSTRACTION

875    Behn, Siegfried. "Ueber Phänomenologie und Abstrktion." *Philosophisches Jarbuch,* vol. 38, 1925, 303-311.

876    Hartmann, Klaus. "Abstraction and existence in Husserl's phenomenological reduction." *Journal of the British Society for Phenomenology,* vol. 2, no. 1, 1971, 10-18.

## ACCIDENTAL

877    Sini, Carlo. "Sul problema dell'accidental." *Aut Aut,* no. 69, 1962, 201-216.

## ACT

878    Caso, Antonio. *El acto ideario y la filosofía de Husserl.* México: Porrua, 1946.

879    de Muralt, André. "La notion d'acte fondé dans les rapports de la raison et de la volonté selon les *Logische Untesuchungen* de Husserl. Les véritables sources scolastiques de l'intentionalité husserliene. Essai d'analyse structurelle des doctrines." *Revue de Métaphysique et de Morale,* vol. 82, 1977, 511-527.

880    Messer, A. "Ueber den Begriff des Aktes." *Archivfür die Gesammte Psychologie,* vol. 24, 245ff.

## ACTION

881 Shmueli, E. "Consciousness and action: Husserl and Marx on theory and praxis." *Analecta Husserliana,* vol. 5, 1976, 343-382.

## AESTHETICS (and ART)

882 Anceschi, Luciano. *Autonomia ed eteronomia dell'arte: saggio di fenomenologia delle poetiche.* 2a ed. riveduta. Firenze: Vallecchi, 1959, 304 p.

883 Dorlfes, G. "Momenti di una ricerca estetica." *Aut Aut,* no. 56, 1960, 81-89.

884 Dufrenne, Mikel. *Phénoménologie de l'expérience esthétique,* I: L'objet esthétique; II: La perception esthétique 9Epimétée). Paris: Presses Universitaires de France, 1953.

885 Lipps, Theodor. *Aesthetik* (2a ed.). Leipzig: Voss, I, 1914; II, 1920.

886 Meckaner, Walter. "Aesthetische Idee und Kunsttheorie." *Kantstudien,* vol. 32.

887 Morris, Bertram. "Intention and fulfillment in art." *Philosophy and Phenomenological Research,* vol. 1, 1940-1941.

888 Neri, G. D. "Fenomenologia ed estetica." *Aut Aut,* no. 72, 1962, 517-522.

889 Odebrecht, Rudolph. *Grundlegung einer ästhetischen Werttheorie.* I: Das äesthetische Welterlebnis. Berlin, 1927, 315 p.

890 Read, W. T. Jr. "Aesthetic emotion." *Philosophy and Phenomenological Research,* Dec. 1940.

891 Schmidt, Herman. "Der Horizontbegriff Husserls in Anwendung auf die äesthetischeErfahrung." *Zeitschrift für Philosophische Forschung,* vol. 21, 1967, 499-511.

892 Taminiaux, Jacques. "Notes sur une phénoménologie de l'expérience esthétique." *Revue Philosophique de Louvain,* vol. 55, 1957, 93-110.

893 Zecchi, Stefano. "Note di estetica fenomenologica [Husserl]." *Aut Aut,* no. 102, 1967, 63-87.

894 Ziegenfuss, Werner. *Die phänomenologische Äesthetik.* Berlin: Collignon, 1928.

## ALTER EGO see also: OTHER

895 Danek, Jaromir. "Méditation husserlienne sur l'*Alter Ego.*" *Laval Théologique et Philosophique,* vol. 31, June 1975, 175-191.

896 Waelhens, Alphonse de. "Beschouwing over de historische ontwikkeling van de ervaring van het alter-ego." *Tijdschrift voor Filosofie,* vol. 13, 1951, 667-685.

## ANALYSIS

897 Schmitt, Richard. "Phenomenology and analysis." *Philosophy and Phenomenological Research,* vol. 23, 1962-1963, 101-110.

ANALYTIC (Philosophy)

898     *Analytic philosophy and phenomenology.* Harold A. Durfee (ed.) (American University Publications in Philosophy, 2). The Hague: Martinus Nijhoff, 1976, viii-278.

ANTHROPOLOGY *See also:* MAN, HUMAN SCIENCES, PSYCHOLOGY

899     Allen, Jeffner. "Husserl's philosophical anthropology." *Philosophy Today,* vol. 21, Winter 1977, 347-355.

900     Bidney, D. "Phenomenological method and the anthropological science of the cultural life-world," in *Phenomenology and the social sciences,* Mauice Natanson (ed.). Evanston, Ill.: Northwestern University Press, 1973, vol. I, 109-140.

901     Caruso, Paolo. "Ragione analitica e ragione dialettica nella nuova antropologia." *Aut Aut,* no. 82, 1964, 93-103.

902     Paci, Enzo. *Fenomenologia e antropologia.* Milano, 1962 (Dispense universitaire a cura di C. Sini).

903     Paci, Enzo. "Fenomenologia e antropologia culturale." *Aut Aut,* no. 77, 1963, 9-11.

904     Renzi, Emilio. "Per un'antropologia fenomenologica." *Aut Aut,* no. 67, 1962, 80-89.

905     Scanlon, John D. "The epoche and phenomenological anthropology." *Research in Phenomenology,* vol. 2, 1972, 95-110.

906     Strasser, Stephan. *Bouwstenen voor een filosofische anthropologie.* Hilversum-Antwerpen: Paul Brand, 1965.

907     Toldo, Sisto. *Ontologia trascendentale e antropologia in Edmund Husserl* (Collana di studi filosofici, 25). Padova: Gregoriana, 1973,189 p.

908     Wild. John. "L'anthropologie philosophique et la crise des sciences humaines," in *Husserl* (Cahiers de Royaumont, 3). Paris: Editions de Minuit, 1959, 271-292 [Discussion, 293-306].

APODICTICITY

909     Strasser, Stephan. "Beschouwingen over 't vraagstuk van de apodicticiteit en de critische verantwoording van de phenomenologie." *Tijdschrift voor Filosofie,* vol. 8, 1946, 226-270.

A PRIORI

910     Brand Gerd. "The material *apriori* and the foundation for its analyses in Husserl." *Analecta Husserliana,* vol. 2, 1972, 128-148.

911     Eley, Lothar. *Die Krise des Apriori in der transzendentalen Phänomenologie Edmund Husserls* (Phaenomenologica, 10). The Hague: Martinus Nijhoff, 1962, viii-146.

912 Ingarden, Roman. "*A priori* knowledge in Kant versus *a priori* knowledge in Husserl," Ewa Hoffman Szczepanek (trans.). *Dialectics and Humanism,* 1973, 5-18.

913 Maxsein, Agnes. *Die Entwicklung des Begriffs a priori von Bolzano über Lotze zu Husserl und den von ihm beeinflussten Phänomenologen.* Fulda, 1933.

914 Mohanty, J. N. "Life-world and *a priori* in Husserl's later thought." *Analecta Husserliana,* vol. 3, 1974, 46-65.

915 Murphy, Richard T. "The transcendental *a priori* in Husserl and Kant." *Analecta Husserliana,* vol. 3, 1974, 66-79.

916 Gallagher, Kenneth T. "Kant and Husserl on the synthetic *a priori.*" *Kantstudien,* vol. 63, 1972, 341-353.

917 Pentzopoulou-Valalas, Thérèse. "Réflexions sur le fondement du rapport entre *l'a priori* et *l'eidos* dans la Phénoménologie de Husserl." *Kantstudien,* vol. 65, 1974, 135-151.

ARCHIVES (Husserl)

918 Martínez G., L. "El archivo de Husserl en Lovaina." *Pensamiento,* vol. 13, 1957, 117-118.

919 Sokolowski, Robert. "The Husserl Archives and the edition of Husserl's works." *New Scholasticism,* vol. 38, 1964, 473-482.

920 S. T. "Os arquivos de Husserl." *Revista Portuguesa de Filosofia,* vol. 2, 1946, 304-307.

921 Van Breda, Herman Leo. "Hedendaagsch phaenomenologische Strooming. I. Husserl-Archiev te Leuven. 2. International Phenomenological Society. Buffalo." *Tijdschrift voor Filosofie,* vol. 7, 1945, 195-202.

922 Van Breda, Herman Leo. "Les archives Husserl à Louvain. Leur état actuel." *Revue Philosophique de Louvain,* vol. 43, 1945, 346-350.

923 Van Breda, Herman Leo. "The Husserl Archives in Louvain." *Philosophy and Phenomenological Research,* vol. 7, 1946-1947, 487-491.

924 Van Breda, Herman Leo. "Notes from the Husserl Archives." *Philosophy and Phenomenological Research,* vol. 8, 1947-1948, 302-304.

925 Van Breda, Herman Leo. "Das Husserl-Archiv zu Löwen." *Zeitschrift für Philosophische Forschung,* vol. 2, 1947, 172-176.

926 Van Breda, Herman Leo. "Les archives Husserl à Louvain." *Theoria,* vol. 13, 1947, 65-70.

927 Van Breda, Herman Leo. "Notes sur les Archives Husserl à Louvain," in *Problèmes actuels de la phénoménologie.* Paris: Desclée de Brouwer, 1952, 155-159.

928 Van Breda, Herman Leo, und Boehm, Rudolf. "Aus dem Husserl-Archiv zu Löwen." *Philosophisches Jahrbuch,* vol. 62, 1953, 241-252.

929 Van Breda, Herman Leo, et Boehm, Rudolf. "Les Archives Husserl à Louvain (Traduction française de Jacques Ridé)." *Etudes Philosophiques,* vol. 9, 1954, 3-20.

930    Van Breda, Herman Leo, and Boehm, Rudolf. "O Arquivo de Husserl em Lovaina." *Revista Portuguesa de Filosofia,* vol. 12, 1956, 29-44.

931    Van Breda, Herman Leo. "Geist und Bedeutung des Husserl-Archivs," in *Edmund Husserl 1859-1959* (Phaenomenologica, 4). The Hague: Martinus Nijhoff, 1959, 116-122.

932    Van Breda, Herman Leo. "Le sauvetage de l'héritage husserlien et la fondation des Archives-Husserl;" "Die Rettung von Husserl Nachlass und die Gründung des Husserl-Archivs [Uebersetzt von Rudolf Boehm)," in *Husserl et la pensée moderne* (Phaenomenologica, 2). The Hague: Martinus Nijhoff, 1959, 42-77.

933    Van Breda, Herman Leo. "Maurice Merleau-Ponty et les Archives-Husserl à Louvain." *Revue de Métaphysique et de Morale,* vol. 67, 1962, 410-430.

ARITHMETIC

934    Torretti, Roberto. "La filosofía de la arithmética de Husserl." *Studi Internazionali di Filosofia,* vol. 4, 1972, 183-206.

ASSOCIATION

935    Holenstein, Elmar. *Phänomenologie der Assoziation.* Zur Struktur und Funktion eines Grundprinzips der passiven Genesis bei Edmund Husserl (Phaenomenologica, 44). The Hague: Martinus Nijhoff, 1972, xxvi-370.

936    Walton, Roberto Juan, - Pirk, Andrés. "Associación y sintesis pasiva [Husserl]." *Cuadernos de Filosofía,* 11 (sic for: 13), 1973, 433-446.

AUTHENTICITY

937    Van Breda, Herman Leo. "Réduction et authenticité d'après Husserl." *Revue de Métaphysique et de Morale,* vol. 56, 1951, 4-5. "A note on reduction and authenticity," in *Husserl. Expositions and appraisals,* F. Elliston and P. McCormick (eds.). Notre Dame, Ind.-London: University of Notre Dame Press, 1977, 124-125.

AUTONOMY

938    De Boer, Theodor. "De idee der autonomie bij Husserl." *Annales Genootsch. Wetenschap. Philosophie,* vol. 37, 1966, 169-186.

BEING

939    Ferrari, Oward. "El ser en la fenomenología de Husserl y de Heidegger." *Philosophía,* no. 35, 1969, 65-110.

940    Lafont, Ghislain. "Genèse de la métaphysique [Husserl et l'être]." *Témoignages,* cahier 29, 1951, 214-223.

941    Mayer-Hillebrand, Franziska. "Franz Brentanos ursprüngliche und spätere Seinslehre und ihre Beiziehugen zu Husserls Phänomenologie." *Zeitschrift für Philosophische Forschung,* vol. 13, no. 2, [Husserl], 1959, 316-339.

942    Millán Puelles, A. *El problema del ente ideal.* Un examen através de Husserl y Hartman. Madrid: Instituto "Luis Vives," C. S. I. c., 1947, 194 p.

943    Salmerón, Fernando. "El ser ideal en las *Investigaciones lógicas* de Husserl." *Diánoia* (México), vol. 12, 1966, 132-154.

944    Smith, F. Joseph. "Being and subjectivity: Heidegger and Husserl," in *Phenomenology in perspective,* F. J. Smith (ed.). The Hague: Martinus Nijhoff, 1970, 122-156.

## BIBLIOGRAPHY

945    Allen, Jeffner. "Husserl: Bibliography of English translations." *The Monist,* vol. 59, Jan. 1975, 133-137.

946    Brand, Gerd. "Husserl-Literatur und Husserl." *Philosophische Rundschau,* vol. 8, 1960, 261-289.

947    De Lellis, Enzo. "Bibliografia delgi studi husserliani in Italia: 1960-1964 (La fenomenologia in Italia, II)." *Revue Internationale de Philosophie,* vol. 19, no. 71-72, 1965, 140-152.

948    Eley, Lothar. "Husserl-Bibliographie 1945-1959." *Zeitschrift für Philosophische Forschung,* vol. 13, no. 2, [Husserl], 1959, 357-367.

949    Eley, Lothar. "Berichtigugen zur Husserl-Bibliographie." *Zeitschrift für Philosophische Forschung,* vol. 13, no. 2 [Husserl], 1959, 475.

950    Maschke, Gerhard, and Kern, Iso. "Husserl. Bibliographie." *Revue Internationale de Philosophie,* vol. 19, no. 71-72, 1965, 153-202.

951    Noack,H. "Bibliographie," in *Husserl* (Wege der Forschung, 40). Hrsg. von H. Noack. Darmstadt: Wissenshcatliche Buchgesellschaft, 1973, 325-331.

952    Patocka, Jan. "Bibliographie" im Gedachtnisheft der *Revue Internationale de Philosophie,* 1939, 374-397.

953    Raes,J. "Ergänzung und Erweiterung dieser Bibliographie." *Revue Internationale de Philosophie,* 1950, 469-475.

954    Robert, Jean-Dominique. "Eléments de bibliographie husserlienne." *Tijdschrift voor Filosofie,* vol. 20, 1958, 534-544.

955    Van Breda, Herman Leo. "Bibliographie [sur la phénoménologie rente]," in *La philosophie au milieu du vingtième siècle.* Tome II. Par les soins de Raymond Klibanski. Firenze: La Nuova Italia Editrice, 1958, 65-70.

956    Van Breda, Herman Leo. and Paci, Enzo. "Bibliographie," in *Les grands courants de la pensée mondiale contemporaine* (Ouvrage publié soux la direction de M. F. Sciacca). Les tendances principales, Vol. I. Paris-Milano: Fischbacher-Marzorati, 1961, 441-464.

957    Van de Pitte. M. M. "Husserl Literatur 1965-1971." *Archiv für Geschichte der Philosophie,* vol. 57, 1975, 36-53.

958    Varet, Gilbert. *Manuel de bibliographie philosophique.* Paris: Presses Universaitires de France, t. II, 654-656, et 877-881.

## BODY

959    Kessler, Gary E. "Pragmatic bodies versus transcendental egos." *Transaction of the Peirce Society,* vol. 14, Spring 1978, 101-119.

960    Lingis, Alphonso. "Intentionality and corporeity." *Analecta Husserliana,* vol. 1, 1971, 75-90.

961    Panish, Theodore M. "Phenomenology and the human body." Ph.D. Dissertation, University of Missouri-Columbia, 1970. Ann Arbor, Mich.-London: University Microfilms International, 1977, v-135.

962    Presas, Mario A. "Corporalidad e historia en Husserl." *Revista Latinoamericana de Filosofía,* vol. 2, July 1976, 167-178.

963    Tymieniecka, Anna-Teresa. "Die phänomenologische Selbstbesinnung, I: Der Leib und die Transzendentalität in der gegenwartigen phänomenologischen und psychiatrischen Forschung." *Analecta Husserliana,* vol. 1, 1971, 1-10.

964    Van Haecht, Louis. "Phenomenologische analyse van 't menschelijke licaam naar Edmund Husserl." *Tijdschrift voor Filosofie,* vol. 6, 1944, 135-190.

965    Waelhens, Alphonse de. "La phénoménologie du corps." *Revue Philosophique de Louvain,* vol. 48, 1950, 371-397. "The phenomenology of the body," in *Readings in existential phenomenology,* N. Lawrence and D. O'Connor (eds. and trans.). Englewood Cliffs, N.J.: Prentice Hall, 1967, 149-167.

966    Wild, John. "Husserl's life-world and the lived body," in *Phenomenology pure and applied,* Erwin Strauss (ed.). Pittsburgh, Pa.: Duquesne University Press, 1964, 10-28 [Discussion, Theodor de Boer, 28-40].

CARTESIANISM *See also:* DESCARTES

967    Fulton, James Street. "The Cartesianism of phenomenology." *Philosophical Review,* vol. 49, 1940. Reprinted in *Essays in phenomenology,* Maurice Natanson (ed.). The Hague: Martinus Nijhoff, 1966, 58-78.

968    Landgrebe, Ludwig. "Husserls Abschied vom Cartesianismus." *Philosphische Rundschau,* vol. 9, 1962. "Husserl's departure from Cartesianism," in *The phenomenology of Husserl,* R. O. Elveton (ed. and trans.). Chicago: Quadrangle Books, 1970, 259-306.

969    Praetorius, H. M. "Escape from the evil demon. A discourse on the Cartesianism of phenomenology," Ph.D. Dissertation Claremont Graduate School, 1969.

CAUSALITY

970    Zecchi, Stefano. "Causalità e percezione." *Aut Aut,* no. 105-106, 1968, 66-90.

CHILD

971    Allen, Jeffner. "A Husserlian phenomenology of the child." *Journal of Phenomenological Psychology,* vol. 6, 1975-1976, 164-179.

CERTAINTY

972    Volkelt, Johannes. "Die phänomenologische Gewissheit." *Zeitschrift für Philosophie und Philosophische Kritik,* vol. 165, 1918, 124-189. Abgedruckt in his *Gewissheit und Warheit,* 433-454.

COGITO

973 Berger, Gaston. *Le cogito de Husserl.* Paris: Aubier, 1941, 190 p. *The cogito in Husserl's philosophy.* K. McLaughlin (trans.), introd. by James M. Edie. Evanston, Ill.: Northwestern University Press, 1972, xxvii-159.

974 Gurwitsch, Aron. "The cogito in Husserl's philosophy [On G. Berger, 973]," *Philosophy and Phenomenological Research,* vol. 7, 1946-1947, 649-654. "Das Cogito in Husserls Philosophie," (aus dem Englischen übersetzt von Ursula Beul)," in *Husserl.* Hrsg. von H. Noack (Wege der Forschung, 40). Darmstadt: Wissenschaftliche Buchgesellschaft, 1973, 222-230.

975 Merleau-Ponty, Maurice. *Phénoménologie de la perception.* Paris: Gallimard, 1945, 423-468. Various translations in English, German, Italian, etc.

976 Miéville, Henri. "Le cogito de la phénoménologie de Husserl et le cogito de Descartes." *Jahrbuch Schweizer Philosophische Gesselschaft,* vol. 1, 1941.

977 Reymond, A. "A propos du cogito de Descartes." *Annales de la Société Suisse de Philosophie,* vol. 2, 1942, 78-84.

978 Vanni-Rovighi, Sofia. "Il 'cogito' di Cartesio ed il 'cogito' di Husserl," in *Cartesio,* I, 1937, 767-780.

COGNITIVE SUBJECT & TYPE

979 Motroshilova, N. V. "The problem of the cognitive subject as viewed by Husserl and Ingarden." *Dialectics and Humanism,* vol. 2, no. 3, 1975, 17-31.

980 Orth, Ernst Wolfgang. "Husserls Begriff der cogitativen Typen und seine methodologische Reichweite," in *Phenomenologie heute.* Festschrift für Ludwig Landgrebe (Phaenomenologica, 51). The Hague: Martinus Nijhoff, 1972, 138-167.

COMMUNAL SPIRIT

981 Allen, Jeffner. "Husserl's communal spirit." *Philosophy and Social Criticism* (formerly, *Cultural Hermeneutics*), vol. 5, no. 1, Jan. 1978.

COMMUNICATION

982 Orth, Ernst Wolfgang. "Anthropologie und Intesubjektivität. Zur Frage von Transzendentalität oder Phanomenalität der Kommunikation [Husserl]," in *Mensch, Welt, Verständigung.* Beiträge von Helmut Rombach, u.a. (Phänomenologische Forschungen, 4). Freiburg-München: Alber, 1977, 103-129.

CONCEPT

983 Heinrich, E. *Untersuchungen zur Lehre vom Begriff.* Göttingen, 1910.

984 Thyssen, Johannes. "Husserls Lehre von den 'Bedeutungen' und das Begriffsproblem." *Zeitschrift für Philosophische Forschung,* vol. 13, 1959.

CONSCIOUSNESS *see also:* INTENTIONALITY

985 Ales Bello, Angela. "Conscienza e soggettivtà nella fenomenologia di Husserl." *Incontri Culturali,* vol. 3, 1970, 69-78.

986    Bosio, Franco. "L'intenzionalità e il concetto di coscienza nella *Logische Untersuchungen.*" *Aut Aut,* no. 72, 1962, 479-504.

987    Bowes, Pratima. *Consciousness and freedom.* Three views. London: Methuen-New York: Barnes and Noble, 1971, 230 p.

988    Breton, Stanislas. "Conscience et intentionalité selon Husserl." *Archives de Philosophie,* vol. 1, no. 4, 1956, 55-97.

989    Breton, Stanislas. *Conscience et intentionalité* (Problèmes et doctrines). Lyon-Paris, Viatte, 1956.

990    Brough, John B. "The emergence of an absolute consciousness in Husserl's early writings on time-consciousness." *Man and World,* vol. 5, 1972, 298-326. Reprinted in *Husserl. Expositions an appraisals,* F. Elliston and P. McCormick (eds.). Notre Dame, Ind.-London: University of Notre Dame Press, 1977, 83-100.

991    Cairns, Dorion. "The many senses and denotations of the word *Bewusstsein* (Consciousness) in Edmund Husserl," in *Life-world and consciousness.* Essays for Aron Gurwitsch, Lester E. Embree (ed.). Evanston, Ill.: Northwestern University Press, 1972, 19-32.

992    Funke, Gerhard. "Bewusstseinswissenschaft. Evidenz und Reflexion als Implikate der Verifikation." *Kantstudien,* vol. 61, 1970, 433-466.

993    Giorda, Renato and Cimico, Luigi. *La conscienza nel pensiero moderno e contemporaneo.* Roma: Città Nuova, 1978, 278 p.

994    Gorsen, F. *Zur Phänomenologie des Bewusstseinsstroms.* Bergson, Dilthey, Husserl, Simmel und die lebensphilosphischen Antinomien. Bonn: Bouvier, 1966, 243 p.

995    Gurwitsch, Aron. "A non-egological conception of consciousness." *Philosophy and Phenomenological Research,* vol. 1, 1940-1941, 325-338. Reprinted in his *Studies in phenomenology and psychology.* Evanston, Ill.: Northwestern University Press, 1966, 287-301.

996    Gurwitsch, Aron. *Théorie du champ de la conscience* Paris: Desclée de Brouwer, 1957, *The field of consciousness.* Pittsburgh, Pa.: Duquesne University Press, 1964.

        **Book Reviews:**

        A. Kockelmans, "Phaenomenologie van de waarneming volgens Aron Gurwitsch." *Tijdschrift voor Filosofie,* vol. 20, 1958, 57-113 [Summary, 113-114].

997    Gurwitsch, Aron. "L'approche phénoménologique et psychologique de la conscience." *Iyyun,* 1953, 193-202.

998    Gurwitsch, Aron. "The phenomenological and the psychological approach to consciousness." *Philosophy and Phenomenological Research,* vol. 15, 1954-1955, 303-319. Reprinted in his *Studies in phenomenology and psychology.* Evanston, Ill.: Northwestern University Press, 1966, 89-106.

999    Gurwitsch, Aron. "Der Begriff des Bewusstsein bei Kant und Husserl." *Kantstudien,* vol. 55, 1964, 410-427. Reprinted in his *Studies in phenomenology and psychology.* Evanston, Ill.: Northwestern University Press, 1966, 148-175, "The Kantian and Husserlian conceptions of consciousness," 148-175.

1000    Gurwitsch, Aron. "The Husserlian conception of the intentionality of consciousness." *The Isenberg Memorial lecture series, 1965-1966,* Michigan State University Press, 1969, 145-162.

1001    Gurwitsch, Aron. "On the intentionality of consciousness," in *Philosophical essays in memory of Edmund Husserl,* Marvin Farber (ed.). Cambridge, Mass.: Harvard University Press, 1940. Reprinted in his *Studies in phenomenology and psychology.* Evanston, Ill.: Northwestern University Press, 1966, 124-140.

1002    Kumar, Jitendra. "Consciousness and its correlatives: Eliot and Husserl." *Philosophy and Phenomenological Research,* vol. 18, 1967-1968, 332-352.

1003    Laskey, Dallas. "Embodied consciousness and the human spirit." *Analecta Husserliana,* vol. 1, 1971, 197-207.

1004    Malmgren, H. "Internal relations in the analysis of consciousness." *Theoria,* vol. 41, 1975, 61-83.

1005    Margolin, Julius. "Grundphänomene des intentionalen Bewusstseins." Dissertation, Berlin, 1929.

1006    Murphy, Richard T. "Consciousness in Brentano and Husserl." *Modern Schoolman,* vol. 45, March 1968, 227-241.

1007    Olafson, Frederick A. "Consciousness and intentionality in Heidegger's thought." *American Philosophical Quarterly,* vol. 12, April 1975, 91-103.

1008    Oxenhandler, Neal. "The quest for pure consciousness in Husserl and Mallarmé," in *The quest for imagination,* O. B. Hardison (ed.). Press of Case Western Reserve University, 1971, 149-166.

1009    Paci, Enzo. "Coscienza fenomenologica e coscienza idealistica." *Il Verri,* no. 4, 1960, 3-15.

1010    Pantaleo, P. *La direzione coscienza-intenzione nella filosofia di Kant e Husserl.* Bari: Arti grifiche Laterza e Polo, 1967, 363 p.

1011    Poltawski, Andrzej. *Swiat, spostrzetenie,* swiadomsc. Fenomenologiczna koncepcja swiadomosci a realizm. Warszawa: Panstwowe Wydawnictwo Nakowe, 1973, 474 p.

1012    Rodríguez Sández, José Luis. "El ser absoluto de la conciencia. U. análisis de su sentido en la filosofíía de E. Husserl." Madrid: Edit. Gredos, [s.a.] 39 p.

1013    Sancipriano, Mario. "The activity of consciousness: Husserl and Bergson." *Analecta Husserliana,* vol. 3, 1974, 161-167.

1014    Schönrock, W. "Das Bewusstsein. Ein psychologisch-phänomenologischer Versuch." Dissertation, Erlangen, 1924.

1015     Shmueli, E. "Consciousness and action: Husserl and Marx on theory and praxis." *Analecta Husserliana,* vol. 5, 1976, 343-382.

1016     Smith, Quentin. "On Husserl's theory of consciousness in the Fifth *Logical investigations.*" *Philosophy and Phenomenological Research,* vol. 37, June 1977, 482-497.

1017     Sukale, Michael. "The ego and consciousness in rival perspectives. A study of Husserl and the early Sartre [in Hebrew]." *Iyyun,* vol. 22, 1971, 193-214. [Summary, 276-274].

1018     Zaner, Richard M. "Passivity and activity of consciousness in Husserl." *Analecta Husserliana,* vol. 3, 1974, 199-202. [Discussion: A.-T. Tymieniecka, M. R. Barral, E. Straus, R. M. Zaner, S. Morin, W. Ver Eecke, E. Eng, A. Poltawski, M. Sancipriano, J. N. Mohanty, H. Köchler, 202-226].

CONSTITUTION

1019     Bosio, Franco. "Costituzione statica e costituzione genetica." *Archivo di Filosofia,* no. 1, 1960, 73-88.

1020     Calvi, L. A. "Sulla costituzione dell'oggetto fobico come 'esercizio fenomenologico'. *Psichiatria* (Padova), no. 1, 1963, 38-74.

1021     Hartmann, P. "Die Rolle der Sprache in Husserls Lehre von der Konstitution," in *Der Deutschunterricht,* vol. 6, 1956.

1022     Ingarden, Roman. "Le problème de la constitution e le sens de la réflexion constitutive chez Edmund Husserl," in *Huserl* (Cahiers de Royaumont, 3). Paris: Editions de Minuit, 1959, 242-264. [Discussion: 265-270].

1023     Landgrebe, Ludwig. "Reflexionen zu Husserls Konstitutionslehre." *Tijdschrift voor Filosofie,* vol. 36, 1974, 466-482.

1024     Mays Vallenilla, Ernesto. *Fenomenología del concimiento.* El problema de la constitución del objeto en la filosofía de Husserl (Coleccion de tesis doctorales, 1). Caracas, Facultad de Humanidades y Educacion, Universidad Central de Venezuela. [Buenos Aires: Imprenta López, 1956], 372 p.

1025     Murphy, Richard T. "Husserl and the pre-reflexive constitution." *Philosophy and Phenomenological Research,* vol. 26, 1965-1966, 100-105.

1026     Oosthuizen, D. C. S. "Die transendentaal-fenomenologiese Idealisme. 'n Aspek van die konstitutie-probleem in die filosofie van Edmund Husserl," in *Festschrift H. J. de Vleeschauwer* (Communications of the University of South Africa, Supplement 1). Pretoria: Publications Committee of the University of South Africa, 1960, 180-194.

1027     Paci, Enzo. La formazione del pensiero di Husserl e il problema della costituzione della natura materiale e della natura animale. Corso di filosofia teoretica. Anno accademico 1966-1967 (Università delgi studi di Milano). Milano: La Goliardica, 1967, 201 p.

1028    Prufer, Thomas. "Reduction and constitution," in *Ancients and moderns,* John
        K. Ryan (ed.). Washington, D.C.: The Catholic University of America
        Press, 1970, 341-343.

1029    Rotenstreich, Nathan. "Ambiguities of Husserl's notion of constitution," in
        *Phenomenology and natural existence.* Essays in honor of Marvin Farber,
        Dale Relpe (ed.). Albany, N.Y.: State University of New York Press, 1973,
        151-170.

1030    Sini, Carlo. "Genesi e costituzione in riferimento al secondo libro di *Idee.* "
        *Aut Aut,* no. 105-106, 1968, 91-99.

1031    Sokolowski, Robert. "Immanent constitution in Husserl's lectures on time."
        *Philosophy and Phenomenological Research,* vol. 24, 1963-1964, 530-551.

1032    Sokolowski, Robert. *The formation of Husserl's concept of constitution*
        (Phaenomenologica, 18). The Hague: Martinus Nijhoff, 1964, xii-250.

1033    Tarnowski, Karol. "Roman Ingarden's critique of transcendental
        constitution." *Dialectics and Humanism,* vol. 3, Winter 1976, 111-119.

CONTINGENCY

1034    Kim, Sang-ki. "The problem of the contingency of the world in Husserl's
        phenomenology." Ph.D. Dissertation, SUNY at Buffalo, 1973, 173 p.
        *Dissertation Abstracts,* vol. 34, no. 9, March 1974, 6045-A.

1035    Kim, Sang Ki. *The problem of the contingency of the world in Husserl's
        phenomenology* (Philosophical currents, 17). Atlantic Highlands, N.J.:
        Humanities Press, 1977, 102 p.

CREATIVITY

1036    Ales Bello,Angela. "Fenomenologia e creatività." *Sapienza,* vol. 28, April-June
        1975.

CHRISTIANITY

1037    Hourton, Jorge. "Husserl. La fenomenología y el pensamiento cristiano." *Finis
        Terrae,* vol. 10, no. 40, 1963, 187-204.

1038    Paci, Enzo. "Husserl e il cristianesimo." *Aut Aut,* no. 1974, 133-134.

1039    Piana, Giovani. "Husserl e la cultura cattolica." *Aut Aut,* no. 67, 1962.

EDUCATION

1040    Bertolini, Piero. *Fenomenologia e pedagogia.* Bologna: Malipiero, 1958, 245
        p.

1041    Chamberlin, J. G. "Phenomenological methodology and understanding
        education," in *Existentialism and phenomenology in education:* Collected
        essays, D. E. Benton (ed.). New York: Teachers College Press, 1974,
        119-138.

1042    Palermo, James. "Direct experience in the open classroom: A
        phenomenological description." *Proceedings of Philosophy of Education,*
        vol. 30, 1974, 241-254.

1043   Russo, G. "Fenomenologia e pedagogia." *Nuova Rivista Pedogogica* (Roma), agosto 1961, 3-13.

1044   Troutner, Leroy F. "Toward a phenomenology of education: An exercise in the foundations." *Proceedings of Philosophy of Education,* vol. 30, 1974, 148-164.

DIALECTICS

1045   Chiodi, Pietro. "Esistenzialismo e marxismo. Contributo a un dibattito sulla dialettica." *Rivista di Filosofia,* no. 2, 1963, 164-190.

1046   Paci, Enzo. "Tempo e dialettica in Husserl." *Il Pensiero,* vol. 4, 1959, 129-150.

1047   Strasser, Stephan. "Intuition und Dialektik in der Philosophie Edmund Husserls," in *Husserl* (Cahiers de Royaumont, 3). Paris: Editions de Minuit, 1959, 148-153.

1048   Zecchi, Stefano. "Dialettica: possibilità e realtà [Huserl]." *Aut Aut,* no. 111, 1969, 40-72.

EGO

1049   Banja, John D. "Ego and reduction: A key to the development of Husserl's phenomenology." Ph.D. Dissertation, Fordham University, 1975, 281 p. *Dissertation Abstracts,* vol. 37, no. 2, Aug. 1976, 1017-A.

1050   Bergoffen, Debra B. "Sartre's transcendence of the ego: A methodological reading." *Philosophy Today,* vol. 22, no. 4, Fall 1978, 244-251.

1051   Broekman, Jan M. *Phänomenologie und Egologie.* Faktisches und transzendentales Ego bei Edmund Husserl (Phaenomenologica, 12). The Hague: Martinus Nijhoff, 1963, x-224.

1052   Carr, David. "Kant, Husserl and the nonempirical ego." *Journal of Philosophy,* vol. 74, Nov. 1977, 682-690.

1053   Caruso, Paolo. "L'Io trascendentale come 'durata esplosiva'. Intenzionalità e tempo nella fenomenologia di Husserl." *Archivo di Filosofia,* no. 1, 1960, 49-72 [Tempo e intenzionalità].

1054   Doran, Robert M. "Sartre's critique of the Husserlian ego." *Modern Schoolman,* vol. 44, 1966-1967, 307-317.

1055   Elkin, Henry. "Towards a development phenomenology: Transcendental-*ego* and body-*ego*." *Analecta Husserliana,* vol. 2, 1972, 256-266.

1056   Embree, Lester E. "An interpretation of the doctrine of the ego in Husserl's *Ideen*," in *Phenomenology. Continuation and criticism,* F. Kesten and R. M. Zaner (eds.) (Phaenomenologica 50). The Hague: Martinus Nijhoff, 1973, 24-32.

1057   Feidmann, H. "Zur phänomenologischen Strukturanalyse der Störungen des Ichbewusstseins." *Archiv für Psychiatrie und Zeitschrift für d. ges. Neurologie,* vol. 198, 1958.

1058   Filippini, E. "Ego ed alter-ego nella *Krisis* di Husserl," in *Ommagio a* Husserl. Milano: 1960, 213-230.

1059    Gurwitsch, Aron. "Phänomenologie der Thematik und des reinen Ich. Studien über Beziehungen von Gestalttheorie und Phänomenologie." Ph.D. Dissertation, Göttingen, 1928. Published in *Psychologische Forschung,* vol. 12, 1929. "Phenomenology of thematics and of the pure ego. Studies of the relation between Gestalt theory and phenomenology," in his *Studies in phenomenology and psychology.* Evanston, Ill.: Northwestern University Press, 1966, 175-286.

1060    Gurwitsch, Aron. "A non-egological conception of consciousness." *Philosophy and Phenomenological Research,* vol. 1940-1941, 325-338. Reprinted in his *Studies in phenomenology an psychology.* Evanston, Ill.: Northwestern University Press, 1966, 287-301.

1061    Held, Klaus. *Lebedige Gegenwart.* Die Frage nach des Seinsweise des transzendentalen Ich bei Edmund Husserl, entwickelt amLeitfaden der Zeitsproblematik (Phaenomenologica, 23). The Hague: Martinus Nijhoff, 1966, xvii-190.

1062    Horosz, William. "Does Husserl's reach exceed his grasp? A critique of the transcendental ego." *Philosophy Today,* vol. 18, 1974, 181-197.

1063    Kessler, Gary E. "Pragmatic bodies versus transcendental egos." *Transactions of the Peirce Society,* vol. 14, Spring 1978, 101-119.

1064    Kockelmans, Joseph J. "Husserl and Kant on the pure ego," in *Husserl. Expositions and appraisals,* F. Elliston and P. McCormick (eds.). Notre Dame, Ind.-London: University of Notre Dame Press, 1977, 269-285.

1065    Lapointe, François H. "Psicología fenomenológica de Husserl y Sartre." *Revista Latinoamericana de Psicología,* vol. 2, no. 3, 1970, 377-385.

1066    Marbach, Eduard. *Das Problem des Ich in der Phänomenologie Husserls* (Phaenomenologica, 59). The Hague: Martinus Nijhoff, 1974, xvi-348.

1067    Natanson, Maurice. "The empirical and transcendental ego," in *For Roman Ingarden: Nine essays in phemoneology,* A.-T. Timieniecka (ed.). The Hague: Martinus Nijhoff, 1959. Reprinted in his *Literature, philosophy, and the social sciences.* The Hague: Martinus Nijhoff, 1962, 44-54.

1068    Prezioso, Antonio F. "Immagine, coscienza ed Io in Sartre." *Sapienza,* vol. 2, April-June 1976, 206-217.

1069    Pucci, Raffaele. *Io trascendentale e mondo della vita nella fenomenologia di Husserl.* Napoli: Libreria Scientifica Editrice, 1962, 26 p.

1070    Pucci, Raffaele. "Io trscendnetale e mondo della vita nella fenomenologia di Husserl." *Rassegna di Scienze Filosofiche,* vol. 16, 1963, 67-89.

1071    Rábade Romeo, Sergio. "El sujeto trascendental en Husserl." *Anales del Seminar de Metafísica,* vol. 2, 1966, 7-27.

1072    Sala, Javier San Martín. "La teoría del yo trascendental en Kant y Husserl." *Anales del Seminar de Metafísica,* vol. 9, 1974, 123-143.

1073    Sartre, Jean-Paul. "La transcendance de l'ego. Esquisse d'une description phénoménologique." *Recherches Philosophiques,* vol. 6, 1938, 85-123. *The transcendence of the ego.* An existentialist theory of consciousness.

Annotated with an introd. by Forrest Williams and Robert Kirkpatrick (trans.). New York: The Noonday Press, a Division of Farrar, Straus and Giroux, 1957.

1074    Seifert, Josef. Relativismus und Immanentismus in Edmund Husserls *Cartesianischen Meditationen.* Die Äquivokation im Ausdruk transzendentales Ego an der Basis jedes transzendentalen Idealismus." *Salzburger Jahrbuch für Philosophie,* vol. 14, 1970, 85-109.

1075    Stone, Robert V. "The self as agent-in-the-world. An alternative to Husserl's and Sartre's accounts of the ego." Ph.D. Dissertation, University of Texas at Austin, 1972, 240 p. *Dissertation Abstracts,* vol. 34, no. 9, March 1974, 6051-A.

1076    Sukale, Michael. "The ego and the consciousness in rival perspectives. A study of Husserl and the early Sartre [in Hebrew]." *Iyyun,* vol. 22, 1971, 193-214.

1077    Van Peursen, Cornelis. "Some remarks on the Ego in the phenomenology of Husserl," J. W. M. Verhaar (trans.), in *For Roman Ingarden.* Nine essays in phenomenology, A.-T. Tymieniecka (ed.). The Hague: Martinus Nijhoff, 1959, 1-15.

1078    Van Peursen, Cornelis. "La notion de temps et de l'ego transcendental chez Husserl," in *Husserl* (Cahiers de Royaumont, 3). Paris: Editions de Minuit, 1959.

1079    Vélez, Danilo Cruz. "Vicisitudes del yo en Husserl." *Man and World,* vol. 1, 1968, 540-652.

EGOCENTRIC PREDICAMENT

1080    Kim, Chin Tai. "Husserl and the egocentric predicament [Abstract]." *Journal of Philosophy,* vol. 67, 1970, 821-822.

EIDETIC VARIATION

1081    Levin, David Michael. "Induction and Husserl's theory of eidetic variation." *Philosophy and Phenomenological Research,* vol. 29, 1968, 1-15.

EIDOS

1082    Pentzopoulou-Valalas, Thérèse. "Réflexions sur le fondement du rapport entre l'*a priori* et l'*eidos* dans la phénoménologie de Husserl." *Kantstudien,* vol. 65, 1974, 135-151.

EINFÜHLUNG

1083    Hartmann, Klaus. Husserls Einfühlungstheorie auf monadologischer Grundlage. Bonn: 1953 [multigraphié].

1084    Renzi, E. "Ricoeur e l'Einfühlung husserliana." *Il Verri,* no. 4, 1960, 131-138.

1085    Stein, Edith. "Zum Problem der Einfühlung." Dissertation, Freiburg, Halle, 1917.

EMPATHY

1086    Elliston, Frederick A. "Husserl's phenomenology of empathy," in *Husserl.*
        *Expositions and appraisals,* F. A. Elliston and P. McCormick (eds.). Notre
        Dame, Ind.-London: Notre Dame University Press, 1977, 213-231.

EMOTIONS

1087    Guthrie, Hunter. "Max Scheler's epistemology of the emotions." *Modern
        Schoolman,* vol. 16, 1939.

EMPIRICISM  *see also:* LOCKE, HUME, PEIRCE

1088    Dougherty, Charles J. "Phenomenological critiques of empiricism. A study
        in the philosophies of Husserl and Peirce." Ph.D. Dissertation, University
        of Notre Dame, 1975, 245 p. *Dissertation Abstracts,* vol. 36, no. 3, Sept.
        1975, 1576-A.

1089    Heffner, John. "Husserl's critique of traditional empiricism." *Journal of the
        British Society for Phenomenology,* vol. 5, 1974, 159-162.

EPOCHÉ

1090    Abustan, R. L. "Edmund Husserl's epoché and St. Thomas' metaphysical
        abstraction." *Unitas* (Manilla), vol. 44, no. 4, 1971, 59-94.

1091    Bossert, Philip J. "The sense of 'epoché' and 'reduction' in Husserl's
        philosophy [H. Spiegelberg, 'Is the reduction necessary for phenomenology'.
        *See* 1099]." *Journal of the British Society for Phenomenology,* vol. 5, 1974,
        243-255.

1092    Guaraldi, Antonella. "La modificazione di neutralità comme epoché
        naturale." *Revue Internationale de Philosophie,* vol. 19, no. 71-72, 1965,
        74-106.

1093    Kohark, Erazim V. "Existence and the phenomenological epoché." *Journal
        of Existentialism,* vol. 8, Fall 1967, 19-47.

1094    Kuspit, D. B. "Parmenidean tendencies in the epoché [Husserl." *Review of
        Metaphysics,* vol. 18, 1964-1965, 739-770.

1095    Lowit, Alexandre. "L"epoché' de Husserl et le doute de Descartes." *Revue
        de Métaphysique et de Morale,* vol. 62, 1957, no. 4, 399-415.

1096    Paci, Enzo. "Il senso delle parole (Epoché, transcendentale)." *Aut Aut,* no.
        74, 1963, 108-111.

1097    Reiman, Jeffrey H. "Time and the epoché of Husserl." Ph.D. Dissertation,
        Pennsylvania State University, 1968, 206 p. *Dissertation Abstracts,* vol. 30,
        no. 3, 1969, 1205-A.

1098    Scanlon, John D. "The epoché and phenomenological anthropology."
        *Research in Phenomenology,* vol. 2, 1972, 95-110.

1099    Spiegelberg, Herbert. "'Epoché' without reduction: Some replies to my critics
        [*see* Bossert 1091]." *Journal of the British Society for Phenomenology,* vol.
        5, 1974, 256-261.

1100    Ströker, Elisabeth. "Das Problem der $\pi o \xi$ in der Philosophie Edmund
        Husserls." *Analecta Husserliana,* vol. 1, 1971, 170-185.

1101      Van de Pitte, M. M. "On bracketing the epoché." *Dialogue*, vol. 11, no. 4, Dec. 1972, 535-545.

ERROR

1102      Winthrop, Henry. "The constitution of error in the phenomenological reduction." *Philosophy and Phenomenological Research*, vol. 9, 1949-1949, 741-748.

ESSENCE

1103      Ashmore, Jerome. "Essence in recent philosophy: Husserl, Whitehead, Santayana." *Philosophy Today*, vol. 18, Fall 1974, 198-210.

1104      Kersten, Fred. "On understanding idea and essence in Husserl and Ingarden." *Analecta Husserliana*, vol. 2, 1972, 55-63.

1105      Kersten, Fred. "The occasion and novelty of Husserl's phenomenology of essence," in *Phenomenological perspectives*, Philip Bossert (ed.) (Phaenomenologica, 62). The Hague: Martinus Nijhoff, 1975, 61-92.

1106      Solomon, Robert C. "Sense and essence: Frege and Husserl." *International Philosophical Quarterly*, vol. 10, 1970, 379-401. Reprinted in his *Phenomenology and existentialism*, Robert C. Solomon (ed.). New York: Harper & Row, 1970.

1107      Mohanty, J. N. "Individual fact and essence in Husserl's philosophy," in his *Phenomenology and ontology*, (Phaenomenologica, 37). The Hague: Martinus Nijhoff, 1970, 152-161.

ETHICS

1108      Kogan, Jacobo. "Etica y metafísica en Husserl." *Revista de Filosofía* (La Plata), no. 11, 1962, 42-65.

1109      Löwith, Karl. *Das Invididuum in der Rolle des Mitmenschen.* Ein Beitrag zur anthropologischen Grundlegung des ethischen Problems. München, 1928, xvi-180.
         **Book Reviews:**
         F. Kaufmann, *Kantstudien*, vol. 37, 150-151. [Zusammenhang mit Husserl hervorgehoben].

1111      Mijuskovic, Ben. "The simplicity argument and absolute morality." *Journal of Thought*, vol. 10, April 1975, 123-135.

1112      Morra, Gianfranco. "L'etica materiale del valore nel pensiero di E. Husserl." *Ethica*, vol. 3, 1964, 33-46.

1113      Robberechts, Ludovic. "Réflexion phénoménologique et réflexion éthique [J. Nabert and E. Husserl]." *Etudes Philosophiques*, vol. 17, 1962, 403-420.

1114      Roth, Alois. *Edmund Husserls ethische Untersuchungen.* Dargestellt anhand seiner Vorlesungsmanuskripte (Phaenomenologica, 7). The Hague: Martinus Nijhoff, 1960, xviii-171.

1115      Sancipriano, Mario. *L'ethos di Husserl.* Communicazione intersoggettiva ed etica sociale, I. Torino: Giappichelli, 1967, 136 p.

1116    Soloviov, E. Y. "Phenomenology and ethics." *Dialectics and Humanism,* vol. 2, Aut. 1975, 51-58.

EVIDENCE

1117    Arata, Carlo. "Evidenza e metafisica." *Rivista di Filosofia Neo-Scolastica,* no.2-3, 1960, 168-205.

1118    Hemmendinger, D. "Husserl's concepts of evidence and science." *The Monist,* vol. 59, Jan. 1975, 81-97.

1119    Jolivet, Régis. "Le problème de l'évidence du jugement et l'évidence antéprédicative d'après Husserl." *Revue de l'Université d'Ottawa,* vol. 21, [section spéciale], 1951, 235-253.

1120    Levin, David Michael. "Husserl's notion of self-evidence," in *Phenomenology and philosophical understanding,* Edo Pivcevic (ed.). Cambridge University Press, 1975, 53-77.

1121    Levin, David Michael. *Reason and evidence in Husserl's phenomenology.* Evanston, Ill.: Northwestern University Press, 1970, xxv-232.

1122    Levin, David Michael. "A critique of Edmond Husserl's theory of adequate apodictic evidence." Ph.D. Dissertation, Columbia University, 1967, 360 p. *Dissertation Abstracts,* vol. 28, no. 10, 1968, 4213-A.

1123    Marina Torres, José Antonio. "Fenomenología crítica y teoría de la evidencia en Husserl." *Anales del Seminar de Metafísica,* vol. 3, 1967, 7-46.

1124    Patzig, Günther. "Kritische Bemerkungen zu Husserls Theses über das Verhältnis vom Wahrheit und Evidenz." *Neue Heffe für Philosophie,* no. 1, 1971, 12-32.

1125    Reimer, W. "Der phänomenologische Evidenzbegriff." *Kantstudien,* vol. 23, 1919, 269-301.

1126    Rosen, Klaus. *Evidenz in Husserls deskriptiver Transzendentalphilosophie.* Meisenheim am Glan: Anton Hain, 1977, 177 p.

1127    McGill, V. J. "Evidence in Husserl's phenomenology," in *Phenomenology. Continuation and criticism.* Essays in memory of Dorion Cairns (Phaenomenologica, 50). The Hague: Martinus Nijhoff, 1973, 145-166.

1128    Pietersma, Henry. "Husserl's views on the evident and the true," in *Husserl. Expositions and appraisals,* F. Elliston and P. McCormick (eds.). Notre Dame, Ind.-London: University of Notre Dame Press, 1977, 38-53.

1129    Valori, Paolo. "Evidenza e verità nella fenomenologia huserliana." *Aquinas,* vol. 1, 1958, 224-240.

EXISTENCE

1130    Gurwitsch, Aron. "The problem of existence in constitutive phenomenology." *Journal of Philosophy,* vol. 58, 1961, 625-632. Reprinted in his *Studies in phenomenology and psychology.* Evanston, Ill.: Northwestern University Press, 1966, 116-123.

1131   Hartmann, Klaus. "Abstraction and existence in Husserl's phenomenological reduction." *Journal of the British Society for Phenomenology*, vol. 2, no. 1, 1971, 10-18.

1132   Kohak, Erazim V. "Existence and the phenomenological epokhé." *Journal of Existentialism*, vol. 8, Fall 1967, 19-47.

1133   Morgenstern, Georg. "Der Begriff des Existenz in der modernen Philosophie." Leipziger Dissertation, Weida, 1917.

1134   Ricci, Louis M. "Independent existence in Royce, Perry and Husserl." Ph.D. Dissertation, SUNY at Buffalo, 1970, 172 p. *Dissertation Abstracts*, vol. 31, no. 9, March 1971, 4844-A.

1135   Sciacca, Giuseppe Maria. *Esistenza e realtà in Husserl.* Palmero: Palumbo, 1960, 126 p.

EXISTENTIALISM

1136   Chiodi, Pietro. *Esistenzialismo e fenomenologia.* Milano, 1963.

1137   Edie, James M. "Transcendental phenomenology and existentialism." *Philosophy and Phenomenological Research*, vol. 25, 1964-1965, 52-63.

1138   Fragata, Júlio. "Husserl e a filosofia da existência." *Revista Portuguesa de Filosofia*, vol. 21, 1965, 17-35.

1139   Licciardello, N. "L'esistenzialismo in Italia." *Teoresi*, vol. 16, 1961, 111-114.

1140   Madison, Gary B. "Phenomenology and existentialism: Husserl and the end of idealism," in *Husserl. Expositions and appraisals*, F. Elliston and P. McCormick (eds.). Notre Dame, Ind.-London: University of Notre Dame Press, 1977, 247-268.

1141   Mihalich, Joseph C. "Husserl and the rise of continental existentialism," in his *Existentialism and thomism.* New York: Philosophical Library, 1960, 51-62.

1142   Spiegelberg, Herbert. "Husserl's phenomenology and existentialism." *Journal of Philosophy*, vol. 57, 1960, 62-74.

1143   Vernaux, Roger. *Leçons sur l'existentialisme et ses formes principales.* Paris: 1948, 41-58.

1144   Waelhens, Alphonse de. "De la phénoménologie à l'existentialisme," in *Le choix, le monde, l'existence.* Cahiers du Collège Philosophique, Paris: Arthaud, 1974, 37-82.

FACT

1145   Strasser, Stephan. "Misère et grandeur du 'fait': une méditation phénoménologique," in *Husserl* (Cahiers de Royaumont, 3). Paris: Editions de Minuit, 1959, 170-184 [Discussion, 185-195].

1146   Mohanty, J. N. "Individual fact and essence in Husserl's philosophy," in his *Phenomenology and ontology.* The Hague: Martinus Nijhoff, 1970, 152-161.

FAITH

1147 Dupré, Louis. "Husserl's thought on God and faith." *Philosophy and Phenomenological Research,* vol. 29, 1968-1969, 201-215.

FEELING

1148 Smith, Quentin P. "The phenomenology of feeling: A critical development of the theories of feeling in Husserl, Scheler and Sartre." Ph.D. Dissertation, Boston College, 1977, 479 p. *Dissertation Abstracts,* vol. 38, no. 3, Sept. 1977, 1457-A.

1149 Smith, Quentin P. "Husserl and the inner structure of feeling-acts." *Research in Phenomenology,* vol. 6, 1976, 84-104.

FICTION

1150 Kuspit, Donald B. "Fiction and phenomenology." *Philosophy and Phenomenological Research,* vol. 29, Sept. 1968, 16-33.

FREE-PHANTASY Variation

1151 Zaner, Richard M. "Examples and possibilities A criticism of Husserl's theory of free-phantasy variation." *Research in Phenomenology,* vol. 3, 1973, 29-43.

FREEDOM

1152 Bowes, Pratima. *Consciousness and freedom.* Three views. London: Methuen; New York: Barnes & Noble, 1971, 230 p.

1153 Reiner, Hans. "Freiheit, Wollen und Aktivität. Phänomenologische Untersuchungen in der Richtung auf das Problem der Willensfreiheit." Ph.D. Dissertation, Freiburg, Halle, 1927, vi-172.

1154 Semerari, G. "Verità e libertà." *Aut Aut,* no. 57, 1970, 175-180.

1155 Van Breda, Herman Leo. "Husserl et le problème de la liberté," in *Actes du IVe* Congrès des Sociétés de philosophie de langue française, Etre et Penser, no. 29. NeucÂtel: Editions de la Baconnière, 1949, 377-381. "Husserl und das Problem der Freiheit," [Aus dem Französischen übersetzt von Katharina Arndt]," in *Husserl.* Hrsg. von H. Noack (Wege der Forschung, 40). Darmstadt: Wissenschaftliche Buchgesellschaft, 1973, 277-281.

GEIST

1156 Rovatti, Pier Aldo. "'*Geist*' e '*Lebenswelt*' nella filosofia di Husserl." *Aut Aut,* no. 105-106, 1968, 44-65.

GENESIS

1157 Holenstein, Elmar. "Passive Genesis. Eine begriffsanalytische Studie. *Tijdschrift voor Filosofie,* vol. 33, 1971, 112-153.

1158 Holenstein, Elmar. *Phänomenologie der Assoziation.* Zu Struktur und Funktion eines Grundprinzips der passiven Genesis bei E. Husserl (Phaenomenologica, 44). The Hague: Martinus Nijhoff, xxvi-370.

1159   Sini, Carlo. "Genesi e costituzione in riferimento al secondo libro di *Idee*." *Aut Aut,* no 105-106, 91-99.

1160   Welton, D. "Structure and genesis in Husserl's phenomenology," in *Husserl. Expositions and appraisals,* F. Elliston and P. McCormick (ed.). Notre Dame, Ind.-London: University of Notre Dame Press, 1977, 54-69.

GEOMETRY

1161   Grieder, Alfons. "Geometry and the life-world in Husserl's later philosophy." *Journal of the British Society for Phenomenology,* vol. 8, no. 2, May 1977, 119-122.

GIVEN

1162   Hartjes, John F. "The critique of the 'given' in Wilfrid Sellars and Edmund Husserl." Ph.D. Dissertation, The Catholic University of America, 1974, 280 p. *Dissertation Abstracts,* vol. 35, no. 3, Sept. 1974, 1701-A.

1163   Wild, John. "The concept of the given in contemporary philosophy." *Philosophy and Phenomenological Research,* vol. 1, 1940-1941.

GOD *see also:* RELIGION, THEOLOGY

1164   Ales Bello, Angela. "L'uomo e Dio nella fenomenologia di Husserl," in *Ristrutturazione antropologica dell'insegnamento filosofico. Sapienza,* vol. 24, no. 3-4, 1969, 556-569.

1165   Dupré, Louis. "Husserl's thought on God and faith." *Philosophy and Phenomenological Research,* vol. 29, 1968-1969, 201-215.

1166   Fragata, Júlio. "O problema de Deus na fenomenologia de Husserl." *Revista Portuguesa de Filosofia,* vol. 17, 1961, 113-126.

1167   Le Blond, M. "Quelques documents actuels sur le problème de Dieu." *Archives de Philosophie,* vol. 30, Jan.-March 1967, 89-105.

1168   Ponsetto, Antonio. "Edmund Husserl: dalla critica alla società alla domanda intorno a Dio." *Civiltà Cattolica,* vol. 121, no. 4, 1970, 233-239.

1169   Strasser, Stephan. "Das Gottesproblem in der Spätphilosophie Edmund Husserls." *Philosophisches Jahrbuch,* vol. 67, 1958 [1959], 130-142. Reprinted in his *Bouwstenen voor een filosofische anthropologie.* Hilversum-Antwerpen: Paul Brand, 1965, 293-311.

1170   Van Breda, Herman Leo. "Husserl et le problème de Dieu," in *Proceedings of the Xth international Congress of Philosophy.* Amsterdam, 1948, 1210-1212.

GRAMMAR, GRAMMATICAL

1171   Bar-Hillel, Yehoshua. "Husserls' conception of a purely logical grammar." *Philosophy and Phenomenological Research,* vol. 17, 1956-1957, 362-369.

1172   Edie, James M. "Husserl's conception of '*the grammatical*' and contemporary linguistics," in *Life-world and consciousness.* Essays for Aron Gurwitsch, Lester E. Embree (ed.). Evanston, Ill.: Northwestern University Press, 1972,

233-263. Reprinted in his *Speaking and meaning. The phenomenology of language.* Bloomington, Ind.: Indiana University Press, 1976, 45-71.

**Book Reviews:**

J. E. Atwell, *Journal of Aesthetics and Art Criticism,* vol. 35, Summer, 1977, 478-480.

## HERMENEUTICS

1173 Gadamer, Hans-Georg. "Hermeneutics and social science." *Cultural Hermeneutics,* vol. 2, Fall 1976, 307-316.

1174 Kuypers, K. "Hermeneutik und die Interpretation der Logos-Idee." *Revue Internationale de Philosophie,* vol. 29, 1975, 52-77.

1175 Ricoeur, Paul. "Phénoménologie et herméneutique." *Man and World,* vol. 7, Aug. 1974, 223-253. "Phenomenology and Hermeneutics." *Nous,* vol. 9, April 1975, 85-102.

## HISTORY

1176 Ales Bello, Angela. *Edmund Husserl et la storia.* Parma: Nuovi Quaderni, 1972, xv-186.

1177 Bakker, Reinout. "Husserl. De fenomenologie van het wezen," in his *De geschiedenis van het fenomenologisch denken.* Utrecht-Antwerpen: Aula-Boeken, 1964, 69-108.

1178 Beerling, R. F. "Husserl, de geschiedenis en het absolute." *Tidjschrift voor Filosofie,* vol. 29, 1967, 353-394. [Zusammenfassung: Husserl. Die Geschichte und das Abjsolute, 395]

1179 Boehm, Rudolf. "Die Phänomenologie der Geschichte," in *Vom Geschichtsprunkt der Phänomenologie.* Husserl-Studien (Phaenomenologica, 16). The Hague: Martinus Nijhoff, 1968, 237-256.

1180 Boehm, Rudolf. "La phénoménologie de l'histoire." *Revue Internationale de Philosophie,* vol. 19, no. 71-72, 1965, 55-73.

1181 Brand, Gerd. "Horizont, Welt, Geschichte [Husserl]," in *Kommunikationskultur und Weltverständnis.* Beitrage von Gerd Brand, Joseph Kockelmans. Redaktion und Einleitung von E. W. Orth (Phänomenologische Forschungen, 5). Freiburg i. Br.: Verlag Karl Alber, 1977, 14-89.

1182 Brand, Gerd. "Interpretationen von Husserls Ansäntzen zu Praxis und Geschichte," in his *Welt, Geschichte, Mythos.* Trier: NCO-Verlag, 1977.

1183 Brüning, Walther. "La filosofía de la historia en Husserl y Heidegger. (Trad. del alemán: Katrin Goethe)." *Humanitas* (Tucumám), vol. 7, no. 11, 1959, 65-78.

1184 Carr, David. *Phenomenology an the problem of history.* A study of Husserl's transcendental philosophy. Evanston, Ill.: Northwestern University Press, 1974, xxvi-283.

1185 Carr, David. "Husserl's *Crisis* and the problem of history." *Southwestern Journal of Philosophy,* vol. 5, 1974, 127-148.

1186 De Crescenzio, G. "I valori nella husserliana filosofia della storia." *Sapienza,* vol. 13, 1960, 427-429.

1187 D'Ippolito, Bianca Maria. *Ontologia e storia in Edmund Husserl* (Saggi, 1). Salerno: Rumma, 1968, 354 p.

1188 Dondeyne, Albert. "L'historicité dans la philosophie contemporaine." *Revue Philosophique de Louvain,* vol. 54, 1956, 5-25; and 456-477.

1189 Fink, Eugen. "Monde et historie (Traduit par Jean Ladrière et Jacques Taminiaux)," in *Husserl et la pensée moderne* (Phaenomenologica, 2). The Hague: Martinus Nijhoff, 1959, 159-172. "Welt und Geschichte," in *Ibid.*

1190 Flynn, Bernard Charles. "Michel Foucault and the Husserlian problematic of a transcendental philosophy of history." *Philosophy Today,* vol. 22, no. 4, Fall 1978, 224-238.

1191 Forni, Guglielmo. "Fenomenologia della storia e idealismo intenzionale in Husserl." *Giornale di Metafisica,* vol. 23, 1968, 408-428.

1192 Forni, Guglielmo. *Il soggetto e la storia.* Bologna: Il Mulino, 1972, 260 p. ["Fenomenologia e filosofia della storia." "Commento alla *Crisi* delle scienze europee, I e II." "Problema della storia nell'ultimo Husserl."]

1193 Garulli, Enrico. *Coscienza e storia in Husserl.* Urbino: S.T.E.U., 1964, 180 p.

1194 Hindess, Barry. "Transcendentalism and history: The problem of history of philosophy and the science in the later philosophy of Husserl." *Economics and Society,* vol. 2, no. 3, Aug. 1973, 309-342.

1195 Hohl, Hubert. *Lebenswelt und Geschichte.* Grundzüge der Spätphilosophie E. Husserls (Symposion 7). Freiburg-Munchen: Karl Alber, 1962, 122 p.

1196 Hohl, Hubert. "Geschichte und Geschichtlichkeit. Ein Beitrag zur Spätphilosophie E. Husserls." *Philosophisches Jahrbuch,* vol. 69, 1961, 101-124.

1197 Janssen, Paul. *Geschichte und Lebnswelt.* Ein Beitrag sur Diskussion von Husserls Spätwerk (Phaenomenologica, 35). The Hague: Martinus Nijhoff, 1970, xxii-218.

1198 Janssen, Paul. "Ontologie, Wissenschaftstheorie und Geschichte im Spätwerk Husserls," in *Perkpektiven transzendentalphänomenolgischer Forschung* (Phaenomenologica, 49). Hrsg. von U. Claesges und K. Held. The Hague: Martinus Nijhoff, 1972, 145-163.

1199 Jordan, Robert W. "Vico and Husserl: History and historical science," in *Giambattista Vico's view of humanity,* Giorgio Tagliacozzo (ed.). Baltimore: The Johns Hopkins University Press, 1976, 251-261.

1200 Landgrebe, Ludwig. *Phänomenologie und Geschichte.* Gutersloh: Gutersloher Verlagshaus G. Mohn, 1967, 206 p.

1201 Landgrebe, Ludwig. "Meditation über Husserls Wort 'Die Geschichte ist das grosse Faktum des absoluten Seins'." *Tijdschrift voor Filosofie,* vol. 36, 1974, 107-126. "A meditation on Husserl's statement: "History is the grand fact of absolute Being." *Southerwestern Journal of Philosophy,* vol. 5, no. 3, 1974, 111-125.

1202    Landgrebe, Ludwig. "Die Phänomenologie als transzendentale Theorie des Geschichte," in *Phänomenologie udn Praxis* (Phänomenologische Forschung, 3). Freiburg-München: Karl Alber, 1976, 17-47.

1203    Melandri, Enzo. "Husserl: la filosofia della storia. Genesi e sviluppo di un problema." Tesi di laurea, Bologna, 1958.

1204    Miguelez, Roberto. *Sujet et histoire.* Ottawa: Les Editions de l'Université d'Ottawa, 1973, 22 p. [*Krisis*]

1205    Morrison, James C. "Husserl's *Crisis* Reflections on the relationship of philosophy and history." *Philosophy and Phenomenological Research*, vol. 37, March 1977, 312-320.

1206    Pazanin, Ante. "Das Problem der Geschichte bei Husserl, Hegel und Marx," in *Phänomenologie heute.* Festschrift für Ludwig Landgrebe. Hrsg. von Walter Biemel (Phaenomenologica, 51). The Hague: Martinus Nijhoff, 1972, 173-203.

1207    Pazanin, Ante. *Wissenschaft und Geschichte in der Phänomenologie Edmund Husserls* (Phaenomenologica, 46). The Hague: Martinus Nijhoff, 1972, xii-192.

1208    Presas, Mario A. "Corporalidad e historia en Husserl." *Revista Latinoamericana de Filosofía*, vol. 2, July 1976, 167-178.

1209    Pucci, Raffaele. "Il mondo-della-vita e la storia [Husserl]" *Rassegna di Scienze Filosofiche*, vol. 16, 1963, 327-356.

1210    Ricoeur, Paul. "Husserl et le sense de l'historie." *Revue de Métaphysique et de Morale*, vol. 54, 1949, 280-316. "Husserl's and the sense of History," in his *Husserl.* An analysis of his phenomenology. Edward G. Ballard and Lester E. Embree (trans.). Evanston, Ill.: Northwestern University Press, 1967, 143-174. "Husserl und der Sinn der Geschichte. (Aus dem Französischen übersetzt von Klaus Stickweh)," in *Husserl.* Hrsg. von H. Noack. (Wege der Forschung, 40). Darmstadt: Wissenschaftliche Buchgesellschaft, 1973, 231-276.

1211    Schmueli, Efraim. "Critical reflections of Husserl's philosophy of history." *Journal of the British Society for Phenomenology*, vol. 2, no. 1, 1971, 35-51.

1212    Shiner, L. E. "Husserl and historical science." *Social Research*, vol. 37, no. 4, 1970, 511-532.

1213    Siegfried, Theodor. *Phänomenologie und Geschichte.* Kairos, 1926, 92-231.

1214    Valori, Paolo. "Inediti Husserliani sulla teologia della storia." *Archivo di Filosofia*, vol. 1, 1954 [Filosofia della storia della filosofia], 1954, 165-167.

1215    Valori, Paolo. "Inédits husserliens sur la téléologie de l'historie," in *La philosophie de l'histoire de la philosophie, Archives de Philosophie*, 1954, 121-123.

## HISTORICISM

1216    Wagner, Helmut R. "Husserl and historicism." *Social Research*, vol. 39, no. 4, 1972, 696-719.

## HORIZON

1217    Brand, Gerd. "Horizont, Welt, Geschichte [Husserl]," in *Kommunikationskultur und Weltverständnis*. Beitrage von Gerd Brand, Joseph Kockelmans. Redaktion und Einleitung von E. W. Orth (Phänomenologische Forschungen, 5). Freiburg-Munchen: Karl Alber, 1977, 14-89.

1218    Pietersma, Henry. "The concept of horizon." *Analecta Husserliana,* vol. 2, 1972, 278-282.

1219    Schmidt, Hermann. "Der Horizontbegriff Husserls in Anwendung auf die ästhetische Erfahrung." *Zeitschrift für Philosophische Forschung,* vol. 21, 1967, 499-511.

1220    Van Peursen, Cornelis. "The horizon," in *Husserl. Expositions and appraisals,* F. Elliston and P. McCormick (eds.). Notre Dame, Ind.-London: University of Notre Dame Press, 1977, 182-201.

## HYLE-HYLETIC DATA

1221    Larrabee, Mary Jeanne. "Husserl on sensation: Notes on the theory of hyle." *New Scholasticism,* vol. 47, 1973, 179-203.

1222    Lingis, Alphonso. "Hyletic data." *Analecta Husserliana,* vol. 2, 1972, 96-101.

1223    Smith, Quentin. "A phenomenological examination of Husserl's theory of hyletic data." *Philosophy Today,* vol. 21, Winter 1977, 356-367.

## IDEALISM

1224    Adorno, Theodore W. "Husserl and the problem of idealism." *Journal of Philosophy,* vol. 37, 1940, 5-18. [*see:* F. Kaufmann 1235]

1225    Baratta, Giorgio. *L'Idealismo fenomenologico di Edmund Husserl* (Pubblicazioni dell'Universita di Urbino. Testi e saggi). Urbino: Argalia, 1969, 244 p.

1226    Boehm, Rudolf. "Husserl und der klassische Idealismus," in his *Vom Gesichtspunkt der Phänomenologie.* Husserl-Studien (Phaenomenologica, 26). The Hague: Martinus Nijhoff, 1968, 18-71. "Husserl et l'idéalisme classique." *Convivium,* vol. 3, 1958, 53-93.

1227    Casaubön, Juan Alfredo. "Gérmenes de idealismo en las *Investigaciones lógica de Husserl.*" *Sapientia,* vol. 11, 1956, 250-280.

1228    Celms, Theodor. *Der phänomenologische Idealimus Husserls.* Riga, 1928.

1229    De Boer, Theodor. "The meaning of Husserl's idealism in the light of his development." *Analecta Husserliana,* vol. 2, 1972, 322-333.

1230    Holmes, R. H. "Is transcendental phenomenology committed to idealism?" *The Monist,* vol. 59, Jan. 1975, 98-114.

1231    Ingarden, Roman. *On the motives which lead Husserl to transcendental idealism.* Arnór Hannibalsson (trans. from the Polish) (Phaenomenologica, 64). The Hague: Martinus Nijhoff, 1975, 72 p.

**Book Reviews:**

R. Sokolowski, *Journal of Philosophy,* vol. 74, March 1977, 176-180.

1232      Ingarden, Roman. "About the motives which lead Husserl to transcendental idealism," in *Phenomenology and natural existence.* Essays in honor of Marvin Farber, Dale Riepe (ed.). Albany, N.Y.: State University of New York Press, 1973, 95-117.

1233      Ingarden, Roman. "Ueber den transzendentalen Idealismus bei E. Husserl," in *Husserl et la pensée moderne* (Phaenomenoligica, 2). The Hague: Martinus Nijhoff, 1959, 19-204. "De l'idéalisme transcendental chez E. Husserl (Traduit par Jacques Taminiaux)," in *Ibid.,* 205-215.

1234      Ingarden, Roman. "Bermerkungen zum Problem 'Idealismus-Realismus'." *Jahrbuch für Philosophie und Phänomenologische Forschung,* 1929 (Ergänzungsband Edmund Husserl zum 70. Geburtstag gewidmet), 159-190.

1235      Kaufmann, Fritz. "Review of T. W. Adorno, 'Husserl and the problem of idealism'," [*see:* 1225] *Philosophy and Phenomenological Research,* vol. 1, 1940-1941, 123-125.

1236      Kockelmans, A. "Realisme-idealisme en Husserls phaenomenologie." *Tijdschrift voor Filosofie,* vol. 20, 1958, 395-441 [Survey, 441-442].

1237      Kockelmans, Joseph J. "World-constitution. Reflections on Husserl's transcendental idealism." *Analecta Husserliana,* vol. 1, 1971, 11-35.

1238      Madison, Gary B. "'Phenomenology and existentialism': Husserl and the end of idealism," in *Husserl. Expositions and appraisals,* F. Elliston and P. McCormick (eds.). Notre Dame, Ind.-London: University of Notre Dame Press, 1977, 247-268.

1239      Merlan, Philip. "Idélisme, Réalisme, phénoménologie," in *Husserl* (Cahiers de Royaumont, 3). Paris: Editions de Minuit, 1959, 382-410.

1240      Minozzi, B. *L'idealismo fenomenologico di Husserl.* Bologna, 1962.

1241      Mohanty, J. N. "Husserl's phenomenology and Indian realism." *Philosophical Quarterly, A.,* vol. 24, 1951, 147-156.

1242      Morriston, Wesley. "Intentionality and the phenomenological method: A Critique of Husserl's transcendental idealism." *Journal of the British Society for Phenomenology,* vol. 7, Jan. 1976, 33-43.

1243      Nahmke, D. *Das unsichbare Konigreich des deutschen Idealismus.* Halle, 1920.

1244      Oosthuizen, D. C. S. "Die transendentaal-fenomenologiese Idealisme. 's Aspek van die konstitusie-probleem in die filosofie van Edmund Husserl," in *Festschrift H. J. de Vleeschauwer,* Pretoria: Publications Committee of the University of South Africa, 1960, 180-194.

1245      Siméon, J.-P. "Maurice Merleau-Ponty et l'idéalisme." *Revue de Métaphysique et de Morale,* vol. 82, July-Sept. 1977, 296-311.

1246    Tymieniecka, Anna-Teresa. "Beyond Ingarden's idealism/realism controversy with Husserl. The new contextual phase of phenomenology." *Analecta Husserliana*, vol. 4, 1976, 241-418.

1247    Van de Pitte, M.M. "Husserl: the idealist malgré lui." *Philosophy and Phenomenological Research*, vol. 37, 1976-1977, 70-78.

IDEATION *see also:* THINKING

1248    Enyvari, E. "Zur Phänomenologie der Ideation." *Zeitschrift für Philosophie und Philosophische Kritik*, 1914.

INDUCTION

1249    Levin, David Michael. "Induction and Husserl's theory of eidetic variation." *Philosophy and Phenomenological Research*, vol. 29. 1968-1969, 1-15.

1250    Mall, R. A. "Der induktionsbegriff. Hume und Husserl." *Zeitschrift fur Philosophische Forschung*, vol. 29, 1975, 34-62.

1251    Palermo, James. "Apodictic truth: Husserl's eidetic reduction versus induction." *Notre Dame Journal of Formal Logic*, vol. 19, Jan. 1978, 69-80.

INFINITY

1252    Lingis, Alphonso. "The origin of infinity." *Research in Phenomenology*, vol. 6, 1976, 27-46.

1253    Melandri, E. "I paradossi del'infinito nell'orizzonte fenomenologico," in *Omaggio a Husserl.* Milano, 1960, 81-120.

IMAGE

1254    Casey, Edward S. "The image/sign relation in Husserl and Freud." *Review of Metaphysics*, vol. 30, Dec. 1976, 207-225.

1255    Feldman-Comiti, Yanne. "Structures intellectuelles. Introduction à l'étude phénoménologique de l'image." *Revue de Métaphysique et de Morale*, vol. 44, no. 4, 1937, 767-779.

1256    Sallis, John. "Image and phenomenon." *Research in Phenomenology*, vol. 5, 1975, 61-75.

1257    Sartre, Jean-Paul. "Structure intentionnelle de l'image." *Revue de Métaphysique et de Morale*, vol. 45, 1938, 543-609.

IMAGINATION

1258    Casey, Edward S. *Imagination.* A phenomenological study. Bloomington, Ind.: Indiana University Press, 1976, 240 p.

1259    Casey, Edward S. "Imagination and phenomenological method," in *Husserl. Expositions and appraisals,* F. Elliston and P. McCormick (eds.). Notre Dame, Ind.-London: Notre Dame University Press, 1977, 70-82.

1260    Russow, Lilly-Marlene. "Some recent works on imagination." *American Philosophical Quarterly*, vol. 15, Jan. 1978, 57-66.

1261    Saraiva, Maria Manuela. *L'imagination selon Husserl.* (Phaenomenologica, 34). The Hague: Martinus Nijhoff, 1970, xvi-280.

1262    Saraiva, Maria Manuela. "L'imagination selon Husserl." Dissertation, Univerité Catholoque de Louvain, Institut Supérieur de Philosophie, 1963, 365 [multigraphié].

1263    Sartre, Jean-Paul. *L'imagination*. Paris: Presses Universitaires de France, 1936. Trans.: *Psychology and Imagination*. New York, Philosophical Library, 1948.

1264    Sartre, Jean-Paul. *L'imaginaire, psychologie phénoménologique de l'imagination*. Paris: Gallimard, 1940. Trans.: *The Psychology of the imagination*. New York: Rider, 1951.

1265    Warnock, Mary. *Imagination [Part IV: The nature of the mental image]*. *London: Faber and Faber, 1976, Los Angeles: University of California Press*.

## IMMANENCE

1266    Boehm, Rudolf. 'Immanenz und Transzendenz," in *Vom Gesichtspunkt der Phaenomenologie*. Husserl-Studien (Phaenoenologica, 26). The Hague: Martinus Nijhoff, 1968, 141-185.

## INTELLIGIBILITY

1267    Galay, Jean-Louis. "Essai sur le problème de l'intelligibilité d'après la *Critique de la raison logique* de Husserl." *Studia Philosophica*, vol. 29, 1969, 25-53.

## INTENTIONALITY

1268    Anzenbacher, Arno. *Die Intentionalität bei Thomas von Aquin und Edmund Husserl*. München: Oldenburg, 1972, 234 p.

1269    Armstrong, Edward G. "Intersubjective intentionality." *Midwest Journal of Philosophy*, vol. 5, Spring 1977, 1-11.

1270    Benedikt, M. "Strukturwandel der Intentionalität, " in *Wiener Jahrbuch für Philosophie*, Hrsg. von Erich Heintel, vol. 5, 1972.

1271    Bosio, Franco. "L'intenzionalità e il concetto di coscienza nella *Logische Untersuchungen*." *Aut Aut*, no. 72, 1972, 479-504.

1272    Breton, Stanislas. *Conscience et intentionalité*. Lyon-Paris: Vitte, 1957, 290 p.

1273    Breton, Stanislas. "Conscience et intentionalité selon Husserl." *Archives de Philosophie*, vol. 19, no. 4, 1956, 55-97.

1274    Breton, Stanislas. "De conceptu intentionalitatis conscientiae juxta thomismum et phenomenologiam Husserl." *Euntes Docete*, vol. 9, no. 1-3, 1956, 394-418.

1275    Carr. David. "Intentionality," in *Phenomenology and philosophical understanding*, Edo Pivcevic (ed.). Cambridge University Press, 1975, 17-36.

1276    Caruso, Paolo. "L'io trascendentale come 'durata explosiva'. Intenzionalità e tempo nella fenomenologia di Husserl." *Archivo di Filosofia*, no. 1, 1960, 49-72.

1277 Cerri, Stefano. "La nozione di intenzionalità in Husserl e S. Tommaso. Appunti per un esame comparativo." *Rivista di Filosofia Neo-Scolastica*, vol. 59, 1967, 700-725.

1278 Christensen, Renate. "Einige Bermerkungen zur Problematik von Intentionatität und Reflexion bei E. Husserl." *Wiener Jahrbuch für Philosophie*, vol. 9, 1976, 73-87.

1279 Cruz Hernändez, Miguel. *La doctrina de la intencionalidad en la fenomenología* (Acta Salmanticensia. Filosofía y Letras, tomo XIV, 2). Universidad de Salamanca, 1958, 116 p.

1280 De Muralt, André. "Les deux dimensions de l'intentionalité husserlienne." *Revue de Théologie et Philosophie*, vol. 8, 1958, 188-202.

1281 De Muralt, André. "La notion d'acte fondé dans les rapports de la raison et de la volonté selon des *Logische Untersuchungen* de Husserl. Les véritables sources scolastiques de l'intentionalité husserlienne. Essai d'analyse structurelle des doctrines." *Revue de Métaphysique et de Morale*, vol. 82, 1977, 511-527.

1282 Díaz Hernández, Carlos. "La intencionalidad en Husserl." *Revista de Filosofía* (Madrid), vol. 28, 1969, 59-76.

1283 Díaz Hernández, Carlos. *La intencionalided en la fenomenología de Husserl* (Extracto de tesis). Madrid: Facultad de Filosofiía y Letras de la Universidad, 1970.

1284 Díaz, Carlos. *Husserl.* Intencionalidad y fenomenología (Biblioteca Promocion del Pueblo. Serie P., 40). Algorta; Editorial Zero, 1971, 128 p.

1285 Ehrlich, W. *Intentionalität und Sinn.* Prolegomena zur Normenlehre. Halle, 1934, 48 p.

1286 Fagone, Virgilio. "Tempo e intenzionalità. Brentano--Husserl--Heidegger." *Archivo di Filosofia*, no. 1, 1960, 105-131.

1287 Fisch, M. P. *Husserls Intentionalitäts-und Urteilslehre.* Bale, 1942.

1288 Gurwitsch, Aron. "The Husserlian conception of the intentionality of consciousness," in *The Isenberg Memorial lecture series,* 1965-1966. Michigan State University Press, 1969, 145-162.

1289 Gurwitsch, Aron. "Husserl's theory of intentionality of consciousness in historical perspective," in *Existentialism and phenomenology,* N. L. Lee and M. Mandelbaum (eds.). Baltimore: The Johns Hopkins University Press, 1967. Reprinted in his *Phenomenology and the theory of science.* Evanston, Ill.: Northwestern University Press, 1974, 210-240.

1290 Joja, Crizantema. "Intentionalité et signification chez Husserl." *Revue Roumaine des Scieces Sociales-Philosophie et Logique,* vol. 20, 1976, 119-126. [Résumé, 119]

1291 Kersten, Frederick. "The originality of Gurwitsch's theory of intentionality." *Research in Phenomenology,* vol. 5, 1975, 19-27.

1292 Kumar, F. L. "Husserlian notion of intentionality." *Midwest Journal of Philosophy,* vol. 4, Spring 1976, 35-42.

1293    Lauer, Quentin. *Phénoménologie de Husserl.* Essai sur la genèse de l'intentionalité. Paris: Presses Universitaires de France, 1955, 441. [Bibliographie, 431-441]

1294    Lazzarini, Renato. *Intenzionalità e estanza metafisica* (Pubblicazioni dell'Instituto di Studi Filosofici-Roma. Serie II, no. 3). Roma: Fratelli Bocca, 1954, 482 p.

1295    Levinas, Emmanuel. "Intentionalité et sensation." *Revue Internationale de Philosophie,* vol. 19, no. 71-72, 1965, 34-54.

1296    Lingis, Alphonso. "Intentionality and corporeity." *Analecta Husserliana,* vol. 1, 1971, 75-90.

1297    Linke, Paul F. "Der Satz des Bewusstseins und die Lehre von der Intentionalität," in *Atti del V Congresso internazionale di filosofia in Napoli,* 1924. Napoli, 1927, 79ff.

1298    Mackie, J. L. "Problems of intentionality," in *Phenomenology and philosophical understanding,* Edo Pivcevic (ed.). Cambridge University Press, 1975, 37-52.

1299    Madden, Robert E. "Husserl and the problem of hidden reason: Intentionality as accomplished life." Ph.D. Dissertation, Duquesne University, 1973, 435 p. *Dissertation Abstracts,* vol. 34, no. 12, June 1974, 7824-A.

1300    Margolin, Julius. "Grundphänomene des intentionalen Bewusstseins." Dissertation, Berlin, 1929.

1301    Mohanty, J. N. *The concept of intentionality.* St. Louis: Warren H. Green, 1971, 213 p.

1302    Mohanty, J. N. "Husserl's concept of intentionality." *Analecta Husserliana,* vol. 1, 1971, 100-132.

1303    Morrison, James C. "Husserl and Brentano on intentionality." *Philosophy and Phenomenological Research,* vol. 31, 1970-1971, 27-46.

1304    Morriston, Wesley. "Intentionality and the phenomenological method: A critique of Husserl's transcendental idealism." *Journal of the British Society for Phenomenology,* vol. 7, Jan. 1976, 33-43.

1305    Morujâo, Alexandre Fradique. "A doutrina da intencionalidade na fenomenologia de Husserl." *Biblos* (Coimbra), vol. 30, 1954, 53-190.

1306    Morujâo, Alexandre Fragique. *A doutrina da intencionalidade na fenomenologia de Husserl.* Das *Investigaçoes lógicas às Meditaçoes cartesianas* [Separata de *Biblos,* vol XXX]. Coimbra: Coimbra Editors, 1955, 144 p.

1307    Natanson, Maurice. "Phenomenology and existentialism: Husserl and Sartre on intentionality." *Modern Schoolman,* vol. 37, Nov. 1959, 1-10. Reprinted in his *Literature, philosophy, and the social sciences.* The Hague: Martinus Nijhoff, 1962, 26-33. Also reprinted in *Philosophy Today,* Jerry H. Gill (ed.), no. 3. New York: Macmillan, 1970, 61-71.

1308     Null, Gilbert T. "Generalizing abstraction and the judgment of subsumption in Aron Gurwitsch's version of Husserl's theory of intentionality." *Philosophy and Phenomenological Research,* vol. 38, June 1978, 469-488.

1309     Olafson, Frederick A. "Husserl's theory of intentionality in contemporary perspective." *Nous,* vol. 9, March 1975, 73-83. Reprinted in *Husserl. Expositions and appraisals,* F. Elliston and P. McCormick (eds.). Notre Dame, Ind.-London: University of Notre Dame Press 1977, 160-167.

1310     Patocka, Jan. "Der Geist und dis zwei Grundschichten der Intentionalität." *Philosophia,* vol. 1, 1936.

1311     Prezioso, Faustino Antonio. "L'intenzionalità della conscienza nella fenomenologia di E. Husserl." *Rassegna di Scienze Filosofiche,* vol. 22, 1969, 187-220.

1312     Ryan, William F. J. "Intentionality in Edmund Husserl and Bernard Lonergan." *International Philosophical Quarterly,* vol. 13, 1973, 173-190.

1313     Ryan, William F. J. "Passive and active elements in Husserl's notion of intentionality." *Modern Schoolman,* vol. 54, no. 1, Nov. 1977, 37-56.

1314     Satue Alvarez, A. *La doctrina de la intencionalidad en Franz Brentano.* Barcelona: C.S.I.C. Instituto Luis Vives de Filosofía, 1961, 228 p.

1315     Sartre, Jean-Paul. "Une idée fondamentale de la philosophie de Husserl: l'intentionalité." *Nouvelle Revue Francçaise,* vol. 17, no. 304, 1939, 129-132. Reprinted in his *Situations, I.* Paris: Gallimard, 1947. "Intentionality: A fundamental idea of Husserl's phenomenology. P. Fell (trans.), in *J.-P. Sartre, Perspectives. Journal of the British Society for Phenomenology,* vol. 1, no. 2, 1970, 4-5.

1316     Smith, David Woodruff. "Intentionality, noemata, and individuation. The role of individuation in Husserl's theory of intentionality." Ph.D. Dissertation, Stanford University 1971, 267 p. *Dissertation Abstracts,* vol. 32, no. 2, Aug. 1971, 1023-A.

1317     Souches-Dagues, D. *Le développement de l'intentionalité dans la phénoménologie husserlienne* (Phaenomenologica, 52). The Hague: Martinus Nijhoff, 1972, vi-306.

1318     Spiegelberg, Herbert. "Der Begriff der Intentionalität in der Scholastik, bei Brentano und Bei Husserl." *Philosophische Hefte,* vol. 5, 1936, 75-91.

1319     Spiegelberg, Herbert. "'Intention' and 'Intentionalität' in der Scholastik, bei Brentano und Husserl." *Studia Philosophica,* vol. 29, 1969, 189-216. "'Intention' and 'intentionality' in Scholastics, Brentano and Husserl," Linda L. McAlister and Margarate Schalte (trans. from the German) in *The philosophy of Brentano,* with an introduction by Linda McAlister (ed.). London: G. Duckworth and Co., 1976, 108-127.

1320     Smith, David and McIntyre, Ronald. "Intentionality via intensions." *Journal of Philosophy,* vol. 68, 1971, 541-561.

1321    Snowball, K. R. "The nature of intentionality." Ph.D. Dissertation, Queen's University of Belfast, 1976, 324 p. *Dissertation Abstracts, Int. European,* vol. 37, no. 3, Spring 1977, 479.

3122    Strasser, Stephan. "Problemen rondom het begrip der intentionaliteit [E. Husserl]." *Nederlands Tijdschrift voor Pyschologie,* vol. 20, 1965, 1-20.

1323    Vasquéz, G. H. "Intentionalität als Verantwortung. Geschichtsteleologie und Teleologie der Intentionalität." Ph.D. Dissertation, Koln, 1973, 256 p. *Dissertation Abstracts Int. European,* vol. 37, no. 3, Spring 1977, 480.

1324    Vasquéz Hoyos, Guillermo. *Intentionalität als Verantwortung.* Geschichtsteleologie und Teleologie der Intentionalität bei Husserl (Phaenomenologica, 67). The Hague: Martinus Nijhoff, 1976, viii-212.

1325    Van Breda, Herman Leo. "La phénoménologie husserlienne comme philosophie de l'itentionalité," in *La Fenomenologia.* Atti dell'XI Convegno del Centro di Studi Filosofici tra Professori Universitari--Gallarate, 1955. Brescia: Morcelliana, 1956, 41-48.

1326    Vanni-Rovighi, Sofia. "Una fonte remota della teoria husserliana dell'intenzionalità," in *Omaggio a Husserl.* Milano, 1960, 47-65. Reprinted in her *Studi di filosofia medioevale.* Vol. II: Secoli XIII e XIV (Scienzefilosofiche, 20). Milano: Vita E Pensiero 1978, 283-298.

1327    Vanni-Rovighi, Sofia. "La teoria dell'intenzionalità nella filosofia di Husserl." *Rivista di Filosofia Neo-Scholastic,* vol. 50, 1958, 197-211.

1328    Vuillemin, Jules. "Le problème phénoménologique: intentionalité et réflexion." *Revue Philosophique de la France et de l'Etranger,* vol. 84, no. 4, [Edmund Husserl], 1959, 463-470.

1329    Waelhens, Alphonse de. "L'idée phénoménologique d'intentionalité," in *Husserl et la pensée moderne* (Phaenomenologica, 2). The Hague: Martinus Nijhoff, 1959, 115-129. "Die phänomenologische Idee der Intentionalität (Übersetzt von Rudolf Boehm)," in *Ibid,* 129-142.

1330    Welton, Donn. "Intentionality and language in Husserl's phenomenology." *Review of Metaphysics,* vol. 27, 1973-1974, 260-297.

1331    Wilming, Josef. "Husserls Lehre von dem intentionellen Erlebnissen." Dissertation, Leipzig, 1925.

INTERSUBJECTIVITY *see also:* ALTER EGO, COMMUNICATION, OTHER

1332    Allen, Jeffner M. "Husserl and intersubjectivity: A phenomenological investigation of the analogical structure of intersubjectivity: A phenomenological investigation of the analogical structure of intersubjectivity." Ph.D. Dissertation, Duquesne University, 1973, 590 p. *Dissertation Abstracts,* vol. 34, no. 12, June 1974, 7816-A.

1333    Armstrong, Edward E. "Intersubjective intentionality." *Midwest Journal of Philosophy,* vol. 5, Spring 1977, 1-11.

1334    Ballard, Edward G. "Husserls philosophy of intersubjectivity in relation to his rational ideal." *Tulane Studies in Philosophy,* vol. 12. The Hague: Martinus Nijhoff, 1962, 3-38.

1335    Brand, Gerd. "Husserl. Zu Phänomenologie der intersubjektivität." *Philosophische Rundschau,* vol. 25, no. 1-2, 1978, 54-79.

1336    Cunningham, Suzanne. "Language and intersubjectivity in the phenomenology of E. Husserl." Ph.D. Dissertation, Florida State University, 1972, 155 p. *Dissertation Abstracts,* vol. 33, no. 5, 1972, 2423-A.

1337    Garulli, Enrico. "L'intersoggettività nella V *Meditazione cartesiana* di Husserl." *Nuova Rivista di Pedagogia* (Roma), dicembre 1960, 97-108.

1338    Harland, Robert M. "The I and the other: A reformulation of Husserl's Fifth *Cartesian meditation.*" Ph.D. Dissertation, New School for Social Research, 1978.

1339    Held, Klaus. "Das Problem der Intersubjektivität und die Idee einer phänomenologischen Transzendentalphilosophie," in *Perspektivien transzendentalphänomenologischer Forschung (Phaenomenologica, 49). Hrsg. von U. Claesges und K. Held. The Hague: Martinus Nijhoff, 1972, 3-61.*

1340    Hoffmann, Gisbert. "Zur Phänomenologie der Intersubjektivität. Kritische Bermerkungen zu Texten aus Husserls Nachlass." *Zeitschrift für Philosophische Forschung,* vol. 29, 1975, 138-149.

1341    Hyppolite, Jean. "L'intersubjectivité chez Husserl, in his *Figures de la pensée philosophique. Ecrits (1938-1968).* Paris: Presses Universitaires de France, 1968, vol. I, 499-512.

1342    Masullo, Aldo. *Lezioni sull'intersoggettività, I: Fichte e Husserl.* Napoli: Libreria Scientifica Editrice, 1964, 140 p. [litografato].

1343    McCormick, Peter. "Husserl and the intersubjectivity materials [E. Husserl, *Zur Phänomenologie der Intersubjektivität.* Hrsg. von Iso Kern]." *Research in Phenomenology,* vol. 6, 1976, 167-189.

1344    MarujÂo, Alexandre Fradique. "Subjectividade e intersubjectividade em Husserl," in *Actas da Assmebleia internacional de estudios filosoficos.* Braga: Faculdade Filosofia, 1969, 81-10. *Revista Portuguesa de Filosofia,* vol. 25, no. 3-4, 1969, 81-100.

1345    Schütz, Alfred. "Das Problem der transzendentalen Intersubjektivität bei Husserl." *Philosophische Rundschau,* vol. 5, 1957, 82-107.

1346    Schütz, Alfred. "Le problème de l'intersubjectivité transcendentale chez Husserl" in *Husserl* (Cahiers de Royaumont. Philosophie no. 3). Paris: Editions de Minuit, 1959, 334-365 [Discussion, 366-381].

1347    Schütz, Alfred. "The problem of transcendental intersubjectivity in Husserl," in his *Collected Papers III: Studies in phenomenological philosophy.* The Hague: Martinus Nijhoff, 1970, 51-83. [Including "Discussion by Eugen Fink an response by the author to Fink and other critics," 84-91].

1348   Sinn, Dieter. "Die transzendentale Intersubjektivität bei Edmund Husserl mit ihren Seinshorizonten." Dissertation, Heidelberg, 1958.

1349   Strasser, Stephan. "En andere Husserl. Verkenningstochten door Husserl's fenomenologie der intersubjectiviteit [E. Husserl, *Zur Phänomenologie der Intersubjektivität,* I-III]." *Tijdschrift voor Filosofie,* vol. 35, 1973, 617-630.

1350   Strasser, Stephan. *The idea of dialogal phenomenology.* Pittsburgh, Pa.: Duquesne University Press, 1973, 136 p. [Inability of Husserl's transcendental phenomenology of solve the problem of intersubjectivity].

1351   Theunissen, Michael. "Die destruierende Wiederholung der transzendentalen Intersubjectivitätstheorie Husserls in der Sozialontologie Sartres," in *Der Andere: Studien zur Sozialontologie der Gegenwart.* Berlin: Walter de Gruyter, 1965, 187-240.

1352   Van de Pitte, Margaret M. "The epistemological function of an affective principle in the phenomenology of intersubjectivity." Ph.D. Dissertation, University of Southern California, 1966. Ann Arbor, Mich.-London: University Microfilms International, 1977, ii-244.

## INTUITION - INTUITIONISM

1353   de Marneffe, J., S.J. "Bergson's and Husserl's concepts of intuition." *Philosophical Quarterly, A.,* vol. 33, 1960-1961, 169-180.

1354   Hufnagel, A. *Intuition und Erkenntnis nach Thomas von Aquin.* Münster, 1932.

1355   König, Josef. *Der Bergriff des Intuition Dissertation, Göttingen, Halle, 1926, bes. 290-367].* Halle: Niemeyer, 1926, bes. 290-367.

1356   Levinas, Emmanuel. *Théorie de l'intuition dans la phénoménologie de Husserl* (Bibliothèque d'histoire de la philosophie). Nouvelle édition conforme à la première. Paris: J. Vrin, 1963, 224 p. *The theory of intuition in Husserl's phenomenology* André Orianne (trans.). Evanston, Ill.: Northwestern University Press, 1973. [Originally published by Alcan, 1930].

1357   Patocka, Jan. "La doctrine husserlienne de l'intuition eidétique et ses critiques récents." *Revue Internationale de Philosophie,* vol. 19, no. 71-721, 1965, 17-33. "The Husserlian doctrine of eidetic intuition and its recent critics," in *Husserl. Expositions and appraisals,* F. Elliston and P.McCormick (eds.). Notre Dame, Ind.-London: University of Notre Dame Press, 1977, 150-159.

1358   Pietersma, Henry. "Intuition and horizon in the philosophy of Husserl [Abstract]." *Journal of Philosophy,* vol. 67, 1970, 822-823.

1359   Sinha, Debabrata. "Phenomenology: A break-through to a new intuitionism," in *Phänomenologie heute.* Festschrift für Ludwig Landgrebe, (Phaenomenologica, 51). Hrsg. von W. Biemel. The Hague: Martinus Nijhoff, 1972, 27-48.

1360   Strasser, Stephan. "Intuition und Dialektik in der Philosophie Husserls," in *Husserl* (Cahiers de Royaumont, 3). Paris: Editions de Minuit, 1959, 148-153.

## JUDGMENT

1361    De Muralt, André. "Adéquation et intentions secondes. Essai de confrontation de la phénoménologie husserliene et de la philosophie thomiste sur le point du judement." *Studia Philosophica,* vol. 20, 1960, 88-114.

1362    Fisch, M. P. *Husserls Intentionalitäts-und Urteilslehre.* Bale, 1942.

1363    Garulli, Enrico. "Realtà e giudizio nella logica husserliana." *Studia Urbinati,* vol. 36, 1962, 282-298.

1364    Hoche, Hans-Ulrich. *Nichtempirische Erkenntnis.* Analytische und synthetische Urteile bei Kant und bei Kant. Meisenheim am Glan: Anton Hain, 1964, 208 p.

1365    Jolivet, Régis. "Le problème de l'évidence du judgment et l'évidence antéprédicative d'après Husserl." *Revue de l'Université d'Ottawa,* vol. 21, 1951, 235-253.

1366    Kelly, Francis Joseph. "The structural and the developmental aspects of the formulation of categorial judgments in the philosophy of Edmund Husserl." Ph.D. Dissertation, Georgetown University, 1978.

1367    Langsdorf, Lenore. "Husserl on judging: A critique of the theory of ideal objects." Ph.D. Dissertation, SUNY at Stony Brook, 1978.

1368    Sallis, John C. "The problem of judgment in Husserl's later thought." *Tulane Studies in Philosophy,* 1967, 129-152.

## KNOWLEDGE

1369    Adorno, Theodor W. *Zur Metakritik der Erkenntnistheorie.* Studien über Husserl und die phänomenologischen Antinomien. Stuttgart, 1956. [Edition Suhrkamp, 590. Frankfurt am Main: Suhrkamp, 1972, 245 p.] *Sulla metacritica della gnoseologia.* Studi su Husserl e sulle antinomie fenomenologiche. Trad. it di Alba Burger Cori. Milano: Sugar, 1964, 248 p.

1370    Banfi, A. "Sulla conoscenza intuitiva." *Aut Aut,* no. 54, 363-373.

1371    Bjelke, J. Fr. "Der Ausgangspunkt der Erkenntnistheorie. Eine Auseinandersetzung mit Husserl." *Kantstudien,* vol. 55, 1964, 3-19.

1372    Boelaars, H. "De intentionaliteit der kennis bij Ed. Husserl." *Bijdragen,* 3, 1940, 111-161, and 221-264.

1373    Cammarota, Pasquale. "Revisione odierna del problema gnoseologica. Le conclusioni fenomenologiche della Husserl." *Studia Patavina,* vol. 10, 1963, 450-457.

1374    Campanale, D. *Problemi epistemologici da Hume all'ultimo Wittgenstein.* Bari, 1961.

1375    Casaubón, Juan A. "Examen de al doctrina husserliana sobre el conocimiento como constitución de su objeto." *Sapientia,* vol. 14, 1959, 179-187.

1376 Casaubón, Juan A. "Examen de la teoría de Husserl acerca del conocimiento como constitución activa y originaria de su objeto," in *Atti XII Congresso internazionale di Filosofia*, XII: Storia della filosofia moderna e contemporanea. Firenze: Sansoni, 1961, 63-69.

1377 Chestov, Leo. "Memento mori (A propos de la théorie de la connaissance d'Edmond Husserl," in his *Le pouvoir des clefs* (*Potestas clavium*) (Traduction de B. de Schloezer. Paris: J. Schiffren, Editions de la Pléiade, 1928, 307-396. [*see* Jean Héring, 1383].

1378 Cohen, Hermann. *Logik der reinen Erkenntnis.* Berlin, 3. A., 55-57.

1379 Ehrlich, W. *Das unpersonale Erlebnis.* Einführung in eine neue Erkenntnislehre. Halle, 1927.

1380 Funke, Gerhard. "Seinsgebundenheit der Erkenntnis und phänomenologische Kritik." *Dialectics and Humanism*, vol. 3, Winter 1976, 73-89.

1381 Geyser, Josef. *Neue und alte Wege der Philosophie.* Eine Erörterung der Grundlagen der Erkenntnis im Hinblick auf Edmund Husserls Versuch ihrer Neubegründung. Münster i. W., 1916, 302 p.

**Book Reviews:**

W. Meckauer, *Kantstudien*, vol. 34, 1929, 433-435.

1383 Héring, Jean. "Sub specie aeterni." *Revue Philosophique de la France et de l'Etranger,* VII, 1927. [Critique of Chestov. *see:* 1377].

1384 Hoche, Hans-Ulrich. *Nichtempirische Erkenntnis.* Analytische und synthetische Urteile bei Kant und bie Husserl. Meisenheim am Glan: Anton Hain, 1964, 208 p.

1385 Ingarden, Roman. *Ueber die Stellung der Erkenntnistheorie im System der Philosophie.* Halle, 1926, 36 p.

1386 Ingarden, Roman. "*A priori* knowledge in Kant vs. *a priori* knowledge in Husserl." Ewa Hoffman Szcepanek (trans.). *Dialectics and Humanism,* 1973, 5-18.

1387 Kynast, R. "Intuitive Erkenntnis." Dissertation, Breslau, 1919.

1388 Landgrebe, Ludwig. "Formale und materiale Normen der Erkenntnis," in *Travaux du IXe Congrès international de Philosophie,* Paris, 1937, XI, 34-38.

1389 Landmann, Edith. *Die Transzendenz des Erkennens.* Berlin, 1923.

1390 Linke, Paul F. "Die Minderwertigkeit der Erfahrung in der Theorie der Erkenntnis. Phänomenologische Randglossen zu H. Cornelius' *Transcendentaler Systematik.*" *Kantstudien,* vol. 23, 1918, 426-443.

1391 Mall, Ram Adhar. "Husserl's criticism of Kant's theory of knowledge." *Journal of Indian Academy of Philosophy,* vol. 6, 21-31.

1392 Maritain, Jacques. "Notes sur la connaissance." *Rivista di Filosofia Neo-Scholastica,* vol. 24, fasc. 1, 1932, 13-23.

1393 Mayz Vallenilla, Ernesto. *Fenomenología del conocimineto.* El problema de la constitución del objeto en la filosofía de Husserl. Buenos Aires: Imprenta López, 1956, 372 p.

1394 Orth, Ernst W. "Husserls Begriff der cogitativen Typen und seine methodologische Reichweite," in *Phänomenologie heute*. Grundlagen und Methodenprobleme. Hrsg. von der Deutschen Gesselschaft für phänomenologische Forschung, vol. 1, 1975.

1395 Port, K. "Bertrachtungen zu Husserls Einteilung der Denkakte und ihrer erkenntnistheoretischen Bedeutung." *Archiv für die Gesammte Psychologie,* vol. LXVI.

1396 Rickert, Henrich. "Zwei Wege der Erkenntnistheorie." *Kantstudien,* vol. 14, 1909.

1397 Schunk, K. *Verstehen und Einsehen.* Eine philosophische Besinnung in Form einer Abhandlung über Wesen, Arten und Bedingungen der Erkenntnis. Halle, 1926.

1398 Somogyi, Joseph. "Das Problem der intuitiven Erkenntnis." *Philosophia Perenis,* Regensburg: Habbel, 1931.

1399 Temuralq, T. *Ueber die Grezen der Erkennbarkeit bei Husserl und Scheler.* Berlin, 1937.

1400 Vanni-Rovighi, Sofia. "Riflessioni sul problema della conoscenza." *Rivista di Filosofia Neo-Scolastica,* no. 2-3, 1960, 157-167.

1401 Wilhelm, Frederick E. "Theory of knowing in Husserl's phenomenology." Ph.D. Dissertation, University of California at Los Angeles, 1974, 592 p.

## LANGUAGE

1402 Ammann, Herman. *Die menschliche Rede,* I. T. Lahr i. B., 1925. II. T. *Ibid.,* 1927.

1403 Ammann, Herman. *Vom Ursprung der Sprache.* Lahr i. B., 1929.

1404 Bühler, F. *Sprachtheorie* (Die Darstellungsfunktion der Sprache). Jena, 1934, besonders, 9-11, 63-68, 228-233, 292.

1405 Carruba, Gerald J. "Some phenomenological aspects of a Marxist philosophy of language." *Kinesis,* vol. 10, Spring 1974, 37-55.

1406 Chatterjee, Margaret. "Language as phenomenon," *Philosophy and Phenomenological Research,* vol. 30, Sept. 1969, 116-121.

1407 Cunningham, Suzanne. "Language and intersubjectivity in the phenomenology of Edmund Husserl." Ph.D. Dissertation, Florida State University, 1972, 155 p. *Dissertation Abstracts,* vol. 33, no. 5, Nov. 1972, 2423-A.

1408 Cunningham, Suzanne. *Language and the phenomenological reductions of Edmund Husserl* (Phaenomenologica, 70). The Hague: Martinus Nijhoff, 1976, x-102.

1409 Dauenhauer, Bernard P. "On speech and temporality: Jacques Derrida and Edmund Husserl." *Philosophy Today,* vol. 18, 1974, 171-180.

1410 Derrida, Jacques. *Speech and phenomena,* and other essays on Husserl's theory of signs. With an introduction by David B. Allison (trans.). Pref. by Newton Garver. Evanston, Ill.: Northwestern University Press, 1973, xlii-166.

1411 Derrida, Jacques. "La forme et le vouloir-dire. Note sur la phénoménologie du langage." *Revue Internationale de Philosophie,* vol. 21, 1967, 277-299.

1412 Duval, R. "Parole, expression, silence: Recherche sur la parole comme révélatrice d'autrui." *Revue des Sciences Philosophiques et Théologiques,* vol. 60, April 1976, 226-260.

1413 Edie, James M. "Husserl's conception of the ideality of language." *Humanitas* (Pittsburgh), vol. 11, May 1975, 201-217. "La pertinence de la conception husserliene de l'idélité du language." Traduit de l'anglais par Michel Philibert, in *Sens et existence.* Hommage à Paul Ricoeur, Gary Brent Madison (ed.). Paris: Editions du Seuil, 1975, 107-123.

1414 Eley, Lothar. "Logik und Sprache [Husserl]." *Kantstudien,* vol. 63, 1972, 247-260.

1415 Eley, Lothar. "Konstitutionsverhältnis Intention und Erfullung als eine Sprachhandlung," in *Aspekte und Probleme der Sprachphilosophie,* Hrsg. von Josef Simon. Freiburg-München: Karl Alber, 1974.

1416 Gadamer, Hans-Georg. *Kleine Schriften, III: Idee und Sprache.* Plato--Husserl--Heidegger. Stuttgart: J. C. B. Mohr (P. Siebeck), 1972, 271 p.

1417 Gironella, Juan Roig. "Filosofía del lenguaje y el problema de la analogía: Fundamentación de las matemáticas."

1418 Gironella, Juan Roig. "Un capítulo de filosofía del lenguaje: La metafísica de Santo Tomá y la transcendencia del pensamiento, planteada por la fenomenología." *Espíritu,* vol. 70, 1974, 131-147.

1419 Gonzáaez, Serafín Vegas. "Sobre el sentido y la originariedad del lenguaje." *Pensamiento,* vol. 33, July-Sept. 1977, 297-315.

1420 Hülsmann, Heinz. *Zur Theorie der Sprache bei Edmund Husserl* (Salzburger Studien zur Philosophie, 4). Munchen: Pustet, 1964, 255 p.

1421 Lejewski, Czeslaw. "Syntax and semantics of ordinary language: Part I." *Aristotelian Society,* vol. 49, 1975, 127-146.

1422 Luckmann, Thomas. "The constitution of language in the world of everyday life," in *Life-world and consciousness.* Essays for Aron Gurwitsch, Lester E. Embree (ed.). Evanston, Ill.: Northwestern University Press, 1972, 469-488.

1423 Martínez Bonati, Félix. *La concepción del lenguaje en la filosofía de Husserl* (Serie negra, 6). Santiago (Chile): Ediciones de los Anales de la Universidad de Chile, 1960, 98 p.

1424 Merleau-Ponty, Maurice. "Sur la phénoménologie du language," in *Problèmes actuels de la phénoménologie.* Paris: Desclée de Brouwer, 1951, 89-110. Reprinted in his *Signes.* Paris: Gallimard, 1959. Richard C. McCleary (English trans.), *Signs.* Evanston, Ill.: Northwestern University Press, 1964, 84-97.

1425 Montero Moliner, Fernando. "El análisis del lenguaje y la reducción eidetica." *Convivium,* 34, 1971, 5-22.

1426    Orth, Ernst Wolfgang. *Bedeutung, Sinn, Gegenstand*. Studien zur Sprachphilosophie Edmund Husserls und Richard Hönigswalds (Conscientia, 3). Bonn: Bouvier, 1967, xiv-269.

1427    Paci, Enzo. "Tre paragrafi per una fenomenologia del linguaggio." *Il Pensiero*, no. 2, 1960, 145-156.

1428    Parret, Herman. "Husserl and the neo-Humboldtians on language." *International Philosophical Quarterly*, vol. 12, 1972, 43-68.

1429    Parret, Herman. "Expression et articulation. Une confrontation des points de vue husserlien et saussurien concernant la langue et le discours." *Revue Philosophique de Louvain*, vol. 71, 1973, 72-112. [Résumé: 113]

1430    Parret, Herman. "Le débat de la psychologie et de la logique concernant le langage: Marty et Husserl," in *History of linguistic thought and contemporary linguistics*, Herman Parret (ed.) (Foundations of communications). Berlin-New York: Walter de Gruyter, 1976, 732-771.

1431    Pos, H. J. "Phénoménologie et linguistique." *Revue Internationale de Philosophie*, 2, 1939, 354-363.

1432    Raggio, Andrés. "Una ambigüedad en la filosofía del lenguage de Husserl." *Cuadernos de Filosofía*, vol. 8, 1968, 21-26.

1433    Reeder, Harry P. "Public and private aspects of language in Husserl and Wittgenstein." Ph.D. Dissertation, University of Waterloo (Canada), 1977. *Dissertation Abstracts*, vol. 38, no. 5, Nov. 1977, 2852-A.

1434    Ricoeur, Paul. "Husserl and Wittgenstein on language," in *Phenomenology and existentialism*, N. Lee and M. Mandelbaum (eds.). Baltimore: The Johns Hopkins University Press, 1967, 207-217.

1435    Solomon, Robert. "Husserl's private language." *Southwestern Journal of Philosophy*, vol. 5, no. 3, 1974, 203-228.

1436    Stenzel, Julius. "Philosophie der Sprache," in *Handbuch der Philosophie*, vol. II, München-Berlin, 1934, vol. II, bes. 60-72.

1437    Welton, Donn. "Intentionality and language in Husserl's phenomenology." *Review of Metaphysics*, vol. 27, 1973-1974, 260-297.

LAW

1438    Boehm, Rudolf. "Zur Phänomenologie der Gemeinschaft. Edmund Husserls Grundgedanken," in *Phänomenologie, Rechtsphilosophie, Jurisprudenz, Festschrift für Gerhart Husserl* zum 75. Geburtstag. Hrsg. von Thomas Wurtenberger. Frankfurt am Main: V. Klostermann, 1969

1439    Cossio, Carlos. "La posibilidades de la lógica juridica según la lógica de Husserl." *Revista de la Facultad de Derecho y Ciencias Sociales* (Buenos Aires, vol. 6, no. 23, 1951, 201-241.

1440    Cossio, Carlos. "La norma y el imperativo en Husserl." *Revista Brasileira de Filosofia*, vol. 10, 1960, 43-90.

1441    Husserl, Gerhardt. *Rechtskraft und Rechtsgeltung*. Berlin, 1925.

1442     Husserl, Gerhardt. *Recht und Zeit.* 5 Rechtsphilosophische Essays. Frankfurt
         am Main: Klosterman, 1955, 225 p.
         **Book Reviews:**
         W. Wieland, *Philosophische Rundschau,* vol. 4, 1956, 97-104.

1443     Kaufmann, Felix. *Logik und Rechtswissenschaft.* Tübingen, 1922.

1444     *Philosophes d'aujourd'hui en présence du droit.* Sartre, Husserl, Gabriel
         Marcel, Teilhard de Chardin, Ernst Bloch, S. Reinach (*Archives de
         philosophie du droit,* 10). Paris: Sirey, 1965, viii-375.

1445     Schreier, F. *Grundbegriffe und Grundnormen des Rechts.* Leipzig-Wien 1924.

1446     Schupp, W. *Die neue Wissenschaft vom Relcht.* Eine phänomenologische
         Untersuchung. Berlin-Grunewald, 1930.

1447     Strenger, I. "Influências de Husserl no pensamento jusfilosófico brasileiro
         actua." *Revista Brasileira de Filosofia,* vol. 9, 1959, 569-576.

1448     Vierwec, Theodor. "Husserl, Hauriou und die deutsche Rechtswissenschaft."
         *Archiv für Rechts-und Sozialphilosophie* (Bern), vol. 31, 1937, 84-89.

LEBENSPHILOSOPHIE *see also:* DILTHEY
1449     Misch, Georg. *Lebensphilosophie und Phänomenologie.* Eine
         Auseinandersetzung d. Diltheyschen Richtung mit Heidegger und Husserl.
         Leipzig-Berlin, 1930 [Reprint of 1931 ed.]. Stuttgart: Teubner, 1967, x-328.
         **Book Reviews:**
         A. Kojevnikoff, *Recherches Philosophiques,* vol. 2, 1934, 470-475.
         A. Spaier, *Recherches Philosophiques,* vol. 3, 1935, 431-432.

LEBENSWELT
1450     Biemel, Walter. "Réflexions à propos des recherches husserliennes de la
         Lebenswelt." *Tijdschrift voor Filosofie,* vol. 33, 1971, 659-683.

1451     Biemel, Walter. "Reflexionen zur Lebenswelt-Thematik," in *Phänomenologie
         heute.* Festschrift für Ludwig Landgrebe (Phaenomenologica, 51). Hrsg.
         von W. Biemel. The Hague: Martinus Nijhoff, 1972, 49-77.

1452     Blumenberg, Hans. "The life-world and the concept of reality," Theodore
         Kisiel (trans.), in *The life-world and consciousness.* Essays for Aron
         Gurwitsch, Lester E. Embree (ed.). Evanston, Ill.: Northwestern University
         Press, 1972, 425-444.

1453     Bosio, Franco. "La riduzione al mondo della vita [Husserl]." *Aut Aut,* no. 75,
         1963, 16-27.

1454     Brand, Gerd. "Der Reuckgang auf das weltfahrende Leben und die
         Zeitlichkeit als seine Ur-Form. Nach unveroeffentlichten Manuskripten
         Edmund Husserls." Louvain, Dissertation [pro manuscripto]. 1950,
         viii-208.

1455     Brand, Gerd. "The structure of the life-world according to Husserl." *Man and
         World,* vol. 6, 1973, 143-162.

1456    Carr, David. "Husserl's problematic concept of the life-world." *American Philosophical Quarterly,* vol. 7, 1970, 331-339. Reprinted in *Husserl. Expositions and appraisals,* F. Elliston and P. McCormick (eds.). Notre Dame, Ind.-London: University of Notre Dame Press, 1977, 202-210.

1457    Claesges, Ulrich. "Zweideutigkeiten in Husserls Lebenswelt-Begriff," in *Perspektiven transzendentalphänomenologischer Forschung* (Phaenomenologica, 49). Hrsg. von U. Claesges and K. Held. The Hague: Martinus Nijhoff, 1972, 85-101.

1458    de Boer, Jesse. "Comments on Professor Wild's paper [*see:* 1492]," in *Phenomenolgy pure and applied,* Erwin Strauss (ed.). Pittsburgh, Pa.: Duquesne University Press, 1964, 28-35.

1459    Declève, Henri. "La Lebenswelt selon Husserl." *Laval Théologique et Philosophique,* vol. 27, 1972, 151-161.

1460    Gadamer, Hans-Georg. "The science of the life-world." *Analecta Husserliana,* vol. 2, 1972, 173-185.

1461    Gaos, José. "La Lebenswelt de Husserl." *Revista Méxicana de Filosofía,* no. 5-6, 1963, 73-78.

1462    Gaos, José. "La Lebenswelt de Husserl," in *Symposium sobre la nación husserliana de la 'Lebenswelt'.* México: Universidad Nacional Autónoma de México, 1963, 19-24.

1463    Gurwitsch, Aron. "The life-world and the phenomenological theory of science," in his *Phenomenology and the theory of science.* Evanston, Ill.: Northwestern University Press, 1974, 3-32.

1464    Gurwitsch, Aron. "The last work of Husserl. II: The Lebenswelt." *Philosophy and Phenomenological Research,* vol. 17, 1956-1957, 370-398 [Also in *Ibid.,* vol. 16, 1955-1956, 380-399]. Reprinted in his *Studies in phenomenology an psychology.* Evanston, Ill.: Northwestern University Press, 1966, 397-448.

1465    Hermann, Friedrich-Wilhelm von. "Lebenswelt und In-der-Welt-sein. Zum Ansatz des Weltproblems bie Husserl und Heidegger," in *Weltaspekte der Philosophie.* Hrsg. von Werner Beierwalters und Wiebke Schrader. Amsterdam: Rodopi N.V., 1972, 123-141.

1466    Hohl, H. *Lebenswelt und Geschichte.* Grundzüge der Spätphilosophie Edmund Husserls. München, 1962.

1467    Janssen, Paul. "Geschichte und Lebenswelt. Ein Beitrag zur Diskussion der Husserlschen Spätphilosophie (Inaugural-Dissertation zur Erlangung des Doktorgrades der philosophischen Fakultät der Universitat Köln). Köln, 1964, 239 p. [impr. offset].

1468    Jannsen, Paul. *Geschichte und Lebenswelt.* Ein Beitrag zur Diskussion von Husserls Spätwerk (Phaenomenologica, 35). The Hague: Martinus Nijhoff, 1970, xxii-218.

1469    Kersten, Fred. "The life-world revisited." *Research in Phenomenology,* vol. 1, 1971, 33-62.

1470    Landgrebe, Ludwig. "Das Methodenproblem der transzendentalen
        Wissenschaft vom lebensweltlichen Apriori," in *Symposium sobre la nación
        husserliana de la 'Lebenswelt'.* México: UNAM, 1963, 25-49.

1471    Marx, Werner. "Lebenswelt und Lebenswelten [erschien u.d.T. *Das Problem
        der Sonderwelten bei Husserl,*" in *Gegenwart und Tradition.* Strukturen d.
        Denkens. Eine Festschrift für Bernhard Lakebrink. Hrsg. Cornelio Fabro.
        Frieburg i. Br.: Rombach, 1969], in his *Vernunft und Weit.* Zwischen
        Tradition und anderrem Anfang (Phaenomenologica, 36). The Hague:
        Martinus Nijhoff, 1970, 63-77.

1472    Marx, Werner. "Vernunft und Lebenswelt. Bermerkungen zu Husserls
        'Wissenschaft von der Lebenswelt' [repr. *Hermeneutik und Dialektik.*
        Tubingen: Verlag Mohr, 1970]," in his *Vernunft und Welt.* Zwischen
        Tradition und anderem Anfang (Phaenomenologica, 36). The Hague:
        Martinus Nijhoff, 1970, 45-62.

1473    Marx, Werner. "The life-world and its particular sub-worlds," in his *Reason
        and world.* Between tradition and another beginning. The Hague: Martinus
        Nijhoff, 1971, 62-76.

1474    Mohanty, J. N. "*Life-world* and *a priori* in Husserl's later thought." *Analecta
        Husserliana,* vol. 3, 1974, 46-65.

1475    Natanson, Maurice. "The Lebenswelt," in *Phenomenology: pure and applied,*
        Erwin W. Straus (ed.). Pittsburgh, Pa.: Duquesne University Press, 1964,
        75-93 [Discussion by John Kiuper, 93-100].

1476    Paci, Enzo. "The *Lebenswelt* as ground and as *Leib* in Husserl: somatology,
        psychology, sociology," in *Patterns of the life-world.* Essays in honor of John
        Wild, James M. Edie (ed.), et al. Evanston, Ill.: Northwestern University
        Press, 1974, 123-138.

1477    Paci, Enzo. "Die Lebensweltwissenschaft," in *Symposium sobre la noción
        husserliana de la 'Lebenswelt'.* México: UNAM, 1963, 51-75.

1478    Paci, Enzo. Il senso delle parole (Lebenswelt, Struttura)." *Aut Aut,* no. 73,
        1963, 88-94.

1479    Patocka, Jan. "La philosophie de la crise des sciences d'après Edmund
        Husserlet sa conception d'une phénoménologie du 'monde de la vie'," [text
        in French]," in *Archivum Historii Filozofii i Mysli Spolecznej.* Warszawa:
        Ossolineum, 1972, Andrej Walicki, red.

1480    Pucci, Raffaele. "Io trascendentale e mondo della vita nella fenomenologia di
        Husserl." *Rassegna di Scienze Filosofiche,* vol. 16, 1963, 67-89.

1481    Pucci, Raffaele. "Il mondo-della-vita e la storia." *Rassegna di Scienze
        Filosofiche,* vol. 16, 1963, 327-356.

1482    Quintin, Paul-André. "Le monde du vécu chez Husserl." *Dialogue,* vol. 13,
        1974, 543-559.

1483    Rovatti, Pier Aldo. "'*Geist*' e '*Lebenswelt*'nella filosofia di Husserl." *Aut Aut,*
        no. 105-106, 1968, 44-65.

1484    Schütz, Alfred. "Some structures of the life-world," in his *Collected papers III: Studies in phenomenological philosophy*. The Hague: Martinus Nijhoff 1970, 116-132.

1485    Schrag, Calvin O. "The life-world and its historical horizon," in *Patterns of the life-world*. Essays in honor of John Wild, James M. Edie (ed.), et al. Evanston, Ill.: Northwestern University Press, 1970, 107-122.

1486    Stack, George J. "Husserl. El mundo-vita y las ciencias humanísticas." *Folia Humanistica,* vol. 11, 1973, 525-537.

1487    *Symposium sobre la noción husserliana de la'Lebenswelt'.* [*see:* J. Gaos 1462, L. Landgrebe 1470, E. Paci 1477, L. Villoro 1488, J. Wild 1490]

1488    Villoro, Luis. "Presentacion," in *Symposium sobre la nación husserliana de la 'Lebenswelt'.* México: UNAM, 1963, 7-18.

1489    Veca, Salvatore. "Implicazioni filosofiche della nozione di ambiante [Husserl]." *Aut Aut,* no. 105-106, 1968, 172-182.

1490    Wild, John. "Husserl's life-world and the lived body," in *Symposium sobre la noción husserliana de la 'Lebeswelt'.* México: UNAM, 1963, 77-93.

1491    Wild, John. "Man and his life-world," in *For Roman Ingarden: Nine essays in phenomenology,* A.-T. Tymieniecka (ed.). The Hague: Martinus Nijhoff, 1959.

1492    Wild, John. "Husserl's life-world and the lived body," in *Phenomenology pure and applied,* Erwin Strauss (ed.). Pittsburgh, Pa.: Duquesne University Press, 1964, 10-28 [Commentary by Jessie de Boer, *see:* 458, 28-35; and Wild's reply, 35-42].

## LINGUISTICS

1493    Edie, James M. "Husserl's conception of *the grammatical* and contemporary linguistics," in *Life-world and consciousness,* Lester E. Embree (ed.). Evanston, Ill.: Northwestern University Press, 1972, 233-261.

1494    Pos, H. J. "Phénoménologie et linguistique." *Revue Internationale de Philosophie,* 2, 1939, 354-363.

1495    Tugendhat, E. "Phenomenology and linguistic analysis," in *Husserl. Expositions and appraisals,* F. Elliston and P. McCormick (eds.). Notre Dame, Ind.-London: Notre Dame University Press, 1977, 325-337.

## LITERATURE

1496    Magliola, Robert R. *Phenomenology and literature.* An introduction. West Lafayette, Ind.: Purdue University Press, 1977, 208 p.

LOGIC *see also* in Part VI: *Erfahrung und Urteil, Formal and Transcendental Logic* and *Logische Untersuchungen*

1497    Bachelard, Suzanne. La logique de Husserl. Etude sur *Logique formelle et logique transcendentale* (Epiméthée). Paris: Presses Universitaires de France, 1957, 316 p. *A study of Husserl's Formal and transcendental logic.* Lester E. Embree (trans.). Evanston, Ill.: Northwestern University Press, 1968, ix-230.

1498    Bachelard, Suzanne. "Logique husserlienne et sémantique," in *Vérité et vérification* (Actes du 4e Colloque international de Phénoménologie, H.-L. Van Breda, ed.) (Phaenomenologica, 61). The Hague: Martinus Nijhoff, 1974, 117-129 [Discussion: C. A. Van Peursen, P. Hountondji, J. J. Kockelmans, 129-131]

1499    Banfi, A. "La tendenza logistica della filosofia tedesca contemporanea e le *Richerche logiche* di E. Husserl." *Rivista di Filosofia,* 1923.

1500    Bosio, Franco. "La genesi della logica formale dall'esperienza antpredicativa in *Erfahrung und Urteil* di E. Husserl." *Il Pensiero,* vol. 6, 1961, 334-356.

1501    Bosio, Franco. "Psicologia e logica nella fenomenologia di Husserl." *Aut Aut,* no. 68, 1962, 131-154.

1502    Bosio, Franco. *Fondazione della logica in Husserl* (Biblioteca di filosofia e di cultura. 3). Milano: Lampugnani Nigri, 1966, 232 p.

1503    Bosio, Franco. "La lotta contro lo psicologismo e l'idea della logica pura in Husserl." *Aut Aut,* no. 71, 1962, 373-382.

1504    Casaubón, Juan A. "La lógica de Husserl (Examen crítico desde el punto de vista tomista)." *Sapientia,* vol. 14, 1959, 8-22.

1505    Danek, Jaromir. *Die Weiterentwicklung der Leibnizschen Logik bei Bolzano.* Meisenheim am Glan: Anton Hain, 1970, vii-160.

1506    Danek, Jaromir. "Kant, Husserl et l'histoire de la logique." *Dialogue,* vol. 12, 1973, 110-115.

1507    De Crescenzio, G. *Istituzioni di logica fenomenologica.* Napoli, 1960.

1508    Delbos, Victor. "Husserl. La Critique du psychologisme et sa conception d'une logique pure." *Revue de Métaphysique et de morale,* 1911. Reprinted in his *La philosophie allemande au XIXe siècle.* Paris: Alcan, 1912, Chap. 2.

1509    Eley, Lothar. "Logik und Sprache [Husserl]." *Kantstudien,* vol. 63, 1972, 247-260.

1510    Farber, Marvin. "The idea of a naturalistic logic [Husserl and Dewey]." *Philosophy and Phenomenological Research,* vol. 2, 1968-1969, 598-601.

1511    Garulli, Enrico. "Realtà e giudizio nella logica husserliana." *Studie Urbinati,* vol. 36, 1962, 282-298.

1512    Geyser, J. *Auf dem Kampffelde der Logik.* Freiburg i. Br., 1926.
        **Book Reviews:**
        W. del Negro, *Kantstudien,* vol. 34, 435-437.

003

1513    Ginsburg, E. "Zur Husserlschen Lehre von Ganzen und Teilen." *Archiv für Systematische Philosophie,* 1929.

1514    Gotesky, Rubin. "Husserl's conception of logic as *Kunstlehre* in the *Logische untersuchungen.*" *Philosophical Review,* vol. 47, 1928, 375-389.

1515    Gotesky, Rubin. "Logic as an independent science. An examination of Husserl's conception of pure logic in the 'Prolegomena zur reinen Logik (First volume of the *Logische Untersuchungen.* ) Ph.D. Dissertation, New

York University, 1939, 246 p. Ann Arbor, Mich.-London: University Microfilms International, 1977.

1516 Gurwitsch, Aron. "Présuppositions philosophiques de la logique." *Revue de Métaphysique et de Morale*, 1951, 395-405. Also in *Phénoménologie-Existence*. Recueil d'études par Henri Birault, et al. Paris: Armand Colin, 1953, 11-21. "Philosophical presuppositions of logic," in his *Studies in phenomenology and psychology*. Evanston, Ill.: Northwestern University Press, 1966, 350-358.

1517 Haddock, G. E. Rosado. "Edmund Husserls Philosophie der Logik und Mathematik im Lichte der gegenwartigen Logik und Grundlagenforschng." Ph.D. Dissertation, Bonn, 1973, 160 p. *Dissertation Abstracts, Int. European*, vol. 37, no. 1, Aut. 1976.

1518 Höfler, A. *Logik*, 2.A. Wien-Leipzig, 1922.

1519 Kalinowski, Georges. *Etudes de logique déontique*, T.II (1953-1969). Préface de R. Blanché. Paris: Librairie générale de droit et de jurisprudence, 1972, 270 p. ["La logique des normes d'Edmund Husserl (*Archives de Philosophie du Droit*, vol. 10, 1965), 111-122. "La logique des valeurs d'Edmond Husserl," (*Archives de Philosophie de Droit*, vol. 13, 1968, 267-282), 237-256.

1520 Külpe, Oswald. *Vorlesungen über Logik*. Leipzig, 1923, 139-157.

1521 Linke, Paul F. "The present state of logic and epistemology in Germany." *The Monist*, 1926.

1522 Linke, Paul F. "Logic and epistemology," in *Philosophy to-day*, E. L. Schaub (ed.). Chicago, 1928, 359-392.

1523 Lugarini, Luigi. "La fondazione trascendentale della logica in Husserl," in *Omaggio a Husserl*. Milano, 1960, 163-194.

1524 Maticevic, J. *Zur Grundlegung der Logik*. Ein Beitrag zur Bestimmung des Verhältnisses zwischen Logik und Psychologie. Wien, 1909.

1525 McCarthy, Thomas Anthony. "Husserl's phenomenology and the theory of logic." Ph.D. Dissertation, University of Notre Dame, 1968, 336 p. *Dissertation Abstracts*, vol. 29, no. 9, March 1969, 3184-A. Ann Arbor, Mich.-London: University Microfilms International, 1976, v-330.

1526 Melandri, E. *Logica ed esperienza in Husserl*. Bologna, 1960.

1527 Meyn, Henning Ludwig. "Husserl's transcendental logic and the problem of its justification." Ph.D. Dissertation, Brown University, 1971, 102 p. *Dissertation Abstracts*, vol. 32, no. 9, March 1972, 5288-A.

1528 Noël, L. "Les frontières de la logique." *Revue Néo-Scholastique de Philosophie*, vol. 17, 1910.

1529 Oesterreich, T. K. "Die reine Logik und die Phänomenologie," in Freidrich Ueberweg, *Grundriss der Geschichte der Philosophie* (12th ed.), 1923, vol. IV, 504-514.

1530 Osborn, Andrew D. *Edmund Husserl and his logical investigation*. Cambridge, Mass.: Harvard University Press, 1949, 2nd. ed.

1531    Paci, Enzo. "Per la logica di Husserl." *Aut Aut,* no. 42, 1957, 501-505.

1532    Paci, Enzo. "Per lo studio della logica in Husserl." *Aut Aut,* no. 94, 1966, 7-25.

1533    Palagyi, M. *Der Streit der Psychologisten und Formalisten in der modernen Logik.* Leipzig: Engelmann, 1902.

1534    Petruzzellis, Nicola. "Logica e fenomenologia." *Rassegna di Scienze Filosofiche,* vol. 11, 1958, 161-190.

1535    Pfänder, Alexander. *"Logik."* *Jahrbuch für Philosophie und Phänomenologische Forschung,* vol. 4, 1921, 139-494.

1536    Preti, G. "I fondamenti della logica formale nella *Wissenschaftslehre* di B. Bolzano e nella *Logische Untersuschungen* di E. Husserl." *Sophia,* vol. 3, 1935, 187-194, and 361-376.

1537    Puhakka, Kaisa - Puligandla, R. "Methods and problems in Husserl's transcendental logic." *International Logic Review,* vol. 2, 1971, 202-218.

1538    Rabaeu, Gaston. "La logique d'Edmond Husserl." *Revue des Sciences Philosophiques et Théologiques,* vol. 26, 1932, 5-24.

1539    Raggiunti, Renzo. *Husserl. Dalla logica alla fenomenologia* (Istituto di Filosofia dell'Università di Pisa). Firenze: F. Le Monnier, 1967, 328 p.

1540    Riverso, Emmanuel. "Il valore della logica en Edmondo Husserl." *Sapienza,* vol. 13, 1960, 251-256.

1541    Sancipriano, Mario. *Il logos di Husserl.* Genealogia della logica a dinamica intenzionale. Torino: Bottega d'Erasmo, 1962, 440 p.

1542    Schulz, Julius. "Ueber die Fundamente der formalen Logik." *Vierteljahrsschrift für Wissenschaftliche Philosophie,* vol. 27, 1903, 1-37.

1543    Schrimieri, G. Problemi di logica. Studio sui *Prolegomena zur reinen Logik di E. Husserl.* Con l'ausilio dei manoscritti inediti delgi Archivi Husserl di Louvain. Bari: Levante, 1959, 160 p.

1544    Scrimieri, Giorgio. *I problemi della logica.* Studio sui *Prolegomena sur reinen Logik* di E. Husserl. Alla luce dei manoscritti inediti delgi Archivi Husserl di Louvain. Bari: Tip. Levante, 1958, 124 p.

1545    Serrus, Charles. "Le conflit du logicisme et du psychologisme." *Organe officiel de la Société,* vol. 1, May 1928.

1546    Sigwart, Christian. *Logik,* 5, mit Anmerkungen von Heinrich Maier. Tübingen, 1924, vol. 1, 24ff.

1547    Sokolowski, Robert. "The logic of parts and wholes in Husserl's *Investigations.* " *Philosophy and Phenomenological Research,* vol. 28, 1967-1968, 537-553.

1548    Tragesser, Robert. *Phenomenology and logic.* Ithaca, N.Y.: Cornell University Press, 1977, 138 p.

1549    Veatch, Henry. "Formalism and/or intentionality in logic." *Philosophy and Phenomenological Research,* vol. 11, 1950-1951. [Discussion by Irving M. Copi and response by H. Veatch].

1550    Voltaggio, Franco. *Fondamenti della logica di Husserl* (Saggi di cultua contemporanea, 65). Milano: Edizioni di Comunità, 1965, 237 p.

1551    Watson, Lawrence W. "A study of the origins of formal logic in Husserl's *Formal and transcendental logic.*" Ph.D. Dissertation, De Paul University, 1973, 201 p. *Dissertation Abstracts,* vol. 34, no. 2, Aug. 1973, 826-A.

1552    Ziehen Theodor. *Lehrbuch der Logik.* Bonn, 1920, 184ff.

LOGICAL EMPIRICISM

1553    Gutting, Gary. "Husserl and logical empiricism." *Metaphilosophy,* vol. 2, 1971, 197-226.

LOGOS

1554    Kuypers, K. "Hermeneutik und die Interpretation der Logos-Idee." *Revue Internationale de Philosophie,* vol. 29, 1975, 52-77.

1555    Tommasi, Adriano. "Logos di Husserl." *Rivista Rosminiana,* vol. 57, Oct-Dec. 1963, 282-285.

MAN *see also:* ANTHROPOLOGY, PSYCHOLOGY, SOCIAL SCIENCE

1556    Kuypers, K. "Die Wissenschaften vom Menschen und Husserls Theorie von zwei Einstellungen." *Analecta Husserliana,* vol. 1, 1971, 186-196. "The sciences of man and the theory of Husserl's two attitudes." *Analecta Husserliana,* vol. 2, 1972, 186-196.

1557    Merleau-Ponty, Maurice. *Les sciences de l'homme et la phénoménologie.* Introduction et lre partie: Le problème des sciences de l'homme selon Husserl (Les Cours de Sorbonne). Paris: Tournier et Constans, 1953, 56 p. "Phenomenology and the sciences of man," John Wild (trans.), in his *The primacy of perception. With an introduction by James M. Edie (ed.). Evanston, Ill.: Northwestern University Press, 1964, 43-95.*

1558    Metzger, Arnold. "Die Frage nach dem Menschen in der Philosophie unserer Zeit von Husserl bis Heidegger und Sartre." *Universitas,* vol. 27, no. 1, Jan. 1972, 65-77. "The question of man in the philosophy of our time from Husserl to Heidegger and Sartre." *Universitas,* vol. 14, no. 4, 1972, 339-351.

1559    Paci, Enzo. "Il significato dell'uomo in Marx e in Husserl." *Aut Aut,* no. 73, 1963, 10-21.

1560    Paci, Enzo. *Funzione delle scienze e significato dell'uomo.* Milano: Il Saggiatore, 1963. *The function of the sciences and the meaning of man.* With an introduction by P. Piccone and J. E. Hansen (trans.). Evanston, Ill.: Northwestern University Press, 1972, xxxv-475.

1561    Salvucci, P. *Prospettive sull'uomo nella filosofia francese contemporanea.* Bologna, 1961.

1562    Stack, George J. "Husserl's concept of the human science." *Philosophy Today,* vol. 17, 1973, 52-61.

1563    Vircillo, Domenico. "Le scienze umane e la fenomenologia da Husserl a Merleau-Ponty." *Teoresi,* vol. 25, 1970, 235-273.

1564    Welch, E. P. "Phenomenology and the doctrine of man." *Journal of Liberal Religion,* vol. 1, no. 1, 1939.

## MARXISM see also: K. MARX, LENIN

1564 Caruso, Paolo. "Marxismo e fenomenologia." *Aut Aut,* no. 71, 1962, 369-372.

1565 Lozinski, Jerzy. "On the problems of the relation between Marxism and phenomenology: Truth and revolution - Husserl and Lenin." *Dialectics and Humanism,* vol. 3, Winter 1976, 121-133.

1566 Nemeth, T. "Husserl and Soviet Marxism." *Journal of Soviet Thought,* vol. 15, 1975, 183-196.

1567 Tran-Duc-Thao. "Marxisme et phénoménologie." *Revue Internationale,* 1946.

1568 Tran-Duc-Thao. *PhénomAenologie et Matérialisme dialectique.* Paris, 1951, 368 p.

1569 Wartofsky, M. W. "Consciousness, praxis, and reality. Marxism vs. phenomenology," in *Interdisciplinary phenomenology,* Don Ihde and Richard M. Zaner (eds.). The Hague: Martinus Nijhoff, 1977, 133-151. Also in *Husserl. Expositions and appraisals,* F. Elliston and P. McCormick (eds.). Notre Dame, Ind.-London: Notre Dame University Press, 1977, 304-313.

## MATHEMATICS

1570 Becker, Oskar. "Ueber den sogenannten Anthroplogismus in der Philosophie der Mathematik." *Philosophischer Anzeiger,* vol. 3, 1929, 369-387.

1571 Becker, Oskar. *Mathematische Existenz.* Untersuchungen zur Logik und Ontologie mathemat. Phänomene [SA, aus: *Jahrbuch für Philosophie und Phänomenologische Forschung,* vol. 8, 1927]. 2. unveränd. Aufl. Tübingen: Niemeyer, 1973, vii-369.

1572 Campbell, Robert. "Essai sur la philosophie des mathématiques selon Jean Cavaillès (II)." *Critique,* Jan. 1953, 43-66.

1573 Gagnebin, S. "La mathématique universelle d'après E. Husserl," in *Etudes de philosophie des sciences.* En hommage à Ferdinand Gonseth à l'occasion de son 60e anniversaire. NeuchÂtel: Editions du Griffon, 1950, 99-114.

1574 Granville, C. Henry, Jr. "Aspects of the influence of mathematics on contempoary philosophy." *Zeitschrift fur Philosophie und Mathematik,* vol. 3, Dec. 1966, 17-36.

1575 Gironella, Juan Roig. "Fenomenología de las formas y filosofía de las matemáticas a través del comentario de Tomás de Aquino a la metafísica." *Pensamiento,* vol. 30, July-Sept. 1974, 251-288.

1576 Haddock, G. E. Rosado. "Edmund Husserl's Philosophie der Logik und Mathematik in Lichte der gegenwartigen Logik und Grundlagenforschung." Ph.D. Dissertation, Bonn, 1973, 160 p. *Dissertation Abstracts Int. European,* vol. 37, no. 1, Aut. 1976.

1577 Kaufmann, Felix. *Das Unendliche in der Mathematik und seine Ausschaltung.* Leipzig-Wien, 1930.

1578    Kockelmans, Joseph J. "The mathematization of nature in Husserl's last publication, *Krisis.*" *Journal of the British Society for Phenomenology,* vol. 2, 1971, 45-67.

1579    Martin, Gottfried. "Neuzeit und Gegenwart in der Entwicklung des mathematischen Denkens [Husserl, Whitehead]." *Kantstudien,* vol. 45, 1953-1954, 155-165.

1580    Picker, Bernold. "Die Bedeutung der Mathematik für die Philosophie Edmund Husserls." *Philosophia Naturalis,* vol. 7, 1961-1962, 266-355.

1581    Scrimieri, Giorgio. *La matematica nel pensiero giovanile di E. Husserl.* Bari: F. Cacucci, 1965, 296 p.

1582    Winance, Eleuthere, O.S.B. "Logique, mathématique et ontologie come 'mathesis universalis' chez Edmond Husserl." *Revue Thomiste,* vol. 66, 1966, 410-434.

MEANING *see also:* FREGE, NOEMA, SIGNIFICATION

1583    Aquila, Richard E. "Husserl and Frege on meaning." *Journal of the History of Philosophy,* vol. 12, 1974, 377-383. [Review of Föllesdal and D. W. Smith *see:* 1585 and 1586]

1584    Díaz, Carlos. "La teoría de la significación en Husserl." *Anales del Seminar de Metafísica,* vol. 5, 1969, 41-57.

1585    Föllesdal, Dagfinn. "Husserl's notion of the noema." *Journal of Philosophy,* vol. 66, 1969, 680-687. Reprinted in *Phenomenology and existentialism,* Robert C. Solomon (ed.). New York: Harper & Row, 1970.

1586    McIntyre, R. and Smith, Woodruff, D. "Husserl's identification of meaning and noema." *The Monist,* vol. 59, 1975, 115-132.

1587    Mohanty, J. N. *Edmund Husserl's theory of meaning.* (Phaenomenologia, 14). The Hague: Martinus Nijhoff, 1964, xii-148, 2nd. ed. 1969.

1588    Mohanty, J. N. "On Husserl's theory of meaning." *Southwestern Journal of Philosophy,* vol. 5, no. 3, 1974, 229-244.

1589    Mohanty, J. N. "Husserl's theory of meaning," in *Husserl. Expositions and appraisals,* F. Elliston and P. McCormick (eds.). Notre Dame, Ind.-London: Notre Dame University Press, 1977, 18-37.

1590    Montero Moliner, Fernando. "La teoría de la significación en Husserl y Heidegger." *Revista de Filosofía* (Madrid), vol. 12, 1953, 393-426.

1591    Orianne, André P. "Husserl's theory of meaning. A commentary on the first *Logical investigation.*" Ph.D. Dissertation, University of California at Berkeley, 1971, 265 p.

1592    Ortega Ortiz, José M.a. "Teoría de la significación en las *Investigaciones lógicas de Husserl.*" *Convivium,* no. 37, 1972, 85-118.

1593    Perez, E. P. "La significación en la filosofía de Husserl." *Revista de la Universidad Católica del Perú,* 1942.

1594    Volkmann-Schluck, K. H. "Husserls Lehre von der Idealität der Bedeutung als metaphysisches Problem," in *Husserl et la pensée moderne*

(Phaenomenologica, 2). The Hague: Martinus Nijhoff, 1959, 230-241. "La doctrine de Husserl au sujet de l'idéalité de la signification en tant que problème métaphysique (Traduit par Jean Ladrière)," in *Ibid,*. 241-250.

1595 Welton, Donn Curtis. "The temporality of meaning. A critical study of the structure of meaning an temporality in Husserl's phenomenology." Ph.D. Dissertation, Southern Illinois University, 1973, 314 p. *Dissertation Abstracts,* vol. 34, no. 9, March 1974, 6053-A.

## MEMOIRS, REMINISCENCES, PORTRAIT, OBITUARY, IN MEMORIAM

1596 Agosti, Vittorio. "Brevi note husserliane." *Giornale di Metafisica,* vol. 22, 1967, 493-497.

1597 Aguilar, Francisco. "Edmund Husserl (1859-1959)." *Universidad* (Sante Fe), no. 41, 1959, 61-71.

1598 Ales Bello, Angela. "Husserl filosofo 'borghese'? in *Filosofia e impegno politico,* [L. Landgrebe, Intervento sulle sommunicazioni di A. Ales Bello e i G. Nardone, 284-288]," Atti del Convegno dell'Istituto italiano di fenomenologia. Milano: Editrice Massimo, 1976, 235-246.

1599 Anonymous. "Gedenkfeier für den Philosophen E. Husserl. (Universität Freiburg)." *Universitas,* vol. 14 1959, 993.

1600 Anonymous. "Ed. Husserl." *Revue de Métaphysique et de Morale,* vol. 45, no. 3, 1938, 33-34, Supp.

1601 Anonymous. "Ed. Husserl. Notice." *Rivista di Filosofia,* vol. 27, 1938, 365-369.

1602 Betancour, Cajetano. "Ed. Husserl." *Bolletín de la Universidad Catolica Bolivariana,* 1939, 418-449.

1603 Biemel, Walter. "Edmund Husserl. Persönaliche Aufzeichnungen. Herausgegeben von Walter Biemel." *Philosophy and Phenomenological Research,* vol. 16, 1955-1956, 293-302.

1604 Biermann, K.-R. "Did Husserl take his doctor's degree under Weierstrass' supervision?" *Organon* (Warszawa), no. 6, 1969, 261-264.

1605 Binswanger, Ludwig. "Dank an Edmund Husserl," in *Edmund Husserl 1859-1959* (Phaenomenologica, 4). The Hague: Martinus Nijhoff, 1959, 64-72.

1606 Bobbio, H. "Husserl postumo." *Rivista di Filosofia,* vol. 31, 1940, 37-45.

1607 Brecht, F. J. "Edmund Husserl, zum 70. Geburtstag am 8. April 1929." *Neue Jarbüher für Wissenschaft und Jugenbildung,* vol. 5, 1929, 370-373.

1608 Brecht, F. J. "Festschrift E. Husserl zum 70. Geburstag gewidmet." *Kantstudien,* vol. 36, no. 1-2.

1609 Brecht, F. J. "Edmund Husserl," in *Die grosen Deutschen. Biographien,* Hrsg. von H. Heimpel, Th. Heuss, B. Reifenberg, vol. 5, Berlin, 1957, 436-448.

1610 Cairns, Dorion. *Conversations with Husserl and Fink.* Husserl-Archives in Louvain (ed.). (Phaenomenologica, 66). The Hague: Martinus Nijhoff, 1976, xiv-114.

1611    Cairns, Dorion. "A letter from Husserl," 283-285.

1612    Cairns, Dorion. "My own life," in *Phenomenology.* Continuation and criticism. Essays in memory of Dorion Cairns (Phaenomenologica, 50). F. Kersten and R. M. Zaner (eds.). The Hague: Martinus Nijhoff, 1973, 1-13.

1613    Cairns, Dorion. "A letter to John Wild about Husserl." *Research in Phenomenology,* vol. 5, 1975, 155-181.

1614    Chestov, Leo. "A la mémoire d'un grand philosophe: Edmund Husserl." *Revue Philosophique de la France et del'Entranger,* vol. 129, 1940, 5-32. "In memory of a great philosopher: Edmund Husserl." George L. Kline (trans.). *Philosophy and Phenomenological Research,* vol. 22, 1961-1962, 449-471.

1615    Demetz, Peter. "Kafka, Freud, Husserl: Probleme einer Generation." *Zeitschrift für Religions-und Geistesgeschichte,* vol. 7, 1955, 59-69.

1616    Fink, Eugen. "Totenrede auf Edmund Husserl bei der Einäscherung am 29. April 1938." *Perspektiven Philosophie,* vol. 1, 1975, 285-286.

1617    Gibson, W. R. Boyce. "From Husserl to Heidegger. Excerpts from a 1928 Freiburg diary by W. R. Boyce Gibson," Herbert Spiegelberg (ed.). *Journal of the British Society for Phenomenology,* vol. 2, no. 1, 1971, 58-83.

1618    Groothoff, Hans Hermann. "Edmund Husserl zu Gedächtnis." *Hambger Akademische Rundschau,* vol. 3, 1950, 745-749.

1619    Husserl, Edmund. "A letter from Edmund Husserl to Aron Gurwitsch," in *Life-world and consciousness.* Essays for Aron Gurwitsch, Lester E. Embree (ed.). Evanston, Ill.: Northwestern University Press, 1972, xiv-xvi.

1620    Héring, Jean. "La phénoménologie d'Edmund Husserl il y a trente ans." *Revue Internationale de Philosophie,* no. 2, 1939, 366-373.

1621    Héring, Jean. "Edmund Husserl. Souvenirs et réflexions," in *Edmund Husserl 1859-1959* (Phaenomenologica, 4). The Hague: Martinus Nijhoff, 1959, 26-28.

1622    Hocking, William Ernest. "From the early days of the *Logische Untersuchungen,*" in *Edmund Husserl 1859-1959* (Phaenomenlogica, 4). The Hague: Martinus Nijhoff, 1959, 1-11.

1623    Ingarden, Roman. "Edmund Husserl zum 100 Geburtstag." *Zeitschrift für Philosophique Forschung,* vol. 13, 1959, 459-463.

1624    Ingarden, Roman. "Drei unveröffentlichte Briefe von Husserl an Ingarden." *Zeitschrift für Philosophische Forschung,* vol. 13, no. 2, 1959.

1625    Ingarden, Roman. "Roman Ingarden's letter to Edmund Husserl. A.-T. Tymieniecka, (ed.)." *Analecta Husserliana,* vol. 2, 1972, 357-374.

1626    Ingarden, Roman. "Erlauterungen und Erinnerungen an Husserl," in *Edmund Husserl. Briefe an Romans Ingarden.* Hrsg. von Roman Ingarden. The Hague: Martinus Nijhoff, 1968, 106-184.

1627    Ingarden, Roman. *Edmund Husserl. Briefe an Roman Ingarden.* Hrsg. von Roman Ingarden. The Hague: Martinus Nijhoff, 1968, 186 p.

1628      Ingarden, Roman. "Edith Stein on her activity as an assitant of Edmund Husserl (Extracts from the Letters of Edith Stein with a commentary and introductory remarks)," Janina Makota (English trans.). *Philosophy and Phenomenological Research,* vol. 23, 1962-1963, 155-175.

1629      Kaufmann, Fritz. "In Memoriam Edmund Husserl." *Social Research,* Feb. 1940.

1630      Kühndel, Jan. "Edmund Husserls Heimat und Herkunft." *Archiv für Geschichte der Philosophie,* vol. 51, 1969, 286-290.

1631      Landgrebe, Ludwig and Patocka, Jan. *Edmund Husserl zum Gedächtnis. Schriften des Prager philosophischen Cercles,* vol. 1, 1938, 287-321. Nachdr. d. Ausg. Prag. Academia Verlagsbuchhandlung, 1938.

1632      Löwith, Karl. "Eine Erinnerung an E. Husserl," in *Edmund Husserl 1859-1959* (Phaenomenologica, 4). The Hague: Martinus Nijhoff, 1959, 48-55.

1633      Malavasi, G. "Presencia de Edmund Husserl en Costa Rica." *Revista de Filosofía de la Universidad de Costa Rica,* vol. 3, 1962, 275-278.

1634      Oesterreicher, John M. "Edmund Husserl. Serviteur de la vérité," in *Sept philosophes juifs devant le Christ* (Collection "Foi vivante"). Paris: Editions du Cerf, 1955,93-166. "Edmund Husserl," in *Walls are crumbling.* Seven Jewish philosophers discover Christ. New York: Devin-Adair, 1952. "Edmund Husserl. De dienaar van de waarheid," in *Muren storten in.* ZevenJoodse filosofen vinden de weg naar Christus. Haarlem: Standaardboekerij, 1954, 64-113.

1635      Osborn, Andrew A. "A philosopher's philosopher." *Journal of Philosophy,* vol. 36, 1939, 234-236.

     Patocka, Jan. *see:* L. Landgrebe 1631.

1636      Patocka, Jan. "Erinnerungen an Husserl," in *Die Welt des Mesnchen. Die Welt der Philosophie.* Hrsg. von Walter Biemel (Phaenomenologica, 72). The Hague: Martinus Nijhoff, 1976, vii-xix.

1637      Plessner, Helmut. "Ad memoriam Ed. Husserl." *Gemeenschap,* vol. 14, 1938, 310.

1638      Plessner, Helmut. "Bei Husserl in Göttingen," in *Edmund Husserl 1859-1959* (Phaenomenologica, 4). The Hague: Martinus Nijhoff, 1959, 29-39.

1639      Plessner, Helmut. *Husserl in Göttingen.* Rede zur Feier d. 100. Geburtstages Edmund Husserls (Göttinger Universitatsreden. N. R. H. 24). Göttingen: Vandenhoeck & Ruprecht, 1959, 25 p.

1640      Pollnow, Hans. "Ed. Husserl." *Zeitschrift für Freie Deutsche Forschung,* vol. 1, 1939, 105-108.

1641      Pos, H. J. "In memoriam Ed. Husserl." *Algemeem Nederlands Tijdschrift voor Wijsgebeerte en Psychologie,* vol. 31, 1938, 227.

1642      Schapp, Wilhelm. "Erinnerungen an Husserl," in *Edmund Husserl 1859-1959* (Phaenomenlogica, 4). The Hague: Martinus Nijhoff, 1959, 12-25.

1643    Schuhmann, Karl. *Husserl-Chroniek.* Denk-und Lesensweg Edmund Husserls (Husserliana. Dokumente, I). The Hague: Martinus Nijhoff, 1977, xxi-516.

1644    Schütz, Alfred. "Husserl and his influence on me," in *Interdisciplinary phenomenology,* Don Ihde and Richard M. Zaner (eds.). (Selected studies in phenomenology and existential philosophy, 6). The Hague: Martinus Nijhoff, 1977, 124-129.

        Shestov, Leon. *see:* Chestov 1614.

1645    Simmel, Georg. "Simmels Brief an Paul Ernst, Adolf von Harnack, Edmund Husserl, Heinrich Rickert, an und von Rainer Maria Rilke, Auguste Rodin, Margarete Susman, Max und Marianne Weber," in *Buch des Dankes an G. Simmel.* Briefe, Erinerungen, Bibliographie. Zu seiner 100. Geburtstag. Hrsg. von K. Ganser. Berlin: Duncker & Humblot, 1958, 67-135.

1646    Somogyi, Jozsef. "Ed. Husserl (1859-1938)." *Ateneum* (Warsaw), vol. 24, 1939, 209-224.

1647    Spear, Otto. "Philosophie als Menschheitsaufgabe. Der Philosoph Edmund Husserl in der Situation unserer Zeit." *Universitas,* vol. 24, 1969, 1315-1324.

1648    Spiegelberg, Herbert. "The last portrait of Edmund Husserl by Franz and Ida Brentano," in *Philomathes.* Studies and essays in the humanities in memory of Philip Merlan, Robert B. Palmer (ed.). The Hague: Martinus Nijhoff, 1971, 341-345.

1649    Spiegelberg, Herbert. "Perspektivenwandel: Konstitution eines Husserlbildes," in *Edmund Husserl 1859-1959* (Phaenomenologica, 4). The Hague: Martinus Nijhoff, 1959, 56-63.

1650    Spiegelberg, Herbert. "Husserl in England. Facts and lessons." *Journal of the British Society for Phenomenology,* vol. 1, no. 1, 1971, 4-14 [Postscript, 15].

1651    Tatarkiewicz, V. "Réflexions chronologiques sur l'époque où a vécu Husserl," in *Husserl* (Cahiers de Royaumont, Philosophie, no. III), Paris: Editions de Minuit, 1959, 16-26 [Discussion, 27-31].

1652    Vegetti, M. "L''Ommagio a Husserl' nel centenario della nascità." *Il Pensiero Critico,* no. 3, 1960, 80-96.

1653    Versiani Velloso, Arthur. "Centenários de 1959 [Husserl, Bergson...]." *Kriterion* (Brazil), vol. 12, 1959, 499-516.

1654    Walther, Gerda. "Bei Edmund Husserl in Freiburg i. Br.," in *Zum anderen Ufer. Vom Marxismus und Atheismus zum Christentum.* Remagen: Reichl, 160, 196-220.

MEMORY

1655    Brough, J. B. "Husserl on memory." *The Monist,* vol. 59, Jan. 1975, 40-62.

METAPHILOSOPHY

1656    McCormick, Peter. "Phenomenology and metaphilosophy," in *Husserl. Expositions and appraisals,* F. Elliston and P. McCormick (eds.). Nortre Dame, Ind.-London: Univeristy of Notre Dame Press, 1977, 350-365.

## METAPHYSICS

1657 Seifert, Josef. "Üeber die Möglichkeit einer Metaphysik. Die Antwort der 'Münchener Phänomenologen' auf E. Husserls Transzendentalphilosophie," in *Der Münchener Phänomenologie*, Vorträge des internationalen Kongresses en München 13-18 Avril 1971 (Phaenomenologica, 65). The Hague: Martinus Nijhoff, 1975, 81-104.

## METHOD

1658 Murphy, Richard T. "A metaphysical critique of method. Husserl and Merleau-Ponty." *Boston College Studies in Philosophy*, vol. 1, 1966, 175-207.

1659 Winthrop, Henry. "Phenomenological method from the standpoint of the empiricist bias." *Journal of Philosophy*, vol. 46, 1949, 57-74.

1660 Van de Pitte, Margarete M. "Is there a phenomenological method?" *Metaphilosophy*, vol. 8, Jan. 1977, 21-35.

1661 Zaner, Richard M. "On the sense of method in phenomenology," in *Phenomenology and philosophical understanding*, Edo Pivcevic (ed.). Cambridge University Press, 1975, 125-142.

## MIND-BRAIN RELATION

1662 Engelhardt, H. Tristram, Jr. "Husserl and the mind-brain relation," in *Interdisciplinary phenomenology*, Don Ihde and Richard M. Zaner (eds.). The Hague: Martinus Nijhoff, 1977, 51-70.

## MOTIVATION

1663 Daghini, Giairo. "Motivazione, irreltà e el tema della praxis [Husserl]." *Aut Aut*, no. 105-106, 1968, 7-43.

1664 Nissim-Sabat, Marilyn. "Husserl's theory of motivation." Ph.D. Dissertation, De Paul University, 1977, 266 p. *Dissertation Abstracts*, vol. 37, no. 9, March 1977, 5887-A.

1665 Paci, Enzo and Rovatti, Pier Aldo. "Persona, mondo circostante, motivazione." *Aut Aut*, no. 105-106, 1968, 142-171.

1666 Paci, Enzo. "Motivazione, ragione, enciclopedia fenomenologica." *Aut Aut*, no. 105-106, 1968, 100-128.

1667 Rang, Bernhard. *Kausalität und Motivation*. Untersuchungen zum Verhältnis von Perspektivität und Objektivität in der Phänomenologie Edmund Husserls (Phaenomenologica, 53). The Hague: Martinus Nijhoff, 1973, viii-248.

## MULTIPLICITY

1668 Gauthier, Yvon. "La théorie de toutes les théories possibles est-elle possible?" *Dialogue*, vol. 14, March 1975, 81-87.

MUSIC

1669 Smith, F. Joseph. "Musical sound as a model for Husserliand intuition an time-consciousness." *Journal of Phenomenological Psychology,* vol. 4, 1973-1974, 271-296.

NATURAL ATTITUDE

1670 Cantoni, R. "Edmund Husserl e la critica dell'atteggiamento naturale." *Il Pensiero Critico,* no. 3, 1960, 1-46.

NATURE

1671 Kockelmans, Joseph K. "The mathematization of nature in Husserl's last publication, *Krisis.*" *Journal of the British Society for Phenomenology,* vol. 2, 1971, 45-67.

1672 Merleau-Ponty, Maurice. "Husserl et la notion de nature (Notes prises au cours de Maurice Merleau-Ponty) [deux leçons conjointes prononcées les 14 et 25 mars 1957, transcrites par Xavier Tilliette]." *Revue de Métaphysique et de Morale,* vol. 70, 1965, 257-269.

1673 Paci, Enzo. "Per un'interpretazione della natura materiale in Husserl." *Aut Aut,* no. 100, 1967, 47-73.

NEO-HUMBOLDTIAN

1674P arret, Herman. "Husserl and the neo-Humboldtians on language." *International Philosophical Quarterly,* vol. 12, 1972, 43-68.

NEO-KANTIANISM

1675 Stapleton, Timothy J. "Husserl and neo-Kantianism." *Auslegung,* vol. 4, Fall 1977, 81-104.

NOEMA *see also:* FREGE, INTENTIONALITY, MEANING

1676 Föllesdal, Dagfinn. "Husserl's notion of noema." [Symposium: Phenomenology]. *Journal of Philosophy,* vol. 66, 1969, 680-687. Reprinted in *Phenomenology and existentialism,* Robert C. Solomon (ed.). New York: Harper & Row, 1972, 241-250. [*see:* R. Holmes 1678]

1677 Gurwitsch, Aron. "Husserl's noesis-noema doctrine," in his *Studies in phenomenology and psychology.* Evanston, Ill.: Northwestern University Press, 1966. Also in *Phenomenology an existentialism,* Robert C. Solomon (ed.). New York: Harper & Row, 1972, 231-238.

1678 Holmes, Richard. "An explication of Husserl's theory of the noema." *Research in Phenomenology,* vol. 5, 1975, 143-155. [*see:* Föllesdal 1676]

1679 Kersten, Fred. "Husserl's doctrine of noesis-noema," in *Phenomenology. Continuation and criticism,* F. Kersten and R. M. Zaner (eds.) (Phaenomenoloica, 50). The Hague: Martinus Nijhoff, 1973, 114-144.

1680 McIntyre, Ronald T. "Husserl and referentiality. The role of the noema as an intensional entity." Ph.D. Dissertation, Stanford University, 1971, 267 p.

1681 Mohanty, J. N. "A note on the doctrine of noetic-noematic correlation." *Analecta Husserliana,* vol. 2, 1972, 317-321.

1682    Solomon, Robert C. "Husserl's concept of the noema," in *Husserl. Expositions and appraisals,* F. Elliston and P. McCormick (eds.). Notre Dame, Ind.-London: Notre Dame University Press, 1977, 168-181.

NONEMPIRICAL

1683    Meyn, Henning. "Nonempirical investigations in Husserl and ordinary language philosophy." *Southwestern Journal of Philosophy,* vol. 5, no. 3, Fall 1974, 245-259.

NORM

1684    Cossio, C. "La norma e el imperativo en Husserl." *Revista Brasileira de Filosofia,* vol. 10, 1960, 43-90.

1685    Gioja, Ambrosio Lucas. "Estructura lógica de la norma para E. Husserl." *Ideas y Valores* (Bogotá), Dec. 1951-March 1952, no. 3-4, 245-253.

1686    Kalinowski, Georges. "La logique des normes d'Edmund Husserl." *Archives de Philosophie du Droit,* vol. 10, 1965. Reprinted in his *Etudes de logique déontique,* T. II (1953-1969). Préface de R. Blanché. Paris: Librairie générale et de jurisprudence, 1972, 111-122.

NUMBER

1687    Willard, Dallas. "Concerning Husserl's view of number." *Southwestern Journal of Philosophy,* vol. 5, Fall 1974, 97-109.

OBJECT

1688    Atwell, John E. "Husserl on signification and object." *American Philosophical Quarterly,* vol. 6, 1969, 312-317.

1689    Ingarden, Roman. "Husserls Betrachtungen zur Konstitution des physikalischen Dinges." *Archives de Philosophie,* vol. 27, no. 3-4, 1964, 355-407. [Résumé en français, 407]

1690    Küng, Guido. "Husserl on pictures and intentional objects." *Review of Metaphysics,* vol. 26, 1973, 670-680.

1691    Mayz Vallenille, E. *Fenomenología del conocimiento.* El problema de la constitución del objeto en la filosofía de Husserl. Caracas, 1956.

1692    Mohanty, J. N. "The 'object' in Husserl's phenomenology." *Philosophy and Phenomenological Research,* vol. 14, 1953-1954, 343-353. Reprinted in his *Phenomenology and ontology* (Phaenomenologica, 37). The Hague: Martinus Nijhoff, 1970, 138-151.

1693    Scrimieri, Giorgio. *La formazione della fenomenologia de E. Husserl.* La ' *Dingvorlesung* del 1907. Bari: Edizioni Levante, 1967, viii-494.

1694    Theunissen, Michael. "Internationaler gegenstand und ontologische Differenz. Ansätze zur Fragestellung Heideggers in der Phänomenologie Husserl." *Philosophisches Jahrbuch,* vol. 70, 1963, 344-362. "Objeto intencional y diferencia ontológica. Inicios del planteamiento de Heidegger en la fenomenología de Husserl (Traducción de Ramón Castilla Lázaro). *Diálogos,* vol. 1, no. 2, 1964, 35-59.

OBJECTIVITY

1695   Rang, Bernhard. *Kausalität und Motivation.* Untersuchungen zum Verhältnis von Perspektivität und Objectivität in der Phänomenologie Edmund Husserls (Phaenomenologica, 53). The Hague: Martinus Nijhoff, 1973, viii-248.

1696   Seltzer, Edward C. "The problem of objectivity. A study of objectivity reflected in a comparison of the philosophies of Cassirer, Piaget and Husserl." Ph.D. Dissertation, New School for Social Research, 1969, 196 p. *Dissertation Abstracts,* vol. 30, no. 11, May 1970, 5031-A. Ann Arbor, Mich.-London: University Microfilms Int., 1977.

ONTOLOGY

1697   Altamore, Giovanni. *Dalla fenomenologia all'ontologia.* Saggio interpretativo su Edmund Husserl (Il Pensiero moderno. S. III, 6). Padova: CEDAM, 1969, 184 p.

1698   Bergmann, Gustav. "The ontology of Edmund Husserl." *Methodos,* vol. 12, 1961, 359-392. Reprinted in his *Logic and reality.* Madison: Wisconsin University Press, 1969, 193-224.

1699   Fink, Eugen. "Das Problem der ontologischen Erfahrung," in *Actas del Primer Congresso de Filosofía,* vol. 2, 733-749. Mendoza, 1949.

1700   Fragata, Júlio. "O conceito de ontologia em Husserl." *Kriterion* (Belo Horizonte), vol. 19, no. 66, 1966-1972, 51-74.

1701   Kwant, Remy C. "Phenomenologie en ontologie," in his *Phenomenologie in wijsbegeerte.* Utrecht-Brüssel, 1950, 1-25.

1702   Landgrebe, Ludwig. "Seinsregionen und regionale Ontologien in Husserl's Phänomenologie." *Studium Generale,* vol. 9, 1956, 313-324. Reprinted in his *Den Weg der Phänomenologie.* Gütersloh: Gerd Mohn, 1963.

1703   Müller, Max. "Phänomenologie, Ontologie und Scholastik." *Tijdschrift voor Filosofie,* vol. 14, 1952, 63-86.

1704   Prezioso, Faustino Antonio. "Nuove prospettive ontologiche della fenomenologia di E. Husserl." *Rassegna di Scienze Filosofiche,* vol. 23, 1970, 22-53.

1705   Renzi, E. "Fenomenologia e ontologia." *Aut Aut,* no. 65, 1961, 473-475.

1706   Scanlon, John D. "Formal logic and formal ontology." *Research In Phenomenology,* vol. 5, 1975, 95-107.

1707   Sokolowski, Robert. "Ontological possibilities in phenomenology: The dyad and the on [Husserl]." *Review of Metaphysics,* vol. 29, 1975-1976, 691-701.

1708   Trépanier, Emmanuel. "Phénoménologie et ontologie: Husserl et Heidegger." *Laval Théologique et Philosophique,* vol. 28, 1972, 249-265.

1709   Van Peursen, Cornelis. "Die Phänomenologie Husserls und die Erneuerung der Ontologie." *Zeitschrift für Philosophische Forschung,* vol. 16, 1962, 489-501.

1710    Van Peursen, Cornelis. "Phénoménologie et ontologie," in *Recontre. Begegnung Encounter.* Contributions à une psychologie humaine dédiées au Professeur F. J. J. Buytendijk. Utrecht-Antwerpen: Het Spectrum, 1957, 308-317. "Phenomenology and ontology." *Philosophy Today,* vol. 4, 1959, 35-42.

1711    Van Peursen, Cornelis. "The importance of Husserl's phenomenology for ontology," in his *Phenomenology an reality.* Pittsburgh, Pa.: Duquesne University Press, 1972, 92-112.

## ORDINARY LANGUAGE PHILOSOPHY

1712    Meyn, Henning. "Nonempirical investigations in Husserl and ordinary language philosophy." *Southwestern Journal of Philosophy,* vol. 5, no. 3, Fall 1974, 245-259.

1713    Weinzweig, Marjorie. "Phenomenology and ordianry language philosophy." *Metaphilosophy,* vol. 8, April-June 1977, 116-146.

## OTHER *see also:* ALTER EGO, CARTESIAN MEDITATIONS

1714    Filipini, E. "Ego ed alter ego nella *Krisis* di Husserl," in *Omaggio a Husserl.* Milano, 1960, 213-230.

1715    Downes, Chauncey. "Husserl and the coherence of the other minds problems." *Philosophy and Phenomenological Research,* vol. 26, 1965-1966, 253-259.

1716    Harland, Robert. "The I and the other: A reformulation of Husserl's Fifth *Cartesian meditation.*" Ph.D. Dissertation, New School for Social Research, 1978.

1717    Kelkel, Lothar. "Le problème de l'autre dans la phénoménologie transcendentale de Husserl." *Revue de Métaphysique et de Morale,* vol. 61, 1956, 40-52.

1718    Laín Entralgo, Pedro. "El otro en la reflexión fenomenológica," in his *Teoría y realidad del otro,* vol. I, Madrid: Revista de Occidente, 1961, 156-172.

1719    Lambert, F. "Husserl's constitution of the other in the Fifth *Cartesian meditation.*" *Dialogue,* (*P. S. T.* ), vol. 17, no. 2-3, 1974-1975, 44-51.

1720    Lingis, Alphonso. "The perception of others." *Philosophical Forum* (Boston), vol. 5, Spring 1974, 460-474.

1721    Morriston, Barbara W. "Husserl and other minds." Ph.D. Dissertation, Northwestern University, 1974, 197 p. *Dissertation Abstracts,* vol. 35, no. 6, Dec. 1974, 3815-A.

1722    Sartre, Jean-Paul. *L'être et le néant* [Part 3, chap. i, IV]. Paris: Gallimard, 1943. "Husserl, Hegel, Heidegger," in *Being and nothingness.* With an introduction by Hazel Barnes (trans.). New York: Philosophical Library, Inc., 1956, 233-252.

1723    Zeltner, Herman. "Das Ich und die Andern. Husserls Beitrag zur Grundlegung der Sozialphilosophie." *Zeitschrift für Philosophische Forschung,* vol. 13, no. 2, [Husserl], 1959, 288-315.

## PERCEPTION

1724    Asemissen, Hermann Ulrich. *Strukturanalytische Probleme der Wahrenhmung in der Phänomenologie Husserls* (Kantstudien. Ergänzungshefte, 73). Koln: Kolner Universitats-Verlag, 1957, 100 p.

1725    Dreyfus, Hubert L. "Husserl's phenomenology of perception. From transcendental to existential phenomenology." Ph.D. Dissertation, Harvard University, 1964, 153 p.

1726    Dreyfus, Hubert L. *Husserl's phenomenology of perception.* Evanston, Ill.: Northwestern University Press, 1978.

1727    Drummond, John J. "Presenting and kinaesthetic sensations in Husserl's phenomenology of perception." Ph.D. Disseriation, Georgetown University, 1975, 295 p. *Dissertation Abstracts,* vol. 36, no. 9, March 1976, 6144-A.

1728    Drummond, John J. "On the nature of perceptual appearances, or is Husserl an Aristotelian?" *New Scholasticism,* vol. 52, Winter 1978, 1-22.

1729    Fabro, Cornelio. *La fenomenologia della percezione.* Brescia, 1961.

1730    Föllesdal, Dagfinn. "Husserl's theory of perception," in *Aisthesis.* Essays on the philosophy of perception. Proceedings of an International Colloquium in the philosophy of perception, Helsinki, Sept. 24-26, 1973. *Ajatus,* vol. 36, 1974, 95-105. [*see:* R. Holmes, *Research in Phenomenology,* vol. 5, 1975, 143-155.]

1731    Granel, Gérard. *Le sens du temps et de la perception chez E. Husserl* (Bibliothèque de philosophie). Paris: Gallimard, 1968, 282 p.

1732    Gurwitsch, Aron. "Beitrag zur phänomenologischen Theorie der Wahrnehmung." *Zeitschrift für Philosophische Forschung,* vol. 13, 1959, 419-437. "Contribution to the phenomenological theory of perception," in his *Studies in phenomenology and psychology.* Evanston, Ill.: Northwestern University Press, 1966, 332-349.

1733    Joseph de Sainte Marie, O.C.D. "Le présupposé transcendental dans la phénoménologie de la perception de E. Husserl." *Doctor Communis,* vol. 25, 1972, 169-211.

1734    Kates, Carol A. "Perception and temporality in Husserl's phenomenology." *Philosophy Today,* vol. 14, 1970, 89-100.

1735    Krausser, P. *Untersuchungen uber den grundsätzlichen Anspruch der Wahrnehmung, Wahr-Nehmung zu sein.* Meisenheim am Glan: Anton Hain, 1959.

1736    Linke, Paul F. *Grundfragen der Wahrnehmungslehre.* München, 1918, 129, 2 [mit e. Nachwort über Gegestandsphänomenologie und Gestalttheorie].

1737    Malhotra, M. K. "Die indische Philosophie und die Phänomenologie Husserls. Der Begriff der 'Wahrnehmung' in den beiden Denkrichtngen." *Zeitschrift für Philosophische Forschung,* vol. 19, no. 2 [Husserl], 1959, 339-346.

1738    McCluskey, Frank B. "The perceptual basis of phenomenology in Husserl and Hegel." Ph.D. Dissertation, New School for Social Research, 1978.

1739    Rang, Bernhard. "Repräsentation und Selbstgegebenheit. Die Aporie der Phänomenologie der Wahrnehmung in den Frühschriften Husserls," in *Idealismus und seine Gegenwart*. Festschrift für Werner Marx zum 65 Geburtstag. Hrsg. von U. Guzzoni, u. a. Hamburg: Felix Meiner Verlag, 1976, 378-397. Also in *Phänomenologie heute*. The Hague: Martinus Nijhoff, 1976, 105-137.

1740    Routila, Lauri. "Wahrenhmung und Interpretation." *Ajatus,* vol. 36, 1974, 125-141.

1741    Schapp, W. *Beiträge zur Phänomenologie der Wahrnehmung.* Halle, 1910.

1742    Ströker, Elisabeth. "Zur phänomenologischen Theorie der Wahrnehmung." *Ajatus,* vol. 36, 1974, 106-124.

1743    Zecchi, Stefano. "Causalità e percezione." *Aut Aut,* no. 105-106 [Husserl], 1968, 66-90.

PERSON

1744    Kumar, Frederick L. "The concept of person in Husserl's phenomenology." *Midwest Journal of Philosophy,* vol. 6, Spring 1978, 21-33.

1745    Paci, Enzo and Rovatti, Pier Aldo. "Persona, mondo circostante, motivazione [E. Husserl]." *Aut Aut,* no. 105-106, 1968, 142-171.

1746    Sinha, Dababrata. "Der Begriff der Person in der Phänomenologie Husserls." *Zeitschrift für Philosophische Forschung,* vol. 18, 1964, 597-613.

1747    Sinha, Dababrata. "'Person' in Husserl's phenomenology." *Philosophical Quarterly* (India), July, 121-129.

1748    Son, B. H. *Science and person.* A study on the idea of 'Philosophy as rigorous science' in Kant and Husserl. Assen: Van Gorcum, 1972, 188 p.

1749    Stack, George J. "Husserl's concept of person." *Idealistic Studies,* vol. 4, 1974, 267-275.

PERSPECTIVE

1750    Graumann, Carl Friedrich. *Grundlagen einer Phänomenologie und Psychologie der Perspektivität* (Phaenomenologisch-psychologische Forschungen, 2). Berlin: Walter de Gruyter, 1960, vi-194.

1751    Rang, Bernhard. *Kausalität und Motivation.* Untersuchungen zum Verhältnis von Perspektivität und Objektivität in der Phänomenologie Edmund Husserls (Phaenomenologica, 53). The Hague: Martinus Nijhoff, 1973, viii-248.

PHENOMENOLOGY *see also:* Section V and VI

1752    Banfi, Antonio. "La fenomenologia pura di E. Husserl e l'autonomia ideale della sfera teorica." *Rivista di Filosofia,* 1923, 209-223.

1753    Banfi, Antonio. "La fenomenologia pura dell'Husserl," in his *Principi di una teoria della ragione.* Firenze, 1926, 555-577.

1754    Banfi, Antonio. "La fenomenologia e il compito del pensiero contemporaneo."
        *Revue Internationale de Philosophie,* no. 2, 1939, 326-341. Reprinted in
        *Omaggio a Husserl.* Milano, 1960, 29-46.

1755    Berger, Gaston. "Les thèmes principaux de la phénoménologie de Husserl."
        *Revue de Métaphysique et de Morale,* vol. 49, 1944, 22-43.

1756    Bertoldi, Eugene F. "Phenomenology of phenomenology." *Canadian Journal
        of Philosophy,* vol. 7, 1977, 239-253.

1757    Cairns, Dorion. "Phenomenology," in *A history of philosophical systems,*
        Vergilius Fern (ed.). New York: Philosophical Library, Inc., 1950, 353-364.

1758    Elliston, Frederick. "Phenomenology reinterpreted: From Husserl to
        Heidegger." *Philosophy Today,* vol. 21, Fall 1977, 273-283.

1759    Farber, Marvin. "Phenomenology," in *Twentieth centuᵗy philosophy,* Dagobert
        Runes (ed.). New York: Philosophical Library, Inc., 1943, 343-370.

1760    Findlay, John N. "Phenomenology," in *Encyclopedia Britannica,* 1964 ed., vol.
        18, 699-702.

1761    Fulda, Hans Friedrich. "Husserls Wege zum Anfang einer transzendentalen
        Phänomenologie," in *Der Idealismun und seine Gegenwart.* Festschrift für
        Werner Marx xum 65 Gebrtstag. Hrsg. von U. Guzzoni, u.a. Hamburg:
        Felix Meiner Verlag, 1976, 147-165.

1762    Ihde, Don. *Experimental phenomenology.* An introduction (Capricorn Book).
        New York: G. P. Putnam's Sons, 177, 154 p.

1763    Larrabee, Mary Jeanne. "Static and genetic phenomenology. A study of two
        methods in Edmund Husserl." Ph.D. Dissertation, University of Toronto,
        1974.

1764    Natanson, Maurice. "Phenomenology: A viewing." *Methods,* vol. 10, 295-318.

1765    Ricoeur, Paul. "Phenomenology," Daniel J. Herman and Donald V. Morano
        (trans.). *Southwestern Journal of Philosophy,* vol. 5, 1974, 149-168.

1766    Schmitt, Richard. "Phenomenology," in *Encyclopedia of Philosophy,* vol. VI.
        New York: Macmillan, 1967, 135-151.

1767    Schütz, Alfred. "Some leading concepts of phenomenology," in *Essays in
        phenomenology,* Maurice Natanson (ed.). The Hague: Martinus Nijhoff,
        1966, 23-39.

1768    Wild, John. "On the nature and aims of phenomenology." *Philosophy and
        Phenomenological Research,* vol. 3, 1942-1943, 85-93.

PHENOMENON

1769    Kunz, Hans. "Die Verfehlung der Phänomene bei Husserl," in *Die Münchener
        Phänomenologie.* Hrsg. von Helmut Kuhn, et al. (Phaenomenologica, 65).
        The Hague: Martinus Nijhoff, 1975, 39-62.

1770    Quinton, Anthony. "The concept of a phenomenon," in *Phenomenology and
        philosophical understanding,* Edo Pivcevic (ed.). Cambridge University
        Press, 1975, 1-16.

PHILOSOPHY

1771    Buck, Wayne F. "Husserl's conception of philosophy." *Kinesis,* vol. 8, Fall 1977, 10-25.

1772    Celms, Theodor. "Wom Wesen der Philosophie," in *Philosophia perenis.* Festgabe für Josef Geyser, II. Regensburg: Habbel, 1930.

1973    Compton, John J. "Hare, Husserl and philosophic discovery." *Dialogue,* vol. 3, no. 1, 1964, 42-51.

1774    Costa, Filippo. *La filosofia come scienza rigorosa* (Saggio su Husserl). Milano: Silva, 1961, 412 p.

1775    Cruz Vélez, Danilo. "Husserl y la filosofía griega." *Idea y Valores* (Bogotá), vol. 4, no. 15-16, 1962-1963, 5-24.

1776    Diemer, Alwin. "La fenomenología y la idea de la filosofía como ciencia rigurosa." (trad: Rafael Carrilo). *Ideas y Valores* (Bogotá), vol. 4, no. 15-16, 1962-1963, 41-52.

1777    Funke, Gerhard. "Transzendentale Phänomenologie als erste Philosophie." *Studium Generale,* vol. 11, no. 9, 1958, 564-582; and *Ibid,* no. 10, 632-647.

1778    Georgoulis, K. D. "O Edmund Husserl καὶ ἡ φενομενολογικὴ φιλοσοφία." Νεα Εγτια, vol. 22, 1943, 243-247, and 434-440.

1779    Heinrich, Dieter. "Ueber die Grundlagen von Husserls Kritik der philosophischen Tradition." *Philosophische Rundschau,* vol. 6, 1958, 1-26.

1780    Kuspit, Donald B. "Hegel and Husserl on the problem of the difficulty of beginning philosophy." *Journal of the British Society for Phenomenology,* vol. 2, no. 1, 1971, 52-57.

1781    Kuypers, K. "La conception de la philosophie comme science rigoureuse et les fondements des sciences chez Husserl." *Algemeen Nederlands Tijdschrift voor Wijsbegeerte en Psychologie,* vol. 51, 158-1959, 225-233. Reprinted in *Husserl* (Cahiers de Royaumont, no. III). Paris: Editions du Seuil, 1959, 72-82 [Discussion, 83-94]. Also in his *Verspreide geschriften II.* Assen: Van Gorcum, 1968, 240-250.

1782    Kuypers, K. "De idee van filosofie als strenge wetenschap bij Husserl." *Tijdschrift voor Filosofie,* vol. 36, Dec. 1974, 673-706.

1783    Landgrebe, Ludwig. "The problem of the beginning of philosophy in Husserl's phenomenology." José Huertas-Jourda (trans.), in *Life-world and consciousness.* Essays for Aron Gurwitsch. Evanston, Ill.: Northwestern University Press, 1972, 33-54. Lester E. Embree (ed.).

1784    Landsberg, Paul. "Husserl et l'idée de la philosophie." *Revue Internationale de Philosophie,* no. 2, 1939, 317-326.

1785    Mende, Georg. "Die Geschichte der Philosophie nach den Auffassungen Edmund Husserls." *Wissenschaftliche Zeitschrift Fr.-Schiller-Universität* Jena (Ges.- u. spr. R.), vol. 13, 1964, 243-248.

1786   Marujao, Alexandre Fradique. "Husserl e la filosofia como ciência rigorosa." *Revista Portuguesa de Filosofia,* vol. 11, no. 3-4, 1955, [Actas do I Congresso Nacional de Filosofia], 80-90.

1787   Nink, C. "Vom Anfang der Philosophie." *Scholastik,* vol. 26, 1951, 177-190.

1788   McCormick, Peter. "Phenomenology and metaphilosophy," in *Husserl. Expositions and appraisals,* F. Elliston and P. McCormick (eds.). Notre Dame, Ind.-London: Notre Dame University Press, 1977, 350-365.

1789   Oiserman, T.I. "Husserl's philosophy of philosophy." *Dialectics and Humanism,* vol. 2, no. 3, 1975, 55-64.

1790   Overhold, Gary E. "Husserl and the science of philosophy." Ph.D. Dissertation, Claremont Graduate School, 1966, 272 p. *Dissertation Abstracts,* vol. 28, no. 2, Aug. 1967, 730-A.

1791   Pazanin, Ante. "Das Problem der Philosophie als strenger Wissenschaft in der Phänomenologie Edmund Husserls (Inaugural-Dissertation, zur Erlangung des Doktorgrades der Philosophischen Fakultät der Universität zu Köln). Köln, 1962, 186 p. [impr. offset]

1792   Pietersma, Henry. "Edmund Husserl's concept of philosophical clarification. Its development from 1887 to 1913." Ph.D. Dissertation, University of Toronto, 1962, 152 p.

1793   Pietersma, Henry. "Husserl's concept of philosophy." *Dialogue,* vol. 5, 1966, 425-442.

1794   Pucciarelli, Eugenio. "La idea de filosofía en Husserl." *Humanitas* (Tucumán), no. 13, 1960, 29-35.

1795   Pucciarelli, Eugenio. "Husserl y la actitud científica en filosofía." *Buenos Aires. Revista de Humanidades,* vol. 2, no. 2, 1962, 257-280.

1796   Scanlon, John D. "Husserl's conception of philosophy as a rigorous science." Ph.D. Dissertation, Tulane University, 1968, 304 p. *Dissertation Abstracts,* vol. 29, no. 5, Nov. 1968, 1573-A.

1797   Sokolowski, Robert. "Husserl's interpretation of the history of philosophy." *Franciscan Studies,* vol. 24, 1964, 261-180.

1798   Stern, Alfred. "Husserl's phenomenology an the scope of philosophy." *The Personalist,* vol. 35, 1954, 267-284.

1799   Strauss, Leo. "Philosophy as a rigorous science and political philosophy [in Hebrew]." *Iyyun,* vol. 20, 1969, 14-22, [Summary, 315].

1800   Valori, Paolo. "Il punto di partenza della filosofia in Giuseppe Zamboni ed Edmund Husserl," in *Studi sul pensiero di Giuseppe Zamboni.* Milano: Marzorati, 1957, 667-674.

1801   Valori, Paolo. *Il metodo fenomenologico e la fondazione della filosofia* (Collectio philosophica lateranensis, 2). Roma: Desclee et C., 1959, 22 p.

1802   Vancourt, R. "Deux conceptions de la philosophie: Husserl et Kierkegaard." *Mélanges des Sciences Religieuses,* vol. 1, 1944, 193-240.

## PICTURE

1803  Küng, Guido. "Husserl on pictures and intentional objects." *Review of Metaphysics,* vol. 26, 1972-1973, 670-680.

## PLATONISM

1804  Berl, H. "E. Husserl oder die Judaisierung des Platonismus." *Menorah* (Wien), vol. 10, 1932, 321-331.

1805  Findlay, John N. *Plato, the written and unwritten doctrines.* London: Routledge & Kegan Paul, 1974, 484 p.

1806  Lowit, Alexandre. "Pourquoi Husserl n'est pas platonicien." *Etudes Philosophiques,* vol. 9, 1954, 324-336.

1807  Paci, Enzo. "Sul significato del 'platonismo' di Husserl." *Acme,* vol. 10, 1957, 135-151.

1808  Souche-Dagues, D. "Le platonisme de Husserl." *Analecta Husserliana,* vol. 3, 1974, 335-360.

## POLITICAL

1809  Jung, Hwa Yol. "The hermeneutics of political ideaology and cultural change: Maoism at the sinicization of Marxism." *Cultural Hermeneutics,* vol. 3, Aug. 1975, 165-188.

1810  Kim, Hong-Woo. "Phenomenology and political philosophy. A study of the political implications of Husserl's account of the life-world." Ph.D. Dissertation, University of Georgia, 1975, 240 p. *Dissertation Abstracts,* vol. 37, no. 2, Aug. 1976, 1023-A.

1811  Strauss, Leo. "Philosophy as a rigorous science and political philosophy," [in Hebrew]. *Iyyun,* vol. 20, 1969, 14-22 [Summary, 315-314].

## POSITIVISM

1812  Sinha, Debabrata. "Phenomenology and positivism." *Philosophy and Phenomenological Research,* vol. 23, 1962-1963, 562-57.

## POSSIBILITY

1813  Baumgardt, H. Das Möglichkeitsproblem in der *Kritik der reinen Vernunft,* der modernen Phänomenologie und der Gegenstandstheorie. *Kantstudien,* Erg.-Heft 51, 1920, 64 p.

## POSTHUMOUS WRITINGS

1814  Wagner, Hans. "Kritische Bemerkungen zu Husserls Nachlass." *Philosophische Rundschau,* vol. 1, 1953-1954, 1-22. *Critical observations concerning Husserl's posthumous writings,* " in The phenomenology of Husserl, R. O. Elveton (ed. and trans.). Chicago: Quadrangle Books, 1970, 204-258.

PRAGMATISM

1815     Corello, Anthony V. "Some structural parallels in phenomenology and
         pragmatism," in *Life-world and consciousness.* Essays for Aron Gurwitsch,
         Lester E. Embree (ed.). Evanston, Ill.: Northwestern University Press, 1972,
         367-388.

PRAXIS

1816     Brand, Gerd. "Interpretation von Husserls Ansätzen zu Praxis und
         Geschichte," in his *Welt, Geschichte, Mythos.* Trier: NCO Verlag, 1977.

1817     Daghini, Giairo. "Motivazione, irrealtà e il tema della praxis." Aut Aut, no.
         105-106 [Husserl], 1968, 7-43.

1818     Desanti, Jean T. *Phénoménologie et praxis.* Paris: Editions Sociales, 1963, 149
         p.

1819     Menéndez-Urenña, Enrique. "Teoría y praxis en la fenomenología
         trascendental (E. Husserl) y en la teoría crítica (J. Habermas)."
         *Pensamiento,* vol. 31, 1975, 231-244.

1820     Shmueli, E. "Consciousness and action. Husserl and Marx on theory of
         praxis." *Analecta Husserliana,* vol. 5, 1975, 367-388.

1821     Wartofsky, M. W. "Consciousness, praxis, and reality: Marxism vs.
         phenomenology," in *Husserl. Expositions and appraisals,* F. Elliston and P.
         McCormick (eds.). Notre Dame, Ind.-London: Notre Dame University
         Press, 1977, 304-313.

PREPREDICATIVE

1822     Harrison, R. "The concept of prepredicative experience," in *Phenomenology
         and philosophical understanding,* Edo Pivcevic (ed.). Cambridge University
         Press, 1975, 93-108.

1823     Jolivet, Régis. "Le problème de l'évidence ju jugement et l'évidence
         antéprédicative d'après Husserl." *Revue de l'Université d'Ottawa,* vol. 21,
         1951, 235-253.

PREREFLEXIVE CONSCIOUSNESS

1824     Murphy, Richard T. "Phenomenology and the dialectic of pre-reflexive
         consciousness in the phenomenological theories of Husserl, Sartre, and
         Merleau-Ponty." Ph.D. Dissertation, Fordham University, 1963, 294 p.
         *Dissertation Abstracts,* vol. 24, no. 2, Aug. 1963, 779-A. Ann Arbor,
         Mich.-London: University Microfilms International, 1977.

1825     Murphy, Richard T. "Husserl and the pre-reflexive constitution." *Philosophy
         and Phenomenological Research,* vol. 26, 1965-1966, 100-105.

PRESENCE

1826     Allison, David Blair. "Derrida's critique of Husserl. The philosophy of
         presence." Ph.D. Dissertation, The Pennsylvania State University, 1974,
         201 p. *Dissertation Abstracts,* vol. 35, no. 6, Dec. 1974, 3803-A.

1827    Fuchs, Wolfgang Walter. "Phenomenology and the metaphysics of presence. An essay in the philosophy of Edmund Husserl." The Pennsylvania State University, 1971, 148 p. Dissertatin Abstracts, vol. 32, no. 9, March 1972, 5283-A.

1828    Paci, Enzo. "Sulla Presenza Comme Centro relazionale in Husserl." Aut Aut, no. 58, 1960, 236-241.

PSYCHOLOGISM

1829    Ballanti, G. "Psicologismo ed esistenzialismo." Revista di Filosofia Neo-Scolastica, vol. 43, 1951, 421-435.

1830    Bosio, Franco. "Lo lotta contro lo psicologismo e l'idea della logica pura in Husserl." Aut Aut, no. 71, 373-382.

1831    Buczynaska-Garewicz, H. "Husserl's critique of psychologism in axiology." [In Polish]. Etyka, 1975, 211-228.

1832    Delbos, Victor. "Husserl. La critique du psychologisme et sa conception d'une logique pure." Revue de Métaphysique et de Morale, 1911. Reprinted in his La philosophie alleande contemporaine. Paris: Alcan, 1912.

1833    Gaos, José. "La crítica del psychologismo en Husserl." Universidad, vol. 8, 1931, 3-26; and Ibid., vol. 9, 1932, 625-645, and 877-904.

1834    Heim, K. Psychologismus oder Antipsychologismus? Berlin, 1902.

1835    Meiland, Jack W. "Psychologism is logic. Husserl's critique." Inquiry, vol. 19, no. 3, Aut. 1976, 325-340.

1836    Moog, Willy. "Die Kritik des Psychologismus." Archiv für die Gesammte Psychologie, vol. 37, 341ff.

1837    Mortán, Günter. "Einige Bemerkungen zur Überwindung des Psychologismus durch Gottlob Frege und Edmund Husserl," in Atti XII Congresso internazionale di Filosofia, vol. XII: Storia della filosofia moderna e contemporanea. Firenze: Sansoni, 1961, 327-334.

1838    Ribeiro da Silva, Isidro. "O antipsicologismo de Husserl segundo o 1 volume das Investigaçoes lógicas." Revista Portuguesa de Filosofia, vol. 18, 1962, 278-308.

1839    Richir, Marc. "Le problème du psychologisme: quelques réflexions préliminaires." Annales de l'Institut de Philosophie, 1969, 109-137.

1840    Schuppe, Wilhelm. "Zum Psychologismus und zum Normcharakter des Logik. Eine Erganzung zum Husserls Logischen Untersuchungen," in Husserl. Hrsg. von H. Noack (Wege der Forscung, 40). Darmstadt: Wissenschaftliche Buchgesellschaft, 1975, 16-35.

PSYCHOLOGISM

1841    Serrus, Charles. "Le conflit du logicisme et du psychologisme." Etudes Philosophiques, vol. 2, no. 1, 1928, 9-18.

1842    Wagner de Reyna, Alberto. "La refutación del psicologismo por Husserl." Revista de la Universidad Católica del Perú, vol. 17, no. 1, 1944, 1-17.

1843 Wild, John. "Husserl's critique of psychologism: Its historic and contemporary relevance," in *Philosophical essays in memory of Edmund Husserl,* Marvin Farber (ed.). Cambridge, Mass.: Harvard University Press, 1940, 19-43.

1844 Willard, Dallas. "The paradox of logical psychologism: Husserl's way out." *American Philosophical Quarterly,* vol. 9, 1972, 94-100. Reprinted in *Husserl. Expositions and appraisals,* F. Elliston and P. McCormick (eds.). Notre Dame, Ind.-London: Notre Dame University Press, 1977, 10-17.

PSYCHOLOGY

1845 Allen, Jeffner. "A Husserlian phenomenology of the child." *Journal of Phenomenological Psychology,* vol. 6, 1975-1976, 164-179.

1846 Anschütz, G. *Spekulative, exakte und angewandte Psychologie.* Leipzig, 1912, 320ff.

1847 Baade, W. "Aufgaben und Begriff der 'darstellenden' Psychologie." *Zeitschrift für Psychologie,* vol. 71, 356ff.

1848 Binswanger, Ludwig. *Einführung in die Probleme der allgemeinen Psychologie.* Berlin, 1922.

1849 Binswanger, Ludwig. "On the relationship between Husserl's phenomenology and psychological insight." *Philosophy and Phenomenlogical Research,* vol. 3, 1942-1943.

1850 Bona, J. "L'interesse e la fenomenologia del sonno." *Aut Aut,* no. 64, 1961, 363-365.

1851 Borrello, O. "L'intuizione nella psicologia fenomenologica di J.-P. Sartre." *Rivista di Filosofia,* no. 2, 1962, 128-158.

1852 Bosio, Franco. "Psicologia e logica nella fenomenologia di Husserl." *Aut Aut,* no. 68, 1962, 131-154.

1853 Brück, Maria. *Ueber das Verhältnis Edmund Husserls zu Franz Brentano vornhmlich mit Rücksicht auf Brentanos Psychologie.* Würzburg: Konrad Triltsch, 1933.

1854 Buytendijk, Frederik J. J. *Theorie der menschlichen Haltung und Bewegung.* Berlin, 1956.

1855 Buytendijk, Frederik J. J. "Die Bedeutung der Phänomenologie Husserls für die Psychologie der Gegenwart," in *Husserl et la pensee moderne* (Phaenomenologica, 2). The Hague: Martinus Nijhoff, 1959, 78-98. "La signification de la phénomenénologie husserlienne pour la psychologie actuelle (Traduit par Georges Thinès)," in *Ibid.,* 98-114. "Husserl's phenomenology and its significance for contemporary psychology," *Readings in existential phenomenology,* Nathaniel Lawrence (trans.). Englewood Cliffs, N.J.: Prentice-Hall, 1967, 352-364.

1856 Campos, Milton. *O metodo fenomenologico na psicologia.* Rio de Janeiro, 1945, ix-94.

1857	Carentini, E. "La signification transcedantale de la psychologie chez E. Husserl." *Revue de Psychologie et des Sciences de l'Education* (Liège), vol. 7 1972, 471-493 [Résumé, Samenvattig, summary, 493-494].

1858	Cornelius, H. "Psychologische Principienfragen." *Zeitschrift für Psychologie,* vol. 42-43.

1859	Dorfles, G. "Fenomenologia e psichiatria." *Aut Aut,* no. 64, 1961, 368-376.

1860	Drüe, Hermann. *Edmund Husserls System der phänomenologischen Psychologie* (Phaenomenologisch-psychologische Forschungen, 4). Berlin: Walter de Gruyter, 1963, xvi-326.

1861	Foulquié, Paul and Deledalle, Gérard. *La psychologie contemporaine.* Paris: Presses Universitaires de France, 1951, 350-412.

1862	Frischeisen-Köhler, Max. "Philosophie und Psychologie." *Die Geistewissenschaften,* vol. 1, 1914, 371-373, and 400-403.

1863	Funari, E. A. "Fenomenologia e psicologia della visione." *Aut Aut,* no. 74, 1963, 95-103.

1864	Giorgi, Amedeo. *Psychology as a human science.* A phenomenologically based approach. New York: Harper & Row, 1970.

1865	Golomb, Jacob. "Psychology from the phenomenological standpoint of Husserl." *Philosophy and Phenomenological Research,* vol. 36, June 1976, 451-471.

1866	Gurwitsch, Aron. "Edmund Husserl's conception of phenomenological psychology." *Review of Metaphysics,* vol. 19, 1965-1966, 689-727. Reprinted in his *Phenomenology and the theory of science.* Evanston, Ill.: Northwestern University Press, 1974, 77-112.

1867	Gurwitsch, Aron. "The place of psychology in the system of sciences," in his *Studies in phenomenology and psychology.* Evanston, Ill.: Northwestern University Press, 1964, 56-68.

1868	Hamilton, Kenneth. "Ed. Husserl's contribution to psychology." *Journal of Philosophy,* vol. 36, 139, 225-232.

1869	Hegg, Hans. *Das Verhältnis der phänomenologislchen Lehre von Husserl zur empirischen Psychologie* (Ph.D. Dissertation, Bern, 1919). Heidelberg: Hahn, 1919, 59 p.

1870	Kockelmans, Joseph J. *De fenomenologische psychologie volgens Husserl.* Een historisch kritische studie. Tielt: Lannoo; s'-Gravenhage: Anna Paulownastraat, 73, 1964, 397 p. *Edmund Husserl's phenomenological psychology.* A historico-critical study. Bernd Jager (trans. from Dutch) and revised by the author (Duquesne studies. Psychological series, 4). Pittsburgh, Pa.: Duquesne University Press, 1967, 359 p.; Louvain: E. Nauwelaerts.

1871	Kockelmans, Joseph J. "Theoretical problems in phenomenological psychology," in *Phenomenology and the social sciences,* vol. I, Maurice Natanson (ed.). Evanston, Ill.: Northwestern University Press, 1973, 225-280.

1872 Köhler, Wolfgang. "Wesen und Tatsachen." *Forschung und Fortschritte.* Nachrichtenblatt der Deutschen Wissenschaft und Technik, vol. 8, no. 12.

1873 Köhler, Wolfgang. *Dynamics in psychology.* New York: Liveright, 1940.

1874 Landgrebe, Ludwig. "Das Problem der phänomenologischen Psychologie bei Husserl," in *Akten des XIV. International Kongress für Philosophie,* II. Wien: Herder, 1968, 151-163. [See Richard M. Zaner 1909].

1875 Lannoy, Christian. "Phaenomenologie, ontologie en psychologie in t' werk van Ed. Husserl." *Tijdschrift voor Filosofie,* vol. 11, 1949, 391-416.

1876 Lanteri-Laura, Georges. *La psychiatrie phénoménologique.* Fondements philosophiques (Bibliothèque de pschiatrie). Paris: Presses Universitaires de France, 1963, 208 p.

1877 Linschoten, Johannes. *Auf dem Wege zu einer phänomenologischen Psychologie.* Die Psychologie von William James. Ins Deutsche übertragen von Franz Mönks (Phänomenologisch-psychologische Forschungen, 3). Berlin: Walter de Gruyter, 1961, vii-254.

1878 Maier, H. "Logik und Psychologie," in *Festschrift für Alois Riehl.* Halle, 1914.

1879 Marini, A. "Psicologia e fenomenologia in Husserl e in Merleau-Ponty." *Aut Aut,* no. 66, 1961, 539-551.

1880 Merleau-Ponty, Maurice. *Phénoménologie de la perception.* Paris: Gallimard, 1945. Various translations.

1881 Messer, A. "Husserls Phänomenologie in ihrem Verhältnis zur Psychologie." *Archiv für die Gesammte Psychologie,* vol. 22, 1912, and vol. 32, 1914.

1882 Moog, W. *Logik, Psychologie und Psychologismus* (Wissenschaftssystematische Untersuchungen), Halle, 1919, vii-306.

1883 Müller-Freienfels, Richard. *The evolution of modern psychology.* W. Beran Wolfe (trans.). New Haven: Yale University Press, 1935.

1884 Murphy, Gardner. *An historical introduction to modern psychology.* New York: Harcourt, Brace and Co., 1932.

1885 Natorp, Paul. *Allgemeine Psychologie,* I, Tübingen, 1912, 280-290.

1885 Nudler, Oscar. "La psicología y la crisis de la ciencia según Husserl." *Cultura Universitaira* (Caracas), no. 96-97, 1967, 100-104.

1886 Paci, Enzo. "Fenomenologia, psicologia e unita delle scienze [Husserl]." *Aut Aut,* no. 63, 1961, 214-234.

1887 Paci, Enzo. "La psicologia fenomenologica e la fondazione della psicologia come scienza [Husserl]." *Aut Aut,* no. 74, 1963, 7-19.

1888 Paci, Enzo. "The *Lebenswelt* as ground and as *Leib* in Husserl: Somatology, psychology, sociology," in *Patterns of the life-world.* Essays in honor of John Wild, James M. Edie (eds.) et al. Evanston, Ill.: Northwestern University Press, 1973, 123-138.

1889 Pfänder, Alexander. *Einführung in die Psychologie.* Leipzig, 1920.

1890 Pucci, Raffaele. "Fenomenologia e psicologia," in *Omaggio a Husserl.* Milano: 1960, 227-262.

1891 Reyer, W. "Untersuchungen zur Phänomenologie des begrifflichen Gestaltens. Beitrage zur Grundlegung einer eidetischen Interntionalpsychologie." Ph.D. Dissertation, Hamburg, 1924.

1892 Schmid-Kowarzik, W. *Umriss einer neuen analytischen Psychologie und ihr Verhältnis zur empirischen Psychologie,* 1912, 52ff.

1893 Schmid-Kowarzik, W. *Phänomenologie und nichtempirische Psychologie.* Einführung in die neuere Psychologie. 5th ed. Osterwieck-Harz: A. W. Zickfeldt, 1931.

1894 Sjaardema, Hendrikus. "A critical examination of the concept of understanding in the psychologies of Wilhelm Dilthey, Eduard Spranger, and Karl Jaspers." Ph.D. Dissertation, University of Southern California, 1939.

1895 Spicker, Stuart F. "Shadworth Hodgson's reduction as an anticipation of Husserl's phenomenological psychology." *Journal of the British Society for Phenomenology,* vol. 2, no. 2, 1971, 57-73.

1896 Spiegelberg, Herbert. "The revelance of phenomenological philosophy for psychology," in *Phenomenology an existentialism,* N. Lee and M. Mandelbaum (eds.). Baltimore: The Johns Hopkins University Press, 1967, 219-241.

1897 Stein, Edith. "Beiträge zur philosphischen Begründung der Psychologie und der Geistewsissenschaften." *Jahrbuch für Philosophie und Phänomenologische Forschung,* vol. 5, 1922, 1-116.

1898 Strasser, Stephan. "Fenomenologieën en psychologieën." *Algemeen Nederlands Tijdschrift voor Wijsbegeerte en Psychologie,* vol. 55, 1962, 1-20.

1899 Strasser, Stephan. *Le problème de l'Âme.* Etudes sur l'objet respectif de la psychologie métaphysique et de la psychologie empirique. Traduit par J.-P. Wurtz, Louvain-Paris: Publications universitaires de Louvain; Desclée de Brouwer, 1953.

Book Reviews:

P. Ricoeur, *Esprit,* 1955, 721-726.

D. De Petter, *Tijdschrift voor Filosofie,* 1951, 686-723.

J. Dubois, *Revue des Sciences Philosophiques et Théologiques,* 1957, 459-462.

J. Dubois, *Revue de Métaphysique et de Morale,* 1956, 87-91. English trans. *The soul in metaphysical and empirical Psychology.* Pittsburgh, Pa.: Duquesne University Press, 1962.

1900 Strasser, Stephan. "Phenomenological trends in European psychology." *Philosophy and Phenomenological Research,* vol. 18, 1957-1958, 18-34.

1901 Strasser, Stephan. "Phenomenologies and psychologies." *Review of Existential Psychology and Psychiatry,* vol. v, no. 1, Winter 1965, 80-105. Reprinted in *Readings in existential phenomenology,* N. Lawrence and D. O'Connor (eds.). Englewood Cliffs, N.J.: Prentice-Hall, 1967, 331-351.

1902    Titchener, Edward B. *Systematic Psychology: Prolegomena.* New York: Macmillan, 1929, 213-218.

1903    Uhler, Kathleen J. "A clarification of Husserl's distinction between phenomenological psychology and transcendental phenomenology." Ph.D. Dissertation, Georgetown University, 1975, 163 p. *Dissertation Abstracts,* vol. 37, no. 1, June 1976, 388-A.

1904    Van den Berg, J. H. *The phenomenological approach to psychiatry:* An introduction to recent phenomenological psychopathology. Springfield, Ill.: C. C. Thomas, 1955. *Fenomenologia e psichiatria.* Trad. it. di E. Spagnol. Milano: 1960.

1905    Vircillo, Domenico. "I problemi della psicologia e l'unità del sapere in Dewey e Husserl." *Teoresi,* vol. 24, 1969, 83-105.

1906    Vuorinen, Risto. "Edmund Husserl and the quest for a rigorous science of psychology." *Ajatus,* vol. 33, 1971, 64-105.

1907    Waelhens, Alphonse de. *Actes du VIIe Congrès des Sociétés* de philosophie de langue française. Paris, 1956, vol. II: Psychologie et phénoménologie, 45-100.

1908    Yee, Stevan T. "Husserl's idea of phenomenological psychology and the problem of its relation to transcendental phenomenology." The Pennsyvlania State University, 1976, 286 p. *Dissertation Abstracts,* vol. 37, no. 11, May 1977, 7169-A.

1909    Zaner, Richard M. "Critical commentary on Ludwig Landgrebe: Das Problem der phänomenologischen Psychologie bei Husserl," in *Akten des XIV. Internationalen Kongress für Philosophie,* Wien: Herder, 1968, vol. II, 227-230. [*see:* Landgrebe 1874].

REAL

1910    Gibson, R. Boyce. "The problem of the real and ideal in the phenomenology of Husserl." *Mind,* vol. 34, 1925, 311-333.

REALISM *see also:* IDEALISM

1911    Ameriks, Karl. "Husserl's realism." *Philosophical Review,* vol. 86, Oct. 1977, 498-517.

1912    Chapman, R. M. "Realism and phenomenology," in *The return to reason,* J. Wild (ed.). Chicago: Henry Regnery, 1953, 3-35.

1913    De Muralt, André. "La solution husserliene du débat entre le rélisme et l'idéalisme." *Revue Philosophique de la France et de l'Entranger,* vol. 84, no. 4, 1959, 545-552. [Edm. Husserl].

1914    Findlay, John M. "Phenomenology and the meaning of realism," in *Phenomenology and philosophical understanding,* Edo Pivcevic (ed.). Cambridge University Press, 1975, 143-158.

1915    Kockelmans, A. "Realisme-idealisme en Husserls phaenomenologie." *Tijdschrift voor Filosofie,* vol. 20, 1958, 395-441 [Survey, 441-442].

1916    Ingarden, Roman. "Bermerkungen zum Problem 'Idealismus-Realismus'."
        *Jahrbuch für Philosophie und Phänomenologische Forschung,* 1929
        (Ergänzungsband, Edmund Husserl zum 70. Geburtstag gewidmet),
        159-190.

1917    Llambías de Azevedo, Juan. "La contribución del idealismo fenomenológico
        a la restauración del realismo [Husserl]." *Cuadernos Uruguayos de Filosofía,*
        vol. 1, 1961, 23-43.

1918    Merlan, Philip. "Idéalisme, réalisme, phénoménologie," in *Husserl* (Cahiers
        de Royaumont, no. III). Paris: Editions de Minuit, 1959, 382-410.

1919    Thyssen, Johannes. "Zur Neubegründung des Realismus in
        Auseinandersetzung mit Husserl." *Zeitschrift für Philosophische Forschung,*
        vol. 7, 1953, 145-170, and 368-385.

1920    Tymieniecka, Anna-Teresa. "Beyond Ingarden's idealism/realism controversy
        with Husserl. The new contextual phase of phenomenology." *Analecta
        Husserliana,* vol. 4, 1976, 241-418.

1921    Van Riet, Georges. "Réalisme thomiste et phénoménologie husserlienne,"
        *Revue Philosophique de Louvain,* vol. 55, 1957, 58-92. Reprinted in his
        *Problèmes d'épistémologie* (Bibliothèque philosophique de Louvain, 20).
        Louvain: Publications universitaires de Louvain; Paris: Nauwelaerts, 1960,
        170-206.

1922    Waelhens, Alphonse de. "Phénoménologie et réalisme." *RNP,* 1936, 497-517.

REALITY

1923    Blumemberg, Hans. "The life-world and the concept of reality," T. Kisiel
        (trans.), in *The life-world and consciousness,* Lester E. Embree (ed.).
        Evanston, Ill.: Northwestern University Press, 1972, 425-444.

1924    Garulli, Enrico. "Realita e giudizio nella logica husserliana." *Studi Urbinati,*
        vol. 36, 1962, 282-298.

1925    Sciacca, Giuseppe Maria. *Esistenzà e realtà* in Husserl. Palermo: Palumbo,
        1960, 126 p.

1926    Senn, Silvio. *La question de la réalité dans la phénoménologie de Husserl* [SA.
        aus *Studia Philosophica,* vol. 36, 1977, 159-181). Basel: Verlag für Recht
        und Gesellschaft, 1977, 159-181.

REDUCTION

1927    Aguirre, Antonio. *Genetische Phänomenologie und Reduktion.* Zur
        Letztbegründung der Wissenschaft aus der radikalen Skeptis im Denken E.
        Husserls (Phaenomenologica, 38). The Hague: Martinus Nijhoff, 1970,
        xxiv-198.

1928    Altamore, Giovanni. "La filosofia come scienza rigorosa e la riduzione
        fenomenologica." *Teoresi,* vol. 20, 1965, 157-194.

1929    Banja, John D. "Ego and reduction: A key to the development of Husserl's
        phenomenology." Ph.D. Dissertation, Fordham University, 1975, 281 p.
        *Dissertation Abstracts,* vol. 37, no. 2, Aug. 1976, 1017-A.

1930     Ballard, Edward G. "On the method of phenomenological reduction, its presuppositons," in *Life-world and consciousness.* Essays for Aron Gurwitsch, Lester E. Embree (ed.). Evanston, Ill.: Northwestern University Press, 1972, 101-124.

1931     Bednarski, Jules. "La réduction husserliene." *Revue de Métaphysique et de Morale,* vol. 62, no. 4, 1957, [Autour de la phénoménologie], 416-435.

1932     Bednarski, Jules. "Deux aspects de la réduction husserlienne: abstention et retour." *Revue de Métaphysique et de Morale,* vol. 64, 1959, 337-355 [Husserl]. "Two aspects of Husserl's reduction." *Philosophy Today,* vol. 4, 1960, 208-223.

1933     Boehm, Rudolf. "Elementare Bemerkungen über Husserls 'phänomenologische Reduktion'." *Bijdragen,* vol. 26, 1965, 193-208. "Basic reflections on Husserl's phenomenological reduction." *International Philosophical Quarterly,* vol. 5, 1965, 183-202. "Die phänomenologische Reduktion," in his *Vom Gesichtspunkt der Phänomenologie.* Husserl-Studien (Phaenomenologica, 26). The Hague: Martinus Nijhoff, 1968, 119-140.

1934     Boelaars, H. "Husserls reducties en haar signification voor 't thomisme." *Tijdschrift voor Filosofie,* vol. 6, 1944, 333-376.

1935     Bosio, Franco. "Problematica della riduzione e costituzione trascendnetale." *Aut Aut,* no. 74, 1963, 62-83.

1935     Bosio, Franco. "La riduzione al mondo della vita." *Aut Aut,* no. 75, 1963, 16-27.

1936     Bossert, Philip J. "The origins and early development of Edmund Husserl's method of phenomenological reduction." Ph.D. Dissertation, Washington University, 1973, 277 p. *Dissertation Abstracts,* vol. 34, no. 5, Nov. 1973, 2692-A.

1937     Bossert, Philip J. "The sense of 'epoche' and 'reduction' in Husserl's philosophy." *Journal of the British Society for Phenomenology,* vol. 5, 1974, 243-255. [*see:* Pettit and Spiegelberg 1954, 1959]

1938     de Fraga, Gustavo. "As duas vias da reduçao fenomenológica." *Filosofia* (Lisboa), vol. 4, 1957, 180-187.

1939     de Fraga, Gustavo. "A reduçao eidética na filosofia de Husserl." *Filosofia,* (Lisboa), vol. 5, no. 18, 1958, 75-86.

1940     De Vidovich, A. "Riduzione eidetica e riduzione trascendentale nell'analisi fenomenologica." *Aut Aut,* no. 59, 1960, 302-315.

1941     Drumond, John J. "Husserl on the ways to the performance of the reduction." *Man and World,* vol. 8, 1975, 47-69.

1942     Deveterre, Raymond. "Merelau-Ponty and the Husserlian reductions." *Philosophy Today,* vol. 17, 1973, 297-310.

1943     Fink, Eugen. "Reflexionen zu Husserls phänomenologischer Reduktion." *Tijdschrift voor Filosofie,* vol. 33, 1971, 540-558. Reprinted in his *Nähe und*

*Distanz.* Phänomenologische Vorträge und Aufsätze. Hrsg. von F.-A. Schwarz. Freiburg-München: Karl Alber Verlag, 1976.

1944    Hartmann, Klaus. "Abstraction and existence in Husserl's phenomenological reduction." *Journal of the British Society for Phenomenology,* vol. 2, no. 1, 1971, 10-18.

1945    Ingarden, Roman. "Probleme der Husserlschen Reduktion. Vorlesung gehalten an der Universität Oslo, Oktober-Novembre 1967," in *Ingardeniana. Analecta Husserliana,* vol. 4, 1976, 1-71.

1946    Kern, Iso. "Die drei Wege zur transzendental-phaenomenologischen Reduktion Edmund Husserls." *Tijdschrift voor Filosofie,* vol. 24, 1962, 303-349. *The three ways to the transcendental phenomenological reduction in the philosophy of Edmund Husserl,"* in *Husserl. Expositions and appraisals,* F. Elliston and P. McCormick (eds.). Notre Dame, Ind.-London: Notre Dame University Press, 1977, 126-149.

1947    Küng, Guido. "Phenomenological reduction as epoché and as explication." *The Monist,* vol. 59, Jan. 1975, 63-89. Reprinted in *Husserl. Expositions and appraisals,* F. Elliston and P. McCormick (eds.). Notre Dame, Ind.-London: Notre Dame University Press, 1977, 338-349.

1948    Kockelmans, Joseph J. "Phenomenologico-psychological and transcendental reductions in Husserl's *Crisis.*" *Analecta Husserliana,* vol. 2, 1972, 78-89.

1949    Macann, Christopher. "Genetic production and the transcendental reduction in Husserl." *Journal of the British Society for Phenomenology,* vol. 2, no. 1, 1971, 28-34.

1950    Montero Moliner, Fernando. "El analisis del lenguaje y la reducción eidetica." *Convivium,* 34, 1971, 5-22.

1951    O'Connor, Tony. "Ambiguity and the search for origins." *Journal of the British Society for Phenomenology,* vol. 9, May 1978, 102-110.

1952    Palermo, James. "Apodictic truth: Husserl's eidetic reduction versus induction." *Notre Dame Journal of Formal Logic,* vol. 19, Jan. 1978, 69-80.

1953    Pucci, Raffaele. "Il metodo della riduzione fenomenologica in Husserl," in *La fenomenologia.* Atti dell'XI Convegno del Centro di Studi Filosofici tra Professori Universitari-Gallarate 1955. Brescia: Morcelliana, 1956, 161-172.

1954    Pettit, Philip. "Is the reduction necessary for phenomenology: Husserl's and Pfänder's replies. A reply to Herbert Spiegelberg." *Journal of the British Society for Phenomenology,* vol. 5, 1974, 16-19. [Klaus Hartman, Comments on Spiegelberg's and Philip Pettit's papers, 45].

1955    Recktenwald, Friederike. *Die phänomenologische Reduktion bei Edmund Husserl.* München, 1929, 30 p.

1956    Russo, Rocco. "Riduzione bonaventuriano e riduzione husserliana." *Miscellenea Francescana,* vol. 75, 1975, 733-744.

1956    Schmitt, Richard. "Husserl's transcendental-phenomenological reduction."
        *Philosophy and Phenomenological Research,* vol. 20, no. 2 [Symposium
        Husserl], 1959-1960, 238-245.

1957    Seeburger, Francis F. "Heidegger and the phenomenological reduction."
        *Philosophy and Phenomenological Research,* vol. 36, 1975-1976, 212-221.

1958    Spicker, Stuart F. "Shadworth Hodgson's reduction as an anticipation of
        Husserl's phenomenological psychology." *Journal of the British Society for
        Phenomenology,* vol. 2, no. 2, 1971, 57-73.

1959    Spiegelberg, Herbert. "'Epoché' without reduction: some replies to my critics."
        *Journal of the British Society for Phenomenology,* vol. 5, 1974, 256-261. [*see:*
        Bossert and Pettit 1937, 1954]

1960    Spiegelberg, Herbert. "Is the reduction necessary for phenomenology?
        Husserl's and Pfänder's replies." *Journal of the British Society for
        Phenomenology,* vol. 5 1974, 315 [K. Hartmann, Comments on H.
        Spiegelberg's and P. Pettit's papers, 45].

1961    Tran-Du-Thao. "Les origines de la réductin phénoménologique chez Husserl."
        *Deucalion,* no. 3, 1950, 128-142.

1962    Van Breda, Herman Leo. "De transcendenteel phenomenologische reductie
        in de Husserl's 'aatste periode (1920-1938)." Dissertation, Louvain, 1941.

1963    Van Breda, Herman Leo. "Réduction et authenticité d'après Husserl." *Revue
        de Métaphysique et de Morale,* 1951, 4-5. "Reduction and authenticity," in
        *Husserl. Expositions and appraisals,* F. Elliston and P. McCormick (eds.).
        Notre Dame, Ind.-London: Notre Dame University Press, 1977, 124-125.

1964    Van Breda, Herman Leo. "La réduction phénoménologique," in *Husserl*
        (Cahiers de Royaumont, no. III). Paris: Editions de Minuit, 307-318
        [Discussion 319-333].

1965    Villoro, Luis. "La 'reducción a la inmanencia' en Husserl." *Diánois* (México),
        vol. 12, 1966, 215-235. Reprinted in his *Estudios sobre Husserl.* México:
        Universidad Nacional Autónoma de México, 1975, chap. 2. "Los
        antecedentes de la reducción fenomenológica," *Ibid.,* chap. 1.

1966    Williams, Forrest. "Doubt and phenomenological reduction: An appendix to
        the Natanson-Ames controversy." *Philosophy and Phenomenological
        Research,* vol. 18, 1957-1958, 379-381.

1967    Winthrop, Henry. "The constitution of error in the phenomenological
        reduction." *Philosophy and Phenomenological Research,* vol. 9, 1948-1949,
        741-748.

## REFLEXION

1968    Berger, Gaston. "Le progrès de al réflelxion chez Bergson et Husserl," in *Henri
        Bergson.* NeuchÂtel: Editions de la Baconnière, 1943, 257-263.

1969    Farber, Marvin. "On the meaning of radical reflection," 154-166.

1970    Grant, Nigel J. "Reflexion and totality in the philosophy of E. Husserl. A reply
        to Thomas M. Seebohm." *Journal of the British Society of Phenomenology,*
        vol. 5, 1974, 31-32. [*see:* Seebohm 1973]

1971    Hoeres, W. "Zur Dialektik der Reflexion bei Husserl." *Salzburger Jahrbuch
        für Philosophie und Psychologie,* vol. 2, 1958, 211-230.

1972    Rotenstreich, Nathan. "Reflection and philosophy." *Ratio,* vol. 17, June 1975,
        1-17.

1973    Seebohm, Thomas E. "Reflexion and totality in the philosophy of E. Husserl."
        *Journal of the British Society for Phenomenology,* vol. 5, 1974, 20-30. [*see:*
        Nigel J. Grant 1970]

1974    Vuillemin, Jules. "Le problème phénoménologique: intentionalité et
        réflexion." *Revue Philosophique de la France et de l'Etranger,* vol. 84, no.
        4 [Ed. Husserl], 1959, 463-470.

RELATIVE

1975    de Boer, Theodor. "Die Begriffe 'absolut' and 'relativ' bei Husserl." *Zeitschrift
        für Philosophische Forschung,* vol. 27, 1973, 514-533.

RELIGION *see also:* CHRISTIANITY, FAITH, GOD, THEOLOGY

1976    Bixler, J. S. "Germany's Quest for an absolute'." *Internatinal Journal of
        Ethics,* vol. 9, 1929, 589-606.

1977    Bixler, J. S. "German phenomenology and its implications for religion."
        *Journal of Philosophy,* vol. 9, 1929.

1978    Bixler, J. S. "A phenomenological approach to religious realism," in *Religious
        realism,* D. C. Macintosh (ed.) et al. New York, 1931.

1979    Duméry, Henry. *Critique et religion.* Problèmes de méthode en philosophie
        de la religion (Collection "Pensée"). Paris: Société d'Edition
        d'Enseignement Supérieur, 1957, 358 p.

1980    Heber, Johannes. "Die phänomenologische Methode in der
        Religionsphilosophie. Ein Beitrag zur Methodologie der
        Wesensbestimmung der Religion." Dissertation, Leipzig, 1929, 59 p.

1981    Héring, Jean. *Phénoménologie et philosophie religieuse.* Paris: Alcan, 1926,
        xii-148.

1982    Köpp, W. *Grundlegung zur induktiven Theologie.* Kritik, Phänomenologie und
        Methode des algemeinen und des theologischen Erkennens. Gütersloh,
        1927, 68 p.

1983    Mager, Alois. "Phänomenologie und Religionsphilosophie." *Hochland,* vol.
        20, 544-546.

1984    Mundle, W. "Recht und Möglichkeit einer phänomenologischen Betrachtung
        der Religion." *Theologische Blätter,* vol. 2, 181-186.

1985    Piana, G. "G. van der Leeuw. *Fenomenologia della religione.*" [*see:* 1988] *Il
        Pensiero,* no. 3, 1961, 104-107.

1986　　Straubinger, Heinrich. *Einführung in die Religionsphilosophie.* Freiburg i. Br.,
　　　　　1929.

1987　　Vancourt, R. *La phénoménologie et la foi.* Paris: Desclée de Brouwer, 1953.

1988　　Van der Leeuw, G. *Phänomenologie der Religion.* Tübingen, 1933, xii-669. *La
　　　　　religion dans son essence et ses manifestations.* Phénoménologie de la religion
　　　　　(traduction par Jacques Marty. Paris: Payot, 1948.

1989　　Winkler, R. "Das religiöse Urphanomen." *Preussische Jahrbücher,* vol. 83.

1990　　Winkler, R. *Phänomenologie und Religion.* Tübingen, 1921.

1991　　Winkler, R. "Husserls Programm der Phänomenologie in seiner Bedeutug für
　　　　　die systematische Theologie." *Zeitschrift für Theologie und Kirche,* 1921.

SCIENCE

1992　　Aguirre, Antonio. *Genetische Phänomenologie und Reduktion.* Zur
　　　　　Letzbegründung der Wissenschaft aus der radikalen Skepsis in Denken E.
　　　　　Husserl (Phaenomenologica, 38). The Hague: Martinus Nijhoff, 1970,
　　　　　xxix-198.

1993　　Astrada, Carlos. "En torno a la *Wissenschaftslehre* de Husserl," in his *Ensayos
　　　　　filosóficos.* Bahia Blanca, Universidad Nacional del sur, Departamento de
　　　　　Humanidades, 1963, 11-58.

1994　　Blanco, F. "La Crisi delle scienze e la fenomenologia." *Civiltà delle Macchine,*
　　　　　May-June 1961, 11-12.

1995　　Boehm, Rudolf. "Les sciences exactes et l'idéal husserlien d'un savoir
　　　　　rigoureux." *Archives de Philosophie,* vol. 27 no. 3-4, 1964, 424-438.

1996　　Dauenhauer, Bernard P. "Husserl's phenomenological justification of
　　　　　universal rigorous science." *International Philosophical Quarterly,* vol. 16,
　　　　　1976, 63-80.

1997　　De Natale, Ferrucio. "Il problema fenomenologico della scienza in Husserl
　　　　　da *Idee II* alla *Crisi."* *Filosofia,* vol. 27, 1976, 241-276.

1998　　Gurwitsch, Aron. *Phenomenology and the theory of science.* Evanston, Ill.:
　　　　　Northwestern University Press, 1974, [Part I: The Project of the
　　　　　Phenomenological Theory of Science, 1-150]

1999　　Hemmendinger, David. "Husserl's concepts of evidence and science." *The
　　　　　Monist,* vol. 59, Jan. 1975, 81-97.

2000　　Herrera, Daniel. "Crítica de Husserl a las ciencias." *Franciscanum* (Bogatá),
　　　　　vol. 6, 1964, 159-164.

2001　　Hindess, Barry. "Transcendentalism and history: The problem of history of
　　　　　philosophy and the sciences in the later philosophy of Husserl." *Economics
　　　　　and Society,* vol. 2, no. 3, Aug. 1973, 309-342.

2002　　Hyppolite, Jean. "L'idée fichtéenne de la doctrine de la science et le projet
　　　　　husserlien," in *Husserl et la pensée moderne* (Phaenomenologica, 2). The
　　　　　Hague: Martinus Nijhoff, 1959, 173-182. "Die fichtescht Idee der
　　　　　Wissenschaftslehre und der Entwurf Husserls (Uebersetz von Walter

Biemel und E. Ch. Schröder), in *Ibid.*, 182-192. "The Fichtean idea of the science of knowledge and the Husserlian project." *Auslegung*, 1-2, 1973-1975, 77-84.

2003  Kattsoff, Louis O. "The relation of science to philosophy in the light of Husserl's thought," in *Philosophical essays in memory of Edmund Husserl*, Marvin Farber (ed.). Cambridge, Mass.: Harvard University Press, 1940, 203-218.

2004  Kisiel, Theodore J. "Husserl on the history of science," in *Phenomenology and the natural sciences*. Essays and translations, Joseph J. Kockelmans and Theodore J. Kisiel (eds.). Evanston, Ill.: Northwestern University Press, 1970, 68-90.

2005  Kisiel, Theodore J. "On the dimensions of a phenomenology of science in Husserl and the young Dr. Heidegger." *Journal of the British Society for Phenomenology*, vol. 4, 1973, 217-234.

2006  Kockelmans,Joseph J. and Kisiel, Theodore J. (ed. & trans.). *Phenomenology and the natural sciences*, essays and translations. Evanston, Ill.: Northwestern University Press, 1970.

2007  Kottje, F. *Illusionen der Wissenschaft.* Stüttgart, 1931, 70-83.

2008  Nudler, Oscar. "La psicología y la crisis de la ciencia según Husserl.: *Cultura Universitaria* (Caracas), no. 96-97, 1967, 100-104.

2009  Null, Gilbert T. "The role of the perceptual world in the Husserlian theory of the sciences." *Journal of the British Society for Phenomenology*, vol. 7, Jan. 1976, 56-59.

2010  Pacchiani, Claudio. *L'idea della scienza in Husserl* (Pubblicazioni della Scuola di Perfezionamento in Filosofia dell'Università di Padova. Quaderni di Storia della filosofia, 5). Padova, CEDAM, 1973, 124 p.

2011  Paci, Enzo. *Funzione delle scienze e significato dell'uomo.* Milano: Il Saggiatore, 1963, 482 p. *The function of the sciences and the significance of man.* P. Piccone and J. Hansen (trans.). Evanston, Ill.: Northwestern University Press, 1972.

2012  Patocka, Jan. "La philosophie de la crise des sciences d'après Edmund Husserl et sa conception d'une phénoménologie du 'monde de la vie'." *Archiwum Filozofii i Mysli Spolecznej*, 1972. [Text in French]

1913  Pirella, A. "Fenomenologia e scienza (Husserl, Merleau-Ponty, Paci)." *Rendiconti* (Bologna), no. 1, 1961, 35-40.

2014  Schwartzmann, Félix. "Husserl y la ciencia moderna." *Revista de Filosofía* (Universidad de Chile), vol. 6, no. 2-3, 1959, 1-27.

2015  Semerari, G. "Scienza e filosofia nella fenomenologia della percezione." *Aut Aut*, no. 66, 1961, 481-497.

2016  Sinha, Debabrata. "The crisis of science and Husserl's phenomenology." *The Journal of the Indian Academy of Philosophy*, vol. 2, 1963, 29-38.

2017  Stack, George J. "Husserl's concept of the human science." *Philosophy Today*, vol. 17, 1973, 52-61.

2018    Ströker, Elisabeth. "Edmund Husserl's phenomenology as foundation of natural science." *Analecta Husserliana,* vol. 2, 1972, 245-257.

2019    Vajda, Mihály. *Zarójelbe telt tudomány* [Science in parenthesis]. *A husserli fenomenológia tudamányfelfogásának brátatához* [A critique of the scientific conception of Husserl's phenomenology]. Budapest: Akadémiai Kiadó, 1968, 175 p.

2020    Vircillo, Domenico. "Sulla neutralizzazione della scienze e della teologia in Husserl." *Teoresi,* vol. 25, 1970, 89-107.

2021    Wagner, Hans. "Husserl's ambiguous philosophy of Science." *Southwestern Journal of Philosophy,* vol. 5, Fall 1974, 169-185.

SECONDARY QUALITIES

2022    Witschel, Günter. "Zwei Beiträge Husserls zum Problem der sekundären Qualitäten." *Zeitschrift für Philosophische Forschung,* vol. 18, 1964, 30-49.

SELF

2023    Ames, Van Meter. "Mead and Husserl on the self." *Philosophy and Phenomenological Research,* vol. 15, 1954-1955, 320-331.

2024    Harris, Errol E. "The problem of self-constitution for idealism and phenomenology." *Idealistic Studies,* vol. 7, Jan. 1977, 1-21.

2025    Oberlander, George E. "The transcendental self in Husserl's phenomenology. Some suggested revisions." *Research in Phenomenology,* vol. 3, 1973, 45-62.

2026    Rawlinson, Mary C. "Identity and differing: Husserl's doctrine of self-constitution." Ph.D. Dissertation, Northwestern University, 1978.

2027    Silverman, Hugh J. "The self in Husserl's *Crisis.*" *Journal of the British Society for Phenomenology,* vol. 7, Jan. 1976, 24-32.

SEMIOTIC

2028    Bachelard, Suzanne. "Logique husserliene et sémantique," in *Vérité et vérification,* Herman Leo Van Breda (ed.) (Phaenomenologica, 61). The Hague: Martinus Nijhoff, 1974, 117-131.

2029    Kaufman, J. N. "Husserl et le projet d'une sémiotique phénoménologique." *Dialogue,* vol. 17, March 1978, 20-34.

SENSATION

2030    Chapman, Harmon C. *Sensations and phenomenology.* Bloomington, Ind.: Indiana University Press, 1966.

2031    Drummond, John H. "Presenting and kinaesthetic sensations in Husserl's phenomenology of Perception." Ph.D. Dissertation, Georgetown University, 1975, 295 p. *Dissertation Abstracts,* vol. 36, no. 9, March 1976, 6144-A.

2032    Larabee, Mary Jeanne. "Husserl on sensation: notes on the theory of hyle." *New Scholasticism,* vol. 47, 1973, 179-203.

2033    Levinas, Emmanuel. "Intentionalité et sensation." *Revue Internationale de Philosophie,* vol. 19, no. 71-72, 1965, 34-54.

2034    Pradines, Maurice. *Le problème de la sensation.* Paris: Les Belles-Lettres, 1928.

SIGN

2035    Derrida, Jacques. *La voix et le phénomène.* Introduction au problème du signe dans la phénoménologie de Husserl (Epiméthée). Paris: Presses Universitaires de France, 1967, xx-120. *Speech and Phenomena* and other essays on Husserl's theory of signs. With an introduction by David B. Allison (trans.). Pref. by Newton Garver. Evanston, Ill.: Northwestern University Press, 1973, xlii-166. *La voce e il fenomena.* Introduzione al problema del segno nella fenomenologia di Husserl. A cura di G. Dalmasso. Milano: Jaca Book, 1968, vii-150.

SIGNIFICATION

2036    Atwell, John E. "Husserl on signification and object." *American Philosophical Quarterly,* vol. 6, 1969, 312-317.

2037    Díaz, Carlos. "La teoría de la significación en Husserl." *Anales del Seminario de Metafísica,* 1969, 41-57.

2038    Ortega Ortiz, José M. "Teoría de la significación en las *Investigaciones lógicas* de Husserl." *Convivium,* 37, 1972 85-118.

2039    Perez, E. P. "La significación en la filosofía de Husserl." *Revista de la Universidad Católica del Perú,* 1942.

2040    Volkmann-Schluck, K. H. "Husserls Lehre von der Idealität der Bedeutung als metaphysisches Problem," in *Husserl et la pensée moderne* (Phaenomenologica, 2). The Hague: Martinus Nijhoff, 1959, 230-241. "La doctrine de Husserl au sujet de l'idéalité de al signification en tant que problème métaphsique (Traduit par Jean Ladrière)," in *Husserl et la pensée moderne,* 241-250.

SLEEP and DREAM

2041    Paci, Enzo. "Problemi di antropologia. Per un'analisi fenomenologica del sonno e del sogno." *Aut Aut,* no. 70, 1962, 275-283.

SOCIAL *see also:* SOCIETY

2042    Toulemont René. "La spécificité du social d'aprés Husserl." *Cahiers Internationaux de Sociologie,* vol. 25, 1958, 135-151.

SOCIAL SCIENCE AND PHILOSOPHY

2043    Beerling, R. F. *De transcendentale vreemdeling.* Een studie over Husserl, fenomenologie en sociale wetenschappen (Wijsgerige verkeningen). Hilversum: W. de Haan; Amsterdam: J.M.Neulenhoff, 1965, 175 p.

2044    Bubner, Rüdiger. "Responses to 'Hermeneutics and social science'." *Cultural Hermeneutics,* vol. 2, Feb. 1975, 327.

SOCIAL STRUCTURE

2045    Hartshorne, Charles. "Husserl and the social structure of immediacy," in *Philosophical essays in memory of Edmund Husserl,* Marvin Farber (ed.). Cambridge, Mass.: Harvard University Press, 1940, 219-230.

2046 Gorman, Robert A. "The phenomenological 'humanization' of social science. A critique." *British Journal of Sociology,* vol. 26, Dec. 1975, 389-403 [*Ideas* ]

2047 Kaufmann, Felix. *Methodenlehre der Sozialwissenschaften.* Wien, 1936, 331 p.

2048 Kaufmann, Felix. "Die Bedeutung der logischen Analyse für die Sozialwissenschaften," in *Actes du VIIIe Congrès international de Philosophie,* Prague, 1936, 209-216.

2049 Natanson, Maurice. "Phenomenology and the social sciences," in *Phenomenology and the social sciences,* Maurice Natanson (ed.), vol. I, 3-44. Evanston, Ill.: Northwestern University Press, 1973.

2050 Neisser, Hans P. "The phenomenological approach in social science." *Philosophy and Phenomenological Research,* vol. 20, 1959-1960, 198-212.

2051 Schütz, Alfred. *Der sinnhafte Aufbau der sozialen Welt.* Wien, 1932, viii-286.

2052 Schütz, Alfred. "Husserl's importance for the social sciences," in *Edmund Husserl 1859-1959* (Phaenomenologica, 4). The Hague: Martinus Nijhoff, 1959, 86-98.

2053 Schäutz, Alfred. *Collected Papers. I: The problem of social reality.* Introduced by Maurice Natanson (ed.), with a preface by H. L. Van Breda (Phaenomenologica, 11). The Hague: Martinus Nijhoff, 1962, xlvii-361. *El problema de la realidad social.* Trad. pro Nestor Miguez. Buenos Aires: Amorrortu, 1974, 327 p.

2054 Schütz, Alfred. "Phenomenology and the foundations of the social science," *Philosophy and Phenomenological Research,* vol. 13, June 1953. Reprinted in his *Collected Papers III.* The Hague: Martinus Nijhoff, 1970, 40-50.

2055 Strasser, Stephan. "Grundgedanken der Sozialontologie Edmund Husserls." *Zeitschrift für Philosophische Forschung,* vol. 29, 1975, 3-33.

2056 Waldenfels, Bernhard. *Das Zwischenreich des Dialogos.* Socialphilosophische Untersuchungen in Anschluss an Edmund Husserl (Phaenomenologica, 41). The Hague: Martinus Nijhoff, 1971, xiv-428.

2057 Zeltner, Hermann. "Das Ich und die Andern. Husserls Beitrag zur Grundlegung der Sozialphilosophie." *Zeitschrift für Philosophische Forschung,* vol. 13, no. 2 [Husserl], 1959, 288-315.

SOCIETY *see also:* COMUNITÀ, GEMEINSCHAFT

2058 Boehm, Rudolf. "Zur Phänomenologie der Gemeinschaft. Edmund Husserls Grundgedanken," in *Phänomenologie, Rechtsphilosophie, Jurisprudenz.* Festschrift für Gerhart Husserl zum 75. Geburtstag. Hrsg. von Thomas Wurtenberger. Frankfurt am Main: V. Klostermann, 1969.

2059 Crespi, F. "Il problema della società nella fenomenologia di Husserl." *Rivista di Sociologia* (Roma), Jan-April 1964, 77-94.

2060 Masullo, Aldo. *La communità come fondamento.* Fichte, Husserl, Sartre (Filosofia e pedagogia). Napoli: Libreria Scientifica Editrice, 1965, 468 p.

2061    Toulemont, René. "La spécificité du social d'après Husserl." *Cahiers Internaltionaux de Sociologie*, vol. 25, 1958, 135-151.

2062    Toulemont, René. *L'essence de la société selon Husserl* (Bibliothèque de philosophie contemporaine). Paris: Presses Universitaires de France, 1962, 348 p.

2063    Uygar, Nermi. "Die Phänoenologie Husserl und die 'Gemeinschaft'." *Kantstudien*, vol. 50, 1958-1959, 439-460.

## SOCIOLOGY

2064    Armstrong, E. G. "New directions in sociological theory." *British Journal of Sociology*, vol. 27, June 1976, 251-254. [Reply to R. E. Best *see:* 2065]

2065    Best, Ron E. "New directions in sociological theory? A critical note on phenomenological sociology and its antecedents." *British Journal of Sociology*, vol. 26, no. 2, June 1975, 133-135.

2066    Gummer, Gillen M. "A critical examination of phenomenological sociology." *Sociological Analysis*, vol. 3, Oct. 1972-1973, 1-15.

2067    Marini, A. "Sociologia e fenomenologia." *Aut Aut*, no. 84, 1964, 68-86.

2068    Paci, Enzo. "Per un sociologia intenzionale." *Aut Aut*, no. 71, 1962, 359-367.

2069    Renzi, E. "Sociologia e fenomenologia." *Aut Aut*, no. 68, 1962, 155-159.

## SOLIPSISM

2070    Dauenhauer, Bernard P. "A comment on Husserl and solipsism." *Modern Schoolman*, vol. 52, 1974-1975, 189-193.

2071    Strasser, Stephan. "Het vraagstuk van t' solipsism bij Ed. Husserl." *Tijdschrift voor Filosofie*, vol. 7, 1945, 3-78.

## SPACE

2072    Claesges, Ulrich. *Edmund Husserls Theorie der Raumkonstitution* (Phaenomenologica, 19). The Hague: Martinus Nijhoff, 1964, ix-148.

2073    Kersten, Frederick I. "Husserl's investigations toward a phenomenology of space." Ph.D. Dissertation, New School for Social Research, 1964, 259 p. *Dissertation Abstracts*, vol. 25, no. 10, April 1965, 5988-A.

2074    Scrimieri, G. "Introduzione allo studio della fenomenologia dello spazio di E. Husserl," in *Annali della Facoltà di Lettere e Filosofia* (Pubblicazioni dell' Università di Bari), vol. 8, 1962, 102-162.

## SPECIES

2075    Adorno, Theodor W. "Spezies und Intention." *Archiv für Philosophie*, vol. 6, no. 1-2, 1956, 14-41.

## STRUCTURALISM

2076    Cohen, Sande. "Structuralism and the writing of intellectual history." *History and Theory*, vol. 17, May 1978, 175-206.

2077    Hollenstein, Elmar. "Jakobson und Husserl. Ein Beitrag zur Genealogie des Strukturalismus." *Tijdschrift voor Filosofie*, vol. 35, 1973, 560-607.

2078    Holenstein, Elmar. "Jakobson and Husserl. A contribution to the genealogy of structuralism." *Human Context-Le Domain Humain,* vol. 7, Spring 1975, 61-83.

2079    Holenstein, Elmar. *Jakobson ou le structuralisme phénoménologique.* Paris: Seghers, 1974, 247 p.

SUBJECT

2080    Medina Angel. "Husserl on the nature of the subject." *New Scholasticism,* vol. 45, 1971, 547-572.

2081    Warnke, Camilla. "Husserl's transcendental subject." *Dialectics and Humanism,* Winter 1976, 103-109.

SUBJECTIVE

2082    Spiegelberg, Herbert. "How subjective is phenomenology?" in *Essays in phenomenology,* Maurice Natanson (ed.). The Hague: Martinus Nijhoff, 1966, 137-143.

2083    Farber, Marvin. *Naturalism and subjectivism.* (American Lectures Series, 367). (A monograph in the Bannerstone division of American Lectures in Philosophy). Springfield, Ill.: Charles C. Thomas, 1959, xvi-389.

SUBJECTIVITY

2084    Ales Bello, Angela. "Coscienza e soggettività nella fenomenologia di Husserl." *Incontri Culturali,* vol. 3, 1970, 69-78.

2085    Bosio, Franco. "Il paradosso della soggettività." *Aut Aut,* no. 76, 1963, 17-35.

2086    Lübbe, Hermann. "Die geschichtliche Bedeutung der Subjektivitätstheorie Edmund Husserls." *Neue Zeitschrift für Systematische Theologie,* vol. 2, 1960, 300-319.

2087    Pos, H.J. "Methodisch verschil tusschen Natorp en Husserl inzake de subjectiviteit." *Algemeen Nederlands Tijschrfit voor Wijsgebeerte en Psychologie,* vol. 18, 1925.

2088    Roig Gironella, Juan. "Dudas acerca de la noción de 'sujetividad transcendental'." *Giornale di Metafisica,* vol. 13, 1958, 425-438.

2089    Lauer, Quentin. "The subjectivity of objectivity," in *Edmund Husserl 1858-1959* (Phaenomenologica, 4). The Hague: Martinus Nijhoff, 1959, 167-174.

TELEOLOGY

2090    Ales Bello, Angela. "Teologia e teleologia nella fenomenologia di Husserl." *Vita Sociale,* vol. 26, 1969, 167-177.

2091    Hoyos, Guillermo. "Zum Teologiebegriff in der Phänomenologie Husserls," in *Perspektiven transzendentalphänomenologischer Forschung* (Phaenomenologica, 49). Hrsg. von U. Claesges und K. Held. The Hague: Martinus Nijhoff, 1972, 61-84.

THEOLOGY *see also:* CHRIST, GOD

2092   Ales Bello, Angela. "Teologia e teleologia nella fenomenologia di Husserl." *Vita Sociale,* vol. 26, 1969, 167-177.

2093   Farley, Edward. *Ecclesial man.* A social phenomenology of faith and reality. Philadelphia: Fortress Press, 1975. *See:* R. Williams 2094

2094   Williams, Robert. "*Ecclesial man:* A radical approach to theology through Husserl's phenomenology." *Philosophy Today,* vol. 19, 1975, 369-375. *see:* E. Farley 2093.

2095   Vircillo, Domenico. "Sulla neutralizazzione delle scienze e della teologia in Husserl." *Teoresi,* vol. 25, 1970, 89-107.

THEORY *see also:* PRAXIS

2096   Embree, Lester E. "Toward a phenomenology of theoria," in *Life-world and consciousness.* Essays for Aron Gurwitsch, Lester E. Embree (ed.). Evanston, Ill.: Northwestern University Press, 1972, 191-207.

2097   Menéndez-Ureña, Enrique. "Teoría y praxis en la fenomenología trascendental (E. Husserl) y en la teoría crítica (J. Habermas)." *Pensamiento,* vol. 31, 1975, 231-244.

THING *see:* OBJECT

THINKING

2098   Burloud, A. *La pensée d'après les recherches expérimentales* de H. J. Watt, de Messer et de Bühler. Paris: 1927.

2099   Düsing, Klaus. "Das Problem der Denkökonomie bei Husserl und Mach," in *Perspektiven transzendentalphänomenologischer Forschung* (Phaenomenologica, 49). Hrsg. von U. Claesges und K. Held. The Hague: Martinus Nijhoff, 1972, 225-254.

2100   Messer, A. *Empfindung und Denken.* Leipzig, 1908.

2101   Ortega y Gasset, José. "Notes on thinking: its creation of the world and its creation of God," in his *Concord and liberty.* New York: Norton, 1968.

2102   Port, K. "Betrachtungen zu Husserls Einteilung der Denkakte und ihrer enkenntnisstheoretischen Bedeutung." *Archiv für die Gesammte Psychologie,* vol. 63, 369-412.

2103   Schräder, Herta. "Die Theorie des denkens bei Külpe und Husserl." Dissertation, Münster i. W., 1924, 46 p.

2104   Schuwer, André. "Remarks on the idea of authentic thinking in the *Logical investigations." Research in Phenomenology,* vol. 1, 1971, 17-32.

2105   Spaier, André. *La pesée concrète.* Paris: Alcan, 1927.

THOMISM *see also:* THOMAS AQUINAS, INTENTIONALITY

2106   Anzenbacher, Arno. "Thomism and the I-Thou philosophy." *Philosophy Today,* vol. 11, Winter 1967, 238-256.

2107    Boelaars, H. "Husserls reducties en haar signification voor 't thomisme."
        *Tijschrift voor Filosofie,* vol. 6, 1944, 333-376.

2108    Breton, Stanislaus. "De conceptu intentionalitatis conscientiae justo
        thomismum et phenomenologiam Husserl." *Eunts Docete,* vol. 9, no. 1-3,
        1959, 394-418.

2109    De Muralt, André. "Adéquation et intentions secondes. Essai de confrontation
        de la phénoménologie husserlienne et de la philosophie thomiste sur le point
        du jugement." *Studia Philosophica,* vol. 20, 1960, 88-114.

2110    Orlando, P. "Verso un tomismo esistenziale." *Aquinas,* vol. 14, 1971, 381-410.

2111    Reinhardt, Kurt. "Husserl's phenomenology and thomistic philosophy." *New
        Scholasticism,* vol. 11, 1937, 320-331.

2112    Van Riet, Georges. "Réalisme thomiste et phénoménologie husserlienne."
        *Revue Philosophique de Louvain,* vol. 55, 1957, 58-92. Reprinted in his
        *Problèmes d'épistémologie* (Bibliothèque philosophique de Louvain, 20).
        Louvain: Publications universitaires de Louvain; Paris: Beatrice
        Nauwelaerts, 1960, 170-206.

TIME

2113    Abba, Boris. *Vor- und Selbstzeitigung als Versuch der Vermenschlichung in
        der Phänomenologie Husserls* (Monographien zur philosophischen
        Forschung, 104). Meisenheim am Glan: Anton Haim, 1972, 161 p.

2114    Alexander, Meena. "Inner time and a phenomenology of existence." *Indian
        Philosophical Quarterly,* vol. 2, July 1975, 319-339.

2115    Berger, Gaston. *Phénoménologie du temps et prospective.* I: La méthode
        phénoménologique. II: La situation de l'homme. III: Phénoménologie du
        temps, IV: La prospective. Avant-propos par Edouard Morot-Sir. Paris:
        Universitaires de France, 1964, viii-280.

2116    Berger, Gaston. "Approche phénoménologique u problème du temps."
        *Bulletin de la Société française de Philosophie,* 1950.

2117    Boehm, Rudolf. "Zijn en tijd in de filosofie van Husserl." *Tijdschrift voor
        Filosofie,* vol. 21, 1959, 243-275 [Zusammenfassung, 275-276].

2118    Brand, Gerd. *Welt, Ich, und Zeit.* Nach unveröffentlichten Manuskripten
        Edmund Husserls (Phaenomenologica). The Hague: Martinus Nijhoff,
        1955, xiv-147. *Mondo, io e tempo nei manoscritti inediti di Husserl.* Trad.
        it. a cura di E. Filipini. Introd. di Enzo Paci. Milano: 1960.

2119    Brocker, Walter. "Husserls Lehre von der Zeit." *Philosophia Naturalis,* vol.
        4, 1957, 374-379.

2120    Brough, John B. "A study of the logic and evolution of Edmund Husserl's
        theory of the time-consciousness, 1893-1917." Ph.D. Dissertation,
        Georgetown University, 1970, 503 p. *Dissertation Abstracts,* vol. 31, no. 5,
        Nov. 1970, 2433-A.

2121    Brough, John B. "The emergence of an absolute consciousness in Husserl's early writings on time-consciousness." *Man and World,* vol. 5, 1972, 298-326. Reprinted in *Husserl. Expositions and appraisals,* F. Elliston and P. McCormick (eds.). Notre Dame, Ind.-London: Notre Dame University Press, 1977, 83-100.

2122    Caruso, Paolo. L'io trascendentale come 'durata esplosiva'. Intenzionalità e tempo nella fenomenologia di Husserl." *Archivo di Filosofia,* no. 1, 1960, 49-72.

2123    Cost, Filippo. "Sulla evoluzione del problema del tempo in Edmund Husserl." *Filosofia,* vol. 20, 1969, 473-502.

2124    Costa, Margarita. "En torno a *La fenomenología de la conciencia inmanente del tiempo.*" *Revista de Filosofiía* (La Plata, no. 17, 1966, 31-48.

2125    Eigler, Günther. *Metaphysische voraussetzungen in Husserls Zeitanalysen* (Monographien zur philosophische Forschung, 24). Meisenheim am Glan: Anton Hain, 1961, 117 p.

2126    Eley, Lothar. "Zeitlichkeit und Protologik," in *Perspektiven transzendentalphänomenologischer Forschung* (Phaenomenologica, 49). The Hague: Martinus Nijhoff, 1972, 164-188.

2127    Fanizza, Franco. "Tempo e verità nella fenomenologia di Husserl." *Giornale Cirtico della Filosofia Italiana,* vol. 41, 405-417.

2128    Findlay, John N. "Husserl's analysis of the inner time-consciousness." *The Monist,* vol. 59, Jan. 1975, 3-20.

2129    Granel, Gérard. *Le sens du temps et de la perception chez Edmond Husserl* (Bibliothèque de Philosophie). Paris: Gallimard, 1968, 282 p.

2130    Huertas-Jourda, José. "Structures of the living present: Husserl and Proust," in *The study of time,* II: Proceedings of the second conference of the International conference for the study of time, J. T. Fraser and N. Lawrence (eds.). Berlin-New York: Springer Verlag, 1975, 163-195.

2131    Held, Klaus. *Lebendige Gegenwart.* Die Frage nach des Seinsweise des transzendentalen Ich bei Edmund Husserl, entwickelt am Faden der Zeitproblematik. The Hague: Martinus Nijhoff, 1966, 190 p.

2132    Hoy, Ronald C. "Time and the mental. An examination of Broad's and Husserl's theories of temporal consciousness." Ph.D. Dissertation, University of Pittsburgh, 1973, 215 p. *Dissertation Abstracts,* vol. 35, no. 2, Aug. 1974, 1160-A.

2133    Jacobelli Isoldi, Angela Maria. *Il tempo in Kant e suoi sviluppi in Husserl e in Heidegger.* Romas: Editrice E. de Santis, 1963, 168 p.

2134    Kouropoulos, Pétros. "Remarques sur le temps de l'homme selon Heidegger et "Husserl" (Les Cahiers du Centre d'Etudes et de Recherches marxistes). Paris: Centre d'Etudes et de Recherches marxistes, 1967, 1-33 [multigraphié]

2135    Merlan, Philip. "Time consciousness in Husserl and Heidegger." *Philosophy and Phenomenological Research,* vol. 8, 1947-1948, 23-54.

2136    Mohanty, J. N. "Notas a las lecciones de Husserl sobre la conciencia del tiempo." *Diánoia* (México), vol. 14, 1968, 82-95.

2137    Paci, Enzo. *Tempo e verità nella fenomenologia di Husserl* (Biblioteca di cultura moderna, 559). Bari: Laterza, 1961, 280 p.

2138    Paci, Enzo. *Il problema del tempo nella fenomenologia di Husserl.* Corso di filosofia teoretica. Anno accademico 1959-1960 (Università delgi studi di Milano. Facoltà di Lettere e Filosofia). Milano: La Goliardica, 1960, 232 p.

2139    Paci, Enzo. "Tempo e relazione intenzionale in Husserl." *Archivo di Filosofia,* no. 1 [Tempo e intenzionalità], 1960, 23-48.

2140    Paci, Enzo. "Tempo e riduzione." *Rivista di Filosofia,* vol. 50, 1959, 146-179.

2141    Paci, Enzo. "Teempo e dialettica in Husserl." *Il Pensiero,* vol. 4, 1959, 129-150.

2142    Picard, Yvonne. "Le temps chez Husserl et Heidegger." *Deucalion,* vol. 1, 1946, 93-124.

2143    Reiman, Jeffrey H. "Time and the epoché of Husserl." Ph.D. Dissertation, The Pennsylvania State University, 1968, 206 p. *Dissertation Abstracts,* vol. 30, no. 3, Sept. 1969, 1205-A.

2144    Sánchez Ortiz de Urbina, Ricardo. "Conciencia y temporalidad (Un análisis fenomenológico de Husserl)." *Aporía,* vol. 1, 1965, 356-374.

2145    Spicker, Stuart F. "Inner time and lived-through time: Husserl and Merleau-Ponty." *Journal of the British Society for Phenomenology,* vol. 4, 1973, 235-247.

2146    Van Peursen, Cornelis. *De tijd bij Augustinus en Husserl.* Groningen: J. B. Wolters, 1953, 20 p.

2147    Van Peursen, Cornelis. "Augustine's phenomenology of time," in *Phenomenology and reality.* Pittsburgh, Pa.: Duquesne University Press, 1972, 113-133.

2148    Van Peursen, Cornelis. "La notion du temps et de l'ego transcendental chez Husserl," in *Husserl* (Cahiers de Royaumont, no. III). Paris: Editions du Seuil, 1959, 196-207. [Discussion, 208-213]

2149    Welton, Donn C. "The temporality of meaning. A critical study of the structure of meaning and temporality in Husserl's phenomenology." Ph.D. Dissertation, Southern Illinois University, 1973, 314 p. *Dissertation Abstracts,* vol. 34, no. 9, March 1974, 6053-A.

2150    Winter, Michael F. "Lived time in Husserl and Whitehead: A comparative study." Ph.D. Dissertation, Northwestern University, 1975, 165 p. *Dissertation Abstracts,* vol. 36, no. 7, Jan. 1976, 4568-A.

TRANSCENDENCE-TRANSCENDENTAL

2151    Boehm, Rudolf. "Les ambigüities des concepts husserliens d'"immanence' et de 'transcendance'." *Revue Philosophique de la France et de l'Etranger,* vol. 84, no. 4 [Edm Husserl], 1959, 481-526. "Immanenz und Transzendenz," in his *Vom Geschitspunkt der Phänomenologie.* Husserl-Studien (Phaenomenologica, 26). The Hague: Martinus Nijhoff, 1968, 141-185.

2152 Boehm, Rudolf. "Omlijning van een nieuw begrip van transcendentaalfilosofie. Een kritiek op Husserls reductie van de fenomenologie tot een transcendentale." *Tijdschrift voor Filosofie,* vol. 34, 1972, 407-432. [Zusammenfasung: Umschreibung einer neunen Idee der Transzendentalphilosophie, 432-433]

2153 Brüning, Walther. "Der Ansatz der Transzendentalphilosophie in Husserls *Cartesianischen Meditationen.*" *Zeitschrift für Philosophische Forschung,* vol. 20, 1966, 185-196.

2154 Conrad-Martinus, Hedwig. "Die transzendentale und die ontologische Phänomenologie," in *Edmund Husserl 1859-1959* (Phaenomenologica, 4). The Hague: Martinus Nijhoff, 1959, 175-184.

2155 Edie, James M. "Transcendental phenomenology and existentialism." *Philosophy and Phenomenological Research,* vol. 25, 1964-1965, 52-63.

2156 Eley, Lothar. "Zum Begriff des Transzendentalen, eine kritische Studie zu Th. W. Adorno: *Zur Metakritik der Erkenntnistheorie. Studien über Husserl und die phänomenologischen Antinomine.*" *Zeitschrift für Philosophischen Forschung,* vol. 13, no. 3, [Husserl], 1959, 351-357.

2157 Funke, Gerhard. "Transzendentale Phänomenologie als erste Philosophie." *Studium Generale,* vol. 11, 1958, 564-582 and 632-646. "Fenomenología trascendental y 'filosofía primera'. Observaciones al 'Ensayo de una histtoria crítica de las indeas' de Husserl." (Trad. José Gaos). *Diánois* (México), vol. 5, 1959, 150-194.

2158 Ingarden, Roman. "Die vier Begriffe der Transzendenz und das Problem des Idealismus in Husserl." *Analecta Husserliana,* vol. 1, 1971, 36-74.

2159 Landgrebe, Ludwig. "La phénoménologie de Husserl est-elle une philosophie transcendentale?" *Etudes Philosophiques,* vol. 9, 1954, 315-323. "Ist Husserls Phänomenologie eine Transzendentalphilosophie?" in *Husserl.* Hrsg. von H. Noack (Wege der Forschung, 40). Darmstadt: Wissenschaftliche Buchgesellschaft, 1973, 316-324.

2160 Market, Oswaldo. "Meditaciones husserlianas. El descubrimiento del plano trascendental [resumen]." *Revista de Filosofía* (Madrid), vol. 20, 1961, 423-426.

2161 Miéville, Henri-Louis. "Du 'cogito' au transcendental et au métaphysique." *Revue de Théologie et de Philosophie,* vol. 92, 1964, 265-287.

2162 Schérer, René. "Sur la philosophie transcendentale et l'objectivité de la connaissance scientifique." *Revue de Métaphysique et de Morale,* vol. 62, no. 4, 1957, 436-464.

2163 Schmitt, Richard. "Transcendental phenomenology: Muddle or mystery?" *Journal of the British Society for Phenomenology,* vol. 2, Jan. 1971, 19-27. Reprinted in *Phenomenology an existentialism,* Robert C. Solomon (ed.). New York: Harper & Row, 1972, 127-144.

2164 Schrader-Klebert, Karin. "Der Begriff des Transcendentalen bei Jürgen Haberman." *Soziale Welt,* vol. 19, no. 3-4, 1968, 342-459.

2165 Spencer, James C. "Husserl's conception of the transcendental: A critical analysis." Ph.D. Dissertation, SUNY at Buffalo, 1974, 217 p. *Dissertation Abstracts,* vol. 35, no. 3, Sept. 1974, 1710-A.

2166 Tillman, Frank. "Transcendental phenomenology and analytic philosophy." *International Philosophical Quarterly,* vol. 7, March 1967, 31-40.

## TRUTH

2167 Babolin, Albino. "Verità e verificazine (IV Colloquio internazionale di fenomenologia, Schwäbisch-Hall)." *Rivista di Filosofia Neo-Scolastica,* vol. 61, 1969, 743-749.

2168 Casares, Angel Jorge. "El problema de la verdad en Husserl." *Diálogos,* vol. 1, 1964, no. 2, 61-86.

2169 Chestov, Léon. "Qu'est-ce que la vérité?" *Revue Philosophique de la France et de l'Entranger,* vol. 53, 1927. Reprinted in his *Le ouvoir des cleá.* Trad. de B. de Schlozer. Paris: J. Schriffin, Editions de la Pléiade, 1928, 397-456.

2170 Downes, Chauncey. "On Husserl's approach to necessary truth." *The Monist,* vol. 49, 1965, 87-105.

2171 Dupré, Louis. "The concept of truth in Husserl's *Logical investigations.*" *Philosophy and Phenomenological Research,* vol. 24, 1963-1964, 345-354.

2172 Dupré, Louis. "Husserl's notion of truth--via media between idealism and realism? Four lectures on the *Logical investigations* and *Ideas,*" in *Teaching Thomism Today,* Washington, D.C. The Catholic University of America Press, 1964, 405-417.

2173 Fanizza, Franco. "Tempo e verità nella fenomenologia di Husserl." *Giornale Critico della Filosofia Italiana,* vol. 41, 1962, 405-417.

2174 Hein, K. F. "Husserl's criterion of truth." *The Journal of Critical Analysis* Jersey City, N. J., vol. 3, no. 3, 1971, 125-136.

2175 IJsseling, Samuel. "De waarheid bij Husserl en Heidegger [E. Tugenhat, *Der Wahrheitsbegriff bei Husserl und Heidegger].*" *Tijdschrift voor Filosofie,* vol. 31, 1969, 771-785.

2176 Krämer, Ernst. *Benno Erdmans Warheitsauffassung und ihre Krtik durch Husserl.* Blaubeuren, 1930.

2177 Lapp, Adolf. *Versuch über den Wahrheitsbegriff mit besonderer Berücksichtigugn von Rickert, Husserl und Vaihinger.* Erlangen, 1912.

2178 Linke, Paul F. "Die Existentialtheorie der Wahrheit und der Psychologismus der Geltungslogik." *Kantstudien,* vol. 29, 1924, 395-415.

2179 Lugo, Elena. "Dos conceptos de la verdad en las *Investigationes lógicas* de Husserl." *Anuario Filosófico,* vol. 3, 1970, 169-183.

2180 Meiland, Jack W. "Concepts of relative truth." *The Monist,* vol. 60, Oct. 1977, 568-582.

2181 Paci, Enzo *Tempo e verità nella fenomenologia di Husserl* (Biblioteca di cultura moderna, 559). Bari: Laterza, 1961, 280 p.

2182 Palermo, James. "Apodictic truth: Husserl's eidetic reduction vs. induction." *Notre Dame Journal of Formal Logic,* vol. 19, Jan. 1978, 69-80.

2183 Pazanin, Ante. "Wahrheit und Lebenswelt beim späten Husserl," in *Vérité vérification,* H.-L. Van Breda (ed.) (Phaenomenologica, 61). The Hague: Martinus Nijhoff, 1974, 71-90 [Discussion: W. Marx, E. W. Straus, R. Ingarden, L. Landgrebe, H. Reiner, Th. M. Seebohm, K. H. Volkmann-Schuluck, D. Carr, K. Kuypers, G. Semerari, H. Barreau, F. F. Hrubi, J. J. Kockelmans, D. Howard, P. Janssen, J. C. Bouman, G. Brand, S. Krohn, 91-116].

2184 Patzig, Günther. "Kritische Bemerkungen zu Husserls Thesen über das Verhátnis von Wahrheit und Evidenz." *Neue Hefte für Philosophie,* no. 1, 1971, 12-32.

2185 Pietersma, Henry. "Husserl's views on the evident and the true," in *Husserl. Expositions and appraisals,* F. Elliston and P. McCormick (eds.). Notre Dame, Ind.-London: Notre Dame University Press, 1977, 38-53.

2186 Robert, Jean-Dominique. "Le problème du fondement de la vérité chez Husserl, dans les *Logische Untersuchungen* et la *Formale und transzendentale Logik.*" *Archives de Philosophie,* vol. 23, 1960, 608-632.

2187 Ruggenini, Mario. *Verità e soggettività.* L'idealismo fenomenologico di Edmund Husserl (Quaderni veronesi di varia letteratura, 8). Verona: Fiorini, 1972, vii-110. 2a ed., 1974, xvii-601.

2188 Sánches Oritz de Urbina Ricardo. "Introducción al concepto e verdad en la filosofía de Husserl." *Aporía,* vol. 1, 1964-1965, 205-251.

2189 Street, Fulton. "Husserl's significance for the theory of truth." *The Monist,* vol. 45, 1935.

2190 Tugendhat, Ernst. *Der Wahrheitsbegriff bei Husserl und Heidegger.* Berlin: Walter de Gruyter, 1967, xii-416. (2., unveränd. Aufl., 1970).

2191 Valori, Paolo. "Evidenza e verità nella fenomenologia husserliana." *Aquinas,* vol. 1, 1958, 224-240.

2192 Waelhens, Alphonse de. "Phénoménologie et vérité. Essai sur l'évolution de l'idée de vérité chez Husserl et Heidegger (Collection "Epiméthée"). Paris: Presses Universitaires de France, 1953, 168 p.

UNCONSCIOUS

2193 Geiger, Moritz. "Fragment über den Befriff des Unbewussten und die psychische Realität." *Jahrbuch für Philosophie und Phänomenologische Forschung,* vol. 4, 1921, 1-137.

2194 Waelhens, Alphonse de. "Réflexions sur une problématique husserlienne de l'inconscient, Husserl et Hegel," in *Edmond Husserl 1859-1959* (Phaenomenologica 4). The Hague: Martinus Nijhoff, 1959, 221-237.

## UNIVERSALS

2195    Chandler, Albert R. "Plato's theory of ideas studied in the light of Husserl's theory of universals." Ph.D. Dissertation, Harvard University, 1913, 167 p.

2196    Kersten, Fred. "Universals." *Research in Phenomenology,* vol. 4, 1974, 29-33.

2197    Wolter, J. "Het universale in de philosophia perennis en bij Husserl." *Studia Catholica,* vol. 16, 1940, 347-371.

## VALUE

2198    De Crescenzo, Giovanni. "Il valori nella husserliana filosofia della storia." *Sapienza,* vol. 13, 1960, 427-429.

2199    Farber, Marvin. "The phenomenological view of values [A. Roth *see:* 2202]." *Philosophy and Phenomenlogical Research,* vol. 24, 1963-1964, 552-560.

2200    Kalinowski, Georges. "La logique des valeurs d'Edmond Husserl." *Archives de Philosophie du Droit,* vol. 13, 1968, 267-282. Reprinted in his *Etudes de logique déontique, T: II (1953-1969).* Preface de R. Blanche. Paris: Librarie générale de droit et de jurisprudence, 1972, 237-256.

2201    Morra, Gianfranco. "L'etica materiale del valore nel pensiero di E. Husserl." *Ethica,* vol. 3, 1964, 33-46.

2202    Roth, Alois. *Edmund Husserls ethische Untersuchungen.* Dargestellt anhand seiner Vorlesungsmanuskripte (Phaenomenologica, 7). The Hague: Martinus Nijhoff, 1960, xvii-171. [*see:* Farber 2199]

## WORLD

2203    Bednarski, Jules. "La teneur phénoménologique du monde constitué chez Husserl." *Etudes Philosophiques,* vol. 19, 1964, 49-56.

2204    Brand, Gerd. *Welt, Ich und Zeit.* The Hague: Martinus Nijhoff, 1955. *Mondo, io e tempo* nei manoscritti inediti di Husserl. Trad. it. a cura di E. Filipini. Introd. di Enzo Paci. Milano: 1960.

2205    Brand, Gerd. "Horizont, Welt, Geschichte," in *Kommunikationskultur un Weltverständnis.* Beitrage von G. Brand, J. Kockelmans. Redaktion und Einleitung von E. W. Orth (Phaenomenologische Forschung, 5). Freiburg-München: Karl Alber, 1977, 14-89.

2206    Burke, John P. "The concept of world in Husserl's transcendental phenomenology." Ph.D. Dissertation, University of California at San Diego, 1974, 495 p. *Dissertation Abstracts,* vol. 35, no. 2, Aug. 1974, 1154-A.

2207    Dreyfus, Hubert L. "The priority of *the* world to *my* world. Heidegger's answer to Husserl (and Sartre)." *Man and World,* vol. 8, no. 2, May 1975, 121-130.

2208    Farber, Marvin. "First philosophy and the problem of the world [Husserl]." *Philosophy and Phenomenological Research,* vol. 23, 1962-1963, 315-334.

2209    Fink, Eugen. "Welt und Geschichte," in *Husserl et la pensée moerne* (Phaenomenologica, 4). The Hague: Martinus Nijhoff, 1959, 143-159. "Monde et histoire," in *Ibid.*, (traduit par Jean Ladrière et J. Taminiaux).

2210    Guilead, Reuben. "Le concept de monde selon Husserl." *Revue de Métaphysique et de Morale*, vol. 82, 1977, 345-364.

2211    Hermann, Friedrich-Wilhelm von. "Lebenswelt und In-der-Welt-sein. Zum Ansatz es Weltproblems bei Husserl und Heidegger," in *Weltaspekte der Philosophie* Hrsg. von Werner Beierwalters und Weibke Schrader. Amsterdam: Rodopi N. V., 1972, 123-141.

2212    Kim, Sang-Ki. "The problem of contingency of the world in Husserl's phenomenology." Ph.D. Dissertation, SUNY at Buffalo, 1973, 173 p. *Dissertation Abstracts*, vol. 334, no. 9, March 1974, 6045-A.

2213    Kim, Sang-Ki. *The problem of the contingency of the world in Husserl's phenomenology*. (Philosophical currents, 17). Atlantic Highlands, N.J.: Humanities Press, 1977, 102 p.

2214    Klein Jr., Theodore E. "The world as horizon. Husserl's constitutional theory of the objective world." Ph.D. Dissertation, Rice University, 1967, 198 p. *Dissertation Abstracts*, vol. 28, no. 4, Oct. 1967, 1469-A.

2215    Kockelmans, Joseph J. "World constitution. Reflections on Husserl's transcendental idealism." *Analecta Husserliana*, vol. 1, 1971, 11-35.

2216    Landgrebe, Ludwig. "The world concept," in his *Major problems in conntemporary European philosophy*, Kurt F. Reinhardt (trans.). New York: Frederick Ungar, 1966, 56-83.

2217    Marx, Werner. "Das Problem der Sonderwelten bei Husserl," in *Gegenwart und Tradition*. Hrsg. von C. Fabro. Freiburg i. Br.: Rombach, 1969. Reprinted in his *Vernunft un Welt*. The Hague: Martinus Nijhoff, 1970, 63-77.

2218    Morujño, Alexandre Fradique. *Mundo e intencionalidade*. Ensaio sobre o conceito de mundo na fenomenologia de Husserl (Instituto de Estudo filosóficos. Serie de Filosofia). Coimbra: Universidade de Coimbra, 1961, 274 p.

2219    Paci, Enzo. "Relazionismo e significato fenomenologico del mondo [Husserl]." *Il Pensiero*, vol. 6, 1961, 28-51.

2220    Patocka, Jan. *Prirozeny svèt jako filosoficky problém* (Die natürliche Welt als philosophisches Problem). Prag, 1936.

2221    Schuhmann, Karl. *Die Fundamentalbetrachtung der Phänomenologie.* Zum Weltproblem in der Philosophie Edmund Husserls (Phaenomenologica, 42). The Hague: Martinus Nijhoff, 1971, xlvii-201.

2222    Strasser, Stephan. "Der Begriff der Welt in der phänomenologischen Philosophie [E. Husserl]," in *Phänomenologie und Praxis* (Phänomenologische Forschungen, 3). Freiburg-München: Karl Alber, 1976, 151-179.

2223 Yagüe, Joaquin. "El concepto de mundo en Husserl." *Crisis,* vol. 22, no. 86-88, 1975, 315-331.

## Section 5

## General Discussion of Husserl

2224 Abba, Boris. "La autoenaanación de la experiencia trascendental en la fenomenología de Husserl, como autocrítica humanizante." *Diánoia,* vol. 17, 1971, 129-140.

2225 Adorno, Theodor W. "Zur Philosophie Husserls." *Archiv für Philosophie,* vol. 3, 1949, 339-378.

2226 Aguilar, F. "Edmund Husserl, 1859-1959." *Universidad* (Sante Fe, no. 41, 1959, 61-72.

2227 Aguirre, Antonio. "Transzendentalphänomenologischer Rationalismus," in *Perspektiven transzendentalpháomenologischer Forschung,* hrsg. von U. Claesges und K. Held (Phaenomenologica, 49). Festschrift für Ludwig Landgrebe 70. Geburtstag. The Hague: Martinus Nijhoff, 1972, 102-128.

2228 Ales Bello, Angela. "L'uomo e Dio nela fenomenologia di Husserl," in *Ristrutturazione antropologica del'insegnamento filosofico.* Atti del II Convegno nazionale dei docenti italiane di filosofia nella Facoltà, Seminari e Studentati d'Italia (*Sapienza,* 1969, vol. 24, no. 3-4, 556-559.

2229 Ales Bello, Angela. "Teologia e teleologia nella fenomenologia di Husserl." *Vita Sociale,* vol. 26, 1969, 167-177.

2230 Ales Bello, Angela. "Ragione e utopia nella prospettiva fenomenologica [Husserl]." *Incontri Culturali,* vol. 4, 1971, 190-198.

2231 Ales Bello, Angela. "Husserl filosofo 'borghese'?" in *Filosofia e impegno politico,* [L. Landgrebe, intervento sulle commmunicazioni di A. Alex Bello e di G. Nardone, 284-288]," Atti del Convengo dell'Istituto italiano di fenomenologia. Milano: Editrice Massimo, 1976, 235-246.

2232 Ameriks, Karl. "Husserl's realism." *Philosophical Review,* vol. 86, 1977, 498-519.

2233 Astrada, Carlos. *Fenomenología y praxis.* Buenos Aires: Ed. Siglo veine, 1967, 110 p.

2234 Atwell, John E. "Husserl on signification and object." *American Philosophical Quarterly,* vol. 6, 1969, 312-317.

2235 Bachelard, Suzanne. "Logique husserlienne et sémantique," in *Vérité et vérification.* (Phaenomenologica, 61). The Hague: Martinus Nijhoff, 1974, 117-129. [Discussion: C. A. van Peursen, P. Hountondji, J. J. Kockelmans, 129-131]

2236 Bagdasar, N. "Edmund Husserl." *Revista e Filosofie* (Bukarest), 1928.

2237 Ballard, Edward G. "Husserl's philosophy of intersubjectivity in relation to his rational ideal." *Tulane Studies in Philosophy,* vol. 12. New Orleans: Tulane University, The Hague: Martinus Nijhoff, 1962, 3-38.

2238 Ballard, Edward G. "Objectivity and rationality in Husserl's philosophy," in his *Philosophy at the crossroads.* Baton Rouge, La.: Louisiana State University Press, 1971, 172-215.

2239 Banfi, Antonio. "La tenndenza logistica della filosofia tedesca contemporanea e le *Ricerche logiche* de Edmund Husserl." *Rivista di Filosofia,* 1923, 115-133.

2240 Banfi, Antonio. "La fenomenologia pura di Edmund Husserl e l'autunomia ideale della sfera teorica." *Rivista di Filosofia,* 1923, 209-223.

2241 Banfi, Antonio. "La fenomenologia pura dell' Husserl," in *Principi di una teoria della ragione,* Firenze, 1926, 557-577.

2242 Banfi, Antonio. "Filosofia fenomenologica." *La Cultura,* n.s. vol. 10, 1931, 463-472.

2243 Banfi, Antonio. "Edmund Husserl." *Civiltà Moderna,* vol. 1, 1939.

2244 Banfi, Antonio. "La fenomenologia e il compito el pensiero contemporaneo." *Revue Internationale de Philosophie,* 2, 1939, 326-341.

2245 Banfi, Antonio. "La fenomenologia e il compito del pensiero contemporaneo," in *Omaggio a Husserl.* Milano, 1960, 29-46.

2246 Banfi, Antonio. "Edmundo Husserl." *Rivista di Filosofia,* 1939, no. 1, 30.

2247 Banfi, Antonio. "Husserl et la crise de la civilisation eurpéene," in *Husserl* (Cahiers de Royaumont. Philosophie no. III). Paris: Les Editions de Minuit, 1959, 411-427.

2248 Banfi, Antonio. "Husserl e la crisi della civiltà europea." *Aut Aut,* no. 43-44, 1958.

2249 Banfi Antonio. *Filosofi contemporanei.* Firenze, 1961.

2250 Bar-Hillel, Y. "Husserl's conception of a purely logical grammar." *Philosophy and Phenomenological Research,* vol. 17, 1956-1957, 362-369.

2251 Beck, Maximilian. "The last phase of Husserl's phenomenology." *Philsophy and Phenomenological Research,* vol. 1, 1940-1941, 479-491. [*see:* Dorion Cairns 2294] "La última fase de la fenomenología de Husserl (Trad. del inglés por el Prof. Angel Jorge Casares)." *Humanitas* (Tucumán), vol. 3, no. 7, 1956, 135-160. [objeciones del prof. Dorion Cairns, 149-156; respuesta de Beck, 156-157]

2252 Beck, Maximilian. "Neue Problemlage der Erkenntnistheorie." *Deutsche Vierteljahrschrift für Literaturwissenschaft und Geistegeschichte,* 1928.

2253 Beck, Maximilian. "Ideelle Existenz." *Philosophische Hefte,* vol. 1, 1929-1930.

2254 Beck, Maximilian. "Der phänomenologische Idealismus, die phänomenlogische Methode and die Hermeneutik (NB. Heideggers) Im Anschluss an Theodor Celms, "Der phänomenologische Idealisme Husserls'." *Philosophische Hefte,* vol. II, no. 2, 1930-1931, 97-101.

2255    Beck, Maximilian. *Psychologie.* Leiden, 1938.

2256    Beck, Oskar. "Die Philosophie Edmund Husserls (anlässlich seines 70.
        Geburtstags.) *Kantstudien,* vol. 35, 1929, 119-150. Reprinted in *Husserl.*
        Hrsg. von H. Noack (Wege der Forschung 40). Darmstadt:
        Wissenschaftliche Buchgesellschaft, 1973, 129-167. English trans. "The
        philosophy of Edmund Husserl," in *The Phenomenology of Husserl,* R. O.
        Elveton (ed. & trans.). Chicago: Quadrangle Books, 1970, 40-72.

2257    Bednarski, Jules. "La réduction husserliene." *Revue de Métaphysique et de
        Morale,* vol. 62, no. 4, 1957, 416-435 [Autour de la phénoménologie].

2258    Bednarski, Jules. "Deux aspects de la réduction husserlienne: abstention et
        retour." *Revue de Métaphysique et de Morale,* vol. 64, 1959, 337-355.

2259    Bednarski, Jules. "La teneur phénoménologique du monde constitué chez
        Husserl." *Etudes Philosophique,* vol. 19, 1964, 49-56.

2260    Beerling, R. F. "Spanningen bij Husserl." *Algemeen Nederlands Tijdschrift
        voor Wijsbegeerte en Psychologie,* vol. 55, 1962-1963, 239-253. [*see:* J. J.
        Poortman 2592]

2261    Bénézé, Georges. "Au-delà de Husserl, I-II." *Etudes Philosophiques,* vol. 14,
        1959, 191-201, and 449-468.

2262    Bense, Max. "Bemerkungen über die Gesamtausgabe der Werke Husserls."
        *Merkur,* vol. 5, no. 10, 1951, 987-990.

2263    Berger, Gaston. "Quelques aspects de la philosophie allemande
        contemporaine." *Etudes Philosophiques,* 3-4, 10, 1936, 68-74.

2264    Berger, Gaston. "Les thèmes principaux de la phénoménolgie de Husserl."
        *Revue de Métaphysique et de Morale,* vol. 49, 1944, 22-43.

2265    Berger, Gaston. "La phénoménologie transcendentale" in *Encyclopédie
        Française,* t. XIX, 1957, 19.10-6 a 19.10-8. Paris: Larousse, 1957.

2266    Bergmann, Gustav. "The ontology of Edmund Husserl," in his *Logic and
        reality.* Madison, Wis.: Wisconsin University Press, 193-224.

2267    Bergmann, Samuel Hugo. "Metaphysical implications of Husserl's
        phenomenology." *Scripta Hierosolymitana,* vol. 2, 1955, 220-230.

2268    Berl, H. "E. Husserl oder die Judaisierung des Platonismus." *Menorah,*
        (Wien), vol. 10, 1932, 321-331.

2269    Betancourt, Cajetano. "Ed. Husserl." *Boletín de al Universidad Catholica
        Bolivariana,* 1938, 418-419.

2270    Beyer, Wilhelm Raimund. "Im Schatten Husserls," in *Vier Kritiken:
        Heidegger, Sartre, Adorno, Lukács.* Koln: Pahl Rugenstein, 1970, 146-149.

2271    Biemel, Walter. "Die entsceideden Phasen der Entfaltung von Husserls
        Philosophie." *Zeitschrift für Philosophische Forschung,* vol. 13, no. 2, 1959,
        187-213. "Les phases décisives dans le développement de la philosophie de
        Husserl," in *Husserl* (Cahiers de Royaumont). Paris: Les Editions de
        Minuit, 1960, 32-62 [Discussion, 63-71]. "The decisive phases in the
        development of Husserl's philosophy," in *The phenomenology of Husserl,*

R.O. Elveton (ed. & trans). Chicago: Quadrangle Books, 1970, 148-173. "Las fases decisivas del desarollo de la filosofía de Husserl." *Convivium,* vol. 3, 1958, 3-35.

2272    Biemel, Walter. "Husserls *Encyclopaedia Britianica* Artikel und Heideggers Anmerkungen dazu." *Tijdschrift voor Filosofia,* vol. 12, 1950. "Husserl's *Encyclopaedia Britannica* article and Heidegger's remarks thereon," in *Husserl. Expositions and appraisals,* F. A. Elliston and P. McCormick (eds.). Notre Dame, Ind.-London: University of Notre Dame Press, 1977, 286-303.

2273    Biemel, Walter. "Edmund Husserl: Persönliche Aufzeichnungen 1906-1908." *Philosophy and Phenomenological Research,* vol. 3, 1942-1943.

2274    Blanco, Julio Enrique. "Tres lecciones sobre Husserl." *Universidad Bolivariana,* 1941, 5-17.

2275    Blanco, Julio Enrique. "Una vez mas Husserl y Plotino." *Universidad Bolivariana,* 12, 1946, 471-490.

2276    Bobbio, P. "La filosofia di Husserl e la tendenza fenomenologica." *Rivista di Filosofia,* vol. 26, 1935, 47ff.

2277    Bobbio, P. "Husserl postumo." *Rivista di Filosofia,* vol. 31, 1940, 37-45.

2278    Bochenski, J.-M. *Europäische Philosophise der Gegenwart.* 2. Aufl. Bern: Francke, 1951, 142-150. *La philosophie contemporaine en Europe.* Trad. par François Vaudou. Paris: Payot, 1951, 116-134. *Contemporary European philosophy.* Los Angeles, Cal.: University of California Press, 1956.

2279    Boehm, Rudolf. "Une introduction à la philosophie phénoménologique [à propos de *Die Krisis der europíschen Wissenschaften...*]." *Archives e Philosophie,* no. 2, 1954, 169-172.

2280    Boehm, Rudolf. "Les ambigüités des concepts husserliens d"immanence' et e 'transcendence'." *Revue Philosophique de la France et de l'Etranger,* vol. 84, no. 4, 481-526. [Edmund Husserl]. "Immanenz und Transzendenz," in his *Gesichtspunkt der Phänomenologie. Husserl-Studien* (Phaenomenologica, 26). The Hague: Martinus Nijhoff, 1968, 141-185.

2281    Boehm, Rudolf. "Zur Phänomenologie der Gemeinschaft. Edmund Husserl Grundgedanken," in *Phänomenologie, Rechtsphilosophie. Jurisprudenz.* Festschrift für Gerhardt Husserl zum 75. Geburtstag. Hrsg. von Thomas Wurtenberger. Frankfurt am am Main: V. Klostermann, 1969, 1-26.

2282    Bosio, Franco. "Psicologia e logica nella fenomenologia di Husserl." *Aut Aut,* no. 68, 1962, 131-154.

2283    Bosio, Franco. "La lotta contro lo psicologismo e l'idea logica pura in Husserl." *Aut Aut,* no. 71, 1962, 373-382.

2284    Bosio. Franco. "Problematica della riduzione e costituzione trascendentale." *Aut Aut,* no. 74, 1963, 62-83.

2285    Bosio, Franco. "La riduzione al mondo della vita [Husserl]." *Aut Aut,* no. 75, 1963, 16-27.

2286    Bosio, Franco. "La costituzione fenomenologica del mondo dello spirito nelle "*Ideen*' di Ed. Husserl." *Il Pensiero,* vol. 12, 1967, 56-65.

2287    Brand, Gerd. "Horizont, Welt, Geschichte," in *Kommunikationskultur und Weltverständnis.* Beiträge von Gerd Brand, Joseph Kockelmans. Redaktion u. Einleitung von E. W. Orth (Phänomenologische Forschungen, 5). Freiburg i. Br.-Munchen: Verlag Karl Alber, 1977, 14-89.

2288    Brand, Gerd. "Die wichtigsten Grundlagen der Phänomenologie Husserls," in his *Welt, Geschichte, Mythos.* Trier: NCO-Verlag, 1977.

2289    Brand, Gerd. "Interpretationen von Husserls Ansatzen zu Praxis und Geschichte," in his *Welt, Geschichte, Mythos.* Trier: NCO-Verlag, 1977.

2290    Bréhier, Emile. *Histoire de la philosophie,* t. II, Philosophie moderne, Paris: Vrin 1932, 1108-1116.

2291    Bréhier, Emile, et Ricoeur, Paul. *Histoire de la philosophie allemande.* Paris: Vrin, 1954. Troisième édition mise à jour par P. Ricoeur (Bibliothèque d'Histoire de la Philosophie), P. Ricoeur, "Quelques figures contemporaines (Husserl, Scheler, Jaspers, Heidegger).

2292    Brock, Werner. *Beginnings of Contemporary Germany philosophy.* Cambridge University Press, 1935, 1-44.

2293    Brunner, Auguste. S.J. *La personne incarnée.* Etude sur la phénoménologie et la philosophie existentialiste. Paris: Beauchesne, 1947. Contient une importante étude critique de points fondamentaux chez Husserl.

2294    Cairns, Dorion. "Concerning Beck's 'The last phase of Husserl's phenomenology'." *Philosophy and Phenomenological Research,* vol. 1, 1940-1941, 492-498 [*see:* Beck 2251].

2295    Cairns, Dorion. "Some results of Husserl's investigations." *Journal of Philosophy,* vol. 36, 1939, 236-238.

2296    Cairns, Dorion. "An approach to Husserlian phenomenology [published under the title 'An approach to phenomenology', in *Philosophical essays in memory of Edmund Husserl,* Marvin Farber (ed.). Cambridge, Mass.: Harvard University Press, 1940, 3-18]," in *Phenomenology. Continuation an criticism.* Essays in memory of Dorion Cairns, F. Kersten and R. Zaner (eds.) (Phaenomenologica, 50). The Hague: Martinus Nijhoff, 1973, 223-238.

2297    Cairns, Dorion. "An approach to Husserlian phenomenology," in *Phenomenology and existentialism,* Richard M. Zaner and Don Ihde (eds.). New York: Putnam's Sons, Capricorn Books, 1973, 31-46.

2298    Campanale, Domenico. "L'interpreetazione husserliana di Cartesio" in *Problemi epistemologici da Hume all'ultimo Wittgenstein* (Universita di Bari. Pubblicazioni dell'Istituto di Filosofia, 4). Bari: Andriatica Editrice, 1961, 241-278. Originally published in *Rassegna di Scienze filosofiche,* no. 3-4, 1952.

2299    Cantoni, R. "Edmund Husserl e la critica del'atteggiamento naturale." *Il Pensiero Critico,* no. 3, 1960, 1-46.

2300    Capalbo, Creusa. "A fenomenologia segundo Husserl." *Revista Brasileira de Filosofia,* vol. 21, 1971 39-46.

2301   Caponigri, Robert A. "Phenomenology," Part I, chap. VII, 152-182, in his *A history of Western philosophy*, vol. V, Philosophy from the age of positivism to the age of analysis. South Bend, Ind.: University of Notre Dame Press, 1971, 152-182, vol. V.

2302   Casaubón, Juan Alfredo. "Examen de la doctrina husserliana sobre el conocimiento como constitución de su objeto." *Sapientia*, vol. 14, 1959, 179-187.

2303   Casaubón, Juan Alfredo. "La experiencia humana e la intencioalidad constituyente de Husserl idealista." *Sapientia*, vol. 31, 1976, 29-46.

2304   Caso, Antonio. "E. Husserl y la filosofía inglesa." *Luminar* (México), 2, 1938, 177-183.

2305   Cavailllès, Jean. *Sur la logique et la théorie de la science.* Paris: Presses Universitaires de France, 1947, 44-78.

2306   Celms, Theodor. "Der phänomenologische Idealismus Husserls." *Acta Universitatis Latviensis,* Riga, vol. 19, 1928. [*see:* Maximilian Beck 2254]

2307   Ceñal, Ramón. "La fenomenología de Husserl: su propósito fundamental." *Revista de Filosofía* (Madrid), vol. 15, 1956, 102-106.

2308   Chandler, A. "Professor Husserl's program of philosophical reform." *Philosophical Review,* vol. 26, 1917, 634-648.

2309   Chandravarty, H. "Husserl, la phénoménologie et la recherche occidentale du soi." *Age Nouveau,* no. 110, 1960, 37-50.

2310   Chapman, H. M. "Realism and phenomenology," in *The return to reason,* John Wild (ed.). Chicago: Henry Regnery, 1953, 3-35.

2311   Chestov, Léon. "Memento mori." *Revue Philosophique e la France et de l'Entranger,* 1926, 5-62. [A propos de al théorie de la connaissance de Husserl]. [Reprinted in his *Les pouvoirs des clefs,* Oeuvres de Léon Chestov, tomes V et VI. Paris: J. Schriffrin, Editions de la Pléiade, 307-395]

2312   Chestov, Léon. "A la mémoire d'un grand philosophie: E. Husserl." *Revue Philosophique e la France et de l'Etranger,* 129, 1940, 5-32.

2313   Chisholm, R. M. "Introduction," to his *Realism and the background of phenomenology.* New York: Free Press of Glencoe-London: Allen and Unwin, 1960.

2314   Cho, Kah Kyung. "Mediation and immediacy for Husserl," in *Phenomenology and natural existence.* Essays in honor of Marvin Farber, Dale Riepe (ed.). State University of New York Press, 1973, 56-82.

2315   Collins, James. "Husserl," in his *The existentialists.* A critical study. Chicago: Henry Regnery, 1959, 26-38.

2316   Conrad-Martius, Hedwig. "Die transzendentale und die ontologische Phänomenologie," in *Edmund Husserl 1859-1959* (Phaenomenologica, 4). The Hague: Martinus Nijhoff, 1960, 175-184.

2317   Cossio, C. "La norma e el imperativo en Husserl." *Revista Braisileira de Filosofia,* vol. 10, 1960, 43-90.

2318  Costa, Filippo. "Sulla evoluzione del problema del tempo in Edmund Husserl." *Filosofia*, vol. 20, 1969, 473-502.

2319  Costa, Margarita. "En torno a *La fenomenología de la conciencia inmanente del tiempo.*" *Revista de Filosofía* (La Plata), no. 17, 1966, 31-48.

2320  Cruz Vélez, D. "Supuestos en la filosofía de Husserl." *Bolívar* (Bogotá), vol. 11, 1959, 441-457.

2321  Dartigues, André. "Husserl," in his *La phénoménologie.* Toulouse: Privat, 1972. *La fenomenología,* trad. por J. A. Pombo. Barcelona: Editorial Herder, 1975.

2322  Dauenhauer, Bernard P. "Husserl's phenomenological justification of universal rigorous science." *International Philosophical Quarterly,* vol. 16, 1976, 63-80.

2323  de Boer, Th. "Edmund Husserl," in *Filosofen van de 20e eeuw.* Onder redactie van C. P. Bertels en E. Petersma. Assen, Amsterdam: Van Gorcum-Amsterdam, Brussel: Intemediair, 1972, 87-98.

2324  de Carvalho, Antônio Pinto. "O apriorismo fenomenológico de Husserl." *Kriterion* (Brazil), vol. 10, no. 39-40, 1957, 36-55.

2325  De Crescenzio, G. "I valori nella husserliana filosofia della storia." *Sapienza,* vol. 13, 1960, 427-429.

2326  Delbos, Victor. "Husserl, sa critique du psychologisme et sa conception d'une logique pure." *Revue de Métaphysique et de Morale,* vol. 16, 1911. Reprinted in his *La philosophie allemande au XIXe siècle.* Paris: Alcan, 1912, chap. II.

2327  Del-Negro, Walter. "Von Brentano über Husserl zu Heidegger." *Zeitschrift für Philosophische Forschung,* vol. 7, 1953, 571-585. Also in *Zeitschrift für Religions- und Geistesgeschichte,* vol. 7, 1955, 59-69.

2328  De Muralt, André. "La solution husserlienne du débat entre le réalisme et l'idéalisme." *Revue Philosophique de la France et de l'Etranger,* vol. 84, no. 1, 1959, 545-552. [Edmund Husserl]

2329  De Muralt, André. "Epoché-Malin Génie-Théologie de la tout-puissance divine 'Husserl, Descartes, Occam'." *Studia Philosophica,* vol. 26, 1966, 159-191.

2330  Demuth, M. "E. Husserl." *Lektorenkonferenz der deutschen Frankziskaner für Philosophie und Theologie,* vol. 3, Werl, 1926, 66-79.

2331  De Natale, Ferruccio. "Il problema fenomenologico della scienza in Husserl da '*Idee II*' alla '*Crisi*'." *Filosofia,* vol. 27, 1976, 241-276.

2332  Derisi, Octavio Nicolás. "El ámbito del objeto de la fenomenología en E. Husserl." *Sapientia,* vol. 26, 1971, 273-290.

2333  Dessoir, Max. "La phénoménologie de Husserl." *Revue Internationale de Philosophie,* 2, 1939, 271-276.

2334  De Vidovich, A. "Riduzione eidetica e riduzione trascendentale nell'analisi fenomenologica." *Aut Aut,* no. 59, 1960, 302-315.

2335 Di Carlo, E. "Intorno alla filosofia dello Husserl." *Sociologia,* (Roma), genn.-dic., 1961, 447-458.

2336 Diemer, Alwin. "La phénoménologie de Husserl comme metáphysique." (Texte traduit par Jacques Ridé. Notes tradutes par Alexandre Lovit et Henri Colombié). *Etudes Philosophiques,* vol. 9, 1954, 21-49.

2337 Dovydaitis, P. "Ed. Husserl." *Logos,* vol. 18, 1939, 187-190.

2338 Drummond, John J. "On the nature of perceptual appearances, or is Husserl an Aristotelian?" *New Scholalsticism,* vol. 52, Winter 1978, 1-22.

2339 Duméry, Henri. *Critique et religion.* Paris: Sedes, 1957. Chap. V: La description phénoménologique, 135-178 [Contient une étude et une critique de la méthode de Husserl]

2340 Dupré, Louis. "Husserl's notion of truth-via media between idealism and realism? Four lectures on the *Logical investigations* and *Ideas,*" in *Teaching Thomism today.* Washington, D.C.: Catholic University of America Press, 1968, 150-182.

2341 Dussort, Henri. "Introduction au 'Projet d'un livre sur Husserl," (Texte recueilli et présenté par Bernard Teyssèdre). *Revue de Métaphysique et de Morale,* vol. 66, 1961, 233-236.

2342 Ehrlich, Walter. *Intentionalität und Sinn.* Prolegomena zur Normenlehre. Halle, 1934.

2343 Eley, Lothar. "Zeitlichkeit und Protologik," in *Perspektiven transzendentalphänomenologischer Forschung* (Phaenomenologica, 49). Hrsg. von K. Held und U. Claesges. The Hague: Martinus Nijhoff, 1972, 164-188.

2344 Elveton, R. O. "Introduction," to *The phenomenology of Husserl,* R. O. Elveton (ed. & trans.). Chicago: Quadrangle Books, 1970, 3-39.

2345 Erckmann, R. "Husserl und Hans Hörbiger." *Schlüssel zum Weltgeschehen,* vol. 5, 1919, 150-154, 184-188.

2346 Eschke, Hans-Günter. "Bermerkungen zur Phänomenologie Edmund Husserls." *Deutsche Zeitschrift für Philosophie,* vol. 12, 1964, 596-611.

2347 Essen, J. van. "Husserl's phaenomenologie." N. T. P., 1938, 5; *Algemeen Nederlands Tijdschrift voor Wijsgebeerte en Psychologie,* 1938, 270.

2348 Eyser, Ulrich. "Phänomenologie. Das Werk E. Husserls." *Mass und Wert,* vol. 2, 1938, 8-30.

2349 Fagone, Virgilio. "Tempo e intenzionalità. Brentano, Husserl, Heidegger." *Archivo di Filosofia,* no. 1, 1960, 105-131.

2350 Farber, Marvin. "Edmund Husserl and the background of his philosophy." *Philosophy and Phenomenological Research,* vol. 1, 1940-1941. Reprinted in his *The foundation of phenomenology.* New York, 1943, 3-24.

2351 Farber, Marvin. "The ideal of a presuppositionless philosophy," in *Philosophical essays in memory of Edmund Husserl,* Marvin Farber (ed.). Cambridge, Mass.: Harvard University Press, 1940, 44-64.

2352    Farber, Marvin. "The goal of a complete philosophy of experience," in *Phänomenologie heute*. Festschrift für Ludwig Landgrebe (Phaenomenologica, 51). The Hague: Martinus Nijhoff, 1972, 14-26.

2353    Farber, Marvin. "Edmund Husserl," in *Collier's Encyclopedia*, vol. 12, 1965.

2354    Farber, Marvin. "The ideal of a naturalistic logic. [Husserl and Dewey]." *Philosophy and Phenomenological Research*, vol. 29, 1968-1969, 598-601.

2355    Filipini, E. "Nota su Husserl e Heidegger." *Rivista di Filosofia*, no. 2, 1961, 212-216.

2356    Fink, Eugen. "Die phänomenologische Philosophie Edmund Husserls in der gegenwärtigen Kritik." *Kantstudien*, vol. 38, 1933, 319-383. English trans., "The phenomenological philosophy of Edmund Husserl and contemporary criticism," in *The phenomenology of Husserl*, R. O. Elveton (ed.). Chicago: Quadrangle Books, 1970, 73-147. [Reprinted in his *Studien zur Phanomenologie*]

2357    Fink, Eugen. "Was will die Phänomenologie Edmund Husserls." *Die Tatwelt*, vol. 10, 1934, 15-32. English trans. in *Research in Phenomenology*, vol. 2, 1972, 5-27, "What does the phenomenology of Edmund Husserl want to accomplish? (The phenomenological idea of laying-a-ground)." Arthur Grugan (trans.).

2358    Fink, Eugen. "Das Problem der Phänomenologie Edmund Husserls." *Revue International de Philosophie*, Jan. 15, 1939, vol. 1, 1938-1938, 226-270.

2359    Fink, Eugen. "L'analyse intentionnelle et le problème de la pensée spéculative," in *Problèmes actuels de la phénoménologie*. Paris: Desclée de Brouwer, 1952, 53-88.

2360    Fink, Eugen. "Operative Begriffe in Husserls Phänomenologie" (Vortrag auf dem "III. colloque international de phénoménologie" in Royaumont). *Zeitschrift für Philosophische Forschung*, vol. 11, 1957, 321-337.

2361    Fink, Eugen, u.a. *Phänomenologie, lebendig oder tot?* Zum 30. Todesjahr Edmund Husserls. (Veröffentlichungen der katholischen Akademie der Erzdiözese Freiburg, 18). Karlsruhe: Badenia-Verlag, 1969, 48 p.

2362    Fink, Eugen. "Die Spätphilosophie Husserls in der Freiburger Zeit," in *Edmund Husserl 1859-1959* (Phaenomenologica, 4). The Hague: Martinus Nijhoff, 1959, 99-115.

2363    Fischer, Alden L. "Some basic themes in the phenomenology of Edmund Husserl." *Modern Schoolman*, vol. 43, 1965-1966, 347-363.

2364    Flory, M. "Notas críticas sobre la 'Introduccion a la fenomenologiía' de Husserl." *Estudios Ecclesiasticos*, vol. 13, 1934, 155-174.

2365    Forni, Guglielmo. "Fenomenologia della storia e idealismo intenzionale in Husserl." *Giornale di Metafisica*, vol. 23, 1968, 408-428.

2366    Fragata, Julio. "A fenomenologia de Husserl." *Revista Portuguesa de Filosofia*, vol. 11, 1955, 3-35.

2367    Fragata, Julio. "Husserl e a fundamentaçño das ciências." *Revista Portuguesa de Filosofia*, vol. 13, 1957, 44-51.

2368 Fragata, Julio. "A filosofia de Edmund Husserl." *Filosofia L.,* vol. 8, 1961, 283-300.

2369 Franchi, Attilio. "Realtà e mediocrità della filosofia di Husserl." *Giornale di Metafisica,* vol. 18, 1963, 561-575.

2370 Frezioso, Antonio F. "A propositi della 'Fenomenologia di Husserl'." *Sapienza,* vol. 28, April-June 1975, 219-228.

2371 Fulda, Hans Friedrich. "Husserls Wege zum Anfang einer transcendentalen Phänomenologie," in *Der Idealismus und seine Gegenwart,* Fetschrift für Werner Marx zum 65 Geburtstag. Hrsg. U. Guzzoni u.a. Hamburg: Felix Meiner Verlag, 1976, 147-165.

2372 Funke, Gerhard. "Transzendentale Phänomenologie als erste Philosophie." *Studium Generale,* vol. 11, 1958, 564-582; 632-646. Fenomenología trascendental y 'filosofía primera.... Observaciones al 'Ensayo de una historia crítica de las ideas', de Husserl (Trad. José Gaos)." *Diánoia,* (México), vol. 5, 1959, 150-194.

2373 Funke, Gerhard. "Bewusstseinswissenschaft. Evidenz und Reflexion als Implikate der Verifikation [Husserl]." *Kantstudien,* vol. 61, 1970, 433-466.

2374 Funke, Gerhard. "Husserl's phenomenology as the foundational science." *Southwestern Journal of Philosophy,* vol. 5, no. 3, 1973, 187-201.

2375 Gadamer, Hans-Georg. *Wahrheit und Methode.* Grundzüge einer philosophischen Hermeneutik. Tübingen: J. C. B. Mohr, 1960, xvii-486.

2376 Gadamer, Hans-Gejorg. "Die phänomenologische Bewegung." *Philosophische Rundschau,* vol. 11, 1963-1964, 1-45.

2377 Gadamer, Hans-Georg. *Kleine Schriften, III: Idee und Sprache.* Plato. Husserl. Heidegger. Tübingen: J.B.C. Mohr, 1972.

2378 Gagnebin, S. "La mathématique universelle d'après Edmund Husserl," in *Etudes de philosophie des sciences en l'honneur de Gonseth,* 1950, 175-215.

2379 Galay, Jean-Louis. "Essai sur le problème de l'intelligibilité d'après la *Critique de la raison logique* de Husserl." *Studia Philosophica,* vol. 29, 1969, 25-53.

2380 García Bacca, Juan David. "Husserl, modelo del método fenomenológico de filosofar," in *Siete modelos de filósofar.* Caracas: Universidad Central, Faculdad de Filosofía y Letras, 1950, 115-128.

2381 Garin, Eugenio. "Introduzione storica," in *Bilancio della fenomenologia e dell' esistenzialismo,* 7-47 [Interventi, risposte e chiarimenti, 47-72]. Padova: Liviana Editrice, 1960.

2382 Garroni, E. "Ipotesi per una 'pittura husserliana'," in Crispolti-Garroni, *Alfredo del Greco.* Roma, 1962, 9-13.

2383 Garulli, Enrico. "Fenomenologia, logica e storia in Husserl." *Il Dialogo* (Bologna), ottobre 1960, 21-43.

2384 Garulli, Enrico. "Due fasi del pensiero husserliano: le *Ricerche logiche* e la *Krisis." Studi Urbaniti,* n.s. B, vol. 35, 1961, 192-235.

2385 Garulli, Enrico. "Le ragioni di una ripresa della filosofia husserliana." *Nuova Rivista Pedogogica* (Roma), agosto 1963, 69-86.

2386 Garulli, Enrico. "Problemi della filosofia husserliana, I-II." *Studi Urbinati di Storia, Filosofia e Letteratura,* n.s. B, vol. 38, 1964, 235-299, and *Ibid.,* vol. 39, 1965, 450-472.

2387 Gatta, Ernesto A. "I temi della fenomenologia e l'*Origine della geometria* [Husserl]." *Annali della Facoltà di Lettere e Filosofia di Bari,* vol. 8, 1962, 5-26.

2388 Georgoulis, K. D. "Ο Edmund Husserl καὶ ἡ φενομενολογικὴ φιλοσοφία." Νεα Εγτια, 1943, 22, 243-247 et 434-440.

2389 Giacon, Carlo. "Husserl al Convegno di Gallarate." *L'Italia che Scrive,* vol. 12, 1955.

2390 Gibson, R. Boyce. "The problem of real and ideal in the phenomenology of Husserl." *Mind,* vol. 34, 1925, 311-333.

2391 Gilles, Richard. "Phenomenology: A non-alternative to empiricism," in *Phenomenology, structuralism, semiology,* Harry R. Garvin (ed.). *Bucknell Review,* April 1976, Lewisburg, Pa.: Bucknell University Press, 1976, 71-98.

2392 Giordani, Máio Curtis. "Husserl, o filósofo das essências puras." *Vozes,* vol. 58, 1964, 750-765.

2393 Granel, Gérard. "La gigantomachie," in *Traditionis traditio.* Essais. Paris: Gallimard, 1972, 315 p. [Etudes sur Husserl, Heidegger, une analyse du rapport entre *Sein und Zeit* et la phénoménologie husserlienne]

2394 Grassi, E. "La fenomenologia di E. Husserl," in *Dell'apparire e dell'essere.* Firenze, 67-77.

2395 Grimme, A. "Die frohe Botschaft der Husserlschen Philosophie." *Der Falke,* vol. 1, 1917, 224-231.

2396 Groethuysen, Bernard. *La philosophie allemande depuis Nietzsche.* Paris, 1926, 88-103.

2397 Gronau, G. *Die Philosophie der Gegenwart.* Langensalza, 1922, 1-11.

2398 Guaraldi, Antonella. "La modificazione di neutralità comme epochè naturale." *Revue Internationale de Philosophie,* vol. 19, no. 71-72, 1965, 74-106.

2399 Gurvitch, Georges. "La philosophie phénoménologique en Allemagne: Edmund Husserl." *Revue de Métaphysique et de Morale,* vol. 33, 1928.

2400 Gurvitch, Georges. "Edmund Husserl," in *Les tendances actuelles de la philosophie allelmande.* Paris: Vrin, 3e ed., 1951, 11-66.

2401 Gurwitsch, Aron. "Présuppositions philosophiques de la logique [Husserl]," in *Phénoménologie-Existence, Revue de Métaphysique et de Morale,* 1953, vol. 58, 11-21.

2402 Gurwitsch, Aron. Review of Jean Hering, "La phénoménologie d'Edmund Husserl il y a trente ans," [*Revue Internationale de Philosophie,* vol. 1, no.

2, 1939, 366-373]." *Philosophy and Phenomenological Research,* vol. 1, 1940-1941, 253-254.

2403    Gurwitsch, Aron. "Review of Paul L. Lansberg, "Husserl et l'idée de la phénoménologie," [*Revue Internationale de Philosophie,* vol. 1, 1939, 317-326]." *Philosophy and Phenomenological Research,* vol. 1, 1940-1941, 513-515.

2404    Gurwitsch, Aron. *Théorie du champ de la conscience* ("Textes et Etudes anthropologiques"). Paris: Desclée de Brouwer, 1957, 353 p. English trans., *The field of consciousness* (Duquesne Studies, Psychological series, 2). Pittsburgh, Pa.: Duquesne University Press; Louvain: Editions Nauwelaerts, 1964, xiv-428.

2405    Gurwitsch, Aron. "The last work of Husserl." *Philosophy and Phenomenological Research,* vol. 17, 1956-1957, 370-398. Reprinted in his *Studies in phenomenology and psychology.* Evanston, Ill.: Northwestern University Press, 1964, 397-447.

2406    Gurwitsch, Aron. "On the intentionality of consciousness," in *Philosophical essays in memory of Edmund Husserl,* Marvin Farber (ed.). Cambridge, Mass.: Harvard University Press, 1940, 65-83.

2407    Gurwitsch, Aron. "Gurwitsch, Aron. 'Husserlian perspectives on Galilean physics'; 'An introduction of constitutive phenomenology'; 'Some fundamental principles of constitutive phenomenology'," in *Phenomenology and the theory of science.* Evanston, Ill.: Northwestern University Press, 1974, 33-59; 153-189; 190-209.

2408    Gurwitsch, Aron. "Critical study of Husserl's *Nachwort,*" in his *Studies in phenomenology and psychology.* Evanston, Ill.: Northwestern University Press, 1964, 107-115.

2409    Guzzoni, G. "Di una posizione 'storicamente' positiva respetto alla fenomenologia di Husserl," in *Omaggio a Husserl.* Milano, 1960, 263-289.

2410    Hachim, André. "Existentialisme et phénoménologie. Trois étapes: Husserl-Heidegger-Sartre." *Bulletin du Cercle Thomiste* (Caen), no. 15, 1953, 25-32.

2411    Haecht, Louis van. "Phenomenologische analyse van 't menschelijke lichaam naar Ed. Husserl." *Tijdschrift voor Filosofie,* vol. 6, 1944, 135-190.

2412    Hamilton, K. G. "Edmund Husserl's contribution to philosophy." *Journal of Philosophy,* vol. 36, 1939.

2413    Hammer, Felix. *Leib und Geschichte.* Philosophischen Perspektiven (no. 240). Bonn: Bouvier, 1974, vii-269.

2414    Hartmann, Klaus. "Abstraction and existence in Husserl's phenomenological reduction." *Journal of the British Society for Phenomenology,* vol. 2, no. 1, 1971, 10-18.

2415    Hartshorne, Charles. "Husserl and the social structure of immediacy," in *Philosophical essays in memory of Edmund Husserl,* Marvin Farber (ed.). Cambridge, Mass.: Harvard University Press, 1940, 219-230.

2416    Heinemann, F. H. "The loneliness of the transcendental ego," in his *Existentialism and the modern predicament*. New York: Harper Torchbooks, 1958, 47-58, and passim.

2417    Heffner, John. "Husserl's critique of traditional empiricism." *Journal of the British Society for Phenomenology*, vol. 5, 1974, 159-162.

2418    Héring, Jean. "Sub specie aeterni." [critique of Chestov, "Memento mori," *see:* 2311]." *Revue Philosophique de la France et de l'Etranger*, VII, 1927.

2419    Héring, Jean. "Bemerkungen über das Wesen, die Wesenheit und die Idee." *Jahrbuch für Philosophie und phänomenologische Forschung*, vol. 4, 1921.

2420    Héring, Jean. "La phénoménologie de Husserl il y a trente ans." *Revue Internationale de Philosophie*, 1939, 366-373. [*see:* A. Gurwitsch 2402]

2421    Herrera, Daniel. "Crítica de Husserl a las ciencias." *Franciscanum* (Bogotá), vol. 6, 1964, 159-166.

2422    Herrera, Daniel. "El pensamiento husserliano anterior a las *Ideas*." *Franciscanum* (Bogotá), vol. 6, 1964, 207-235.

2423    Herrera, Daniel. "Un primer esbozo de la fenomenología de Husserl." *Revista de Filosofía* (Mexico), vol. 2, 1969, 195-207.

2424    Hicks, Georges Dawes. "The philosophy of Husserl." *The Hibbert Journal*, vol. 12, 1914, 198ff.

2425    Hoche, Hans Ulrich. "Bemerkungen zum Problem der Selbst- und Fremderfahrung bei Husserl und Sartre." *Zeitschrift für Philosophische Forschung*, vol. 25, 1971, 172-186.

2426    Hülsmann, Heinz. "Der Systemanspruch der Phänomenologie E. Husserls." *Salzburger Jahrbuch für Philosophie*, vol. 7, 1963, 173-186.

2427    [Husserl, E.]. "Notes concerning Husserl by W. P. Montague, Charles Hartshorne, Andrew D. Osborne, Horace L. Friess, Dorion Cairns." *Journal of Philosophy*, vol. 36, no. 9, 1939.

2428    "Husserl, Edmund," in Ziegenfuss, Werner, *Philosophen-Lexikon* 2 Bd. Berlin, 1950, 569-576, vol. 1.

2429    Hyppolite, Jean. "L'idee fichtéenne de la doctrine de la science et le projet husserlien" and "Die fichtesche Idee der Wissenschaftslehre und der Entwurf Husserls," in *Husserl et la pensée moderne(Phaenomenologica, 2)*. The Hague: Martinus Nijhoff, 1959, 173-182. English trans. Auslegung, vol. 1-2, 1973-1975, 77-84, "The Fichtean idea of the science of knowledge and the Husserlian project."

2430    Hourton, Jorge. "Husserl. La fenomenología y el pensamiento cristiano." *Finis Terrae*, vol. 10, no. 40, 1963, 187-204.

2431    Ihde, Don. "Under the sign of Husserl and Heidegger," in his *Listening and voice*. A phenomenology of sound. Athens, Ohio: Ohio University Press, 1976, 17-25.

2432    Ingarden, Roman. "Die Bedeutung der Phänomenologie Husserls für die Selbstbestimmung der Gegenwart," in *Husserl et la pensée moderne* (Phaenomenologica, 2). The Hague: Martinus Nijhoff, 1959.

2433    Ingarden, Roman. "Bermerkungen zum Problem 'Idealismus-Realismus'." *Jahrbuch für Philosophie und Phänomenologische Forschung,* 1929 (Ergänzungsband, Edmund Husserl zum 70. Gebutstag gewidmet), 159-190.

2434    Ingarden, Roman. "Husserls Betrachtungen zu Konstitution des physikalischen Dinges." *Archives de Philosophie,* vol. 27, no. 3-4, 1964, 355-407. [résumé en français]

2435    Ingarden, Roman. "Die vier Begriffe der Transzendenz und das Problem des Idealismus in Husserl." *Analecta Husserliana,* vol. 1, 1971, 36-74.

2436    Ingarden, Roman. "The letter of Husserl about the VI [*Logical] investigation* and 'idealism'." Helmut Girndt (trans. from the German) [with Ingarden's own introduction, conclusion and comments to the same letter, A.-T. Tymieniecka (trans.).] *Ingardeniana, Analecta Husserliana,* 1976, vol. 4, 418-438.

2437    Jakowenko, B. "Filosofija E. Husserlja," in *Novyja idei v filozofii,* II. St. Petersbourg, 1912.

2438    Jakowenko, B. "Edmund Husserl und die russische Philosophie," in *Der Russische Gedanke,* 1929, vol. 1, 210ff.

2439    Janssen, Paul. "Ontologie, Wissenschaftstheorie und Geschichte im Spätwerk Husserls," in *Perspektiven transzendental-phänomenologischer Forschung* (Phaenomenologica, 49), Hrsg. von U. Claesges und K. Held. The Hague: Martinus Nijhoff, 1972, 145-163.

2440    Jeanson, Francis. *La phénoménologie.* Paris: Téqui, 1951.
        **Book Reviews:**
        E. Brisbois, *Nouvelle evue de Théologie,* vol. 74, 1952, 769.
        J. Collins, *Modern Schoolman,* vol. 30, 1953, 240-241.
        J.-M. Grévillot, *Revue Nouvelle,* vol. 17, 1953, 106-107.
        G. Lafont, *Témoignages,* cahier 37, no. 97, 1953, 97.
        O. Mannoni, *Espíritu,* vol. 20, no. 8-9, 1952, 401-402.
        F. Romano, *Sophia,* vol. 20, 1952, 360.
        H. Saint-Denis, *Revue de l'Université d'Ottawa,* vol. 22, 1952, 374-375.

2441    Joja, Crizantema. "Intentionalité et signification chez Husserl." *Philosophie et Logique,* vol. 20, April-June 1976, 119-126.

2442    Jolivet, Régis. "Le probléme de l'évidence du jugement et l'évidence antéprédicative d'après Husserl." *Revue de l'Université d'Ottawa,* vol. 21, 1951, 235-253 [section spéciale].

2443    Jordan, Robert Welsh. "Husserl's phenomenology as an 'historical' science." *Social Research,* vol. 35, no. 2, 1968, 245-259.

2444    Joseph de Sainte Marie, O.C.D. "Le présupposé transcendental dans la
        phénoménologie de la perception de E. Husserl." *Doctor Communis,* vol.
        25, 1972, 169-211.

2445    Kalinowski, Georges. *Etudes de logique déontique,* T. II (1953-1969). Préface
        de R. Blanché. Paris: Librairie générale de droit et de jurisprudence, 1972,
        270 p. Contient:

        "La logique des normes d'Edmund Husserl," (*Archives de Philosophie du
        droit,* 1965), 111-122.

        "La logique des valuers d'Edmond Husserl (*Archives de Philosophie du droit,*
        13, 1968), 237-256.

2446    Kates, Carol A. "Perception and temporality in Husserl's phenomenology."
        *Philosophy Today,* vol. 14, 1970, 89-100.

2447    Kelkel, Arion Lothar. "Avant-propos," vii-xlvi, à Edmund Husserl,
        *Philosophie première (1923-1924).* Première partie: Histoire critique des
        idées; Deuxième partie: Théorie de la réduction phénoménologique, traduit
        de l'allemand par A. L. Kelkel. Paris: Presses Universitaires de France, 1970
        et 1972, 2 vols. [Avant-propos situe le Cours dans l'évolution de Husserl
        qui va des *Idées* à la *Krisis*]

2448    Kelly, Derek. "Metaphysical directive in Husserl's phenomenology." *Modern
        Schoolman,* vol. 48, 1970-1971, 1-18.

2449    Kersten, Fred. "The occasion and novelty of Husserl's phenomenology of
        essence," in *Phenomenological perspectives,* Philip Bossert (ed.)
        (Phaenomenologica, 62). The Hague: Martinus Nijhoff, 1975, 61-92.

2450    Kim, Chin Tai. "Husserl and the egocentric predicament." [Abstract]. *Journal
        of Philosophy,* vol. 67, 1970, 821-822.

2451    Kisiel, Theodore J. "Husserl on the history of science," essays in
        *Phenomenology and the natural sciences.* J. J. Kockelmans and T. J. Kisiel
        (ed. & trans.). Evanston, Ill.: Northwestern University Press, 1970, 68-90.

2452    Knight, Everett W. "Husserl," in his *Literature considered as philosophy.* New
        York: Macmillan, 1950, 3-33.

2453    Kockelmans, A. "Realisme-Idealisme in Husserls Phaenomenologie."
        *Tijdschrift voor Filosofie,* vol. 20, 1958.

2454    Kesten, Fred. "Zur transzendentalen Phänomenologie der Vernunft [E.
        Husserl]." *Perspektiven in Philosophie,* vol. 1, 1975, 57-84.

2455    Kockelmans, Joseph J. "The mathematization of nature in Husserl's last
        publication, *Krisis,*" in *Phenomenology and the natural sciences.* Essays and
        translations. J. J. Kockelmans and T. J. Kisiel (eds.). Northwestern
        University Press, 1970, 45-67.

2456    Kockelmans, Joseph J. "On the meaning and function of experience in
        Husserl's phenomenology," in *Der Idealismus und seine Gegenwart,*
        Festschrift fü Werner Marx. Hrsg. von U. Guzzoni, u.a. Hamburg: Felix
        Meiner Verlag, 1976, 297-317.

2457 Kosik, Karel. *Dialectics of the concrete*. A study of problems of man and world. K. Kovanda and J. Schmidt (trans.). Boston: D. Reidel Pub. Co., 1976.
**Book Reviews:**
M. Bakan, *Telos,* no. 35, Spring 1978, 244-253.

2458 Kraft, Julius. *Von Husserl zu Heidegger.* Kritik der phänomenologischen Philosophie. Leipzig, 1932. 2. Aufl. Frankfurt, 1957.
**Book Reviews:**
V. Springmeyer, *Kantstudien,* vol. 37, 281-284.

2459 Krzemicka, I. "Filosofia Ed. Husserl." *Ateneum* (Varsovie), 1939, 117-125.

2460 Külpe, Oswald. "Husserls Phänomenologie." *Deutschland unter Kaiser Wilhelm II,* 3. Teil, 1914, 15-16.

2461 Külpe, Oswald. *Vorlesungen uber Logik.* Leipzig, 1923, 139-157.

2462 Küng, Guido. "Husserl on pictures and intentional objects." *Journal of Philosophy,* vol. 69, 1972, 677.

2463 Kunz, Hans. "Die Verfehlung der Phänomene bei Edmund Husserl," in *Die Münchener Phänomenologie,* Hrsg. von Helmut Kuhn et al. (Phaenomenologica, 65). The Hague: Martinus Nijhoff, 1975, 39-62.

2464 Kuspit, Donald B. "Fiction and phenomenology [Husserl]." *Philosophy and Phenomenological Research,* vol. 29, 1968-1969, 16-33.

2465 Kuypers, K. "La conception de la philosophie comme science rigoureuse et les fondements des sciences chez Husserl." *Algemeen Nederlands Tijdschrift voor Wijsbegeerte en Psychologie,* vol. 51, 1958-1959, 225-233.

2466 Kwakman, S. "The beginning of philosophy. On the apodictic way to the object of transcendental experience in the philosophy of Edmund Husserl." *Tijdschrift voor Filosofie,* vol. 36, 1974, 521-564.

2467 Ladrière, Jean. "Hegel, Husserl, and reason today." *Modern Schoolman,* vol. 37, 1959-1960, 171-195.

2468 Lafont, Ghislain. "Genèse de la métaphysique [Husserl et l'être]." *Témoignages,* cahier 29, 1951, 214-223.

2469 Landgrebe, Ludwig. "Die Methode der Phänomenologie E. Husserls." *Neue Jahrbücher für Wissenschaft und Jugendbildung,* 1933.

2470 Landgrebe, Ludwig. "Husserls Phänomenologie und die Motive zu ihrer Umbildung." *Revue Internationale de Philosophie,* 1939, 277-316. Reprinted in his *Phänomenologie und Metaphysik.* Hamburg: Marion von Schröder, 1949.

2471 Landgrebe, Ludwig. *Philosophie der Gegenwart.* Bonn, 1952. (wiederveröffentlicht in Ullsein-Bücher, no. 166, 1957). Dutch trans. *Moderne filosofie,* L. Witsenburg (trans.). (Aula-boeken, 79). Utrecht: Het Spectrum 1962, 192 p.

2472 Landgrebe, Ludwig. "Husserls Abschied vom Cartesianismus." *Philosophische Rundschau,* vol. 9, 1962. "Husserl's departure from Cartesianism," in *The phenomenology of Husserl*, R. O. Elveton (ed. & trans.). Chicago: Quadrangle Books, 1970, 259-306. Reprinted in his *Den Weg der Phänomenologie*, 163-206.

2473 Landgrebe, Ludwig. "Lal phénoménologie de Husserl est-elle une philosophie transcendentale?" (Traduction française de M. Henri Colombié). *Etudes Philosophiques*, vol. 9, 1954, 315-323.

2474 Landgrebe, Ludwig. "Seinsregionen und regionale Ontologien in H usserls Phänomenologie." *Studium Generale*, vol. 9, 1956, 313-324. Reprinted in his *Den Weg der Phänomenologei*. Gütersloh: Gerd Mohn, 1963.

2475 Landgrebe, Ludwig. "Die Bedeutung der Phaänomenologie Husserls fur die Selbstbesinnung der Gegenwart"; "La signification de la phénoménologie de Husserl pour la réflelxion de notre époque," *Traduit par J. Taminiaux), in Husserl et la pensée moderne.* The Hague: Martinus Nijhoff, 1959, 216-223, 223-229.

2476 Landgrebe, Ludwig. "Husserl, Heidegger, Sartre. Trois aspects de la phénoménologie." *Revue de Métaphysique et de Morale*, vol. 69, 1964, 365-380.

2477 Landgrebe, Ludwig. "Introduzione alla fenomenologia di Edmund Husserl," in *Filosofi tedeschi d'oggi.* Saggi a cura di Albino Babolin. Bologna: Il Mulino, 1967, 217-241.

2478 Langlois, Jean. "Observations sur Husserl et la phénoménologie," in *La fenomenologia.* Atti dell'XI Convegno del Centro dei studi filosofici tra professori universitari-Gallarate 1955. Brescia: Morcelliana, 1956, 148-150.

2479 Langan, T. "Beyond positivism and psychologism," in *Recent philosophy, Hegel to the present*, E. H. Gilson (ed.). New York, 93-144.

2480 Lannoy, Chrysologus. "Phenomenologie, ontologie en psychologie en het werk van Edmund Husserl." *Tijdschrift voor Filosofie*, vol. 11, 1949, 391-416.

2481 Lansberg, Paul L. "Husserl et l'idée de la phénoménologie." *Revue Internationale de Philosophie*, 1939, 317-326.

2482 Lauer, Quentin. "The subjectivity of objectivity," in *Edmund Husserl 1859-1959.* (Phaenomenologica, 4). The Hague: Martinus Nijhoff, 1960, 167-174.

2483 Lee Kwei-Liang. "Edmund Husserl's phenomenology (in Chinese)." *Contemporary Thought Quarterly* (Taiwan), 1961.

2484 Lehmann, Gerhard. "Edmund Husserl," in *Geschichte der Philosophie*, XI: Die Philosophie im ersten Drittel des zwanzigsten Jahrhundert. Zweiter Teil (Samlung Göschen, 850). Berlin: Walter de Gruyter, 1960, 24-36.

2485 Leiss, William. "Husserl y el dominio de la naturaleza. Traducción: Geoges Delacre." *Diálogos*, vol. 7, no. 19, 1970, 31-52.

2486 Levin, David Michael. "Induction and Husserl's theory of eidetic variation." *Philosophy and Phenomenological Research*, vol. 29, Sept. 1968, 1-15.

2487   Levinas, Emmanuel. "L'oeuvre d'Edmond Husserl." *Revue Philosophique de la France et de l'Etranger,* CXXIX, 1940, 33-85. Reprinted in his *En découvrant l'existence avec Husserl et Heidegger.* Paris: Vrin, 1949, 5-52.

2488   Levinas, Emanuel. *De l'existence à l'existant.* Paris: Fontaine, 1947.

2489   Levinas, Emmanuel. "Intentionalité et métaphysique." *Revue Philosophique de la France et de l'Etranger,* vol. 84, 1959, no. 4, 471-479 [Edmund Husserl].

2490   Levinas, Emanuel. "Le permanent et l'humain chez Husserl." *Age Nouveau,* no. 110, 1960, 51-56.

2491   Levinas, Emmanuel. "De la conscience à la veille. A partir de Husserl." *Bijdragen,* vol. 34, 1974, 235-249.

2492   Levinas, Emmanuel. *Autrement qu'être, ou au-delà de l'essence.* The Hague: Martinus Nijhoff, 1974, x-236.

2493   Llambias de Azevedo, Juan. "La contribución del idealismo fenomenólogico a la restauración del realismo [Husserl]." *Cuadernos Uruguayos de filosofía,* vol. 1, 1961, 23-43.

2494   Lozinski, Jerzy. "On the problems of the relations between Marxism and phenomenology: Truth and revolution--Husserl and Lenin." *Dialectics and Humanism,* vol. 3, Winter 1976, 121-133.

2495   Lübbe, Hermann. "Das Ende des phänomenologislchen Platonismus. Eine kritische Betrachtung aus Anlass eines neuen Buches." *Theologie und Philosophie,* vol. 16, 1954, 639-666.

2496   Lübbe, Hermann. "Die geschichtliche Bedeutung der Subjektivitätstheorie Edmund Husserls." *Neue Zeitschrift für systematische Theologie,* vol. 2, 1960, 300-319.

2497   Lugarini, Leo. "Studi husserliani." *Archivo di Filosofia,* no. 1, 1960, 151-160.

2498   Lyotard, Jean-François. *La phénoménologie.* Paris: Presses Universitaires de France, Que Sais-je?, 1954.

2499   Macann, Christopher. "Genetic production and the transcendental reduction in Husserl." *Journal of the British Society for Phenomenology,* vol. 2, no. 1, 1971, 28-34.

2500   Mahnke, D. "Von Hilbert zu Husserl." *Unterrichtsblätter für Mathematik und Naturissenschaften,* vol. 29, 34-37.

2501   Mall, Ram Adhar. "Phenomenology of reason," in *Perspektiven transzendentalphänomenologischer Forschung* (Phaenomenologica, 49), Hrsg. von U. Claesges und K. Held. The Hague: Martinus Nijhoff, 1972, 129-144.

2502   Marbach, Eduard. "Ichlose Phänomenologie bei Husserl." *Tijdschrift voor Filosofie,* vol. 35, 1973, 518-559.

2503   Marcuse, Herbert. "On science and phenomenology," in *Positivism and sociology,* Anthony Giddens (ed.). London-New York: Heinemann, distributed by Humanities Press, 1974, 225-236. [On *The Crisis of European science and transcendental phenomenology*]

2504	Maréchal, J. "Phénoménologie pure ou philosophie de l'action," in *Festgabe für Geyser*, vol. I, Regensburg: Hebbell, 1931, 379-400. Reprinted in his *Mélanges J. Maréchal.* I. Paris: 1950, 181-206.

2505	Marini, Alfredo. "Edmund Husserl." *Belfagor* (Firenze), vol. 28, 1973, 557-591.

2506	Market, Oswaldo. "Primacia ontológica del 'ordo idearu' en Husserl." *Revista de Filosofía* (Madrid), vol. 19, 1960, 185-197.

2507	Market, Oswaldo. "Meditaciones husserlianas. El descubrimiento del plano trascendental [résumen]." *Revista de Filosofía* (Madrid), vol. 20, 1961, 423-426.

2508	Marx, Werner. "Vernunft und Lebenswelt. Bemerkungen zu Husserls 'Wissenschaft von der Lebenswelt' (reprinted *Hermeneutik und Dialektik*, Verl. Mohr, Tübingen, 1970] in *Vernunft und Welt.* Zwischen Tradition und anderem Anfang (Phaenomenologica, 36). The Hague: Martinus Nijhoff, 1970, 45-62.

2509	Massolo, Arturo. "Husserl e il cartesianismo." *Giornale Critico della Filoofia Italiana*, vol. 20, 1939, 434-452.

2510	Mathur, D. Ch. *Naturalistic philosophies of experience.* Studies in James, Dewey, and Farber against the background of Husserl's phenomenology. St. Louis: Warren H. Green, 1971, 158 p.

2511	Maxsein, Agnes. *Die Entwicklung des Begriffs a priori von Bolzano uber Lotze zu Husserl und den von ihm beeinflussten Phänomenologen.* Fulda, 1933.

2512	Mayer-Hillebrand, Franziska. "Von Brentanos Ursprünglicke und spätere Seinslehre und ihre Beziehungen zu Husserls Phänomenologie." *Zeitschrift für Philosophische Forschung*, vol. 13, no. 2, 1959, 316-339. [Edmund Husserl]

2513	Mays, Wolfe. "Husserl and phenomenology." *Philosophy*, vol. 46, 1971, 262-268.

2514	Mays, Wolfe. "Husserl on Ryle's review of Sein und Zeit." *Journal of the British Society for Phenomenology*, vol. 1, 1970, 14-15.

2515	Mays, Wolfe. "The later Husserl." *Inquiry*, vol. 17, 1974, 113-125.

2516	McCarthy, T. A. "Logic, mathematics and ontology in Husserl." *Journal of the British Society for Phenomenology*, vol. 3, 1972, 158-164.

2517	McGill, V. J. "A materialist approach to Husserl's philosophy," in *Philosophical essays in memory of Edmund Husserl*, Marvin Farber (ed.). Cambridge, Mass.: Harvard University Press, 1940, 231-250.

2518	Merlan, Philip. "Idéalisme, réalisme, phénoménologie," in *Husserl* (Cahiers de Royaumont, no. 3). Paris: Editions de Minuit, 1960, 383-410.

2519	Merleau-Ponty, Maurice. *Phénoménologie de la perception.* Paris: Gallimard, 1945.

2520   Merleau-Ponty, Maurice. *Les sciences de l'homme et la phénoménologie.* Les
       Cous de Sorbonne. Centre de Documentation universitaires a Paris, Tounier
       et Constans, 1951. "Phenomenology and the sciences of man," in his *The
       primacy of perception* and other essays on phenomenological psychology,
       the philosophy of art, history of politics. Evanston, Ill.: Northwestern
       University Press, 1964. Reprinted also in *Phenomenology and the social
       sciences,* Maurice Natanson (ed.). Evanston, Ill.: Northwestern University
       Press, 1973, vol. 1, 47-108.

2521   Merleau-Ponty, Maurice. "Le philosophe et son ombre," in *Edmund Husserl
       1859-1959* (Phaenomenologica, 4). The Hague: Martinus Nijhoff, 1959,
       195-110. Reprinted in his *Signes,* Paris: Gallimard, 1960. "The philosophy
       and his shadow," in *Signs.* Richard C. McLeary (trans.). Evanston, Ill.:
       Northwestern University Press, 1964, 159-181. Also in *Phenomenology and
       existentialism,* Robert C. Solomon (ed.). New York: Harper & Row, 1972,
       121-126.

2522   Messer, A. "Husserls Phänomenologie in ihrem Verhältnis zur Psychologie."
       *Archiv für die Gesammte Psychologie,* vol. 22, 1912 and vol. 32, 1914.

2523   Messer, A. "Ueber den Befriff des Aktes." *Archiv für die Gesammte
       Psychologie,* vol. 24, 1912.

2524   Messerich, Valerius. "An apodictic approach to reality [Husserl]." *Franciscan
       Studies* (St. Bonaventure), vol. 13, no. 2-3, 1953, 1-36.

2525   Metzger, Arnold. "Die Frge nach dem Menschen in der Philosophie unserer
       Zeit von Husserl bis Heidegger und Sartre." *Universitas,* vol. 27, 1972,
       65-72.

2526   Meyer, Rudolf. "Descartes, Valéry, Husserl." *Hamburger Akademische
       Rundschau,* vol. 3, 1950, 753-759.

2527   Meyn, Henning. "Nonempirical investigations in Husserl and ordinary
       language philosophy." *Southwestern Journal of Philosophy,* vol. 5, no.3,
       1974, 245-259.

2528   Micic, Jagorka. "Fenomenologija Edmund Husserla." *Studija iz savremene
       Filozofije* (Beograd), 1937, 176ff.

2529   Minozzi, Bruno. *Saggio di una teoria dell'essere come pesenza pura.* Bologna:
       Il Mulino, 1960, 267 p.

2530   Minozzi, Bruno. *L'idealismo fenomenologico di E. Husserl.* Bologna: Il
       Mulino, 1962, 32 p.

2531   Mohanty, J. N. "Husserl's phenomenology and Indian idealism."
       *Philosophical Quarterly,* vol. 24, 1951, 147-156.

2532   Mohanty, J. N. "Individual fact and essence in Edmund Husserl's
       philosophy," in his *Phenomenology and ontology* (Phaenomenologica, 37).
       The Hague: Martinus Nijhoff, 1970, 152-161.

2533   Mohanty, J. N. "*Life-world* and *a priori* in Husserl's later thought." *Analecta
       Husserliana,* vol. 3, 1974, 46-65.

2534    Molina, Fernando. "The Husserlian ideal of a pure phenomenology," in *An invitation to phenomenology*. Studies in the philosophy of experience, James M. Edie (ed.). Chicago: Quadrangle Books, 1965, 161-179.

2535    Montague, W. P. "Concerning Husserl's phenomenology." *Journal of Philosophy*, vol. 36, 1939, 232-233.

2536    Moore, S. "Is this phenomenology?" *Philosophy and Phenomenological Research*, vol. 3, 1942-1943, 78-84.

2537    Morriston, Wesley. "Intentionality and the phenomenological method: A critique of Husserl's transcendental idealism." *Journal of the British Society for Phenomenology*, vol. 7, Jan. 1976, 33-43.

2538    Morujño, Alexandre Fradique. "O 'fenómeno puro', punto de partida da fenomenologia de Husserl." *Filosofia* (Lisboa), vol. 4, no. 13, 1957, 1-17.

2539    Morujño, Alexandre Fradique. "Subjectividade e intersubjectivadade em Husserl," in *Actas Assemblie int. Estud. filos.*, 81-100.

2540    Müller, Gustav E. "On the historical significnce of Husserl's phenomenology." *Sophia*, vol. 21, 1953, 54-62.

2541    Müller, Max. "Phänomenologie, Ontologie und Scholastik." *Theologie und Philosophie*, 1952, 93-125. Reprinted in his *Crise de la métaphysique*. Paris: Desclée de Brouwer, 1953.

2542    Murphy, Richard T., S.J. "A metaphysical critique of method: Husserl and Merleau-Ponty," in *The quest for the absolute*, P. J. Adelmann (ed.). (Boston College Studies in Philosophy, vol. 1, 1966). The Hague: Martinus Nijhoff, 1966, 175-207.

2543    Mytrowytch, Kyryle. "La philosophie de l'existence et la finitude de la philosophie." *Revue Philosophique de Louvain*, vol. 55, 1957, 470-486.

2544    Naess, Arne. "Husserl on the apodictiv evidence of ideal laws." *Theoria*, vol. 20, 1954, 53-63.

2545    Natanson, Maurice. "Phenomenology from the natural standpoint: A reply to Van Meter Ames." *Philosophy and Phenomenological Research*, vol. 17, 1956-1957, 241-245.

2546    Natanson, Maurice. *Literature, philosophy, and the social sciences.* Essays in existentialism and phenomenology. 3rd printing. The Hague: Martinus Nijhoff, 1968, xii-220.

2547    Naville, Pierre. "Marx ou Husserl." *Revue Internationale de Philosophie*, no. 3, 1946, 227-243 et 414-454.

2548    Negri, Antimo. "Husserl filosofo senza storia?" *Giornale Critico della Filosofia Italiana*, vol. 41, 1962, 177-193.

2549    Neri, G. D. "La filosofia come ontologia universals e le obiezioni del relativismo scettico in Husserl," in *Omaggio a Husserl*. Milano: 1960, 67-79.

2550    Nielsen, H. A. "Is phenomenology based on an oversight?" *New Scholasticism*, vol. 52, Winter 1978, 72-79.

2551    Nieto Arteta, Luis Eduardo. "Husserl y Heidegger." *Cienci Fe,* vol. 8, no. 31-32, 1952, 29-39.

2552    Nieto Arteta, Luis Eduardo. "Husserl y Heidegger: La fenomenología y la analítica de la existencia." *Universidad de Antioquia* (Medellín), no. 114, 1953, 243-262.

2553    Nitta, Y. "Sur l'analytique universelle chez Husserl." (in Japanese). *Bunka,* vol. 19, no. 3, 1955, 69-90.

2554    Nudler, Oscar. "La psicología y la crisis de la ciencia según Husserl." *Cultura Universitaria* (Caracas), no. 96-97, 1967, 100-104.

2555    Null, Gilbert T. "The role of the perceptual world in the Husserlian theory of the sciences." *Journal of the British Society for Phenomenology,* vol. 7, Jan. 1976, 56-59.

2556    Olafson, Frederick F. *Principles and persons.* An ethical interpretation of existentialism. Baltimore: The Johns Hopkins University Press, 1967.

2557    Olvera, Francisco García. "El conocimiento humano y la fenomenología de Husserl." *Logos* (México), vol. 2, Sept.-Dec. 1974, 363-397.

2558    Orth, Wolfgang Ernst. "Husserls Begriff der cogitativen Typen und seine methodologische Reichweite," in *Phänomenologie heute.* Festschrift für L. Landgrebe (Phaenomenologica, 51). The Hague: Martinus Nijhoff, 1972, 138-167.

2559    Orth, Ernest W. "Husserl und Hegel. Ein Beitrag zum Problem des Verhältnisses historische- und systematischer Forschung in der Philosophie," in *Die Welt des Menschen. Die Welt der Philosophie.* Festschrift für Jan Patocka. Hrsg. von Walter Biemel. (Phaenomenologica, 72). The Hague: Martinus Nijhoff, 1976, 213-250.

2560    Osborn, Andrew. "A philosopher's philosopher." *Journal of Philosophy,* vol. 36, 1939, 234-236.

2561    Paci, Enzo. "Tempo e riduzione in Husserl." *Rivista di Filosofia,* vol. 50, 1959, 146-179.

2562    Paci, Enzo. "Sulla presenza come centro relazionale in Husserl." *Aut Aut,* no. 58, 1960, 236-241.

2563    Paci, Enzo. "Doxa e individuazione nella fenomenologia di Husserl." *Rivista di Filosofia,* vol. 51, 1960, 144-161.

2564    Paci, Enzo. "Husserl sempre di nuovo," in *Omaggio a Husserl.* Milano, 1960, 7-27.

2565    Paci, Enzo. "Fenomenologia, psicologia e unità della scienze [Husserl]." *Aut Aut,* no. 63, 1961, 214-234.

2566    Paci, Enzo. "Relazionismo e significato fenomenologico del mondo [Husserl]." *Il Pensiero,* vol. 6, 1961, 28-51.

2567    Paci, Enzo. *Funzione della scienze e significato dell'uomo.* Milano, 1963. *The function of the sciences and the meaning of man.* With an introduction by

P. Piccone and J. E. Hansen (trans.). Evanston, Ill.: Northwestern University Press, 1972, xxxv-475.

2568 Paci, Enzo. "Attualità di Husserl." *Revue Internationale de Philosophie*, vol. 19, no. 71-72, 1965, 5-16.

2569 Paci, Enzo. "Natura animale, uomo concreto e comportamento reale in Husserl." *Aut Aut*, no. 101, 1967, 27-47.

2570 Paci, Enzo. "Il senso delle parole. Fenomenologia della prassi e realta obiettiva [Husserl]." *Aut Aut*, no. 96-97, 1966-1967, 153-154.

2571 Paci, Enzo. "Fondazione e chiarificazione in Husserl." *Aut Aut*, no. 99, 1967, 7-13.

2572 Paci, Enzo. "Per una semplificazione dei temi husserlianai fino al primo volume di *Idee*," in *Studi in onore di Arturo Massolo*, a cura di Livio Sicherollo. Urbino: Argalia, 1967, 767-787.

2573 Paci, Enzo and Rovatti, Pier Aldo. "Persona, mondo circostante, motivazione [E. Husserl]." *Aut Aut*, no. 105-106, 1968, 142-171.

2574 Paci, Enzo. "Life-world, time and liberty in Husserl," in *Life-world and consciousness*. Essays in honor of Aron Gurwitsch, Lester E. Embree (ed.). Evanston, Ill.: Northwestern University Press, 1972, 461-468.

2575 Paci, Enzo. "Husserl: From naturalism to the phenomenological Encyclopedia," in *Phenomenology and natural existence*. Essays in honor of Marvin Farber, Dale Riepe (ed.). State University of New York Press, 1973, 131-154.

2576 Passmore, J. A. "The movement towards objectivity," in *A hundred of years of philosophy*. Hammonsworth, Middlesex: Penguin Books, 1969, 175-202.

2577 Patocka, Jan. "Der Subjectivisumus der Husserlschen und die Möglichkeit einer 'asubjektiven' Phänomenologie." *Philosophische Perspektiven*, vol. 2, 1970, 317-334.

2578 Patocka, Jan. "La philosophie de la crise des sciences d'après Edmond Husserl et sa conception d'une phénoménologie du 'monde de la vie'." *Archiwum Historii filosofii i Másti Spolecznej* (Warszawa), vol. 18, 1972, 3-18.

2579 Pedroli, G. "Realità e prassi in Husserl," in *Omaggio a Husserl*. Milano, 1960, 195-212.

2580 Pentzopoulou-Valalas, Thérèse. "Réflexions sur le fondement du rapport entre l'*a priori* et l'*eidos* dans la phénoménologie de Husserl." *Kantstudien*, vol. 65, 1974, 135-151.

2581 Pettit, Philip. *On the idea of phenomenology*. Dublin: Scepter Books, 1969, 99 p.

2582 Piana, Giovanni. "Husserl e la cultura cattolica." *Aut Aut*, no. 67, 1962, 37-43.

2583 Piana, Giovanni. "Accomunamento, storicità, tradizione nello Husserl inedito." *Aut Aut*, no. 68, 1962, 113-130.

2584 Pietersma, Henry. "Intuition and horizon in the philosophy of Husserl." *Philosophy and Phenomenological Research*, vol. 34, 1973-1974, 95-101.

2585    Piguet, Jean-Claude. *De l'esthéthique à la métaphysique.* (Phaenomenologica, 4). The Hague: Martinus Nijhoff, 1959, 165-175.

2586    Pintor-Ramos, Antonio. "Estudios husserlianos recientes." *Ciudad de Dios,* vol. 184, 1971, 261-270.

2587    Piorkowski, Henry, O.F.M. "The path of phenomenology: Husserl, Heidegger, Sartre, Merleau-Ponty." *Duns Scotus Philosophical Association,* vol. 30, 1966, 177-221.

2588    Pivcevic, Edo. *Von Husserl zu Sartre.* Auf. d. Spuren d. Phänomenologie. Aus d. Engl. von Anne Edwards (List -Taschenbücher der Wissenschaft, 1643: Philosophie). München: List, 1972, 254 p.

2589    Plessner, Helmuth. "Phänomenologie. Das Werk Edmund Husserls (1859-1938)," in *Zwischen Philosophie und Gesellschaft.* Bern: Francke, 1953, 39ff.

2590    Polinov, Hans. "Edmund Husserl." *Zeitschrfit Freie Deutsche Forschung,* 1, 1939, 105-108.

2591    Ponsetto, Antonio. "Edmund Husserl: Dalla critica alla società alla domanda intorno a Dio." *La Civiltà Cattolica,* vol. 121, no. 4, 1970, 233-239.

2592    Poortman, J. J. "De spanning in ieder van ons [*see:* R. F. Beerling 2260] *Algemeen Nederlands Tijdschrift voor Wijsbegeerte en Psychology,* vol. 56, 1963-1964, 87-90.

2593    Port, K. "Betrachtungen zu Husserls Einteilung der Kenkakte und ihrer erkenntnisstheoretischen Bedeutung." *Archiv für die Gesammte Psychologie,* Bd. 63, 369-412.

2594    Postow, B. C. "Husserl's failure to establish a presuppositionless science." *Southern Journal of Philosophy,* vol. 14, Summer, 1976, 179-188.

2595    Presas, Mario A. "Husserl en los límites de la fenomenología," in *Temas de filosofía contemporánea,* Emilio Sosa López (ed.)., Alberto Caturelli (IIo Congreso Nacional de Filosofía). Buenos Aires: Editorial Sud-americana, 1971, 173-184.

2596    Preti, G. "Filosofia e saggezza nel pensiero husserliano." *Archivo di Filosofia,* 1934, 83-88.

2597    Preti, G. "Edmund Husserl." *La Nuova Italia,* vol. 11, 83-85.

2598    Prufer, Thomas. "An outline of some Husserlian distinctions and strategies, especially in '*The Crisis*'," in *Phänomenologie heute,* Festschrift für Ludwig Landgrebe (Phaenomenologica, 51). The Hague: Martinus Nijhoff, 1972, 89-103.

2599    Przywara, Erich. "Edmund Husserl." *Modern Schoolman,* vol. 11, 1934, 57ff.

2600    Pucci, Raffaele. "Il trascendentale e mondo della vita nella fenomenologia di Huserl." *Rassegna di Scienze Filosofiche,* vol. 16, 1963, 67-89.

2601    Pucci, Raffaele. "Il mondo-della-vita e la storia [Husserl]." *Rassegna di Scienze Filosofiche,* vol. 16, 1963, 327-356.

2602    Pucci, Raffaele. "Edmond Husserl," in *Les grands courants de la philosophie contemporaine,* M. F. Sciacca (ed.). *Portraits.* Paris: Fischbacker, 1964, 771-802. Milano: Marzorati., Vol. 1, 771-802.

2603    Pucciarelli, Eugenio. "La idea de filosofía en Husserl." *Humanitas* (Tucumán), no. 13, 1960, 29-35.

2604    Pucciarelli, Eugenio. "Husserl y la actitud científica en filosofía." *Buenos Aires. Revista de Humanidades,* vol. 2, no. 2, 1962, 257-280.

2605    Rang, Bernhard. "Räpresentation und Selbstgegebenheit. Die Aporie der Phänomenologie der Wahrnehmung in den Frühschriften Husserls," in *Phänomenologie heute,* (Phaenomenologica, 51). The Hague: Martinus Nijhoff, 1972, 105-137. Also in *Der Idealismus und seine Gegenwart,* Festschrift für Werner Marx zum 65. Geburtstag. Hrsg. von U. Guzzoni, u.a. Hamburg: Felix Meiner Verlag, 1976, 378-397.

2606    Reboul, Jean. "Husserl et le Vedanta." *Revue de Métaphysique et de Morale,* vol. 64, 1959, 320-336.

2607    Reinach, Adolf. *Was ist Phänomenologie?* München, 1951 [auch in: Reinach: *Gesammelte Werke,* Halle, 1921]

2608    Reiner, Hans. "Sinn und Recht der phänomenologischen Methode," in *Edmund Husserl 1859-1959* (Phaenomenologica, 4). The Hague: Martinus Nijhoff, 1959, 134-147.

2609    Richir, Marc. "Husserl: une pensée sans mesure." *Critique,* vol. 25, 1969, 778-808.

2610    Ricoeur, Paul. "Edmond Husserl," in *Histoire de la philosophie allemande.* Paris: J. Vrin, 1967, 183-197. *See:* Brehier 2291

2611    Ricoeur, Paul. "Analogie et intersubjectivité chez Husserl d'après les Inédits de la périod 1905-1920 (Edition Iso Kern, *Husserliana,* tome XIII, Nijhoff, 1973)," in *Enige facette van opvoeding en onderwijs,* 163-170. [Nederlandse samenvatting door Monica Geertsen-Smits, 171-172]

2612    Ricoeur, Paul. "Phénoménologie existentielle," in *Encyclopédie Française,* t. XIX. Paris: Larousse, 1957, 19.10-8 a 19.10-12.

2613    Riepe, Dale (ed.). *Phenomenology and natural existence.* Essays in honor of Marvin Farber. State University of New York Press, 1973.

2614    Rintelen, Fritz-Joachim von. *Contemporary German philosophy and its background. Deutsche Philosophie der Gegenwart.* Bonn: Bouvier, 1970, 1777 p.

2615    Riverso, E. "Il valore della logica in E. Husserl." *Sapienza,* vol. 13, 1960, 251-256.

2616    Rizo, Urbano. "La fenomenología de Husserl." *Montezuma* (México), no. 104, 1950, 27-36.

2617    Robert, Jean-Dominique. "Approches rétrsopectives de la phénoménologie husserlienne. Rappel de quelques éléments de sa genèse et de son évolution, ses chances d'avenir." *Laval Theologique et Philosophique,* vol. 28, 1972, 27-62.

2618    Roche, Maurice. *Phenomenology, language and the social sciences.* London: Routledge and Kegan Paul, 1973.

2619    Rollin, France. *La phénoménologie au départ.* Husserl, Heidegger, Gaboriau (Trident, 3). Paris: P. Lethielleux, 1967, 200 p.

2620    Rossi, Alejandro. "Sentido y sinsentido en las *Investigaciones lógicas.*" *Diánoia* (México), vol. 6, 1960, 91-114.

2621    Rossi, Mario M. "Die Entwicklung der Lehre von Husserl: Phänomenologie und Phänomenologismus." *Giornale di Metafisicia,* vol. 15, 1960, 492-500.

2622    Rovatti, Pier Aldo. "'Geist' e 'Lebenswelt' nella filosofia di Husserl." *Aut Aut,* no. 105-106, 1968, 44-65.

2623    Rubert y Candau, José Maria. "El campo básico de la filosofía y la intuición. Un diálogo con E. Husserl." *Verdad y Vida,* vol. 18, 1960, 301-320.

2624    Ruggiero, Guido de. "Husserl e la 'Fenomenologia'." *La Critica,* 29, 1931, 100-109. Reprinted in his *Filosofi del novecento,* 1934, 88ff.

2625    Ryle, Gilbert. "Phenomenology." *Proceedings of the Aristotelian Society.* Supplement, 1932, 68-115. Reprinted in part, in *Phenomenology and existentialism,* Robert C. Solomon (ed.). New York: Harper & Row, 1972, 213-226.

2626    Salman, D. H. "La phénoménologie après Husserl." *Revue des Sciences Philosophiques et Théologique,* vol. 31, 1947, 237-240.

2627    Salmon, C. V. "The starting point of Husserl's philosophy." *Proceedings of the Aristotelian Society,* vol. 30, 1930.

2628    Sancipriano, Mario. "Intuizione e possesso nella fenomenologia di Edmondo Husserl," in *La fenomenologia.* Milano, 1960, 151-160.

2629    Sartre, Jean-Paul. "Une idée fondamentale de la philosophie de Husserl." *Nouvelle Revue Francçaise,* no. 304, 1939, vol. 27, 129-132. Reprinted in his *Situations, I.* Paris: Gallimard, 1947.

2630    Sartre, Jean-Paul. *L'être et le néant.* Paris: Gallimard, 1943.

2631    Scanlon, John D. "Formal logic and formal ontology." *Research in Phenomenology,* vol. 5, 1975, 95-108.

2632    Schacht, Robert. "Husserl and Heidegger," in *Hegel and after. Studies in contemporary philosophy between Kant and Sartre.* Pittsburgh, Pa.: University of Pittsburgh Press, 1975, 207-228.

2633    Schérer, René. "Clôture et faille dans la phénoménologie de Husserl." *Revue de Métaphysique et de Morale,* vol. 73, 1968, 344-360.

2634    Schérer, René. "Edmund Husserl, la phénoménologie et ses développements," in *Histoire de la philosophie: idées, doctrines,* éditée sous la direction de François Chatelet. Paris: Hachette, 1972-1973, vol. VI, chap. 9.

2635    Schestow, Leo. *see also:* Chestov. "Memento mori," in *Potestas clavium.* München: Nietzsche Gesellschaft, 1926.

2636    Sjestow, Leo. *Krisis der zekerheden.* Pascal-Dostojewsky-Husserl. [Trans. *Na wesach iowa en Potestas clavium*]. Vert. uit het Russisch door C. I. Spruit, 2e dr. (Parthenon-recks). Bussum: Moussalt, 1958, 220 p.

2637    Schuhmann, Karl. "Over de grondslagen van de fenomenologie [Husserl]. *Tijdschrift voor Filosofie,* vol. 32, 1970, 471-486. [Zusamenfassung: Über die Grundlagen der Phänomenologie, 486-487]

2638    Schütz, Alfred. "Husserl and his influence on me," in *Interdisciplinary phenomenology,* Don Ihde and Richard M. Zaner (eds.). The Hague: Martinus Nijhoff, 1977, 124-129.

2639    Schütz, Alfred. "Type and eidos in Husserl's late philosophy." *Philosophy and Phenomenological Research,* vol. 20, no. 2, 1959-1960, 147-165. Reprinted in his *Collected papers, III:* Studies in phenomenological philosophy, with an introduction by Aron Gurwitsch. The Hague: Martinus Nijhoff, 1970, 92-115.

2640    Schwartzmann, Félix. "Husserl y la ciencia moderna." *Revista de Filosofía* (Universidad e Chile), vol. 6, no. 2-3, 1959, 27 p.

2641    Seebohm, Thomas M. "Reflexion and totality in the philosophy of E. Husserl." *Journal of the British Society for Phenomenology,* vol. 4, 1973, 20-30 [Nigel J. Grant, "A reply to Thomas E. Seebohm," *Ibid,* 31-32. K. Hartmann, "Comments on T. M. Seebohm's paper," *Ibid.,* 45]

2642    Seifert, Josef. "Über die Möglichkeit einer Metaphysik. Die Antwort der ''Münchener Phänomenologen: auf E. Husserls Transzendentalphilosophie," in *Die Münchener Phänomenologie,* Hrsg. von Helmut Kuhn, et al. (Phaenomenologica, 65). The Hague: Martinus Nijhoff, 1975, 81-104.

2643    Semarari, G. *Da Schelling a Merleau-Ponty.* Bologna, 1962.

2644    Serrus, Charles. "L'oeuvre philosophique d'Edmond Husserl." *Etudes Philosophiques,* vol. 4, 1930, 42-46, 126-133; and *Ibid.,* vol. 5, 1931, 18-23.

2645    Serrus, Charles. "E. Husserl's *Nachwort* et *Méditations cartésiennes.*" *Etudes Philosophiques,* vol. 5, 1931.

2646    Sinha, Debabrata. "The phenomenology of Husserl." *The Calcutta Review,* 1960, 241-250.

2647    Sinha, Debabrata. "Theory and practice in Indian thought: Husserl's observations." *Philosophy East and West,* vol. 21, 1971, 255-264.

2648    Sinha, Debabrata. "Phenomenology: A break-through to a new intuitionism," in *Phänomenologie heute.* Festschrift für L. Landgrebe (Phaenomenologica, 51). The Hague: Martinus Nijhoff, 1972, 27-48.

2649    Sini, C. "Husserl e il pensiero moderno." *Il Pensiero,* no. 2, 1961, 203-215.

2650    Sini, C. "Per una propedeutica alla fenomenologia come scienza rigorosa." *Aut Aut,* no. 84, 1964, 19-51.

2651    Sini, C. "Lezioni introduttive alla fenomenologia di Husserl," in Enzo Paci, *Fenomenologia e antropologia.* Milano, 1962, 3-96. (dispense universitaire).

2652 Smith, Joseph. "Being and subjectivity: Heidegger and Husserl," in *Phenomenology in perspective,* F. J. Smith (ed.). The Hague: Martinus Nijhoff, 1970, 122-156.

2653 Sokolowski, Robert. "Edmund Husserl and the principles of phenomenology," in *Twentieth century thinkers,* J. K. Ryan (ed.). New York: Alba House, 1968, 133-157.

2654 Sokolowski, Robert. "Husserl's protreptic," in *Life-world and consciousness.* Essays for Aron Guwitsch, Lester E. Embree (ed.). Evanston, Ill.: Northwestern University Press, 1972, 55-82.

2655 Solomon, Robert C. "Edmund Husserl and phenomenology: The new way of philosophy," in his *From rationalism to existentialism. The existentialists and their ninteenth century backgrounds.* New York: Harper & Row, 1972, 141-173.

2656 Somogyi, Jozscí. "Edmund Husserl (1859-1938)." *Ateneum* (Warsaw), vol. 24, 1939, 209-224.

2657 Spear, Otto. "Philosophie als Menschheitsaufgabe. Der Philosoph Edmund Husserl in der Situation unserer Zeit." *Univeristas,* vol. 24, 1969, 1315-1324.

2658 Spiegelberg, Herbert. "Husserl's way into phenomenology for Americans. A letter an its sequel [German original and translation]," in *Phenomenology. Continuation and criticism. Essays in memory of Dorion Cairns* (Phaenomenologica, 50). The Hague: Martinus Nijhoff, 1973, 168-191.

2659 Stegmüller, Wolfgang. "Edmund Husserl," in *Haptströmungen der Gegenwartsphilosophie. Eine kritisch-historische Einführung* (Sammlung "Die Universität," vol. 32). Wien-Stuttgart: Humbolt Verlag, 1952, 494 p. English translation "Methodological phenomenology: Edmund Husserl," in *Main currents in contemporary German, English and American philosophy.* A. E. Blenberg (trans. from the German). Bloomington, Ind.: Indiana University Press, 1970, chap. 2, 63-108.

2660 Stein, Edith. "Husserls Phänomenologie und die Philosophie des heiligen Thomas von Aquino." *Jahrbuch für Philosophie und Phänomenologische Forschung,* (Husserl Festschrift, 1929), 1929.

2661 Stein, Edith. *Endliches und ewiges Sein.* Louvain: Nauwelaerts, 1950.

2662 Stern, Alfred. "Husserl's phenomenology and the scope of philosophy." *The Personalist,* vol. 35, 1954, 267-284.

2663 Stevens, Richard. "Spatial and temporal models in Husserl's *Ideen II.*" *Cultural Hermeneutics,* vol. 3, 1975-1976, 105-117.

2664 Stewart, David and Mickunas, Algis. *Exploring phenomenology:* A guide to the field and literature. Chicago: America Library Association, 1974, vii-165.

2665 Strasser, Stephan. "Het vraagstuk van t' solipsism bij Ed. Husserl." *Tijdschrift voor Filosofie,* vol. 7, 1945, 3-78.

2666    Strasser, Stephan. "Beschouwingen over 't vraagstuk van de apodicticiteit en de critische verantwoording van de phenomenologie." *Tijdschrift voor Filosofie,* vol. 8, 1946, 226-270.

2667    Strasser, Stephan. "Die doppelte Ich-Spaltung in der transzendentalen Phänomenologie Edmund Husserls." *Seele und Beseeltes,* Vienna, 1955, 45-54.

2668    Strasser, Stephan. *The idea of dialogal phenomenology.* Pittsburgh, Pa.: Duquesne University Press, 1973, 136 p. [Inability of Husserl's transcendental phenomenology to solve the problem of intersubjectivity]

2669    Street, James Fulton. "The Cartesianism of phenomenology." *Philosophical Review,* 1940.

2670    Strenger, I. "Influências de Husserl no pensamento jusfilsoófico brasileiro actual." *Revista Brasileira de Filosofia,* vol. 9, 1959, 569-576.

2671    Szilasi, Wilhelm. "Werk und Wirkung Husserls [Erschienen in *Die neue Rundschau,* no. 4, vol. 70, 1959], in *Philosophie und Naturwissenschaft* (Dalp-Taschenbücher, 347). Bern & München: Francke, 1961, 115-133.

2672    Swiderski, Edward M. "Phenomenology in the *Filosofskaja Enciklopedija.*" *Studies in Soviet Thought,* vol. 18, Feb. 1978, 57-66.

2673    Tertulian, Nicolas. "Camil Petrescu e la fenomenologia di Husserl." *Aut Aut,* no. 112, 1969, 71-86.

2674    Theunissen, Michael. "Objeto intencional y diferencia ontológica. Inicios del planteamineto de Heidegger en la fenomenología de Husserl." (Traducción de Ramon Castilla Lázaro). *Diálogos,* vol. 1, no. 2, 1964, 35-59.

2675    Thévenaz, Pierre. "La question du point de départ radical chez Descartes et Husserl," in *Problèmes actuels de la phénoménologie.* Paris: Desclée de Brouwer, 1952, 9-30. Reprinted in his *L'homme et sa raison.* T. I: Raison et conscience de soi. Préface de Paul Ricoeur ("Etre et penser." Cahiers de philosophie, 46). NeuchÂtel: Editions de la Baconnière, 1956, 147-165.

2676    Thévenaz, Peirre. Qu'est-ce que la phénoménologie? I: La phénoménologie de Husserl." *Revue de Théologie et de Philosophie,* vol. 2, 3e serie, 1952, 9-30. Reprinted in his *De Husserl à Merleau-Ponty.* Qu'est-ce que la phénoménologie? (Coll. "Etre et penser," 52). NeuchÂtel: Editions de la Baconnière, 1966, 120 p. English translation *What is phenomenology,* James M. Edie (ed. & trans.). Chicago: Quadrangle Books, 1966. *La fenomenologia.* Trad. G. Mura.

2677    Thyssen, Johanne. "Husserls Lehre von den "Bedeutungen' und das Begriffskproblem." *Zeitschrift für Philosophische Forschung,* vol. 13, no. 2, 1959, 163-186, and *Ibid.,* 438-458.

2678    Thyssen, Johannes. "Wege aus dem geschlossenen System von Husserls Monadologie," in *Actes du XIe Congrès International de Philosophie,* Bruxelles, 1953, 188-194.

2679    Thyssen, Johannes. "Die Husserlsche Faszination." *Zeitschrift für Philosophische Forschung,* vol. 17, 1963, 553-585.

2680    Tymieniecka, Anna-Teresa. "Husserl's phenomenology opening the field of inquiry," in her *Phenomenology and science in contemporary European thought.* New York: Farrar, Strauss Cudihy, Noonday Press, 1962, 1-17.

2681    Tymieniecka, Anna-Teresa. "Beyond Ingarden's idealism/realism controversy with Husserl--The new contextual phase of phenomenology," in *Ingardeniana. Analecta Husserliana,* vol. 4, 1976, 241-418.

2682    Tymieniecka, Anna-Teresa. "Phenomenology reflects upon itself, II. The ideal of the universal science: The original project of Husserl reinterpreted with reference to the acquisitions of phenomenology and the progress of contemporary science." *Analecta Husserliana,* vol. 2, 1972, 3-17.

2683    Uccelli, Augusta. "Problematica husserliana logico-algebrica." *Aut Aut,* no. 85, 1965, 31-45.

2684    Ueberweg, Freidrich. *Grundriss der Geschichte der Philosophie.* 4. T.: Die deutsche Philosophie des 19. Jahrhunderts und der Gegenwart. Hrsg. von Traugott Konstantin Oesterreich. 13. Aufl., univeränd. Nachdr. d. völlig neubearb. 12. Aufl. Tübingen: Wiss. Buchgemeinschaft, 1951, 503-513.

2685    Ureña, Enrique Menéndez. "Teoriía y praxis en la fenomenología trscendental (E. Husserl) y en la teoría crítica (J. Habermas)." *Pensamiento,* vol. 31, July-Sept. 1975, 231-245.

2686    Uranga,Emilio. "Leyendo a Husserl." *Revista Méxicana de literatura,* mayo-junio 1957, 41-55.

2687    Uygar, Nermi. "Die Phäanomenologie Husserls und die 'Gemeinschaft'." *Kantstudien,* vol. 50, 1958-1959, 439-460.

2688    Valori, Paolo. "Essenza e significto della fenomenologia husserliana." *Giornale di Metafisicia,* vol. 8, 1953, 222-232.

2689    Valori, Paolo. "Inédits husserliens sur la théologie de l'histoire," in *La philosophie et l'histoire de la philosophie.* Roma: Istituto di Studi filosofici; Paris: Vrin, 1956, 121-123.

2690    Valori, Paolo. "Evidenza e verità nella fenomenologia husserliana." *Aquinas,* vol. 1, 1958, 224-240.

2691    Valori, Paolo. "Recenti studi sulla fenomenologia husserliana." *Civiltà Cattolica,* vol. 112, I, 1961, 278-285.

2692    Van Beda, Hermann Leo. "Het 'Zuivere Phaenomeen' volgens Husserl." *Tijdschrift voor Filosofie,* vol. 3, 1941, 477-498.

2693    Van Breda, Hermann Leo. "Note sur E. Husserl," in *Philosophie de la religion,* du R. P. Ortegat. Louvain-Paris: Ed. de l'Institut Supérieur de Philosophie, Vrin, 1948, t. II, 702-705.

2694    Van Breda, Hermann Leo. "La fécondité des grands thèmes husserliens pour le progrès de la recherche philosophique." *Philosophisches Jahrbuch,* vol. 66, 1957 [Festschrift H. Conrad-Martius], 5-11. "Great themes in Husserl's thought: Their fruitfulness and influence." *Philosophy Today,* vol. 3, 1959, 192-198.

2695    Van Breda, Hermann Leo. "La phénoménologie," in *La philosophie au milieu du vingtième siècle*. Tome II: Par les soins de Raymond Klibanski. Firenze: La Nuova Italia Editrice, 1958, 53-70.

2696    Van Breda, Hermann Leo. "L'itinéraire husserlien de la phénoménologie pure à la phénoménologie transcendentale," in *Die Welt des Menschen. Die Welt der Philosophie*. Festschrift für Jan Patocka. Hrsg. von Walter Biemel (Phaenomenologica, 72). The Hague: Martinus Nijhoff, 1976, 301-318.

2697    Van Breda, Hermann Leo. "L'itinéraire husserlien de la phénoménologie pure à la phénoménologie transcendentale. Exposé: Père Hermann Leo Van Breda. Discussion: Mlle. S. Bachelard, MM. Y. Belaval, E. Levinas, R. Ninck, P. Ricoeur, P. M. Schuhl, E. Wolff. *In memoriam:* H. L. Van Breda: E. Levinas, P. Ricoeur. *Bulletin de la Société Française de Philosophie,* vol. 67, no. 4, 1973, 149-187,

2698    Van de Pitte, M. M. "Is there a phenomenological method?" *Metaphilosophy,* vol. 8, Jan. 1977, 21-35.

2699    Vanni Rovighi, Sofia. "Edmund Husserl." *Rivista di Filosofia Neo-Scholstica,* vol. 30, 1938, 338-340.

2700    Vanni-Rovighi, Sofia. "La fenomenologia di Husserl." *Humanitas* (Brescia), vol. 1, 1946, 141-149.

2701    Vanni-Rovighi, Sofia. "Edmund Husserl e la perenita della filosofia," in *Edmund Husserl 1859-1959.* (Phaenomenologica, 4). The Hague: Martinus Nijhoff, 1959, 185-194.

2702    Vanni-Rovighi, Sofia. "Studi husserliani." *Rivista di Filosofia Neo-Scholstica,* vol. 55, 1963, 522-536.

2703    Vanni-Rovighi, Sofia. "La fenomenologia di Husserl." *Verifiche,* vol. 2, no. 1, 1973, 3-17.

2704    Verdenal, René. s "La sémiotique de Husserl: La logique des signes (A propos de certins inéditis)." *Etudes Philosophiques,* no. 4, 1973, 553-564.

2705    Villoro, Luis. "La 'reducción a la inmanencia' en Husserl." *Diánoia* (México), vol. 12, 1966, 215-235. Reprinted in his *Estudios sobre Husserl.* México: UNAM, 1975.

2706    Villoro, Luis. "La constitución de la realidad en la conciencia pura (El segundo tomo de las *Ideen zu einer reinen Phänomenologie und phänomenologischen Philosophie* de Husserl)." *Diánoia* (México), vol. 5, 1959, 195-212. Reprinted in his *Estudios sobre Husserl.* México: UNAM, 1975.

2707    Vuillemin, Jules. "Le problème phénoménologique: intentionalité et réflexion." *Revue Philosophique de la France et de l'Etranger,* vol. 84, no. 4, 1959 [Edmund Husserl], 463-470.

2708    Waelhens, Alphonse de. "Descartes et la pensée phénoménologique." *R. N. S.,* vol. 41, 1938, 571-589.

2709    Waelhens, Alphonse de. "Husserl et la phénoménlogie." *Critique,* vol. 8, no. 55, 1951, 1044-1057.

2710    Waelhens, Alphonse de. "Phénoménologie husserlienne et phénoménologie hégéliene." *Revue Philosophique de Louvain,* vol. 52, 1954, 234-249.

2711    Waelhens, Alphonse de. *Phénoménologie et vérité.* Paris: 1953.

2712    Waelhens, Alphonse de. "Husserl (1859-1938)," in *Les philosophes célèbres.* Ouvrage publié sous la direction de Maurice Merleau-Ponty (La Galerie des hommes célèbres. Collections créeé et dirigée par Lucien Mazenod, vol. 9). Paris: Editions d'art Lucien Mazenod, 1956, 322-329.

2713    Waelhens, Alphonse de. "Kommentaar op *Die Idee der Phaenomenologie.*" *Tijdschrift voor Filosofie,* vol. 19, 1957, 602-620 [Resume on francais, 620].

2714    Wagner, Hans. "Kritische Bemerkungen zu Husserls *Nachlass.*" *Philosophische Rundschau,* vol. 1, 1953-1954, 1-22. "Critical observations concerning Husserl's posthumous writings," in *The phenomenology of Husserl,* R. O. Elveton (ed. & trans.). Chicago: Quadrangle Books, 1970, 204-258.

2715    Wahl, Jean. "Notes sur quelques aspects empiristes de la pensée de Husserl." *Revue de Métaphysique et de Morale,* vol. 57, 1952, 17-45. Reprinted in *Phénoménologie. Existence.* Recueil d'études par Henri Birault, et al. Paris: Armand Colin, 1953, 107-139.

2716    Waldenfels, Bernhard. "Weltliche und soziale Einzigkeit bei Husserl." *Zeitschrift für Philosophische Forschung,* vol. 25, 1971, 157-171.

2717    Waldenfels, Bernhard. "El regreso de Husserl al 'mundo de la vida'." (Trad.por Carmen Rodríguez de Gauger. *Documentación Crítica Iberoamericana de Filosofía y Ciencias Afines,* vol. 2, 1965, 597-601.

2718    Warnke, Camilla. "Husserl's transcendental subject." *Dialectics and Humanism,* Winter 1976, 103-109.

2719    Welch, E. Parl. "Max Scheler's phenomenology of religion." Dissertation, University of Southern California, 1934. [First section deals with Husserl]

2720    Welch, E. Parl. "Edmund Husserl. An appreciation." *The Personalist,* Winter 1940.

2721    Weinzweig, Marjorie. "Phenomenologya and ordinary language philosophy." *Metaphilosophy,* vol. 8, April-June 1977, 116-146.

2722    Welton, Donn. "Intentionality and language in Husserl's phenomenology." *Review of Metaphysics,* vol. 27, 1973-1974, 260-297.

2723    White, David A. "Husserl and the poetic consciousness." *The Personalist,* vol. 53, 1972, 408-424.

2724    White, Morton G. "Phenomenology: Edmund Husserl," in his *Age of analysis.* Boston: Houghton Mifflin, 1955, 100-115.

2725    Winance, Eleuthère, O.S.B. "Logique, Mathématique et ontologie comme 'mathesis universalis' chez Edmond Husserl." *Revue Thomiste,* vol. 66, 1966, 410-434.

Wissengrund, Theodor. [*see:* Adorno, *Dissertation,* 312]

2726 Witschel, Günter. "Zwei Beiträge Husserls zum Problem der sekundären Quälitaten." *Zeitschrift für Philosophische Forschung,* vol. 18, 1964, 30-49.

2727 Wundt, Wilhelm. *Kleine Schriften,* vol. 1, Leipzig, 1910, 511-634.

2728 Xirau, Joaquín. "A crisis. Husserl and Bergson." *The Personalist,* 1946, 27-33, and *Ibid.,* 269-294.

2729 Zaner, Richard M. *The way of phenomenology.* New York: Pegasus Books, 1970. [Chap. 3: on *Ideas* and *Phenomenology of internal time-consciousness.]*

2730 Zaner, Richard M. "Examples and possibles: A criticism of Husserl's theory of free-phantasy variation." *Research in Phenomenology,* vol. 3, 1973, 29-44.

2731 Zubiri, Xavier. "Husserl, la filosofiía como ciencia estricta," in his *Cinco lecciones de filosofía.* Madrid: Sociedad de Estudios y publicaciones, 1963, 213-279.

## Section 6

## Studies and Reviews of Individual Works By Husserl

### 1) *Philosophie der Arithmetik*

2732 Bixio, A. *Rivista Internazionale di Filosofia del Diritto,* vol. 50, 1973, 342-344.

2733 Bosio, Franco. "Gli inizi della fenomenologia. La '*Filosofia dell'aritmetica*'." *Aut Aut,* no. 70, 1962, 294-308.

2734 Couloubaritsis, L. "*Philosophie de l'arithmétique.* Trad. par J. English (1971)." *Cahiers Internationaux du Sybolisme,* no. 22-23, 1973, 114-116.

2735 Elsas, A. "Husserls *Philosophie der Arithmetik.*" *Philosophische Monatshefte,* vol. 30, 1894, 437-440.

2736 Frege, E. Gottlob. *Zeitschrift für Philosophie und Philosophische Kritik,* no. 103, 1894, 313-332. Translated in English and reprinted in *The philosophical writings of Gottlob Frege,* M. Black and P. Geatch (eds.). Oxford: Basil Blackwell, 1960. Partial translation in *Phenomenology and existentialism,* Robert C. Solomon (ed.). New York: Harper & Row, 1972, 96-105. Trans. of E. W. Klug, in *Mind,* vol. 81, 1972, 321-337. Reprinted in *Husserl. Expositions and appraisals,* F. Elliston and P. McCormick (eds.). Notre Dame, Ind.-London: Notre Dame University Press, 1977, 314-324.

2737 Heurtas-Jourda, José. "On the threshold of phenomenology. A study of Edmund Husserl's *Philosophie der Arithmetik.*" Ph.D. Dissertation, New York University, 1969, 209 p. *Dissertation Abstracts,* vol. 30, no. 8, Feb. 1970, 3502-A.

2738 Kluge, E.-H. W. *Dialogue,* vol. 12, 1973,, 147-150.

2739 Torretti, Roberto. "La filosofia de la aritmética de Husserl." *Studi Internzaionali di Filosofia,* vol. 4, 1972, 183-206.

2740 Wussing, H. *Deutsche Literaturseitung* (Berlin), vol. 92, 1971, 745-746.

2) *On the concept of Number.* Psychological analysis.

2741    Husserl, Edmund. "On the concept of number. Psychological analysis. Introduction by Dallas Willard (trans.)." *Philosophia Mathematica,* vol. 9, 1972, 40-52; vol. 10, 1973, 37-87.

2742    Willard, Dallas. "Concerning Husserl's view of number." *Southwestern Journal of Philosophy,* vol. 5, Fall 1974, 97-109.

3) *The origin of geometry*

2743    Bernard-Maître, H. *Revue de Synthèse,* vol. 87, 1966, 106-107.

2744    Deguy, M. *Critique,* vol. 19, no. 192, 1963, 434-448.

2745    Husserl, Edmund. *L'origine de la géométrie.* Traduction et introduction par Jacques Derrida (Epiméthée. Essais philosophiques. Collection dirigée par Jean Hyppolite). Paris: Presses Universitaires de France, 1962, iv-220.

2646    Gatta, Ernesto A. "I temi della fenomenologia e l'*Origine della geometria* [Husserl]." *Annali della Facoltà di Lettere e Filosofia* (Bari), vol. 8, 1962, 5-26.

2747    Jacob, A. *Etudes Philosophiques,* vol. 18, 1963, 465.

2748    Leavy, John P. "Undecidables and old names: Derrida's deconstruction and 'Introduction' to Husserl's *The origin of geometry.*" Ph.D. Dissertation, Emory University, 1976. *Dissertation Abstracts,* vol. 37, no. 9, March 1977, 3886-A.

2749    Lemaigre, B.-M. *Revue des Sciences Philosophiques et Théologiques,* vol. 51, 1967, 298-304.

2750    Sturani, E. *Rivista di Filosofia,* vol. 56, 1965, 101-102.

2751    Wahl, Jean. *Revue de Métaphysique et de Morale,* vol. 70, 1965, 122-123.

4) *Logische Untersuchungen*

2752    Atwell, John E. "A critical exposition of Edmund Husserl's first two *Logical investigations.*" Ph.D. Dissertation, University of Wisconsin, 1964, 208 p. *Dissertation Abstracts,* vol. 25, no. 6, Dec. 1964, 3616-A. Ann Arbor, Mich.-London: University Microfilms International, 1976.

2753    Banfi, A. "La tendenza logistica della filosofia tedesca contemporanea e le *Ricerche logiche* di Edmund Husserl." *Rivista di Filosofia,* vol. 14, 1923.

2754    Bernard-Maître, H. "*Recherches logiques, I-III.*" *Revue de Synthèse,* vol. 87, 1966, 105-106.

2755    Blanché, R. "*Recherches logiques, II:* Recherches pour la phénoménologie... I-II." *Revue Philosophique de la France et de l'Etranger,* vol. 90, 1965, 245-246.

2756    Bosio, Franco. "L'intenzionalità e il concetto di conscienza nella *Logische Untersuchungen* [Husserl]." *Aut Aut,* no. 72, 1962, 479-504.

2757   Busse, L. *Zeitschrift für Philosophie und Psychologie der Sinnersorgane,* vol. 33, 1903, 153-157.

2758   Casaubón, Juan Alfredo. "Gérmenes de idealismo en las *Investigaciones lógicas* de Husserl." *Sapientia,* vol. 11, 1956, 250-280.

2759   Creaven, J. A. "*Logical investigations,* I-II." *Heythrop Journal,* vol. 12, 1971, 192-197.

2760   De Boer, Theodorus. "Das Verhältnis zwischen de ersten und dem zweiten Teil der *Logischen Untersuchungen* Edmund Husserls." *Filosofia,* vol. 18, 1967, 837-859 [Samenvatting, 837]. Also in Saggi filosofici, 27. Torino: Edizioni di "Filosofia," 1967, 28 p.

2761   Delbos, Victor. "Husserl. La critique du psychologisme et sa conception d'une logique pure." *Revue de Métaphysique et de Morale,* 1911. Reprinted in his *La philosophie allemande au 19e siècle.* Paris: Alcan, 1912, chap. II.

2762   de Muralt, A. "La notion d'acte fondé dans les rapport de la raison et de la volonté selon les *Logische Untersuchungen* de Husserl." *Revue de Métaphysique et de Morale,* vol. 82, Oct.-Dec. 1977, 511-527.

2763   Doniela, W. V. "*Logical investigations,* I-II." *Australasian Journal of Philosophy,* vol. 49, 1971, 227-231.

2764   Durpé, Louis. "The concept of truth in Husserl's *Logical investigations.*" *Philosophy and Phenomenological Research,* vol. 24, 1963-1964, 345-354.

2765   Elie, Hubert. "Etude logico-grammaticale sur les *Logische Untersuchungen* de Husserl." *Studia Philosophica,* vol. 23, 1963, 51-89. Also Basel: Verlag für Recht und Gesselschaft, 1963.

2766   Fink, Eugen. "Vorbemerkung zum Entwurf einer Vorrede zu den *Logischen Untersuchungen* (1913)." *Tijdschrift voor Filosofie,* vol. 1, 1939.

2767   Galay, Jean-Louis. "Essai sur le problème de l'intelligibilité d'après la *Critique de la raison logique* de Husserl." *Studia Philosophica,* vol. 29, 1969, 25-53.

2768   Garulli, Enrico. "Due fasi del pensiero husserliano: le *Ricerche logiche* e la *Krisis.*" *Studi Urbinati,* vol. 35, n.s. B, 1961, 192-235.

2769   Gorner, P. "Introduction to the logical investigations. E. Fink (ed.)." *Journal of the British Society for Phenomenology,* vol. 8, 1977, 60-61.

2770   Gorner, Paul. "Husserl's *Logische Untersuchungen.*" *Journal of the British Society for Phenomenology,* vol. 3, 1972, 187-194.

2771   Gotesky, Rubin. "Husserl's conception of logic *als Kunstlehre* in the *Logische Untersuchungen.*" *Philosophical Review,* vol. 47, 1938, 375-389.

2772   Gotesky, Rubin. "Logic as an independent science. An examination of Husserl's conception of pure logic in the Prolegomena zur reinen Logik, first volume of the *Logische Untersuchungen.*" Ph.D. Dissertation, New York University, 1939.

2773   Grünewald, Bernward. *Der phänomenologische Ursprung des Logischen:* ein krit. Analyse d. phänomenolog. Grundlegung d. Logik in Edmund Husserls '*Logischen Untersuchungen.*' Kastellaun: Henn, 1977, 184 p.

2774   Hoeres, Walter. "Zum Begriff der verifizierenden Anschauung in Husserls *Logische Untersuchungen.*" *Archiv für Philosophie*, vol. 7, 1957, 325-334.

2775   Ingarden, Roman. "The letter to Husserl about the VI [*Logical investigation and 'idealism'*. Helmut Girndt (trans. from the German) [with Ingarden's own introduction, conclusion and comments to the same letter, A.-T. Tymieniecka (trans.)]." *Ingardeniana. Analecta Husserliana*, vol. 4, 1976, 418-438.

2776   Jacob, A. "*Recherches logiques*, II. lre partie." *Etudes Philosophiques*, vol. 16, 1961, 454.

2777   Jacob, A. "*Recherches logiques*, III: Elements d'une élucidation phénoménologique." *Etudes Philosophiques*, vol. 20, 1965, 539.

2778   Lemaigre, B.-M. "*Recherches logiques*, II. 1-2, III." *Revue des Sciences Philosophiques et Théologiques*, vol. 51, 1967, 87-88.

2779   Levin, David M. "*Logical investigations*, I-II. J. N. Findlay (trans.)." *Journal of Philosophy*, vol. 69, 1972, 384-398.

2780   Lugo, Elena. "Dos conceptos de la verdad en las *Investigaciones lógicas* de Husserl." *Anuario Filosófico*, vol. 3, 1970, 169-183.

2781   Mays, Wolfe. " *Logical investigations*, I-II. J. N. Findlay (trans.)," *Philosophical Books*, vol. 12, no. 1, 1971, 13-15.

2782   Mensch, James R. "The quest for being in Husserl's *Logical investigations.*" Ph.D., University of Toronto. *Dissertation Abstracts*, vo. 39, no. 4, Oct. 1978, 2340-A.

2783   Meyn, H. *Metaphilosophy*, vol. 4, 1973, 162-172.

2784   Natorp, Paul. "Zur Frage der logischen Methode. Mit Beziehung auf Edmund Husserls *Prolegomena zur reinen Logik*," in *Husserl*. Hrsg. von H. Noack (Wege der Forschung, 40). Darmstadt: Wissenschaftliche Buchgesellschaft, 1973, 1-15.

2785   Oesterreich, T. K. "Die reine Logik und die Phänomenologie," in Friedrich Ueberweg, *Grundriss der Geschichte der Philosophie* (12th ed., 1923), IV, 504-515.

2786   Orianne, André P. "Husserl's theory of meaning. A commentary on the first two *Logical investigations.*" *Ph.D. Dissertation, University of California at Berkeley, 1971, 265 p.*

2787   Ortega Oritz, José M. "Teoría de la significación en las *Investigaciones lógica* de Husserl." *Convivium*, no. 37, 1972, 85-118.

2788   Osborn, Andrew D. "The philosophy of Edmund Husserl in its development from his mathematical interests to his first conception of phenomenology in *Logical investigations.*" Ph.D. Dissertation, Columbia University, 1934.

2789   Pivcevic, Edo. "*Logical investigations.*" *Mind*, vol. 80, 1971, 462-472.

2790   Preti, G. "I fondamenti della logica formale pura nella *Wissenschaftslehre* di B. Bolzano e nella *Logische Untersuchungen* di Edmund Husserl." *Sophia*, vol. 3, 1935, 187-194, and 361-376.

2791   Ribeiro da Silva, Isodro. "O antipsicologismo de Husserl segundo o 1 volume das *Investigacoes lógicas.*" *Revista Portuguesa de Filosofia,* vol. 18, 1962, 178-308.

2792   Rossi, Alejandro. "Sentido y sinsentido en las Investigaciones lógicas." *Diánoia* (México), vol. 6, 1960, 91-114.

2793   Salmerón, Fernando. "El ser ideal en las *Investigaciones lógicas* de Husserl." *Diánoia* (México), vol. 12, 1966, 132-154.

2794   Sandín, T. " *Investigaciones lógicas.*" *Studium,* vol. 8, 1968, 403-404.

2795   Schérer, René. *La phénoménologie des Recherches logiques de Husserl* (Epiméthée). Paris: Presses Universitaires de France, 1967, 372 p. *La fenomenología de las 'Investigaciones lógicas' de Husserl.* Trad. del francés por Jesus Días (Biblioteca hispánica de filosofía, 59). Madrid: Gredos, 1969, 348 p.

2796   Schermann, H. "Husserls II. *logische Untersuchung* und Meinongs-Hume-Studien I," in *Jenseits von Sein und Nichtsein.* Beiträge zur Meinong-Forschung. Hrsg. von Rudolf Haller. Graz: Akademische Druck.- und Verlagsanstalt, 1972, 103-115.

2797   Schuppe, Wilhelm. "Zum Psychologismus und sum Normcharakter der Logik. Eine Ergänzung in Husserl's *Logische Untersuchungen.*" *Archiv für System. Philosophie,* vol. 7, 1901, 1-22. Reprinted in *Husserl.* Hrsg. von H. Noack (Wege der Forschung, 40). Darmstadt: Wissenschaftliche Buchgesellschaft, 1973, 16-35.

2798   Schuwer, André. "Remarks on the idea of authentic thinking in the *Logical investigations.*" *Research in Phenomenology,* vol. 1, 1971, 17-32.

2799   Scrimieri, Giorgi. "Dalle *Logische Untersuchungen* di E. Husserl." *Annali della Facoltà di Lettere e Filosofia* (Bari), vol. 6, 1960, 169-204.

2800   Scrimieri, Girogio. *Problemi di logica.* Studio sui *Prolegomena zur reinen Logik* di E. Husserl. Bari: Levante, 1959, 160 p.

2801   Smith, Quentin. "On Husserl's theory of consciousness in the fifth *Logical investigation.*" *Philosophy and Phenomenological Research,* vol. 37, 1976-1977, 482-497.

2802   Sokolowski, Robert. "The logic of part and wholes in Husserl's *Investigations.* " *Philosophy and Phenomenological Research,* vol. 28, 1967-1968, 537-553.

2803   Sokolowski, Robert. "The structure and content of Husserl's *Logical investigations.*" *Inquiry,* vol. 14, 1971, 318-347.

2804   Spiegelbert, Herbert. "Remarks on Findlay's translation of Edmund Husserl's *Logical investigations.*" *Journal of the British Society for Phenomenology,* vol. 3, 1972, 195-196.

2805   Stephens, James W. "Phenomenology and realism. An essay on Husserl's *Logical investigations.*" Ph.D. Dissertation, Princeton University, 1978. *Dissertation Abstracts,* vol. 39, no. 4, Oct. 1978, 2345-A.

2806    Taminiaux, Jacques. "Le regard et l'excédent. Remarques sur Heidegger et
        les *Recherches logiques* de Husserl." *Revue Philosophique de Louvain,* vol.
        75, Feb. 1977. Reprinted in his *Le regard et l'excédent* (Phaenomenologica,
        75). The Hague: Martinus Nijhoff, 1977, xii-182.

2807    Tatemastsu, Hirotaka. *Ronri-gaku Kenkyu,* 2 (Husserl, *Logical investigations*
        ). Tokyo: Misuzu-shobo, 1970, 308 p.

2808    Vandenbussche, F. "Recherches logique, I-II." *International Philosophical
        Quarterly,* vol. 1, 1961, 539-540.

2809    Vela, Fernando. *Abreviature de Investigaciones logicas de E. Husserl.* Buenos
        Aires: Revista de Occidente, Argentina, 1949, 507 p.

2810    Willard, Dallas A. "Meaning and universals in Husserl's *Logische
        Untersuchungen.*" Ph.D. Dissertation, University of Wisconsin, 1964, 284
        p. *Dissertation Abstracts,* vol. 25, no. 6, Dec. 1964, 3672-A.

## 5) *Philosophie als strenge Wissenschaft*

2811    Biemel, W. "Die Phänomenologie und die Idee der Philosophie als strenge
        Wissenschaft." *Zeitschrift für Philosophische Forschung,* vol. 13, no. 2, 1959.

2812    Boehm, Rudolf. "*Die Philosophie als strenge Wissenschaft,*" in *Vom
        Gesichtspuunkt der Phänomenologie.* Husserl-Studien (Phaenomenologica,
        26). The Hague: Martinus Nijhoff, 1968, 1-17.

2813    B., J. "*Philosophie als strenge Wissenschaft.*" *Philosophisches Jahrbuch,* vol. 73,
        1966, 213-214.

2814    Collins, J. "*La philosophie comme science exacte.*" *Modern Schoolman,* vol.
        33, 1956, 281-284.

2815    Conci, Domenico. "A proposito della '*Filosofia come scienza rigorosa*' di E.
        Husserl." *Giornale di Metafisica,* vol. 23, 1968, 186-207.

2816    Corona, N. A. "*Philosophie als strenge Wissenschaft.*" *Sapienza,* vol. 28, 1973,
        221-224.

2817    de Vries, J. "*La philosophie come science rigoureuse.* Introduction, traduction
        et commentaire par Quentin Lauer." *Scholastik,* vol. 36, 1961, 448-449.

2818    Dilthey,-Husserl. "En torno a la filosofia como ciencia estricta y al alcance
        del historicismo. Correspondencia entre Dilthey y Husserl, 1911 [Edición,
        introducción, y notas por Walter Biemel]. *Revista de Filosofía de la
        Universidad de Costa Rica,* vol. 1, no. 2, 101-124.

2819    Ecole, Jean. "*La philosophie come science exacte.*" *Etudes Philosophiques,* vol.
        10, 1955, 514.

2820    Fragata, J. "*A filosoia como ciência de rigor.*" *Revista Portuguesa de Filosofia,*
        vol. 9, 1953, 217-218.

2821    Kuypers, K. "De idee van filosofie als strenge wetenschap bij Husserl."
        *Tijdschrift voor Filosofie,* vol. 36, 1974, 673-704 [Zusammenfassung:
        Husserls *Idee der Philosophie als strenge Wissenschaft,* 704-706].

2822    Lauer, Quentin. "Introduction" à l'édition de *La philosophie comme science
        rigoureuse de E. Husserl.* Paris: Presses Universitaires de France, 1955, 1-50.
        Bibliographie, 193-199. "Introduction," Husserl, *Phenomenology and the
        crisis of philosophy.* New York: Harper Torchbooks, TB 1170, 1965, 1-70.

2823    Ledrut, R. "*La philosophie comme science rigoureuse.*" *Critique,* no. 117, 1957,
        123-151.

2824    McGill, V. J. "*La filosofia como ciencia estricta.*" *Journal of Philosophy,* vol.
        50, 1953, 78-79.

2825    McGill, V. J. "*La philosophie comme science exacte.*" *Journal of Philosophy,*
        vol. 53, 1956, 843-849.

2826    MorujÂo, Alexandre Fradique. "Husserl e a *filosofia como ciência rigorosa.*"
        *Revista Portuguesa de Filosofia,* vol. 11, no. 3-4, 1955, 80-90.

2827    Muñoz-Alonso, A. "*La philosophie come science exacte.*" *Crisis,* vol. 3, 1956,
        121.

2828    Pazanin, Ante. Das Problem der Philosophie als strenger Wissenschaft in der
        Phänomenologie Edmund Husserls (Inaugural-Dissertation zur Erlangung
        des Kotrogrades der Philosophischen Fakultät der Universität zu Köln).
        Köln, 1962, 186 p. [impr. off-set]

2829    Son, B. H. *Science and person.* A study on the idea of *Philosophy as rigorous
        science* in Kant and Husserl. Assen: Van Gorcum, 1973.

2830    Thompson, M. M. "*La filosofia como ciencia estricta.*" *The Personalist,* vol.
        34, 1953, 90.

2831    Versiani Velloso, A. "*A filosofia como ciencia de rigor.*" *Kriterion* (Minas
        Gerais), vol. 5, 1952, 534-536.

6) *Die Krisis der europäischen Wissenschaften*

2832    Anceschi, Luciano. "*Krisis,* Beilage III zu s. 9 a." *Il Verri,* no. 4, Aug. 1960,
        54-77.

2833    Banfi, A. "Husserl et la crise de la civilisation européenne," in *Husserl*(Cahiers
        de Royaumont, III). Paris: editions de Minuit, 1959, 411-427. "Husserl e
        la crisi della civiltà europea." *Aut Aut,* no. 43-44, 1958.

2834    Bennett, John B. "Husserl's *Crisis* and Whitehead's process philosophy." *The
        Personalist,* vol. 56, Summer 1975, 289-300.

2835    Bianco, F. "La crisi delle scienze e la fenomenologia." *Civilta delle Macchine,*
        May-June 1961, 11-12.

2836    Boehm, Rudolf. "Une introduction à la philosophie phénoménologique [à
        propos de l'oeuvre de Husserl: *Die Krisis der europäischen Wissenschaften*
        ]." *Archives de Philosophie,* no. 2, 1954, 169-172.

2837    Bossert, Philip J. "A common understanding concerning Husserl's *Crisis*text."
        *Philosophy and Phenomenological Research,* vol. 35, 1974-1975, 20-33.

2838    Brecht, F. J. "*Die Krisis der europäischen Wissenschaften.*" *Universitas,* vol.
        10, 1955, 975.

2839 Carr, David. "Husserl's *Crisis* and the problem of history." *Southwestern Journal of Philosophy,* vol. 5, Fall 1974, 127-148.

2840 de Muralt, A. "*Die Krisis der europaischen Wissenschaften.*" *Revue de Théologie et de Philosophie,* vol. 7, 1957, 309-311.

2841 Devivaise, Charles. "Le testament philosophique de Husserl." *Etudes Philosophiques,* vol. 9, 1954, 352-359.

2842 Dussort, Henri. "Deux textes de Husserl sur la méthode et le sens de la phénoménologie. I: Marche de la pensée phénoménologique (1907). II: Avant-propos à la suite de la *Crisis* (1937) (Textes traduits et présentés par H. Dussort." *Revue Philosophique de la France et de l'Etranger,* vol. 84, no. 4, [Husserl], 1959, 433-462.

2843 Faggiotto, Pietro. *L'interpretazione husserliana del pensiero moderno.* Guiida alla luttura della parte I et II della *Crisi.* Padova: Gregoriana, 1971, 54 p.

2844 Filippini, E. "Ego ed alter-ego nella *Krisis* di Husserl," in Omaggio a Husserl. Milano, 1960, 213-225.

2845 Fisher, Alden L. "*The crisis of European sciences.*" *Modern Schoolman,* vol. 48, 1970-1971, 293-297.

2846 Forni, Guglielmo. "Commento alla *Crisi* di E. Husserl." [I]. *Girnale di Metafisica,* vol. 26, 1971, 137-170. "Commento alla *Crisi* di E. Husserl, II." *Ibid.,* 453-476. Reprinted in his *Il soggetto e la storia.* Bologna: Il Mulino, 1972.

2847 Fragata, J. "*Die Krisis der europäischen Wissenschaften.*" *Revista Portuguesa de Filosofia,* Supl. bibl., vol. 2, 1955, 328-329.

2848 Garulli, Enrico. "Due fasi del pensiero husserliano: le *Richerche logiche* e la *Krisis.*" *Studi Urbinati,* vol. 35, n.s. B., 1961, 192-235.

2849 Guerra, Augusto. "La *Krisis* di Edmund Husserl." *De Homine,* vol. 1, no. 2-3, 1962, 183-205. [*see:* F.L. 2864]

2850 Gurwitsch, Aron. "The last work of Edmund Husserl." *Philosophy and Phenomenological Research,* vol. 16, 1955-1956, 380-399, vol. 17, 1956-1957, 370-398. Reprinted in his *Studies in phenomenology and psychology.* Evanston, Ill.: Northwestern University Press, 1966, 397-448.

2851 G., H.-D. "Die Krisis...." *Revue des Sciences Philosophiques et Theologiques,* vol. 41, 1957, 196.

2852 Hindess, Barry. "Transcendentalism and history. The problem of the history of philosophy and the sciences in the later philosophy of Husserl." *Economy and Society,* vol. 2, no. 3, Aug. 1973, 309-342.

2853 Ingarden, Roman. "What is new in Husserl's *Crisis?* Rolf George (trans. from the German text)." *Analecta Husserliana,* vol. 2, 1972, 23-47.

2854 Kockelmans, Joseph J. "Phenomenologico-psychological and transcendental reductions in Husserl's *Crisis.*" *Analecta Husserliana,* vol. 2, 1972, 78-89.

2855    Kockelmans, Joseph J. "The mathematization of nature in Husserl's last publication, *Krisis.*" *Journal of the British Society for Phenomenology,* vol. 2, no. 1, 1971, 45-67.

2856    *Krisis* di Husserl (La). *Recenzione a cura di vari autori. De Homine,* vol. 1, no. 2-3, 1962, 183-228. [*see:* A. Guerra, F.L. 2849, 2864]

2857    Kunz, H. "*Die Krisis....*" *Studia Philosphica,* vol. 15, 1955, 238-239.

2858    Lehmann, G. "*Die Krisis....*" *Deutsche Literaturzeitung,* vol. 77, 1956, 10-13.

2859    Lübbe, Hermann. "Husserl und die Europäische Krise." *Kantstudien., vol. 49, 1957, 225-237.*

2860    Marcuse, Herbert. "*Die Krisis....*" *Zeitschrift für Sozialforschung,* vol. 6, 1937, 415-415.

2861    Marcuse, Herbert. "On science and phenomenology," in *Positivism and sociology,* Anthony Giddens (ed.). London: Heinemann, dist. by Humanities Press, 1975, 225-236.

2862    Martínez Gómez, L. "*Die Krisis....*" *Pensamiento,* vol. 11, 1955, 83-85.

2863    Miguelez, Roberto. *Sujet et histoire.* Ottawa: Les Editions de l'Université d'Ottawa, 1973, 222 p.

2864    F. L. "Postilla [a proposito della *Krisis*]." *De Homine,* vol. 1, no. 2-3, 1962, 211-218. [*see:* A. Guerra 2849]

2865    Morrison, James C. "Husserl's '*crisis*'. Reflections on the relationship of philosophy and history." *Philosophy and Phenomenological Research,* vol. 37, 1976-1977, 312-320.

2866    P. M. "*Phenomenology and the crisis of philosophy..*" *Review of Metaphysics,* vol. 19, 1965-1966, 590.

2867    K. K. "Die Krisis...." *Algemeen Nederlands Tijdschrift voor Wijsgebeerte en Psychologie,* vol. 47, 1954-1955, 50-51.

2868    Paci, Enzo. "*Die Krisis....*" *Aut Aut,* no. 38, 1957, 185-187.

2869    Pozzan, A. M. "La *Krisis* nell'ambito delle correnti fenomenologische europee e americane." *De Homine,* vol. 1, no. 2-3, 1962, 205-211.

2870    Prufer, Thomas. "An outline of some Husserlian distinctions and strategies, especially in the *Crisis,*" in *Phänomenologie heute.* Grundlagen und Methodenprobleme. Hrsg. von der Deutscher Gesellschaft für phänomenologische Forschung, Ernst Wolfgang Orth, Hrsg. Freiburg-München: Karl Alber, 1975.

2871    Riverso, E. "*La crisi delle scienze europee....*" *Rivista Critica di Storia della Filosofia,* vol. 15, 1962, 370-371.

2872    Scrimieri, Giorgio. "I sensi della *Krisis der europäischen Wissenschaften und die transzendentale Phänomenologie* di Edmund Husserl e la mia prospettiva filosofica." *Annali della Facoltà di Lettere e Filosofia* (Bari), vol. 7, 1961, 271-284.

2873    Silverman, Hugh J. "The self in Husserl's *Crisis.*" *Journal of the British Society for Phenomenology,* vol. 7, Jan. 1976, 24-32.

2874    Wagner, H. "Die *Krisis....*" *Philosophische Rundschau,* vol. 2, 1954-1955, 222-224.

2875    Wahl, Jean. *L'ouvrage posthume de Husserl: La Krisis.* La crise des sciences européennes et la phénoménologie transcendentale. Paris: Centre de Documentation Universitaire, 1958.

### 7) *Erfahrung und Urteil*

2876    Bertman, Martin A. *"Experience and judgment."* *Modern Schoolman,* vol. 53.

2877    Bosio, Franco. "La genesi della logica formale dall'esperienza antepredicativa in *Erfahrung und Urteil* di E. Husserl." *Il Pensiero,* vol. 6, 1961, 334-356.

2878    Schilling, K. *"Erfahrung...."* *Philosophische Literaturanzeiger,* vol. 1, 1949-1950, 150-153.

2879    de Vries, J. *"Erfahrung...."* *Scholastik,* vol. 25, 1950, 404-406.

2880    H. D. *"Erfahrung...."* *Philosophisches Jahrbuch,* vol. 65, 1956 [1957], 433.

2881    Farber, Marvin. *"Erfahrung und Urteil* (résumé)." *Journal of Philosophy,* vol. 36, 1939, 247-249.

2882    Findlay, J. N. *"Erfahrung..."* *Mind,* vol. 59, 1950, 262-268.

2883    Geiger, L. B. *"Erfahrung...."* *Revue des Sciences Philosophiques et Théologiques,* vol. 35, 1951, 83.

2884    Harrison, R. "The concept of prepredicative experience," in *Phenomenology and philosophical understanding,* Edo Pivcevic (ed.). Cambridge University Press, 1975, 93-107.

2885    K. K. *"Erfahrung...."* *Algemeen Nederlands Tijdschrift voor Wijsbegeerte en Psychologie,* vol. 43, 1951, 112.

2886    Landgrebe, Ludwig. "Lettre sur un article de M. Jean Wahl concernant *Erfahrung und Ureil* de Husserl." *Revue de Métaphysique et de Morale,* vol. 57, 1952, 282-283. [*see:* J. Wahl 2892]

2887    Null, Gilbert T. *"Experience and judgment.* J. S. Churchill (trans.)." *Man and World,* vol. 7, no. 2, 1974, 182-192.

2888    Ogiermann, H. *"Erfahrung."* *Scholastik,* vol. 31, 1956, 134.

2889    P. E. P. *"Expérience et jugement.* " *Dialectica,* vol. 23, 1969, 151-152.

2890    Presas, Mario A. *"Erfahrung...."* *Revista Latinoamericana de Filosofía,* vol. 1, March 1975, 65-69.

2891    Pucciarelli, E. *"Experienza e giudizio."* *Buenos Aires,* vol. 2, no. 2, 1962, 366-369.

2892    Wahl, Jean. "Notes sur la première partie de *Erfahrung und Urteil de Husserl."* *Revue de Métaphysique et de Morale,* vol. 56, 1951. Reprinted in *Phénoménologie et existence.* Paris: Armand Colin, 1953, 77-106.

8) *Erste Philosophie, I-II.*

2893 Anonymous. "*Erste Philosophie. II.*" *Revue de Métphysique et de Morale,* vol. 64, 1959, 485.

2894 Anonymous. "*Erste Philosophie, I.*" *Tijdschrift voor Filosofie,* vol. 18, 1956, 308-309.

2895 Anonymous. "*Erste Philosophie, II.*" *Tijdschrift voor Filosofie,* vol. 21, 1959, 367-368.

2896 Boehm, Rudolf. "Einleitung" zu *Husserliana,* Bd VIII, 1: *Erste Philosophie.* The Hague: Martinus Nijhoff, 1956. Reprinted, "Die '*Erste Philosophie*' und die Wege zur Reduktion," in his *Vom Gesichtspunkt der Phänomenologie.* Husserl-Studien (Phaenomenologica, 26). The Hague: Martinus Nijhoff, 1968, 186-216.

2897 Farber, Marvin. "First philosophy and the problem of the world." *Philosophy and Phenomenological Research,* vol. 23, 1962-1963, 315-334.

2898 Fragata, J. "*Erste Philosophie, II.*" *Revista Portuguesa de Filosofia,* vol. 17, 1961, 217-218.

2899 García Bacca, Juan David. "*Erste Philosophie, I.*" *Revista Nacional de Cultura* (Caracas), vol. 18, no. 116, 1956, 149.

2900 Heinemann, F. H. "*Erste Philosophie, II.*" *Philosophy,* vol. 34, 1959, 355-356.

2901 Héring, Jean. "*Erste Philosophie, I.*" *Etudes Philosophiques,* vol. 11, 1956, 505-506.

2902 Heinrich, D. "*Erste Philosophie.* I. Teil: Kritische Ideengeschichte." *Philosophische Rundschau,* vol. 6, 1958, 1-26.

2903 Kelkel, Arion L. "Avant-propos," a *Philosophie première (1923-1924). Première partie: Histoire critique des idées: Deuxième partie: Théorie de la réduction phénoménologique. Traduit de l'allemand par Arion L. Kelkel. Paris: Presses Universitaires de France, 1970et 1972, vii-xlvi.*

2904 Kunz, H. "*Erste Philosophie. II.*" *Studia Philosophica,* vol. 20, 1960, 161-162.

2905 Landgrebe, Ludwig. "Husserls Abschied vom Cartesianismus [*Erste Philosophie,* II]." *Philosohische Rundschau,* vol. 9, no. 2-3, 1961-1962, 133-177. "Husserl's departure from Cartesianism," in *The phenomenology of Edmund Husserl,* R. O. Elveton (ed. & trans.). Chicago: Quadrangle Books, 1970, 259-303.

2906 Lugarini, Leo. "La problematica husserliana della '*filosofia prima*'." *Il Pensiero,* vol. 5, no. 2, 1960, 248-260.

2907 Paci, Enzo. "*Erste Philosophie. I.*" *Aut Aut,* no. 38, 1957, 185-187.

2908 Pirard, R. "*Philosophie première, II.*" *Revue Philosophique de Louvain,* vol. 71, 1973, 595-597.

2909 Roëls, Claude. "*Philosophie première, I.*" *Etudes Philosophiques,* vol. 4, 1972, 545-547.

2910 Roëls, Claude. "*Philosophie première, II.*" *Etudes Philosophiques,* no. 1, 1974, 117-119.

2911   Villoro, Luis. "*Erste Philosophie. II.*" *Diánoia* (México), vol. 6, 1960, 231-235.

2912   Wahl, Jean. *La Philosophie première. Erste Philosophie* (Les Cours de Sorbonne). Paris: Centre de Documentation Universitaire, 1961, 144 p.

### 9) *Die Idee der Phänomenologie*

2913   Anonymous. *Revue de Métaphysique et de Morale,* vol. 57, 1952, 95-96.

2914   Anonymous. *Rivista di Filosofia,* April-June 1951.

2915   Berger, G. *Etudes Philosophiques,* 1950, 265-266.

2916   Brecht, F. J. *Universitas* (Tübingen), vol. 6, 1951, 1021-1022.

2917   Derrida, Jacques. "The idea of phenomenology." *Etudes Philosophiques,* vol. 20, 1965, 538.

2918   Endres, J. *Divus Thomas* (Freiburg, Switzerland), vol. 30, 1952, 241-242.

2919   Gessani, Alberto. "Il significato de *L'idea della fenomenologia* nello sviluppo el pensiero di Edmund Husserl." *Proteus,* vol. 2, no. 6, 1971, 95-112.

2920   Giannini, G. "Idee per una fenomenologia...." *Humanitas* (Brescia), vol. 7, 1952, 999-1001.

2921   Holz, H. H. *Deutsche Literaturzeitung,* vol. 77, 486-493.

2922   Kahl-Furthmann, G. *Philosophische Literaturanzeiger,* vol. 3, 1951, 193-194.

2923   Kunz, H. *Studia Philosophica,* vol. 10, 1950, 171.

2924   K. K. *Algemeen Nederlands Tijdschrift voor Wijsbegeerte* en *Psychologie,* vol. 43, 1951, 111-112.

2925   Lowit, Alelxandre. "Sur les 'Cinq Leçons' de Husserl. (2de partie de la préface de *L'idée de la phénoménologie,* trad. par A. Lowit (Epiéthée). Paris: Presses Universitaires de France, 1970)." *Revue de Métaphysique et de Morale,* vol. 76, 1971, 226-236. [*see:* K. Schuhmann 2937]

2926   Machado Neto, A. L. "*L'idee....*" *Revista Brasileira de Filosofia,* vol. 21, 1971, 339-341.

2927   Millá Puelles, A. "*Die Idee....*" *Revista de Filosofía* (Madrid), vol. 10, 1951, 217-219.

2928   P. M. "*The idea of phenomenology.*" *Review of Metaphysics,* vol. 19, 1965-1966, 589-590.

2929   Nakhnikian, George. "Introduction," to *The idea of phenomenology.* William P. Alston ad George Nakhinikian (trans.). New York: Humanities Press, 1966, xxii-60.

2930   Nota, J. "*Die Idee....*" *Bijdragen,* vol. 13, 1952, 200.

2931   Paumen, J. "*Die Idee....*" *Revue Internationale de Philosophie,* vol. 5, 1951, 400-404.

2932   Picard, N. "*Die Idee....*" *Antonianum,* vol. 26, 1951, 332-334.

2933   Picard, N. "*Die Idee....*" *Antonianum,* vol. 27, 1952, 204-205.

2934    Pinto de Carvalho, A. *"Die Idee...." Revista da Faculdade de Letras* (Lisboa), vol. 17, 1951, 265-266.

2935    Mitchells, K. *Philosophy,* vol. 40, 1965, 174-176. [*The idea of phenomenology*]

2936    Rawlins, F.I.G. *"Die Idee...." Nature,* vol. 166, 1950, 919-921.

2937    Schuhmann, Karl. "Alexandre Lowit als vertaler en interpretator van Husserl [*see:* 2905]." *Tijdschrift voor Filosofie,* vol. 34, 1972, 348-353.

2938    Tavares, S. *"Die Idee...." Revista Portugues de Filosofia,* Supl. bibl. vol. 1, 1951, 162-163.

2939    Waelhens, Alphonse de. "Kommentaar op *Die Idee der Phänomenologie.*" *Tijdschrift voor Filosofie.* vol. 19, 1957, 602-620 [Résumé en français, 620].

**10)** *Formale und transzendental Logik*

2940    Bachelard, Suzanne. "Introduction," to *Logique formelle et logique transcendentale.* Paris: Presses Universitaires de France, 1957, 3-25.

2941    Bachelard, Suzanne. *La logique de Husserl.* Etude sur la *Logique formele et transcendentale.* (Epiméthée). Paris: Presses Universitaires de France, 1957, 316 p. Lester E. Embree (trans.). Evanston, Ill.: Northwestern University Press, 1968, lx-230.

2942    de Muralt, A. *"Logique formelle...." Studia Philosophica,* vol. 17, 1957, 140-149.

2943    Ecole, Jean. *"Logique formelle...." Etudes Philosophiques,* vol. 13, no. 1, 1958, 76.

2944    Forni, G. and Gatta, E. A. *"Formale und transzendentale Logik.* " (Sguardi su la filosofia contemporanea, 88). Torino: Ed. di Filosofia, 1969, 18 p.

2945    Gatta, E. A. *"Logica formale e trascendentale.* Trad. G. D. Neri." *Filosofia,* vol. 18, 1967, 536-545.

2946    Ingarden, Roman. " *Formale und transzendentale Logik,* " in *Husserl.* Hrsg. von H. Noack (Wege der Forschung, 40). Darmstadt: Wissenschatliche Buchgesellschaft, 1973, 168-173.

2947    McCormick, P. *"Formale and transcendental logic.* D. Cairns (trans.)." *Journal of the British Society for Phenomenology,* vol. 2, 1971, 87-92.

2948    Paci, Enzo. "Prefazione" in *Logica formale e trascendentale.* Saggio di critica della ragione logica. *Traduzione, avvertenza, nota agguiunta e note a cura di Guido Neri. (Classici della filosofia moderna). Bari: Laterza, 1966, xvi-432.*

2949    Pudda, M. R. *"Logica formale...." Giornale di Metaficisca,* vol. 23, 1968, 67-68.

2950    Russo, F. *"Logique formelle...." Etudes,* 298, 1958, 130-131.

2951    Stack, George J. *"Formal and transcendental logic." Modern Schoolman,* vol. 48, 1970-1971, 385-387.

2952 Waston, Lawrence. "A study of the origins of formal logic in Husserl's *Formal and transcendental logic.*" Ph.D. Dissertation, de Paul University, 1973, 201 p. *Dissertation Abstracts,* vol. 34, no. 2, Aug. 1973, 826-A.

2953 Wood, A. W. "*Formal and....*" *Philosophical Review,* vol. 80, 1971, 267-273.

## 11) Husserls *Encyclopaedia Britannica* Artikel

2954 Biemel, Walter. "Husserls Encyclopaedia-Britiannica Artikel und Heideggers Anmerkungen dazu." *Tijdschrift voor Filosofie,* vol. 12, 1950, 246-280. Reprinted in *Husserl.* Hrsg. von H. Noack (Wege der Forschung, 40). Darmstadt: Wissenschaftliche Buchgesellslchaft, 1973, 282-315. " *Phenomenology.* Edmund Husserls article for the *Encyclopaedia Britiannica* (1927). Richard E. Palmer (trans.)." *Journal of the British Society for Phenomenology,* vol. 2, no. 2, 1971, 77-90. "Husserl's *Encyclopaedia Britannica* article and Heidegger's remarks thereon," in *Husserl. Expositions and appraisals,* F. Elliston and P. McCormick (eds.). Notre Dame, Ind.-London: Notre Dame University Press, 1977, 286-303.

2955 Oehme, H. "Husserls Encyclopaedia-Britannica Artikel...." *Psyche* (Heidelberg), vol. 5, no. 8, 1951, 155-159.

2956 Spiegelberg, Herbert. "On the misfortunes of Edmund Husserl's *Encyclopedia Britannica* article *Phenomenology.*" *Journal of the British Society for Phenomenology,* vol. 2, 1971, 74-76.

## 12) *Cartesianische Meditationen*

2957 Attig, Thomas W. "Cartesianism, certainty and the coigto in Husserl's *Cartesian meditations.*" Ph.D. Dissertation, Washington University, 1973, 342 p. *Dissertation Abstracts,* vol. 34, no. 12, June 1972, 7818-A.

2958 Attig, Thomas W. "How definitive is the text of Husserl's *Cartesian meditations.*" *Journal of the British Society for Phenomenology,* vol. 7, Jan. 1976, 3-11.

2959 Bastable, J. D. "*Cartesian meditations....*" *Philosophical Studies* (Maynooth), vol. 11, 1961-1962, 246-247.

2960 Berger, G. "*Cartesianische....*" *Etudes Philosophiques,* 1950, 265-266.

2961 Brecht, F. J. "*Cartesianische....*" *Universitas* (Tübingen), vol. 6, 1951, 1021-1022.

2962 Brüning, Walther. "Der Ansatz der Transzendentalphilosophie in Husserls *Cartesianischen Meditationen.*" *Zeitschrfit für Philosophische Forschung,* vol. 20, 1966, 185-196.

2963 Carr, David. "The 'Fifth Meditation' and Husserl's Cartesianism." *Philosophy and Phenomenological Research,* vol. 34, 1973-1974, 14-35.

2964 Downes, Chauncey B. "Husserl's theory of other minds. A study of the *Cartesian meditations.*" Ph.D. Dissertation, New York University, 1963,

354 p. *Dissertation Abstracts,* vol. 25, no. 1, July 1964, 536-A. Ann Arbor, Mich.-London: University Microfilms International, 1976.

2965    Endres, J. *"Cartesianische...." Divus Thomas* (Freiburg), vol. 30, 1952, 241-242.

2966    Farber, Marvin. "Husserl's *Méditations cartésiennes." Philosophical Review,* vol. 44, July 1935.

2967    Fisher, Alden L. *"Cartesian meditations...." Modern Schoolman,* vol. 39, 1961-1962, 417-418.

2968    Franchini, R. *"Meditazioni cartesiane...." Il Pensiero,* vol. 6, 1961, 105-109.

2969    Garulli, E. "L'intersoggettività nella V *Meditazione cartesiana* di Husserl." *Nuova Rivista di Pedagogia,* (Roma), Dec. 1960, 97-108.

2970    Harlan, Robert M. "The I and the other. A reformulation of Husserl's Fifth *Cartesian meditation.* " Ph.D. Dissertation, New School for Social Research, 1978.

2971    Hermann, Friedrich-Wilhelm von. *Husserl und die Meditationen des Descartes* (Antrittsvorlesung) (Wissenschaft und Gegenwart. Geisteswissenschaft Reihe H. 48). Frankfurt am Main: Klostermann, 1971, 29 p.

2972    Holveck, Eleanore W. "Edmund Husserl's concept of the ego in the *Cartesian meditations."* Ph.D. Dissertation, University of North Carolina at Chapel Hill, 1970, 179 p. *Dissertation Abstracts,* vol. 31, no. 11, June 1971, 6111-A.

2973    Kuhn, Helmut. "Méditations cartésiennes." *Kantstudien,* vol. 39, 1933, 210-216. Reprinted in *Husserl.* Hrsg. von H. Noack (Wege der Forschung, 40). Darmstadt: Wissenschaftliche Buchgesellschaft, 1973, 174-187.

2974    Kunz, H. *"Cartesianische...." Studia Philosophica,* vol. 10, 1950, 171.

2975    Lambert, F. "Husserl's constitution of the other in the Fifth *Cartesian meditation." Dialogue, Journal of Phi Sigma Tau,* vol. 17, no. 2-3, 1974-1975, 44-51.

2976    Lauer, Quentin. *"Cartesian meditations." Thought,* vol. 36, 1961, 468-469.

2977    Lavelle, Louis. *"Méditations cartésiennes,"* in his *Panorama des doctrines philosophiques.* Paris: Albin Michel, 1967, 153-162.

2978    Market, Oswaldo. "Meditaciones husserlianas. El descubrimiento del plano transcendental [resumen]." *Revista de Filosofía* (Madrid), vol. 20, 1961, 423-436.

2979    McGill, V. J. *"Cartesianische...." Journal of Philosophy,* vol. 48, 1951, 362-368.

2980    Millán Puelles, A. *"Cartesianische...." Revista de Filosofía* (Madrid), vol. 10, 1951, 217-219.

2981    Paumen, Jean. *"Cartesianische...." Revue Internationale de Philosophie,* vol. 5, 1951, 400-404.

2982    Pérez Espejo, Sergio. *La reducción trascendental y el problema del alter ego in las Meditaciones cartesianas* de Husserl (Colección 'Lectio philosóphica'). *Cartagena: Athena Ediciones, 1959, 33 p.*

2983    Picard, N. *"Cartesianische...." Antonianum,* vol. 26, 1951, 332-334.

2984  Ricoeur, Paul. "Etude sur les *Méditations cartésiennes* de Husserl." *Revue Philosophique de Louvain,* vol. 52, 75-109. "A study of Husserl's *Cartesian meditations,*" in his *Husserl.* An analysis of his phenomenology. Edward G. Ballard and Lester E. Embree (trans.). Evanston, Ill.: Northwestern University Press, 1967, 82-114. "Husserl's Fifth *Cartesian meditation.*" in *Ibid.,* 115-142.

2985  Rhees, Rush. "*Cartesianische....*" *Mind,* vol. 60, 1951, 60.

2986  Röttges, Heinz. *Evidenz und Solipsismus in Husserls Cartesianischen Meditationen* (Philosophie als Beziehungswissenschaft, 9) (Eidos, 12). Frankfurt am Main: Heiderhoff, 1971, 23 p.

2987  Schütz, Alfred. "Edmund Husserl's *Cartesianische Meditationen* und Pariser Vorträge." *Philosophy and Phenomenological Research,* vol. 11, 1950, 1951, 421-423.

2988  Seifert, Josef. "Kritik am Relativismus und Immanentismus in E. Husserls *Cartesianischen Meditationen.* Die Äquivokationen im Ausdruck *transzendentales ego* as der Basis jedes transzendentalen Idealismus." *Salzburger Jahrbuch für Philosophie,* vol. 14, 1970, 85-109.

2989  Serrus, Charles. "E. Husserl, Nachwort et *Méditations cartésiennes.*" *Etudes Philosophiques,* vol. 5, 1931, 127-131.

2990  Rawlins, F. I.G. "*Cartesianische....*" *Nature,* vol. 166, 1950, 919-921.

2991  Strasser, Stephan. "Introduction," *Cartesianische Meditationen und Pariser Vorträge.* Hrsg. und eingeleitet von S. Strasser (*Husserliana.* Gesammelt Werke. The Hague: Martinus Nijhoff, 1963, xxxiii-249.

2992  Stratton, Melville J. "The immanent and the transcendent in Husserl's *Cartesian meditations.*" Ph.D. Dissertation, State University of New York at Buffalo, 1970, 273 p. *Dissertation Abstracts,* vol. 31, no. 9, 1971, 4846-A.

2993  Tavares, S. "*Cartesianische....*" *Revista Portuguesa de Filosofia,* Supl. bibl. vol. 1, 1951, 162-163.

2994  Vásquez, Juan Adolfo. "Las *Meditaciones cartesianas* de Husserl." *Notas Estudios Filosóficos,* vol. 4, no. 13, 1953, 53-56.

2995  Werkmeister, W. H. "*Cartesian meditations.*" *The Personalist,* vol. 43, 1962, 405-406.

### 13) *Ideen zu einer reinen Phänomenologie*

2996  Anonymous. "*Idee per una fenomenologia....*" *Sophia,* vol. 19, 1951, 395-396.

2997  Berger, Gaston. "*Ideen directrices....*" *Etudes Philosophiques,* 1950, 265-266.

2998  Bosio, Franco. "La costituzione fenomenologica del mondo dello spirito nelle *Ideen* di E. Husserl." *Il Pensiero,* vol. 12, 1967, 56-65.

2999  Brecht, F. J. "*Ideen...* II-III." *Universitas,* vol. 7, 1952, 1231-1232.

3000  Casaubón, J. A. "Ideas relativas a una fenomenologia pura." *Sapienta,* vol. 18, 1963, 284-286.

3001 Chandler, A. "Prof. Husserl's program of philosophical reform." *Philosophical Review,* vol. 26, 1917, 534-648.

3002 Debus, Ute I. "A critical analysis of Husserl's *Ideen I.* " Ph.D. Dissertation, The Johns Hopkins University, 1971, 250 p. *Dissertation Abstracts,* vol. 32, no. 5, Nov. 1971, 2741-A.

3003 De Natale, Ferruccio. "Il problema fenomenologica della scienza in Husserl da *Idee II* alla *Crisi."* *Filosofia,* vol. 27, April 1976, 241-276.

3004 Embree, Lester E. "An interpretation of the doctrine of the ego in Husserl's *Ideen,*" in *Phenomenology.* Continuation and criticism. Essays in memory of Dorion Cairns, F. Kersten and R. M. Zaner (eds.). (Phaenomenologica, 50). The Hague: Martinus Nijhoff, 1973, 24-32.

3005 Gurwitsch, Aron. "Critical study of Husserl's *Nachwort.* Frederick Kersten (trans.) in Gurwitsch, *Studies in phenomenology and psychology.* Evanston, Ill.: Northwestern University Press, 1966, 107-115.

3006 Holz, H. H. "*Ideen I-III.*" *Deutsche Literaturzeitung,* vol. 77, 1956, 486-493.

3007 Kattsoff, L. O. "Husserls, *ideen... I.*" *Philosophy and Phenomenological Research,* vol. 12, 1951-1952, 139.

3008 Kaufmann, P. "*Idées directrices....*" *Revue Philosophique de la France et de France et de l'Entranger,* vol. 79, 1954, 474-479.

3009 Kunz, H. "*Ideen... II-III.*" *Studia Philosophica,* vol. 15, 1955, 238-239.

3010 Léger, G. " *Ideen... I.*" *Revue des Sciences Philosophiques et Théologiques,* vol. 37, 1953, 478.

3011 Leroux, Henri. "Sur la publication complète des *Ideen* de Husserl." *Etudes Philosophiques,* vol. 7, 1952, 261-277.

3012 Levinas, Emmanuel. "Sur les *Ideen* de E. Husserl." *Revue Philosophique de la France et de l'Etranger,* 1929. "Las *Ideen* de E. Husserl." *Letras,* 1937. "Uber die *Ideen* Edmund Husserls (Aus dem Französischen übersetzt von Herbert Backes)," in *Husserl.* Hrsg. von H. Noack (Wege der Forschung, 40). Darmstadt: Wissenschaftliche Buchgesellsachaft, 1973, 87-128.

3013 Llorente, Bartha. "Resumen de *Idées directrices pour une phénoménologie* d'Edmund Husserl," *Ideas y Valores* (Bogotá), vol. 2, no. 7-8, 1952-1953, 692-700.

3014 Long, W. "*Ideas....*" *The Personalist,* vol. 35, 1954, 165-166.

3015 McGill, V. J. "*Ideen....*" *Journal of Philosophy,* vol. 48, 1951, 362-368.

3016 Natorp, Paul. "Husserls *Ideen zu einer reinen Phänomenologie.*" *Logos,* 1917-1918. Reprinted in *Husserl.* Hrsg. von H. Noack (Wege der Forschung, 40). Darmstadt: Wissenschaftliche Buchgesellschat, 1973, 36-60.

3017 Nink, H. "*Ideen... I.*" *Scholastik,* vol. 27, 1952, 441-442.

3018 Paci, Enzo. "Per una semplificazione dei temi husserliani fino al primo volume di *Ideen,*" in *Studi in onere di Arturo Massolo,* a cura di Livio Sicherollo. Urbino: Argalia, 1967, 767-787.

3019 Paci, Enzo. "*Ideen... I-III.*" *Aut Aut,* no. 38, 1957, 185-187.

3020 Paumen, Jean. "*Ideen....* " *Revue Internationale de Philosophie,* vol. 5, 1951, 400-404.

3021 Rawlings, F. I. G. "*Ideen... I-III.* " *Nature,* vol. 170, 1952, 470-471.

3022 Ricoeur, Paul. "Introduction" à *Ideen I* de E. Husserl, in *Idées directrices pour une phénoménologie* de E. Husserl. Paris: Gallimard, 1950. [Traduction et notes de Paul Ricoeur]. [see next item for translation into English]

3023 Ricoeur, Paul. "Analyses et problèmes dans *Ideen II* de Husserl." *Revue de Métaphysique et de Morale,* vol. 56, 1951, 357-394; vol. 57, 1952, 1-16. Reprinted in Phénoménologie-Existence. Paris: Collin, 1953, 23-76. "An introduction to Husserl's *Ideas I,*" and "Husserl's *Ideas I,*" and "Husserl's *Ideas II:* Analyses and problems," in his *Husserl.* An analysis of his phenomenology. Edward G. Ballard and Lester E. Embree (trans.). Evanston, Ill.: Northwestern University Press,

3024 Schuhmann, Karl. *Die Dialektik der Phénomenologie.* Vol. II: Reine Phänomenologie und phänomenologische Philosophie. Historisch-analytische Monographie uber Husserls *Ideen I* (Phaenomenologica, 57). The Hague: Martinus Nijhoff, 1973, vii-107.

3025 Schütz, Alfred. "Edmund Husserl's *Ideas,* volume II." *Philosophy and Phenomenological Research,* vol. 13, 1952-1953, 394-413. Reprinted in his *Collected papers,* III: Studies in phenomenological philosophy. The Hague: Martinus Nijhoff, 1970, 15-39. (Phaenomenologica, 22)

3026 Schütz, Alfred. "*Ideen.... III.* " *Philosophy and Phenomenological Research,* vol. 13, 1952-1953, 506-514. "Phenomenology and the foundations of the social sciences," reprinted in his *Collected papers, III.* The Hague: Martinus Nijhoff, 1970, 40-50, (Phaenomenologica, 22).

3027 Sini, Carolo. "Genesi e costituzione in referimento al secondo libro di *Idee.*" *Aut Aut,* no. 105-106, 1968, 91-99.

3028 Stevens, Richard. "Spatial and temporal models in Husserls *Ideen II.*" *Cultural Hermeneutics,* vol. 3, 1975-1976, 105-117.

3029 Tavares, S. "*Ideen... I.*" *Revista Portuguesa de Filosofia,* Supl. bibl. vol. 1, 1952, 233.

3030 Tavares, S. "*Ideen... II-III.*" *Revista Portuguesa de Filosofia,* Supl. bibl. vol. 2, 1954, 181.

3031 Tielsch, E. "*Ideen... II-III.*" *Philosophische Literaturanzeiger,* vol. 6, 1953-1954, 3-8.

3032 Tomassini, Roberta. "Il papragrafo 64 di *Idee II.*" *Aut Aut,* no. 105-106, 1968, 183-191.

3033 Villoro, Luis. "La constitutción de la realidad en la conciencia pura (El segundo tomo de las *Ideen zu einer reinen Phänomenologie und phänomenologische Philosophie*)." *Diánoia* (México), vol. 5, 1959, 195-212.

3034 Vita, L. W. "*Ideas relativas a una fenomenologia pura....*" *Revista Brasileira de Filosofia,* vol. 13, 1963, 297-299.

**14)** *Zur Phänomenologie des inneren Zeitbewusstseins*

3035      Bernard-Maitre, H. "*Leçons pour une phénoménologie* de la conscience intime du temps. Traduction H. Dussort." *Revue de Synthèse*, vol. 87, 1966, 107.

3036      Biral, A. "*Zur Phänomenologie....*" *Giornale di Metafasica*, vol. 23, 1968, 64-66.

3037      Boehm, Rudolf. "Das Konstitutionsproblem und das Zeitbewusstsein [Einleitung zu Husserl, *Zur Phänomenologie....*]," in his *Vom Geischtspunkt der Phänomenologie*. Husserl-Studien (Phaenomenologica, 26). The Hague: Martinus Nijhoff 1968, 106-118.

3038      Colbert Jr., J. G. "*The phenomenology of internal time-consciousness*." *Documentación Crítica Iberoamerican de Filosof*, vol. 2, 1965, 541-543.

3039      Costa, Margarita. "En torno a *La fenomenología de la conciencia inmanente del tiempo*." *Revista de Filosofía* (La Plata), no. 17, 1966, 31-48.

3040      Derrida, Jacques. "*Zur Phänomenologie....*" *Etudes Philosophiques*, vol. 22, 1967, 94.

3041      Dupré, Louis. "*The phenomenology....*" *New Scholasticism*, vol. 40, 1966, 199-203.

3042      Fortuny, N. A. "*Fenomenologia de la conciencia del tiempo inmanente*." *Revista de Filosofía* (La Plata), no. 11, 1962, 141-143.

3043      Henning, J. "Zur Phänomenologie...." *Deutsche Literaturzeitung*, vol. 88, 1967, 783-785.

3044      Mitchells, K. "*The phenomenology....*" *Philosophy*, vol. 40, 1965, 174-176.

3045      Mundle, C. W. K. "*The phenomenology....* " *Philosophical Quarterly*, vol. 16, 1966, 185-186.

3046      Piaciola, C. "*Leçons pour une....*" *Rivista di Filosofia*, vol. 57, 1966, 111-112.

3047      Picard, Ivonne. "El tiempo en Husserl y en Heidegger," in *Fenomenología de la conciencia del tiempo inmanente*, de E. Husserl. Trad. de O. E. Lafgelder. Buenos Aires: Edit. Nova, 1959, 212 p.

3048      Schrag, Calvin O. "Introduction," to *The phenomenology of internal time-consciousness*, of E. Husserl. M. Heidegger (ed.). James S. Chirchill (trans.). Bloomington, Ind.: Indiana University Press, 1964, 188 p.

3049      Schuhl, P.-M. "Sur un problème d'édition husserlienne." *Revue Philosophique de la France et de l'Etranger*, vol. 91, 497-498 [*Lecons pour....*].

3050      Sokolowski, Robert. "Immanent constitution in Husserl's lectures on time." *Philosophy and Phenomenological Research*, vol. 24, 1963-1964, 530-551.

## 15) Phänomenologische Psychologie

3051 Bianco, F. "*Phänomenologische Psychologie.*" *Archivio di Filosofia,* no. 3, 1965, 148-149.

3052 Blanchard, Y. "*Phänomenologische Psychologie.*" *Dialogue,* vol. 3, 1964-1965, 451-452.

3053 Brecht, F. J. "*Phänomenologische Psychologie.*" *Universitas,* vol. 18, 1963, 424-425.

3054 Cerf, W. "*Phänomenologische Psychologie.*" *Philosophy and Phenomenological Research,* vol. 27, 1966-1967, 110-114.

3055 Derrida, Jacques. "*Phänomenologische....*" *Etudes Philosophiques,* vol. 18, 1963, 203-206.

3056 Drue, Hermann. *Edmund Husserls System der phänomenologischen Psychologie.* Berlin: Walter de Gruyter, 1963.

3057 Gilen, L. "*Phänomenologische....*" *Scholastik,* vol. 40, 1965, 104-108.

3058 Heinemann, F. H. "*Phänomenologische....*" *Philosophy,* vol. 38, 1963, 84-85.

3059 Kockelmans, Joseph J. *De fenomenologische psychologie volgens Husserl.* Tielt: Lannoo; 1964. *Edmund Husserl's phenomenological psychology.* Pittsburgh, Pa.: Duquesne University Press, 1967, 359 p.

3060 Riverso, E. "*Phänomenologische....* " *Rivista Critica di Storia della Filosofia,* vol. 17, 1964, 76-77.

3061 Unsigned. *Tijdschrift voor Filosofie,* vol. 24, 1962, 779-780.

3062 Kunz, H. *Studia Philosophica,* vol. 23, 1963, 230-231.

## 16) The Paris Lectures

3063 Blanché, R. "*The Paris lectures.*" *Revue Philosophique de la France et de l'Etranger,* vol. 91, 1966, 512-513.

3064 Derrida, Jacques. *Etudes Philosophiques,* vol. 20, 1965, 539.

3065 Koestenbaum, Peter. "Introduction," to *The Paris lectures.* Peter Koestenbaum (trans. from the German). The Hague: Martinus Nijhoff, 1967-1968, lxxvii-39.

3066 Obertello, L. *Giornale di Metafisica,* vol. 21, 1966, 405-407.

3067 Husserl, Edmund. "Syllabus of a course of four lectures on 'Phenommenological method and phenomenological philosophy'. Delivered at University College, London, June 6, 8, 9, 12, 1922." *Journal of the British Society for Phenomenology,* vol. 1, no. 1, 1970, 18-23. [*see:* Spiegelberg 3068]

3068 Spiegelberg, Herbert. "Notes on the text of Husserl's Syllabus." *Journal of the British Society for Phenomenology,* vol. 1, no. 1, 1970, 16-17. [*see:* 2956]

**17)** *Ding und Raum.* Hrsg. von U. Claesges.

3069     Scanlon, John D. "Radical geometry: *Ding un Raum.*" *Research in Phenomenology,* vol. 4, 1974, 129-136.

3070     Scrimieri, Giorgio. "Introduzione" allo studio sulla *Dingvorlesung* del 1907 di E. Husserl." *Annali della Facoltà di Lettere e Filosofia* (Bari). vol. 8, 1962, 60 p.

3071     Scrimieri, Giorgio. *La formazione della fenomenologia di E. Husserl. La Dingvorlesung* del 1907. Bari: Edizioni Levnate, 1967, xiii-494.

3072     Sokolowski, Robert. *Review of Metaphysics,* vol. 27, 1973-1974, 796-797.

3073     Strube, C. *Archiv für Geschichte der Philosophie,* vol. 58, no. 3, 1976, 309-313.

**18)** *Zur Phänomenologie der Intersubjektivität,* I-III.

3074     McCormick, Peter. "Husserl and the intersubjectivity materials. Review of *Zur Phänomenologie der Intersubjektivität.*" *Research in Phenomenology,* vol. 6, 1976, 167-190.

3075     Strasser, Stepha. *Tijdschrfit voor Filosofia,* vol. 35, 1973, 617-630.

**19)** *Analysen zur passiven Synthesis*

3076     Brand, Gerd. *Philosophische Rundschau,* vol. 17, 1970, 57-77.

3077     Forni, Guglielmo. *Giornale di Metafisica,* vol. 22, 1967, 552-557.

3078     Martínez-Gómez, L. *Pensamiento,* vol. 23, 1967, 217-218.

3079     Wahl, Jean. *Revue de Métaphysique et de Morale,* vol. 73, 1968, 127-128.

3080     K. K. *Algemeen Nederands Tijdschrift voor Wijsbegeerte en Psychologie,* vol. 58, 1966, 253-254.

3081     M. J. V. *Review of Metaphysics,* vol. 22, 1969, 571.

**20)** *Briefe an Roman Ingarden*

3082     Brough, J. B. *New Scholalsticism,* vol. 45, 1971, 154-156.

3083     Gorner, Paul. *Journal of the British Society for Phenomenology,* vol. 2, 1971, 84-87.

3084     Kalinowski, G. *Etudes Philosophiques,* no. 3, 1969, 405-406.

3085     Kalinowski, G. *Archives de Philosophie,* vol. 33, 1970, 161-162.

3086     Kuhn, H. *Philosophische Rundschau,* vol. 19, 1972, 161-162.

3087     Periera de Freitas, J. *Revista da Faculdade de Letras.* Serie de Filosofia (Porto), vol. 1, 1971, 306-308.

3088     Steinbach, H. *Philosophische Literaturanzeiger,* vol. 23, 1970, 88-91.

## 21) *Inedita - Husserliana*

3089 Bense, Max. "Bermerkungen über die Gesamtausgabe der Werke Husserls." *Merkur,* vol. 5, no. 10, 1951, 987-990.

3090 Bona, Ida. "Su alcuni manoscritti di Husserl." *Aut Aut,* no. 75, 1963, 7-15, 16-27.

3091 Fries, Horace L. "Husserl unpublished manuscripts." *Journal of Philosophy,* vol. 36, 1939, 238-239.

3092 Herrera Restrepo, D. "Teología de la razón y filosofía. Estudio de un inédito husserliano de 1911." *Ideas y Valores* (Bogotá), no. 13, 1962, 29-42.

3093 Melandri, E. "Gli inediti di Husserl." Il Mulino, Bologna, 1959, (VIII), 529-534.

3094 Paci, Enzo. "Commento al Manoscritto E III 5 (della Teoleologia di Husserl)." *Archivio di Filosofia,* no. 1, 1960 [Tempo e intenzionalita], 17-22.

3095 Piana, Giovanni. *Esistenza e storia negli inediti di Husserl.* Prefazione di Enzo Paci Milano: Lampugnani Nigri, 1965, xvi-114.

3096 Piana, Giovanni. "Accomunamento, storicità, tradizione nella Husserl inedito." *Aut Aut,* no. 68, 1962, 113-130.

3097 Piana, Giovanni. "L'inedito husserliana C 8 1." *Aut Aut,* no. 70, 1962, 284-293.

3098 Ricoeur, Paul. "Analogie et intersubjectivité chez Husserl d'après les Inédits de la période 1905-1920 (Edition Iso Kern, *Husserliana,* tome XIII. Nijhoff, 1973)," in *Enige facetten van opvoeding en onderwijs,* 163-170.

3099 Sancipriano, Maril (ed.). "L"Urkind' di Husserl [pagine centrali di un inedito de Husserl, introdotto e tradotto da M. Sancipriano]." *Aut Aut,* no. 86, 1965, 7-26.

3100 Valori, Paolo. "Inediti Husserliana sulla teologia della storia." *Archivio di Filosofia,* no. 1, 1954, 165-167.

3101 Valori, Paolo. "Inédits husserliens sur la téléologie de l'histoire," in *La philosophie de l'histoire de la philosophie.* Roma: Istituto di Studi Filosofia; Paris: J. Vrin, 1956, 121-123.

3102 Van Breda, Herman Leo. "The actual state of the work on Husserl's *inedita:* achievements and projects." *Analecta Husserliana,* vol. 2, 1972, 149-159.

3103 Verdénal, René. "La sémiotique de Husserl: la logique des signes (à propos de certains inédi)." *Etudes Philosophiques,* no. 4, 1973, 553-564.

## Section 7
### Brief Discussion of Husserl and Phenomenology

3104 Abbagnano, Nicolà. *Dizionario di filosofia.* Torino, 1961.

3105 Accattatis, Vincenzo. "Il gatto e il triangolo." *Rivista di Studi Crociani,* vol. 4, Jan.-March 1967, 95-100.

3106 Adorno, Theodor W. "Spezies und Intention." *Archiv für Philosophie,* vol. 6, no. 1-2, 1956, 14-41.

3107 Ames, Van Meter. "Reply to Maurice Natanson's reply [*see:* Maurice Natanson 3410] *Philosophy and Phenomenological Research., vol. 17, 1956-1957, 246-247.*

3108 Ammann, Herman. *Die menschliche Rede.* Lahre i. Br., vol. 1, 1925, vol. II, 1927.

**Book Reviews:**

F. Kreis, "Die Idee der Sprache und das Wesen der Wortbedeutung." *Kantstudien,* vol. 32.

3110 Ammann, Herman. *Vom Ursprung der Sprache.* Lahre i. B., 1929.

3111 Anceschi, Luciano (ed.). *Arte, critica, filosofia.* Bologna: Pàtron, 1965, 348 p.

3112 Anschütz, G. *Spekulative, exakte und angewandte Psychologie.* Leipzig, 1912, 320ff.

3113 Apel, Karl-Otto. "The problem of (philosophical) ultimate justification in the light of a transcendental pragmatic of language." *Ajatus,* vol. 36, 1974, 142-165.

3114 Arata, C. "Evidenza e metafisica." *Rivista di Filosofia Neo-Scholastica,* no. 2-3, 1960, 168-205.

3115 Asemissen, H. U. "Egologische Reflexion." *Kantstudien,* vol. 50, no. 3, 1958-1959.

3116 Asemissen, H. U. "Phénomenalité et transcendence." *Archives de Philosophie,* vol. 32, no. 1, 1959. English trans. in *Philosophy and Phenomenological Research,* vol. 20, no. 2, 1959.

3117 Aster, E. von. *Prinzipien der Erkenntnislehre.* Leipzig, 1913.

3118 Aster, E. von. *Geschichte der Philosophie.* Leipzig, 1932, 373ff.

3119 Aster, E. von. *Philosophie der Gegenwart.* Leiden, 1935.

3120 Astrada, Carlos. *Idealismo fenomenológico y metafísica existencial.* Buenos Aires, 1936, 132.

3121 Astrada, Carlos. *Fenomenología y praxis.* Buenos Aires: Ed. Siglo Veinte, 1967, 110.

3122 Babolin, Albino. "Verità e verificazione (IV Colloquio internazionale di fenomenologia)." *Rivista di Filosofia Neo-Scholastica,* vol. 61, 1969, 743-749.

3123 Bagolini, L. "Sociologia e fenomenologia del potere politico. Probleme di metodo." *Rivista Internzaionale di Filosofia del Diritto,* no. 3, 1964, 364-401.

3124 Ballanti, G. "Psicologismo ed esistenzialismo." *Rivista di Filosofia Neo-Scholastica,* vol. 43, 1951, 421-435.

3125 Banfi, A. "La fenomenologia e il compito del pensiero contemporaneo," in *Omaggio a Husserl.* Milano: Il Saggiatore, 1960, 29-46.

3126 Banfi, A. "Filosofia fenomenologica." *La Cultura,* vol. 10, 1931.

3127 Banfi, A. *Principi di una teoria della ragione* (Opera di A. Banfi, I). Milano: Parenti, 1960, 566.

3128 Banfi, A. *Filosofi contemporanei.* Firenze, 1961.

3129 Banfi, A. *La ricerca della realtà* (Pubblicazioni della Facoltà di Lettere e Filosofia dell'Università di Milano, 28) [2 vol.]. Firenze: Sansoni, 1959.

3130 Barilli, R. "Chiave fenomenologica per due narratori (Saint-Exupéry e Robbe-Grillet)." *Aut Aut,* no. 57, 1960, 143-161.

3131 Barilli, R. "L'estetica fenomenologica di Anceschi." *Aut Aut,* no. 83, 1964, 51-61.

3132 Barth, E. M. "Phenomenology, grammar, or theory of argumentation." *Cultural Hermeneutics,* vol. 4, April 1977, 163-182.

3133 Bartlett, Steven. "Phenomenology of the implicit." *Dialectica,* vol. 29, 1975, 173-188.

3134 Baumgardt, D. *Das Möglichkeitsproblem in der Kritik der reinen Vernunft, der modernen Phänomenologie und er Gegenstandstheorie. Kantstudien* (ergänzungsheft, no. 51, 1920, 64 p.

3135 Berger, Gaston. "L'éstablissement de la phénoménologie par Marvin Farber." *Revue Philosophique de la France et de l'Etranger,* 138, 1948, 92-95.

3136 Berger, Gaston. "L'attitude phénoménologique," in *Encyclopédie Française,* t. XIX, Paris: Larousse, 19.10-6 a 19.10-8.

3137 Berger, Gaston. *Phénoménologie du temps et prospective.* I: La Méthode phénoménologique. II: La situation de l'homme. III: Phénoménologie du temps. IV: La prospective. Paris: Presses Universitaires de France, 1964, 280 p.

3138 Berger, Gaston. "Quelques aspects de la philosophie allemande contemporaine." *Etudes Philosophiques,* vol. 10, no. 3-4, 1936, 68-74.

3139 Berger, Gaston. "L'originalité de la phénoménologie." *Etudes Philosophiques,* 1954, 249-259.

3140 Berger, Herman. *Op zoek naar identiteit.* Het Aristotelisch substanteibegrip en de mogeltijiceid van een hedengaagse metafysiek. Nijmegen: dekker & Van de Vegt, 1968, 259 p.

3141 *Bilancio della fenomenologia e dell'esistenzialismo.* Realizioni di E. Garin, E. Paci, P. Prini. Padova, 1960.

3142 Bixler, Seelye. "Germany's 'Quest for an absolute'." *International Journal of Ethics,* vol. 41, 1930.

3143   Binswanger, Ludwig. "Ueber Phänomenologie." *Zeitschrift für gesamte Neurologie und Psychiatrie,* vol. 82, 10-45.

3144   Binswanger, Ludwig. *Ueber Ideenflucht.* Zürich, 1933.

3145   Blanco, F. "Intorno al rapporto tra l'ontologia fenomenologica e il problema della demitizzazione." *Archivio di Filosofia,* no. 1, 1960, 161-171.

3146   Boehm, Rudolf. "Une introduction à la philosophie phénoménologique." *Archivio di Filosofia,* vol. 2, 1954, 169-172.

3147   Boehm, Rudolf. "Bewusstsein als gegenwart des vergangenen." *The Monist,* vol. 59, Jan. 1975, 21-39.

3148   Bonomi, A. "Elementi per una fenomenologia del linguaggio filmico." *Aut Aut,* no. 57, 1960, 187-191.

3149   Bonomi, A. "Un filosofo e la politica." *Aut Aut,* no. 82, 1964, 40-57.

3150   Bosanquet, Bernard. *The Meeting of extremes in contemporary philosophy.* London, 1924.

3151   Bosio, F. "Costituzione statica e costituzione genetica." *Archivio di Filosofia,* no. 1, 1960, 73-88.

3152   Bosio, F. "Fenomenologia e criticismo." *Aut Aut,* no. 60, 1960, 392-395.

3153   Bosio, F. "La riduzione al mondo della vita." *Aut Aut,* no. 75, 1963, 16-27.

3154   Bosio, F. "Il paradosso della soggettività." *Aut Aut,* no. 76, 1963, 17-35.

3155   Bosio, F. "Opere recenti sulla fenomenologia." *Aut Aut,* no. 79-80, 1964, 115-127.

3156   Bozzi, P. "Fenomenologia del movimento e dinamica pregalileina." *Aut Aut,* no. 64, 1961, 377-393.

3157   Bossert, Philip J. "Paradox and enlightenment in Zen dialogue and phenomenological description." *Journal of Chinese Philosophy,* vol. 3, June 1976, 269-280.

3158   Brecht, Franz Josef. *Bewusstsein und Existenz.* Wesen und Wege der Phänomenologie. Bremen: Storm, 1948 (verfasst 1932).

3159   Brock, Eric. *An Introduction to contemporary German philosophy.* Cambridge University Press, 1935, 164ff.

3160   Brunner, Auguste, S.J. *La connaissance humaine.* Paris: Aubier, 1953.

3161   Burgert, Helmut. "Zur Kritik der Phänomenologie." *Philosophisches Jahrbuch,* vol. 38, 1925, 226-230.

3162   Buttemeyer, Wilhelm. "Der Streit um 'positivistische' Erziehungswissenschaft in Deutschland." *Scientia,* vol. 110, 1975, 419-468.

3163   Buytendijk, Frederik. *Phénoménologie de la reconte* (texte fraçaise de Jean Knapp). Paris: Textes et études philosophiques, 1952.

3164   Cairns, Dorion. "The ideality of verbal expressions." *Philosophy and Phenomenological Research,* vol. 1, 1940-1941. Reprinted in *Phenomenology. Continuation and criticism.* Essays in memory of Dorion

Cairns. F. Kersten and R. Zaner (eds.) (Phaenomenologica, 50). The Hague: Martinus Nijhoff, 1973, 239-250.

3165 Cairns, Dorion. "Phenomenology," in *The Dictionary of philosophy*, Dagobert Runes (ed.). New York: Philosophical Library, Inc., 1942.

3166 Calvi, L. A. "Sulla costituzione dell'oggetto fobico come 'esercizio fenomenologico'." *Psichaitria* (Padova), no. 1, 1963, 38-74.

3167 Cantoni, R. "Senso comune e filosofia." *Il Pensiero Critico*, no. 1, 1961, 1-25.

3168 Catoni, R. "Antropologia e partecipazione." *Il Pensiero Critico*, no. 4, 1961, 1-29.

3169 Capuuto, John D. "The nothingness of the intellect in Meister Eckhart's *Parisian questions*." *The Thomist*, vol. 39, Jan. 1975, 85-115.

3170 Caruso, P. "Ragione analitica e ragione dialettica nella nuova natropologia." *Aut Aut*, no. 82, 1964, 93-103.

3171 Caruso, P. "Dalla fenomenologia al relazionismo." *Aut Aut*, no. 56, 1960, 108-109.

3172 Caspary, Adolph. "Ueber Phänomenologie." *Geisteskultur*, vol. 36, 1927, 234-243.

3173 Celms, Theodor. "Vom Wesen der Philosophie," in *Philosophia perennis*. Festgabe für Josef Geyer, II, Regensburg: Habbel, 1930.

3174 Chapman, Harmon C. *Sensations and phenomenology*. Bloomington, Ind.: Indiana University Press, 1966.

3175 Chisholm, R. M. "Introduction," to *Realism and the background of phenomenology*. New York: The Free Press of Glencoe-London: Allen and Unwin, 1960.

3176 Chiodi, Pietro. Esistenzialismo e marxismo. Contributo a un diabattito sulla dialettica." *Rivista di Filosofia*, no. 2, 1963, 164-190.

3177 Chiodi, Pietro. *Esistenzialismo e fenomenologia*. Milano, 1963.

3178 Claesges, Ulrich. "Intentionality and transcendnece. On the constitution of material nature." *Analecta Husserliana*, vol. 2, 1972, 283-291. German text, "Intentionalität und Transzendenz. Zur Konstitution des materielle Natur." *Analecta Husserliana*, vol. 1, 1971, 91-99.

3179 Clauss, F. *Die nordische Seele*. Halle, 1923.

3180 Cohen, Hermann. *Logik der reinen Erkenntnis*. Berlin, 3rd. ed., 55ff.

3181 Colette, J. "Chronique de phénoménologie." *Revue des Sciences Philosophiques et Théologiques*, vol. 59, Oct. 1975, 613-644.

3182 Conrad-Martius, Hedwig. "Zur Ontologie und Erscheinungslehre der realen Aussenwelt." *Jahrbuch für Philosophie und Phänomenologische Forschung*, vol. 3, 1916.

3183 Cornelius, H. "Psychologische Principienfragen." *Zeitschrift für Psychologie*, vol. 42-43.

3184 Costa, Margarita. "El método fenomenológica." *Cuadernos de Filosofía*, vol. 12, 1972, 93-110.

3185 Daghini, Giairo. "Materialismo obiettivate ed esistenzialismo dialettico." *Aut Aut,* no. 82, 1964, 18-39.

3186 Daghini, Giairo. "Motivazione, irrealta e il tema della praxis." *Aut Aut,* no. 105-107, 1968, 7-43.

3187 Dallmayr, Fred R. "Phenomenology and critical theory." *Cultural Hermeneutics,* vol. 3, July 1976, 367-406.

3188 de Araújo Figueiredo, P. "Cinco apontamentos sobre fenomenologia." *Revista da faculdade de Letras.* Serie de Filosofia (Porto), vol. 2, no. 1-2, 1972, 69-78.

3189 De Crescenzio, G. *Istituzioni di logica fenomenoligica.* Napoli, 1960.

3190 de Fraga, Gustavo. "Fenomenologia e cartesianismo." *Filosofia* (Lisboa), vol. 4, no. 14, 1957, 89-97.

3191 de Muralt, André. "Epoché - Malin Génie - Théologie de la toute-puissance divine - Le concept objectif sans object - Recherche d'une structure de pensée." *Studia Philosophica,* vol. 26, 1966, 159-191.

3192 Desanti, Jean. T. *Phénoénologie et praxis.* Paris: Editions Sociales, 1963, 149.

3193 De Vleeschauwer, H. "La philosophie contemporaine et le criticisme kantien." *Etudes Philosophiques,* vol. 11, 1937, no. 3-4, 9-14. and *Ibid.,* vol. 12, no. 1-2, 1938, 29-31.

3194 Diemer, Alwin. "Ziele und Aufgaben einer phänomenologischen Philosophie." *Zeitschrift für Philosophische Forschung,* vol. 9, 1955, 315-320.

3195 Dondeyne, Albert. "Psychologie et phénoménologie," in *Recherches et Débats,* Cahier no. 3, 1953, 187-203, Foi, théologie de la foi et phénoménologie, Supl. à *Recherches et Débats,* Paris: C.C.I.F., 1951, 32-38.

3196 Dorlfes, G. "Fenomenologia e psichiatria." *Aut Aut,* no. 64, 1961, 368-376.

3197 Dorfles, g. "Tecnica e intenzionalita alla XXXII Biennale." *Aut Aut,* no. 83, 1964, 53-61.

3198 Driesch, Hans. *Die Logik als Aufgabe.* Tübingen: J.C.B. Mohr, 1913.

3199 Driesch, Hans. *Philosophische Forschungswege.* Leipzig, 1930, 17-49.

3200D riesch, Hans. "Die Phänomenologie und ihre Vieldeutigkeit." *Proceedings 7th International Congress of Philosophy,* Oxford University Press, 1931.

3201 Edie, James M. "Phenomenology as a rigorous science." *International Philosophical Quarterly,* vol. 7, March 1967, 21-30.

3202 Edie, James M. "Phenomenology in the United States [1974]." *Journal of the British Society for Phenomenology,* vol. 5, Oct. 1974, 199-211.

3203 Eisler, Rudolph. "Phänomenologie," in *Handwörtebuch der Philosophie,* 2nd. ed. Berlin: E. S. Mittler & Son, 1922.

3204 Eley, Lothar. "*Life-world* constitution of propositional logic and elementary predicate logic.". *Analecta Husserliana,* vol. 2, 1972, 333-353.

3205 Elsenhabs, Theodor. "Phänomenologie, Psychologie, Erkenntnistheorie." *Kantstudien,* vol. 20, 1924, 224-275.

3206 Elsenhans, Theodor. "Phänomenologie und Empirie." *Kantstudien,* vol. 22, 1918, 243-261.

3207 Elliston, Frederick. "Phenomenology reinterpreted: From Husserl to Heidegger." *Philosophy Today,* vol. 21, Fall 1977, 273-284.

3208 Ehrlich, W. *Das unpersonale Erlebnis.* Einführung in eine neue Erkenntnislehre. Halle, 1927, 624 p.

3209 Ehrlich, W. *Intentionalität und Sinn.* Prolegomena zur Normenlehre. Halle, 1934, 48 p.

3210 Embree, Lester E. "Toward a phenomenology of theoria," in *Life-world and consciousness.* Essays in honor of Aron Gurwitsch, Lester E. Embree (ed.). Evanston, Ill.: Northwestern University Press, 1972, 191-208.

3211 Eng, Erling. "Body, consciousness, and violence." *Analecta Husserliana,* vol. 2, 1972, 267-277.

3212 Enyvari, E. "Zur Phänomenologie der Ideation." *Zeitschrift für Philosophie und Philosophische Kritik,* 1924, 153ff.

3213 Ettlinger, Max. *Geschichte der Philosophie von der Romantik zur Gegenwart* (Philos. Handbibliothek, vol. 8,) München, 1928, 308ff.

3214 Ewald, O. "Die deutsche Philosophie im Jahre 1907." *Kantstudien,* vol. 13, 1908, 197-237. [bes. 227-228]

3215 Fabro, Cornelio. *La fenomenologia della percezione.* Brescia, 1961.

3216 Fanizza F. "Il 'nuoveau roman' francese contemporaneo e la fenomenologia." *Il Pensiero,* no. 3, 1960, 372-386.

3217 Fanizza, F. "Di una recente apertura metodologica." *Aut Aut,* no. 56, 1960, 115-124.

3218 Farber, Marvin. "Remarks about the phenomenological program." *Philosophy and Phenomenological Research,* vol. 6, 1945-1946, 1-10.

3219 Farber, Marvin. "Experience and transcendence, a chapter in recent phenomenology an existentialism." *Philosophy and Phenomenological Research,* vol. 12, 1951-1952, 1-23.

3220 Farber, Marvin. "Phenomenology" in *Twentieth century philosophy,* Dagobert Runes (ed.). New York: Philosophical Library, 1943; 2nd ed. *Living schools of philosophy.* Ames, Iowa: Littlefield, Adams & Co., 1956.

3221 Farber, Marvin. "La philosophie descriptive et la nature de l'existence humaine," in *L'activité philosophique contemporaine en France et aux Etats-Unis.* Paris: Presses Universitaires de France, t. I, 1950, 67-94. English version, "Descriptive philosophy and the nature of human existence," in *Philosophic thought in France and the United States.* New York: Philosophical Library, 1950, 419-441.

3222 Farber, Marvin. "Theses concerning the foundation of logic." *Philosophical Review,* vol. 38, 1929.

3223 Farber, Marvin. "Relational categories and the quest for unity." *Philosophical Review,* vol. 44, 1934.

3224    Farber, Marvin. "The function of phenomenological analysis." *Philosophy and Phenomenological Research*, vol. 1, 1940-1941.

3225    Farber, Marvin. "Modes of reflection inscribed to the memory of Ed. Husserl." *Philosophy and Phenomenological Research*, vol. 8, 1947-1948 588-600.

3226    Farber, Marvin. "Phenomenology." *Collier's Encyclopedia*, vol. 18, 1965.

3227    Farber, Marvin. "Phenomenology," in *The concise encyclopedia of Western philosophy and philosophers*, J. O. Urmson (ed.). New York: Hawthorn Books, Inc., 1960.

3228    Feldkeller P. *Sinn, Echthiet Liebe nach P. Hoffmans Sinnanalyse.* Berlin, 1931.

3229    Filiasi Gargono, Paolo. "La funzione metodologica della fenomenologia," chap. 7, in *La metodologia nel rinnovarsi del pernsiero contemporaneo* ("Filosofia e pedagogia"). Napoli: Libreria Scientifica Editrice, 1957, xii-450.

3230    Filipovic, Vladimir. "Die Sendung der Philosophie in unserer Zeit nach Marx und Husserl." *Praxis,* vol. 3, 1967, 346-351.

3231    Findlay, J. N. "Phenomenology and the meaning of realism," in *Phenomenology and philosophical understanding,* E. Pivcevic (ed.). Cambridge University Press, 1976, 146-158.

3232    Fink, Eugen. "Das Problem der ontologischen Erfahrung," in *Actas del primer congresso de filosofía,* vol. 2, 733-747. Medoza, 1949.

3233    Fink, Eugen. "L'analyse intentionnelle et le problème de la pensée spéculative," in *Problemes actuale de la phénoménologie.* Paris: Desclée de Brouwer, 1952, 53-88.

3234    Fink, Eugene. "Vergegnewartigung und Bild. Beitrage zur Phänomenologie der Unwirklichkeit. Tiel I." *Jahrbuch für Philosophie und Phänomenologische Forschung,* 1930.

3235    Fischl, Johann. *Geschichte der Philosophie.* Bd. 5: Idealismus, Realismus und Existentialismus der Gegenwrt (Philosophie in Einzeldarstellungen, Bd. 14) Graz-Wien-Köln: Verlag Styria, 1954, 194-204.

3236    Fondane, Benjamin. *La conscience malheureuse.* Paris, 1936, xxv-307.

3237    Formaggio, D. "Estetica e metafisica (Una discussione)." *Aut Aut,* no. 63, 1961, 275-282.

3238    Forni, Guglielmo. *Fenomenologia.* Brentano, Husserl, Scheler, Hartmann, Fink, Merleau-Ponty, Ricoeur. Milano: Marzorati Editore, 1973, 230.

3239    Freudn, Ludwig. *Philosophie ein unlösbares Problem Abrechnung mit einer Illusion.* München, 1932.

3240    Fulton, James Street. "The Cartesianism of phenomenology." *Philosophical Review,* vol. 49, 1940.

3241    Funari, E. A. "Fenomenoloiga e psicologia della visione." *Aut Aut,* no. 74, 1963, 95-103.

3242    Funke, Gerhard. "Bewusstseinswissenschaft. Evidenz und Reflexion als Implikate der Verifikation." *Kantstudien,* vol. 61, 1970, 433-466.

3243 Funke, Gerhard. "Seinsgebundenheit der Erkenntnis und phänomenologische Kritik." *Dialectics and Humanism,* vol. 3, Winter 1976, 73-89.

3244 Funke, Gerhard. "Mundane Geschichte, ontologische Erfhrung und transzendentale Subjektivität. Eine transcendental-phänomenologische Untersuchung." *Philosophisches Jahrbuch,* vol. 61, 1956, 117-154.

3245 Funke, Gerhard. "Transzendentale Phänomenologie als erste Philosophie." *Studium Generale,* vol. 11, II, no. 9, 564-582; and *Ibid.,* no. 10, 632-647.

3246 Funke, Gerhard. "Transzendental-phänomenologische Untersuchung über 'universalen Idealismus', 'Intentionaanalyse' und 'Habitusgenese' [con traduzione italiana]," in *Il compito ella fenomenologia,* 117-154. Padova: CEDAM, 1957, 117-154.

3247 Garica Bacca, Juan David. "E. Husserl and J. Joyce. Theory and practice of the phenomenological attitude." *Philosophy and Phenomenological Research,* vol. 9, 1948-1949, 588-594.

3248 Garin, E. *La cultura italiana tra '800 e '900.* Bari, 1962.

3249 Gehlen, Arnold. *Wirklicher und unwirklicher Geist.* Leipzig, 1932.

3250 Geiger, Moritz. "Beitrage zur Phänomenologie des ésthetischen Genusses." *Jahrbuch für Philosophie und Phänomenologische Forschung,* vol. 1, 1913.

3251 Geiger, Moritz. "The philosophical attitudes and the problem of subsistence and essence," in *Proceedings 6th International Congress of Philosophy,* London, 1926.

3252 Geiger, Moritz. "Zum Problem der Stimmungseinfuhlung." *Zeitschrift für Aesthetik und allgemeiner Kurstwisenschaft,* vol. 6.

3253 Geyser, Josef. *Ueber Wahrheit und Evidenz.* Freiburg, 1918, Herber.

3254 Geyser, Josef. *Eidologie.* Freiburg, 1921, Herder.

3255 Geyser, Josef. *Erkenntnistheorie.* Freiburg, 1922, Herder.

3256 Geyser, Josef. "Ueber Begriff und Wesensschau." *Philosophisches Jahrbuch,* vol. 39, 1924.

3257 Geyser, Josef. *Auf dem Kampffelde der Logik.* Freiburg i. Br., 1926, Herder.

3258 Geyser, Josef. *Neue und alte Wege der Philosophie.* Münster: Aschendorff, 1916, 302ff.

3259 Gérard, Jean. *L'être et la pensée.* Paris, 1954.

3260 Glockner, Hermann. *Die europäische Philosophie von den Anfingen bis zur Gegenwart.* Stuttgart: Reclam, 1958.

3261 Grassi, E. "Sviluppo e significato della scuola fenomenologica nella filosofia tedesca contemporanea." *Rivista di Filosofia,* 1929, 129ff.

3262 Grieder, Alfons. "Philosophy in a technological age." *Journal of the British Society for Phenomenology,* vol. 6, Ja. 1975, 3-12.

3263 Gronau, G. *Die Philosophie der Gegenwart.* Langensalza, 1922.

3264 Groethuyssen, Bernard. *La philosophie allemande depuis Nietzsche.* Paris, 1927.

3265 Gründler, Otto. *Elemente zu einer Religionsphilosophie auf phänomenologischer Grundlage.* München, 1922, 136 p.
**Book Reviews:**
Ch. Herrmann, *Kantstudien,* vol. 33, 316-317.

3266 Gründler, Otto. "Die Bedeutung der Phänomenologie für das Seelenleben." *Hockland,* vol. 19, 1921-1922.

3267 Gurwitsch, Aron. "Review of 'The Cartesianism of phenomenology' by J. Fulton [*see:* 3240]. *Philosophy and Phenomenological Research,* vol. 2, 1941-1942.

3268 Gurwitsch, Aron. "Gelb-Goldstein's concept of 'concrete' and 'categorial attitude' and the phenomenology of ideation." *Philosophy and Phenomenological Research,* vol. 10, 1949-1950, 172-196.

3269 Haecht, L. van. "Les racines communes de la phénoménologie, de la psychanalyse, et de l'art contemporain." *Revue Philosophique de Louvain,* vol. 51, 1953, 568-590.

3270 Haman, R. "The concept of prepredicative experience," in *Phenomenology and philosophical understanding,* E. Pivcevic (ed.). Cambridge University Press, 1975, 93-107.

3271 Hamer, Felix. *Leib und Geschichte.* Philosophischen Perspektiven. Bonn: Bouvier, 1974, vii-269.

3272 Hartmann, Nicolai. *Grundzüge einer Metaphysik der Erkenntnis.* Berlin: W. de Gruyter, 1925.

3273 Hartmann, Nicolai. *Zur Grundlegung der Ontologie.* 1935.

3274 Hartmann, Nicolai. *Der Aufbau der realen Welt.* Misenheim am Glan, 1949.

3275 Hartmann, Nicolai. "Ueber die Erkennbarkeit des Apriorischen." *Logos,* 1915, vol. 5, 290ff.

3276 Hartmann, Nicolai. *Metaphysik der Erkenntnis.* Berlin: W. de Gruyter, 1925.

3277 Hartmann, Nicolai. *Teleologisches Denken.* Berlin: W. de Gruyter, 1951.

3278 Hartshorne, Charles. "The method of imaginative variations." *Journal of Philosophy,* vol. 36, 1939, 233-234.

3279 Heim, K. *Psychologismus oder Antipsychologismus?* Berlin, 1902.

3280 Heimsöth, H. "Die Philosophie im XX. Jahrhundert," in W. Windleband, ed., *Lehrbuch der Gesichichte der Philosophie.* Tübingen, 1935, vol. 13, 571-610.

3281 Heinemann, Fritz. *Neue Wege der Philosophie.* Geist-Leben-Existenz. Eine Einführung in die Philosophie der Gegenwart. Leipzig, 1929.

3282 Heinemann, Fritz. "Les problèmes et la valeur d'une phénoménologie comme théorie de la réalité. Etre et apparaitre," in *Travuax IXc Congrés international de Philosophie,* Paris, 1937, 69-71.

3283 Heinrich, E. *Untersuchungen zur Lehre vom Begriff.* Göttingen, 1910.

3284 Henry, Michel. *L'essence de la manifestation.* Paris: Presses Universitaires de France, 1963, viii-908. (2 tomes).

3285 Héring, Jean. "Von den phänomenologischen Bewegung. Ein Beitrag zur zeitgenössischen Philosophiegeschichte." *Theologische Zeitschrift,* 1946, no. 2, 292-296.

3286 Héring, Jean. "La phénoménologie en France," in *L'activité philosophique contemporaine en France et aux Etats-Unis.* Paris: Presses Universitaires de France, 1951, t. II, 76-95.

3287 Hicks, George Dawes. "The philosophy of Husserl." *The Hibbert Journal,* vol. 12.

3288 Hicks, George Dawes. "Survey of recent philosophical literature." *The Hibbert Journal,* vol. 37, Oct. 1938.

3289 Hofmann, H. "Ueber den Empfindungsbegriff." Dissertation, Göttingen. *Archiv für die gesammte Psychologie,* 1913.

3290 Hohler, Thomas P. "Seeing and saying: Phenomenology's contention." *Philosophy Today,* vol. 21, Winter 1977, 327-346.

3291 IJselling, Samuel. "Heidegger en de fenomenologie." *Tijdschrift voor Filosofie,* vol. 38, Dec. 1976, 511-536.

3292 Illeman, Werner. *Die vorphanomenologische Philosophie.* Leipzig, 1932.

3293 Inciarte, Fernando. *Eindeutigkeit und Vairation.* Die Wahrung der Phänomene und des Problem des Reduktionismus. Freiburg-München: Karl Alber, 1973, 261 p.

3294 Ingarden, Roman. *O pozanwaniu dziela literackiego.* Lwów, 1927, 150 p.

3295 Ingarden, Roman. *Grenzgebiet der Ontologie, Logik und Literaturwissenschaft.* Halle, 1931, 398 p.

3296 Metzger, A. *Phänomenologie und Metaphysik.* Das Problem des Relativismus und seine Ueberwindung. Halle, 1934, xvi-269.
Book Reviews:
A. Kojevnikoff, *Recherches Philosophiques,* vol. 2, 480-486.

3297 Ingarden, Roman. *Untersuchungen zur Ontologie der Kunst.* Musikwerk - Bild - Architektur - Film. Tübingen: Max Niemeyer Verlag, 1962, x-342.
Book Reviews:
A. Guy, *Etudes Philosophiques,* vol. 22, 1967, 475.
G. Küng, *Zeitschrift für Philosophische Forschung,* vol. 17, 1963, 179-181.

3298 Ingarden, Roman. *Der Streit um die Existenz der Welt, I: Existentialontologie.* Tübingen: Max Niemeyer Verlag, 1964, xvi-267.
Book Reviews:
J. de Vries, *Theologie und Philosophie,* vol. 44, 1969, 138-139.

3299 Ingarden, Roman. *Das literarische Kunstwerk.* Mit e. Anh. von den funktionen d. Sprache in Theaterschauspiel. 3 durchges. Aufl. Tübingen: Max Niemeyer, 1965, xxiii-430. English trans. *The Literary work of art.* Evanston, Ill.: Northwestern University Press, 1973, lxxxiii-415.

**Book Reviews:**

C. F. Breslin, *Review of Metaphysics,* vol. 28, 1974-1975, 555-556.

H. G. Gadamer, *Philosophische Rundschau,* vol. 11, 1963, 17-19.

G. Kalinowski, *Archives de Philosophie,* vol. 31, 1968, 281-287.

3300      Ingarden, Roman. *The Cognition of the literary work of art.* Ruth A. Crowley and Kenneth R. Olson (trans.). Evanston, Ill.: Northwestern University Press, 1973, xxx-436.

**Book Reviews:**

E. T. Long, *Review of Metaphysics,* vol. 28, 1974-1975, 554-555.

3301      Janssen, D. *Vorstudien zur Metaphysik.* Halle, 1921.

3302      Jaspers, Karl. *Psychologie der Weltanschauungen.* Berlin, 1919.

3303      Jakowenko, Boris. "Was ist die tranzendentale Methode?" *Bericht über den III. international Philosophenkongress in Heidelberg.* Heidelberg, 1909, 787-799.

3304      Jakowenko, Boris. "Filozofija E. Husserlja." *Novyja idei v filozofii,* vol. 2, St. Petersbourg, 1912.

3305      Jakowenko, Boris. "Il cammino della conoscenza filosofica." *Logos,* vol. 5, 1922.

3306      Jakowenko, Boris. *Wom Wesen des Pluralismus.* Prague, 1928, 65ff.

3307      Jakowenko, Boris. "Edmund Husserl und die russische Philosophie," in *Der russische Gedanke,* 1929, vol. 1, 210ff.

3308      Jakowenko, Boris. "Kritische Bemerkungen uber die Phänomenologie," in *Proceedings of the Seventh International Congress of Philosophy,* 1930.

3309      Jakowenko, Boris. "Zur Kritik der Logistik der Dialektik und der Phänomenologie." Bibliothèque internationale de Philosophie, Prag, 1936.

3310      Jeanson, Francis. *La fenomenologia,* trad. e prefaz, di R. Barilli. Milano: 1962.

3311      Jerusalem, W. *Der kritische Idealismus und die reine Logik.* Ein Ruf in Streite. Wien, 1905.

3312      Joël, K. "Die Ueberwindung des XIX. Jahrhunderts im Denken der Gegenwart." *Kantstudien,* vol. 35.

3313      Joël, K. "Die philosophische Krisis der Gegenwart." Rektoratsrede, 1914.

3314      Kaufmann, Felix. *Logik und Rechtswissenschaft.* Tübingen, 1922.

3315      Kaufmann, Felix. *Die Kriterien des Rechts.* Tübingen, 1924.

3316      Kaufmann, Felix. *Das Unendliche in der Mathematik und seine Ausschaltung.* Leipzig-Wien, 1930.

3317      Kaufmann, Felix. "Die Bedeutung der logischen Analyse für die Socialwissenschaften," *Actes du VIIIe Congrès international de Philosophie.* Prague, 1936.

3318      Kaufmann, Felix. *Methodenlehre der Sozialwissenschaften.* Wien, 1936, 331ff.

3319    Kaufmann, Felix. "Truth and logic." *Philosophy and Phenomenological Research,* vol. 1, Sept. 1940.

3320    Kerler, Dietrich H. *Die auferstandene Metaphysik.* Ulm, 1921, 283ff.

3321    Kockelmans, Joseph J. "Het standpunt van de phaenomenologie met betrekling tot de vraag over de vorhousing tussen zijn en verschijnen." *Tijdschrift voor Filosofie,* vol. 22, no. 4, 1960.

3322    Kockelmans, Joseph J. *The world in science and philosophy.* Milwaukee: Bruce Pub., 1969 ("Horizons in Philosophy").

3323    Köpp, W. *Grundlegung zur induktiven Theologie.* Kritik, Phänomenologie und Methode des allgemeinen und theologischen Erkennens. Güterslch, 1927.

3324    Kottje, F. *Illusionen der Wissenschaft.* Stuttgart: J. G. Gottasche Buchhandlung, 1931, 70-83.

3325    Kozak, J.-B. "Das Wesen der geistigen Intention: das transzendierende Meinen." *Philosophia,* vol. 1, 1936.

3326    Kraft, Julius. *Die Grundformen der wissenschaftlichen Methoden.* Wien, 1926. Sitzungsberichte der Akademie der Wissenschaften, hist-phil. Klasse, vol. 23, 1926, 304.

3327    Kraft, Julius. "Die wissenschaftliche Bedeutung der phänomenologischen Rechtsphilosophie." *Kantstudien,* vol. 31, 286-296.

3328    Kreis, Friedrich. *Phänomenologie und Kritizismus.* Tübingen, Mohr, 1930.
**Book Reviews:**

F. Blaschke, *Blätter für deutsche Philosophie,* vol. 5, 1931-1932, 335-336.

3329    Krejcf, Fr. *Filosofie poslednich let pred valkou.* Prag, 1930, 297-306.

3330    Kröner, Franz. *Die Anarchie der philosophischen Systeme.* Leipzig, 1929, bes. 57ff, 237ff, 295ff.

3331    Kuntze, Fr. *Die kritische Lehre von der Objectivität.* 193ff.

3332    Kuspit, Donald B. "Fiction and phenomenology." *Philosophy and Phenomenological Research,* vol. 29, Sept. 1968, 16-33.

3333    Kuypers, K. "Fenomenologie en metafysica." *Algemeen Nederlands Tijdschrift voor Wijsbegeerte en Psychologie,* vol. 52, 1960, 143-156.

3334    Kuznitzky, G. *Naturerlebnis und Wirklichkeitsbewusstseins.* Breslau, 1919.
**Book Reviews:**

Edith Stein, *Kantstudien,* vol. 24, 402-405.

3335    Kwant, Remy C. "Phenomenologie en ontologie." *Phenomenologie en Wijsbegeerte.* Utrecht und Brüssel, 1950, 1-25.

3336    Kynast, Reihard. *Das Problem der Phänomenologie.* Eine wissenschaftstheoretische Untersuchung. Breslau, 1917.

3337    Kynast, Reihard. "Intuitive Erkenntnis." Dissertation, Breslau, 1919.

3338    Landgrebe, Ludwig. "Phenomenology and metaphysics." *Philosophy and Phenomenological Research,* vol. 10, 1949-1950, 197-205.

3339   Landgrebe, Ludwig. *Phänomenologie und Metaphysik.* (Sammelband verschiedener Arbeiten des Verfassers). Hamburg, 1949.

3340   Landgrebe, Ludwig. "Geist und Transzendenz des Bewusstseins." *Philosophia,* vol. 1, 1936.

3341   Landgrebe, Ludwig. "The world as a phenomenological problem." *Philosophy and Phenomenological Research,* vol. 1, 1940-1941.

3342   Landgrebe, Ludwig. *Philosophie der Gegenwart.* Wiesbaden: Atheneum, 1953.

3343   Landgrebe, Ludwig. "Principien der Lehre vom Empfinden." *Zeitschrift für Philosophisches Forschung,* vol. 8, 1954, 195-209.

3344   Landmann, Edith. *Die Transzendenz des Erkennens.* Berlin, 1923.

3345   Lanteri Laura, Georges. "L'usage de l'exemple dans la phhénoménologie." *Etudes Philosophiques,* vol. 9, 1954, 57-72.

3346   Larrabee, Mary Jeanne. "Husserls static and genetic phenomenology." *Man and World,* vol. 9, June 1976, 163-174.

3347   Lazzarini, R. *Situazione unama e il senso della storia e del tempo.* Milano, 1961.

3348   Ledrut, Raymond. "Phénoménologie et rationalisme." *Critique,* no. 117, 1957, 151-223.

3349   Legendecker, H. *Zur Phänomenologie der Täuschungen.* Halle, 1913.

3350   Lehmann, Gerhard. *Die Ontologie der Gegenwart in ihren Grundgestalten.* Halle, 1933, 42 p.

3351   Lehsegang, H. *Deutsche Philosophie im 20, Jahrhundert.* Breslau, 1928.

3352   Lejewski, Grzeslaw. "Syntax and semantics of ordinary language: Part I." *Aristotelian Society,* vol. 49, 1975, 127-146.

3353   Levinas, Emmanuel. "Intentionalité et métaphysique." *Revue Philosophique de la France et de l'Etranger,* vol. 84, 1959, no. 4, 471-479.

3354   Levinas, Emmanuel. "De la conscience à la veille. à partir de Husserl." *Bijdragen,* vol. 34, 1974, 235-249.

3355   Levinas, Emmanuel. "Reflexions sur la 'technique' phénoménologique," 95-107 [Discussion, 108-117]," in *Husserl* (Cahiers de Royaumont).

3356   Liebert, Arthur. "Das problem der Geltung." *Kantstudien,* vol. 32, 1914.

3357   Linke, Paul F. *Die phänomenale Sphäre und das reele Bewusstsein.* Halle, 1912.

3358   Linke, Paul F. "Das Recht der Phänomenologie. Eine Auseinandersetzung mit Theodor Elsehans." *Kantstudien,* vol. 21, 1916, 163-221.

3359   Linke, Paul F. *Niedergangserscheinungen in der Philosophie der Gegenwart.* Wege zu ihrer Überwindung. München-Basel: Ernst Reinhardt-Verlag, 1961, 154 p.

3360   Linke, Paul F. "Die Minderwertigkeit der Erfahrung in der Theorie der Erkenntnis." *Kantstudien,* vol. 23, 1918.

3361   Linke, Paul F. *Grundfragen der Wahrnehmungslehre.* München, 1918, vol. I, 1929, vol. II.

3362 Linke, Paul F. "Die Exlistentialtheorie der Wahrheit und der Psychologismus der Geltungslogik." *Kantstudien,* vol. 29, 1924.

3363 Linke, Paul F. "Beobchten und Schauen." *Vierteljahrsschrift für philosophische Pädogogik,* vol. 2, 44ff.

3364 Linke, Paul F. "The present status of logik and epistemology in Germany." *The Monist,* vol. 36, 1926.

3365 Linke, Paul F. "Der Staz des Bewusstseins und die Lehre von der Intentionalität." *Atti del V Congresso internazionale di filosofia in Napoli,* 1924. Napoli, 1927.

3366 Linke, Paul F. "Logic and epistemology," in *Philosophy Today,* E. L. Schaub (ed.). Chicago, 1928.

3367 Linke, Paul F. "Gegenstandsphänologie." *Philosophische Hefte,* vol. 2, 1930-1931, 79ff.

3368 Linke, Paul F. "Auseinandersetzung: Fr. Krejci, 'Parallelistische Phanomenologie' (Paralelistická fenomenologie)." *Ceskà Mysl,* 1931, 3-17.

3369 Lombardi, F. *Discorrendo di filosofia e di sociologia e di altre poche cose.* Bari, 1962.

3370 Lombardi, F. "A che punto siamo in filosofia?" *De Homine,* no. 1, 1962, 1-32.

3371 Löwenstein, K. "Sätze uber Phänomenologie." *Zeitschrift für Philosophie und Philosophische Kritik,* vol. 148, 1912, 17-41.

3372 Löwith, Karl. "Grundzüge der Entwicklung der Phänomenologie zur Philosophie und ihr Verhältnis zur protestantischen Theologie." *Theologische Rundschau,* 1930.

3373 Löwith, Karl. *Das Individuum in der Rolle des Mitmenschen.* Munchen, 1928.

3374 Lozinski, Jerzy. "Some remarks concerning David Rasmussen's 'The Marxist critique of phenomenology'." *Dialectics and Humanism,* vol. 2, Aut. 1975, 71-75. see: 3482

3375 Lübbe, Hermann. "Das Ende des phänomenologischen Platonismus. Eine kritische Betrachtung aus Anlass eines neuen Buches [W. Schapp, *In Geschichten verstrickt*] *Tijdschrift voor Filosofie,* vol. 16, 1954, 639-666.

3376 Lugarini, L. "Ragione critical e ragione fenomenologica." *Giornale Criticao della Filosofia Italiana,* no. 4, 1961, 443-461.

3377 Mahnke, D. "Eine neue Monadologie." *Kantstudien,* Erganzungsheft, vol. 39, 1917.

3378 Mahnke, D. *Der Wille zur Ewigkeit.* Halle, 1917, 127 p.

3379 Mahnke, D. *Das unsichbare Königreich des deutschem Idealismus.* Halle, 1920.

3380 Maier, H. "Logik und Psychologie," in *Festschrift für Alois Riehl.* Halle, 1914.

3381 Maréchal, J. "Phénoménologie pure ou philosophie de l'action," in *Festgabe für Geyser,* vol. 1, 1931. Regensburg, 379-400. Reprinted in *Mélanges Maréchal,* vol. 1, 1950.

3382 Marini, A. "Sociologia e fenomenologia." *Aut Aut,* no. 84, 1964, 68-86.

3383  Maritain, Jacques. "Notes sur al connaissance." *Rivista di Filosofia Neo-Scholastic,* vol. 24, 1932, fasc. 1, 13-23.

3384  Masullo, Aldo. *Struttura soggetto prassi.* Napoli: Libreria Scientifica, 1962, 364 p.

3385  Maticevic, J. *Zur Grundlegung der Logik.* Ein Beitrag zur Bestimmung des Verhältnisses zwischen Logik und Psychologie. Wien, 1909.

3386  Mays, Wolfe and Brown, S. C. (eds.). *Linguistic analysis and phenomenology.* Lewisburg, Pa.: Bucknell University Press, 1972.

3387  Menzer, Paul. *Deutsche Metaphysik der Gegnwart.* Berlin: Mittler und Sohn, 1931, 59ff.

3388  Mertens, Paul. "Zur Phänomenologie des Glaubens." Dissertation, Bonn, 1927, 40 p.

3389  Messer, A. *Empfindung und Denken.* Leipzig, 1908.

3390  Messer, A. "Husserls Phänomenologie in ihrem Verhältnis zur Psychologie." *Archiv für Gesammte Psychologie,* vol. 22, 1912; vol. 32, 1914.

3391  Messer, A. "Ueber den Begriff des Aktes." *Archiv für Gesammte Psychologie,* vol. 24, 1913.

3392  Messer, A. *Philosophie der Gegenwart in Deutschland.* Leipzig, 1931.

3393  Melandri, E. "I paradossi dell'infinito nell'orizzonte fenomenologico," in *Omaggio a Husserl.* Milano, 1960,, 81-120.

3394  Messerich, Valerius. "An apodictic approach to reality." *Franciscan Studies,* vol. 13, no. 2-3, 1953, 1-36.

3395  Metzger, A. "La situación presente de la fenomenológia." *Revista de Occidente,* vol. 22, 1928, 177-201.

3396  Metzger A. *Phänomenologie und Metaphysik.* Das Problem des Relativismus und seine Ueberwindung. Halle, 1934, xvi-269.
**Book Reviews:**
E. Levinas, *Revue Philosophique,* vol. 62, 1935, 258-262.
H. Corbin, *Recherches Philosophiques,* vol. 4, 1936, 411-412.

3397  Michaltschew, D. *Philosophische Studien.* Leipzig, 1912.

3398  Miéville, Henri-Louis. "Du 'cogito' au transcendental et au métaphysique." *Reuve de Théologie et de Philosophie,* vol. 92, 1964, 265-287.

3399  Mijuskovic, Ben. "The simplicity argument and absolute morality." *Journal of Thought,* vol. 10, April 1975, 123-135.

3400  Minkowski, Eugène. *Esquisses phénoménologiques.* Paris: Boivin, 1935.

3401  Monetta, Giusepina Chiara. "The foundation of predictive experience and the spontaneity of consciousness," in *Life world and consciousness.* Essays in honor of Aron Gurwitsch, Lester E. Embre (ed.). Evanston, Ill.: Northwestern University Press, 1972, 171-190.

3402  Moog, Willy. "Die Kritik des Psychologismus." *Archiv für die Gesammte Psychologie,* vol. 37, 341ff.

3403   Moog, Willy. *Psychologie und Psychologismus* (Wissenschaftssystematische Untersuchungen). Halle, 1919, viii-306.

3404   Moog, Willy. *Die deutsche Philosophie des XX. Jarhrhunderts.* Stuttgart, 1922, 248ff.

3405   Moore, Jared S. "Is this phenomenology?" *Philosophy and Phenomenological Research,* vol. 3, 1942-1943.

3406   Morpurgo-Tagliabue, Guido. "Fenomenologia del processo semantico e struttura dei linguaggi artistici." *Rivista di Estetica,* no. 1, 1962, 19-57.

3407   Morris, Charles W. *Six theories of mind.* Chicago: University of Chicago Press, 1932.

3408   Müller, A. *Einleitung in die Philosophie.* Berlin, 1931.

3409   Müller, Max. "Phänomenologie, Ontologie und Scholastik." *Tijdschrift voor Filosofie,* vol. 14, 1952, 63-86. Reprinted in *Existenzphilosophie im geistigen Leben der Gegenwart,* 2. Aufl., Heidelberg: Kerle, 1958, 107-134.

3410   Natanson,, Maurice. "Phenomenology from the natural standpoint: A reply to Van Meter Ames." *Philosophy and Phenomenological Research,* vol. 17, 1956-1957, 241-245. [*see:* Ames 3107]

3411   Natanson, Maurice. "Phenomenology as a rigorous science." *International Philosophical Quarterly,* vol. 7, 1967, 5-20.

3412   Natanson, Maurice. *Literature, philosophy, and the social sciences.* Essays in existentialism and phenomenology. 3rd printing. The Hague: Martinus Nijhoff, 1968, xii-220.

3413   Negri, A. "Attualismo e fenomenologia." *Giornale Critico della Filosofia Italiana,* no. 2, 1964, 216-250.

3414   Negri, G. D. "Fenomenologia ed estetica." *Aut Aut,* no. 72, 1962, 517-522.

3415   Nielsen, H. A. "Is phenomenology based on an oversight?" *New Scholasticism,* vol. 52, Winter 1978, 72-79.

3416   Nink, Caspar. *Grundlegung der Erkenntnistheorie.* Frankfurt am Main, 1930.

3417   Nink, Caspar. "Vom Anfang der Philosophie'." *Scholastik,* vol. 26, 1951, 177-190.

3418   Nink, Caspar. *Ontologie,* Freiburg, 1952.

3419   Noél, L. "Les frontières de la logique." *Revue Néo-scolastique de Philosophie,* vol. 17, 1910.

3420   Nota, J. "Phaenomenologie als methode." *Tijdschrift voor Filosofie,* vol. 3, 1941.

3421   Odebrecht, Rudolph. *Grundlegung einer ästhetischen Werttheorie. I: Das ästhetische Welterlebnis.* Berlin, 1927.

3422   Otaka, T. *Die Lehre vom sozialen Verband.* Wien, 1932, xi-280.

3423   Paci, Enzo. *Diario fenomenologico.* Milano: 1961.

3424   Paci, Enzo. *Scienza e fenomenologia.* Milano, 1961 (dispense universitaire).

3425   Paci, Enzo. *La filosofia contemporanea.* Milano, 1961, (2a ed.).

3426　Paci, Enzo and Rovatti, Pier Aldo. "Persona, mondo circostante, motivazione," 142-171.

3427　Paci, Enzo. "Aspetti di una problematica filosofica." *Aut Aut,* no. 55, 1960, 1-9.

3428　Paci, Enzo. "Indicazioni fenomenologische per il romanzo." *Quaderni Mialanesi,* Autunno 1960.

3429　Paci, Enzo. "Coscienza fenomenologica e coscienza idealistica." *Il Verri,* no. 4, 1960, 3-15.

3430　Paci, Enzo. "Sullo stile della fenomenlogia." *Aut Aut,* no. 57, 1960, 265-282.

3431　Paci, Enzo. "Tecnica feticizzata e linguaggio." *L'Europa Letteraria,* no. 9-10, 1961.

3432　Paci, Enzo. "Qualque osservzaione filosofica sulla critica e sulla poesia." *Aut Aut,* no. 61-62, 1961, 1-21.

3433　Paci, Enzo. "Espressione e significato." *Aut Aut,* no. 61-62, 1961, 162-167.

3434　Paci, Enzo. "Per una fenomenologia dell'Eros." *Nuovi Argomenti,* no. 51-52, 1961, 52-76.

3435　Paci, Enzo. "Nuove ricerche fenomenologiche." *Aut Aut,* no. 68, 1962, 99-112.

3436　Paci, Enzo. "Problemi di antropologia. Per un'analisi fenomenologica del sonno e del sogno." *Aut Aut,* no. 70, 1962, 275-283.

3437　Paci, Enzo. "Strutta e lavoro vivente." *Aut Aut,* no. 71, 1962, 453-457.

3437　Paci, Enzo. "Bomba atomica e significato di verità." *Il Verri,* no. 6, 1962, 159-162.

3439　Paci, Enzo. "Bomba atomica e significato di verità." *Il Verri,* no. 6, 1962, 159-162.

3440　Paci, Enzo. "In un rapporto intenzionale." *Questo e Altro,* no. 2, 1963, 25-41.

3441　Paci, Enzo. "Il senso delle parole (Lebenswelt, Struttura)." *Aut Aut,* no. 73, 1963, 88-94.

3442　Paci, Enzo. "Il senso delle parole (Epoché, Trascendentale)." *Aut Aut,* no. 74, 1963, 108-111.

3443　Paci, Enzo. "Sociologia e condizione umana." *Aut Aut,* no. 76, 1963, 7-16.

3444　Paci, Enzo. "Il senso delle parole (Riconsiderazione, Senso, Causa, Il Cogito e la Monade)." *Aut Aut,* no. 76, 1963, 106-108.

3445　Paci, Enzo. "Fenomenologia e antropologia culturale." *Aut Aut,* no. 77, 1963, 91-111.

3446　Paci, Enzo. "Il senso delle parole (Sprachleib, Soggettività linguistica, Langue et parole, Strutturalismo fonologia e antropologia)." *Aut Aut,* no. 77, 1963, 100-103.

3447　Paci, Enzo. "Il senso delle parole (Gradi dell'alienazione, Strumentalismo, Il corpo proprio inorganico, Informale e nuova figurazione, Tradizione e avanguardia)." *Aut Aut,* no. 78, 1963, 91-94.

3448 Paci, Enzo. "Annotazioni per una fenomenologia della musica." *Aut Aut,* no. 79-80, 54-66.

3449 Paci, Enzo. "Il senso delle parole (Scientificità, Irreversibilità, Entropia e informazione, Operazionismo, Musica e modalità temporali)." *Aut Aut,* no. 79-80, 132-138.

3450 Paci, Enzo. "Teatro, funzione delle scienze e riflessione." *Aut Aut,* no. 81, 1964, 7-14.

3451 Paci, Enzo. "Le parole." *Aut Aut,* no. 82, 1964, 7-17.

3452 Paci, Enzo. "Il senso delle parole (Linguaggio oggettivato, Soggeto e comportamento, La scienza e la vita)." *Aut Aut,* no. 82, 1964, 104-107.

3453 Paci, Enzo. "Fenomenologia e cibernetica." *Aut Aut,* no. 83, 1964, 33-41.

3354 Paci, Enzo. "Il senso delle parole (Introduzione, Cose e problemi, Forme categoriali)." *Aut Aut,* no. 83, 1964, 93-95.

3455 Paci, Enzo. "Il senso delle parole (Prima persona, Fenomenologia e fisiologia, Dualismo teatro personaggi)." *Aut Aut,* no. 81, 1964, 108-112.

3456 Paci, Enzo. "Struttura temporale e orizzonte storico." *Aut Aut,* no. 87, 1965, 7-19.

3457 Paci, Enzo. "Il senso delle parole. (Fenomenologia della prassi e realtà obiettiva [Husserl])." *Aut Aut,* no. 96-97, 1966-1967, 153-154.

3458 Palagyi, Melchior. *Der Streit der Psychologisten und der Formalischen in der modernen Logik.* Leipzig, 1902, 94 p [bes. 8-10].

3459 Passmore, J. A. "The movement towards objectivity," in *A Hundred years of philosophy.* Hamonsworth: Peguin Books, 1970, 175-202.

3460 Patocka, Jan. *Prirozeny svèt jako filosoficky problem.* Prag, 1936.

3461 Penati, Girogio. "Il rapporto datità-metafisica e le sue consequenze metodologiche." *Rivista di Filosofia Neo-Scholastica,* no. 6, 1961.

3462 Perry, Ralph B. *Philosophy of the recent past.* New York: Scribner's, 1926.

3463 Petruzzellis, Nicolà. "Logica e fenomenologai." *Rassegna di Scienze Filosofiche,* vol. 2, 1958, 161-190.

3464 Pegis, Anton C. "Medalist's address." *Proceedings of Catholic Philosophical Association,* vol. 49, 1975, 228-238.

3465 Pfänder, Alexander. "Logik." *Jahrbuch für Philosophie und Phänomenologische Forschung,* vol. 4, 1921, 139-494.

3466 Pfänder, Alexander. "Zur Psychologiie der Gesinnungen." *Jahrbuch für Philosophie und Phänomenologische Forschung,* vol. 1, 1913, and vol. 3, 1916.

3467 Piana, G. "Un recente libro sulla fenomenologia." *Aut Aut,* no. 59, 1960, 322-325.

3468 Piana, Giovanni. "Un'analisi husserliana del colore." *Aut Aut,* no. 92, 1966, 21-30.

3469 Piana, Giovanni. "Saggi di fenomenologia." *Archivio di Filosofia*, no. 1, 1960, 99-103.

3470 Piovesan, R. *Analisi filosofica e fenomenologia linguistica.* Padova, 1961.

3471 Pivcevic, Edo (ed.). "Editor's introduction," to *Phenomenology and philosophical understanding.* Cambridge University Press, 1975; and Chap. 15, "Concept, phenomenology and philosophy," 271-285.

3472 Pettit, Philip. "The life world and role theory," in *Phenomenology and philosophical understanding,* Edo Pivcevic (ed.). Cambridge University Press, 1975, 251-270.

3473 Poltawski, Andrezej. "Constitutive phenomenology and intentional object." *Analecta Husserliana,* vol. 2, 1972, 90-95.

3474 Pos, H.J. "Valeur et limits de la phénoménologie," in *Problèmes actuels de la phénoménologie,* 31-52. Paris: Desclée de Brouwer, 1952, 31-52.

3475 Prini, Pietro. *Discorso e situazione.* Roma, 1961.

3476 Prufer, Thomas. "Reduction and constitutiion," in *Ancients and moderns,* John K. Ryan (ed.). Washington, D. C.: Catholic University of America Press, 1970, 341-353.

3477 Przywara, Erich. *Gott.* Fünf Vorträge uber die religionsphilosophischen *Probleme.* München, 1926.

3478 Przywara, Erich. "Drei Richtungen der Phänomenologie." *Stimmen der Zeit,* 1928.

3479 Przywara, Erich. "Die Wende zum Menschen." *Stimmen der Zeit,* 1929-1930.

3480 Pucci, R. "Fenomenologia e psicologia," in *Omaggio a Husserl.* Milano, 1960, 227-262.

3481 Pucci, R. "Il mondo-della-vita e la storia." *Rassegna di Scienze Filosofiche,* 16, 1963, 327-356.

3482 Rasmussen, David. "The Marxist critique of phenomenology." *Dialectics and Humanism,* no. 2, Aut. 1975, 59-70. [*see:* Lozinski 3374]

3483 Reinach, Adolf. *Gesammelte Schriften,* Halle, 1922.

3484 Reinach, Adolf. *Was ist Phänomenologie?* [auch in *Gesammelte Werke*] München: Kösel, 1951.

3485 Reiner, Hans. "Sinn und Recht der phänomenologischen Methode," in *Edmund Husserl 1859-1959* (Phaenomenologica, 4). The Hague: Martinus Nijhoff, 1960, 134-147.

3486 Reiner, Hans. "Freiheit. Wollen und Aktivität. Phänomenologische Untersuchungen in der Richtung auf das Problem der Willensfreiheit." Dissertation, Freiburg, Halle, 1927, vi-172.

3487 Renzi, E., Garin, Paci, Prini. "Bilancio dell'esistenzialismo e della fenomenologia." *Il Verri,* no. 4, 1960, 123-130.

3488 Renzi, E. "Sociologia e fenomenologia." *Aut Aut,* no. 68, 1962, 155-159.

3489    Reyer, W. "Untersuchungen zur Phänomenologie des begrifflichen Gestaltens. Beiträge zur Grundlegung einer eidetischen Intentionalpsychologie." Dissertation, Hamburg 1924.

3490    Reyer, W. "Ueber das Wesen und die Bedeutung der phänomenologischen Forschung." *Hamburger Universitatszeitung,* vol. 8, 1926, 77-79.

3491    Reyer, B. *Einführung in die Phänomenologie.* Leipzig, 1926, xiv-465.

3492    Rickert, Heinrich. "Zwei Wege der Erkenntnistheorie." *Kantstudien,* vol. 14, 1909, 169-228.

3493    Rickert, Heinrich. "Das Unmittelbare." *Logos,* vol. 12, 1923.

3494    Rickert, Heinrich. *Das Eine, die Enheit und die Eins.* Tübingen, 1923.

3495    Ricoeur, Paul. *Philosophie de la volonté,* t. I. Paris: Aubier, 1949. "La méthode descriptive et ses limites," 8-23.

3496    Ricoeur, Paul. "Sympathie et respect." *Revue de Métaphysique et de Morale,* 1954, 380-397. [Réflexions sur les limits de la méthode phénoménologique]

3497    Ricoeur, Paul. "Sur la phénoménologie, I & II." *Esprit,* 1953, 821-839, et *Ibid.,* 1955, 722-726. [Translated in *Southwestern Journal of Philosophy, see:* 3499].

3498    Ricoeur, Paul. "Méthode et taches d'une phénoménologie de la volonté," in *Problems actuels de la phénoménologie.* Paris: Desclée de Brouwer, 1952, 111-140.

3499    Ricoeur, Paul. "Phenomenology." [Translation of *Esprit,* 1953, 821-839]. *Southwestern Journal of Philosophy,* vol. 5, Fall, 1974, 149-168.

3500    Ricoeur, Paul. "Phénoménologie et herméneutique." *Man and World,* vol. 7, Aug. 1974, 223-253.

3501    Ricoeur, Paul, et le Centre de Phénoménologie. *La sémantique de l'action.* Paris: Editions du CNRS, 1977, 301 p.

3502    Robert, Jean-D. "Le sort de la philosophie à l'heure des sciences de l'homme." *Revue des Sciences Philosophiques et Théologique,* vol. 41, Oct. 1967, 573-616.

3503    Roberts, Carl. "Husserlian phenomenology and Parsonian functionalism in juxtaposition." *Dialogue* (P.S.T.), vol. 18, April 1976, 60-65.

3504    Rogoni, L. "Alienazione e intenzionalità." *Aut Aut,* no. 79-80, 1964, 7-14.

3505    Rombach, Heinrich. "Ueber Ursprung und Wesen der Frage," *Symposion,* vol. 3, 1952.

3506    Rotenstreich, Nathan. "Reflections and philosophy." *Ratio,* vol. 17, June 1975, 1-17.

3507    Rotenstreich, Nathan. "The forms of sensibility and transcendental phenomenology," in *Life world and consciousness.* Essays in honor of Aron Gurwitsch, Lester E. Embree (ed.). Evanston, Ill.: Northwestern University Press, 1972, 389-406.

3508    Rovatti, P. "Per un discorso fenomenologico sul teatro (In collab. con S. Veca)." *Aut Aut,* no. 81, 1964, 15-54.

3509 Sainati, Vittorio. "La fenomenologia o la conclusione della filosofia metafisica," in *La fenomenologia*. Gallarate, 1955, 172-182.

3510 Sallis, John. "On the ideal of phenomenology," in *Life world and consciousness*. Essays in honor of Aron Gurwitsch, Lester E. Embree (ed.). Evanston, Ill.: Northwestern University Press, 1972, 125-134.

3511 Salvucci, P. *Prospettive sull'uomo nella filosofia francese contemporanea*. Bologna, 1961.

3512 Sancipriano, Mario. "Il mondo, l'io e il temp nella fenomenologia." *Filosofia e Vita*, vol. 1, 1960, 74-80.

3513 Schaerer, René. "Points de repère et points de vue sur le cheminement philosophique." *Studia Philosophica*, vol. 30, 1970-1971, 244-271.

3514 Schaff, W. *Beiträge zur Phänomenologie der Wahrnehmung*. Halle, 1910.

3515 Scheler, Max. "Idealismus-Realismus." *Philosophischer Anzeiger*, vol. 2, 1927.

3516 Scheler, Max. *Philosophische Weltanschauung*. Bonn, 1929, 158 p.

3517 Scheler, Max. *Wesen und Formen der Sympathie*. Frankfurt am Main: Schulte-Bulmke, 1948, 5th ed.

3518 Schérer, René. "Sur la philosophie transcendentale et l'objectivité de al connaissance scientifique." *Revue de Métaphysique et de Morale*, vol. 62, no. 4, 1957, 436-464.

3519 Schilpp, Paul. *Commemorative essays*. Stockton, Cal., 1930.

3520 Schmalenbach, H. "Neues zum Problem der Phänomenologie." *Deutsche Literaturzeitung*, vol. 43, 1922.

3521 Schmitt, Richard. "Transcendental phenomenology: Muddle or mystery?" *Journal of the British Society for Phenomenology*, vol. 2, no. 1, 1971, 19-27.

3522 Schreier, F. *Grundbegriffe und Grundnormen des Rechts*. Leipzig-Wien, 1924.

3523 Schunk, K. *Verstehen und Einsehen*. Eine philosophische Besinnung in Form einer Abhandlung uber Wesen, Arten und Bedingungen der Erkenntnis. Halle, 1926, vi-71.

3524 Schupp, W. *Die neue Wissenschaft vom Recht*. Eine phänomenologische Untersuchung. Berlin: Grunewald, 1930.

3525 Scrimieri, G. *Problemi di logica*. Bari, 1960.

3526 Seebohm, Thomas. *Die Bedingungen der Möglichkeit der Transcendental-Philosophie*. Bonn, 1962.

3527 Seebohm, Thomas. *Zur Kritik der hermeneutischen Vernunft*. Bonn: Bouvier Verlag H. Grundman, 1972, 164 p.

3528 Seidler, Michael J. "Philosophy as a rigorous science: An introduction to Husserlian phenomenology." *Philosophy Today*, vol. 21, Winter 1977, 302-326.

3529 Semarari, G. *La filosofia come relazione*. Sapri, 1961.

3530 Semarari, G. *Scienza nuova e ragione*. Bari, 1961.

3531 Semarari, G. "Aporetica della comunicazione." *Giornale Critico della Filosofia Italiana,* no. 3, 1961, 287-309.

3532 Semerari, G. "La intenzionalità tecnica." *Aut Aut,* no. 72, 1962, 458-478.

3533 Semerari, G. "Civiltà dei mezi e civiltà dei fini." *Aut Aut,* no. 77, 1963, 12-26.

3534 Semerari, G. "Il carattere del filosofare contemporaneo." *Giornale Critico della Filosofia Italiana,* no. 3, 1962, 283-305.

3535 Semerari, G. "Esistenzialismo e marxismo nella fenomenologia della percezione." *Rivista di Filosofia,* no. 2, 1961, 167-191 & no. 3, *Ibid.,* 1961, 331-353.

3536 Semerari, G. "Verità e libertà." *Aut Aut,* no. 57, 1960, 175-180.

3537 Serrus, Charles. "Le conflit du logicisme et du psychologisme." *Etudes Philosophiques,* vol. 2, 1928, 9-18.

3538 Serrus, Charles. "Catégories grammaticales et catégories logiques." *Etudes Philosophiques,* vol. 3, 1929, 20-30.

3539 Serrus, Charles. *Le parallélisme logico-grammatical.* Paris: 1934, 520 p.

3540 Sigwart, Chr. *Logik,* mit Anmerkungen v. Heinrich Maier. Tübingen, 1924, vol. 1, 24ff.

3541 Sini, C. "Sul problema dell'accidentale." *Aut Aut,* no. 69, 1962, 201-216.

3542 Sini, C. "Il melodramma e la sua 'crisi'." *Aut Aut,* no. 81, 1964, 102-105.

3543 Sini, C. "Per una propedeutica alla fenomenologia come scienza rigorosa." *Aut Aut,* no. 84, 1964, 19-51.

3544 Société Thomiste. *La Phénoménologie* (Journées d'études de la Société Thomiste, 1, Juvisy, 1932, 115).
**Book Reviews:**
A. Kojevnikoff, *Recherches philosophiques,* vol. 3, 1935, 429-431.
L. Landgrebe, *Kantstudien,* 1933, 357.

3545 Siegfried, Th. Phänomenologie und Geschichte. Kairos, 1926.

3546 Smith, F. Joseph. "Musical sound as a model for Husserlian intuition and time-consciousness." *Journal of Phenomenological Psychology,* vol. 4, 1973-1974, 271-296.

3547 Soehngen, Gottlieb. *Sein und Gegenstand.* Münster: Aschendorff, 1930.

3548 Sollers, Philippe. *Sur le matérialisme.* De l'atomisme à la dialectique révolutionnaire. Paris: Les Editions du Seuil, 1974, 190 p.

3549 Somogyi, Joseph. "Das Problem der intuitiven Erkenntnis," in *Philosophia perennis.* Regensburg: Habbel, 1931.

3550 Souriau, M. "La matière et le concret." *Recherches Philosophiques,* vol. 2, 1932, 81-111.

3551 Spaier, A. *La pensée concrète.* Paris, 1927.

3552 Spet, G. *Javlenie i Smysl.* Fenomenologija kak osnovnaja nauka i jeja problemy. Moskva, 1914, 219 p.

3553 Spiegelberg, Herbert. "Der Begriff der Intentionalität in der Scholastik, bei Brentano und bei Husserl." *Philosophische Hefte,* vol. 5, 1936.

3554 Spiegelberg, Herbert. "Critical phenomenological realism." *Philosophy and Phenomenological Research,* vol. 1, Dec. 1940.

3555 Spiegelberg, Herbert. "Ueber das Wesen der Idee." *Jahrbuch für Philosophie und Phänomenologische Forschung,* vol. 11, 1930.

3556 Spiegelberg, Herbert. "Phenomenology of direct evidence." *Philosophy and Phenomenological Research,* vol. 2, 1941-1942.

3557 Spiegelberg, Herbert. *Doing phenomenology* (Phaenomenologica, 63). The Hague: Martinus Nijhoff, 1975, xxv-290.

3558 Ssalagoff, Leo. "Vom Begriff des Geltens in der modernen Logik." Dissertation, Heidelberg, 1910.

3559 Steigerwald, Robert. *Herbert Marcuses dritter Weg.* Berlin: Akademie-Verlag, 1969.

3560 Stein, Edith. "Zum Problem der Einfühlung." Dissertation, Freiburg, Halle, 1917.

3561 Stein, Edith. "Husserls Phänomenologie und die Philosophie des heil Thomas von Aquino," in *Husserl-Fetschrift, Jahrbuch für Philosophie und Phänomenologische Forschung,* 1929, 315-318.

3562 Steinmann, H. "Die systematische Stellung der Phänomenologie." *Archiv für die Gesammte Psychologie,* vol. 36, 1917, 391ff.

3563 Strasser, Stephan. "Beschouwingen over 't vraagstuk van de apodicticiteit en de critische verantwoording van de phenomenologie." *Tijdschrift voor Filosofie,* vol. 8, 1946, 226-270.

3564 Strasser, Stephan. "Phenomenological trends in European psychology." *Philosophy and Phenomenological Research,* vol. 18, 1957-1958, 18-34.

3565 Strasser, Stephan. *The soul in metaphysical and empirical psychology.* Pittsburgh, Pa.: Duquesne University Press, 1962.

3566 Szilasi, W. *Macht und Ohrmacht des Geistes.* Freiburg, 1946.

3567 Tannery, Jules. *Science et philosophie.* Paris: Alcan, 1912, 336 p.

3568 Thabet al-Fandi, Muhammad. *Ma' al Faylasuf* [With the Philosopher]. Beyrouth: Dar al-Nahda al-'Arabiyya, 1974, 285 p. [ch. 5, inter alia, Husserl].

3569 Tymieniecka, Anna-Teresa. *Phenomenology and science in contemporary European thought.* With a foreword by I. M. Bochenski. New York: Farrar, Strauss; Toronto: Ambassador, 1962, xxii-198.

3570 Ueberweg, Friedrich. *Friedrich Ueberwegs Grundriss der Geschichte der Philosophie.* 4. T.: Die deutsche Philosophie des 19. Jahrhunderts und der Gegenwart. Hrsg. von Traugott Konstantin Oesterreich. 13. Aufl., univeränd. Nachrd. d. völlig neubearb. 12. Aufl. Tübingen, Wiss, Buchgemeinschaft, 1951, 503-513.

3571 Valdinoci, Serge. "Décomposition et recomposition phénoménologique." *Etudes Philosophiques,* no. 1, 1977, 95-110.

3572 Valori, Paolo. "Storia della fenomenologia husserliana," in *La fenomenologia* (Atti dell'XI Convegno del Centro di Studi Filosofici tra Professori universitari). Gallarate, 1955, 68-84.

3573 Valori, Paolo. "Fenomenologia e filosofia italiana d'oggi." *Huamanitas* (Brescia), 18, 1963, 604-612.

3574 Vancourt, R. *La philosophie et sa structure, I.:* Philosophie et phénoménologie. Paris: Bloud et Gay, 1952.

3575 Vanni-Rovighi, Sofia. "Il movimento fenomenologico." *Rivista di Filosofia Neo-Scholastica,* vol. 38, 1946, 207-211.

3576 Van Peursen, Cornelis. "Wijsgerige fenomenologie." *Wijsgerig Perspectief,* vol. 1, 1960-1961.

3577 Vasoli, C. "A che servono i filosofi in Itali." *Itinerari,* no. 49, 1961, 96-101.

3578 Veatch, Henry. "Formalism and/or intentionality in logic." *Philosophy and Phenomenological Research,* vol. 11, 1950-1951. [Discussion by M. Copi and reply by Veatch]

3579 Veca, S. "Per un discorso fenomenologico sul teatro." (in Collab. con P. Rovati) *Aut Aut,* no. 81, 1964, 15-54. *see:* Rovati 3508

3580 Veca, Salvatore. "Implicazioni filosofiche della nozione di ambiente." *Aut Aut,* no. 105-106, 1968, 172-182.

3581 Vegas González, Serafin. "El sueño de la fenomenología de Husserl." *Estudios Filosóficos,* vol. 26, 1977, 511-528.

3582 Van Breda, Hermann Leo. "Hedendaagsche phaenomenologische strooming. 1. Husserl-Archiv te Leven. 2. International Phenomenological Society, Buffalo." *Tijdschrift voor Filosofie,* vol. 7, 1945, 195-202.

3583 Volkelt, J. "Die phänomenologische Gewissheit." *Zeitschrift für Philosophie und Philosophische Kritik,* vol. 165, 1918, 124-189.

3584 Vollmer, R. *Beiträge zur Kritik der phänomenologische Methode vom Standpunkte der Friesschen Schule aus.* Jena, 1929.

3585 Vorläner, Karl. *Geschichte der Philosophie,* 7. Leipzig, 1927, III, 235ff.

3586 Vuillemin, Jules. "Le problème phénoménologique: intentionalité et réflexion." *Revue Philosophique de la France et de l'Etranger,* vol. 84, 1959, no. 4, 463-470.

3587 Waelhens, Alphonse de. "Phénoménologie et réalisme." *RNP,* 1936, 497-517.

3588 Waelhens, Alphonse de. "Descartes et la pensée phénoménologique." *RNP,* 1938, 571-589.

3589 Waelhens, Alphonse de. "De la phénoménologie à l'existentialisme," in *Le Choix, le monde, l'existence.* Cahiers du Collège Philosophique, Paris: Arthaud, 1947.

3590 Waelhens, Alphonse de. "Phénoménologie et métaphysique." *Revue Philosophique de Louvain,* vol. 47, 1949, 366-376.

3591   Waelhens, Alphonse de. "Fenomenologia e sociologia." *Archivio di Filosofia,* 1951.

3592   Waelhens, Alphonse de. "Beschouwing over de historische ontwikkeling van de evaring van het alter-ego." *Tijdschrift voor Filosofie,* vol. 13, 1951, 667-685.

3593   Waelhens, Alphonse de. "Die Bedeutung der Phänomenologie." *Diogenes,* 1954, 610-631.

3594   Walehens, Alphonse de. "La fenomenologia," in *Atti dell'XI Convegno* del Centro di Studi filosofici, Gallarate, 1955. Brescia, 1956.

3595   Waelhens, Alphonse de. "Signification de la phénoménologie." *Diogène,* 1954, 49-70.

3596   Waelhens, Alphonse de. "Science, phénoménologie, ontologie." *Revue Internationale de Philosophie,* no. 29, 1954, 254-265.

3597   Waelhens, Alphonse de. "Psychologie et phénoménologie," in *Actes* du VIIe Congrès des Sociétés de philosophie de langue française. Paris, 1956, vol. II, 45-100.

3598   Wallton, Roberto J. "Asociación y sintesis pasiva." *Cuadernos de Filosofía,* vol. 13, 1973, 433-446.

3599   Wallton, Roberto J. "Cultura, existencia y logica trascendental: Apofantica formal en la fenomenología." *ITA Humanidades,* vol. 9, 1973, 41-60.

3600   Wassmer, Thomas A. "Phenomenology: Its method and influence." *Science et Esprit,* vol. 21, 1969, 149-161.

3601   Welton, D. "Structure and genesis in Husserl's phenomenology," in *Husserl. Expositions and appraisals,* F. Elliston and P. McCormick (eds.). Notre Dame, Ind.: University of Notre Dame Press, 1977, 54-69.

3602   Weyl, H. *Raum, Zeit, Materie.* Vorlesung über allgemeine Relativitätstheorie. Berlin, 1918, 2-6.

3603   Widmer, Hans. "Anmerkungen zum Zeitdiagnostischen Anspruch der Philosophie." *Studia Philosophica,* vol. 36, 1976, 204-225.

3604   Winthrop, Henry. "The constitution of error in the phenomenological reduction." *Philosophy and Phenomenological Research,* vol. 9, 1948-1949.

3605   Wolf, Gustav. *Leben und Erkennen.* Vorabeiten zu einer biologischen *Philosophie.* München, 1933.

3606   Wust, Peter. *Die Auferstehung der Metaphysik.* Leipzig, 1920.

3607   Zaner, Richard M. "Examples and possibles." *Research in Phenomenology,* vol. 3, 1973, 29-43.

3608   Zaner, Richard M. "The art of free phantasy in rigorous phenomenological science," in *Phenomenology.* Continuation and criticism. Essays in memory of Dorion Cairns (Phaenomenologica, 50). The Hague: Martinus Nijhoff, 1973, 192-219.

3609   Zecchi, Stefano. "Causalità e percezione." *Aut Aut,* no. 105-106, 1968, 66-90.

3610    Zecchi, Stefano. "Dialecttica: possibilità e realtà." *Aut Aut,* no. 111, 1969,
        40-72.
3611    Zecchi, Stefano. "Note di estetica fenomenologica." *Aut Aut,* no. 102, 1967,
        63-87.
3612    Ziehen, Theodor. *Lehrbuch der Logik.* Bonn, 1920, 184ff.

# PART THREE
# APPENDIX

## Addendum

### Books

3613     Aschenberg, Beidi. *Phänomenologische Philosophie und Sprache*. Grundzüge
         der Sprachtheorien von Husserl, Pos und Merleau-Ponty (Tübinger
         Beiträge zur Linguistik, 96). Tübingen: Verlag Gunter Narr, 1978, 104 p.

3613     Braumer, Hilmar. *Die Phänomenologie Edmund Husserls und ihre Bedeutung
         für soziologische Theorien*. Meisenheim a. Glan, Hain, 1978, 158 p.

3614     Brus, Bernard Theodoor. *Zoekend naar een derde weg*. Studies met betrekking
         tot de betekenis van wetenschappelijk onderzoek voor de onderwijspraktijk.
         Deel I. Deel II: Didaktiek naar menselijke maat. Een perspektief? 3e druk.
         Deel III: Leren bij Husserl. Tilburg: Utig. Zwijsen B. V., 1978, 214 p., 148
         p., 264 p.

3615     Christoff, Daniel. *Husserl*. Trad. Isidro Gómez Romero (Col. Filósofos de
         todos los tiempos). Madrid: Edaf, 1978, 320 p.

3616     de Boer, Theodore. *The development of Husserl's thought*. Theodore Plantinga
         (trans.). (Phaenomenologica, 76). The Hague, Boston, London: Martinus
         Nijhoff, 1978, xxii-545.

3617     Dentoni, Francesco. *La formazione e la problematic filosofica del primo
         Husserl* (Il primo progetto husserliano di filosofia della matematica). Roma:
         L. Lucarini, 1977, 211 p.

3618     Derrida, Jacques. *Edmund Husserl's Origin of geometry*. An introduction.
         With a preface by John P. Leavy, Jr. (trans.). David B. Allison (ed.).
         Appendix: *The origin of geometry*, by E. Husserl. New York: Nicolas Hays:
         Hassocks (Sussex): The Harvester Press, 1978, 207 p.
    **Book Reviews:**
         J. Barnouw, *Review of Metaphysics*, vol. 33, no. 1, Sept. 1979, 168-173.

3619     Dreyfus, Hubert L. *Husserl's phenomenology of perception* (Northwestern
         University studies in phenomenology and existential philosophy). Evanston,
         Ill.: Northwestern University Press, 1979.

3620     Gui Hyun Shin. *Die Struktur des inneren Zeitbuwusstseins:* e. Studie über d.
         Begriff d. Protention in d. veröff. Schriften Edmund Husserls (Europäische
         Hochschulschriften: Reihe 20, Philosophie, 26). Bern, Frankfurt a. M.:
         Lang, 1978, 190 p.

3621     Haglund, Dick A. R. *Perception, time and the unity of mind*. Problems in
         Edmund Husserl's philosophy. Part I (Philosophical communications. Red
         series, 4). Gothenburg: University of Gothenburg, Department of
         Philosophy, 1977, vii-205-xp.

3622 Kalsi, Marie-Luise Schubert. *Alexius Meinong on objects of higher order and Husserl's phenomenology.* The Hague: Martinus Nijhoff, 1979, 252 p.

3623 Kohák, Erazim Vaclav. *Idea and experience.* Edmund Husserl's project of phenomenology in *Ideas I.* Chicago, Ill.: University of Chicago Press, 1978, 249 p.

3624 Kolakowski, Leszek. *Die Suche nach der verlorenen Gewissheit.* Denk-Wege mit Edmund Husserl. Übers. aus. d. Engl. von Jürgen Söring. Stuttgart: Kohlhammer, 1977, 99 p.

3625 Levinas, Emmanuel. *Théorie de l'intuition dans la phénoménologie de Husserl* (Bibliothèque d'histoire de la philosophie). Paris: J. Vrin, 1978, 224 p.

3626 Ponsetto, Antonio. *Die Tradition in der Phänomenologie Husserls.* Ihre Bedeutung f5Dur d. Entwicklung d. Philosophiegeschichte (Monographien zur philosophischen Forschung, 157). Meisenheim a. Glan: Hain, 1978, 188 p.

3627 Zecchi, Stefano. *La fenomenologia dopo Husserl nella cultura contemporanea.* Vol. I: Sviluppi critici della fenomenologia. Vol. II: Fenomenologia e sapere scientifico (Strumenti, 92-93. Filosofia). Firenze: La Nuova Italia Editrice, 1978, 98 p., 164 p.

## Dissertations

3628 Adriaanse, H. J. "Zu en Sachen selbst." Rijksuniversiteit te Leiden, 1974, 263 p. *Dissertation Abstracts Int., European,* vol. 38, no. 4, Summer 1978, 543.

3629 Bersley, William John. "The origins of consciousness: Husserl and Sartre on the 'cogito'." University of Colorado at Boulder, 1978, 309 p. *Dissertation Abstracts,* vol. 39, no. 8, Feb. 1979, 4975-A.

3630 Bodnar, Joanne. "Bolzano and Husserl. Logic and phenomenology." State University of New York at Buffalo, 1976, 169 p. *Dissertation Abstracts,* vol. 37, no. 8, Feb. 1977, 5178-A. Ann Arbor, Mich., London: University Microfilms International, 1979, iii-168.

3631 Haddock, G. E. R. "Edmund Husserls Philosophie der Logik und Mathematik im Lichte der gegenwartigen Logik und Grundlagenforschung." Bonn University, 1973, 160 p. *Dissertation Abstracts Int., European,* vol. 37, no. 1, Aut. 1976.

3632 Harlan, Robert M. "The I and the other: A reformulation of Husserl's Fifth Cartesian Meditation." New School for Social Research, 1978, 260 p. *Dissertation Abstracts,* vol. 39, no. 6, Dec. 1978, 3632-A.

3233 Kelly, Francis J. "The structural and developmental aspects of the formulation of categorial judgments in the philosophy of Edmund Husserl." Georgetown University, 1978, 399 p. *Dissertation Abstracts,* vol. 39, no. 11, May 1979, 6810-A.

3634    Kim, Y.-H. "Husserl und Natorp. Zur Problematik der Letzegründung der Philosophie bei Husserls Phänomenologie und Natorps neukantianischer Theorie." Heidelberg University, 1974, 292 p. *Dissertation Abstracts, European,* vol. 39, no. 2, Winter 1978-79, 194.

3635    Köppel, M. "Zur Analyse von Husserls Welt-Begriff." Zürich, 1977, 245 p. *Dissertation Abstract, European,* vol. 39, no. 2, Winter 1978-79, 194

3636    Langsdorf, Lenore. "Husserl on judging. A critique of the theory of ideal objects." State University of New York at Stony Brook, 1977, 304 p. *Dissertation Abstracts Int.,* vol. 38, no. 6, Dec. 1977, 3560-A. Ann Arbor, Mich., London: University Microfilms International, 1979, x-294.

3636    Leland, Dorothy J. "Phenomenology and the crisis of language," in *Consciousness, language and world: Four essays of contemporary thought.* Purdue University, 1978, 141 p. *Dissertation Abstracts Int.,* vol. 40, no. 1, July 1979, 308-A.

3637    Nissim-Sabat, Marilyn. "Edmund Husserl's theory of motivation." De Paul University, 1977, 266 p. *Dissertation Abstract Int.,* vol. 37, no. 9, March 1977, 5887-A. Ann Arbor, Mich., London: University Microfilms International, 1979, vi-255.

3638    Ponsetto, Antonio. "Die Tradition in der Pháomenologie Husserls." Köln, 1974, 254 p. *Dissertation Abstracts Int., European,* vol. 38, no. 4, Summer 1978, 542.

3639    Rawlinson, Mary Crenshaw. "Identity and differing: Husserl's doctrine of self-constitution." Northwestern University, 1978, 201 p. *Dissertation Abstracts Int,* vol. 39, no. 10, April 1979, 6176-A.

3640    Smith, Quentin Persifor. "The phenomenology of feeling. A critical development of the theories of feeling in Husserl, Scheler and Sartre." Boston College, 1977, 479 p. *Dissertation Abstracts Int.,* vol. 38, no. 3, Sept. 1977, 1457-A. Ann Arbor, Mich., London: University Microfilms International, 1979, xx-467.

3641    Stapleton, Timothy J. "Husserl and Heidegger: The question of a phenomenological beginning." The Pennsylvania State University, 1978, 235 p. *Dissertation Abstracts Int.,* vol. 39, no. 10, April 1979, 6176-A.

3642    Stephens, James Whyte. "Phenomenology an realism. An essay on Husserl's *Logical Investigations."* Princeton University, 1978. *Dissertation Abstracts Int.,* vol. 39, no. 4, Oct. 1978, 2345-A. Ann Arbor, Mich., London: University Microfilms International, 1979, vi-243.

3643    Wolters, P. "Lebenswelt und Wissenschaft. Sozialtheoretische Ansätze unter Aspekten der Phänomenologie." Münster, 1976, 112 p. *Dissertation Abstracts Int.,* vol. 39, no. 2, Winter 1978-79, 196.

3644    Yee, Stevan S. T. "Edmund Husserl's idea of phenomenological psychology an the problem of its relation to transcendental phenomenological philosophy." The Pennsylvania State University, 1976, 286 p. *Dissertation*

*Abstracts Int.,* vol. 37, no. 11, May 1977, 7169-A. Ann Arbor, Mich., London: University Microfilms International, 1979, vii-278.

3645 Yuasa, Shin-Ichi. "Der Leib: Studien zu einer Phänomenologie des Leibes." Köln, 1976, 156 p. *Dissertation Abstracts Int., European,* vol. 37, no. 1, Aut. 1976, 27.

## Essays and Articles

3646 Adorno, Theodor W. "Metacritique of epistemology." *Telos,* no. 38, Winter 1978-79, 77-103.

3647 Aguirre, Antonio. "Consideraciones sobre el mundo de la vida." *Revista Venezolana de Filosofía,* 1979, 7-32.

3648 Ales Bello, Angela. "L'uomo e Dio nella fenomenologia di Husserl," in *Ristrutturazione Antropologia Insegnamento Filosofia.* Atti e II Convegno dei docenti etaliani di filosofia nelle Facoltà e Seminari e Studentati d'Italia. *Sapienza,* vol. 22, no. 3-4, 1969, 556-559.

3649 Ales Bello, Angela. "Il recupero dell'intersoggettività per un mondo umano in E. Husserl." *Fenomenologia e Società* (Milano), vol. 1, no. 3-4, 1977-1978, 290-301.

3650 Allen, Jeffner. "Husserl's philosophical anthropology." *Philosophy Today,* vol. 31, 1977, 347-355.

3651 Allison, David B. "Derrida and Wittgenstein: Playing the game." *Research in Phenomenology,* vol. 8, 1978, 93-109.

3652 Angus, Ian H. "Rationality in the life-world. The interface of scientific knowledge and social action." Paper presented at the 9th World Congress International Sociological Association. Abstract in *Sociological Abstracts,* 1979, 116.

3653 Baekers, S. F. "Dupliek op de kanttekeningen van H. Philipse bij 'Fenomenologie en moderne wetenschapsfilosofie'." *Alg. Ned. Tijds. Wijs.,* vol. 71, Jan. 1971, 52-57. [*See:* H. Philipse 3754]

3654 Bakan, Mildred. "Of language, work and things." *Human Studies,* vol. 1, July 1978, 221-243.

3655 Bartels, Martin. "Identität und Individualitá. Überlegungen zur Problematik der Egologie Edmund Husserls." *Archiv für Geschichte der Philosophie,* vol. 61, no. 1, 1979, 52-67.

3656 Bergoffen, Debra B. "Sartre's transcendence of the ego: A methodological reading." *Philosophy Today,* vol. 22, Fall 1978, 224-251.

3657 Bernet, Rudolf. "Endlichkeit und Unendlichkeit in Husserls Phaenomenologie der Wahrnehmung." *Tijdschrift voor Filosofie,* vol. 40, 1978, 251-269. [*See:* R. Boehm 3661]

3658 Bernet, Rudolf. "Zur Teologie der Erkenntnis. Eine Antwort an Rudolf Boehm." *Tijdschrift voor Filosofie,* vol. 40, 1978, 662-668. [*See:* R. Boehm 3661]

3659   Blanco, Julio E. "Mr. Romanell's review of my 'Tres lecciones sobre Husserl'."
       *Philosophy and Phenomenological Research,* 1945, 437-440. [*See:* P.
       Romanell 3764]

3660   Blandino, Giovanni. "L'esistenza di altri soggetti cocoscenti umani." *Aquinas,*
       vol. 21, May-Dec. 1978, 167-182.

3661   Boehm, Rudolf. "Das 'Ding-an'sich' als Erkenntnisziel. Fragen zu Rudolf
       Bernets Aufsatz 'Endlichkeit und Unendlichkeit in Husserls
       Phänomenologie der Wahrnehmung" [*See:* 3657]." *Tijdschrift voor
       Filosofie,* vol. 40, 1978, 659-661. [*See:* 3657 and 3658]

3662   Bosio, Franco. "La teleologia della teoresi e della prassi nel pensiero
       fenomenologico husserliano." *Raccoltà di Studi e Ricerche,* vol. 2, 1978,
       9-17.

3663   Brand, Gerd. "Edmund Husserl: *Zur Phänomenologie der Intersubjektivität.*
       " *Philosophische Rundschau,* vol. 25, 1978, 54-80.

3664   Brand, Gerd. [Kritische Studie zu:] E. Husserl, *Zur Phänomenologie der
       Intersubjektivität,*" in *Husserl, Scheler, Heidegger in der Sicht neuer Quellen.*
       Beiträge von E. W Orth u.a. (Phänomenologische Forschungen, 6/7).
       Freiburg i. Br.: Verlag Karl Alber, 1978, 28-117.

3666   Buck, Wayne F. "Husserl's conception of philosophy." *Kinesis. Graduate
       Journal in Philosophy,* vol. 8, no. 1, 1977, 10-25.

3667   Caputo, John D. "The question of being and transcendental phenomenology:
       Reflections on Heidegger's relationship to Husserl." *Research in
       Phenomenology,* vol. 7, 1977, 84-105.

3668   Caputo, John D. "Transcendence and the transcendental in Husserl's
       phenomenology." *Philosophy Today,* vol. 23, no. 3, Fall 1979, 205-216.

3669   Carr, David. "Interpretation und Evidenz." *Freiburger Zeitschrift für
       Philosophie und Theologie,* vol. 23, 1976, 253-268.

3670   Carr, David. "Zum Problem des nichtempirischen Ich." *Zeitschrift für
       Philosophische Forschung,* vol. 32, April-June 1978, 163-182.

3671   Carr, David. "Kant, Husserl, and the nonempirical ego." *Journal of
       Philosophy,* vol. 74, Nov. 1977, 682-690.

3672   Carrington, Peter J. "Schütz on transcendental intersubjectivity in Husserl."
       *Human Studies,* vol. 2, April 1979, 95-110.

3673   Casey, Edward S. "Perceiving and remembering." *Review of Metaphysics,* vol.
       32, March 1979, 407-432.

3674   Célis, Raphael. "La mondanité du jeu et de l'image selon Euge Fink." *Revue
       Philosophique de Louvain,* vol. 76, Feb. 1978, 54-66.

3675   Christopher, Dennis. "Husserl and Mill: A rejoinder." *Mill Newsletter,* vol.
       14, Summer 1979, 12-17. [*See:* D. A. Nordquest 3748]

3676   Courtney, Charles. "Phenomenology and Ninian Smart's philosophy of
       religion." *International Journal of Philosophy of Religion,* vol. 9, 1978,
       41-52.

3677 David, G. E. "Edmund Husserl and 'the as yet, in its most important respect, unrecognised greatness of Hume'," in *David Hume. Bicentennary papers.* G. P. Morise (ed.). Edinburgh: Edinburgh University Press, 1977, 69-76. Austin, Texas: University of Texas at Austin Press, 1977, 69-76.

3678 de Boer, Theo. "Heideggers kritiek op Husserl, I-II." *Tijdschrift voor Filosofie,* vol. 40, 1978, 202-249, 452-501. [Résumé: La critique heideggerienne de Husserl, 250, 501]

3679 de Muralt, André. "La notion d'acte fondé dans les rapports de la raison et de la volonté selon les *Logische Untersuchungen* de Husserl." *Revue de Métaphysique et de Morale,* vol. 82, Oct-Dec. 1977, 511-527.

3680 de Muralt, André. "The 'founded act' and the apperception of others. The actual Scholastic sources of Husserlian intentionality. An essay in structural analysis of doctrines." Garry L. Breckon (trans.). *Analecta Husserliana,* vol. 6, 1977, 123-141.

3681 Dentoni, Francesco. "An approach to the philosophical problems of the early Husserl." *Phenomenology Information Bulletin* (Belmont, Mass.), vol. 2, 1978, 58-64.

3681 Derrida, Jacques. "'Genesis and structure' and 'phenomenology' and 'Violence and metaphysics: An essays on the thought of Emmanuel Levinas'," in his *Writing and difference.* With an introduction and additional notes by Alan Bass (trans.). Chicago: University of Chicago Press, 1978, 154-168, 79-153.

3682 Deutscher, Max. "Husserl's transcendental subjectivity." *Canadian Journal of Philosophy,* 1979, [in press]

3683 Di Pinto, Luigia. "Sull'estetica dell'Einfälung in Edmund Husserl: l'opera d'arte come espressione di equilibrio." *Raccoltà di Studi e Ricerche,* vol. 2, 1978, 27-83.

3684 Dougherty, Charles J. 'Significance of Husserl's *Logical Investigations.*" *Philosophy Today,* vol. 23, no. 3, Fall 1979, 217-226.

3685 Drummond, John J. "The phenomenology of perceptual sense." *Southwestern Journal of Philosophy,* vol. 10, Spring 1979, 139-146.

3686 Dubois, M. J. "Etude critique: Réflexions sur *La Structure métaphysique.*" *Revue de Métaphysique et de Morale,* vol. 83, Jan.-March 1978, 102-129.

3687 Dufrenne, Mikel. "Intentionality and aesthetics." *Man and World,* vol. 11, 1978, 401-410.

3688 Ellis, Ralph. "Directionality and fragmentation in the transcendental ego." *Auslegung,* vol. 6, June 1979, 147-160.

3689 Ellis, Ralph. "Directionality and fragmentation in the transcendental ego." *Philosophy Research Archives,* vol. 5, no. 1326, 1979.

3690 Elliston, Frederick. "Phenomenology reinterpreted. From Husserl to Heidegger." *Philosophy Today,* vol. 21, 1977, 273-283.

3691 Embree, Lester. "A note on 'is' and 'ought' in phenomenological perspective." *Philosophy and Phenomenological Research,* vol. 39, June 1979, 595-597.

3692    Farley, Edward. *Ecclesial man*. A social phenomenology of faith and reality. Philadelphia: Fortress Press, 1975.

3693    Fetke, C. B. "Craft and art: A phenomenological distinction." *British Journal of Aesthetics*, vol. 17, no. 2, Spring 1977, 129-137.

3694    Föllesdal, Dagfinn. "Bretano and Husserl on intentional objects of perception," in Die Philosophie Franz Brentanos. Beiträge zur Brentano-Konferenz, Graz, 4.-8 September 1977. Herausgegeben von R. M. Chisholm und R. Haller (*Grazer Philosophische Studien*, vol. 5, 1978. Amsterdam: Rodopi, 1978, 83-94.

3695    Föllesdal, Dagfinn. "Husserl and Heidegger on the role of actions in the constitution of the world," in *Essays in honour of J. Hintikka*, E. Saarinen (ed.), et. al (Synthese Library, 124). Dordrecht, Boston: D. Reidel, 1979, 365-378.

3696    Fogel, Gilvan. "E Husserl e a idéia de regioes ontológicas." *Revista da Universidade Católica de Petrópolis*, no. 3, 1976, 75-84. [Résumé, 85; Summary, 86]

3697    Frings, Manfred S. "Husserl and Scheler: Two views on intersubjectivity." *Journal of the British Society for Phenomenology*, vol. 9, 1978, 143-149.

3698    Funke, Gerhardt. "Die Diskussion um die metaphysiche Kantinterpretation." *Kantstudien*, vol. 67, 1976, 409-424.

3699    Gierulanka, Danuta. "The philosophical work of Roman Ingarden." *Dialectics and Humanism*, vol. 4, Fall 1977, 117-128.

3700    Gilles, Richard. "Phenomenology: A non-alternative to empiricism," in Harry R. Garvin (ed.), Phenomenology, structuralism, semiology. *Bucknell Review*, Lewisburg, Pa.: Bucknell University Press, April 1976, 71-98.

3701    González,Serafín Vegas. "Sobre el sentido y la originariedad del lenguaje." *Pensamiento*, vol. 33, July-Sept. 1977, 297-315.

3702    Gulian, C. I. "'Le monde de la vie' (chez Husserl) en tant que retour à la praxis (in Romanian)." *Rev. Filozofie*, vol. 25, Sept.-Oct. 1978, 609-616.

3703    Gutting, Gary. "Husserl and scientific realism." *Philosophy and Phenomenological Research*, vol. 39, 1978-1979, 42-56.

3704    Hall, Harrison. "Intersubjective phenomenology and Husserl's Cartesianism." *Man and World*, vol. 12, 1979, 13-20.

3705    Hassell, Lewis. "Husserl's theory of meaning and ordinary language." *Graduate Faculty Philosophy Journal*, vol. 3, 1973-1974, 32-41.

3706    Hedwwig, Klaus. "La discussion sur l'origine de l'intentionalité husserlienne." *Etudes Philosophiques*, no. 3, 1978, 259-272

3707    Hedwig, Klaus. "Intention: Outlines for the history of a phenomenological concept." *Philosophy and Phenomenological Research*, vol. 39, March 1979, 326-340.

3708    Hempolinski, M. "Epistemologie und Metaphysik bei Husserl und Ingarden." *Deutsche Zeitschrift für Philosophie*, vol. 24, 1976, 1546-1555.

3709   Hohler, Thomas P. "Seeing and saying: phenomenology's contention [Merleau-Ponty, Ricoeur, Husserl]." *Philosophy Today,* vol. 21, 1977, 327-346.

3710   Hougaard, E. "Some reflexions on the relationship between Freudian psychoanalysis and Husserlian phenomenology." *Psychological Reports Aarhus,* vol. i, no. 1, 111 p. Risskov: Institute of Psychology, University of Aarhus.

3711   Hoy, David Couzens. *The Critical circle.* Literature, history, and philosophical hermeneutics. Berkeley: University of California Press, 1978, vii-182 p.

3712   Hoyos Vásques, Guillermo. "Fenomenología como epistemológia: ruptura del sistema fenomenológico desde la materialidad histórica." *Revista Latinoamericana de Filosofía,* vol. 4, March 1978, 3-20.

3713   Hippolyte, Jean. "The Fichtean idea of the science of knowledge and the Husserlian project." *Auslegung,* vol. 1-2, 1973-1975, 77-84.

3714   Jaspers, Karl. "On Heidegger." *Graduate Faculty Philosophy Journal,* vol. 7, Sept. 1978, 107-128.

3715   Jordan, Robert Welsh. "Vico and Husserl: History and historical science," in *Giambattista Vico's science of history,* Giorgio Tagliacozzo and Roland F. Verene (eds.). Baltimore: Johns Hopkins University Press, 1976.

3716   Jung, Hwa Yol. "A hermeneutical accent on the conduct of political inquiry." *Human Studies,* vol. 1, Jan. 1978, 48-52.

3717   Jung, Hwa Yol. "Two critics of scientism: Leo Strauss and Edmund Husserl." *Independent Journal of Philosophy,* vol. 2, 1978, 81-88.

3718   Jung, Hwa Yol. "The life-world, historicity, and truth. Reflections on Leo Strauss's encounter with Heidegger and Husserl." *Journal of the British Society for Phenomenology,* vol. 9, 1978, 11-25.

3719   Kaufmann, J. N. "Husserl et le projet d'une sémiotique phénoménologique." *Dialogue,* vol. 17, 1978, 20-34.

3720   Kegley, Jacquelyn Ann. "Royce and Husserl: Some parallels and food for thought." *Transactions of Peirce Society,* vol. 14, Summer 1978, 184-199.

3721   Kesler, Gary E. "Pragmatic bodies versus transcendental egos." *Transactions Peirce Society,* vol. 14, Spring 1978, 101-119.

3722   Kojima, H. "Zur philosophischen Erschliesung der religiösen Dimension. Überlegungen im Anschluss an Descartes, Husserl und den Zen-Buddhismus." *Philosophisches Jahrbuch,* vol. 85, 1978, 56-70.

3723   Kühndel, Jan. "Edmund Husserls Heimat und Herkunft." *Archiv für Geschichte der Philosophie,* vol. 51, 1969, 286-290.

3724   Küng, Guido. "Pouvons-nous connaître les choses telles qu'elles sont?" *Freiburger Zeitschrift für Philosophie und Theologie,* vol. 24, 1977, 397-413.

3725   Kultgen, John. "Egological certainty." *Southwestern Journal of Philosophy,* vol. 10, Spring 1979, 117-124.

3726 Landgrebe, Ludwig. "Lebenswelt und Geschichtlichkeit des menschlichen Daseins [E. Husserl]," in *Phänomenologie und Marxismus,* II: Praktische Philosophie. Hrsg. von B. Waldenfels et. al. Frankfurt am Main: Suhrkamp, 1977, 13-58.

3727 Landgrebe, Ludwig. "The problem of passive constitution [Husserl]. Donn Wellan (trans.)." *Analecta Husserliana,* vol. 7, 1978, 23-36.

3628 Lapointe, François H. "The Anglo-American response to Edmund Husserl: A bibliographic essay." *Man and World,* vol. 12, no. 2, 1979, 205-245.

3729 Leland, Dorothy. "Edmund Husserl, phenomenology an the crisis of language." *Philosophy Today,* vol. 23, no. 3, Fall 1979, 226-237.

3730 Lenkowski, William Jon. "What is Husserl's *epoché:* The problem of the beginning of philosophy in a Husserlian context." *Man and World,* vol. 11, no. 3-4, 1978, 299-323.

3731 Leo, John Robert. "Criticism of consciousness in Shelley's *A Defense of poetry.* " *Philosophy and Literature,* vol. 2, Spring 1978, 46-59.

3732 Lippitz, Wilfried. "Der phänomenologische Begriff der 'Lebenswelt': Seine Relevanz für die Sozialwissenschaften." *Zeitschrift für Philosophische Forschung,* vol. 32, July-Sept. 1978, 416-432.

3733 Liversiani, Filippo. "Maréchal ed Husserl," in *Tommaso nel suo settimo centenario,* VI. Napoli: Edizioni Domenicane Italiane, 1977, 524-530.

3734 Madden, Robert E. "Phenomenology in its beginnings." *Research in Phenomenology,* vol. 8, 1978, 203-215.

3735 Mahnke, Dietrich. "From Hilbert to Husserl. First introduction to phenomenology, especially that of formal mathematics. David I. Boyer (trans.)." *Studies in History and Philosophy of Science,* vol. 8, 1977, 71-84.

3736 Marx, Wolfgang. "On the necessity of transformation of the philosophical concept of system." *Ratio,* vol. 20, Dec. 1978, 92-102.

3737 Meiland, Jack W. "Concepts of relative truth." *The Monist,* vol. 60, Oct. 1977, 568-582.

3738 Menges, Karl. "Robert Musil und Edmund Husserl. Über phänomenologische Strukturen im *'Mann ohne Eigenschaften'.*" *Modern Austrian Literature* (Riverside, Cal.), vol. 9, no. 3-4, 1976, 131-154.

3739 Miguelez, Roberto. "Ciencia y valores." *Revista Latinoamericana de Filosofía,* vol. 4, Nov. 1978, 195-211.

3740 Mohanty, J. N. "On the roots of reference: Quine, Piaget, and Husserl." *Southwestern Journal of Philosophy,* vol. 9, Summer 1978, 21-43.

3741 Mohanty, J. N. "Consciousness and existence: Remarks on the relation between Husserl and Heidegger." *Man and World,* vol. 11, 1978, 324-335.

3742 Mohanty, J. N. "Husserl's transcendental phenomenology and essentialism." *Review of Metaphysics,* vol. 32, 1978-1979, 299-321.

3743    Moreira, Mario Humberto. "O problema da intersubjetividade e o ego transcendental em Husserl." *Revista da Universidade Católica de Petrópolis*, no. 3, 1976, 63-73. [Résumé, 74]

3744    Morrison, James C. "Husserl and Heidegger. The parting of the ways," in *Heidegger's existential analytic,* Frederick C. Elliston (ed.). The Hague, Paris, New York: Mouton Publishers, 1978, 47-59.

3745    Morrison, Ronald P. "Kant, Husserl, and Heidegger on time and the unity of consciousness." *Philosophy and Phenomenological Research*, vol. 39, Dec. 1978, 182-198.

3746    Müller, Severin. "Aspekte neuerer Husserl-Forschung." *Philosophisches Jahrbuch,* vol. 84, 1977, 394-419.

3747    Müller, Severin. "Review of E. Marbach, *Das Problem des Ich in der Phänomenologie Husserls.*" [ *See:* 167] *Philosophisches Jahrbuch,* vol. 85, 1978, 426-431.

3748    Nordquest, David A. "Husserl and Mill's 'Psychologism'." *Mill Newsletter,* vol. 14, Winter 1979, 2-9. [*See:* D. Christopher 3675]

3749    O'Connor, Robert. "Ortega's reformulation of Husserlian phenomenology." *Philosophy and Phenomenological Research,* vol. 40, Sept. 1979, 53-64.

3750    Odagawa, Masako. "Reflexion und Welt. Bericht über die Husserl-Interpretation bei einem japanischen Philosophen." *Perspektiven der Philosophie,* vol. 3, 1977, 331-341.

3751    Orth, Ernst Wolfgang. "Husserl, Scheler, Heidegger. Eine Einführung in das Problem der philosophischen Komparatistik," in *Husserl, Scheler, Heidegger in er Sicht neuer Quelen.* Freiburg i. Br.: Verlag Karl Alber, 1978, 7-27.

3752    Palermo, James. "Apodictic truth: Husserl's eidetic reduction versus induction." *Notre Dame Journal of Formal Logic,* vol. 19, Jan. 1978, 69-80.

3753    Pazanin, Ante. "Überwindung des Gegensatzes von Idealismus und Materialismus bei Husserl und Marx," in *Phänomenologie und Marxismus.* I: Konzepte und Methoden. Hrsg. von Berhard Waldenfels, Jan M. Brockman und Ante Pazanin. (Suhrkamp-Taschenbücher Wissenschaft, 195). Frankfurt am Main: Suhrkamp, 1977, 105-127.

3754    Philipse, H. "E. Husserls bounding ten opzichte van de exakte natuurwetenschap." *Alg. Ned. Tijdsch. Wisjg.,* vol. 71, Jan. 1979, 45-51. [ *See:* S. F. Baekers 3653]

3755    Prado, C. G. "Reflexive consciousness." *Dialogue,* vol. 17, 1978, 134-137.

3756    Presas, Mario A. "En torno a las *Meditaciones cartesianas* de Husserl." *Revista Latinoamericana de Filosofía,* vol. 4, 1978, 269-280. [Abstract 280]

3757    Prasas, Mario A. "Leiblichkeit und Geschichte bei Husserl." *Tijdschrift voor Filosofie,* vol. 40, 1978, 111-127.

3758    Presas, Mario A. "Bodilyness (*Leibhaftigkeit*) and history in Husserl. Kenneth L. Heiges (trans.)." *Analecta Husserliana,* vol. 7, 1978, 37-42.

3759 Presas, Mario A. "Corporalidad e historia en Husserl." *Revista Latinoamericana de Filosofía*, vol. 2, 1976, 167-177.

3760 Prauss, Gerold. "Zum Verhältnis innerer und äusserer Erfahrung bei Husserl." *Zeitschrift für Philosophische Forschung*, vol. 31, Jan.-March 1977, 79-84.

3761 Reeder, Harry P. "Language and the phenomenological reduction: A reply to a Wittgensteinian objection." *Man and World*, vol. 12, 1979, 35-46.

3762 Rockmore, Tom. "Fichte, Husserl, and philosophical science." *International Philosophical Quarterly*, vol. 19, March 1979, 15-27.

3763 Roig Gironella, Juan. "El objeto subyacente al lenguaje: A propósito de la relatividad ontológica de W. V. Quine." *Espiritu*, vol. 25, July-Dec. 1976, 163-170.

3764 Romanell, P. "Husserl and Plotinus: A rejoinder to Mr. Blanco." *Philosophy and Phenomenological Research*, vol. 5, March 1945, 441-442. [*See:* 3659]

3765 Rotenstreich, Nathan. "Evidence and the aim of cognitive activity [Husserl]." *Analecta Husserliana*, vol. 7, 1978, 245-258.

3766 Sanchez Puentes, Ricardo. "La intencionalidad fenomenológica." *Revista de Filosofía* (México), vol. 11, May-Aug. 1978, 227-242.

3767 Schneider, Robert O. "Husserl and Heidegger: An essay on the question of intentionality." *Philosophy Today*, vol. 21, 1977, 368-375.

3768 Schöpf, Alfred. "Die Motivation zum sittlichen Handelin: Zur Unterscheidung kognitiver und motivationaler Begründungen der praktischen Philosophie und Ethik." *Zeitschrift für Philosophische Forschung*, vol. 32, Oct.-Dec. 1978, 494-509.

3769 Schuhmann, Karl. "Zu Heideggers Spiegel-Gespräch über Husserl." *Zeitschrift für Philosophische Forschung*, vol. 32, 1978, 591-612.

3770 Scrimieri, Giorgio. "Il problema dell'*immaginario* negli *Studia mathematica* di Edmund Husserl." *Raccoltà di Studi e Ricerche*, vol. 1, 1977, 41-72.

3771 Scrimieri, Giorgio. "Edmund Husserl tra '*Dingvorlesung*' e '*Ding und Raum* '. Inediti sulla cinestesi." *Raccoltà di Studi e Ricerche*, vol. 2, 1978, 119-137.

3772 Seidler, Michael J. "Philosophy as a rigorous science: an introduction to Husserlian phenomenology." *Philosophy Today*, vol. 21, 1977, 306-326.

3773 Seigfried, Hans. "Phenomenology, hermeneutics and poetry." *Journal of the British Society for Phenomenology*, vol. 10, May 1979, 94-100.

3774 Semerari, Giuseppe. "Husserl su Spinoza." *Giornale Critico della Filosofia Italiana*, vol. 56, no. 3-4, Oct.-Dec. 1977, 550-572.

3775 Sheehand, Thomas J. "Heidegger's early years: Fragments for a philosophical biography." *Listening*, vol. 12, Fall 1978, 3-20

3776 Sheehan, Thomas J. "Heidegger's 'Introduction to the phenomenology of religion', 1920-21." *The Personalist*, vol. 60, July 1979, 312-324.

3777 Sini, Carlo. "Il problema del segno in Husserl e in Peirce." *Filosofia*, vol. 29, Oct. 1978, 543-558.

3778    Smith, Quentin. "A phenomenological examination of Husserl's theory of hyletic data." *Philosophy Today,* vol. 21, 1977, 356-367.

3779    Smith, Quentin. "Husserl's theory of the phenomenological reduction in the *Logical investigations.*" *Philosophy and phenomenological Research,* vol. 39, no. 3, March 1979, 433-437.

3780    Sokolowski, Robert. "Making distinctions." *Review of Metaphysics,* vol. 32, June 1979, 639-676.

3781    Spiegelberg, Herbert. "On the significance of the correspondence between F. Brentano and E. Husserl," in Die Philosophie Franz Brentanos. Beiträge zur Brentano-Konferenz, Grz, 4.-8 September 1977. Herausgegeben von R. M. Chisholm und R. Haller ( *Grazer Philosophischen Studien,* 1978, Bd. 5). Amsterdam: Rodopi, 1978, 95-116.

3782    Stack, George J. "Husserl y la paradoja del yo." *Folia Humanistica,* vol. 16, 1978, 533-541.

3783    Strasser, Stephan. "Der Gott des Monadenalls. Gedanken zum Gottesproblem in der Spätphilosophie Husserls." *Perspektiven der Philosophie,* vol. 4, 1978, 361-378.

3784    Ströker, Elisabeth. "Husserls Evidenzprinzip. Sinn und Grenzen einer methodischen Norm der Phänomenologie als Wissenschaft. Für Ludwig Landgrebe zum 75. Geburstag." *Zeitschrift für Philosophische Forschung,* vol. 32, 1978, 3-20.

3785    Struyker, Boudier, C. E. M. "Genese, Struktuur en zin van het verstaan." *Tijdschrift voor Filosofie,* vol. 40, March 1978, 78-110. [Zusammenfassung: Entstehen, Struktur und Sinn des Verstehens, 109]

3786    Taminiaux, Jacques. "Heidegger and Husserl's *Logical investigations.*" *Research in Phenomenology,* vol. 7, 1977, 58-83.

3787    Taylor, Earl. "*Lebenswelt* and *Lebensformen:* Husserl and Wittgenstein on the goal and method of philosophy." *Human Studies,* vol. 1, April 1978, 184-200.

3788    Theodoracopoulos, I. N. "Contemporary philosophy (in Greek)." *Philosophia* (Athens), vol. 7, 1977, 5-12.

3789    Tiryakian, Edward A. "Durkheim and Husserl. A comparison of the spirit of positivism and the spirit of phenomenology," in *Phenomenology and the social sciences: a dialogue.* Joseph Bien (ed.). The Hague: Martinus Nijhoff, 1978, 20-43.

3790    Vadja, Mihaly. "Lukacs' and Husserl's critique of science." *Telos,* no. 38, Winter 1978-79, 104-118.

3791    Vaillancourt, Dan. "The world of Stanislas Breton." *International Philosophical Quarterly,* vol. 19, June 1979, 187-202.

3792    Valdinoci, Serge. "Etude critique: Les incertitudes de l'archéologie: Archè et archive." *Revue de Métaphysique et de Morale,* vol. 83, Jan.-March 1978, 73-101.

3793   Valdinoci, Serge. Review of D. Souche-Dague, *Le développement de l'intentionalité dans la phénoménologie husserlienne.* [*See:* 98] *Revue de Métaphysique et de Morale,* vol. 82, 1977, 123-131.

3794   Valone, James J. "Conflicts in the later Husserl's ontology and theory of knowledge." *Proceedings of the American Catholic Philosophical Association,* vol. 51, 1977, 212-219.

3795   Van de Pitte, M. M. "Is there a phenomenological method." *Metaphilosophy,* vol. 8, 1977, 21-35.

3796   Van de Pitte, M. M. "Husserl's solipsism." *Journal of the British Society for Phenomenology,* vol. 8, 1977, 123-125.

3797   Vanni Rovighi, Sofia. "Una fonte remota della teoria husserliana dell'intenzionalità." *Bolletino di Storia della Filosofia,* vol. 3, 1975, 283-298.

3798   Wallton, Roberto J. "Cultura, existencia y logica trascendental: Apofántica formal y material en la fenomenología." *ITA-Humanidades,* vol. 9, 1973, 41-60.

3798   Waterhouse, Roger. "Husserl and phenomenology." *Radical Philosophy,* vol. 16, Spring 1977.

3799   Weinzweig, Marjorie. "Phenomenology and ordinary language philosophy." *Metaphilosophy,* vol. 8, April-June 1977, 116-146.

3800   Willard, Dallas. "Husserl's critique of extensionalist logic: 'A logic that does not understand itself'." *Idealistic Studies,* vol. 9, May 1979, 143-164.

3801   Zaner, Richrd M. "*Eidos* and science [Husserl]," in *Phenomenology and the social sciences: a dialogue.* Joseph Bien (ed.). The Hague: Martinus Nijhoff, 1978, 1-19.

3802   Zimmerman, Michael E. "Some important themes in current Heidegger research." *Research in Phenomenology,* vol. 7, 1977, 259-281.

## Additional Items

3803   Amado, Georges. *L'Etre et la psychanalyse.* Paris: Presses Universitaires de France, 1978, 288 p.

3804   Aquila, Richard E. *Intentionality. A Study of mental acts.* University Park, Pa.: Pennsylvania State University Press, 1977, xi-168.

3805   Carpio, Adolfo P. *Principios de filosofía. Una introducción a su problemática.* Buenos Aires: Ed. Glauco, 1974, 445 p.

3806   Connell, Desmond. "Substance and subject." *Philosophical Studies* (Maynooth), vol. 26, 1979, 7-25.

3807   Cox, Ronald R. *Schutz's Theory of Relevance. A phenomenological critique* (Phaenomenologica, 77). The Hague: Martinus Nijhoff, 1978, xi-235.

3808   Dallmayr, Fred R. "Husserl, subjectivity and constitutive consciousness vs. Heidegger's 'theory of being'," in *From Contract to Community. Political theory of the community,* Fred. R. Dallmayr (ed.). New York: M. Dekker, 1978.

3809    Dickens, D. R. "Phenomenology," in S. G. McNall (ed.)., *Theoretical Perspectives in Sociology.* New York: St. Martins Press, 1979, 325-347.

3810    Foukes, William. "The concept of the self in Husserl and beyond. The transcendental ego reconsidered." *Philosophy Today,* vol. 24, no. 1, Spring 1980, 44-54.

3811    Fraga, G. de. "Fenomenologia e cartesianismo." *Filosofia* (Lisboa), vol. 4, 1957, 89-97.

3812    Fraga, G. de. "As duas vias da redução fenomenológica." *Filosofia* (Lisboa), vol. 4, 1957, 180-187.

3813    Fragata, Julio A. "A filosofia de Edmund Husserl." *Filosofia* (Lisboa), vol. 8, 1961, 283-300.

3814    Fragta, Julio A. "Metafísica husserliana e metafísica tomista." *Revista Portuguesa de Filosofia,* vol. 15, 1959, 236-242.

3815    Fragata, Julio A. "A possibilidade da filosofia como ciência rigorosa." *Revista Portuguesa de Filosofia,* vol. 11, 1955, 73-79.

3816    Hallen, Barry. "Phenomenology and the exposition of African traditional thought." *Second Order,* vol. 5, July 1976, 45-65.

3817    Hindess, Barry. *Philosophy and Methodology in the Social Sciences.* Sussex: The Harvester Press, 1977, 258 p. [Husserl's concept of the nature of the sciences and of philosophy in *The Crisis*]

3818    Hirsch, Rudolf. "Edmund Husserl and Hugo von Hofmannsthal. Eine Begegnung und ein Brief [vom 12.1.1907]," in Carl-Joachim Freidrich und Benno Reifenberg, Hrsg., *Sprache und Politik.* Festgabe für Dolf Sternberger zum sechzigsten Geburtstag. Heidelberg: Verlag Lambert Schnieder, 1968, 108-115.

3819    Johnson, Galen A. "Husserl and history." *Journal of the British Society for Phenomenology,* vol. 11, no. 1, Jan. 1980.

3820    Kuderowicz, Zbigniew. "Husserl as a critic of historicism." R. Legutko (trans.). *Rep. Phil.,* 1978, 19-29.

3821    Langsdorf, Lenore. "Language, the reductions, and 'immanence'." [Review of *Language and the phenomenological reductions,* by Suzanne Cunningham]. *Research in Phenomenology,* vol. 9, 1970.

3822    Lingis, Alfonso. "L'origine de l'infini," in *Le Savoir philosophique.* Paris: Les Belles Lettres, 1978. Annales de la Faculté des Lettres et Sciences humaines de Nice, no. 32, 1977.

3823    Lynch, Timothy. "Husserl: From logic to philosophy." *Philosophical Studies* (Maynooth), vol. 26, 1979, 26-40.

3824    Lyons, Joseph. "Edmund Husserl," in *The International Encyclopedia of the Social Sciences.* David L. Suls (ed.). New York: The Macmillan Co. & The Free Press, 1968, vol. 7, 27-31.

3825    Marsch, James L. "Inconsistency in Husserl's *Cartesian Meditations.*" *New Scholasticism,* vol. 53, no. 4, Autumn 1979, 460-474.

3826 McMullin, Ernan. "Compton on the philosophy of nature." *Review of Metaphysics,* vol. 33, Sept. 1979, 29-58.

3827 Meder, Norbert. *Prinzip und Faktum. Transzendentalphilosophische Untersuchungen zu Zeit und Gegenständlichkeit im Anschluss an Richard Hönigswald.* Bonn: Bouvier (Grundmann), 1975, 172 p.

3828 Mueller, Fernand-Lucien. *Histoire de la psychologie.* T. II: *La psychologie contemporaine.* Paris: Payot, 1976, Ch. XXIV.

3829 Müller, S. "System und Erfahrung. Metaphysische Aspekte am Problem des Gegebenen bei Edmund Husserl." Ph.D. Dissertation, Univ. München, 1971, 191 p. *Dissertation Abstracts International. C European Abstracts,* vol. 40, no. 1, Autumn 1979, 19.

3830 Null, Gilbert. "On connoting: The relational theory of the concept in Husserlian phenomenology." *Journal of the British Society for Phenomenology,* vol. 11, no. 1, Jan. 1980.

3831 *Perspectivas da fenomenologia de Husserl* (Actas do colóquio fenomenológico de Braga). Centro de Estudos Fenomenológicos, Coimbra, 1965, 112 p.

3832 Pietersma, Henry. "Husserl and Heidegger." *Philosophy and Phenomenological Research,* vol. 40, no. 2, Dec. 1979, 194-211.

3833 Prendergast, Christopher P. "Phenomenology and the problem of foundations. A critique of Edmund Husserl's theory of science." Ph.D. dissertation, Southern Illinois University at Carbondale, 1979, 269 p. *Dissertation Abstracts International,* vol. 40, no. 8, Feb. 1980, 4630-A.

3834 Quintelier, Guy. "Zakalijke evidentie, objectieve wetenschap en technische innovatie." *Tijdschrift voor Filosofie,* vol. 44, June 1979, 301-307.

3835 Rauch, Leo. "Edmund Husserl: *Experience and Judgment.*" *Philosophical Studies* (Maynooth), vol. 25, 1978, 244-253.

3836 Ricoeur, Paul. *Main Trends in Philosophy.* New York: Holmes and Meier Publishers Inc., 1979, xvii-469.

3837 Ricoeur, Paul. "Hegel and Husserl on intersubjectivity," in *Reason, action and experience.* Essays in honor of Raymond Klibanski. Helmut Kohlenberger (ed.). Hamburg: Felix Meiner Verlag, 1979.

3838 Saraiva, M. M. "O primado da percepçño e a concepçño da obra de arte em Husserl," in *Perspectivas da fenomenologia de Husserl.* Coimbra, Centro de Estudos Fenomenológicos, 1965, 73-106. [Résumé en français, Le primat de la perception et la conception de l'oeuvre d'art chez Husserl, 110-112]

3839 Schérer, René. "Sur la philosophie transcendentale et l'objectivité de la connaissance scientifique." *Revue de Métaphysique et de Morale,* vol. 62, 1957, 436-464.

3840 Schroder, William R. "Others: An examination of Sartre and his predecessors. Vol. I: Husserl, Hegel, Heidegger. Vol. II: Sartre." Ph.D. dissertation, University of Michigan, 1979, 882 p. *Dissertation Abstracts International,* vol. 40, no. 2, Aug. 1979, 906-A.

3841 Senn, S. "La question de la realité dans la phénoménologie de Husserl." *Studia Philosophica,* vol. 36, 1976.

3842 Sherover, Charles M. *The Human Experience of Time.* New York: New York University Press, 1975, x-603.

3843 Shin, Gui Hyin. *Die Struktur des inneren Zeitbewusstseins. Eine Studie über d. Begriff d. Protention in d. veröf. Schriften Edmund Husserls.* Bern, Frankfurt am Main, Las Vegas: Lang, 1978, 190 p.

3844 Sinha, Debabrata. *Phenomenology and Existentialism: An Introduction.* Calcutta: Progressive Publishers, 1974, 160 p.

3845 Sinha, Debabrata. "Phenomenology and positivism." *Philosophy and Phenomenological Research,* vol. 23, no. 4, June 1963.

3846 Sinha, Debabrata. "Phenomenology, vis-a-vis Kant and Neo-positivism, on the issue of the *Apriori.*" *Archiv für Geschichte der Philosophie,* vol. 53, no. 1, 1971.

3847 Sinha, Debabrata. "The notion of intentionality and the phenomenological viewpoint." *The Visva-Bharati Journal of Philosophy* (Santiniketan, India), vol. 8, no. 1, Aug. 1971.

3848 Sivak, Joseph. "Review of R. Sokolowski, *Husserlian Meditations.*" *Revue de Métaphysique et de Morale,* vol. 84, avril-juin 1979, 273-274.

3849 Sokolowski, Robert. "Review of Aron Gurwitsch, *Phenomenology and Theory of Science.*" *Man and World,* vol. 11, 1978, 207-211.

3850 Stewart, Roderick M. "The problem of logical psychologism for Husserl and the early Heidegger." *Journal of the British Society for Phenomenology,* vol. 10, no. 3, Oct. 1979, 184-193.

3851 Strauss, D. F. M. *Begrif en Idee.* Assen: Van Gorcum, 1973, 212 p.

3852 Struyker Boudier, C. E. M. "Husserls Bidjrage aan de logika en de genealogie van de vraag." *Tijdschrift voor Filosofie,* vol. 41, June 1979, 217-259.

3853 Tevuzzi, Michael. "A note on Husserl's dependence on William James." *Journal of the British Society for Phenomenology,* vol. 10, no. 3, Oct. 1979, 194-196.

3854 Tischner, J. "Autour de la pensée d'Husserl," in *Archiwum Historii Filozofii y Mysli Spoleczenej.* Andrezej Walicki (ed.). Wroclaw-Warszawa Ossoliveum, 1978.

3855 Tuedio, Jim. "Review of E. Kohak, *Idea and Experience: Edmund Husserl's project of phenomenology in Ideas I.*" *Auslegung,* vol. 6, June 1979, 196-205.

3856 Van Hooft, Stan. "Merleau-Ponty and the problem of intentional explanation." *Philosophy and Phenomenological Research,* vol. 40, Sept. 1979, 33-52.

3857 Willard, Dallas. "Husserl on a logic that failed." *The Philosophical Review,* vol. 89, no. 1, Jan. 1980, 46-64.

3858 Connell, Desmond. "Review of L. Kolakowski, *Husserl and the Search for Certitude.*" *Philosophical Studies* (Maynooth), vol. 25, 1978, 253-257.

## Additional Items

3859    Botero Cadavid, Juan José. "Lógica y realidad en Husserl." *Cuadernos de Filosofie y Letras* (Bogotá), vol. 2, no. 1, 1979, 18-32.

3860    Celms, Theodor. *Der phänomenologische Idealismus Husserls.* Reprint of the 1928 Riga ed. (Phenomenology, Background, foreground, and influences). New York, London: Garland Publishing, 1979.

3861    Denteno, Francesco. *Alle radici della fenomenologia. Husserl 1887-1891.* Dallo scritto di abilitazione *Sul concetto di numero* alla *Filosofia dell'aritmetica* (Guide storiografiche, 6). Roma: Edizioni Abete, 1978, 272 p.

3862    Hall, Harrison. "Intersubjective phenomenology and Husserl's Cartesianism." *Man and World,* vol. 12, 1979, 13-20.

3863    Hougaard, Esben. "Some reflections on the relationship between Freudian psychoanalysis and Husserlian phenomenology." *Journal of Phenomenological Psychology,* vol. 9, 1-83.

3864    Kojima, Hiroshi. "The potential plurality of the transcendental ego of Husserl and its relevance to the theory of space." *Analecta Husserliana,* vol. 8, 1979, 55-61.

3865    Kuroda, Wataru. "Phenomenology and grammar. A consideration of the relation between Husserl's *Logical Investigations* and Wittgenstein's later philosophy." *Analecta Husserliana,* vol. 8, 1979, 89-107.

3866    Libertson, J. "Levinas and Husserl. Sensation and intentionality." *Tijdschrift voor Filosofie,* vol. 41, 1979, 485-502.

3867    Lynch, Timothy J. "Husserl. From logic to philosophy." *Philosophical Studies* (Ireland), vol. 26, 1978, 26-40.

3868    Nitta, Yoshihiro. "Husserl's manuscript 'A nocturnal conversation'. His phenomenology of intersubjectivity. Barbara Haupt Mohr (trans.)." *Analecta Husserliana,* vol. 8, 1979, 21-36.

3869    Ogawa, Tadishi. "The Kyoto School of philosophy and phenomenology [K. Nishida and E. Husserl]. Barbara Haupt Mohr (trans.)." *Analecta Husserliana,* vol. 8, 1979, 207-221.

3870    Paci, Enzo. *Il problema della monadologia da Leibniz a Husserl.* Per uan concezione scientifica e umana della società. Lezioni dell'Anno accademico 1975-1976. A cura di Salvana Merati. Milano: Cuem, 1976, 179 p.

3871    Paci, Enzo. *Il problema della monadologia da Leibniz a Husserl.* Per una concezione scientifica e umana della società (Unicopli universitaria, 7). Milano: Unicopli, 1978, 216 p.

3872    Philipse, H. "E. Husserls houding ten opzichte van de exakte natuurwetenschap. Kanttekeningen bij het artikel van S. F. Baekers: 'Fenomenologie en moderne wetenschapsfilosofie'." *Algemeen Nederlands Tijdschrift Wijsbegeerte,* vol. 71, 1971, 1979, 45-51. [S. F. Baekers, Dupliek op de kanttekeningen van H. Philipse, 52-57]

3873 Quintelier, Guy. "Zakelijke evidentie, objectieve wetenschap en technische innovatie [E. Husserl, *Over de oorsprong van de meetkunde*]." *Tijdschrift voor Filosofie,* vol. 41, 1979, 301-307.

3874 Rockmore, T. "Fichte, Husserl, and philosphical science." *International Philosophical Quarterly,* vol. 19, 1979, 15-27.

3875 Rotenstreich, Nathan. "Exposition of intuition and phenomenology [Kant and Husserl]." *Studi Internazionali di Filosofia,* vol. 9, 1979, 43-84.

3876 Sini, Carlo. "Il problema del segno in Husserl e in Peirce." *Filosofia,* vol. 29, 1978, 543-558.

3877 Struyker Boudier, C. "Husserls bijdrage aan de logika en de genealogie van de vraag." *Tijdschrift voor Filosofie,* vol. 41, 1979, 217-259. [Zusammenfassung: Husserls zur Logik und Genealogie der Frage, 259]

3878 Tatematsu, Hirotaka. "Phänomenologische Betrachtung vom Begriff der Welt [Husserl]." *Analecta Husserliana,* vol. 8, 1979, 109-129.

3879 Wajda, Mihály. "Die Kritik der Tatsachenwissenschaften bei Lukács und Husserl," in *Phanomenologie und Marxismus,* IV: Erkenntnis- und Wissenschaftstheorie. Hrsg. von Bernhard Waldenfels u.a. (Suhrkamp Taschenbücher Wissenschaft, 273). Frankfurt am Main: Suhrkamp, 1979, 46-74.

3878 Miller, Izchak. "The Phenomenology of perception. Husserl's account of our temporal consciousness." Ph.D. dissertation, University of California at Los Angeles, 1979, 218 p. *Dissertation Abstracts Int.,* vol. 40, no. 11, May 1980, 5901A.

3879 Miller, James P. "The presence and absence of number in Husserl's philosophy of mathematics." Ph.D. dissertation, Catholic University of America, 1980, 321 p. *Dissertation Abstracts Int.,* vol. 40, no. 11, May 1980, 5901A.

# PART FOUR
# INDEX OF AUTHORS AND EDITORS

(N. B. - Numbers followed by letter "r" refer to book reviews)

Barth, E. M. 3132

Bartlett, Steven 3133

Bascuñana, Lopéz 263

Basehearts, Sister Mary Catherine 320, 823, 829

Bastable, J. D. 2959

Baudoux, B. 105r

Baumgardt, David 668, 3134

Baumgardt, H. 1813

Bausola, Andriano 226r

Beaufret, Jean 588

Beck, Maximilian 2251, 2252, 2253, 2254, 2255

Beck, R. 111r

Becker, Oskar 14, 141, 157r, 172, 1570, 1571, 2256

Bednarski, Jules 1931, 1932, 2203, 2257, 2258, 2259

Beerling, R. F. 289, 872, 1178, 2043, 2260

Behn, Siegfried 875

Benedikt, M. 1270

Bénézé, Georges 2261

Bennett, John B. 847, 2834

Benoist, J.-M. 97r

Bense, Max 2262, 3089

Berger, Gaston 4, 70, 172, 438, 509, 639, 973, 1755, 1968, 2115, 2116, 2263, 2264, 2265, 2915, 2960, 2997, 3135, 3136, 3137, 3138, 3139, 3140

Berger, Herman 430

Berger, J. 1915

Bergmann, Gustav 1968, 2266

Bergmann, Hugo 119

Bergmann, Samuel Hugl 2267

Bergoffen, Debra B. 1050, 3656

Berl, H. E. 775, 1804, 2268

Bernard-Maitre, Henri 101r, 2743, 2754, 3035

Bernet, Rudolf 321, 520, 3657, 3658

Bersley, William J. 3629

Berte, B. 248r

Bertman, Martin A. 2876

Bertoldi, Eugene F 1756

Caso, Antonio 264, 878, 2304

Caspary, Adolpf 3172

Castro López, O. 575

Cavailles, Jean 2305

Célis, Raphael 3674

Celms, Theodor 125, 1228, 1772, 2306, 3173, 3860

Ceñal, Ramón 103r, 195r, 224r, 2307

Cerf, Walter 129r, 164r, 590, 3054

Cerri, Stefano 833, 1277

Chamberlin, J. G. 1041

Champigny, Robert 69r

Chandler, Albert R. 330, 777, 2195, 2308, 3001

Chandravarty, H. 2309

Chapman, H. M. 45, 1912

Chapman, Harmon C. 2030, 2310, 3174

Chatterjee, Margaret 1406

Chestow, Leo 306, 1377, 1614, 2169, 2311, 2312, 2635, 2636

Chiara Moneta, G. 15

Chiodi, Pietro 55r, 185r, 591, 1045, 1136, 3176, 3177

Chisholm, Roderick M. 2313, 3175

Cho, Kah Kyung 2314

Christensen, Renate 1278

Christoff, Daniel 71, 3615

Christopher, Dennis 3675

Cilleruelo, L. 432

Cimmico, Luigi 993

Cives, G. 226r

Claesges, Ulrich 60, 61, 126, 127, 1457, 2072, 3178

Clauss, F. 3179

Clifford, P. 11r

Cohen, Hermann 1378, 3180

Cohen, Sande 2076

Colbert, J. G. 3038

Colette, Jacques 3181

Collins, James 52r, 69r, 86r, 133r, 167r, 2315, 2440r, 2814

Compton, John J. 570, 1773

Drüe, Hermann 130, 1860, 3056
Drummond, John J. 337, 431, 1727, 1728, 1941, 2031, 2338, 3685
Dubois, J. 1899r
Dubois, M. J. 3686
Ducoin, G. 103r, 105r
Dufrenne, Mikel 64, 856, 884, 3687
Duinter, O. D. 289r
Dumas, J. L. 89r
Duméry, Henry 69r, 1979, 2339
Dupré, Louis 18r, 50r, 52r, 64, 1147, 1165, 2171, 2172, 2340, 2764, 3041
Durño, P. 291r
Durfee, Harold A. 898
Düsing, Klaus 127, 707, 2099
Dussort, Henri 69r, 72r, 456, 671, 2341, 2842
Duval, R. 1412


Ecole, Jean 69r, 80r, 81r, 86r, 103r, 106r, 2819, 2943
Edie, James M. 15, 32, 42r, 43r, 44, 50r, 72r, 179, 840, 1137, 1172, 1413, 1493, 2155, 3201, 3203
Edwards, Anne 179
Ehrhardt, Walter E. 698
Ehrlich, Walter 131, 1285, 2379, 2342, 3208, 3209
Eigler, Günther 132, 2125
Eisler, Rudolph 3203
Eley, Lothar 61, 112r, 127, 133, 911, 948, 949, 1414, 1415, 1509, 2126, 2156, 2343, 3204
Elie, Hubert 74, 2765
Elkin, Henry 61, 1055
Ell, J. 117r
Ellis, Ralph 3688, 3689
Elliston, Frederick A. 13, 1086, 1758, 3207, 3690
Elsas, A. 2735
Elsenhabs, Theodor 3205, 3206
Elveton, R. O. 14, 2344
Embree, Lester E. 15, 1056, 2096, 3004, 3210, 3691
Endres, J. 2918, 2965
Eng, Erling 61, 153r, 3211

Fischer, M. 187r

Fischl, Johann 3235

Fisher, Alden L. 2363, 2845, 2967

Fleming, R. 665

Flew, Anthony 102r

Flynn, Bernard C. 516, 1190

Flory, M. 2364

Fogel, Gilvan 3696

Föllesdal, Dagfinn 42r, 140, 523, 524, 1595, 1676, 1730, 3694, 3695

Folwart, Helmut 141, 340, 599, 672

Fondane, Benjamin 3236

Formaggio, D. 3237

Forni, Guglielmo 210r, 241r, 260r, 1191, 1192, 2365, 2846, 2944, 3077, 3238

Forrest, William 754

Fortuny, N. A. 3042

Foukes, William 3810

Foulquié, Paul 1861

Fragata, Julio A. 69r, 103r, 291, 292, 303r, 1138, 1166, 1700, 2366, 2367, 2368, 2820, 2847, 2898, 3813, 3814, 3815

Francès, R. 103r

Franchi, Attilio 2369

Franchini, R. 209r, 2968

Frege, Gottlob 13, 44, 525, 526, 2736

Freudn, Ludwig 3239

Friess, Horace L. 2427, 3091

Frings, Manfred S. 126r, 3697

Frischeisen-Köhler, Max 1862

Fritsch, W. 142

Fritzsche, Hans-Georg 191r

Füchs, Wolfgang Walter 21, 341, 1827

Fulda, Hans F. 1761, 2371

Fulton, James Street 45, 967, 3240

Funari, E. A. 1863, 3241

Funke, Gerhard 104, 143, 196, 211, 992, 1380, 1777, 2157, 2372, 2373, 2374, 3243, 3244, 3245, 3246, 3698

Hassell, Lewis 3705

Hayen, André 226r

Heber, Johannes 349, 1980

Hedwig, Klaus 3706, 3707

Heffner, John 1089, 2417

Hegg, Hans 147

Heidegger, Martin 32, 603, 604

Heim, Klaus 148, 1834, 3279

Hein, K. F. 2174

Heinemann, Fritz H. 123r, 2416, 2900, 3058, 3281, 3282

Heinrich, D. 2902

Heinrich, E. 983, 3283

Heimsöth, H. 3280

Heintel, E. 195r

Held, Klaus 127, 149, 1061, 1339, 2131

Hemmindinger, David 351, 1118, 1999

Hempel, H.-P. 130r

Hempolinski, Michael 648, 3708

Hems, J. M. 42r

Hems, John M. 857

Hennig, J. 3043

Henning, L. 53r

Henrich, Dieter 1779

Henry, Michel 3284

Héring, Jean 55r, 82, 117r, 1382, 1620, 1621, 1981, 2418, 2419, 2420, 2901, 3284, 3285, 3286

Hermann, Friedrich Wilhelm von 150, 605, 606, 1465, 2211, 2971

Hernandez, Miguel Cruz 1279

Herrera, D. 97r, 2000

Herrera Restrepo, D. 3092

Heyde, G. 352

Hicks, George D. 2424, 3287, 3288

Hindess, Barry 1194, 2001, 2852, 3817

Hines, Thomas J. 23, 825

Hinners, R. C. 35r

Hintikka, J. 527

Leland, Dorothy 3636, 3729

Lemaigre, Bernard 126r, 195r, 2778

Lenkowski, William J. 3730

Lenzen, Wilhelm 372

Leo, John R. 3731

Leroux, Henri 3011

Lévesque, Claude 64

Levin, David Michael 36, 373, 1081, 1120, 1121, 1122, 1249, 2486, 2779

Levinas, Emmanuel 32, 37, 80, 82, 87, 88, 172, 1295, 1356, 2033, 2487, 2488, 2489, 2490,
    2491, 2492, 3353, 3354, 3355, 3396r

Leyvraz, Jean-P. 71r

Libertson, J. 3866

Licciardello, N. 1139

Liebert, Arthur 3356

Lingis, Alphonso 60, 61, 960, 1222, 1252, 1296, 1720, 3822

Linke, Paul F. 1297, 1390, 1521, 1522, 1736, 2178, 3357, 3358, 3359, 3360, 3361, 3362,
    3363, 3364, 3365, 3366, 3367, 3368

Lincschoten, Johannes 299, 662, 1877

Lippitz, Wilfried 3732

Lipps, Theodor 885

Liverziani, Filippo 204r, 3733

Llambías de Azevedo, Juan 1917, 2493

Llorente, Bartha 3013

Lombardi, F. 3369, 3370

Long, E. T. 3300r

Long, W. 55r, 3014

López Quintás, Alfonso 759, 789

Lorenzi, J. L. 103r

Lowenstein, K. 3371

Lowit, Alexandre 484, 1095, 1806, 2295

Löwlith, Karl 82, 1109, 1632, 3372, 3373

Lowry, Atherton C. 734

Lozinski, Jerzy 700, 1565, 2494, 3374

Lübbe, Hermann 166, 178, 708, 2086, 2495, 2496, 2859, 3375

Luckmann, Thomas 1422

Lugarini, Leo 2497, 2906

Montero Moliner, Fernando 615, 1425, 1590, 1950

Montull, Tomás 291r

Mogg, Willy 1836, 1882

Moore, Jared S. 3405

Moore, S. 2536

Moreira, Mario H. 3743

Morel, G. 72r, 84r, 86r

Morgenstern, Georg 380, 1133

Morin, Serge 64

Morpurgo-Tagliabue, Guido 3406

Morra, Gianfranco 1112, 2201

Morris, Bertram 887

Morris, Charles W. 3407

Morrison, James C. 463, 1205, 1303, 2865, 3744

Morrison, Ronald P. 3745

Morriston, Barbara W. 381

Morriston, Wesley 1242, 1304, 2539

Morscher, E. 542

Mortan, Günther 543, 1837

Morujño, Alexandre Fradique 302, 303, 1035, 1306, 2218, 2538, 2539, 2826

Mostroshilova, N. V. 652, 979

Mueller, Fernand-Lucien 3828

Müller, A. 3408

Müller, Gustav E. 2540

Müller, Max 1703, 2541, 3409

Müller, Severin 3746, 3747, 3829

Müller, Wolfgang Hermann 143, 170

Muller-Freienfels, Richard 1883

Mullewie, M. de 82r, 106r

Mundle, C. W. K. 1984, 3045

Muñoz-Alonso, A. 2827

Murphy, Richard T. 62, 382, 464, 686, 737, 778, 915, 1006, 1025, 1658, 1824, 1825, 2542

Muth, Franz 383, 616

Mytrowitch, Kyryle 2543

Piguet, Jean-Claude 72r, 2585
Pinkard, Terry P. 391, 583
Pintor-Ramos, Antonio 282r, 2586
Pinto de Carvalho, A. 2934
Piokorwski, Henry 2587
Piovesan, R. 3470
Pirard, R. 2908
Pirella, A. 739, 2013
Pivcevic, Edo 41r, 49, 179, 544, 800, 2588, 2789, 3471
Piwocki, K. 774
Plebe, Armando 211, 254
Plessner, Helmut 1637, 1638, 1639, 2589
Pleydell-Pearce, H. G. 15r
Pöggeler, Otto 195r
Poggi, S. 51r, 242
Polinov, Hans 2590
Pöll, M. 176, 812
Pollnow, Hans 1640
Poltawski, Andrzej 61, 305, 654, 1011, 3473
Poncelet, A. 296r
Ponsetto, Antonio 206r, 1168, 2591, 3626, 3639
Poole, Roger C. 48r
Poortman, J. J. 2592
Port, K. 1395, 2102, 2593
Pos, H. J. 103, 487, 755, 1431, 1494, 1641, 2087, 3474
Postow, B. C. 2594
Pozzan, A. M. 2869
Pradines, Maurice 2034
Prado, C. G. 3755
Praetorius, H. M. 969
Prauss, Gerold 3760
Prendergast, Christopher P. 3833
Presas, Mario A. 164r, 195r, 962, 1208, 2595, 2890, 3756, 3758, 3759
Preti, G. 451, 1636, 2596, 2597, 2790
Prezioso, Antonio F. 259r, 801, 1311, 1068, 2370
Prezioso, Faustino A. 1704

Reiner, Hans 82, 396, 1153, 2608, 3485, 3486

Reinhardt, Kurt 2111

Renzi, Emilio 207r, 254, 784, 904, 1084, 1705, 2069, 3487, 3488

Reyer, W. 1891, 3489, 3490, 3491

Reymond, A. 488, 977

Rhees, Rush 2985

Riaza, Maria 870

Ribeiro da Silva, Isidro 1838, 2791

Ricci, Louis M. 397, 765, 785, 1134

Rice, L. C. 43r

Richir, Marc 1839, 2609

Rickert, Heinrich 3492, 3493, 3494

Ricoeur, Paul 50, 90, 102r, 103, 104, 172, 196, 624, 688, 713, 862, 1175, 1210, 1434, 1765, 1899r, 2610, 2611, 2612, 2984, 3022, 3023, 3098, 3495, 3496, 3497, 3498, 3499, 3500, 3501, 3836, 3837

Riepe, Dale 2613

Rieser, Max 653

Rintelen, Fritz-J. von 2614

Riverso, Emmanuele 226r, 246r, 1540, 2615, 2871, 3060

Rizo, Urbano 2616

Rizzo, F. 204r

Robberechts, Ludovic 94, 183, 280, 753, 1113

Robert, Carl 762

Robert, Jean-Dominique 73r, 954, 2186, 2617, 3502

Roche, Maurice 2618

Rochot, B. 80r

Rockmore, Tom 3762, 3874

Rodríguez, J. 275r

Rodríguez Sandéz, José Luis 281, 1012

Roels, Claude 2909, 2910

Rognoni, L. 3504

Roig Ginorella, Juan 291r, 835, 836, 1417, 1418, 1575, 2088, 3763

Rollin, France 95, 625, 2619

Romanell, P. 3764

Romano, F. 2440r

Rombach, Heinrich 3505

Sang,-Ki, Kim 8r, 33r, 1034, 1035
San Martín, J. 114r
Santalo, J. 291r
Saraiva, Maria Manuela 96, 404, 1261, 1262, 3838
Sartre, Jean-Paul 32, 1073, 1257, 1263, 1264, 1315, 1722, 2629, 2630
Satue Alvarez, A. 465, 1314
Sauer, Friedrich 645
Savignano, Armando 871
Scanlon, John D. 398, 802, 905, 1098, 1706, 1796, 2069, 2631
Scannone, J. C. 292r
Schacht, Richard 626
Schacht, Robert 2632
Schaerer, René 103r, 3513
Schaff, W. 3514
Schaper, Eva 54r
Schapp, Wilhelm 82, 1642, 1741
Scheler, Max 3515, 3516, 3517
Scherer, P. 71r
Schérer, René 84, 87r, 97, 223, 282, 2162, 2633, 2634, 2795, 3518, 3839
Schermann, Hans 646, 727, 2796
Schiavone, M. 248r
Schilling, K. 193, 2878
Schilpp, Paul A. 3519
Schmalenbach, H. 3520
Schmid-Kowarzik, W. 1892, 1893
Schmidt, Degener H. 399, 779
Schmidt, Hermann 891, 1219
Schmitt, Richard 32, 42, 55r, 400, 897, 1766, 1957, 2163, 3521
Schneider, Robert O. 627, 3767
Schönrock, W. 401, 1014
Schöpf, Alfred 3768
Schräder, H. 402
Schräder, Herta 696, 2103
Schräder-Klebert, Karin 568, 2164
Schrag, Calvin O. 9r, 32, 1485, 3048
Schreier, F. 1445, 3522

Shmueli, E. 1015, 1211, 1820

Siegfried, Theodor 1213

Siegfried, Thomas 192, 3545

Sigwart, Christian 1546, 3540

Silverman, Hugh J. 2027, 2873

Siméon, J.-P. 744, 1245

Simmel, Georg 821, 1645

Simoes Saraiva, Maria Manuela 404

Sinha, Debabrata 51, 1359, 1746, 1747, 1812, 2016, 2646, 2647, 2648, 3844, 3845, 3846, 3847

Sini, Carlo 81r, 235r, 815, 817, 1030, 1159, 2649, 2650, 2651, 3027, 3541, 3542, 3543, 3777, 3876

Sinn, Dieter 405, 1348

Sirchia, F. 239r

Sivak, Joseph 3848

Sjaardema, Henrikus 1894

Smith, Barry 406, 546, 547, 548

Smith, David Woodruff 407, 1316, 1586

Smith, F. Joseph 73r, 479, 630, 944, 1669, 2652, 3546

Smith, Quentin 408, 813, 1016, 1148, 1149, 1223, 2801, 3640, 3778, 3779

Snowball, K. R. 1321

Soehngen, Gottlieb 3547

Sokolowski, Robert 6r, 8r, 11r, 15, 25r, 42r, 44, 52, 53, 120r, 126r, 160r, 188r, 566, 919, 1031, 1032, 1232r, 1547, 1707, 1797, 2653, 2654, 2802, 2803, 3050, 3072, 3780, 3849r

Solaguren, C. 246r

Sollers, Philippe 3548

Solomon, Robert C. 13, 549, 863, 1106, 1435, 1682, 2655

Soloviov, E. Y. 1116

Somogyi, Joseph 1398, 1646, 2656, 3549

Son, B. H. 54, 691, 1748, 2829

Souche-Dagues, D. 62, 98, 1317, 1808

Souriau, M. 3550

Spaier, A. 169r, 1449r, 2105, 3551

Spear, Otto 1647, 2657

Spencer, James C. 409, 2165

Ströker, Elisabeth 60, 61, 1100, 1742, 2018, 3784
Strozewski, W. 64
Strube, C. 3073
Struyker Boudier, C. E. M. 3785, 3852, 3877
Sturani, E. 84r, 94r, 2750
Sukale, Michale 58, 805, 1017, 1076
Sweeney, Robert D. 64
Swiderski, Edward M. 2672
Szilasi, Wilhelm 193, 284, 2671, 3566


Taminiaux, Jacques 80r, 81, 99, 155, 631, 892, 2806, 3786
Tannery, Jules 3567
Tarnowski, Karol 655, 1033
Tatarkiewicz, V. 80, 1651
Tatemastsu, Hirotaka 2807, 3878
Tavares, S. 2938, 2993, 3029, 3030
Tavarez, Barata 311r
Taylor, Charles 55r
Taylor, Darrell D. 416, 746
Taylor, Earl 3787
Temuralq, T. 194, 814, 1399
Tertulian, Nicolas 770, 2673
Terzi, C. 204r
Tevuzzi, Michael 3853
Thabet al-Fandi, Muhammad 3568
Theodorocopoulos, N. 3788
Theunissen, Michael 632, 806, 1351, 1694, 2674
Thévenaz, Pierre 100, 255, 491, 2675, 2676
Thiel, C. 550
Thiele, Joachim 710
Thompson, M. M. 2830
Thyssen, Johannes 984, 1919, 2677, 2678, 2679
Tielsch, E. 3031
Tilliette, Xavier 72r, 121r
Tillman, Frank 2166

Van Breda, Hermann Leo 1, 13, 61, 80, 81, 82, 90, 103, 104, 155, 172, 196, 418, 699, 748, 921, 922, 923, 924, 925, 926, 927, 928, 929, 930, 931, 932, 933, 937, 955, 956, 1155, 1170, 1325, 1962, 1963, 1964, 2692, 2693, 2694, 2695, 2696, 2697, 3102, 3582

Vancourt, Raymond 105, 695, 1802

Vandenbussche, F. 297r, 2808

Van de Pitte, Margaree M. 957, 1101, 1247, 1352, 1660, 2698, 3795, 3796

Van der Berg, J. H. 299r, 1904

Vander Gucht, R. 94r, 297r

Vander Kerken, L. 103r

Van der Leeuw, G. 1988

Van Haecht, Louis 81r, 103r, 964, 2411, 3269

Van Hooft, Stan 3856

Van Lier, Henri 103r, 105r

Vanni-Rovighi, Sofia 55r, 81r, 82, 82r, 229r, 232, 235r, 246r, 257, 258, 259, 492, 978, 1326, 1327, 1400, 2699, 2700, 2701, 2702, 2703, 3575, 3797

Van Peursen, Cornelis 13, 65, 66, 80, 310, 433, 863, 864, 865, 1077, 1078, 1220, 1709, 1710, 1711, 2146, 2147, 2148, 3576

Van Riet, Georges 839, 1921, 2112

Van Schoenborn, A. 46r

Vansteenkiste, C. 28r

Varet, Gilbert 958

Vasoli, G. 3577

Vasquez, Juan Adolfo 2994

Vasquez Hoyos, Guillermo 1323, 1324

Veatch, Henry 1549, 3578

Veca, Salvatore 1489, 3579, 3580

Vegas Gonzáles, Serafín 3581

Vegetti, M. 1652

Verhaak, C. 155r, 191r

Vela, Fernando 285, 2809

Vélez, Danilo Cruz 1079

Veloso, Agostinho 311

Vernaux, Roger 1143

Versiani Velloso, Arthur 1653, 2831

Viano, C. 103r

Vierwec, Theodor 1448

Weiler, G. 495

Weinzweig, Marjorie 1713, 2721, 3799

Welch, E. Parl 67, 68, 1564, 2719, 2720

Welton, Donn 13, 420, 1160, 1330, 1437, 1595, 2149, 2722, 3601

Werkmeister, William H. 82r, 130r, 132r, 137r, 158r, 160r, 587, 2995

Westfall, Richard S. 647

Wetherich, N. E. 29r

Wewel, Meinolf, 200, 703

Weyl, H. 3602

White, David A. 2723

White, Morton G. 2724

Widmer, Hans 569, 3603

Widulski, P. 53r

Wienbruch, Ulrich 178

Wild, John 80, 283, 908, 966, 1163, 1487, 1490, 1491, 1492, 1768, 1843

Wilhelm, Frederick E. 421, 1401

Willard, Dallas 13, 44, 551, 552, 1687, 1844, 2742, 2810, 3800, 3857

Williams, Forrest 1966

Williams, R. 20r

Williams, Robert 2094

Wilshire, Bruce W. 56r

Wilming, Josef 422, 1331

Winance, Eleuthere 53r, 1582, 2725

Winkler, R. 1989, 1990, 1991

Winter, Michael F. 423, 854, 2150

Winthrop, Henry 1102, 1659, 1967, 3604

Witschel, Günter 2022, 2726

Wojtyla, Karol 64

Wolf, Alan E. 424

Wolff, Gustav 3605

Wolters, J. 2197

Wolters, P. 3643

Wood, A. W. 2r, 2953

Woodruff Smith, D. 40, 536, 537, 553

Wundt, Wilhelm 201, 2727

Wussing, H. 2740